WALKING

with

the

INEFFABLE

A SPIRITUAL MEMOIR

(with Cats)

WALKING
WITH THE
INEFFABLE

A SPIRITUAL MEMOIR
(with Cats)

STEPHANI NUR COLBY

GREEN PLACE BOOKS | *Brattleboro, Vermont*

Printed in the United States

10 9 8 7 6 5 4 3 2 1

Green Writers Press is a Vermont-based publisher whose mission is to spread
a message of hope and renewal through the words and images we publish.
Throughout we will adhere to our commitment to preserving and protecting
the natural resources of the earth. To that end, a percentage of our proceeds
will be donated to environmental activist groups and The Southern Poverty
Law Foundation. Green Writers Press gratefully acknowledges support from
individual donors, friends, and readers to help support the environment and
our publishing initiative. Green Place Books curates books that tell literary
and compelling stories with a focus on writing about place—these books are
more personal stories, memoir, and biographies.

GREEN
PLACE
BOOKS

Giving Voice to Writers & Artists Who Will Make the World a Better Place
Green Writers Press | Brattleboro, Vermont
www.greenwriterspress.com

ISBN: 978-1-9505841-2-3

COVER DESIGN: ASHA HOSSAIN DESIGN, LLC

THE PAPER USED IN THIS PUBLICATION IS PRODUCED BY MILLS COMMITTED
TO RESPONSIBLE AND SUSTAINABLE FORESTRY PRACTICES.

A REMEMBRANCE

OF REMEMBRANCE,

DEDICATED WITH LOVE

TO ALL THOSE WHO WISH TO REMEMBER,

AND TO KATHARINE,

WHO STARTED THE BALL ROLLING,

AND TO THE LOVING FRIENDS

WHO SUSTAINED IT TO THE END—

MY DEEPEST THANKS

Good Things to Know

Some names have been changed to protect privacy.

Contents

༄

WALKING
with
the
INEFFABLE

CHAPTER ONE

Catastrophe: Christmas Day—Submerged, Rising

*T*he snow was deep and pure. Our Christmas tree twinkled soothingly. We all would have preferred to spend our Christmas Day sipping coffee and hot cocoa, sharing presents, lazily napping, and sinking into the quiet; or, in the case of my brother and me, running around and playing with our exciting Santa-delivered toys.

But this was not to be. Duty called, even for me at six years of age, and even for my brother at merely three. *Over the turnpike and through the suburbs to Aunt Clare's house we go*, we could have sung, had we felt up to singing. Family awaited and so, with a certain amount of grumbling, we all got dressed in our holiday best. Dad shed his pajamas for a sober dark suit, white shirt, and tie; Mom slipped into a glamorous dress, put on chic black high heels, and carefully painted her face to emphasize her dramatic features. My little brother, Cord, was thrust into a miniature suit and bow tie, his wet hair combed up high and in the center into a baby version of what would later be an Elvis curl, earning him the unfortunate nickname "Kingfish," which, with his still-puffy baby cheeks, he more closely resembled than any singing star. My flyaway dark hair now brushed by my mother into a semblance of shining stillness, I was clad in a chiffonish dress of a soft brown with a delicate pink print of flowers (strangely attractive despite the odd color combination) and tied at the waist with a long, sleek pink ribbon.

Having gotten into my bunchy fawn dress coat with a black velvet collar, I leaned down to pat our white cat, Fluffy, and our small Schnauzer-mix dog, Steamboat, neither of whom were invited to the festivities. Fluffy bore this social lapse with typical cat sangfroid (even though, un-catlike, she enjoyed car rides, her specialty being to lie by the window above the back seat and startle other motorists at lights and stop signs by blinking and licking herself—quite a shock to drivers who assumed she was a Steiff toy). Smart little Steamboat detected the sad signs that she was not going to be included in the family outing. After a few adamant barks were ignored, she settled down with a grim look on her little face. I sighed, knowing this meant we would come home only to receive our just punishment—one of her large gristly bones under each of our pillows. If you forgot to look and just tossed yourself down, you were lucky to avoid a pierced eardrum.

So, polished up as much as possible in honor of the occasion, and laden like camels with innumerable presents for relatives, we set off in our trusty Mercury into the well-tamed wilds of Long Island for the hour-long drive to visit the deluxe digs of my father's sister's clan, the steak-and-potatoes, been-here-since-before-the-Civil-war, firmly American side of the family and their guests.

Holiday observances were tricky, as they had to be shared out between two sides of our family that neither understood each other nor got along particularly well. The most important feast of the year, Pascha (Easter), we spent with the Greeks, my mother's family. Pascha was wondrous and joyful, from the magnificent midnight solemnities of the church to the seemingly endless day of laughing, hugging, dancing, singing *"Christos anesti!"* ("Christ is risen!"), storytelling, red egg breaking, bouzouki music, and consuming vast quantities of lamb, rice, cheese pies, salad, and honeyed cake. It passed in delight and left us feeling gloriously glazed.

Warm, relaxed, and adoring of children, the Greeks let us small ones fall asleep beneath coffee tables on the thick Oriental rugs, comfortably enfolded in family, while they danced and joked, drank ouzo, and told stories late into the night. From time to time we awoke, breathed in the rich, spicy currents of happy family swirling around us, and fell asleep again, contented and safe, like children in a lovely fairy tale, slumbering enfolded in the fragrant petals of an enormous, vivid, magical rose.

But on Christmas we usually visited the Anglo-Germanic—and, in the case of my uncle, Dutch—side of the family. The atmosphere was not cold, exactly, but much more subdued and formal than that of the Greeks. Appearances mattered there, and it seemed suddenly important to have one's party-dress bow tied on straight, one's hair neatly combed, and one's posture straight.

Aunt Clare, my father's smart and gracious sister, and Uncle Dirk, who owned a large corporation or two, were wealthy. This economic largesse spilled over into some rather strange elements of home décor that added to my sense of unease. Many brass lamps bore militant chunky-beaked eagles that looked ready to take a piece out of anyone passing too near them. And, for mysterious reasons best known to my aunt and uncle, immense hand-painted murals of steam locomotives—very *large* steam locomotives—actually, almost life-size steam locomotives—adorned the walls of the living and dining rooms. Chugging right at you, billowing painted smoke, these engines' apparent accelerating momentum could make you hesitate as you lifted a forkful of pumpkin pie to your mouth and wrestle with a brief but strong sensation of dining with certain death.

My aunt always had an astonishingly thick and impressive Christmas tree that seemed half a room wide. Abruptly chopped off mid-trunk, it gave the impression that, if you went upstairs, you would see its pointy top sticking surrealistically through the floor.

Still, the tree was very pretty and, compared to our family's skinny balsam, beguilingly lush and prosperous, festooned with bushels of ornaments and lights, receding—in diminishing perspective—more than a big man's arm length into its far-distant core.

In late afternoon on this particular Christmas, having become bored with the family festivities, my cousin, just a few years older than I, joined me in asking to go out and play in the snow. Although permission was given, my mother, to my dismay, insisted on stuffing me into one of those infamous 1950s snowsuits, thick enough to wear for a moon landing and apparently stuffed with sand. So heavily stuffed were these fabric prisons that, once you were squeezed into them, your arms stood out almost at a scarecrow's angle—it was impossible to flatten them at your sides. An enormous, heavy metal zipper was zipped up and cut into your chin (later it would freeze and leave red blazes there like the official tribal tattoo of an obscure polar people). To this were added big, heavy rubber boots with rows of huge sticking buckles and massive mittens that made it impossible to pick up anything. Lastly, a warm, too-big hat was slipped over your head (and eyes), reducing vision—an accompaniment to the marshmallow-like snowsuit hood that rendered you, for practical purposes, deaf.

Like a small, stiff Frankenstein's monster or, at best, a drunken duckling, you at last reeled uncertainly toward the door, guided by quacking, admonishing mother ducks.

So, now resembling a tottering overstuffed sofa, I waddled along in my cousin's wake, her long blond pigtails flying over her shoulders as she sprinted ahead, a veritable nymph clad in mere winter coat, hat, scarf, gloves, and little boots. Soon we reached the edge of the large pond at the bottom of the sloping backyard that my aunt and uncle shared with several neighbors. My cousin told me excitedly that she sometimes walked on the ice. This seemed like an almost-magical act—rather scary, walking on what was usually unwalkable—but very appealing. I wanted to try it too.

"Okay," she said, and we eased ourselves onto the slick silver pond rim, glazed and smooth as a giant ballroom. We shuffled carefully forward, gradually taking bigger and bigger steps, feeling the thrill of sliding on the enchanted ephemeral floor suspended above dark depths. Soon we were almost at the middle of the pond. I began to feel afraid. I glanced at my cousin, ten or twelve feet away, and started to move slowly sideways toward her, clomping as lightly as I could in my heavy boots. I saw a thrill of fear in her face. "No! Don't come any closer!" she cried.

Too late. The ice beneath my feet broke like shattering glass, and my boots shot down into the frigid, tangled water, their weight hurtling me toward muddy depths. I sank into utter darkness, black, black, black, my snowsuit absorbing water like a sponge and dragging me farther down. Choking on inky water that filled my nose and throat as if trying to erase me by main force, in panic I kicked hard and hard again, enough to break the surface and grab the edge of the ice with trembling mittened hands. I saw my cousin sprinting away. I don't know if I cried out for help or not because I was only in the air for a few seconds, my wet mittens gaining no purchase on the slick ice and slipping backwards almost as fast as I had reached them out. The weight of my snowsuit, transformed now into a terrible sea monster twined around me, pulled me remorselessly under the freezing water again.

The unspeakable cold was numbing my arms and legs. I tried to hold my breath but my eyes were wide and blind with terror. I kicked up again and barely broke the surface to choke and spit out water, gasping a breath. I saw through the surge of silver splashing before my eyes that there was no one around at all. In a moment, I sank again. Everything was becoming cloudy and dim and very, very, very cold. Desperately, weakly, I kicked one more time to the surface, straining as if trying to lift a load of iron, and caught a last breath. I still remember how the black treetops looked sprawled dark and spare against the pearly gray sky as I went down for the last time, my snowsuit now like the muscles of a giant python squeezing me to death, my nose, eyes, and throat drinking strangling darkness. I did not rise again. The blackness took me.

I do not know how much later I awoke. I was lying on my stomach on solid pond ice eight or ten feet from the gaping hole. There was nobody around. As my eyes opened, my body arched, and I retched slimy pond water, over and over, until I fell back down on the ice in exhaustion. It was utterly quiet. I was very, very cold and weak. I lay there like a tossed-away doll, wondering, trying to gather strength to get up, overwhelmed and overjoyed that I was no longer drowning, not trapped beneath the ice like a helpless fly imprisoned forever in the pond's dark amber depths. But how had I gotten out of the water? No one was at hand—no adult, not even a dog or a child. Everything around me was completely still, silent as an empty theater.

I later learned that my cousin, in panic, had gone back to the house but not dared to tell the grownups I had fallen through the ice, fearing she might be blamed. No one knew, so no one had come to help me.

So who *had* done it? Who had pulled me out and set me on safe ice? I knew it was not possible I had gotten myself out— weak, waterlogged, frozen, drowning, and unconscious as I was with nothing with which to grip the ice. I certainly had not managed to escape on my own. But someone had . . . *someone* . . . I cast about me, scenting with my mind. Did I sense a subtle, gentle presence?

If I did, it was now telling me firmly to get up quickly and go inside. I heaved myself to my feet and staggered on wobbling, disobedient legs, tripping and falling on the ice. As I picked myself up again, the tears began to flow. Falling again and rising, falling and rising like a pint-sized drunk, I finally reached the shore, crying hard now. I floundered through snowdrifts, reached the house at last, struggled to turn the doorknob with numb hands and impossible mittens, flung the door open, and rushed wailing into a room where my mother, looking elegant in her low-cut black dress and twinkling earrings, was charming guests, judging from the polite laughter surrounding her.

"Mommy!" I sobbed—a sodden, snotty disaster of a daughter, as her disapproving glance immediately told me. I staggered over to her, leaving a trail of puddles on Aunt Clare's nice carpet.

"Mommy, I fell into the pond!" I cried.

"*Nonsense!*" she said. "Don't be silly! However did you get so wet? What a mess you are! You'll ruin the carpet! Let's get you onto the linoleum." Carefully holding me away from her satiny dress, she guided me into the kitchen where she began to strip off the heavy layers of snowsuit glued to my frigid skin.

"But, Mommy, I fell through the ice!"

"Yes, yes, let's get these boots off," she said, not listening, plainly irritated by the public embarrassment and inconvenience I was creating, the unseemliness of it all reflecting poorly on her skill as a mother. But suddenly she stopped and, after a moment of silence, cried out in alarm and dismay.

I sagged with relief. She finally understood! She had almost lost me. Yes, Mommy, I was almost gone! Now we could comfort one another in joy that we were not parted after all, and that the horror was over. All this passed in a flash through my mind. Trembling, a few quiet tears still sliding down my cheeks, I leaned forward and reached out to her for a warm hug of blissful reunion, only to check myself at seeing her eyes riveted on my feet.

"Your *shoes!*" she cried tragically. "Your beautiful, beautiful shoes! They're *ruined!*" She held up two black velvet strapped shoes looking like small limp gutted fish, the multicolored flowers embroidered on them now running in streaks on their soggy surface. "You'll never be able to wear them again! They're spoiled! They'll shrink! I told you not to wear them in those boots but you insisted! Now they'll shrink! You should have been more careful! What a shame!"

It was useless to speak. Shock and hurt left me voiceless, anyway. She had already decided on the story and was steaming along on her own narrow track, implacable as the painted locomotives that bore down upon me from the dining room walls. I could not turn her from it. I also understood, in the way that children sometimes can, that she could not face what had happened and its terrifying implications—that confusion and a battering of feelings would arise in her if she did—and that she had to trivialize the event and me in order to deny the nightmare. She was upset about the shoes so that she did not have to gaze into the dark maw, the sharp descending teeth of tragedy so close to her, its hot breath on her own throat. She mocked me for "carrying on" and making a spectacle, "being a Sarah Bernhardt," to reduce the possibility that anything serious and life-changing—or life-ending—could really have happened.

Numbly I let her finish undressing, drying, and re-dressing me with brisk efficiency into my older cousin's borrowed clothes. Aunt Clare appeared and kindly offered me hot cocoa, which I gratefully accepted. My mother examined her handiwork—a dry and reorganized daughter, no longer crying—shook her head ruefully, and went off to chat with the guests. Aunt Clare followed her out. I heard them laughing, just outside the doorway, at a funny story.

I felt the hot cocoa tingle all through me with the warmth of a magic elixir, reviving me. No warm liquid had ever before felt so deeply good. It was bringing tender life to my icy core, to interior organs strangely cold in contrast, as if my insides had been left for a while in a freezer. I held the mug in both hands, enjoying its toastiness spreading into my pale, pruney fingers. I sat silent and thoughtful on the kitchen chair, my distress and disappointment at my mother's bizarre reaction becoming gradually eclipsed by my deep gratitude at being alive. At the same time I realized, austerely, perhaps for the first time, that I was truly *alone*. Alone—really, really alone.

Bleak with this new knowledge, I closed the door forever on a certain cherished expectation: that I could trust and depend upon grown-up people, especially my parents, to always care for me, know best, and even somehow save me. Anything might happen, just anything, and perhaps no one at all would understand, even the most important things, the things that mattered more than anything, the things of life and death themselves.

Alone, yes—I was really alone. And yet there had been help, unseen and immediate. True help had come but not waited to receive my thanks.

I put down the cocoa mug, climbed off the tall kitchen chair, and, happy in the light warmth of dry clothes that lay on my still-chilled skin like encouraging blessings received past hope, walked in my younger cousin's fluffy slippers to the living room. People were buzzing, talking, sitting on couches and chairs and rocking chairs, drinking, snacking, doing their grown-up things. They did not attend to me and I was glad, drifting unnoticed past them, breathing in the unexpected peace of the moment and undisturbed by the sea-susurration of their chatter and laughter.

I walked up to the huge stubby Christmas tree and gazed into it. It seemed now extraordinarily beautiful; the sheen of the glossy ornaments were unexpectedly splendid and somehow touching, as if their light came from a long way off, from where the stars are, or farther yet. And that same light was touching me now, making a warm glow in my chest and a peaceful meadow in my mind—a place where I could lie down comforted and at rest. It must have been in that shining moment that my world pivoted on its axis and shifted poles, my allegiance and belief shifting away from dependence on people and, instead, to dependence on the subtle and luminous, invisible but faithful Unseen—upon what had come for me when I was past hope, and that had, so quietly and unassumingly, pulled me out of dark, deadly water and saved my life. Without a sign. Without a word. Without a reason I could see or imagine. Yet it had. Yes, it *had*. And it was Christmas. *Christmas!* I would never be alone again.

CHAPTER TWO

Cataclysm: Jezebel, Angel Face, and the Downfall of Ahriman

T he beginning was Zoroastrian: Jezebel, black as a starless night and sleek as a snake, growling with fangs bared over the food bowl at Angel Face, white as a First Communion dress and fluffy as a cumulus cloud, her delicate pink Angora ears pricked back above an expression of regal disdain. Not much taller than they were at age three, I stood transfixed, my Mary Janes glued to the gray linoleum floor, as this spectacle of primal feline fury threatened to explode the placid Betty Crocker normalcy of our homely kitchen.

Fur began to rise on the unruly tide of arching backs, growls crescendoing to a metallic whine that hurt my ears. *Where was Mommy?!* I knew I was too small to stop this sharp-clawed, fang-toothed fray. My pudgy arms were tattooed with neat patches of red welts where Jezebel, with the casual hostility she was inclined to dispense randomly, had yet again demonstrated that she was queen—or, rather, despot—of the jungle. I don't know where Mommy had gotten the all-too-well-named Jezebel, but she served as a small and persistent reminder to my toddler brain that all was not safe and homey on planet Earth.

Crouching with her ears laid flat on her head, her fur shiny as black glass, Jezebel metamorphosed into a menacing serpent about to strike. Angel Face (or "Fluffy," as I called her with the imperturbable literalism of a small child) sat upright, a miniature heraldic lion, one paw raised, pink pads up, in a stern gesture of defiance. Her face with its noble, delicate lines was as lovely in profile as full-face when you could see both her almond eyes, one blue and one yellow-green, above the perfect petite triangle of her rosebud nose. Looking like a small, lithe female Galahad, steel-strong beneath her soft exterior, Fluffy stared down the iniquitous Jezebel with the pure lance of her righteous glance. She did not go around whacking people, especially human kittens, with unsheathed claws. No! Certainly not! Nor did she capitulate to the intimidations of sordid, disgrace-to-the-feline-world, depraved individuals like Jezebel. *Pas du tout!*

Unnerved by the icily controlled purity of the opposition, Jezebel made one knifelike swat that Fluffy knocked away with a sweep of her front leg—a lightning parry worthy of D'Artagnan. Then she leaned forward to deliver the coup de grâce with one potent pink paw. Turning tail with a last vindictive hiss, the black villainess streaked from the room at tornado speed.

Graceful as a ballerina, Fluffy regained her upright posture, her ears slowly returning from battle to normal position. Nonchalant, already dismissing the unseemly incident from her mind, the snowy victor lifted a slim paw and licked it in a refined manner with her pink tongue, like an unconcerned champion rearranging a gauntlet. Straightening, her toilette complete, she glanced casually around the room in preparation for departure. Our eyes never met, though I knew she was fond of me in her way. Fluffy felt no need for adulation, being, as always, self contained and above the fray. She carried her ivory tower with her, from which her blue eye looked out, dispassionate and clear as a cloudless sky. I expected no acknowledgment. I could only admire. In gratitude and awe, I watched this paragon of beauty, skill, and righteousness—whom I understood to be an adult, even though smaller than I—arise and set off at a serene pace, the glorious plume of her tail waving over her back like a triumphant banner—not vulgarly waving, you understand, only some reserved flicks from the upper third indicating satisfaction with the restoration of harmony and peace to the domain over which she presided as earthly guardian angel. Relaxing, I exhaled. The tom-toms were silenced, the jungle had receded, and Jezebel was no longer within slashing distance. Christianity had triumphed. So much for Ahriman, that Evil God. The Good God *did* win in the end.

مِله

I only wished that this were more apparent elsewhere. God seemed irrelevant in my milieu—a mere condiment, like fancy pickles, at an otherwise mesmerizing meal of materialism, a pale frill of ornamentation orbiting the *real* business: the juicy hamburger of possessions, status, pleasures, and daily exertions of nose-to-the-grindstone survival. Despite His amazing reputation and reputed powers, God seemed to have a less real, less notable impact on the daily lives of most people than Marilyn Monroe or Mickey Mantle—or, among my peers, Mickey Mouse. This seemed peculiar. True, some gave Him a brief acknowledgment with certain formal gestures of recognition, like attending church on Sundays. But there wasn't much obvious spillover from that day to the rest of the week. Was it like curtsying or bowing to the Queen, if you were English? You contributed your mite of respect, God nodded infinitesimally, and that was the extent of your intimacy and communication?

There seemed to be some kind of barrier. It was hard to understand what the grownups really felt and thought about all this. Sometimes I felt about adults like I do now when, visiting the Boston Aquarium, I descend the long spiral walkway winding around the gigantic central sea-life tank, an enormous glass cylinder flowing with marine traffic of all kinds—some of it delightful, some of it awesome and rather frightening. Huge looming creatures swing by within inches of my face: massive turtles weighing hundreds of pounds more than I; giant silver fish like huge platters made of gleaming knights' armor, which has somehow escaped and taken on its own weird, cold-eyed life; large bedecked and dazzling angelfish who have obviously spent hours primping and applying makeup just so, gliding by with their arched French-courtier pompadours, lips in a disapproving pout at their enforced proximity to the hoi polloi; sharks in gray business suits, cutting through the water like silent capos on a deadly mission, looking at you sideways, unblinking, as if sizing you up for cement boots.

Adults loom extra-large like this in the life of a child, flashing by at close quarters, hundreds of secrets gleaming all over them like fish scales, glinting, suggesting, but seldom revealing. Their great shadows loom over you suddenly when least expected. What do they really think about God, about anything? To slow or stop them on their mysterious circlings from which you stand apart invites the disagreeable: you may experience the desolation of the hard, unbreachable barrier through which you cannot touch each other, even when you both wish to, or, worse, cause them to open those huge jaws in displeasure and display dagger teeth surrounding a black, threatening maw.

Raising the subject of God seemed often to have this effect, as if I had jolted the whole tank with electricity or sent seismic waves rocketing through the water, shocking these huge, determined creatures, none too pleased, off their appointed, endlessly repetitive course.

Even my father, a genial and gentle man who, though raised Roman Catholic (it was rumored), never went to church, became uncharacteristically stern on the subject of the Creator: "Religion is just about morality—and that is the beginning and the end of it!" he exclaimed, his pleasant chin suddenly setting hard and grim as a pike's jaws.

Not many years before my birth, Dad had been a skinny, starving, nineteen-year-old paratrooper pinned down in the French trenches in World War II, a helpless witness to his young, downy-cheeked buddies screaming and dying all around him in the blood-soaked mud and the cold. He didn't talk about it, preserving a stiff upper lip, and he never even shouted or raised his voice. The war, I think, had burned all the shout out of him. But every night in the dark, in the quietest hours when birds sleep and monks pray and children trace their parents' nocturnal journeys through the still-sensitive antennae of their tender skins, I could hear the faint rustle of my father's restless arising and then, through the wall, the lonely clink of the ice cubes in his highball glass as he sat alone, drinking in the dark, the roar of his silence deafening.

It was the silence of the dark depths of the ocean tank, where cold creatures circle endlessly, where unspeakable things brood in airless caves, too terrible even to talk about, to chance rousing, a silence of negative alchemy that could change even gold into lead, fill the clear, lilting air with a miasma of sorrow that choked every breath. I learned in time that there is also a silence of peace that lifts all burdens and suffuses everything with a gentle light, fills the air with an ineffable sweetness, and, penetrating into the depths, heals. But our house seemed to be the wrong habitat for that kind of silence—there was no space for it to spread its wings, no nest in which it could shelter its shining eggs. The current of despair was too strong. It swept everything else away, everything except the mechanical grind of daily life and the intermittent, superficial pleasures of suburbia, flat and rootless.

Not that, claustrophobic though it was, I didn't also want to participate in this sterile but lavish middle-class oblivion. I, too, was in love with comfort and not eager to interfere with it and the casual material preoccupations upon which it rested: a kind of mythic, thermostat-regulated secular universe floating in unruffled, air-conditioned space on the backs of staid, lumbering tortoises of narrow rationality, Social Darwinism, and hubris. Even though I could feel its surrealism in my very bones, I was not a totally unwilling participant. It was like being a little bit drugged all the time with assorted goodies: picture (and, later, reading) books, TV shows, movies, toys (especially my complete cowgirl outfit and actually rideable mechanical horse, Mobo—well, okay, you pushed up and down a little on his stirrups and he moved an inch or two), games, steaks and hot-fudge sundaes, ballet tutus, dolls, pretty dresses and shoes, playing with friends, and just generally "fitting in," at least on the surface. Deeper down there was distinct discomfort.

I felt a powerlessness that was not only the standard helpless feeling of a child in a world of giants with their seismic sorrows and draconian rules but rather a sense of powerlessness that came from a lack of engagement with whatever it was I was actually here for on this wild spinning earth—with the Really Real. Even as I learned the codes and rules for The Game that school, family, and my neighborhood were training me to play, I felt that somehow I was never getting to the crux, The Meaning, which, with the dim, blundering, but persistent instinct of a blind kitten rooting for its mother's teat, I knew somehow to be there.

I knew there was a deeper life, crackling with energy, trying to break through, something really Good. God was involved, somehow. Not the pale pasteboard God who seemed just a part of Propriety and not much more, one more tidy and constrained segment of Long Island suburban life like the characterless crew-cut lawns and the scared-to-death azaleas chopped into little hot-pink rectangles and pasted against the front of each bland split-level home.

The cats, in their odd way, cut through this blasé haze. They were so scintillatingly authentic. Nothing was artificial or contrived—even Jezebel's meanness was, in its perverse way, sincere. It never hid itself or pretended to be anything else. There was a certain bedrock quality to the genuineness of their lives. No, they couldn't give me The Answer, but, with their untamped-down vibrancy, the cats could transmit some level of alternative to the anesthetized half-life around me. They helped keep some small part of me—the unbought-out part, the part not scared into unconsciousness—alive until I could stumble my way to The Meaning—or until It could overcome enough of my resistance to draw me to Itself.

There were other helpful things, too, like beckoning lights bobbing on buoys at sea seen through a heavy fog, trying to direct my wayward vessel into the right channel. There was the mysterious, exotic beauty of Greek Orthodox church services, flooding my senses and spirit with a wave of frankincense, graceful ritual, deep eyes of icons, shimmering unseen presences, and glorious chant. There was the Bible, that strange, remarkable, dazzling, and unintelligible book. I had one, of course, my very own Bible, white with a gold zipper around three sides, a cross dangling, charmlike, from the tab. The zipper protected the wafer-thin, transparent sheets, black print with red print for the words of Jesus, rims seductively dipped in pure gold. I liked it very much. It looked so pure, so *clean*, like a fresh start. And I loved the mellow, luxurious shine of the gold-leaf page edges, their smooth, cool feeling beneath my fingers.

It was a King James translation, of course, still my favorite despite certain deficiencies (from an Eastern Orthodox viewpoint). The translators seemed to have made a wonderful flying leap, reaching for the unreachable, and just before gravity overcame them in their almost-hopeless attempt and they hurtled earthward, helping hands from the unseen reached out and grabbed their arms, pulling them so high they breathed light and, then descending, poured out a wild, sweet distillation of divine poetry.

I conspired with this Bible at night with a flashlight under my blankets—"reading" seems too tame a verb, and the heavy, damasked bolts of words—satins, velvets, brocades—unrolling before my astonished mind in my little polyester world seemed inherently subversive. I didn't understand much of it—some stories seemed peculiar indeed, some were quite violent, and most of the lovely, archaic, polysyllabic words were incomprehensible to my young mind, still fenced in by inexperience and inarticulation. But some passages were indisputably beautiful, the words of Jesus terrifying, tender, and wonderful, and—even in the sections I didn't much understand—I could feel an electricity, a spiritual current so strong it was almost physical, emanating from the page, sparking into me and thrilling through my being like secret fire. The current had actual movement. I could feel it but didn't really know what I was being taught. Yet if "the trees of the field [could] clap their hands" and "the hills skip like lambs," why couldn't I learn without rationally understanding? After all, that one whose name itself was music—Isaiah—said that someday "the earth shall be full of the knowledge of the Lord, as the waters cover the sea" (Isa. 11:9). This seemed to depict a kind of learning that would rise up in us all with the same naturalness as the green shoots emerging in the cornfield. Though frustrated somewhat on the surface of my mind, deeper in I was rapt. Every night I was glued to that white-and-gold book and the harps of its mystery.

Unfortunately, Mom noticed this. My early trysts with the Bible had actually been swept in toto out of my mind until a fateful visit my mother made to my husband and me unearthed the memory. After a short stretch of silence as conversation lagged, my mother said, her smile turning a little mean and derisive, "Do you remember, Stephani, when you used to read the Bible under the covers at night with a flashlight?" For a moment I didn't and then—bang!—it hit me, rushing back like a flash flood in full spate down a dry riverbed. I remembered it all: the intensity, the wonder, and my mother like a cold statue in my bedroom doorway, a thwarted avenging pagan goddess, with that eye-boring look she had when she *really* wanted to be obeyed, forbidding me to read the Bible at night. She did not forbid me to read other things (despite the standing, if ignored, parental injunction about not staying up too late reading anything)—just the Bible.

While I was still speechless, struggling with the power of that memory, both the shock of it and the shock of having forgotten it, she added in a tone of great self-satisfaction, "I certainly put an end to *that!*" As I stared at her, wide-eyed, she pressed on, some of her side teeth suddenly showing their sharp points, fox-like, as her lips drew back in a bitter smile. "I was afraid you were going to become a little *nun.*" The word "nun" sounded like spitting. "I would rather you became a *prostitute!*"

Ironically, the Bible had been a gift from my mother. The flyleaf was inscribed to the effect that she "hoped it would become threadbare from [my] using it." Although I thought this message was rather sweet, it did confuse me. My mother, a Greek Orthodox Sunday School teacher for many years, informed me with casual candor one day that she was actually an agnostic. On the one hand, this did not seem strange to me as I never in my life saw either of my parents pray. On the other hand, she did go on merrily teaching Sunday School (and even, I think, serving on the Parish Council) in a very unagnostic Church. I was shocked when one Lenten Sunday morning she whipped out a board game she planned to foist on her third graders. "Going to Gethsemane"—a kind of "Monopoly meets Golgotha"—seemed, even in 1950s America, an epoch not known for its taste, a new low in kitsch and irreverence. What? Throw low on the dice and go back two spaces for a scourging? "*Mom!*" I protested. "It's fine," she said. "I have to keep them entertained."

But what was going on within her soul? How did my mother really handle these contradictions? Or was our life so strange, suburbia so phantasmagoric, that serious contradictions didn't matter, didn't even show up, didn't even make a ding in its hard new-Cadillac surface?

My mother was not a mean person—she was actually a warm, generous, creative, flamboyant personality. Mediterranean and passionate. But it was as if I had a secret lover—which I did—and she not only didn't approve of my affianced, she hated Him. Not with the glacier-like hatred of those who have some idea of Who He is and deliberately turn against Him, those deluded denizens of anti-life, but the common run of hatred, that of those who consciously or unconsciously figure that He is the Suspect to finger in the tragic disasters with which the Creation is awash. I used to feel that way myself on a hidden level, hidden from myself, and it took me years to find this out and be healed of it, even during the many years of running after Him as an adult and actually fancying myself as some kind of lover, even a servant, of His. How little we know of the dark chasms, the shadowy caves of resistance, in our own souls!

So many children have something vital going on in their spiritual lives; this is separate from their imaginative lives, which are fun, creative, but made up. Children are too often frightened out of remembering this vital spiritual element, just what it was, or even that it was at all. That night, solar plexus to solar plexus, my mother wordlessly threatened to withdraw her love from me if I continued dallying with God, that big Criminal, and this was more than I could bear. I stopped reading the Bible at night when the reduced distraction allowed its subtle fires to break out and suffuse my being. I shut down the memory. I shut down the current. That night I broke up with God.

It was years before I came back to my first Love, before I could even remember Him properly. Fortunately, He remained faithful even when I was not. And that's the great thing about the Really Real. It never goes away, even if it is somehow temporarily obscured. At the right moment, an angel rolled the stone away from the tomb. And there I was, face to face, heart to heart, with the Really Real. As fierily beautiful as ever. And I felt the same thrill of awakening—no, more!—as when I had opened my first Bible pages that first night, that first night when the Light sprang out and kissed my mind.

CHAPTER THREE

Catechumen: The Apprenticeship in Love

*L*eo was a big cat. Huge. He lay across the top step of three leading to my grandparents' white front door like an enormous samurai clad in flowing robes of black, gold, and tawny brown. The late-afternoon light amplified his splendor, shooting fiery sparks of reddish gold through the tips of his luxuriant fur, as if glinting off inlaid ceremonial armor. Guarding the threshold, he watched us children from half-closed but alert amber eyes, neither friendly nor unfriendly—just measuring us according to his own inscrutable standards. His potent masculine reserve disinclined us to try to pet him; he might take that for impertinence. And, although it was clear we wanted to go inside, Leo never moved for us. As we got closer, hoping he would arise and stalk away, swinging that massive tail, he never moved a whisker. This worked on the nerves of my brother, my cousins, and me. Was Leo a great feline martial artist who could burst into violent, claw-swinging action in the blink of an eye? Or would he allow us to jump over him through the doorway on our short legs (he was too large to step over) and remain peacefully in his silent, hulking guard pose?

When we got desperate, one of us would take the flying leap. Then the rest of us, one at a time, having seen that the reclining dragon had not even raised his head, followed. *Whew!* Looking behind us, we saw Leo's powerful back still dominating the entrance, unchanged and unmoved as a mountain. Now he seemed not so much a fierce Japanese warrior but rather, in his spreading, luxurious furs, an omnipotent pasha on his dais (the doormat), idly awaiting slaves to bring him his rose sherbet and sweet pine-nut cakes, and to fan him slowly with a peacock-tail fan. So powerful was his majestic motionlessness that a mere blink of his large golden eyes, slanted with the setting sunlight, would signal his orders. *Yes, of course, Leo Efendi! Immediately! Without delay!*

The pasha image was not so far-fetched. My Greek ancestors had lived under the moody rule of the Ottomans for hundreds of years, and my grandfather in his youth had been forced to hastily leave his home of Constantinople (Greeks rarely referred to its "occupation" name, Istanbul) to avoid being drafted by the Turkish army to fight other Greeks.

On highway-strewn, mall-bedecked Long Island, throbbing with the constant staccato cries of TVs and lawn sprinklers amid the bass roar of traffic, a Puritan jungle of asphalt with a parsimonious edging of thin green lawns, I spent my childhood. But I also lived my childhood within an enchanting atmosphere of arching, lyrical bouzouki melodies and floating fragrances of frankincense and lemon in a quiet home a block from the sea-singing beach. That home and that life, though also on Long Island, seemed like something out of a fairy tale, but real. How to explain it? All of it reeked of the mysterious East. The mysterious *Christian* East, that is. All the more mysterious because almost no one in our Wonder Bread Yankee suburban town seemed even to have heard of it. No, the mental habit was that one flew straight from Western Europe to China and Japan and Buddha and all that Eastern stuff, jumping over a little blank spot on the globe (with, perhaps, one brief nod to the Parthenon). A Christian East? Nah!

The only people I knew who seemed even vaguely aware of the particular East my family came from were little Roman Catholic children. We ran around the elementary school playground, esoterically taunting each other: "*You* broke away from *us!*" "No, *you* broke away from *us!*" "No, *you* . . ." This was our theological commentary on the Great Schism of 1054 when the Patriarch of Rome (a.k.a. the Pope) and the Ecumenical Patriarch of Constantinople cheekily ignored Gospel injunctions to turn the other cheek and, in pen swipes of breath-taking hostility, excommunicated each other, thereby tearing in two the one Christian Church. I felt that I had the high ground here, since four of the five Patriarchs (Constantinople, Jerusalem, Alexandria, and Antioch) had chosen to stay together rather than continue with Rome. And also my mother had craftily given me my trump card.

"Oh yeah?" I would reply with a smug smile. "If *we* broke away from *you*, then why do *you* still have Greek in your mass and *we* don't have any Latin in our Divine Liturgy?"

Hot, outraged denials of Greek in the mass followed.

"Is that so?" I beamed upon them. "Then what about *Kyrie eleison?*"

"*That's* Greek?"

"Yup, 'Lord, have mercy.'" And I swaggered, victorious (though, from their point of view, still excommunicate), off the patchy tarmac field.

But otherwise the Orthodox Christian East remained invisible in my workaday world. Or, if vaguely visible, mangled. One crushing day in third or fourth grade, when we were learning European history and had reached the Reformation, one student actually remembered that there had been an Orthodox Church and asked the teacher if *they* had a Reformation too. She looked quite taken aback and stuttered, "N-n-n-no." "How come?" asked the persistent information maven. "Well, um, well," she struggled, trying to find an answer where she had none. "Well, uh, actually, they didn't have a Reformation because—because—they were, um, just too ignorant, illiterate, and uneducated to have one."

Illiterate?! Even though I was not a pint-sized theologian, that sweeping remark almost knocked me out of my chair. Illiterate? To speak was beyond both my strength and my daring. The builders of the glorious Hagia Sophia cathedral? The great eloquent scholar-saints like Saint John Chrysostom and Saint Basil the Great? The refined and elaborate culture of the distinguished Byzantine empire? To think that a teacher could proffer such a bald-faced and dishonoring lie! *Kyrie eleison!*

I felt that the two different worlds I lived in had virtually no points of connection. The snappy, time-clock-driven, goal-obsessed 1950s–1960s American culture did not harmonize with or even relate to the warm-hearted, spacious, accepting, numinous, time-optional Greek world. Entangled with both worlds, I felt like an interloper, or some kind of spy, sure to be found out and accused. Of what? I didn't know. But something. Something dangerous. Because what I *did* know was where my preferences and loyalties lay—decisively in the Greek camp. But, nonetheless, I was forced to perform and belong in the colder Anglo-Teutonic culture around me, reeking of secular materialism, and act as if that were the only possible reality. Which I knew to be untrue.

This became a kind of psychological cramp, dominating my consciousness. It was as if I had to see one way out of one eye and a different way out of the other, struggling to achieve an impossible resolution between the two. It is known that if one is forced to see one sight out of one eye and a different one out of the other, the brain cannot tolerate the contradiction and forces the consciousness to pick and recognize only one of the objects. The other is eliminated, as if it had never been. By the time I was six or so, I felt a growing terror of that exclusion, the potential genocide of a particular beautiful consciousness/ethos. The unbearable split yawned wider and wider in daily life, and I felt powerless, small, and vulnerable, wobbling on the brink.

One day, out of the blue, it dawned on me that the vivid culture of my grandparents' household and the Orthodox Church, complex and inexplicable as the sinuous patterns of the Anatolian carpets under our feet, was unintegrated with the crisp starched whites, plain Puritan-dark suits, drab wall-to-wall carpets, and weak, simpering seersucker pastels of WASP culture because *the Greek culture was actually a secret!* I could not tell you how or why this satisfied my six-year-old brain—but somehow it did. I no longer had to try to integrate these two opposing forces; the oil and the vinegar could remain separate. Secrets were, well, separate, by definition. I did not have to expose my secret to a sharp-toothed predatory culture. I relaxed. Mostly.

Although there was some truth in my revelation, it was also impelled by an interior desperation that I was too young to cope with in any other way. This partitioning with a chosen rationale, however flimsy, seemed the only way to get through the crisis. However, partitioning—or splitting—is a dangerous psychic habit because no real resolution takes place. It often leads to our losing our essential authenticity as the number of psychic rooms in our being begins to rise in a lumbering sequence of conflicting styles commanded by a series of opinionated interior kings, resulting in a discordant palace composed of forgotten, contradictory chambers—an architectural disaster in the soul. But, as a temporary life raft, this did work for a while. Sort of.

❧

Children's yogic struggles to fit into a life and reconcile what they feel with the powerful, projecting lies laced through their culture and surroundings take place on tremendous, savage battlefields. It does not take a cultural divide such as mine to initiate such a struggle. The contrast between what a child intuitively and fundamentally feels and the lies being fed to her by the surrounding culture are enough to set off an interior crisis, acknowledged or not. And the shock and fear engendered for that child most often lead to the preferred and seemingly less dangerous option of *forgetting*.

Organized by irrelevant, abstract principles from large (whole creeds) to small (sitting alphabetically in classrooms), children have orientations chosen by adults, sometimes in a healthy way but often, tragically, from a foundation of the adults' compulsive fears and their subsequent overpowering drives to control others. These are dinned into the children so repeatedly and with so much authority that they become a kind of whiteout blizzard that turns the child's own healthy intuitive knowledge invisible and, for practical purposes, out of her reach. Like the whales and dolphins who have navigated by their own sonar for millennia but now beach themselves—disoriented, blood running out of their ears—due to the overwhelming level of ocean noise created by navy sonar and the propellers of millions of ships, children lose their bearings. Some recover but others carry this interior deafness and blindness for the rest of their lives, wounded and suffering from the wholeness they have lost.

ஃ

I, too, forgot and lost touch with so much, but I had the good fortune to be in contact with a culture that held sympathy for the intuitive and mystical—my Greek family's. Not that Greek culture was perfect—far from it. And, like cats, the character and quality of individuals varied greatly. Yes, there were Angel Faces but there were also Jezebels, and their attractive and unattractive masculine equivalents. But there was something about most of them . . . something . . .

One day when we were junior-high age, I was sitting with my cousin Helen on the crowded floor at a great-aunt's small suburban house. It was a dismal, gray, rainy day, and the windows were shut, making the air stuffy with cooking smells and cigarette smoke. We were there to participate in a *makaria*, a memorial meal, following a funeral for someone I did not know.

From a phonograph player in the corner, the heart-piercing laments of *rebetika*—the bluesy Greek music from the tavernas of the poor and downtrodden, carried on a woman's throaty *mavri* (dark) voice—wound around jazzy, troubled, syncopated riffs of bouzouki and clarinet, cutting like dark lightning through the smoke and chatter. Although most of the older people sat on couches and chairs lining the walls, due to small space and too-great numbers a few more-mature individuals had crammed themselves into the crowd on the floor. Idly chatting and giggling with my cousin, I had not even noticed the thin, elderly man in a dark, shabby suit jacket sitting on the carpet just behind me.

Then, very slowly—but with an electric power that compelled me to turn my face toward him, like a sunflower toward the sun—he rose to his feet. The man raised his arms more slowly yet, with a concentrated masculine grace, until they were high above his head, hands cupped downward, and he looked like a short, light-boned heron ready to strike. He dropped his head upon his chest and then, with hooded, unseeing eyes, began to dance. With no more than a square foot of space beneath his feet—a large napkin would have covered the spot—he dropped to the ground— audibly slapping the carpet—then sprang up, half-turned, kicked one leg backward, and slapped the sole of his shoe in perfect syncopated time. Again he turned and again shot down to the floor to slap the ground. Throughout the long, anguished love-lament, he leapt and turned and dropped with the speed of a falcon plummeting on its prey. Sometimes, as he stood upright in moments of utter stillness, his arms would spread slowly like wings from his sides, his shoulders arch up, his hands—palms down—rise like seabirds riding an updraft, then swiftly retract and cup to his chest as he traveled deeper and deeper into himself.

Kéfi, the Greeks call it. The word can refer to high spirits but also, as here, a mingled joy and sorrow: a solo expression of an unbearable and beautiful passion and longing that consume one— balanced, lyrical, and intense, on the sharp interface of pain and ecstasy. As the last ringing notes of the bouzouki faded away, the old man twirled with the gravitas of a planet, and slowly lowered himself to the carpet again, settling with his arms around one knee, head bowed, in the spacious peace left in the wake of the emptying of his need.

The expression of and broad toleration for *kéfi* and its ilk were two of the many reasons I loved the Greeks and Greek culture. Despite my half-breed status and ignorance of the Hellenic language, I could not help being touched by the beauty that flowed from this unlikely treasure into my arid Anglo suburban life, like spring rain in the desert.

☙

All of us, having left the comforting, encompassing ocean of the womb, with its gentle rhythms and soft tides, in birth find ourselves in shock in a new world. Like Dante we could say, "Midway in the journey of our life, I came to myself in a dark wood, for the straight way was lost." (*Inferno*, Canto 1, lines 1–3) Although Dante was speaking of middle age, when we are born we do find ourselves midway in the journey between earth and heaven, and the straight way is lost indeed—the heavenly womb with all its harmony and our nearness to our former transcendent state are vanished. Instead we find ourselves in a world with edges, still faintly reflecting its transcendent source but full of cold, discomfort, strangeness, hard choices, and even danger. Like Dante, we need a guide or guides to help us. And who will our Virgil be? Everyone we encounter, truly, but most of all those closest to us, from whom we absorb our vital lessons every day.

Fairy tales also speak of this wilderness, the place the young prince or princess or foolish but warmhearted child enters to find their heart's treasure. They would surely perish if they did not encounter guiding forces there—a speaking fox, a bent-over old woman gathering sticks, a strange little man in a bright vest atop a mushroom cap. These guides help the inexperienced fashion a noble protection for their vulnerable, guileless hearts and show them the mysterious, hidden path to their own fulfillment. "Every man's life is a fairy tale written by God's fingers," wrote Hans Christian Andersen. And so it is. Let me introduce you to the guides who appeared to me in the conscious waking world as vital helpers in the dark wood of my own childhood.

The Golden Apple and the Noble King
I am here because of a song
A Greek raised in Constantinople/Istanbul early in the twentieth century, Yorgos Baltas, my grandfather, had to leave Anatolia in his late teens to avoid being drafted by the Turkish army. Despite his youth, he had already seen action against the Bulgarians in war and had even been shot as he galloped on horseback carrying messages between the defenders' camps. He was brave but had no wish to be forced by the Turkish government to fight against other Greeks. And so his parents sent him away, hoping he would be able to continue his education in a Greek university, out of the clutches of the Turks.

As a result, fresh from the teeming streets of the Byzantine capital, Yorgos (George) soon found himself residing on the large Greek island of Samos, a scant mile from the Turkish shore. Its beauty smote him like a physical force. Samos was a gloriously green island with fertile olive-tree-silvered meadows and steep wooded slopes alive with splashing streams, glistening waterfalls, and the fluting songs of nightingales. Pirates, of all unlikely influences, had greatly benefitted the local ecosystem. Their brutal, persistent raids had convinced the locals to abandon the island for almost a hundred years, taking their plant-devouring goats with them. Flora had grown back enthusiastically and lavishly during this hiatus, to the delight of returning settlers. The mountainsides rolling down to the sea were so beautiful that one area on the north shore was aptly christened "Paradise." An island made for romance.

One day, on the way to his studies in Vathi, Yorgos was strolling among the park's tall palms and trees, edged with pink and red rose bushes and the graceful curling leaves of acanthus, when he heard a beautiful voice singing. The voice stopped him in his tracks. An ineffable feeling overcame him, with a conviction that he must follow that voice. Leaving the park behind and walking a few blocks into town, he soon found the singer—a lovely young woman, sitting on her balcony, embroidering as she sang. He stood motionless, starstruck, beneath her. Feeling a stranger's attention, she raised her head. When their eyes met, each experienced a shock of inexplicable recognition and boundless love.

When Yorgos could collect himself to speak, he politely introduced himself to the blushing girl—whose name was Eleni Vourliotis—and requested an introduction to her parents. She invited him in and introduced him to her mother. Her father had gone to America in the hopes of sending money back to support his wife and five children, since he had been unable to keep his family from sinking into poverty in Greece. But some months had passed since they had last heard from him or received a remittance from him. They had no idea what had happened.

Yorgos became a daily visitor at the Vourliotis household and, after a short time elapsed, asked Eleni to marry him. She accepted with joy. Then he asked her mother's blessing, which was gratefully bestowed, and informed Mrs. Vourliotis of his intention to locate Eleni's father to ask his blessing also, for the sake of his beloved's honor. Eleni's mother was taken aback at this heroic gesture and insisted that Yorgos did not need to make such a journey. But he was adamant. His sense of chivalry demanded that he make the attempt.

His adventure was complicated by two things: first, the expense of the journey, and second, the inexplicable fact that no one knew where Eleni's father was or what had happened to him. The family feared the worst. They knew he had written to them from New York City, but they had no other contacts there.

But Yorgos remained determined, despite the discouraging odds, to try to locate this one unknown man, a needle in the immense haystack of New York City. He scraped together enough to pay for his ocean crossing and bid a poignant adieu to his fiancée and her mother.

Yorgos made the long, exhausting steerage trip in the crowded, windowless bowels of the huge ocean liner, uncomplaining and with some gaiety of heart in fellowship with a number of other poor Greeks who hoped to make their fortunes in the New World. Processed at Ellis Island, they soon found themselves in the gray, crowded streets, some still cobbled, of Prohibition-era New York. They possessed little to no English. However, one lad had a friend already living there and, after some struggle, they were able to make their way to his address in a rundown neighborhood. Soon seven or eight Greek youths were living in the one-bedroom apartment of their new friend, filling all the available floor space when they lay down to sleep at night. A roof over their heads was good. But they still needed to eat. That meant work, but how were they to find it without English at their command? Those were hungry days.

Every Sunday morning Yorgos slipped out of the smoky streets of New York to enter the soft incense clouds and haunting chanted prayers of *Orthros* (Matins) and divine liturgy at the local Greek Orthodox services. But after divine liturgy he attended Sunday Mass at a nearby Roman Catholic church. He did so due to a wish that, educated man that he was, he might not lose his Latin.

A family who often shared his pew had a son, a young man about Yorgos's age. Smiling, he and the youth eventually began greeting each other, and a warm feeling developed between them over a few weeks. One day after mass they tried to engage in conversation. But the young man knew only Italian and English, and Yorgos only Greek. Conversation was impossible. However, they ultimately stumbled upon how to communicate—each was fluent in Latin. So, after mass, they sat in the pew, exchanging tales about their lives in the classical "dead" language.

When Yorgos explained his destitute situation, the young man—Giovanni—cut him off to exclaim that he knew where Yorgos could find a job right away. He could work for Giovanni's uncle! But Giovanni would not give his friend any further details. Instead he wrote down an address and instructed the young Greek to report there later that night and knock upon the door.

When Yorgos returned to the shared apartment and told his friends what had befallen him, none of them believed that he could possibly have gotten a job. He insisted that his friend Giovanni would not trick him and, responding to their continued derision, challenged them to accompany him that night. So a ragtag band of semi-starved Greeks followed him to the obscure address and waited across the street to see what would unfold.

Yorgos straightened his shoulders, summoned his courage, and knocked on the dark door. As it opened, music, laughter, and cigarette smoke floated out. Giovanni stood there smiling at him and welcomed him in. Yorgos followed the young Italian downstairs into a large room full of people eating, drinking, and dancing. Giovanni's uncle owned a speakeasy! And Giovanni had arranged for Yorgos to begin work there as a waiter. Giovanni had to leave very soon but introduced the tall, strikingly handsome Greek to the waitresses before he left and asked them to help Yorgos in his work. A good thing as, with little English, it was not possible for him to write down the orders given to him at the various tables of merrymakers. He had to pretend to do so as one of the American waitresses, standing close by, wrote them down in English and slipped the receipts to Yorgos to hand to the bartender. Very late that night after the last glittering flappers had left, Yorgos emerged from the raucous speakeasy.

His determined friends were sitting glumly on stoops across the street, like a murder of morose crows. Laughing aloud, he flashed the doubters the dazzling smile that had already enchanted the speakeasy waitresses. "What? You did not believe? Here!" he cried as, with a flamboyant gesture, he emptied his pockets, casting the many coins of his tips down until gleaming money pooled on the pavement around him. Laughing, his head thrown back, he sauntered off as his disbelieving friends rushed across the street to scramble for the shining coins.

Yorgos continued working at the speakeasy, and his facility with the English language grew rapidly. With his movie-star looks and enchanting, warm manner he became a favorite of both staff and customers. Romantic lures were set for him, but he remained faithful to his beloved Eleni, who was waiting patiently on Samos.

Gradually his savings built up and, eventually, through other connections, he was able to take a well-paid job at a furrier's. As he lived with great thrift, this enabled him to accumulate further savings and also to send some funds to Eleni and her family. But, unfortunately, he could not send them any news about Mr. Vourliotis.

Throughout everything, Yorgos kept searching for Eleni's father. The person now residing at his old address had never heard of him. Searching the Greek community and asking the local priest and any Greek he came across about this Samioti man brought no sign of recognition. Yorgos began to think that perhaps the man had fallen ill somewhere there were no Greek-speakers and, as he was known to possess no English, could not make himself understood. Yorgos acquired a list of the hospitals in New York City and methodically, in his free hours, began combing them, particularly concentrating on the paupers' wards.

A couple of months passed with Yorgos dutifully visiting hospitals and checking one after another off his list. But he did not find the man among the suffering there. He kept praying and trying not to despair but was becoming discouraged. There were only a couple of hospitals, in more outflung locations of the city, left on his list.

Hat in hand, he approached the information desk at the next-to-last hospital and found a kind receptionist who checked her patient list for him. No, there was no one of that name. She was sorry. As Yorgos thanked her, his face sad, and began to turn away, she exclaimed, "Oh, wait a moment! I did hear one of the nurses say they had a foreign patient in one ward whom nobody could speak to because they could not understand his language. Would you perhaps like to see him, just in case?"

"Yes, yes, please!" exclaimed Yorgos, hope springing in his heart. The receptionist called someone else to watch the desk and led Yorgos through the hospital to a long paupers' ward. They traveled to a cot at its far end. A small-boned, white-haired man lay on his side there. Although he looked as if he were in some pain, he was awake and his eyes fixed on them with searching clarity as they stood before him.

"Sir, you have a visitor," said the receptionist and walked away, leaving the tall young man staring down at the sick man.

"Good morning, sir," said Yorgos in his most polite Greek. "I am sorry to see that you are sick. May God grant that you soon recover. I wonder if you happen to know a Mr. Vourliotis for whom I am searching?"

The sick man's face lit up with happiness. He raised himself on one elbow and unleashed a flood of Greek, overjoyed to hear his native language and to be understood at long last. And, yes, he was Mr. Vourliotis from Samos! He had fallen ill and passed out in this distant part of the city months ago. Kind strangers had brought him to the local hospital but no one could understand him. Even worse than the physical pain had been his fear for his family and its survival, and about their bewilderment and pain at not hearing from him. Yorgos reassured him about the family, told him of his love for Eleni and hers for him, and respectfully asked him to grant her hand in marriage. With amazed, joyful tears streaming from his eyes, her father granted his blessing with a full heart. Yorgos thanked him, and the two men embraced. Seeing that this excitement had weakened the sick man as he shakily lowered himself to his pillow, Yorgos reassured him that he was supporting the Vourliotis family now and would continue to do so. Was there anything he could bring Mr. Vourliotis or do for him?

"No," said Mr. Vourliotis through his tears. "You have been like an angel from heaven. I thank God that He has sent you, my son. I can die happy now, knowing that my family will be cared for and that my daughter has such a fine husband to help them all. I cannot thank you enough! May the Lord bless you!"

Yorgos promised to come again the next day and to speak with Mr. Vourliotis's doctors should he wish.

Yorgos returned the next day, bearing flowers and edible delicacies. The sick man smiled his gratitude but could not eat. Yorgos managed to speak to one of the doctors there, who was relieved to have a translator but sadly explained that Mr. Vourliotis was now beyond their help. And, on the third day of Yorgos's visits, Mr. Vourliotis quietly breathed his last, passing away peacefully with Yorgos holding his hand.

Yorgos's prayer had been answered. Had he left this hospital for the very last, their paths would never have crossed.

Yorgos arranged an Orthodox funeral for his father-in-law and wrote to Eleni and her mother to tell them that his quest had been successful but that their loved one had passed away in his presence. However, he told them, Mr. Vourliotis had given his wholehearted blessing to Yorgos's suit and, gratefully, with peace of mind, put his family under Yorgos's protection.

Yorgos soon saved enough to bring the whole family to America. Within a few months he was standing side by side with his beloved Eleni in a Greek Orthodox marriage service in New York City, the sweet fragrance of incense wreathing around them as they became man and wife.

Yorgos continued his work with the furriers, becoming active in the union and supporting Eleni and her family through the depths of the Depression. He brought Eleni's siblings over one by one. His older sister and her family emigrated to the Midwest on their own, and Yorgos brought his younger sister over from Turkey as well.

While they lived in Manhattan and the Bronx, Eleni bore Yorgos two daughters, Loukia and Maritsa. The elder, Loukia, born on the site where the United Nations now stands, was my mother.

Eventually the well-educated, polished young man and his good character came to the attention of prominent Greeks in the area, and Yorgos became president of the Greek Orthodox Church association at Zoodochos Pighi, Our Lady of the Life-Giving Spring church, and principal of the Greek American Institute, the first

Greek American school in New York and the second in the nation. The school spanned first through eighth grade, half the day taught in Greek and the other half in English. Given that all aspects of daily life were provided in the close-knit Greek community, my mother, though born in New York, said she did not begin to speak English until she started to attend this school at age six.

Eventually, in 1941, having saved a substantial amount of money, Yorgos moved his family away from the dirt and noise of the city to a tall white house just a block from the beach in Port Washington on Long Island Sound. He continued to work in the Manhattan furriers' district for a while but eventually moved on to other employment closer to their new home.

And here I also lived for the first two years of my life (and visited almost every weekend for years afterwards, as well as full weeks in the summertime), falling immediately in love with my beautiful Greek grandfather, my Pappou.

❧

As a child I used to love sitting alone at the big dark dining-room table with my tall, noble Pappou as he gracefully and carefully, peeled a large golden apple into one unbroken curling ribbon with a small silver knife. I admired my grandfather's long, beautiful fingers holding the apple gently, as if with a caress, unhurriedly turning and turning it, giving it and me his undivided attention in a most companionable silence. A glowing oval moonstone couched in a simple silver band adorned his smallest finger. That finger, as well as his other pinkie, sported an extra-long, finely shaped nail.

"Why do you have those long nails on your little fingers, Pappou?"

"Because, my Stephania, it shows that I am an educated man who does not work with my hands," he replied. This was a significant social indicator in the culture of his home city of Constantinople / Istanbul.

When Pappou had finished peeling the apple, he cut it into fine slices with the same easy grace, handing them to me one by one with the light of love sparkling in his large, dark almond eyes. Once he said, with a gentle sigh, "On the Other Side (Greece), if you put an apple on the table, it perfumes the whole room." But here we had to make do with the inferior fruit of Long Island, probably bred more for resistance to blemishing and cosmetic appeal than the robust, lyrical fragrance of its wilder nature. Yet Yorgos Markos Baltas treated even this more pallid representation of its race (as he did all people and creatures) with love, care, and respect.

For me, it might as well have been one of the Golden Apples of the Hesperides, exuding the happiness of an undying garden, as I felt the undying flow of his love for me like golden honey pouring into my soul, filling it with a deep peace and inexpressible sweetness. And I loved him as he loved me. We did not need to speak. Just to be together in quietness, with me sitting on his lap as we both drifted in dreamy thoughts, or standing in the garden while he laughingly taught me to drink nectar from a honeysuckle blossom, or wandering hand in hand down to the sea to watch the sun sink beneath the gleaming waves, our eyes lit with an inexpressible joy at the miracle of beauty everywhere and especially in the freely given love that we shared.

His love was an early experience of grace for me. I knew that I did not, could not, have earned this love and its enfolding peace. Yes, I was the oldest grandchild, the first to come forth from his beloved daughters, but this alone could not account for the lavish affection poured onto me. This love was from beyond, from a place we could not cause or control in any way. It was not from our own design but seemed in itself an outpouring of beauty and mercy from a luminous otherworldly fountain.

With each other, we breathed the fragrances of the Garden before the Fall. How many grandparents feel such astonishing, seamless love and sweetness with their grandchildren? As we age, our breath changes; unless we are pushing very hard against it, it becomes softer, more receptive, preparing us for the great letting-go in which there will be less of a striving and more of a giving over—a trusting of what we cannot already know, as we lighten the load we are carrying so that we can cross the river of our mortality in a delicate barque that will bear only our most essential weight and no more. Parents are striving and struggling; in the middle of their lives, they must express strong outward energies in order to survive and provide for their families—and are often also still battling to find out who they themselves are. They love their children, most of them, but the pushing rhythm of their lives does not allow them the deeper quiet of many grandparents' receptivity that attunes to and appreciates the pure crystal essences of their grandchildren. Like the unstruck strings of a sitar that respond with their own shimmering sound when the strings near them are struck, the unique character and purity of each grandchild awaken those same eager resonances in the heart of the grandparent.

Pappou was my hero, my gentle and strong king, and the Noah of our little ark of hope and generosity that extended shelter and laughing love to dozens of Greeks arriving bewildered and homeless in the New World. The Port Washington house on Long Island's north shore, ringed with rambling gardens, became their welcoming refuge.

The deepest security I craved I could find resting in Pappou's arms, because—a rare thing—Yorgos Markos Baltas knew who he was. He did not have to search to "find himself." Surrounded by the compensatory, neurotic materialism of 1950s suburban America where men strove to define themselves through their possessions or bank accounts or positions—or putting down women or anyone else in their way—I felt grief for the ghostly quality of their self-esteem. A child feels the pain underneath, the haunting, bedeviling fears, and learns to be cautious about trusting such essentially homeless wanderers, no matter how secure their outward deportment and circumstances may seem. Unless there is a deep awakening, they remain essentially ghost-ridden, with traces of the life-draining, gloomy atmosphere of the cemetery about them, like a psychic smell of formaldehyde. Having lost rites of passage and values rooted in the Really Real, they stumble through life, grasping at shadows, miserable but with a rigid bravado that damages both themselves and others.

Even my father, a good, gentle man, partook of this lostness and its attendant cynicism. When as a child I once asked him who were his heroes, one corner of his mouth twitched up in a sardonic smile and he emitted a short, un-funny laugh. After a pause, he offered flatly, "Dean Martin." I was dismayed. I had seen this boozing, slicked-hair singer lolling around the TV screen arm-in-arm with cookie-cutter scantily clad blondes, a vacuous, dissipated expression on his self-satisfied face, and had averted my eyes in disgust. I wandered off numbly, realizing that my father had just told me he had no heroes at all, and that an important life question only summoned up an unsatisfied envy of some of the worst qualities of the culture.

Shell-shocked from World War II, the spirits of so many men of that time were marooned in a horror they could not overcome and took desperate steps to forget. They could not find the guides they needed to make their way back to their own true natures and the Really Real, and so in many important and fundamental ways they could not be the guides we children needed and instinctively sought.

My Pappou, on the other hand, manifested an inner quiet and security rooted in the unconflicting qualities of his values, his enjoyments, and his soul—a deep alignment tangible in its beauty. I knew who his hero was without having to ask: Jesus Christ. Indeed, in his youth he had felt a yearning to become a priest. Pappou was a warm, manly man without ostentation—a comfort and a teaching to any child's wondering soul, its psychic fingers constantly palpating the unspoken core of complex adult behavior and social values, trying to find the places, if any, that were firm enough to stand in and grow.

و۔

The love I rejoiced in was also spread with a generous hand over friend and stranger alike. During summer late afternoons Pappou and I would often stand in the front garden by the gate of the white picket fence, waiting for a stranger to stroll by on the sidewalk. When this innocent individual appeared, he would be warmly greeted by my Pappou, his hand clasped in friendship. Not relinquishing the stranger's hand, Pappou would genially invite him in to dine with us. Startled, the passerby would object, but his attempts to refuse only brought out a still more golden, melting charm from my grandfather, the embracing warmth of his smile, and the glad light in his eyes. The stranger's resistance would begin to wear down until it seemed churlish to say no to this glowing man with his little granddaughter smiling up invitingly.

Soon the gaping guest was whisked through the gate and successive gardens to the back of the house. There he found himself in an Anatolian scene that might have been sourced from *The Arabian Nights*, and was seated in the backyard at a long damask-covered outdoor table beside a grapevine flourishing over a white trellis.

Smiling Greek women of assorted ages suddenly appeared, mysteriously propelled out of the trellis like Athena, fully formed, emerging miraculously from Zeus's forehead. The women greeted the astonished visitor warmly, presenting him with a royal feast that spilled down the long table as if overflowing from a mythic cornucopia: platters of lamb-stuffed grape leaves garlanded with lemon slices; feta cheese triangles in flaky, golden-brown dough; bowls of glistening dark olives; tiny spicy meatballs rich in cumin; mounds of fresh fish swathed in lemon juice and fragrant olive oil; big bowls of colorful salad with feta cheese cubes and tangy dressing; fire-grilled lamb souvlaki with tomatoes, green peppers, and onions, all bursting with flavor from an intense oregano-rich herbal marinade; pasta casseroles with ground beef in a velvety, rich cheese-and-tomato custard sauce; crusty roasted potatoes like little browned boats; and huge bowls of hot, pearly rice cooked mouthwateringly in chicken broth, lemon juice, and spices.

Grinning men also appeared from nowhere, bearing bottles of red and white wine, filling his glass while patting him fondly on the back and joking, as if he were a beloved returning relative.

Bouzouki music swirling from the house tingled in the warm air lit by slanting rays of the setting sun as all settled in to eat, laugh, and make the honored guest feel at home, embracing him as family.

Later, after tiny cups of strong Greek coffee had been drunk and delicious, honeyed baklava and fruit had been eaten, the first stars appeared and the guest was escorted back down the wisteria-roofed path, the warm cries of the family entreating him to come again whenever he liked, to come back soon. His arm gently laid across the guest's back, guiding him to the gate, my grandfather thanked him for coming to dinner and honoring his house and entreated him to not be shy about returning soon. "My house is your house," Yorgos would say, spreading his arms wide. In gentle delight, Pappou and I would watch the man stumble off (perhaps having imbibed just a bit too much wine) with a dazed, amazed, happy look on his face, having found himself so unexpectedly beloved, startlingly cherished—into the warm night, now dark and tumbling with stars.

I participated in this spontaneous act of hospitality with my Pappou many times. It was a delight and also funny to watch the reluctant bewilderment of the embraced guest change into pure wonder and at last into joy. You can fall into a happy fairy tale at any time, when least expected, the guest discovered. And I learned that sharing joy and everything good even with—and perhaps especially with—a stranger was one of the main reasons we were put on this marvelous spinning green earth.

His family's original name, Pappou told me, was Theodorou— "gift of God." But somewhere in the family line, he said, was a great-great-great-great ancestor who came to be called "Balta"—a variation on a Turkish word for "axe"—a commentary on his notably sharp tongue. And so the family name evolved into "Baltas." But Yorgos and Eleni remained "gifts of God" for countless people.

My grandparents' hospitality extended beyond dinner invitations to giving shelter to needy Greeks for weeks, months, sometimes years. My father used to say that when homeless Greek immigrants arrived on the docks in New York, they encountered a man there giving out handbills that read, "Come to Baltas's." They even gave Eleni's family's property on Samos to a poor family in great need. Their American house was not huge. To this day my cousin Helen and I, counting over and over the small number of available bedrooms in that house, cannot figure out how so many people at one time were sheltered within it—and without a sense of being cramped! It was like a magic purse in a fairy tale that miraculously expanded and contracted to comfortably encompass those who needed its protection. Helen and I remain happily bewildered to this day by its apparent ability to exceed the laws of physics!

Pappou adored his smiling wife, Eleni. I loved to see them dancing in a line dance in the living room with a dozen Greeks, Pappou leading, twirling a white handkerchief high as he made the occasional fancy squat or turn, kicking out his leg. There was often such enjoyment but I remember it particularly on New Year's Eve, when, after the dancing, we followed an old Hellenic tradition where we waited breathlessly in silence and stillness for midnight and, as the first chimes struck, we all began kissing and hugging each other to ensure a happy family life in the next year. It was believed that whatever one was doing as midnight struck, one would do much of in the coming year—hence it was important not to be caught up in argument or unhappiness or unkind feelings. To this day, I follow this custom, usually praying and singing hymns at my candlelit shrine as the midnight bells sing out, just as my husband and I did together for so many years.

Sadly, my grandmother died relatively young of a stroke. In many ways, Pappou never recovered. His eyes always filled with tears whenever her name was mentioned. He never remarried, though many widows indicated their interest to him on his numerous return trips to Greece. "There can be no one ever for me but your Yiayia," he would say sorrowfully.

Pappou loved his two beautiful daughters and the six grandchildren they gave him. He said, "When Maritsa comes into a room, the moon comes out. And when Loukia comes into a room, the sun comes out." And this did reflect their natures. Loukia was his favorite, more fiery and extroverted in temperament—and, like him, stubborn! Maritsa was gentler and less willful, her mother's favorite. Both girls were intelligent and lovely, their charms enhanced by the family's impish sense of humor.

But Yorgos and Loukia frequently went to war with each other. My mother felt that he was too highhanded, and he that she was insufficiently respectful. One excruciating year in my teens they got into a heated argument—who knows about what?—with the result that they did not talk to each other for a year, even though Pappou and my Uncle Demetrius came to our house almost every Sunday throughout this time (this was after my grandmother's passing). The upshot? I was brought into indentured servitude as the official message bearer. For example:

"Stephania, tell your mother that she should call Costas very soon."

"Stephani, tell your grandfather that dinner is ready and that he should come."

"Stephania, tell your mother that I have brought retsina for us."

"Stephani, tell your grandfather that I am not going to go there!"

"Stephania, tell your mother that she should be more respectful and obey her father!"

By the end of the year, I was ready to murder them both! And then they mysteriously made up about whatever absurdity had set them off, and it was as if the whole year of tense messaging had never occurred.

Loving the Greek Orthodox Church, Pappou was faithful in his attendance at the many long, beautiful services of Holy Week. Both his daughters had dropped away from the Church, which gave him great sorrow. I remember, as a young teenager, sitting with him in a pew on Holy Thursday evening, at a Matins service where the Lord's Passion was dramatically commemorated, him looking at me with tears in his eyes and shaking his head, saying, "The only one! The only one!" Loneliness was closing in on him from all sides.

He and Uncle Demetrius eventually moved into Aunt Maritsa's and Uncle Jack's home in wooded Northport, where they could spend time with her and my four younger cousins and conserve their funds and energy.

Living in Boston by this time as a young adult, I was seldom able to make trips down to Long Island but occasionally managed to come south to see them. Once, at the end of a weekend visit, I was about to leave. Pappou and I were standing in his doorway. We gave each other a big, heartfelt hug and, as we parted, he said with a look of shock and great sadness in his eyes, "I will never see you again!" I also felt a momentary shock. But, of course, in my young, ignorant way I tried to deny and minimize this notion. Waving and smiling, I left him standing there, heartbroken.

Indeed, I never saw him again. A few months later, Pappou went to the hospital for what my aunt said was a routine procedure on a minor problem with his leg. Somehow, complications arose, my aunt attributing them to medical error. Unexpectedly, my beautiful, glowing Pappou passed away. I sorrowed but somehow never understood its depth until one day, three years later, standing in the produce section of a supermarket, I found myself staring at heaps of glossy red grapes that I had been mysteriously unable to eat for all that time and remembered that they were Pappou's favorite grape. The grief quietly lodged in my throat had not allowed their passage. Like an ancient harper's lays playing incessantly below conscious hearing, such inarticulate markers held the memory of an inextinguishable grief for a noble, deeply beloved guide, true mentor in love, and graceful hero, gone forever out of this world.

True to his sixth sense, Pappou left the family icons to me, including the large one of the Virgin and Child painted in 1842 and set within a border of mother-of-pearl in a dark, glass-topped wooden box that had been charred by some ancient fire. This inheritance annoyed my mother, and she was even more resentful that he had left me a large reliquary cross, made of what was probably a silver alloy, large enough for a priest to wear, on its big chain. Both his daughters had fallen away from the Orthodox Church, and he knew that I too had left it. But apparently he also knew, in his visionary way, that I would return. Foreknowledge ran strongly in his side of the family—both his daughters had waves of it, his younger sister was rich with it, and it was also passed down to some of us grandchildren. His heart perhaps saw my return before my own heart reawakened. Well, he had always, from the very beginning, from the great fullness of his own, known the depths of my heart.

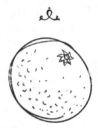

The Flying Orange and the Joyful Elf
What I remember best about my grandmother, my Yiayia, are her laughing brown eyes, sparkling with happy mischief. Kind, warm, and welcoming, she also could not resist teasing and joking. One day a pretentious guest, a bamboozling talker and flashy dresser, came down to breakfast after having used an inferior dye to transform his increasingly gray hair to what he regarded as a seductive black. Unfortunately, the treacherous dye had instead turned his hair a strange murky shade that would have suited a not-too-fastidious vampire, overlaid with the shimmering, startling sheen and colors of the aurora borealis. As all of us at the breakfast table gazed raptly, struck wordless, at this pre-punk purple and green apparition, Yiayia let out a great burbling laugh. "You look like a pheasant!" she cried. He did. And we all broke down. Even the pheasant, helplessly. We laughed until we cried.

Perhaps, given her whimsical temperament, it should not be a surprise that the child Eleni was thrown out of the nuns' school on Samos (where she studied Esperanto, among other esoterica) because one day she took it into her head, for unknown reasons, to climb a tree and happily pelt the nuns with oranges—a feat she still recounted with glee as a grandmother. She also quite ruined her white gloves in the exercise!

All four of the petite Vourliotis sisters married and established themselves in the New World—three in the U.S. (as well as the youngest sibling, a brother, Costas) and one in Mexico. They all had very different temperaments. My Yiayia, Eleni (Helen), was the oldest. Felice (Eftihía), the next, the family beauty with huge blue eyes, had a warm and pious disposition (when I was twelve, she gave me St. Augustine's autobiography, gently recommending that I read it). The next, lively Mary, managed to keep her own goat (Beulah!) in a little house in her Long Island suburban backyard. And then there was Sophia, the "mad" sister.

Whenever Sophie's name was mentioned, the family rolled their eyes. I didn't really understand why, even though one of my "toys" was a small, exceedingly heavy tomato-red safe, painted with flowers and leaves, that Sophie had sent as a wedding present to my parents from Mexico—C.O.D.! And without the combination!

However, when I was a young girl, Sophie did send me a pretty embroidered white Mexican blouse, a long colorful skirt with sequins, a fancy tortoiseshell hair comb that I could not keep in my shortish, fine straight hair, and even a pair of castanets. I was enchanted with this romantic costume. Thea Sophie also included a packet of red lollipops. I wanted to try them. My mother was dubious. "I don't know," she said. "They are from Sophie. It might not be a good idea." But insisting that lollipops are harmless, I convinced her to let me try one—and wound up dashing for the sink to get water after just a couple of licks. They were actually red-hot lollipops. As in chile peppers. And water, paradoxically, only intensified the heat! A localized forest fire, glued to my tongue with its hard-to-eradicate melted sweet paste, burned my tender pink skin to rose madder for a surprisingly long time. I grew a bit pensive contemplating the puzzling character of an adult who would knowingly send mouth-burning lollipops to a five-year-old.

♃

My Yiayia was attractive and chic. When she dressed up, every detail was attended to and in place—shoes, hat, gloves, jewelry, handbag, accessories. The only distressing note was a peculiar fox fur she sometimes wore, with the two grimacing heads and front legs of the unfortunate foxes sacrificed to fashion hanging down on one side of her torso, their limp back legs and tails on the other. This savage display, worn so carelessly and even proudly over her handsome tailored suits, shocked me. Whenever she wore it, I had to look away, feeling terrible pity for the foxes. Even as a child I reflected that, rather than the pert hat with a small net veil tipped becomingly on her head and the stylish, delicate heels gracing her tiny feet (size three and a half—she sometimes modeled shoes), a bone through my otherwise-kindly Yiayia's nose would be the only appropriate accessory for this bewildering ensemble. Although my family was not vegetarian, my brother and I had been raised from our earliest ages to be gentle and considerate with animals. My mother was extremely firm on this subject and felt that there was no age too young to learn to be kind to our fellow creatures; even at two years of age, I'm sure we never pulled a cat's tail! And our Yiayia was also fond of animals. However, those foxes looked distinctly displeased. How to understand how all these contradictory practices fit together? I did not have a clue. This was just one of the thousands of unexplained inconsistencies of grown-ups that one had to bewilderedly swim through, as if in a murky pond overgrown with algae and water weeds with visibility nearly nil, hoping that someday, somehow, the water would at last become clear.

I recently learned from my aunt that my grandmother Eleni also worked in the furriers' industry in Manhattan. During tumultuous years of strikes, this tiny woman, as a union member, sometimes walked the picket lines in her dainty high heels, holding the hand of little Maritsa trotting along beside her.

But as a child I knew only that she was my charming Yiayia, joyful and fun, always ready for us with a smile. She used to take my cousin Helen, my brother, and me down to the beach with our little metal buckets to go clamming. This was more an exercise in hilarity than foraging, as often when we bent over to dig for a clam with our small shovels, another clam, safe and unseen in its damp, sandy den, would impudently squirt us on our up-ended backsides, to our great, mirth.

Or my grandmother would go wading and swimming in the water with us, gleaming like a playful seal. Afterward, warm, sandy, and relaxed, we might all stroll, hand in hand, down the hot sidewalk to a little store that sold delicious sour-lemon Italian ices, and wander back to the big white house, joking, laughing, and bright-eyed.

I liked to watch my grandmother swiftly and precisely embroider whole pillow covers, the needle flashing in her hand, covering them in dazzling geometric designs of red and green or yellow and blue like cross-stitch Oriental carpets. Their surfaces looked perfect but Yiayia told me that she always, always, left the last stitch undone. This was important, she insisted, gently serious for once, because only God is perfect and we should remember that we are not. Thus, we thwart hubris, a deadly sin, by avoiding the illusion that our own works are perfect—the witness being the tangible humility of the unfinished stitch.

Once, when I was around eight years old, she made me a very lovely pinafore apron, too beautiful to use in the kitchen or elsewhere. The cotton fabric was a particularly fetching shade of lavender mauve, and Yiayia had carefully embroidered elegant sprays of lilac flowers and lithe green leaves here and there in unusual, evocative stitches. I never wore this apron but I liked to hold it in my hands and admire it, as if it were a soft, treasured letter I was perusing, feeling a deep love rising up from it like the numinous perfume of lilacs.

The perfume my grandmother herself liked best was a relic of the Victorian age, the powder-puff scent of hothouse Parma violets. She liked violet candies, too, and kept a little foil-wrapped roll of dark-purple square ones, along with small, opaque glass perfume bottles, on her bureau. These treasures I used to note, along with her beautiful scrolled silver brushes and combs—the secretly observed museum display of adulthood—as I glided by before dawn in my bathrobe, having tiptoed into my grandparents' bedroom and crept quietly past them.

I never woke them, only admired their sleeping peace—the tall, relaxed form of my grandfather, faintly snoring, and my grandmother's hair like a shining silver bobbed wave on a small white satin pillow, rolled and round. I enjoyed the gentle comfort of their presence, but my object was to reach the petite cast-iron balcony that extended from their bedroom. Being careful not to let the narrow door creak, I would step out and close it behind me delicately, hold the balcony railing, and breathe in the deliriously beautiful new morning, full of rapturous scent rising voluptuously up from dew-heavy roses and a fresh, salty sea breeze, and everything, everything reverberating with a thunderous praise of bird song. Their music came down over me like a silver shower of sound.

Shivering but happy, I awaited the completion of the matinal performance: the climax, the sky lightening from dark gray to insouciant robin's-egg blue and the gay yellow streaks spreading from the rising sun now leaping up magnificently over the shining waves that I could not see but could hear softly in the distance, like the contented, rhythmic thrumming purr of a gigantic, comforting cat. Folding all this enlivening beauty into my thrilled and grateful heart, feeling like one joyous and peaceful part of it all, I would tiptoe out again, cast a last loving look at the sleeping couple who appeared to be the innocent epicenter of all this magic, and wend my way into the promising, lovely day.

In her early sixties, my grandmother suffered a succession of strokes from which she never completely recovered and fell into a dark depression. Her own mother, lost in dementia and already in a nursing home, was not there to care for her as she had done throughout Eleni's life, happily shouldering all the cooking, cleaning, and domestic work. The tall white house with its lovely gardens was quickly sold, and Pappou and Uncle Demetrius moved with Eleni to a small wan house in another town, nearer us. The house repelled me. I could hardly believe that my beautiful grandparents had fallen so abruptly and tragically out of their lyrical lives, like Alice falling down the rabbit hole—and not into wonder but rather into this blank cottage cheese container of a house set in a tiny stubble of dry lawn. The house was so pale, so colorless, with no purpose beyond bleak containment. It possessed not a single distinguishing feature capable of creating enough interest to encourage the enclosed sick woman to try to hold onto life. It was as if some vicious person had come and ripped out all the red and green and blue and yellow stitches from Yiayia's pillows, tossed the lovely threads in the garbage, and left the aging, darkening sacks of the covers piled, dishonored, on a refuse heap.

My mother and I would frequently visit Yiayia in that bland box and try to bear her company, but she remained listless. I remember doing the dishes there one night when I was fifteen, singing "Samiotissa" ("The Girl from Samos") in an attempt to cheer her. Yiayia remained silent and brooding in her bedroom. She died that night in the dark and quiet, at only sixty-four.

Pappou and Uncle Demetrius being away on a trip, it was my poor mother who found her—still, cold, and white in the morning.

Within a month my mother tried to commit suicide, swallowing too many pills—I knew because, though revived, my mother did not know me when I came into her bedroom, despite my father's nervous lies that she was "just sick." An actor in her amateur theater troupe, with whom I believe my mother was having an affair (my parents' marriage had been on the rocks for some time), told me the truth. Grief, shock, serious financial worries, the many sorrows of her life, and now somehow, I felt, the peculiar, doom-like knowledge that there was no time left at all in which to ever become her mother's favorite daughter—a gnawing, perpetual, and impossible craving—had laid Loukia low. We all knew that in this life, to our impoverishment, none of us would ever hear Eleni's rippling, open-hearted laughter again.

The Swinging Brass Censer and the Dawn Priestess

Every morning in the cool, darkened house I crouched in my footsie pajamas on the narrow stairway, waiting.

Dawn was breaking over the chanting ocean a block away, but its wild sea scent did not penetrate the tall white sleeping house, all of its denizens still wrapped in dreams, sighing on soft pillows as, unwitting, they explored unknown lands, met strange beasts, encountered messengers—all soon to be forgotten. But two of us were awake, sharply awake. In unspoken agreement, we awoke to greet the holy sun in its new shining: me—small, huddled against the chill—and she—great, small in stature, unassuming yet a vessel of wisdom, dressed always in widow's black, her gray hair bound in a humble bun which, when untied in the privacy of her room, lapped against her ankles like a secret silver sea tide.

The first narrow beams of light pierced the small, high window at the top of the stairs. A crown-of-thorns plant filled its shelf space, twisting tortuously in overlapping spirals as if painted in a Celtic manuscript, its tiny flowers red as blood, its thorns dark and huge. The light beams lay on its stems like ribbons of pale gold silk and cascaded down to the floor in long, straight lines, as if shining through a cathedral window.

The silence was stirred by a soft, padding sound—the gentle flapping of my great-grandmother's house slippers as she rose and slowly paced down the dreaming hallway, accompanied by a light metallic music, slowly rising and subsiding, as if of distant miniature bells. I hugged myself tightly in anticipation. Yes, now the first dancing curls of frankincense, silver-blue in the early light, wreathed and climbed toward the scrolled plant, lit golden among drifting dust motes where the new light barred them in splendor. The ancient, spicy, sacred smoke filled not only my lungs but my being to the top with a physical touch of consecrating silence and a holy awareness and sobriety beyond my childhood age.

Solemnly, I waited as the shining brass censer full of smoldering red embers swung forward on gleaming chains into the light, heralding the small bent form of the Old Yiayia stepping onto the landing, wrinkled face and pale blue eyes intent and silent. As she carefully descended, I squeezed myself against the wall to leave room for her and her censer's passage. When she passed me, we nodded to each other. We never, ever spoke. Once she reached the bottom of the stairs, I followed her down at a respectful distance as she began to chant prayers in Greek in a cracked, tired voice, yet quietly vigorous with the certainty of blessing. We paced through every room, she censing in all directions, the prayers flowing from her fluent and heartfelt, as if from an undying spring, wreathing around us like the sacred smoke. Once every room and every icon had been blessed, the house thus purified and prepared for the new day, we bowed once to each other, and she and her censer slowly climbed the stair to the solitude of her small room.

I went to my room to change into play clothes and then, filled with the mysterious blessings of the high priestess of the dawn, the handmaiden of Jesus Christ, my hair brushing my face with a lingering memory of frankincense, I slipped out into the dew-fresh garden. Breathing deeply, every cell alive, of its rich incense of wild sea scent and velvet-deep rose fragrances, my heart high in hope, I entered the adventure of the blessed and waiting day, eager and newly purified, like a questing knight going forth arrayed in arms of holy perfume and light.

The Old Yiayia and I never spoke, except for the few basic phrases of my less-than-pidgin Greek. She had lived in America for forty-five years and never learned a word of English. Most of what she communicated to me I have no words for, and most of it she did not tell me in words. Kalliopeia cooked, cleaned, and sang (sometimes even bawdy Turkish songs, I was told), taking good care of her lively daughter Eleni, her lordly, leonine son-in-law, our family, and the throngs of Greeks, friends and strangers, who passed through the ever-hospitable household.

She had a reputation for incisive wit, which I could only appreciate when a kind adult translated for me. Once at dinner, when a mischievous guest, flashily dressed and unctuous, hair slicked and gleaming like a mallard's feathers, offered his opinions, she fixed him with a crisp, assessing eye and issued a dry comment in Greek which made all the guests roar. What was it? "She said, 'There are three bags of lies in this world—and you have two of them!'" When one day I asked her through my mother why she had blue eyes, since most Greeks I knew had brown, she laughed and answered, "I guess the Danes must have invaded!"

Every night, once the Old Yiayia and I had changed into our nightgowns, I would go to her small whitewashed room, climb onto her narrow high bed in an alcove by the window, and watch her brush out the torrents of her extraordinarily long hair with an old scrolled silver brush, as if she were an ancient Rapunzel. It looked like magic; I had no idea hair could grow so long—this enchanting mystery was always hidden within the day's mundane bun, so unnoticeable it seemed it must be concealed by a spell.

Then the Old Yiayia also climbed onto the bed and turned to point to the embroidered cross amidst flowers, her own handiwork, which hung in a frame above her pillow. "*Kaló*," she intoned. "*Kaló*," I agreed, nodding—which means both "good" and "beautiful." Having acknowledged our Savior's preciousness and worth in grateful joy, we then turned to the window to admire the Creator's glorious stars. We both sighed in deep appreciation. I don't remember ever again seeing so many vivid colors in the stars—green, blue, gold, red, white, rose, lavender. We pointed out particularly entrancing ones to each other in gentle eagerness, uttering "*Oraio!*" ("beautiful") and nodding each time in happy agreement, sitting silent together at the last, as if in unspoken prayer of thanksgiving at the wonders of the cosmos.

Thus the oldest one and the youngest one began and ended each day in quietness and wordless communion, celebrating and remembering the light. A sweet, dry kiss, a brief hug, and then I clambered down. "*Kalí níkta*," we wished each other. "A good and beautiful night." And then we parted on earth, taking that light and love onwards in our linked but separate ways into the paths of mystery and dreaming. And though she has gone on ahead into the light and life to come, her memory yet lingers as a strong incense of praise. *Oraio, oraio, oraio. Kaló.*

CHAPTER FOUR

Catechesis: The Apprenticeship in Knowledge

The Flowering Broken Branch and the Wizard

Demetrius Caradjas had been a schoolteacher from the precocious age of sixteen. This was an honored post in Greece, ranking with the local priest and village mayor, but, having come to the New World as a young, bright-eyed, voracious intellectual, Demetrius found himself emerging from the chrysalis of drastic cultural transition as a different creature: a bohemian professional photographer nesting in Greenwich Village, a card-carrying Communist (although he said he had never been a true believer but was merely swept away by the Zeitgeist of his artistic cronies), and a man deeply in love, living with a beautiful ballerina.

One day Demetrius returned from some errands to see a small crowd gathered in the street outside the building where he and the ballerina lived in a tiny apartment on the fourth floor. Trying to see what had drawn the crowd, he moved into it. It parted for him. Some neighbors who knew him turned toward him wordlessly with pale faces of dread. Reaching the center, he found his ballerina lying in a strange broken position on the road, her spirit already flown. She was subject to depression, and on this day the darkness had at last overwhelmed her. His dancer had thrown

46

herself from a fourth-floor window. Unbelieving, Demetrius knelt to caress her face, sobs racking his thin, shuddering body.

His life fell apart. But he did, after a period of numbness and withdrawal, begin to resume some of his contacts with the intellectual and spiritual life of the New York Greek community. In this fashion he met my Pappou, whom he respected as a cultured man and the superintendent of the Greek school, as well as president of the Greek Orthodox Church organization.

Yorgos Baltas, in turn, was deeply appreciative of Demetrius's vast erudition. Not only widely read, this omnivorous scholar also had a photographic memory and was able to offer a pertinent comment and helpful information on virtually any subject. Yorgos felt great compassion for his suffering young countryman. So, realizing that Demetrius was barely scraping by with his photography, Yorgos set out to find more lucrative employment for him. He succeeded in getting him an office-management and accounting position with the furriers' union. And the two young men, Yorgos and Demetrius, became fast friends.

Little did either know that Demetrius's boss, who presented an appearance of respectability, was a crook and an embezzler. Not only that, this man framed the innocent Demetrius with embezzling thousands of dollars in union funds. It was skillfully done, and the blameless intellectual, who would never have touched a penny not his own, went to trial and then to jail in the dank, overcrowded Manhattan prison, built on an unsuccessfully drained swamp, called all-too-appropriately The Tombs.

We can only imagine what this slender, fine-boned scholar must have endured in jail. He was no match for any prison bully. His expansive forehead dominated his delicate, high-cheekboned face with small, deeply set dark eyes that sparkled with intelligence. He looked exactly like an ascetic saint from a Greek Orthodox icon. Dress him in priestly robes and you had a mustached but beardless St. John Chrysostom, aside from wire-rim glasses on his narrow nose. But instead he who bore the name Caradjas of a princely Byzantine line was forced to wear rough prison garb and undergo daily humiliations.

As a child, although I loved "Uncle D's" company, I did find his overly ripe smell hard to take. When I asked my mother about this, she explained his sad prison history, saying that the convicts were forced to take ice-cold showers every morning, a particularly taxing part of his nightmare years. On his own again, Demetrius was disinclined to wash, telling her, sadly, "my own smell comforts me." When Demetrius's sentence finally ended, he left prison a shattered man.

Horrified at what had happened as the result of his trying to help Demetrius, Yorgos agreed with Eleni to offer Demetrius a permanent home with them. So Demetrius joined their household, finding lowly work as a cashier, "Jimmy," in a diner, since his prison record meant he could no longer teach. But Demetrius taught anyway, since it was the core of his nature—without pay, as he helped raise my mother, her sister, and at last me, my brother, and our cousins.

Already treated like a princess in my grandparents' magical household, I was thus further benefitted by having a "royal tutor," conversant in a wide range of subjects and, despite his harrowing life experiences, possessed of an unquenchable delight and enthusiasm for all knowledge. Uncle D, my own personal wizard, took me to museums and cultural events from my earliest days, unfurling richly worked banners of all colors of the human mind to my wondering eyes. My overworked parents (my father slaving endless hours as an aeronautical engineer, my mother hating her tedious job as an office manager for a soft-serve ice cream company) had no apparent cultural interests, aside from my mother's involvement in amateur theater, and I might have remained in the void of TV-show desolation and not much beyond that without his lively, cosmopolitan instruction.

Hopping on the Long Island Railroad, he and I were regular visitors to the wondrous Metropolitan Museum of Art and the Museum of Natural History in New York City. He would talk fluently and interestingly about all we observed, enjoying my naïve, childish comments on the artwork (for example, as we admired a Renaissance painting, I asked him, "Uncle D, why are those women wearing those big hats and necklaces but no other clothes at all?").

I remembered a cafeteria at the Metropolitan as a place of palatial elegance, centered on a huge rectangular pool of dark marble, edged by large pots of towering exotic plants, where we, mere commoners, were honored to be able to lunch. Returning as an adult, I was shocked to find that same pool magically shrunken to the size of a large living room rug and its lush jungle now reduced to handsome but mundane peace plants!

I adored the rainbow-colored, exuberantly unlikely looking preserved birds of paradise with their curling, fluting tails and showy, arching head feathers at the Museum of Natural History; the dramatic dioramas of saber-toothed tigers leaning threateningly over stony precipices; and the magnificent mineral and gem display of startling, varied, and perfectly geometric rock structures, not to mention the emeralds, sapphires, and diamonds seemingly lambent with their own mysterious light from the heart of the earth. In the gift shop, Uncle D bought me rock and mineral sets, and I treasured my charming samples of pyrite and beryl, onyx and malachite, pouring over them in curiosity and delight at home.

Uncle D also took me to the ballet and concerts. He felt that one was never too young to imbibe such richness. I remember sitting on a plush red theater seat, my short legs barely stretching over the cushion, to watching a Japanese Kabuki drama. Uncle D struggled to shorten a pair of earphones to fit me so that I could listen to an English narrator explain the dramatic events executed in mannered, angular gestures by fantastically robed actors, their faces painted white, red, and black—and even green, blue, and purple!—and their heads crowned with intricate headdresses and elaborate black topknots, or wide, wildly colored (blood-red, poison-green) hedge-like manes of hair. Plinking string instruments and small drums hiccupped busily beneath the actors' strange wailing / growling / speaking / chanting / singing. Like some fantastic drama for the entertainment of fabulously wealthy trolls! Although the play remained obscure, I loved it.

Uncle D's generous sharing of knowledge and artistic experience of all kinds continued well into my teens. I remember him dropping me off at a New York theater to watch the magnetic Richard Burton and lovely Julie Andrews star in the enchanting *Camelot*. I was thrilled, but sad that Uncle D had only been able to afford one ticket and missed the wonderful performance himself.

Knowledgeable in electronics, our Renaissance man also built me my own tall record player and painted it pink to match my room. He showered me with records of classical, Baroque (except Bach, whom, oddly, he did not care for: "It sounds like piano exercises to me!"), and early music, with some good Greek authentic folk music thrown in. So began my love affair with Medieval and Renaissance music, among many other enjoyments.

The only enthusiasms of his that I did not share were the music of Gustav Mahler, watching baseball games on TV, electronics, and the art of Cezanne, reproductions of which lined his tiny dungeon cell of a basement room with its one small window. I found the heavy brushstrokes and preponderance of gray among the slabs of color depressing and, in his tiny cave overly redolent of his personal marinating scent, they made me feel even further closed in.

However, I still gladly sat there for hours as, from his photographic memory, he recited *The Iliad* to me in the original Homeric Greek. It never occurred to him that this might be too much for a six-year-old, so it wasn't. The very sounds of this powerful ancient language were stirring, and his rhythmic declamation soothing. His omnivorous intellectual enjoyment was not snobbish, though. He also loaded me with science fiction and elegant mystery novels.

My cousin Helen told me of a sideline unknown to me: that Uncle D and the family happily made bootleg *ouzo*, the Greek hard liquor, in the labyrinthine bowels of the cellar.

Uncle D continued his photographic artwork, usually dramatic black-and-white shots of plants, cats, and children, especially me, developing them himself in a basement darkroom. As I got older, he would take me with him in winter, trudging through the snow, to the huge, steaming Brooklyn Botanic Garden tropical green-house. There I was transformed into our resident bearer, carrying our bunched-up coats, hats, scarves, and whatever else we had brought along while Uncle D arranged his cameras and lenses. Struggling to hold up our jackets with one small arm, I had to keep one hand always free to wipe the mist and drops running down his lenses with a handkerchief as he shot multiple photos of dramatic plants and rare blooms. Our perspiring bodies melted in the intense heat that kept this wonderland of greenery thriving amidst the snows of icy New York, but Demetrius Caradjas, epic explorer, was tireless and self-denying in the pursuit of rare beauty wherever he could find it.

A few times I was able to travel with him up to Brockton, Massachusetts, to see my beloved cousin Helen Gioulis and her family. Helen and I were less than two months apart in age and always craved each other's company. Clever and kind, Helen was serious and sensitive but also quick to laugh and, even at an early age, possessed of a sparkling dry wit. In the summers, Helen came with her great-aunt Eleni (my Pappou's youngest sister, who had adopted her mother), to spend weeks visiting at the Port Washington house, to my great joy. But otherwise we saw each other only on occasional special feast days, so these rare trips to Massachusetts were red-letter days for me.

Both of Helen's parents were Greek—Helen herself had been born in Greece—and I'm sure Uncle D must have greatly enjoyed conversing with her father, Vasilaki, a refined, gracious, and gentlemanly intellectual who ran his own pizza parlor, while his warm-hearted wife, Chryssoula, bustled about to make us all comfortable.

Once, Uncle D and I went off on our own to eastern Massachusetts. He showed me the classic New England patina-ed handsomeness of Marblehead, its pale Colonial-era buildings wrapping around an indigo harbor. We then went into Boston to the Museum of Fine Arts where we spent a rapt afternoon gazing at huge, dazzling

Oriental screens: black-brushed on cream paper, tall fairy-tale mountain humps drowned in mists and swirling rivers, and rioting dragons and tigers were painted in brisk, dancing strokes, almost leaping off the screen at us with fierce predatory elegance. In piquant contrast, we then bowed our heads together over the tiny animals and ornamental objects, carved in glossy wood and bone, of their charming netsuke collection.

My Aunt Maritsa has a favorite photo of mine of Uncle D. Well into middle age, standing in his perpetual loose, worn corduroy pants the color of dust, of earth, and one of his open, casual brown sweaters over a pale, experienced shirt with a fraying collar, he is caught in a trickle of a gentle, laughing smile. Next to him, standing about as tall as he, are his companions, sprays of Madonna lilies towering from the earth in their medieval splendor, rightful companions of the Holy Virgin and her angels, and the graceful stars of so many glorious Renaissance paintings.

But the lilies look happy in their partnership with this keen, rumpled man. One gets the impression that he and they are holding hands somehow, perhaps swinging them in the sun, like good friends. A love, a rightness, flows between them.

Demetrius Caradjas loved nothing so much as the natural world, especially its flowers. He grew a border of amazing gardens on the acre of land on which the Baltas house was set like a white moonstone bezel in a ring. Fragrance-drenched roses were everywhere—and nowhere more charming and magical than on the thick, intertwined branches of red and pink blooms that formed a Sleeping Beauty's cave-like roof over the big white metal sofa swing with its plump cushions on which Helen and I loved to rock and whisper and laugh secretly together, reclining like a pasha's daughters in a blossom-canopied royal garden. There were honeysuckles and clematis, tulips, crocuses, and jonquils, lordly delphiniums, cheeky snapdragons and daisies, silken poppies, sparky zinnias, aristocratic lilies, flowers for which I had no names, and, of course, the charming hoi polloi of plebeian dandelions and violets running amuck in the grass.

Trotting down a narrow, bumpy herringbone-brick path, huge moss-seamed clusters of lavender wisteria blooms from a trellised roof almost brushing our heads, Helen and I ran forward into the sub-gardens, past the curling grapevines lush on white latticework on the flagstone terrace near the red-brick grill, past the cherry trees among the vegetable beds and the wired enclosure for chickens and one large ill-tempered duck whose red carunculated beak always snapped too close to my small heels as he chased me out of his minute, rigidly ruled dukedom until, laughing, we reached the two guardian mulberry trees, one white-fruited and one red-, by the picket fence, where we threw ourselves, gasping, onto the grass and dyed our clothes and faces with their delicious juices.

There was also the sweet haven of a small greenhouse, its white paint chafed and streaked, its floor dirt, built by Uncle D. It poured out vibrant emerald life wherever your eyes turned: pastel and wine-colored sweetpeas sprawled across the floor and walls like an engulfing tide, and lavender, blue, crimson, and maroon pinwheels of passion flowers spun up to the hazy glass of the ceiling and intertwined with star-white jasmine blossoms breathing out fragrant breaths of pure heaven, which were trapped in the warm, sultry air of the greenhouse so that I felt as if I were breathing in a wizardly potion. On a waist-high shelf lining one wall, a whole triumphant tribe of miniature lemon and fig trees stood proudly in their pots, displaying a wealth of pale green or rich-brown figs and ridiculously large golden globes of lemons hanging from narrow but sinewy branches. Before the Jupiter-like explosion of enormous lemons there were waxy white blossoms, flooding the greenhouse with their intoxicating bridal scent, driving the avid sniffer to delirium when combined recklessly with the jasmine's bold perfume. I used to love to sitting alone on the dirt floor on hot summer days, dreaming and enjoying the companionable, happily drugged buzzing of meandering bees who couldn't believe their good fortune at having discovered this Oriental paradise in the midst of their more spartan temperate world. Even the dust motes floating lazily through the soft golden haze of sloping sunlight seemed a comforting cloud making gently visible the peace of this deeply restful place.

But the flowers Uncle D loved best and grew in abundance were chrysanthemums. Not just any chrysanthemums (though the usual ones appeared too) but enormous, elegant Japanese ones, the kind I would usually only see in photographs of stately ikebana arrangements. They had narrow, spiky or curving petals like fireworks in flower form and were of all colors, though mostly white or yellow. No visitor left the Baltas household in the growing season without being ambushed by Uncle D on the way to the car, his hands overflowing with heavy-headed roses, chrysanthemums, snapdragons, lilies, and whatever else was in bloom, his eyes bright with delight as he bequeathed his lavish bouquet on the departing guest, as if he or she were leaving on an ocean liner for a distant port and deserved the fanfare of a ceremonial farewell gift.

He must have grown camellias, too, or known where to locate them. When my grandmother died—my mother said she thought that Uncle D, a celibate man who needed women, had been in love with her—he gently placed a pink camellia blossom between her still, pale hands as she lay in her coffin, stepping away sorrowful and white-faced. Camellias were her favorite flowers.

His wizardry with plants he once demonstrated to me in a memorable way. I had a favorite spot in my family's backyard that I called the Wishing Rock. This isolated boulder, sparkling with mica romantically strewn over its pale gray granite-and-quartz body, must have been thrust into the outlier of our wooded hill by a backhoe when the foundation to my parents' home was dug. It was left beneath the gently spreading branches of our lone pink dogwood tree (my parents said they had arrived one day during construction to see strangers carting off topsoil and dogwood trees from their yard!). The Wishing Rock was my place of refuge when I needed to be alone. I would climb onto it bearing a book or other treasure (like the lovely silver flute in its blue-velvet case I could never learn to play), sit, or stretch out and think. The pink dogwood had lowered a blossom-bedecked branch close over me through which I peered, as if through an elegantly carved screen, at the swatches of blue sky peering back at me through their screen of lordly oak leaves high overhead.

One day, when I went out to play, I saw a small airplane flying low above the neighborhood, a strange dark spray raining down from it. It gave me a bad feeling somehow. I went in to tell my mother. She came out, looked up, and hustled me into the house. She forbade me to go out again that day, looking troubled, but explained nothing. The next morning, when I went out to play, I noticed odd little brown lumps scattered all over the ground and way up the hill beneath the tall trees. When I went to examine one lump, I was shocked to see that it was a dead sparrow. And, as I wandered from lump to lump, I discovered that they were all dead sparrows, scores of them. I felt as if I were walking in a waking nightmare in an ornithological Armageddon. In shock, I stumbled over to my comforting Wishing Rock. Bright on its gray surface, the pink-blossomed dogwood branch framing them, lay three pure-yellow dead goldfinches. Staggering as if with a spear in my heart, I scrambled back to the house, calling for my mother. She went outside and looked, returning with a sad expression, and told me that this slaughter was due to the DDT the plane had sprayed to kill insects. Apparently this poison had also killed almost everything else. She kept me in the house again that day. Later, my father went out with his heavy work gloves to fill a big bag with small dead birds.

Aghast as I was that grown-ups could perpetrate such a rain of death, it was quite awhile before I could bring myself to return to my dear Wishing Rock and comforting dogwood tree; the mind-photo of three rigid, cold little goldfinch bodies arrayed funereally on the sparkling mica always leapt up, causing a catch in my throat and a need to turn away. A short time after I finally did resume my companionship with the rock and tree, a particularly violent thunderstorm struck. To my distress, the next day I found the main bough of the dogwood, as thick as a man's wrist, broken off, with only some thin shreds of bark maintaining their connection with the mother tree. The nearness of the supporting Wishing Rock alone had kept the branch from breaking off altogether. I felt so sad, as if I were losing a dear friend. All treasured life now seemed so nakedly vulnerable to destruction at any time.

But, fortunately, Uncle D came visiting that day and examined the forlorn branch. "Don't be sad," he said, smiling gently, "we can fix this." This was a wizardly remark, indeed. It certainly looked impossible to me! But Uncle D fetched some scissors and a wide roll of shiny black tape. He delicately raised the branch until the ripped parts matched perfectly, again forming a whole. Then he had me hold the branch tightly in place and began to carefully wind the heavy black tape around it, evenly, over and over, beyond the full length of the damage. It seemed to me as if the tape— harsh-looking, ugly stuff—would not stick. But, sure enough, when Uncle D and I finally loosed the branch, it held together!

"Now we will just let it heal. It may take some time. And you must not bump it."

I couldn't believe that this makeshift effort could lead to the healing of my beloved tree but, over the course of two years, I watched the rough gray bark magically begin to creep like an extra-slow, grainy inchworm over the shiny black tape, farther and farther. Finally only one little strip of black showed and then, suddenly, nothing at all. The bark and bough looked completely whole. You would never know about the tight black sling inside it. The branch had a new skin, and I had a new marvel. Out of death and destruction, Uncle D had brought life and healing. Like the branch of his own life, shattered so cruelly and early in its flowering, he had yet been able to bring forth something of wholeness and loveliness, despite pain and despair. In him I saw the triumph of life in the recognition and rescue of beauty out of darkness.

And his wise treatment of the branch showed me that it is always too early to despair. So I am honored and grateful to call him, as I do and always will in my heart, the father of my mind.

The Piercing Spear and the Socratic Philosopher-Queen
There was also a mother of my mind, but she was neither Greek
nor of my household. Yet she had an unswerving respect for ancient
Greek culture. I met her as a senior in high school but I include
her here because a year with her yielded one of the most powerful encounters I would ever have as a youth in the unpredictable
adventures of the dark wood.

Helen Flavia Wyeth looked rather like George Washington and
had the same hairdo. She taught the Advanced Placement senior
English class at Huntington High School in a classroom draped
with black velvet, the better to display her striking collection of
reproduction ancient Greek sculpture. The dominant presence was
the Winged Victory (Nike), an imposing four-foot-tall headless
woman, looming forward over us, rushing urgently to triumph
with her wings outspread. Thin, sculpted windswept draperies
swirlingly revealed much of her semi-naked body on her pedestal
in a front corner by the prudishly silent blackboard. Statues, moon-
pale, stared at us with serious stony expressions from every direction. Even Miss Wyeth's innocuous wooden desk bore a snowy
bust of her beloved Hermes, wing-helmeted, waiting to spark us
forcibly into a life of swift intellect. One day an unfortunate janitor
accidentally knocked Hermes to the floor, fatally. Ms. Wyeth was
volubly indignant at this desecration, threatening the janitor's exile,
but I believe the man was able to retain his post.

Ms. Wyeth was not warm and fuzzy. Although she would
sometimes smile, she mostly did not and ruled us with a benign
austerity. This austerity was shaped by the fact that she almost
never made statements to us. Instead, she asked endless strands of
questions in a strict Socratic style, forcing us to answer and then to
find the reason behind that answer and then the reason behind that
answer and on and on, in a diminishing perspective disappearing
into an infinite horizon. She was an implacable taskmaster. We
were regularly required to rewrite our papers six or eight times or
more, seeing what we could improve each time. She was always
pushing us beyond what we believed to be our strength, a philosophical Marine sergeant determined to whip her wimpy recruits'
minds into intellects of steel, come hell or high water.

Every class began with her strolling the aisles, sternly holding a basket full of cartoons clipped from the *New Yorker*. We were each required to fish one out. Being the angular, whimsical, wordless cartoons of Saul Steinberg, fantasies of esoteric leaping lines and squiggles, these were hard to comprehend. Looking at her watch, Miss Wyeth, a field marshal issuing orders, would announce, "Five minutes to determine your interpretation! And then you must defend it!"

We all struggled to comprehend our enigmatic cartoons. In the blink of an eye, our brief analysis time was gone, and we each sat clammy-handed, hoping we would not be chosen. But every day, one at a time, two or three of us were called up front to stand before the class and explain and justify our interpretations of our selected cartoons. The class, in turn, was required to attack the interpretation in as many ways as possible and to offer alternate interpretations. You learned not be too thin-skinned about your precious ideas here, as the Socratic goddess urged the class, now steely-eyed Achillean warriors and Amazons, to spear your interpretation and lay it low in the dust. You also learned to think—a painful and wonderful thing—and to make a graceful recovery, even if the walls of your own personal Troy had been scaled and razed in the brutal intellectual attack. Perforce, you learned to think about issues from many different sides. We soon discovered that Miss Wyeth was stimulating us to develop effective intellectual muscles with which to engage in heavier struggles than the quixotic Steinberg cartoons.

She was striving to free us from the tyranny of a host of devils: easy assumptions; the blinding load of our parents' opinions and so-called "popular wisdom"; the spiky adolescent resistances and resentments with which we cosseted our personal menageries of immature, idiosyncratic views. Miss Wyeth was aided in this by our excellent world- and American-history teachers, who shook us down from common assumptions to the meaty pursuit of primary and secondary sources, teaching us the difference and how to read the significance of the sometimes misleading discrepancies between the two. Too often in our culture the pursuit of truth is given little attention in public education. As a result, many youths find themselves lost and disoriented. In reaction and desperation, they become cynical or wander into someone else's prison of an idea, fearfully signing on for life. But Miss Wyeth's radical method, inherited from Socrates, kept us awake and alive to possibilities. And this constant, deep-seated questioning did not make us cynical or distrustful—rather, it enflamed our ardor to pursue and know the greatest things, not shunning the necessary rigors and keeping an open mind for the dangers of our own fixed ideas and possible fallacies.

To this end of preparing us for mature intellectual engagement, Ms. Wyeth had us read and report on numerous "great books," many of them utopias. The one that stands out was Plato's *Republic*, which we applied ourselves to rigorously. A year-long project, which would represent a significant portion of our grade, was to write our own utopia—and, of course, be ready to defend it. This could be rendered in media other than the written word, such as painting or sculpture, but it would still have to be explained and defended in equal detail.

I struggled with this assignment for most of the year, trying out different societal systems and making up my own. But each of them seemed to possess irremediable flaws. Eventually I came to the conclusion that the problem lay not so much in the systems as in the variable natures of the individuals who made up these model societies. If the individuals were uncultivated, inadequately educated, had not been raised with a deep-rooted moral code, and had not learned how to think (not an obvious art!), then any political and societal system would run off the rails. For example, how could a populace resist the lies and blandishments of a demagogue who appealed to their unexamined, knee-jerk opinions and emotions in a persuasive, manipulative manner if it had not been taught the disciplines and arts of clear, detached thought processes and research? Or, when such deficiencies were compounded with the lack of a wise, considerate moral code, leading to poor evaluations and impulsive, short-term-gains conclusions that did harm to others and the world, how could a society survive? The pitfalls were enormous. Because I felt that no utopian society could stand without the wise, careful cultivation and education of each individual within it, in the end I gave up on creating a complete societal utopia and, to the best of my ability, wrote instead an elaborate utopian educational system focused on the enlightened and harmonious development of the individual.

Although the intense discipline of Miss Wyeth's English class could at times be harrowing, the light that was shed in some of the dark recesses of our minds and the excitement that such powerful engagement with great ideas and thought processes generated drove our "Peacock Class," as our teacher called it (I think supposedly reflecting our "cream-of-the-crop" student group), to vote to come in one night every week for an extra class! Though it was inconvenient and demanding, we felt the extra time was well used; we craved as much time as we could get with our Socrates before the short school year was over and we enjoyed the rousing, keen exchanges on weighty, meaningful matters with our classmates. I will always be grateful for the way Miss Wyeth awakened our sleeping minds.

What children drink in during early life is critically formative. We are all much more sensitive organisms than we usually acknowledge. And never more so than in childhood, when the doors of perception are open wide. What we give our children perceptually—what we share with them artistically, spiritually, emotionally, and intellectually—is at least as essential to their health and survival as food and drink. These inner nutrients—which can be powerfully good, powerfully bad, and everything in between—will help shape the trajectories of their lives and works.

There are many fathers and mothers of our minds. Some of them can be despots, wreaking harm. Some of those entered my life, too, as must happen to all of us. But how fortunate I feel, how blessed, to have sat at the knees of two greatly gifted teachers, true parents to be forever honored and remembered. As a child, from Uncle D I received a broad mountaintop view of a landscape full of rich culture, amazing colors, and fertile heterodox variety; he seeded my young life as if it were a garden to be filled with worthy delights. From Miss Wyeth, I received instruction in how to delve into the hidden mines of that same mountain, uncover with intellectual sweat its beautiful, sustaining gems, and learn to throw the detritus, no matter how treasured, away. I valued equally the wizard's magic wand/healed dogwood branch and the Philosopher Queen's keen-edged, revealing spear, with its surgical precision for cutting out the inessential and shallow, opinionated stances of immature minds, leading us to transforming depths of discovery that would forever shape our lives toward usefulness, clarity, and good.

CHAPTER FIVE

Katholikón*: *The Mystery Calls*

The One

The chapel was empty and quiet. I was waiting for my mother to return from some busy grown-ups' meeting after Divine Liturgy that Sunday. I was fiddling with a bow that held my shiny black dress shoes onto my short white socks, crook-legged on a pew, when I suddenly looked up—as if called—to focus on the poor, nearly naked figure hung on the big cross above the altar.

The altar was splendid enough for a king, all rich gold-and-white brocades and embroidered linens. Two tall, finely wrought angelic standards—gold-plated brass halos with a many-winged seraph centered in each—stood on long varnished wooden poles guarding the altar. The sanctuary itself was enclosed by the carved *iconostásis*, the icon screen, adorned with jewel-toned full-length portraits of great saints and holy feasts. The low, graceful gates of the Royal Doors in the center, bearing icons of the Virgin Mary and the Archangel Gabriel in mystical communion at the Annunciation, revealed the altar, crucified body, and Cross. Holy persons portrayed in vivid tableaus were frescoed on walls all around, and a contemplative and mighty Christ Pantocrator surrounded by angels and a circling cosmos looked down from the ceiling. Sparkling chandeliers hung above. Oriental patterned carpets spread below. A fragrance of precious incense and the honey of beeswax candles lingered. Everywhere you looked was sumptuous beauty.

How strange then was that poor, suffering, abandoned figure nailed to the Cross, his body red with wounds. He had nothing,

* Greek for a cathedral church.

only a bare loincloth, in the midst of an astonishing emperor's treasury of riches. I felt compassion for him and his hurt, his poverty. And then I felt something else. Suddenly I saw that all the glory surrounding him came swirling out of Himself alone. He was the cause and sustaining force of every magnificence around Him—and of more, of the whole world, of the sumptuous, burgeoning Creation. I could not tear my eyes away from Him and from the unseen but interiorly tangible generating force pouring out of Him, more powerful than the fiercest cyclone but, nonetheless, exquisitely refined and gentle, endlessly flowing. Wide-eyed, breathing it all in, wordlessly I perceived, with the open mind of a child, the mystical paradox between His utter powerlessness and immeasurable, all-things-generating power.

God and man, man and God. I felt both, keenly, sharply, but harmoniously. In the Eastern fashion, the face of Jesus, despite the torment of the Cross, was quiet and serene—the peace of the Godhead illuminating it. He was both dead and alive. He was both suffering mortal man and transcendent cosmos-generating God. And the glorious beauty of it would have stopped my breath, had I not somehow been breathing in a kind of harmonious kinship with the swirl of power cascading out of Him, bending to it, floating upon it as if on a strong tide. The moments when the veil was lifted were brief but I have remembered them all my life. Like most children, though, I never spoke of them. And there have been times in my life I have hidden them in a dark dusty closet in a far corner of my mind. But then, in those gleaming moments, as I sat transfixed on a hard, lonely pew, a precious and indelible gift of utter conviction and profound spiritual beauty was given. It remained waiting for me in my soul until I could bear it again.

"Thou wast transfigured on the mountain, O Christ our God. Thou didst show Thy glory to Thy disciples as far as they could bear it," begins the main hymn for the Feast of the Transfiguration commemorating when Jesus Christ, still in the body, appeared on Mount Tabor in transcendent light, accompanied by the Prophets Moses and Elijah, showing His dual nature, God and man. Overwhelmed, the Apostles Peter, James, and John fell to the earth in ecstasy (Matt. 17:1–8). They were in communion with and overpowered by His Presence.

It is no small thing to draw near the Presence of the living God. At times when we feel a certain personal distance from God, it can be easy to blame Him, interpreting our lack of conscious intimate contact as somehow His fault or even as proof of His nonexistence. Sometimes this unproven conviction carries to irrational extremes, as in the case of a then-atheist friend of mine who one day exclaimed in irritation, "I am just so *angry* at God for not existing!" Gently drawing her attention to what she had said, I watched her get quiet and at last say softly, "Oh." It was a rational epiphany. But the way she ultimately, after many years of disbelief, came to believe in God was from a day she went swimming with manatees. Those big gray gentle creatures somehow, in an inexplicable manner, tenderly bumped her into belief. Their soft touches transcended the harsh lines her burdened heart and storming intellect had drawn around the subject of God. I often say that God is the elephant in the room. But He / She is also in all things. In this case, God was in the manatee in the bay.

Children have not yet made up their minds about what is possible and thus can be innocently receptive to divine Power. "To receive the kingdom of heaven you must become as a little child." The insight I was vouchsafed that day was not a result of my being a particularly virtuous child. Hardly! It happened through ever-inexplicable grace shining through a spiritually evocative environment, a kind of three-dimensional primer of holiness. And, yes, also because there was still some space in me not already filled up with a bustling herd of fiercely tended sacred cows, chewing a tough cud of obstinate reworked opinions regarding Reality and lowering their horns threateningly at the hint of any new idea.

☙

Deprivation

A few years later, proud of my green Girl Scout uniform and sash of colorful badges, I went with my white-gloved troop to attend a Protestant Sunday morning church service. I don't remember why. Perhaps as part of a project for some badge? I had only been in Orthodox churches and was shocked by the plainness and austerity of the interior of the tall, white-steepled church. The walls were stark as snow, fresco-free, and only a small simple wooden cross stood before us, marooned on a plain wooden altar.

The worship service consisted mainly of grown-ups talking and occasionally standing up from the creaking pews to sing monotonous (to my ears, used to the soaring, lyrical flourishes of Byzantine chant) hymns of repetitive simplicity. Even though I was accustomed to a morning hour and a half of Sunday School (held during *Orthros*—Matins, before Divine Liturgy, the Eucharistic mass), always something of an endurance challenge as, to prepare for Holy Communion, we neither ate nor drank (even water) before or during these services—I had trouble staying awake and undistracted, despite the Protestant service being so much shorter. I was glad it was short, thinking with sorrowful pity of the children in that congregation. They had nothing beautiful to look at or hear or smell or touch or taste. What deprivation! I felt like a North American tourist in culture shock encountering rampant poverty in my first developing country, a reaction that I'm sure would have shocked the prosperous, confident, lily-white members of that congregation. Although there must have been people of piety and devotion in that group, all the real action seemed to me to pass from "head to head, mind to mind"—long, lonely strings of words hanging in the air unsupported, untinged by the heart's luminous, passionate pieties. Like an orchestra playing a whole symphony but with only one class of instruments—say, woodwinds—engaged. Bereft of the richness of the whole, there seemed to be enormous holes, blanks, absences.

Although there is an ancient and honored tradition of starving the senses in order to concentrate the powers of the mind—ideally the mind of the heart, the *nous*—to bring forth an awareness of Presence from at least the earliest Orthodox Christian ascetic practices to modern day Quaker custom (and which is found in many other religious traditions as well), this is not the only effective approach to enhancing our personal encounter with God so that we experience greater intimacy with His Presence. Regardless of its inherent value, perhaps this spiritual approach seems so attractive and right to many contemporary seekers because most of us in the West are deeply dyed with the values and perceptions of secular humanism, whether we wish to be or not. Minimalism in worship and practice may seem more reasonable to us, to the semi-hidden, flint-eyed materialist within us who may fear expressiveness and artistic enhancement in worship.

Christopher Hill, understanding our need for a deeper relationship with the tangible Presence of God, writes, "The Church is the great repository of mystery, but for the last century or so, the face of the mainstream churches has been pretty much the rational, main-street, daylight face of God—theology, ethics, charity, and social outreach. Paul would have called it 'law and works.' The sixties awakened a thirst for the face of God that the churches had long ceded to the arts, folklore, and popular culture—the night side of God. When we are cut off from the moon, the night, and the waters of mystery, the spiritual world is blinding and blisteringly arid. Mystery refreshes us. Mystery is a cool dark underground stream, a tributary of living water that bubbled up into the well in a dusty Middle Eastern village where Jesus stopped at midday and spoke to a Samaritan woman. When our roots are sunk in mystery, we flourish like trees planted by a stream."

لـه

The Forest of Candles

We knew not whether we were in heaven or on earth, for surely there
is no such splendor or beauty anywhere upon earth. We cannot describe
it to you. Only we know that God dwells there among men, and that
their service surpasses the worship of all other places. We cannot forget
that beauty.

I cannot forget that beauty either (though for many years I
stored that singing memory away in a distant, soundproof closet
in my mind).

Quoted above are the famous words addressed to the Russian
pagan emperor Vladimir from emissaries he sent out in the
tenth century to examine the religions of Europe—Judaism,
Islam, Roman Catholicism, and Greek Orthodox Christianity—
to help him choose a religion under which to unite his people.
Overwhelmed by the stupendous beauty, splendor, and mystical
Presence they experienced while attending the magnificent Divine
Liturgy in the great Hagia Sophia cathedral in Constantinople,
these nobles recommended Greek Orthodox Christianity to their
emperor. Vladimir agreed and, in 988, he and his people were
baptized. Those men who had attended the Hagia Sophia service
had been lifted out of themselves by worship and surroundings
designed as an antidote to our mundane earthbound sense of limitation and possibility, to enable us by evocative inspiration to lower
the interior walls between us and divinity. Their blessing was that
at times they did not know where they were, only that their souls
might, indeed, be tasting heaven.

I remember being held in the arms of an adult as a small child,
in church in the middle of the night, while all around me a forest
of big, golden candles was rising and falling, rising and falling, all
at slightly different rhythms, slightly different paces, in dozens of
hands—old hands, young hands—a sea of light, a forest of light,
bending and shining in the wind of the Spirit, illuminating the
faces of their holders, and making them beautiful with an incandescent Paschal joy. Some were making the sign of the Cross in
light and fire; others were raising their candles up and down, up
and down, signifying our Beloved's miraculous resurrection from
the dead. All were singing with an outpouring of joy, a blessed and indescribable relief, the ancient hymn I learned in Greek
even before I learned "Row, Row, Row Your Boat" in English:
"*Christos Anesti.*" "*Christos anesti eknekron, thanato, thanaton, pateesas*
ke tees entees mni masee zoeen, haris amenos"—"Christ is risen from

the dead, trampling down death by death, and upon those in the tombs bestowing life." The rhythms of the flowing light and the heartfelt singing, the dance of the blessing hands, blended into a mysterious ocean in which I floated, as happy and natural as a fish in its true home. The evocative, inspired services and our yearning faith newly gave us gills with which to breathe in the formerly unattainable depths of the sea of this overpowering mystery. And our waving candles were the signs of celestial fire with us and within us, and of our great hope, pouring out of a chalice of love and happiness, as we celebrated our Beloved's Resurrection from the dead in the transformed church—and our own promised resurrection to come.

⚓

When I was a young reporter, I was assigned to cover a local museum's exhibit of the work of Ruth Vollmer, a seventy-one-year-old German woman artist. Her unusual and striking work included drawings but was mainly sculptural, concentrating on pure geometric forms of all kinds. These were rendered in various metals, woods, and ceramics and ranged in size from very small to very large. I went from case to case, stand to stand, making notes and enjoying the sense of being suddenly adrift among an airy world of ideas, of manifesting Platonic archetypes. But I kept being drawn back to a huge silver sphere, perhaps five feet in diameter, in the center of the gallery. This magical moonlike globe had such an inexplicable magnetic attraction that I could not stay away from it. The gray-haired artist had been observing us viewers ambling around her work and, after watching me head back for at least the fourth time to the enchanting sphere, she came and stood beside me.

"Do you know," she asked, her keen pale blue eyes penetrating, "why you are so attracted to this sphere?"

"No, I don't—although it is very beautiful."

"I will tell you. I always work with a team of mathematicians and technicians to create my sculptures. Sometimes it takes us many months of calculations and technical adjustments to express my intent. On earth it is not possible to find a perfect sphere. There will always be some irregularity in its form. My engineers and I set out to make as perfect a sphere as it is possible to make on earth. It took us many months of calculating and casting. But we very nearly achieved our goal. This is the most perfect sphere you will ever see in your life, even though it is not absolutely perfect. But it looks strikingly perfect, different from all the other spheres you have ever seen, and the harmony of the pure form is irresistible to you."

She was right. I felt like a fish unthinkingly drawn up through the waters toward the quiet glory of the full moon. There was something unearthly about it, tugging subtly but persistently at my heart like a buried memory, both unfamiliar and yet deeply loved in some quiet, unfathomed place in my soul. I could almost—but not quite—hear its music. How amazed I was to feel so much so powerfully from what was, after all, "just" a geometric shape!

The unseen world of vivid, living spiritual life, with its great beauties and powers in constant movement around us, has just such a potent, entrancing inner tide operating within us. We feel its luminous magnetism tantalizingly near us. But we are often blind to it in our souls, though we need not be. There are an infinite number of roads to approaching its heart-filling radiance. One way is through the divine "poem of the soul" of inspired services with all their layers of beauty for the heart, for the mind, for the body, entrancing and speaking to us on all the levels of our being. Their resonance, both subtle and magnificent, sweeps away our tiresome, mundane thoughts and our endlessly circling self-preoccupations, making room for what really matters and what we cannot circum-scribe: the Divine Presence.

Rather than clinging feverishly to our intellectual ideas about God (which we can misconstrue as faith, though true faith is a much deeper, transformative, and less rational quality) and to our sentimental preoccupation with ourselves that sets up a series of interior roadblocks toward genuine encounters with God, we need to make space for newness, for the glory that wishes to make itself known to us in freshness and in truth. As the wise twelfth-century Sufi poet Farid Ud-din Attar wrote, "*You must know God by Himself and not by you; it is He who opens the way that leads to Him, not human wisdom* (italics mine)."

There is a bare manger bed within us waiting to be filled with the presence of the radiant Christ Child, glorious in both His human and divine attributes. But often this poor manger bed, meant to stay empty until the true moment of birth arrives—a moment of God's choosing, with our cooperation—is already full of an absurd clutter of ideas, emotions, half-digested books, mar-inating resentments and disappointments, vainglorious thoughts, emotions of self-hatred and self-rejection, shallow and pietistic ideas, and half-baked theories. The quiet elegance of the simple, bare, and receptive manger bed has become a city garbage dump. Small wonder that we keep asking ourselves, "Where is God?" We ourselves have blocked His way! As so many these days recommend, we may, with efforts of mindfulness, be able, especially with help, to begin to identify and eliminate some of this ungodly trash and to make space for a new and tangible spiritual birth. Although this is a valuable approach, it is not the only effective one. In an issue of the magazine *Ruminate*, the eloquent pastor and poet Jeff Reed contributed a few astonishing, counterintuitive words about efficacious "clearing out":

> *I am amazed how sticky and resilient disturbing mental images can be clinging to the rusted metal hangers in the deep and busy closet of my middle-aged mind. Clearing out these unwanted spoilers is not nearly as easy as cleaning out the junk in my real-life closets and actually requires an opposite strategy.*
>
> *Instead of the clumsy and tedious attempt to rid these poisonous memories by extraction, it seems better to pursue a course of extinction by stuffing my mind-closet with more stuff—really good, rich, noble, elegant, pure stuff—cram it so full of fresh air and bright colors that the moldy images begin to suffocate and implode for lack of breathing room and attention.*

Eastern Orthodox Christian services, biblically based and generated also from ancient Jewish practices, adorned with the enlightened prayers of a host of saints attuned to the Really Real throughout the ages, full of angelic music transcribed by receptive singers and composers for two thousand years, glorified in art and visual detail springing from acute mystical perception, and revolving around the infinite well—full of life-giving water—of the Holy Mysteries (the Sacraments), have the capacity to fill both our senses and our spirit to an overflowing reception of and participation in—even a healing merging with—the Divine Presence, through grace and our capacity at that given time "We knew not whether we were in heaven or on earth. . . . Only we know that God dwells there among men. . . . We cannot forget that beauty."

ԟ

The Dance of Isaiah
Peeping out from behind the knees of an accompanying grown-up in the packed chapel, I leaned into the church aisle and glimpsed the two young adults standing up front, facing the priest and the altar. I could only see their backs. The woman wore a long gown, gleaming satin-white. The tall man beside her wore a dark suit. They were both adorned with white crowns of flowers. *They are wearing my name!* I thought. For I knew that *stéphana* meant the

white-flowered wedding crowns of fragrant, tubular stephanotis blossoms. But what struck me most deeply, in a flash of insight, was that both crowns were linked by a long, snowy satin ribbon hanging in a graceful loop between them. There was no knot in the ribbon except where it attached to each crown. It was one and seamless! *Oh, so that's what it's about!* Any verbal explanation of marriage would have seemed galumphing to my child mind beside this clear, transcendent image of the meaning of the action that these two young people, under the guiding hand of the priest, attended by their witnesses, were about to take.

Fascinated and quiet, I watched the priest and the *koumbáros*, the best man, exchange the crowns several times on the heads of the bride and groom, and then, the priest holding the Gospel book, followed by the linked newlyweds and their two witnesses, all holding white lit candles, began to tread the slow, graceful Dance of Isaiah. As cantors sang a haunting melody, they passed three times around the small table that had held the Gospel book, the crowns and candles, and a cup of sweet wine from which the bride and groom had just sipped to confirm the shared sweetness of their love and the beginning of their life together. Since the singing was in Greek, it was only years later that I learned the words that undergirded the holy dance in this great sacrament:

(First circling:) *Rejoice* (Dance), *O Isaiah, a Virgin is with child, and shall call His name Emmanuel, both God and man. And Orient is His name, Whom magnifying, we call the Virgin blessed.*

(Second circling:) *O holy martyrs, who fought the good fight and have received your crowns, entreat ye the Lord that He will have mercy on our souls.*

(Last circling:) *Glory to Thee, O Christ God, the Apostles' boast, the Martyrs' joy, whose preaching was the Consubstantial Trinity.*

Years later, when I learned the meaning of the Greek words of this hymn, I was at first surprised. Thrust into such an intimate service, the words themselves sound like cold theology—but, as I soon discovered, only to the uninitiated ear. The couple is not being bypassed or ignored in the interests of proclaiming points of doctrine. Rather, they are being honored and included in all this exalted holiness as real and effective participants in it. When the priest first puts the crowns on their heads, he exclaims, "Oh Lord our God, crown them in glory and honor!"

By here taking on martyric crowns ("martyr" means "witness"), the man and woman are witnessing to their love for one another and commitment to bearing their mutual sufferings and joys in life in oneness with Jesus Christ. Jesus Himself leads their sacred dance of commitment; He is symbolized by the Gospel book carried by the priest as they go round and round in a circle-dance of eternity.

The very same hymns also accompany ordinations. The two people are appointed to a royal place and a specific, greatly blessed calling. They are taking a deeper step into holiness in a mystery that will change them, as every mystery does. But, as in everything in Orthodox Christianity, the mystery is expressed not in words alone but magnified through physical symbols that reach and eloquently teach the soul.

Despite popular misconceptions, the traditional Christian Church does not despise the body and the material world as lower than the soul and unworthy of honor. Relegating the material to the category of "bad" and viewing soul/nonmaterial as the only "good" is actually an ancient heresy. Not only, as we see in Genesis, did God declare all He had made "good", but the incarnation of Jesus Christ in the flesh thoroughly resanctified the material world and blessed it.

This is one of the main reasons such bitter internal wars were fought in the Christian East over the existence of sacred icons. Influenced by both Jewish and Muslim orientations that forbade representations of people and especially of the Godhead in any form, certain Orthodox Christians pursued their own strain of fundamentalism, calling for the destruction of icons.

The iconophiles, friends of the icons, who ultimately won out, asserted that it was essential to show icons representing the Lord and other holy figures, for not to do so would be to deny His incarnation, since He was not only truly God but also truly man. I was taught the truth of this ineffably when, staring at His icon on the crucifix as a small child, I had the experience that begins this chapter. Had the iconoclasts, the destroyers of the icons, won and forbade physical representation, the opportunity for that revelation—that powerful and drastic insight—to leap out at me from His icon would not have existed.

♫

The Tomb of Flowers

One Holy Friday afternoon as a small child, I remember entering the church nave with my mother. For some reason we had come early, before the evening service had begun.

My mother opened the large chapel doors, and I stared into the big empty nave. The heat and lights not yet turned on, it was filled with the damp coolness of early spring. My eyes traveled down the long central aisle until, before the sanctuary, they met a marvel! It seemed like something too rich and fanciful for our world, like an exquisite emanation of the kind only ever encountered in fairy tales. Its fragrance filled my senses, a tidal wave of scent rolling over me like a physical shock, even before the sight fully registered. Full-bodied roses, white and pink Oriental lilies, spicy carnations, graceful freesias, voluptuous gardenias—hundreds of fresh flowers—embedded in delicate ferns and winding greens completely covered what looked like a small, high canopy-bed frame with a domed top. The "bed surface" was empty, but later that day it would contain the Epitáphios, a beautiful embroidered fabric icon of our dead Lord, His head in his grieving mother's lap, surrounded by weeping disciples and sorrowing angels. This was the Lord's Tomb, the holy place of the most terrible, despairing grief but also of the most radiant, redeeming joy.

I felt stunned by the beauty of the offering. Grown-ups must have spent hours and hours lovingly adorning the Tomb with this beautiful waterfall of living flowers, inserting each one patiently by hand. They must have gone to great expense and effort to create such a magnificent yet ephemeral tribute to His preciousness and sacrifice. *How they must love Him!* I thought in amazement. So much work and outlay for something that would exist for one day and never be seen again. I felt as if I were catching a glimpse of a beautiful secret, a brief sighting of a veiled, pure, and reverent chamber deep within the adults' hearts.

That evening, we would follow the lovely Tomb, now bearing the cloth icon of our sacrificed Lord in its simple interior, borne by strong men, and the priest, altar servers, choir members, and fellow parishioners out into the night as mourners circling round the church in sacred procession while the cantors and choir sang a heart-piercing funeral dirge. Before we re-entered the church we would pass underneath the Tomb itself, held high by the strong young men, to receive the blessing of the downward emanation of its holiness.

One day, at my current church, the weather outside was so stormy that the funeral procession on Holy Friday took place inside instead. As I passed under the Tomb and reached over my head for the customary touch of the blessed wood, I paused for a moment, something I normally did not do as, when coming in from outside, I am usually preoccupied with negotiating the stairs, keeping my candle lit, and not getting in anyone's way. During the unaccustomed luxury of a brief two-second pause beneath the Tomb, I felt as if a bolt of lightning passed down my arm with that brief touch, and then I moved on, electric with blessing.

A few years ago, Pat Pasternak, a Roman Catholic friend of mine, visiting the island of Patmos on a Greek-island cruise, found herself in the ancient Cave of the Apocalypse, now a small Orthodox church, where St. John the Theologian and Evangelist received the Book of Revelation in his exile.

Tradition teaches that the low cave roof, strangely split in three, divided in the Apocalyptic moment when the voice of Jesus Christ, as the blazing Ancient of Days, sounded in St. John's ears. Pat, passing beneath, impulsively reached up to touch the crack in the roof and was shocked by the lightning energy that poured down her arm. Her husband spontaneously did likewise and also received a startling, fiery rush of power and blessing flowing down his hand and arm.

It is easy, in our secular modern world, in our lonely unrooted life of the intellect, to disdain touch as something lesser, insignificant. But the Bible itself contradicts this view:

> *A woman having an issue of blood twelve years, which had spent of her living upon physicians, neither could be healed of any, came behind him, and touched the border of his garment: and immediately her issue of blood stanched. And Jesus said, Who touched me? Somebody has touched me: for I perceive that virtue has gone out of me.* (Luke 8:43–45, 46)

And let us note that the woman touched only the border of His garment, not Him Himself; the very fabric had effectively absorbed power.

Objects can absorb and communicate this live wire of holy transmission, as we see also with the apostles and other saints:

> *And God wrought special miracles by the hands of Paul: So that from his body were brought unto the sick handkerchiefs or aprons, and the diseases departed from them, and the evil spirits went out of them.* (Acts 19:11–12)

To this day relics are treasured as possible gateways for the transmission of divine power and healing blessing.

ﻋﻠﻰ

Often criticized by some groups of Protestant Christians and others for indulging in unnecessary pomp, expense, and splendor, the sensory details of Orthodox Christian services, to the contrary, stem from a deep sobriety and sophisticated understanding of human nature. None of the beauty and magnificence is random, as if proliferating from some spoiled, wealthy king's love of luxury, greed, and sensual excess. Nor is it a display of power. All is offered as, in the Bible, Abel offered his first fruits (Exod. 3:2–4) and as the penitent woman poured out the precious, expensive oil of spikenard upon the Lord's head, then washed his feet with her tears and dryed them with the long locks of her hair (John 12:3–8). This splendor is a great gift of love offered in tribute for the gift that is above all price, our Lord's coming to us in humility and love to effect our salvation and renew all life.

There is also meaning in every sensory detail, from the incense rising, symbolic of our prayers, and the censing we receive, symbolic of grace and blessing descending upon us from above, to the beautiful robes worn by bishops, priests, deacons, and altar servers. This rich clothing is not meant to be a glorification of any of these persons but rather a reminder to both clergy and parishioners that a heavenly mystery is being represented in the sacred tabernacle in our midst by inadequate human beings. Indeed, each time the priests and deacons vest they say prayers that remind them of their own lowliness and call upon the grace of heaven to help them, though unworthy, fittingly represent such ineffable forces. As for the congregation—certainly the children—our attention is drawn to the shining robes and graceful gestures as a hint of the heavenly reality that we are all swimming in, though unseen, and the mystical presence and actions of the holy angels, the forces of light.

Christmas Pageant I

My Greek Orthodox Sunday School, probably as a gesture of see-we-belong-and-are-normal acculturation to America, held a Christmas pageant every year during Advent. I remember this as taking place in the church proper, the nave. Our little play was offered below the imposing presence and penetrating dark-eyed gaze of tall men and women saints, their full-length icons looming over us from the carved screen before the altar in silence as deep as a crater lake. Dangerously close, just behind them, lay the bubbling and potent mystical ambience of the sanctuary and altar itself, semi-enclosed but sending out magnetic spumes of holiness at unexpected moments, like solar flares that could whip through our prayerful silence or wandering thoughts with spiritual fire, startling our rigid atoms into unexpected epiphanies.

As a seven-year-old shepherdess slowly pacing down the central aisle with a rocking gait meant to convey both reverence and hard traveling, as dictated by the pageant director, I could not express this. Yet I sensed the hovering mystical presence that always inhabited the chapel, like the beating of thousands of wings in the air, as in the filmed scenes of multitudes of pigeons erupting in ululating clouds from the stones of St. Mark's Square, fanning the gaping tourists into invisibility and oblivion. At that moment, however, my nascent spiritual awareness was dimmed, and the beating wings held at bay, as I desperately tried to figure out how to stem the remorseless falling of my slippery homespun polyester headdress as it slipped in torturous slow motion beneath the skewed yarn rope which slid teasingly back and forth on my too-smooth, too-round head like a planetary orbit gone berserk. Would my shepherd hat fall off, triggering a group snigger from the smiling adults lining the pews? Or, worse, would the rope, dragging the brown cloth, descend over my eyes so that, blinded, I crashed into the shepherd in front of me, bringing down the line of closely packed pilgrims like a row of dominoes? What a disgrace! What a disrespectful indignity in the presence of all those beating wings! And what a ripple of poorly concealed amusement would spread through the congregation, to be ever remembered in later years.

What to do? Just hope and pray—although currently my fear and irritation were quenching the delicate flame of prayer—that the slippage would be slow enough that I could navigate safely until the moment came to fall on my knees before the Baby Jesus, uncondemned by His unseeing baby-doll eyes which would be totally, refreshingly indifferent to the state of my headdress. Then, shielded from prying adult eyes by the concealing bunker of my robe-swathed backside, while pressing my forehead to the floor in adoration, I could give my insolent headgear a quick, admonitory tweak and arise with unstained shepherdly dignity, solemnly giving place to the next adorer. If only . . .

Oh please, please, just a few more feet! Please! The wretched yarn jolted down a half-inch farther! *Oh no! Almost—almost! Yes, yes, thank you, Jesus!* I collapsed to my knees with one eye still able to locate Mary's blue robe! With the grace of God, Who apparently didn't want me to ruin His pageant, I had made it, bursting with relief, not yet burdened by the knowledge that this presaged my growing into a woman who could never keep a scarf or shawl in place. I just seemed to be all slippery slope. To this day I suffer from what I view as "The Curse of the Shepherdess's Headdress"— already feeling odd and awkward among the tightly coiffed, make-up-enhanced, nyloned women moving through the perplexing Tai Chi of daily banality with seemingly effortless mastery, I thump along, my defiant scarves and shawls sliding and colliding wretchedly at inappropriate angles on my bewildered torso, as if expressing outrage at my incompetence: "See, this is a weird one, all right. Can't even keep her scarf on. You know, even as a child kept losing her shepherdess headdress. What can you expect?"

For those of you struck dumb with boredom, I shall move on (and for those others, you scarfistas—you know who you are— please tell me what the immobile-scarf secret is—unless, of course, it involves esoteric, horrific rites with bizarre initiations like having to wear a white Peter Pan-collar blouse with a gold circle pin and a madras wraparound skirt—in which case, never mind. Some prices are just too high to pay and were even in the 1950s. And for those few women—say, cradle Eastern Orthodox of a certain age—with a visceral interest in the head-covering issue, much as I would like to explore the symbolically loaded arcana of this potentially hot—in the ancient sense of the word—phenomenon, I must abandon you here, moved by deep pangs of compassion for our other readers).

Now kneeling, marginally less nervous, in the semicircle of other adoring shepherds, I could breathe again—slightly, anyway. Fortunately, I was ignorant of the fact that, due to both their remoteness from shepherding experience and their overwhelming preoccupation with financial modesty, our suburban parents had decked us out as synthetic-clad budget shepherds, our costumes bearing only the most tenuous relationship to gear worn by any real shepherd, modern or ancient. Scabbed erratically with fake lamb fleece as we were, collectively we resembled a wilted crescent of woebegone shaggy cap mushrooms suffering from some as-yet-undetermined fungal illness. But, humble and scabby as we may have appeared, we were smug in the knowledge that we were one-up on those Johnny-come-latelies, the three kings, lugubriously wandering down the aisle in construction-paper crowns, probably fighting the urge to scratch itches beneath their wool-yarn beards, and trying not to drop the myrrh, frankincense, and gold carried unsteadily in precious papier-maché boxes.

The kings were notably camel-less. As we shepherds were notably sheepless. The dangers of having livestock in our little production—even though it would have been more historically accurate—were too well known. Even at my tender age I had witnessed, in a production of *The Rose Tattoo* by my mother's amateur theater company, a slinky, conspicuously ripe actress downstage left in a tight black slip—Serafina? some Italian-ish name like that—being irremediably upstaged during a tragic soliloquy by a live black goat center stage deciding to add to the verisimilitude obviously craved by the director by improvising, with studied nonchalance, a fragrant pile carefully and very slowly dropped during the actress's most fraught and tearful moments. Some of the audience actually fell out of their seats laughing, holding their sides in pain. Such experiences sear the young mind, and I was in complete agreement with the grownups when they quashed the fervent pleas for real live animals in the cast.

As I knelt, trying to maintain the requisite degree of adoration toward the Baby Jesus—I was aware of my responsibilities—I could not help stealing adoring glances instead at a small boy, also a shepherd, kneeling alongside me, on whom whom I had a crush. Perhaps Athanasius (not his real name—but it could have been; this was, after all, a Greek church!) might never notice me, but here we were, side by side, two warm, squirmy little bodies rapt in the quiet, preternatural stillness, as companionably close and quiet as if we really were in some way intermingled—a wistful hope that, I'm sure, emanated only from me. Even though my knees ached, it was worth it. Here I was, next to Athanasius in the homely crowded stable while the greatest event in human history unfolded before us, and my mind—maybe this was why my scarves always fall off—was on him instead of Him.

Yes, we were all there, all the necessary witnesses: the angels' blessing hands hypnotically swaying, and their coat-hanger-and-silver-garland haloes twinkling above us as Mary, a vision in blue with a Minnie Mouse barrette peeking out slightly from her veil, rested by the unblinking Baby. Joseph, looking tired as if from a long and frustrating day over the lathe, stood stolidly, occasionally fidgeting with his bamboo staff ("When are they going to stop taking the group pictures so we can get out the mule and get on the road?"). Perhaps the occasional nose was picked but, overall, we fulfilled our duties.

Carols were probably playing or being sung—oddly, my Christmas pageant memories take place in total silence, which is unlikely. At least I can be fairly certain that our tableau was not accompanied by the usual nasal Byzantine chant, its piercing minor melodies cutting like scimitars through fluff and idle fantasy. My bones knew that vibrant chant, formally controlled yet as expressively ascending and variegated as the liquid cries of a jungle night, emerged from some unknown territory in close proximity to the sanctuary's fiery fountain: a wild and strange land from which it poured like the awesome but melodic growlings of celestial lions stepping winged and light-footed from mountaintop caves to greet the ruby dawn in an expansive landscape of sparkling violet, gold, and crystal, which sighed and sang of itself, being so full of life.

Western Christmas carols must have wreathed around our snuffling (a cold was going around) little tableau. I did and do love these carols dearly, with their sweet, haunting melodies as caressing and gentle as healing balm on a wound, relieving pain and lifting us up with poignant tenderness. They were as lovely and harmonious as the fine-woven web of Nature itself with its curling ivy tendrils and sparkling stars. As a child I felt that I floated through Christmastime on these dancing, spiraling hymns. They were like gentle hands placed on my shoulders in times of sadness or need, which turned me delicately but firmly toward the Light and a warmth and kindness that transcended all trouble.

However, to really get spiritual business done, give me Byzantine chant every time. You may not be charmed (especially in the beginning), but, given a basic willingness, you will be ripped from the nonessentials and thrust toward that cave mouth where the winged lions are.

I don't remember the journey back over the dusty Judaean hills to the church hall where the celebratory baklava dwelt, nor the later behavior of my headdress (probably fine or I would remember), nor the reaction of my mother (my father, not Orthodox and still quite irritated with God about his experiences in World War II, never came to church). And, alas, regarding Athanasius: our brief forced rapport as co-shepherds never bloomed into the boyfriend/girlfriend relationship I had enjoyed imagining. Perhaps real sheep would have helped. He could have saved me from being butted by a ram, or I could have saved him! But, clearly, it was not God's will.

By now all those none-too-spiffy pageant costumes, including the "dreaddress," have moldered into dust. But the winged lions are still alive and singing in the altar, the thousand-wings are still threshing the air above the blue fire, and an undying voice is calling from the midst of the flame to anyone who will stop walking away, ignore her headdress, drop her mask—and hear.

Christmas Pageant II

Leaping five years forward, it's Christmas-pageant season again. Bits of conversation between my Sunday School teacher and my mother, huddled in a corner, floated over my head one day after class like those streaming TV-weather-show pictures of clouds crossing the sky abnormally fast, mesmerizing but too quick to discern with clarity.

"Long dark hair . . ." whisper, whisper, whisper . . . "will look lovely in blue . . ." whisper some more . . . "and I'm so proud that she finally learned the whole Creed in Greek!"

Yes, I had, and it had taken me a whole year of misery, too. I then—oh, how briefly, Lord!—had 479 syllables of Church Greek clunking around in my head in correct chronological order and could reel them off, with occasional constipated pauses, before the encouraging smile of our kind Sunday School teacher, my friend Argie's mother. But the clattering Greek syllables had no direct connection with any real words or thoughts for me, and the hours spent committing them to memory, like lining up nonsense blocks in a dank mental cell, had been spiritually desolating. What one must do to appease grown-ups! Perhaps this was what they meant by Christian charity.

But I would have done almost anything to please Mrs. Contogine, one of those quick, delicate-featured Greeks. As someone once wrote (who must have also known my lovely teacher), "sweetness of character rose off her in waves like other women's perfume." And years later, even during the time I was not a believer anymore, the memory of the way she used to utter the name of Jesus, with pure accents of humble and tender love, gave me occasional pause in my feckless agnosticism. I could not help but feel its hidden root, tingling with life.

"And she's such a sweet, good girl . . . all right?"

Within moments my mother was standing beside me, a tight, triumphant smile on her face, as if her 4-H heifer had just won first prize at the county fair.

"They want you to be Mary," she blurted out.

"What?"

"They want you to be Mary, Mary in the Christmas pageant."

"Me? Mary? Are you sure?"

"Yes, yes, of course. We have to get you some blue robes."

And a head veil! *Ai yai yai!* But I was honored, deeply honored, although, up to rehearsals, I kept thinking there must be some mistake—me? Not only could I not keep a headdress on, I couldn't even speak Greek. Surrounded by fluent Greek-speaking children far younger than me, I felt somehow disabled by this—clumsy and stupid. This impression was strengthened by the pitying glances of Greek adults who learned, to their shock, that I was, for practical purposes, Hellenically dumb. "What a shame! And your mother speaks such beautiful, charming Samian Greek!" And, long-faced, they would wander off to seek the company of a worthier child, shaking their heads and "Po-po-po"-ing tragically in the approved traditional manner of the sadly, sadly disappointed Greek. Me? Mary?

And I was scared. How could I possibly pretend to represent . . . in front of everybody . . . had I known the word *chutzpah*, I would have used it.

However, my emotional and metaphysical struggle was soon miraculously relieved by good tidings of great joy—guess who would be playing Joseph? Athanasius! Thank you, Lord! Another chance! What was it I had been worrying about anyway? Still, both the thought of playing the Virgin Mary and the one of holy proximity to Athanasius as Joseph made me blush. Though bold in the land of fantasy, I was shy in everyday life. My introversion would definitely be put to the test by this public challenge.

In rehearsals I had nothing much to do but look lovingly at the baby-doll Jesus in his manger straw, surreptitiously peeking at Athanasius during the hundred interruptions which stormed and whimpered through rehearsals as cranky children got bored, restless, and sleepy. But he was a solid, serious Joseph, staring straight ahead as if already contemplating the dangers to come—given his dour expression, a premonition of the flight into Egypt, for example, could have been weighing on his mind. He rarely looked around. Sigh.

Pageant Sunday arrived. Assorted adults fussed over us in the changing rooms. Somehow—*mirabile visu!* (and, alas, never to be repeated)—they managed to get my long azure veil to stay draped politely on my head.

Joseph, the Baby, and I were settled in our places on the heaped straw at the top of the nave before the sanctuary. The church was full. Hundreds of eyes stared at us like silent psychic jackhammers, boring into our not-ready-for-prime-time childish souls. As the narration began, to my surprise my thoughts were not on Athanasius at all. I was praying, begging God, our Lord Jesus, the *Panaghía* (the All-Pure Virgin), the saints, and the angels to help us do well. I especially implored the Holy Virgin Mary to be with me and to help me represent her in a good manner—and to help us avoid disasters. And I wasn't thinking of my headdress at all. As the shepherds began their long journey down the nave with their familiar rocking gaits, I silently invoked her. Part of me, less piously engaged, observed that, as well as being an honor, being Mary had its advantages—you didn't have to move around.

But then I did. No, I didn't visibly move. But I felt the hairs on the back of my neck stand up of their own volition, like a pack of obedient dogs. Something came down over Joseph, the Baby, and me, like a kind of invisible bubble. And suddenly I didn't care about Athanasius—well, I didn't not care about him—but he, I, and the Baby Jesus doll had become ciphers, sanded smooth of personal quirks, so that we could serve as small placeholders in a brief portrait of a big mystery, its awesome, timeless breath flowing over our necks and filling the air around us with invisible sparks of power.

I felt afraid and I didn't feel afraid. It was good and it was terrible. The former I could not explain except it seemed as if those we were representing had perhaps showed up after all or, if not them, someone or something closely allied to them, someone from a mountaintop that sang. It was terrible because it was so much larger than we were, though not maleficent. And it was terrible because I trembled uncontrollably in its presence. From that point on through the whole pageant my consciousness was somewhat removed from the proceedings, although I was still aware of them. I was there but it was as if I were also somewhere else, breathing in cold, piercingly pure mountain air laced with loving daggers of starlight that flayed and cherished me at the same time. Part of me tried to still my physical body that in its weakness could not remain stable in the flow of this refined fire and shook and shook and shook.

When the pageant ended, my mother rushed up to me, her eyebrows v-ed down to her nose in disapproval. "Whatever was the matter with you, Stephania?!" (My full baptismal name was only used in moments of supreme irritation.) "You shook through the whole thing! Really, how ridiculous! There was no reason to be nervous! All you had to do was sit there, you silly girl, not ruin it all with shaking. Really, I don't know what's the matter with you!"

I was already distressed because I was worried I had spoiled the pageant and now my cheeks burned with shame. But, at the same time, I knew that something strange and special and deep had happened there—someone, something, had come and given some kind of potent blessing. The blessing was almost too big to bear, however, so I in my weakness had trembled like a sapling in a high wind the whole time it was there. Someone sturdier probably would not have flinched. But even my failure to accomplish my duty and its attendant disgrace could not make me wish that the big mystery had not visited.

Later I could sympathize with the apostle Peter's confusion on Mount Tabor when the Lord manifested Himself in His Holy Light, flanked in His cloud of brightness by the Prophets Moses and Elijah. Peter managed to cry out an offer to make three tabernacles for the Lord and the prophets before falling on his face in terror. I bet that the hairs stood up on Peter's neck and I bet that even that big tough fisherman shook like a leaf. But he and James and John were grown-ups, hard-tried and virtuous, though, as the Bible makes clear, also fallible. And they were facing the full fire of God's incarnation and manifestation on earth. I, on the other hand, was just a silly little girl, short on both virtue and understanding, and even a whisper of this mystery, gentled and attenuated to be bearable to a puppy like me, I could not endure unmoved. I don't know what God did that day with me and with all the other people, but He did something.

Years later, as a tonsured *Psáltria* (Psalmist / Cantor / Reader), in the candle-starred darkness of a church awash with frankincense and reverence, when chanting and singing my favorite service—the ancient Presanctified Liturgy—each year, I trembled uncontrollably throughout the first and sometimes all of the succeeding eleven Presanctified Liturgies of Lent.

The shaking did not seem to interfere with my ability to perform the service, even when I led the team of Readers. I tried but never could stop the shivering through force of will, feeling that same strange sensation on the back of my neck that I had as a child in the Christmas pageant. My poor fellow Readers, banded close together on the *klíros*, endured this with the patient stoicism of the mystical MASH unit we formed, weaving our way through complicated services in which we chanted and sang for sometimes as many as six hours straight, desperately hoping that nothing would blow up, and that the exacting, even tenor of the congregation's worship would be sustained.

In the last few years I chanted the Presanctified, the trembling stopped altogether. I was relieved but also, after so long, couldn't help but wonder if this indicated that part of me had in some way tuned out of something vital—if I had become complacent and allowed this thing of transcendent beauty to become old-hat ("no problem, done that before") instead of proffering the inner bended knee of "we who mystically represent the cherubim," as the solemn Divine Liturgy hymn describes it, the singers and servants of the Mystery. I didn't and don't know. Perhaps it was so. I don't think I had gained much in stability or virtue but I may well have decreased in sensitivity and fervor. I'm sorry, my God, for all my inadequacies and sins—the trembling ones and the untrembling ones as well.

Still, when one day I found myself in Jerusalem, in the tiny innermost chamber of the Holy Sepulchre, the Tomb of Christ, facing the myrrh-fragranced stone slab from which He arose, as I bent to kiss it in the shadow of the shimmering golden oil lamps above, their glow filling the cell and firing the precious metal *rizas* of the icons all around, not only did I tremble uncontrollably again but my heart itself leapt and danced and ran like a wild thing, flying, battering the air with its wings, into the arms of the Beloved.

ﷻ

The Essence vs. the Caricature
Throughout my life I have encountered both the sublime and the absurd in my life in the Orthodox Church. We stumble around in our human imperfections trying to reach, to evoke the Divine Presence and its perfection. Through grace, often our puny efforts are rewarded far beyond our conceptions and we are expanded. But sometimes we fall on our faces instead, reducing the potentially glorious and ineffable to the mouse-like height of our own combative, self-centered egos.

Twelve Great Feasts a year, vessels of grace and mystical insight, are celebrated in the Orthodox Church. One of these is Theophany (most often called "Epiphany" in the West), celebrated not long after Christmas. Theophany primarily commemorates the baptism of Jesus Christ in the Jordan by St. John the Baptist and Forerunner (although it is also associated with the visit of the Three Kings). Unsurprisingly, this feast centers around the blessing of water. Carried out in church as well as outside in lakes, rivers, and the ocean, this blessing custom extends to individual homes in the parish that the priest visits to bless and renew with the holy water of Theophany. This is usually a lovely and refreshing practice (despite the embarrassment of over-stuffed closets that must also be sprinkled and blessed), but we, in our feckless manner, are quite capable of getting majorly in the way of the blessing trying to descend upon us.

Splash! Theophany Blessings!
Father Akilas (as we will call him) was a determined man. Determined, but not particularly endearing, at least to the little child that I was. He was not especially cold but neither was he especially warm. Somehow I always had the feeling when I was around him that I was a nonentity, didn't exist somehow, a small, insignificant pimple in a dull landscape. Like most Orthodox parish priests, Fr. Akilas was married and had some children of his own. This fact, as far as I could detect, had not noticeably enlarged his paternal sense toward other children. To be fair, I'm sure he was—what priest is not?—severely overworked. And it is true that my somewhat uncharitable view of him could have something to do with my only intense personal interaction with him: the disaster of my one and only Saturday Greek School class, a rite of passage for little Greek-American children that was, for me, about as relaxing as running a ring of fire. To say he was an insensitive teacher would be an understatement.

We were told that most words in other languages (like that tardy entry, English) descended (in every sense of the word) from Our Glorious Language. For those of you who have seen the film *My Big Fat Greek Wedding* (my cousin Helen's astute review: "It's not a comedy, it's a documentary!"), perhaps you remember the Greek School scene near the beginning where a large big-nosed man's face of the funhouse-mirror type is leaning down close to our small heroine's eyes, loudly enunciating Greek syllables that she and the class repeat. It was the same for me except that in my case the teacher was wearing a *ráso* (a priest's cassock), and he did not know how to deal with the catastrophic situation that I was the only child in the class who didn't already speak and read Greek. When Father Akilas discovered this loathsome fact, he immediately stiffened, taking on the posture of an irritated great blue heron in a small, fish-poor creek, and tried to overcome my ineptitude by making me repeat his sentences over and over. And over and over. And over and over, while the rest of the class smirked behind their hands. Not much time passed before I was further humiliated by my own choking sobs. Looking terminally offended by my obviously willful ignorance and stupidity, the frustrated priest at last moved on. "I will never go back there!" I told my mother in tears. And I didn't.

My mother was not fond of Father Akilas either; they had clashed on several issues. Thus it was very unfortunate that on one cold January day Father Akilas decided it was time to give us and our house a Theophany blessing. He did not bother to announce this to my mother in advance, as she had told him many times she did not want him to come. In true Hellenic warrior style, rejecting elementary sensitivity, he ignored this trifling difference of opinion, determined to overcome, one way or another, that woman's unreasonable and impious resistance.

As I was in my bedroom doing homework, I missed—thank you, thank you, dear God!—the first phase of the battle. As I later learned, Father Akilas rang the doorbell, Loukia answered, he tried to enter, and she definitively refused him. Quite definitively, as in closing the door in his face. Father Akilas apparently had quick reflexes, though, and managed to stick one foot in the door.

My mother was outraged. "No!" she exclaimed, leaning hard on the door.

"Yes!" he declared as he pushed, twisting the knob and refusing to withdraw his big, shiny black shoe from the threshold. Two Greeks at war! Athens and Sparta had been at it for years! I was grateful not to have been close at hand when the spears began flying. Anyone brash enough to contend with my mother was reckless to the point of idiocy. But, wily as Odysseus, Father Akilas outsmarted Loukia in the end, gambling that, even at the height of her simmering Hellenic indignation, she would eventually have to open the door to forestall gangrene claiming the sacerdotal foot. He was right. Exasperated but outmaneuvered, she at last caved, uttering curses, and opened the door a crack wider. One hard, fast push and he was inside.

Triumphant over the enemy forces, Father. Akilas flung himself into our house with his white-and-gold *epitrachelion*—the long fringed stole of his office—flying over his black *ráso's* skirts, a spray of green bay leaves clutched in one hairy fist above his crisscross-tied damask cuff and a big bowl of holy water sloshing in the other. Chanting prayers and blessings in Greek, his thick dark eyebrows working up and down, he flew from room to room, startling cats, dogs, and me—my father and brother presciently having gone out on errands—with unexpected rain from heaven. I was lying on my bed, pencil in hand, concentrating on geometry homework, when my bedroom door flew open and, before I could respectfully scramble to my feet, Father Akilas, bellowing incomprehensible prayers, had thoroughly sprinkled me, my room, and my homework with wet, sparkling beatitude.

In a daze, unsure if I might perhaps be having a hallucination, I rose to my feet and followed him in numb surprise to my parents' bedroom, which he then proceeded to douse with the insouciant delight of a toddler with a bucket at the beach. My mother stood in a corner, glowering, her arms folded tight, one foot tapping with dangerous impatience, ready to explode into tempest. Then, suddenly, she went rigid and motionless. Fixing her alarmed eyes on mine, she began tensely mouthing words at me over the deliriously splashing priest's shoulder. I couldn't make them out. Exasperated by my density, she tried again, repeating more emphatically and pointing fiercely at my father's bathroom. Fittingly, an epiphany exploded in my brain. Oh no! My father's magazines! Surely she wouldn't be worried about *Popular Mechanics,* so "PLAYBOY!!!" was the alarm siren she was blasting at my recalcitrant consciousness.

Glibly chanting and unaware of lurking dangers, the priest was now speeding toward my father's private masculine sanctuary. I leapt into life, lightly slipping past him and saying in tones of unctuous consideration, "Please let me get that door for you, Father!"

Opening the door with one hand while reaching for a towel with the other, I scoped out the scene. Of course, on top of the magazine pile by the toilet was not, this time, the staid cover of a laudable *Scientific American* but, rather, a busty, bare-breasted babe reaching out, smiling seductively, as if to welcome the unsuspecting splashing priest to an excessively intimate pool party. My arm shot out and the towel flew over the pile. I whipped around, bestowing a bright, glazed smile upon the advancing pastor, for which I was instantly rewarded with soaked bangs. I didn't care, staggering back into my parents' bedroom with water droplets blurring my sight. I nodded reassurance to my incensed mother. Disgusted, she closed her eyes in deep relief, slowly shaking her head from side to side.

Father Akilas rushed past again, now hurtling down the hall, still tossing chants like bright primroses along his heedless path to the front door, my mother hard on his heels like a small, grim hunting dog. At the door, Father Akilas turned, slightly raising his chin and his eyebrows, and, as their eyes met, splashed a beatific smile on my mother, thereby upping the ante. Loukia regarded him in furious silence with a look that could char his baklava to ashes in a twinkling. At this, his smile glowed and widened. "You're WELCOME!" he chortled gaily, swung open the door, and was gone like a holy tornado or, rather, waterspout. My mother, quivering with rage, and I, damply bewildered, regarded each other for a few mute moments.

"What happened?" I asked at last.

"Oh, that Father Akilas!" she spat. "He always wants to come and give the blessings and I never let him. I told him not to come. This house is a mess and I don't want him in here!"

"Then how—"

"Oh, that *priest!*" she cried, making it sound like the worst possible insult. "When I tried to shut him out, he stuck his foot in the door! *His foot!* Can you believe it? What could I do? Chop off his foot? Oh, I thought about it, all right! *I thought about it!* Oh, that Father Akilas!" And she whirled off down the hall to her room, muttering Greek imprecations, and slammed the door.

I just stood there, blinking. The cats, with their usual fine instincts, were nowhere to be seen. I was grateful that my mother's pet skunk, Joy (named for the perfume, not the emotion), was no longer with us, feeling that he might have misunderstood the beneficence of this unusual blessing and stuck a sharp tooth in Father Akilas's thumb, as he had to my cousin Louise when she foolishly cornered him in a closet. There had been enough chaos today without the further complication of actual bloodshed.

The two dogs, however, whose naps had been interrupted by Father Akilas flinging water on their heads, had trotted to the door to enjoy the excitement but had instantly been overawed into polite silence by the intensity of the colliding Greek tropical storms. They now sat on their haunches in the hall, looking at me expectantly, as if awaiting my translation of the scene they had just witnessed. Had the man in the shiny clothes perhaps stolen the Lady Loukia's bone? We looked gravely into each other's eyes for a moment while I thought it over.

"It's better not to know," I said to them apologetically and went back to my room. Drying my geometry homework with a hair-dryer, I reflected that Father Akilas, perhaps in imitation of God, Who shines and rains on both the just and unjust, sprinkled both the grateful and ungrateful, whether they liked it or not, by God.

Such shenanigans did not rob the Church of the potency of its mysteries, however, but instead underlined the power of the grace that could descend on even our fumbling, confused selves. And grace was everywhere, not only in Church services, though I believe attendance at those services helped raise our personal attunement and availability to such mysteries.

𐡀𐡋

My parents' marriage was an unhappy one. Though they were initially attracted by each other's exoticism (a shy, restrained Yankee man drawn to a flamboyant, extroverted Greek and vice versa; my mother had already broken two engagements to Greeks before she met my father), this same difference in temperament and backgrounds led over the years to an ever-increasing divide in their mutual affection. They tried not to fight in front of us children. However, I could hear them at night through the bedroom wall we shared, my bed right against it. Their pain and sadness were terrible; my heart was wrung for them. And they seemed unaware of any way to staunch the constant bloodletting. One night when I was perhaps ten or so, hearing them claw at each other wildly on the other side of the wall, my heart breaking for their agony, I could bear it no longer. I centered myself with the unanticipated power of childhood concentration and silently addressed myself in an imploring, rock-solid prayer to God. I asked God to let me take on their suffering and allow them to be free of it. I asked this with my whole heart and felt as if I were making this prayer in a depth dive somewhere I had never been before; I felt stirrings in the solar plexus of my will, knowing I was about to take an ineradicable step. But just as I was about to take the last determined step, a

ball of light, maybe two or three feet wide, floated in through my
unopened bedroom window, hung high in the air, and commanded me to stop, lovingly but with implacable firmness. I stared at
it, blinking, for a few moments. And then it gently flew away. I
knew I would never act against its command; it seemed too full of
holiness and wisdom.

&

When I was very small, I used to help myself go to sleep by
imagining myself curled up comfortably in the huge hand, tender
and sheltering, of God. There was a way in which this seemed
quite real. The Mystery was all around, everywhere, night and day.

I also had a strong feeling that the altar in my church was the
"lap of God," and I knew myself to be welcome in His loving lap.
So, one day when I was maybe six years old, at the end of a Sunday
Divine Liturgy, I wandered up onto the *ambo*, the low stairs before
the Royal Doors of the icon screen where normally only the priest
stands. I was not planning on going into the empty Sanctuary,
just wishing to peek over the low gate of the Royal Doors to get a
better look at the altar and the inside. Suddenly there was a flurry
of panicky adult activity, as if a flock of frightened sparrows had
been startled by a swiftly descending hawk. Big hands grabbed
me, pulling me away from the Sanctuary, their owners clucking
disapprovingly. Among them was my mother, visibly upset. "You
can't go in there!" she hissed. *"Never go in there!* If you do, you'll
pollute it, and it will take priests hours and hours of services to
cleanse it!" I was amazed. I also knew it was not true, that part
about me polluting it; I knew this not in a self-righteous way but in
a clear, fundamental way, the way I knew the earth was under my
feet. But I was embarrassed and distressed by the incident, taking
note of the need to be more aware of adult taboos and to try harder
not to run afoul of them. No further explanation was given. Later
in life I learned more about the origin of such superstitions and
dealt with people of a broader, more nuanced theological understanding. But, as a child, it was just another weird adult thing to
deal with, something trying to teach me that somehow I was not
good enough, and, inexplicably, never would be.

I did become somewhat wary of adults as a small child. Upon
first seeing an adult, I usually, at first glance, got a geometric
image in my mind, outlined in light, of his or her psyche. There
were broad places within the shape and narrow places. Quickly I
learned to translate these shapes into the more easygoing and the
more compulsive, fear-filled sides of their psyches. Over time I
wondered if adults were crazy, because the narrow, fearful side in

one person's psyche did not match up with the narrow, fear-filled side in another person's psyche. How could they all be scared of different things and also open in different ways? So strange! But I learned to maneuver by these images. If a conversation was being held, I could feel an adult whose narrow part was about to be triggered by the subject begin to tense up. This was an early-warning system by which I learned to avoid collisions with the adult's particular "stuff." I tended to get on extremely well with adults, probably in part because I often knew ahead of time where not to tread. By the time I was ten or so I became completely and self-reflectively conscious of this ability and, with a shock of fear at my own apparent abnormality, cut the capacity off.

A certain psychic tendency was rampant on my mother's side of the family. Once my mother and I took an "ESP test" in a magazine together and, of course, got perfect scores. There were also strange other uses. When I was enrolled, not very voluntarily, in a summer day camp focused on athleticism and competition, there was a critical basketball game that would help determine the summer's standings between my team and the other girls' team in our age group. I was assigned to guard Glenda, the opposing team's leading forward and quite a big girl compared to my own shrimpiness. The contest was heated and Glenda was scoring more points than anyone, but somehow she seemed to find me increasingly in her way. This was because, paying close attention, I could usually pick up in advance from my psychic sense where she would decide to move in the next moment. Wherever she went, I was also suddenly, in her view inexplicably, there. At one point I had blocked so many of her shots, though without touching her (I did not want to foul), that Glenda lost her temper, pulled back her arm, and slapped me hard across the face. It was a glorious moment, despite my ringing cheek, because, of course, the shouting ref threw her right out of the game! Without Glenda's abilities in offense, her team could not overcome mine, and we won. But still I feel strange and perhaps a little unsafe revealing even to you, dear reader, to whom I have already revealed so much and plan to share so much more, the little secret of my psychic tendencies. There is a sense of danger in putting it boldly out there, and also a sense of something like shame—as if this capacity shouldn't have been at all, and also because I could use it in small ways at times to my advantage, unbeknownst to others, as in the game with Glenda. This is one of the ways knowledge turns into guilt, real or imagined. Those of you who have lived with similar tendencies will understand me. And those of you who think you have not, perhaps you should think again. We are all built on a similar model; this capacity you also have, though it may be well-veiled. Perhaps you have even noticed and used it—but forced yourself, out of fear, to *forget*. However, the opportunity still exists for you to remember it, to remember yourself, to explore this awakened and subtle side of your own being. Who knows what you might discover?

Such a psychic bent is not uncommon among Greeks, Italians, and others of a Mediterranean temperament and bloodline. Also, Irish and Hispanics, very often. And, I'm sure, others. Among ourselves, we are not surprised at its manifestations but most of us are wise enough to conceal it from the frowning Anglo-Teutonic, control-crazy Western culture. It is neither some wizardly ability nor insanity nor clairvoyance (though some people do exist with that gift)—just a level or two of veiling removed between us and the Really Real that gives a certain ability to see what is more subtle. And you can see its overt manifestation in the complex, mystical subtleties of our Churches.

و۔

Pascha: Soaring and Bumbling
Pascha, the Holy Resurrection of our Lord Jesus Christ, was the greatest feast of the year by far. Holy Week itself and Pascha contain twenty-one services within seven days, each of them different, each one eloquent and moving. They compose a long, powerful, extended meditation on the Passion and Resurrection of Jesus Christ. Attending them is like stepping out of the mundane onto a pilgrimage ship heading for the Holy Land. As on physical pilgrimages, there will be joys and there will be sufferings. Anything can happen.

When I was a child, my family only ever attended four of them, but those were moving and magnificent and drenched in grace. We went to Palm Sunday Divine Liturgy. Usually it was only my Pappou and I who attended the Thursday evening service where the "Twelve Passion Gospels" were read, and the priest enacted Jesus dragging His Cross to Golgotha—a heartbreaking evening. But no one would have missed either Holy Friday evening, when the Lamentations were sung and the Lord's Body carried outside in His flower-adorned Tomb, or Saturday night, when the main Paschal service (there were two other ones) was held. From the pitch-blackness of the empty tomb at midnight (all the lights in the church having been completely doused), a light would start to flicker hazily behind the curtain above the Royal Doors of the sanctuary and a soft singing begin to arise. Soon the Royal Doors were flung open and the priest emerged, bearing flower-bedecked candles blazing with light. "Christ is risen!" he shouted. "Come receive the

Light from the Unwaning Light!" And we rushed forward, candles in hand, to light them from his and spread the joy of our Lord's miraculous Resurrection from the dead to all there. A long and gorgeous service rolled out from that point in magnificent waves as we sang and shouted "*Christos anesti!*" ("Christ is risen!") many times, surfed through the mystical glories of the feast, and celebrated in ancient poems, prayers, and biblical passages soaring on the soul-piercing music of inspired saints. But it was not necessary to understand the language to be lifted on this ineffable mystical tide, its luminous breath filling the sails of our hearts.

Comprised of two parts, the service had Paschal Matins and Paschal Divine Liturgy back to back. My family, as is often the case, did not remain for the Divine Liturgy but left after the beautiful Paschal Matins. Although not generally approved, many people did likewise, nonetheless. This meant we left the church around one A.M. (as opposed to possibly three A.M. had we also attended the Divine Liturgy), our lit candles in hand, and drove off to find an all-night diner where we could have our celebratory Paschal breakfast.

Here I must explain about our lit candles. It is an ancient, highly observed tradition in Greek Orthodox churches that you carry home the new Paschal Fire to light and bless your home shrine and your house. So we sometimes take lanterns but often only our large lit beeswax candles, sheltered by a rounded red or white plastic cup against the wind, with us into our cars where we strive to keep them lit. When we arrive home, singing "Christ is risen," one of us carefully marks the lintel above the door to our home with a cross of soot from the holy flame, blessing our house with its protection. Once, in later years, my husband and I were waiting to meet a landlord in the Boston area to look at an apartment we were considering renting. We waited in the small lobby that was surrounded by the doors to four apartments. We noticed that one of the apartment doors had three distinct black soot crosses on its lintel. Ah, we ascertained, Greeks have lived here for three years—three Paschas. We examined the mailboxes and saw that one had a distinctly Greek name. Bingo!

But, as I was saying, this trip home from church was, in our case, interrupted by a stop at an all-night deli for Paschal breakfast. We were often a large party, since non-Orthodox guests frequently accompanied us (including, always, my faithful, long-suffering best friends, Juanita Huber and Roberta "Bird" Grosso), so we would often have to line up a number of tables side by side. Once, when we crowded into a diner, a cheerful waitress scurried up to us and our lit candles, loudly exclaiming, "Oh! Whose birthday is it?!"

We found that what worked best was two or three of those large, heavy glass malted milkshake containers set in the middle of the table to hold our bouquets of big flaming candles. When the food arrived, the Lord's blessing was asked, we sang "*Christos Anesti*" three times, and then feasted. My own small immediate biological family did not follow the prescribed Lenten fasts (my mother, who had to do so as a child, said she never wanted to see another lentil again in her life), but breakfast was much enjoyed by all. The next day we would have a major feast with all the relatives and some friends, usually at Thea Felice's home; this sultan's festival always seemed to me to last for three joyous days.

Of course, there were the occasional snafus. Anyone traveling with my incident-prone mother knew to be wary when in her company, even—or especially—on Pascha. On one Pascha, as we all stood expectantly in the silent, crowded church in the pitch-black darkness of the Tomb, awaiting the Holy Light, my mother exclaimed, "Oh no! I've lost my contact lens! Get down on the floor, Stephani, and see if you can find it!" Soon Mom had most of the people in the first three rows of pews down on the floor in the dark, fumbling around trying to find her lens. Unaware of the chaos awaiting him, the poor priest flung open the Royal Doors at the appointed moment to dramatically announce the Resurrection and share the Holy Fire only to see three rows of people scrabbling around on the floor right before him, like overzealous bargain hunters at a Macy's basement sale. Worse, as worshippers tried to pass the Holy Fire with one hand while still palpating the linoleum with the other, candles got held at odd angles and the rancid smell of burning hair rose to do battle with the sweet fragrance of incense. At last my mother found her lens—between her feet, of course—and, with a certain amount of headshaking, Paschal decorum was restored. This probably didn't endear my mother further to our priest, whose eyebrows had popped with alarm as he viewed the pulsating mob on the church floor when he first brought out the Holy Light.

Another time as we stood during Paschal Matins, my mother at one end of our long pew and me at the other, the eight actor friends she had brought along who stood between us began to behave strangely. One after another, like a line of falling dominoes, they each began to take off their shoes, drawing disapproving snorts and jabberings from the little old black-clad Yiayias near us. What was going on? My mother, tired of standing in her four-inch heels, had slipped off her shoes. The innocent actors, earnestly trying to conform to our local customs, thought this must be what one did in that part of the service and each took off their shoes (a hassle for the men what with untying shoelaces and all), creating a quiet but conspicuous disturbance. I gave my mother an alarmed look. She just smirked back at me, finding all of it highly amusing. At least from the far end of the pew, I could try to ignore the scandalized Yiayias and pretend I did not know that woman and her very strange friends!

There was an art to carrying the Holy Fire home. You had to pull the plastic vase-shaped holder well up around the flame to guard it from wind and also take extra care getting into the car with it so that the rush of air from closing the door did not put it out. There was an old superstition that if your candle blew out before you got home, you would have bad luck that year, as my mother teasingly reminded my friend Bird when hers blew out as she closed the car door one Pascha. We laughed it off. That night, at home in her bedroom, Bird relit her candle to enjoy its light and the memory of the splendor of the service. She was very tired and put it in a loving cup she had won in a spelling bee on her bureau. Unfortunately, it was a low-budget spelling bee, the loving cup was plastic, and the candle burned down, melting it as she dozed. Bird awoke with a start to find her bureau on fire and, without thinking, slapped at the flames, burning her hand. She and her father quickly put out the fire. But Bird was enormously careful the next year as she maneuvered into our car with her candle, my mother watching her with a mischievous, I-told-you-so grin.

و۶

As I got older I became more aware of certain things I did not like in church—like misogyny and sexism. Women definitely seemed to be second-class citizens. Growing up in church, I never heard a woman's voice contributing to the service except that of a particularly pure-voiced soprano who flung her heart up to God during part of the *Anaphora* (the consecration of the bread and wine) in a moving solo. This absence of the female voice puzzled me exceedingly as I stood for hours in church, staring straight ahead at the full-length icon of Saint Paraskevi, to whom our church was dedicated. An early Greek martyr, this beautiful, nobly born young woman gave all her goods away to the poor after her parents' death and, spurning suitors, took to the road, preaching Jesus Christ and converting many. For this she was pursued and tortured by pagan emperors, but she never lost her faith and also manifested gifts of healing, famously of the

eyes, quite actively down to this day. At last she received martyrdom by beheading in the year 140. It made no sense to me that
our whole church was dedicated to and came under the mantle
of this powerful, luminous healer and preacher of Christ who
happened to be a woman, yet there was no indication around me
that women, ecclesiastically mute, could do anything more, ever,
than make *loukoumades* for coffee hour. Sadly, I'd never seen an
Orthodox nun, some of whom (especially abbesses), can give the
rare permitted cameo sermon in churches.

I was also increasingly disturbed by the pomposity, the old boys'
club feeling, exuded by some of the clergy. I found the tendency
toward flowery smugness suffocating and offensive, the self-preen-
ing certainty of some of these prelates that they were the ultimate
and highly laudable authorities on everything and lords over everyone else ugly and offensive. Not to mention, delusional! But there
were good priests, too, fresh and warm like spring meadows, light
bright in their eyes, a feeling of blessing around them. But a child
could not choose which clergy to be around and, regrettably, my
exposure to the latter was limited.

Although there was real piety in our congregation, there was
also a strain of cynicism that became more noticeable to me as I
got older, the bitter cynicism of Greeks who feel they have been
mistreated by other Greeks. One event that displayed this to my
amazed teenaged eyes took place on Pascha itself.

A stranger, a guest priest, was concelebrating with our own
priest at the midnight Matins and Divine Liturgy. The Holy Fire
came out and lit the dark, we sang, we processed, we rejoiced.
Everything was going fine. Then, toward the end of Matins, the
strange priest pulled our pastor aside for a moment and told him
that he would like to address the congregation. Courteously, our
priest allowed him. We listened expectantly as this priest began
his harangue. I could tell it was a harangue—an odd time for
one—by his tone and by his loud but pinched voice, as if he were
smelling something bad while speaking, but I had no idea what
he was saying. A dangerous rumbling murmur began to rise
from the congregation, like the earth preparing a major earthquake, and it grew and grew. "What's he saying?" I implored my
mother. "He is saying," she replied through gritted teeth, her
eyes fixed on the apparently suicidal priest in a most unfriendly
way, "that anyone who leaves after *Orthros* (Matins) and before
Divine Liturgy is like *Judas* who betrayed our Lord!" My eyes
must have been little pinwheels of amazement. It was hard to
imagine a priest so possessed of a death wish as to speak like

that to a bunch of Greeks! He must have been out of his mind. Telling them what to do and calling them names?! Not to mention, four Greeks—nine opinions! I'd say he was very lucky not to be stoned out of the church.

Instead, the vast majority of parishioners stood up abruptly and, carefully guarding their candle flames, stalked out of the church. The noise level was terrible, the indignation flaming as much as the candles. Many people who normally did stay for Paschal Divine Liturgy stomped out, too, in solidarity. No little pipsqueak of a priest was going to talk to them and their friends like that! Fortunately, I was as ignorant of the more colorful Greek expressions as I was of the mundane variety.

This church had a big parking lot surrounded by lawns, within a stone's throw of a major highway. Soon the parking lot looked as if it were hosting a cross between a bumper-cars carnival and a black mass as dozens of people drove around and around with their lit candles flaming, leaning out their windows into the warm spring air and bellowing *"Judas! Judas!"* at each other, laughing uproariously. What innocent drivers passing on the highway that night must have thought, I shudder to think! Odds are probably good that none of them would be too keen on attending an Orthodox service after *that*. But, all in all, despite the downsides, the grievously offended Greeks, never shy about squeezing all possible juice out of any situation, enjoyed themselves enormously!

⚓

Desertion: The Prodigal Journeys to the Uncertain
As an adult I remember standing one day in another Orthodox church with a ten-year-old girl whose golden hair was glowing in the multicolored light of a stained glass window. She looked at me, a powerful radiance in her eyes that outshone the physical light. With conviction she said, "How can anyone *not* believe in God?" Five years later I reminded her of the incident. She said, disbelievingly, "I said *that*?" She had moved into the cynical byways of the teenage landscape by then and was battling with contrary currents—though in this case she did, in the end, retrieve her deeper faith. Not all are so fortunate.

I was no exception to this. I also experienced a movement away from what I intuitively knew about the Really Real and instead was carried off by a chaos of flood waters pouring out of the cultural contradictions I observed and the differing views of others. I lost focus, tossed back and forth on these waves of uncertainty. The misery of this confusion had a sharp edge, and I wanted to get away from it as soon as possible.

The Presence of a loving and trustworthy God faded into the background of a Gestalt that focused on contradictions, competing ideas, and hurt and disappointed feelings run amuck. These contenders made a lot of noise, and the more subtle, serene harmonies of Presence began to disappear from my conscious mind and even, most sadly, from my memory.

If we load tragic life events and shocking experiences on all of this our faith may go down in flames. Sometimes it is the unexpected, truly terrible things that shatter and challenge us and our views. Sometimes it's only going away to college and encountering a host of different views from one's own and one's family's and neighbors', which may seem tragic and shocking enough. The problem of the reason for suffering in the Creation may loom very large, pressing, and unresolved for a long, troubling time.

The events themselves and the often-unripe conclusions we draw from them can become conflated: the difficult experience with the negative metaphysical views we assume as a result. The views can then become the dominant Gestalt, the most prominent pattern in our consciousness. We may even become proud of these beliefs, never giving them and our inner spiritual orientation a chance at coming back to life and being examined in a fresh way. I am not saying that many of these events and shocks are not genuinely tragic and hurtful. But that our compulsive tendency to seize on them and claim them as the rock-bottom foundations of our beliefs forever after can be a disservice to ourselves, especially if we are interested in the Really Real (which tends eternally to be a surprise).

We may decide that we need to be a "free spirit," without spiritual affiliation and without dogma. At least three problems arise with this approach: (1) that we cut ourselves off from the deeper learning paths of the ancient, hard-won wisdom carried distilled within these ancient, blessed roads, just beneath the surface—a wisdom and a way that can transform us, even though we may currently recognize neither the need nor the way; (2) we will still *have* dogma—since dogma is a worldview, everyone of necessity has it, including atheists—however, our current dogma may not stretch us into new realization and life as the inspired dogmas of some of the spiritual paths can—it may just leave us in stalemate; (3) without commitment to a way, teachers, and a community greater than ourselves, we may find ourselves awash in purposelessness, indulging ourselves aimlessly in what we already know rather than in the Spirit-driven stimulation of what we are meant to be, learn, and become. "You must know God by Himself and not by you," says wise Attar. But, of course, my callow soul was unaware of this at the time.

The last day I remember being at church was when I was fifteen. The archbishop was visiting and part of his mission that day was to help auction off the honor of laying the first cornerstone for our new church building—an event that involved holding the congregation hostage for what felt like hours as the church authorities tried to get parishioners to make high bids for the honor of digging the first shovelful of dirt. I was disgusted by this cynical, mercenary effort and decided that I had at last had enough.

So, what to do? What was the furthest away I could imagine from my own church? Ah, simple! The Unitarians! My Roman Catholic friend Bird had come to the same unhappy breaking point with her church so we set off together down the yellow brick road to the Land of the Unitarians. It was lovely—at first. The kind, sophisticated, socially conscious Unitarians treated us with the respect we thought we truly deserved and warmly flattered our ignorance. I still to this day wince at remembering myself introducing Bird as a "recently disillusioned Catholic." *Aaagh!* What a pretentious little twerp I was! And how kindly they smiled at us, as if we were all sharing together, in our enlightened God-optional enclave, a superior secret of understanding.

There was the question of the "services," however. I remember that one Sunday a nuclear physicist gave a talk on, um, nuclear physics. The next Sunday a really good black modern dance troupe from New York performed. And so on. Always interesting but always, somehow, deeply lacking. This strange hollow of absence crystallized one Sunday for Bird and me during fellowship time when a woman archly cooed at us, "Well, you know what the Unitarian sacrament is, don't you?"

"No," we said, amazed.

"*Coffee*, of course!" she chortled, raising her steaming cup to us.

Bird's and my eyes met in the "Uh-oh!" look. Coming from churches that, for all their faults, actually had sacraments and knew what they were, this smug ignorance seemed neither clever nor attractive. And, actually, sad. Nice people, yes, but it seemed things could be a bit too empty and self-congratulatory there. We decided this was not a suitable haven for our questing souls.

For some time, I just wandered around alone in my daze, deciding that I guessed I didn't really believe in God after all. What *did* I believe in? Well, I believed in "Love." Yes, "Love." Seemed good enough for someone not really wishing to examine the issue. And so it remained for a number of years, from age fifteen into my twenties.

Certain things stuck, though, that I couldn't quite shake, like undercover agents in enemy territory. Trained in them from infancy by loving grandparents and even my mother, I still automatically did them. Like always shampooing my hair three times—in honor of the Holy Trinity. Like when bringing someone a glass of water, filling it and pouring it out three times first (also in honor of the Holy Trinity but also quite reminiscent of ancient respectful libations to the gods. Many years later a Christian but non-Orthodox pastor caught me doing this in the church kitchen; "What are you *doing*?!" he said; I stumbled through some vague answer, and he pointed out that pouring out water like that was ecologically wasteful; I stopped doing it).

I did not experience these practices as lingering superstitions; I did not fear that something bad would happen to me if I stopped doing them. These practices felt more like old friends, perhaps elderly relatives who did not speak English too well but who were nice to have around in their vague way. Underlying this may have been a healthy instinct for the wisdom of a traditional culture that reflected in remembrance practices the nearness, the relevance, and the immanence of the helping, healing Divine Presence. God was not an abstraction but there, present, to be remembered and honored even in all the mundane details of daily life. And the reminder was a good one: God could *happen* to you at any moment!

Nonetheless, I stumbled on until, I guess, God felt that He had had enough of my dithering inanity. I was visiting home from college, and my mother, also no longer a believer, insisted that I accompany her to a Greek bake sale at our old church. We walked into the big, empty narthex, me following a few reluctant steps behind my brisk, trotting mother, hearing our footsteps echo hollowly. Suddenly God *happened* to me: I found myself unable to move forward, even when I pressed as hard as I could, against an implacable, invisible barrier in front of me. I couldn't believe it. How could this be? But several attempts on my part failed. Was I having a nervous breakdown? I was horrified.

My mother, now several feet ahead, feeling something wrong, turned suddenly. "Stephani! What is the matter with you?!" I'm sure I must have been white as a sheet. In my disordered panic and disbelief, I could not find words and, instead, burst into tears. Desperately searching for the source of the forbidding force, I found that, although it was impossible to move forward, I could move a little to my right. Following that line of direction, I looked to see what was there. There was nothing—except, several feet away, an *analogion* (icon stand) bearing the icon of St. Paraskevi. Testing as I moved, I found I could continue to move to my right and, as I got closer, felt power emanating, like strong sunlight beating on one's skin on a hot day. It pulsed from Saint Paraskevi's icon. When I reached her portrait, dropping tears on its varnished surface, I humbly bent and kissed it, venerating as I had not done for many years. At that moment, the restraining force vanished, and, shaken but now able to move, I tried to clear my head and followed my incredulous mother to the bake sale.

Did I become a believer again? Nope. I was a bit too shallow and foolish to begin to work with the implications of this experience. But I never forgot it. Many years later, when I became an Orthodox Christian again, I was reacquainted with the hagiography of the great Saint Mary of Egypt, a sixth-century desert mother. I probably never learned this story in Sunday School, as our lessons tended to avoid controversial topics like nymphomaniacs becoming great miracle-working ascetic saints. Well, this was what Mary was, according to her history. Having ensured her passage on a pilgrim ship from Alexandria to the Holy Land by seducing and then sharing herself lavishly with some of the young passengers, Mary felt a strong desire to enter the Church of the Holy Sepulchre in Jerusalem. This massive church shelters both Calvary and the Holy Tomb where Jesus Christ was laid to rest and rose from the dead. Mary reached its great doors and, full of anticipation, tried to enter with a horde of pilgrims. To her horror, she could only proceed a short distance before an invisible wall stopped her on the doorstep, even though other pilgrims were streaming in on either side of her. This was a terrible shock to her soul; forced to contemplate her life, she found herself filled with unexpected remorse. Anguished, she cried out for help to the Virgin Mary, whose icon hung not far from her. The Mother of God responded, telling her what she must do to cleanse her own soul. Mary tearfully assented, and suddenly the restraining force dropped away, and she was able to go forward to venerate the holy shrines. The next day she, obedient to her instructions, took three loaves of bread (a stranger mysteriously gave her three coins to buy them) and some water and crossed the Jordan River, entering the desert. Nothing was heard of her for forty-seven years, until a priest-monk on a Lenten retreat discovered her in the dunes, radiant with holy power. Father Zosimas became Mary's obedient disciple. Their conversation, recorded by a monk in his monastery when Father Zosimas returned, is one of the most beautiful and moving in all accounts of the lives of saints. And the Church dedicates a Sunday and a particular week to her remembrance each Lent.

When I re-encountered this story in my thirties, it held so much visceral meaning for me. Mary of Egypt was a great soul, meant for a great destiny. I don't want to draw any strong parallels to her experience with my own; her experience transformed her life and impelled her to seek the deepest union with God. I was merely discomfited. I nervously turned away from the startling experience, trying to ignore it, powerful though it had been. I couldn't make any sense of it. Two things I did retain, however: that this event had been merciful, a strong—if ignored—corrective from Saint Paraskevi to let me know that, no matter what I believed, she was with me and loved me and also not to dare write off the mystical life altogether; and that God-in-Whom-I-no-longer-believed had a wicked sense of humor. So watch out, all! Fair warning!

CHAPTER SIX

Catalyst: My Cocoon is on Fire

*T*he taxi driver and the Information Man were driving us in their yellow cab high into the green jungles of the hills of Acapulco. The blue sea, wan with the oppressive heat, was dropping rapidly away below us. It was so hot that even the surrounding forests of green trees looked to me like melted emeralds in a lava flow. Sitting in the back seat, I wrapped my arm protectively around the shoulders of my roommate, Jeannie, who was feeling so sick after our long hours on a hot and stuffy bus coming down from the heights and thin air of Mexico City that she was nearly fainting, her face colorless, in the muffling blanket of squalid Acapulcan heat. Freshmen students at the University of the Americas, located about fourteen kilometers above Mexico City, Jeannie and I had decided to use our break time between trimesters to come down to the ocean for refreshment. So far refreshment was the last thing we were getting.

Urged by Mexican friends to visit Acapulco, and assured that a certain guesthouse always had vacancies available, we had dragged our luggage on foot in the drugging heat to this inn, as we were dogged and heckled by a car full of lustful policemen rolling slowly alongside us, only to discover that there was definitely no room. Half dead, we hauled our luggage back to the bus station and, heads swimming, tried to decide what to do next.

We were not new to the possibility of danger. We lived with it every day. Our culture shock at living in Mexico had been drastic. I felt as if the protective cocoon in which my young, tender self was slowly forming its wings and gathering strength to become an adult had been shredded. It felt as if it were on fire, and that I was being forced to leap out of it, half formed, or else dissolve in flames. Culture shock can be like a forest fire, scary and overwhelming, but it does consume the dead wood in your being, often against your desire and will. Suddenly, at seventeen, I found most of the things by which I had known myself falling off me like burnt ash, one after another—nice girl, good student, respected person, safe person—and I had no idea what, if anything, lay beneath them. Was there a ground floor beneath these apparently flimsy structural walls of my persona? Where did the bedrock begin? Was there bedrock? I didn't know. Terrifying! Now I was regarded as a rich (I was the opposite), loose *gringa* whore—not due to anything I had done but because I was tarred and feathered by the Ugly American reputation and the controlling prejudices of a puritanical Roman Catholic culture and government so conservative they had even banned the Beatles from their country.

Our reluctant familiarity with the aggressive *machismo* of the Mexican environment, where walking down any street meant passing through a gauntlet of men "*echando flores*," as they put it, grew daily. This euphemism of "throwing flowers" could hardly disguise the stink of lewd comments and men crowding us and trailing us. After our first trimester, Jeannie and I thought we had developed a certain amount of street smarts, enough to survive the wolf packs, at least in best-case scenarios. But we had not yet learned all their tricks.

ele

Back at the bus station we had dropped wearily into sticky plastic basket chairs, our luggage leaning against us, and tried to make a plan. Even after we both drank some water, Jeannie was still too faint to be able to meaningfully confer, so I knew I had to take charge. I dragged a crumpled little piece of paper out of my pocket with the names of a few alternative guesthouses and hotels our Mexican friends had said were both decent and inexpensive. I looked around for a phone. There was just one, on a wall.

The wall was behind the Information Desk. I had had a helpful encounter at just such a desk at the Mexico City airport on the day of my arrival when an English-speaking Information Lady helped rescue me from being stranded, rideless, at the airport. So I was happy to see an Information Desk here. A fortyish man was standing behind the desk, unusually dressed in a neat suit and tie despite the broiling heat. As I walked around the desk to reach the wall phone, the man stopped me, saying in polite Spanish that he was at my service and could he help me. Naïvely assuming that he was the Information Man, I told him I just wanted to make a couple of calls.

"No, no, *señorita!*" he exclaimed. "You and your friend are so hot and tired. Please sit down and allow me." He waved at the phone with a proprietary air. Perhaps it was the Information Desk phone? I told him we needed a good, inexpensive place to stay and handed him our list. He took it back to the phone and pretended to dial a number from it. We were sitting too far away to hear his conversation. He made a second call, then came over to us, smiling.

"*Señoritas*, I have made a reservation for you at a lovely place. And I have also called a cab to take you there. It will be here in just a few minutes."

We thanked him profusely and limped, pulling our bags, out the front door of the bus station. In an amazingly short time, a taxi pulled up. The driver put our bags in his trunk and, as we got in the back seat, we were surprised to see the Information Man exit the bus station and smoothly slip into the front seat next to the driver. Jeannie was almost unconscious, and I was bewildered. I asked the Information Man in Spanish why he was coming with us.

"Ah, *señoritas*, I wish to show you the beautiful place I have found for you."

I was starting to get worried but thought that it was still possible this could be some innocent Acapulcan practice I was not familiar with. Maybe. So Jeannie and I sat silently in the car as we drove far—and then farther—and then farther still—from Acapulco and its gleaming aquamarine waves, higher and higher into the jungle hills.

Becoming seriously alarmed as habitations dropped out of sight and tropical forests hemmed us in on all sides, I questioned the Information Man with an angry edge in my voice. "Where are you taking us? This is too far. This is no good. Please take us back!"

"*Señorita, señorita*, don't worry!" he said. "You'll see—it is very nice, and we are almost there."

That we were almost there was the only true thing he said. Suddenly the driver pulled the cab over on a narrow grassy verge bordering the jungle. "Get out, *señoritas*," said the Information Man. We stepped out of the cab, and I saw that we were in real trouble. High on this hillside, there was nothing to be seen anywhere but jungle and more jungle.

"There is nothing here! How could this be the place?" I protested.

"You will see, you will see," answered the Information Man. "It is very close now. Come!" And he parted the branches of two bushes by the side of the road. I could see a flagstone path that had been masked by the bushes leading into the jungle. Although scared and wanting to get myself and Jeannie away as quickly as possible, I knew there was no way we could overpower two big men in the middle of nowhere, so I decided it was best to play along with them for the time being. What choice did we have? The Information Man leading and the taxi driver following us, we set off on the jungle path.

After walking a short distance through the shadowy jungle, my heart beating fast, we came upon a clearing. A strange, long house stood in it—one story, with a number of doors fronting a deck that ran its full length. The whole thing was on stilts.

An even stranger figure stood on the deck—a woman, whom the Information Man introduced to us as the "house mother." Russet-skinned and with a face suggesting strong *india* ancestry, "mother" had hair bleached a drastic yellow, piled on top of her head, and held with shiny, rhinestone-studded combs supplemented by a small fortune in hair spray. She wore three women's worth of makeup, and her glaringly red lips looked like warning lights in the jungle dimness. Large hoop earrings swung from her lobes. She wore a sleeveless, very low-cut and clingy purple blouse revealing a large expanse of robust bosom, sandal-style six-inch heels (obviously perfect for walks in the jungle), and, pushing the caricature to its extreme edge, actual gold-lamé toreador pants! I was speechless. She was just short of a hallucination—a cartoon leaping off a *New Yorker* page into terrifying three-dimensional life. It took all my self-control to keep my eyebrows from shooting up into my hairline. And poor Jeannie was now even closer to unconsciousness, not registering our surroundings or the—excuse me—brazen trull who stood before us, reaching out her arms to invite us in.

As the men herded Jeannie and me onto the deck, the "house mother" prattled on in Spanish about how comfortable we were going to be there and how we would love it, how pleased she was to have us girls at her *pensión*, and on and on. We were midway down the deck when "mother" said she would like to show us our room. She opened a door and began to push Jeannie through it. In a flash, alerted by some angel, I saw three things: that there was a padlock hanging on the outside of the door, that there was no light in the room (and possibly no windows), and that, deep within, a naked man was standing with his back to us.

As the woman tried to push the uncomprehending Jeannie into the room by one shoulder, I firmly pulled Jeannie back by

the other and turned to face the "mother." There was not a milli-
second to think about rape, slavery, and the likelihood of Jeannie
and me disappearing into the jungle forever; taking that much
time would be fatal. Fortunately, my shell-shocked consciousness had not a moment to react before an action-oriented angel
stepped into the breach and, keeping my face passive, filled my
mouth with words. Acting as if I had noticed nothing, I found
myself babbling away in Spanish, just a silly *gringa* making
demands, improvising, and ending with this zinger: "*¡Ah, Señora,
lo siento pero necesitamos un teléfono!*" Her expression turned grim
when I demanded a telephone. She quickly closed the door. The
two men, who had been lounging a few feet away, edged up
behind her. The woman tartly replied that they did not have a
telephone and that we would not need one. The angel did not
desert me. I heard myself chattering on, lying in Spanish with a
glossy smoothness that shocked me. "Our family has friends in
Acapulco, *Señora*, and they must approve anywhere we stay, so I
must call them now."

"That is not possible."

"Then we will have to leave," I said firmly.

There was no answer, but all three of our kidnappers' faces
became storm clouds. The Information Man hissed something I
could not make out into the others' ears and, giving me black looks
over their shoulders, they all descended into the clearing and had
a heated, arm-waving discussion about what to do with us. They
were too far away for me to hear what they were saying, but once,
when the taxi driver waved his arms in the air to expostulate,
thus lifting his jacket, I saw a holstered gun hanging beneath his
shoulder.

The stormy discussion went on for some time. At last the
three trooped back up the stairs, looking at us with expressions
of gloomy anger. "So," the Information Man said in a tone indicating that we had ruthlessly wounded his delicate honor, "since
you young ladies are so fussy and so unreasonable and will not
stay in this fine *pensión*, I will have to take you elsewhere. Come!"
With an abrupt gesture he swung on his heel, and he and the taxi
man led us away, back through the jungle, as the "house mother"
glowered darkly at us from the deck. In the end, these kidnappers
had decided not to take a chance in case my wild story, delivered
calmly, might just be true. In Mexico, who you know is critically
important. To possibly offend someone with power was not worth
the risk. They decided not to gamble. The flimsy thread of the
improvised narrative I had fed them, with the grace of God in

Whom at that time I did not believe, raised just enough anxious doubt in their minds to save us.

Back in the taxi, we sped down the twisting jungle roads until at last the Acapulco houses began to appear. We arrived at a small hotel that actually had a beach right across the street. This even turned out to be one of the suitable habitations from our list, and possessed a basic lobby, without a "*madre de la casa*" in sight! My relief was profound.

While the taxi driver rudely tossed our luggage onto the sidewalk (I left Jeannie sitting on it as guard), I entered the lobby to register us. To my displeasure, the Information Man accompanied me. Ignoring my efforts to wave him off, he stood right beside me at the desk while the clerk was checking us in. The Information Man then demanded an exorbitant sum as his rightful pay for "showing you *señoritas* around Acapulco." The basilisk look I turned upon him should have, if karmic consequences only registered more quickly, turned him to stone or, ideally, incinerated him altogether. He was not slow to sum up my sentiments, so even as the words, "No! Certainly not!" in Spanish left my lips, he began shouting.

The clerk and the astonished five or six people rambling around the lobby got to hear the Information Man's outraged denunciation of "cheating *gringas*" who, despite his hospitable efforts, would not pay the basic costs of the working men who had, out of their own goodness, deigned to show these "bad *gringas*" (redundant?) a wonderful tour of Acapulco. He had amazing powers of vocal projection and was working himself up to a higher register. I realized (and so did he) that I just had to get rid of him as quickly as possible. Angrily, I reached into my purse and shoved a very small wad of cash into his hand. It was far, far less than he had been demanding, but I believe he correctly assessed that it was all he would get from me, and, after all, there was that suggestion that we had friends. . . . Cursing me and waving his arms indignantly in the air, the Information Man pounded out of the lobby, and I could breathe again.

Trembling with exhaustion and late-hitting emotion, I collected Jeannie and our luggage, and the clerk showed us to our room. It was even more basic than the lobby—a small square, clean but furnished with only twin beds and a bare light bulb hanging from the ceiling. At that point, we didn't care. We each flung ourselves onto a bed and slept like the dead for a couple of hours.

Waking as if from a hallucinatory dream, I lay there staring at the ceiling, the pastel-tinged rays coming through the window showing that sunset had arrived. I woke up Jeannie, who was feeling much better but still had very little recall of our traumatic day. We decided to refresh ourselves by swimming in the sea and soon, bathing-suit-clad, entered the soft waves of the beach across the street. Although the water was warm, swimming was still refreshing. Soothed, we left the sea. Only to discover why we had not seen anyone else on the beach at our arrival or during our swim time. Big patches of black tar were now sticking to both of us! Apparently, trickster currents carried tar from ships moored in the Acapulco area to this one particular beach. Of course! A fitting end to our disastrous day: we spent our first "spectacular" evening in Acapulco in the pitifully dripping shower, trying to scrub tar off one another while a large green gecko surveyed us with benign interest from the top of the shower stall.

Really, I wasn't supposed to be in Mexico at all. I had been accepted by George Washington University, which callously informed me in May of my senior high school year that, alas, they had over-accepted candidates for their freshman class. And that my parents, having not sent my dorm deposit in on time, had effectively x-ed me out of the class, as the school had to expeditiously shed quite a number of students. Well, actually, I could attend, they amended sanctimoniously, if I had a relative in Washington, D.C., with whom I could live (because no freshmen were allowed to live off campus otherwise). As the shock hit me, I began to wonder frantically where I could find a college acceptance at the eleventh hour. My thoughts drifted to Mexico. I had hoped to study Spanish for a summer at the University of the Americas above Mexico City (a very unlikely dream, as I had to work summers). I thought I probably could get accepted there, even this late, for the full year. And tuition would be low too. Indeed, very soon it was all arranged. Thankfully, neither my parents nor I had any idea how dangerous and insane it was to send a seventeen-year-old girl alone to Mexico City.

Mexico City was like the Wild West in the pre-law-and-order era. It was not like sending your daughter to Paris. Or London. Or Munich. Mexico itself was incredibly untamed. My parents and I, used to the dim suburban normalcy of Long Island, were like people who assume they are adopting a house cat and instead find themselves helplessly wrestling with a saber-toothed puma from the wilds. Well, I wrestled, anyway. Just as soon as I set foot on Mexican soil—or, rather, airport linoleum.

Exhausted and emotionally worn, not having slept in twenty-four hours and suffering my first serious parting from my family and high school boyfriend, I was pretty shaky on arrival. And immediately fell into the clutches of two customs officials who sent me back and forth between their lines until I was the only person left in the big echoing room, an innocent lamb alone with two wolves. Clutching my passport and visa to his chest, leering through his moustache, one official tried to pressure me into going out to dinner with him that night, implying that he would not process my documents until I agreed. My horrified refusal did not sit well with him. I escaped from him and his predatory colleague with difficulty after threatening to call the American embassy and having ultimately to snatch my official papers from the snarling wolf and run as best I could, dragging my luggage and guitar case in awkward haste into the hall.

Further scary confrontations awaited me in the airport, not least because the Greeks, family friends of Pappou's, who were supposed to pick me up did not materialize. My parents and I had no idea that communications to and from Mexico in this precomputer era had to pass through a kind of time-bending Bermuda Triangle—in this case, with the result that the telegram my parents sent to the Greeks three days before my arrival did not show up until two weeks later!

Completely unfamiliar with the social norms (as in the necessity of never making eye contact with any Mexican man) and foolishly unfamiliar with the currency (a massive redcap who grabbed my luggage without a word, tossed it on his cart, and raced off with it, me trotting at his heels, screamed at me, cursing at the top of his lungs, when I offered him an inadequate tip), I was soon completely fried and shaking. Fortunately for me, there was a kind English-speaking young woman behind an Information Desk in the concourse who did her best to see that I was rescued, calling the Greeks—without result—for hours on end while storing my luggage behind her desk. I had no choice but to wander on, circumambulating the concourse like an erratic meteor and, although quite modestly dressed, relentlessly pursued by importuning men who seemed all too aware of my vulnerable, unprotected state.

After a long period of being followed by one pair of footsteps in a lonely area, I at last swung around in anger and fear in front of a column, determined to confront and rebuke my latest pursuer. Instead, the sight of him left me speechless. I found myself staring at a tall eighteen-year-old Mexican Eagle Scout in full regalia— shorts, knee socks, politely knotted bandanna, and pointy khaki hat. Even in my fragile, nerve-reverberating state, I just somehow could *not* be afraid of an *Eagle Scout*. His dark eyes sparkling in a mild, friendly manner, the scout asked me gently in Spanish if he could be of service to me.

So began my first Mexican friendship. Fernando was a premed college student. He took me under his wing, staved off the other hunting men, bought me a milkshake, and hovered over me protectively until the near-hysterical Greeks, finally apprised of the fact that I was in the airport *unchaperoned*, burst into the terminal like a supernova going rogue. This indignant couple dragged me off, rudely shouldering Fernando away, not letting him say goodbye to me or acquire any contact information. But Fernando outsmarted them, later getting my address from my university and connecting with me. Even though he had no English and I barely any Spanish, I enjoyed his company, dictionary in hand, very much; he introduced me to his family, taught me about his culture, serenaded me with his guitar in his car, and taught me many beautiful Mexican love songs. The one thing I didn't find out until months into the relationship—and which put an end to it, as I could not reciprocate in kind—was his telling me that he had fallen in love with me at first sight at the airport and had determined from that moment to marry me.

๛

Cramped in the Greeks' little car as we raced away from the airport, I began to feel ominous cramps gaining momentum in my suddenly troubled digestive system. That milkshake! Oh no! The Greeks were a kindly couple, both lawyers in their early forties, but they displayed a certain dimness around dealing with an exhausted foreign teenage girl. This was not helped by the fact that they spoke only Greek and Spanish. How to communicate? The husband insisted on giving me an evening tour of some of the gigantic city's highlights, which I saw dim and blurred, whipping by in the night, as I desperately tried to calm my nether regions. At least the pain helped keep me awake!

The wife would turn from time to time to stare pityingly at my crumpled self in the back seat and intone, like a doleful Greek chorus, "*¡Pobrecíta! ¡Tan sola! ¡Sin tu madre! ¡Tan sola, tan sola! ¡Sin tu madre!*" I understood enough Spanish from my pathetic three years of high school studies to ascertain that she thought it was a tragic disgrace to be a girl of my tender age "all alone, all alone, without your mother" in Mexico City, adding how much I must miss my *mamá*, etc. This did not cheer me up.

We reached their house, I rushed in, and with unspeakable relief made the acquaintance of their bathroom. The acquaintance of their two teenage children, slightly older than I, a boy and a girl, was less delightful. These two were supercilious and completely uninterested in me in any way. They did not speak English either. But they assessed me with a calculating eye, like two crows deciding whether to dive on a paper bag that was worthless but perhaps might just hold a sandwich.

I spent a miserable few days captive with this family, the well-meaning mother moaning to me about my lamentable state (*"muy triste, muy triste"*—"so sad, so sad") over every meal, though occasionally varying this discourse with her only English phrase—"hoppy [happy] endeeng!" (don't ask)—while her children pressured their parents to allow them to go out to young people's parties normally forbidden them. Providing hospitality to me was the winning excuse. Once we were ensconced in one of these dreadful pretentious-child cocktail parties, the twosome dropped me like a hot potato, leaving me to fend for myself with randy Mexican youths moving in to make toasts to my eyes in the ardent hope of getting their hands on more substantial portions of my anatomy. These parties were long, and I was completely drained at the end of each one, exhausted both by struggling with the Spanish language and fending off would-be Romeos.

اگ

Finally the merciful moment of release arrived: the Greeks, still shaking their heads disapprovingly, had to take me to the apartment on the western side of the city approved by my university for my stay that year. A three-story cube, plastered in pale yellow and angled slightly down at one corner (due to subsidence in the soft soil from Mexico City's frequent earthquakes), sat on an innocuous treeless street, Calle Londres, in a humbler part of the flashy Colonia Roma neighborhood where the streets were named for European cities (hence ours: London), and expensive leather goods, chic perfumes, gem-studded bangles, and fine restaurants abounded. Underclassmen were allowed to stay only in such approved apartments scattered throughout the city; there was no housing for us at the university itself.

And so I met my landlady, the elderly but hale *Señora* Rook, a handsome, formidable Venezuelan widow with an imperious air and a ponderous lacquered gray bun. *Señora* had married into the British diplomatic corps, and seemed to feel that this honor had forever after draped her substantial form with aristocratic glory, before which we mere mortals should feel humbly abased. But, fortunately, she did speak English. After I had a stuffy interview with *Señora* in her small dun living room, she showed me to my bedroom. Without knocking, she swung open a door, revealing a tiny room containing two single beds, upon one of which lay a delicate-boned young woman as crumpled as myself. A very white oval face, framed in blond hair escaping a ponytail, raised itself up and stared at me with pale, exhausted blue eyes. "This is your roommate, Jeanne Stanford," announced *Señora* in a colorless voice, then whisked herself from the room, closing the door.

"Hi!" we both said at the same time, shyly smiling. They were good smiles. Warm sparkles seemed to fly between us. Within minutes we could both see that we were going to be good friends. What a relief! Had I believed in God at the time, I would have been grateful to Him.

Jeannie had arrived at *Señora's* a couple of days before me and quickly gave me the lay of the land. *Señora* was temperamental and a bit difficult but tolerable, usually.

We were forbidden to enter the kitchen, and all meals were cooked and served by a rota of Mexican Indian maids, Jeannie said. She rolled her eyes about the food—enough to sustain life but neither plentiful nor particularly tasty, with a menu running heavily toward whatever was the cheapest food on the market at the time. Unfortunately, this was usually guavas. To this day, I cannot look a guava in the pit. We remade their acquaintance nightly—fresh, stewed, candied, fried, pureed, creamed, and in various other loathsome forms, including on liver as a ghastly sauce. It got to the point that I actually had a nightmare one night of a giant guava chasing me through the jungle!

Of course, we also had to adapt to the spicy Mexican food. It took us some time, and for many months we kept an oversized jar of Tums on the stand between our beds, eating whole handfuls, especially at bedtime. At least the food at *Señora* Rook's was relatively mildly spiced, so we had the opportunity to ease our way in. However, we came to love the spiciness of the cuisine, and, when we returned home, plain food upset my stomach for about the first six months!

But our tribulations in the apartment were relatively minor, and we had the whole wide, exciting world of Mexico City to explore. Even in the 1960s it was one of the largest cities in the world, its dusty streets reaching out for hundreds of square miles in crowded shantytowns, soaring palaces and museums, noble pyramids, beautiful colonial blue-and-white-tile buildings, ancient stone churches, and the crowded, smudged pastel cubes of plastered storefronts leaning against one another, always adorned after dark with locked covers of protective lacy iron grillwork.

Nestled as it was in an ancient drained lake bed at an altitude of over seven thousand feet, it took Jeannie and me a while to acclimate to this lofty city, both because of the heavy smog often trapped in the vast valley by the ring of surrounding mountains and because of the thinness of the air.

Not far from where we lived was the hemisphere's largest city park (almost 1,700 acres), lovely green Chapultepec, decked with statues and crowned with the ill-fated Emperor Maximilian I's decaying but impressive palace. Close by us, the imposing ten-lane Paseo de la Reforma angled diagonally like a long, straight sword through some of the city's most vibrant neighborhoods. La Reforma was anchored dramatically by the twenty-two-foot statue of a large golden winged victory (though female, known universally as *El Ángel*) on its white 148-foot column surrounded by many lesser statues and embraced by a busy traffic circle. The downtown end of la Reforma deposited you at the frothy marble wedding cake of Bellas Artes, the domed city opera house.

I gaped at palm trees, fir trees, eucalyptus, pines, cacti, deciduous trees of all kinds growing together, and fuschia and coral bougainvillea pouring in torrents over courtyard walls. The subtropical highland climate here allowed a lively variety of unlike flora to grow side by side, as if painted fancifully by Henri Rousseau.

Living at such a high altitude often felt exhilarating, as if I were rocketing into the sky like a hawk. And I was breathing in a subtle, unfamiliar energy—a very attractive blend of the Spanish and Indian temperaments and culture—like a wind blowing in from a new direction on a completely new compass in a completely different world. This wild-feeling fusion seemed to reverberate out of the powerful, untamed land itself, both formal and dignified as a Spanish Baroque concerto anchored by round, velvety viola da gamba chords and eagle-shrill, improvised, and irrepressibly soaring as Indian pipes.

There were so many novel colors and sensations that it seemed as if I could never take them all in, hard as I tried. Never had I been anywhere so layered at every turn by elaborate ancient cultures and yet so unflattened, unvanquished, by their weighty presences. The earth itself felt like a huge wild beast, a great puma, and, though it allowed us to sit on its massive mountain shoulders, we could feel the beat of its great unsubdued heart, ready at any time, according to its changing moods, to leap into movement and single-minded life, regardless of our petty human wills and desires. And, indeed, the earth frequently did move.

Exhausted, I actually slept through one of the many minor

temblors to shake the city. Coming into the living room in the morning, I discovered this by the sight of the chandelier rattled overnight into a new and odd angle and a few books on the floor, fallen from a shelf.

Due to the city having been built on fathoms of soft lake-bed sand, all its buildings were slowly sinking; some of the earliest from the colonial era were now thirty feet below the surface. The great doors of one ancient conquistador-era church Jeannie and I sometimes visited were so far underground that we had to enter by tall windows more than one story up and then walk down an interior inserted stairway to reach the nave far below.

There was both squalor and beauty all around, often side by side, such as refuse strewn on the sidewalk in front of aging, decrepit *tiendas*—small stores with hand-lettered cardboard signs in their mostly bare windows—alongside elegant colonial buildings, their outside walls covered in marvelous patterned tiles in white, blue, and yellow.

Beggars, clean and colorfully dressed in skirts and blouses bright with native embroidery, appeared on almost every corner. These Indian women, half a head or more shorter than even short me, stood with one hand outstretched while cuddling their little children clustered around their skirts. Even after our pesos had reached their palms, they did not seem inclined to talk with us. Mexican women of all classes shunned us. It was "known" that *gringas* were whores, so no respectable Mexican woman would be seen with us, much less befriend us. This was very lonely for us, even more so because of the constant harrying by predatory men.

۔لم

A woman, however, became one of my greatest comforts— Iztaccíhuatl, the White Lady. An enormous dormant volcano at over seventeen thousand feet, she lies like a sleeping princess high above the city to the southeast, not far from her companion active volcano, the Popocatépetl. Looking exactly like a huge, glorious woman lying on her back, her head, breasts, torso, knees, and feet plainly to be seen, she is clad in snow streaming down like a gown or long hair into steep ravines, lit purple, amber, and rose by the sunset glow. The White Lady was my unfading inspiration, always lifting me up from whatever dark mood I may have fallen into. Seeing her was endlessly inspiring and comforting, even though the valley's heavy smog often veiled her from view. In the midst of struggling with cultural clashes and drastic change, I was deeply grateful for her unchanging presence of majesty and peace.

چگ

When we were lucky on less smoggy days, rushing off to catch a bus to our school, Jeannie and I might catch an occasional glimpse of the White Lady or the Popo. I loved breathing in the freshness of the early morning as we hurried along, each munching on a steaming-hot, freshly baked *bolillo*—a crusty roll with tender insides, shaped like a little golden boat, purchased from a tiny Indian woman on the street who kept her rolls warm in cloths in a basket hooked over one arm. The streets were full of small-boned Indian maids in simple cotton dresses and aprons, shod in sandals or flip-flops, their long double braids tied with ribbons behind their backs, as they poured soapy water on the sidewalks and scrubbed them with mops, as if washing away all the city's bad dreams of the night in the new gleaming sunlight. My heart always lifted at the sight. It seemed as if they washed my own heart.

But we had to pay careful attention and not get distracted. It took me over a week to learn how to cross the dizzying ten lanes of the Paseo de la Reforma and arrive in one piece at our bus stop. Aside from the generally crazy driving of the cars and even the buses, this was the first time I had ever seen drivers speed up rather than slow down at the sight of a crossing pedestrian! Their intent seemed to be to come as close to grazing you as possible without actually hitting you. Some of these madmen would even shout "*¡Olé!*" as they just skimmed by you. I thought these daredevil drivers must keep competitive scratch-mark charts of their victims on their dashboards. But, thankfully, we always made it to the plain yellow school bus waiting to carry students up higher into the mountains.

Three days after we met, Jeannie and I caught this bus for the first time, peering out its windows in wide-eyed wonder as we left the crowded city behind and the ever-rising road grew narrow and swooping. Far below us we could see deep mountainside barrancas full of dry dirt, grasses, shrubs, and weedy trees, and also, to our horror, two buses from the Toluca line (all too accurately known as the "Toluca Rocket") that had made the hundred-foot plunge and now lay on their battered sides like fallen warriors. This was not as infrequent an occurrence as one might hope! Sobered, we sat quietly for the rest of the ride.

If that sight had been sobering, our orientation lecture was enough to make us catatonic. We just thanked our stars that our parents could not hear it. Let me say that it bore no resemblance whatsoever to the white-gloved Vassar orientation tea my guidance counselor had pressured me into attending the year before.

Welcoming us briefly, the dean quickly abandoned niceties, and with little preamble and unruffled cool, launched into a series of warnings about living safely in Mexico City.

Her topics:

(1) *Never* call the police if there is any problem. They are underpaid, usually corrupt, and will only make the situation worse—at the least, demanding bribes, and sometimes much more (two of their students had been raped by police the year before). Hoping to get more money out of you, they might even put you in jail. Sometimes they are even in on the crime.

(2) Should you be hurt in an accident, crawl into the bushes, if necessary, until you can see which ambulances were sent for. Never *ever* allow yourself to be placed in an ambulance marked with a green cross. Stay in the bushes rather than permit this. These ambulances belong to Mexican hospitals where the sanitary conditions are so bad that, even if you would normally recover, you might be carried off by an infection contracted in that hospital. No matter what, wait for an ambulance with a red cross; that one will take you to the good and sanitary British hospital. (Bear in mind, dear reader, this was advice given in the 1960s, and may no longer apply.)

(3) *Mordidas* ("little bites"), or bribes, are customary here, though not legal. Try to avoid giving them, though in some cases you may not be able to avoid them.

(4) Women students should never wear slacks. This is regarded as signaling that you are a prostitute (in that era, this was quite true).

(5) Never eat from food stands, avoid uncooked fruits and vegetables even in most restaurants, and drink only bottled water. Typhoid and other noxious illnesses periodically sweep through the city.

I think there were more instructions but at some point my eyes and, more to the point, my ears glazed over. What had I done in coming to this crazy, danger-strewn country?! Well, I certainly would *not* be writing to my parents about our orientation because, frightening as it all was, I was already, nonetheless, acquiring a taste for the wild freedom and piquant atmosphere of this fascinating country, so challenging and enlivening to my dull Long Island-anesthetized senses. Jeannie and I both wanted to stay and see how the adventure would unfold.

بؤ

Jeannie and I had hoped that *Señora* Rook might take us under her wing a bit and coach us because we knew that we were dangerously ignorant. But *Señora* brushed us off as if she were too busy for our

questions—not too busy, however, to refrain from often command-
ing me to bring my guitar to the living room and demanding that
we both sing to entertain her. We began to feel like minstrels in
a feudal court.

Unfortunately, *Señora* was "too busy" to counsel us the first
night we decided to go to the movies, so we made a disastrous
choice. Mexican movie theaters were insanely huge—a bit like
roofed-over football fields with odd giant sculptures and other
eccentric ornamental gestures tossed in as surrealistically as in a
dream. They were also very, very dark. As in night black.

There were first-, second-, and third-class movie theaters.
Respectable women only patronized the first-class theaters. Too
bad we didn't know that. We went, of course, to a second-class
movie theater, arriving a little late. We struggled down one of the
huge long aisles in the dark and found two seats by feel.

Partway through the movie, my leg started to feel a bit odd, as
if a small insect was perhaps crawling lightly under my skirt. The
slowly skittering touch was so ephemeral, I wasn't always sure it
was there, especially clad as I was, before the advent of pantyhose,
in one of the era's torture-of-women devices, a rubberized girdle
that held my stockings up. I kept shifting around. The skittering would back off and then return, stop and return. A terrible
moment of clarity crystallized when I suddenly realized that the
touching, growing slowly more purposeful, was not, after all, some
bug but an unseen man's hand under my skirt! I jolted to my feet,
electrified.

"Jeannie, we have to go! Right away!"

"Okay. Are you all right?"

"No!"

As we barged down the aisle, the seated men began to
laugh, guessing all too well the reason for our precipitate flight.
Unfortunately, before we got to the lobby, which seemed to be a
few acres away, an intermission began. Some men came hoot-
ing into the lobby at our heels and chased us out into the street,
accompanied by others who had just been lounging around the
lobby before we provided additional entertainment. This lustful
host followed us for blocks, cheering and catcalling. We felt like
foxes being run down by a pack of hounds, but at last we managed
to lose them. It is amazing how fast you can run when you have to!

Disheveled and sweating, we limped back to *Señora*'s apartment and sat down at her table to drink some water. *Señora* joined
us, inquiring disapprovingly about our disarray. We told her our
tale, watching a delighted grin begin to spread across her face. *I*

can't believe she's that cruel! I thought. But a moment later, all was revealed.

"Yes, this also happened to me," she said, startling us. "Well, you know it is so dark in the theaters they could not tell that I was old. So a man began, you know, to do like that. But I was ready for him! You see this?" she asked, pulling a lethal eight-inch hairpin from her bun and smiling beatifically. "I wait and then I—"she raised her arm high and stabbed hard at the table with the sharp pin, like a karate expert breaking wooden blocks with her hand. "'Ai', he screamed! He screamed! He jumped up and ran away. All the audience was laughing and applauding me! Yes, they clapped and clapped! And then I watched the movie.

"So, girls, remember always to carry hairpins. Sharp ones!" And standing up with the dignity of a reigning queen, having generously shared her largesse of wisdom, she processed back to the royal bedroom.

꧁

Jeannie and I were pretty homesick that fall—it was our first time away from our families, with every day spent stressfully dealing with a challenging foreign culture and language. November rolled around, and we began to think wistfully of the holidays. It would soon be Thanksgiving.

To our surprise, *Señora* started to make glancing references to Thanksgiving dinner, smilingly listing its traditional components. We were amazed. Might she actually be thinking of providing us a real Thanksgiving dinner? How lovely that would be! Especially as her current meals were only enough to sustain life and not much more. Lately, she had even taken to gradually reducing the size of our milk glasses, week after week. We were down to almost shot size.

It must be that we were to have a real Thanksgiving dinner, otherwise why would she keep slyly mentioning it? "Mmmm . . . turkey. Mmmm . . . gravy. Mmmm . . . mashed potatoes. Yes, and pie! Thanksgiving! Right, girls?"

We got more and more excited as the weeks passed. Finally, the great day came. Although we did not smell any of the familiar savory Thanksgiving odors in the apartment, still hoping, we hastened to the dinner table. As we unfolded our napkins, that night's Indian maid carried in two plates of nondescript fritters, also balancing two tiny bowls of—oh yes! Just stick the knife in our chests and get it over with!—candied guavas! And set this feast before us. We were aghast.

At that moment, *Señora*, dressed up and chic in a coat and little hat, her pocketbook swinging from her arm, flounced out of her room. "Goodbye, girls!" she cried. "I am going to Sanborn's to have a *real* American Thanksgiving dinner with my friends!" And sailed out the door.

We were speechless and sat there stunned, drowning in a pool of homesickness. Our disappointment was inexpressible. Two large tears began to roll slowly down Jeannie's face.

"Oh, Jeannie!"

She started to sob. "Oh, this is so terrible!" Pausing to try to control her tears, she then added hopelessly, "I wish that at least, at least, I could have another glass of milk!" She was desperately clutching her shot glass with the hand not wiping her face.

"You will!" I said. I got up and, with stormy brow, stalked into the forbidden kitchen. The maid tried to fend me off but I politely insisted. Getting two big glasses, I filled them with milk and brought them back to the table. "Now, drink that, Jeannie!" I growled. "And then we are going out to eat! Just leave this stuff!"

We drank our milk, got our coats, and went out. Being quite poor, we could not afford the festivities at Sanborn's café but settled for "Thanksgiving tacos" in a local eatery. At least we were not being force-fed guavas! We lingered and had a nice walk, returning to the apartment feeling, if not satisfied, at least calm.

Señora had returned before us, as we discovered when she sprang out of her bedroom like a malevolent jack-in-the-box the moment we entered. "How dare you!" she cried. "I allow you to live under my roof and you steal from my kitchen! Ungrateful, thieving girls!"

"What do you mean, *Señora?*" I replied with dangerous, frozen politeness.

"You know what I mean! The maid told me that you went into the kitchen and took milk!"

"That's right," I agreed. "You have been giving us smaller and smaller glasses, *Señora*. We need the larger size of glasses we originally had. We are paying you for room *and* board!"

She looked at us as if we were loathsome squashed insects she had just found on the bottom of her shoe. Drawing in a deep breath and pulling herself up to her full height, she glared at us and delivered her ultimate masterly thrust, slowly enunciating each word with heavy emphasis: "Do—you—know—why—Mexicans—*hate*—Americans?!"

"No," we responded, mystified.

"It is because they smell like MILK!" she yelled, stepping back into her room and slamming the door.

Jeannie and I, our hands over our mouths, dashed for our room. Closing the door, we threw ourselves on our beds and put pillows over our heads to drown out the sounds of our uncontrollable laughter. When we could finally stop and lay there gasping, aching with hilarity, I grinned at Jeannie and said, "That was almost worth it! After all, who knew?"

"Right." She chuckled. "Mystery solved. Someone should tell the diplomats!"

۞

If Jeannie and I had not had each other, I'm not sure either of us would have survived the loneliness of that year. But we weren't entirely alone. Family appeared fairly early in our stay in the whimsical person of Tío Pepe (Uncle Joe), a longtime resident of Mexico City and the man who had rashly married my Greek grandmother's temperamental (a euphemism the family didn't usually bother with) sister, Sophie. They had now been separated for many years.

Tío Pepe, a short, gray-haired, balding Spaniard with Coke-bottle eyeglasses, who often flourished a lisping Castilian accent (that Mexicans seem to find pretentious), showed up in a neat gray suit and 1940s-style tie and tiepin one day to take Jeannie and me out to lunch. He spoke good English, having lived in the States for many years, which is where he met Sophie. He was retired but neither Jeannie nor I can recall what his profession had been, although I think he might have been an engineer.

More recently he had retired from singing in Mexico City's Bellas Artes opera chorus. He often took us to churches where we could hear him sing on Sundays. Proud of his tenor voice, he made the most of any opportunity to carol aloud, including when we were walking about the city with him, one of us on each arm.

"*La donna è mobile*," sang out Tío Pepe, head thrown back and eyes to the sky, as we three traversed a crowded downtown sidewalk, Jeannie and me watching the ground to keep him from tripping. "*Qual piuma al vento, muta d'accen-en-en-en-to!*" He was so busy hitting the aria's high notes that he didn't seem to notice when passing men would throw a smooch near our faces, try to cop a feel, or lean in to whisper intensely into our ears what beauties we were.

It was deeply distressing to us to have our normally limited freedom further reduced by being attached to Tío Pepe's arms and thus unable to maneuver away from these unwanted attentions. My great-uncle, however, pretended he did not notice the passing brouhaha in the least, and we were reluctant to bring the subject up for fear of embarrassing him. We knew he had masculine vanity enough to feel proud to be swinging along with two young women on his arms, and suspected he ignored the men's provocations for fear that his growing age and waning strength might not be enough to fend off these unpleasant suitors. We sensed that his pride must have suffered significantly somewhere in his life and so we stayed mum rather than inflict another possible wound. But even our gentle suggestions that we walk a bit faster always fell on deaf ears.

ﷺ

Tío Pepe phoned one day to tell us he had great news: we were invited to attend a stylish Spanish wedding with him. The bride and groom were stars of the opera company. We tried to refuse but he would not take no for an answer.

So Tío Pepe appeared at the appointed time and date, grinning broadly, and introduced us to a friend of his, Jorge, a jovial man in his early fifties. Jorge was also a guest and would drive us to the reception (I have no memory of attending the wedding itself).

It was a big wedding reception, apparently no expense spared. Numberless long tables were lined up end to end in an enormous ballroom, set with sparkling glass, shining silver, lavish flowers, and spotless white linen. We were among the last of the two hundred guests to arrive, and Tío Pepe settled us at a table near the bottom of the hall, across from himself and Jorge.

Jeannie and I, after surveying the opulent table settings, looked at each other in consternation. There were seven or eight elegant glasses of various sizes and shapes at each place setting, some of them fancily engraved. This did not bode well. Already excessive by number alone, this many alcoholic drinks at this high altitude would probably knock us unconscious in no time. Wordlessly, we nodded at each other, both thinking the same thing—we would only pretend to drink.

But then the toasts to the bride and groom, a striking young couple, began—they were endless and with each one we had to stand, raise the appropriate glass, and drink. This went on with a different high-octane beverage, poured by waiters, for each of seven or eight courses! Not to mention the lovely apple-scented champagne! Our plan to only pretend was foiled immediately by Tío Pepe who, keeping a close eye on us, noted that we were not really drinking but only raising the glasses to our lips. His face scrunched in disapproval, he gave us a sharp bottoms-up sign each time to make us drink, implying that we were being rude in refusing. This drew attention too. So, sighing, we drank. And drank. And drank.

By the fifth course, we both needed to use the ladies' room but found that our knees were quite wobbly. We managed to climb out of our chairs, leaning on each other.

"Jeannie," I slurred at close range, "There ish no color in your fayshe. Even your lipsh are white."

"Yessh," she mumbled distractedly. "You alsho."

We got free of the table and stood there, embracing each other and swaying. Then, as if making our way on a schooner deck in a storm, we staggered, supporting each other, what seemed like a vast, deck-shifting distance to the ladies' room. We managed to finish our business there and arrived back at the table, me silently cursing to see people swaying to their feet for the sixth-course toast.

Eventually rich wedding cake was served with yet more champagne toasts, and we were relieved to hear Tío Pepe announcing to us that we were finally leaving. He was going downstairs with Jorge to get the car and, after we paid a last trip to the ladies' room, we would meet them in the street below.

We went downstairs and were about to leave when we heard some noises behind us and turned to look. Four Mexican men were carefully carrying the remains of the enormous seven-layer wedding cake, four and a half of the huge layers still intact, down some rather steep, narrow stairs. The cake was about four feet across on the bottom so it was a bit tricky for the large men and the large cake to descend together. Hence, the men were climbing down very attentively and slowly, two to a side.

My state of inebriation had, at that point, passed from catatonia to impish merriment and, on impulse, I said to them cheerily, "*¡Buena suerte!*" (Good luck!)

Fatal. They all laughed. And dropped the cake! (I'm sure that there were no sober people left in that building anyway but still. . . .) It sat at a horrid sharp angle on the steep stairs, melting.

Jeannie and I and the men watched in fascinated horror as the four-plus layers of cake began separating as if in a slow-motion Disney documentary on glaciers, each section descending at its own increasingly mushy, messy pace, calving sugared roses and icing bows, slipping steadily off the gigantic platter and onto the dirty steps. A growl of anger began to rise from the men's throats. Jeannie and I did not hesitate. We did not apologize. We had been in Mexico long enough to know not to lose a second. We were off and running like greyhounds as their protests rose behind us, our fear acting as a tonic to clear our muzzy minds. We arrived, panting, at Jorge's car, threw ourselves into the back seat, slammed the doors, and were off!

Tío Pepe sat, cheerful and unconcerned, in the front seat, alternately serenading us with opera arias and making jokes. Jorge, who obviously had drunk very deep of the libation for each course, had a wild gleam in his eye and was taking half the corners on two wheels only. Jeannie and I were flung back and forth across the back seat (yes, this was in ancient pre-seat belt days) as if we really were riding out a storm at sea. Tío Pepe remained grinning and oblivious while Jorge, ignoring our pleas to slow down, began, to our disbelieving ears, an impassioned rant in Spanish about how "*los Japonéses*" (the Japanese) were the *worst* drivers in the world, and how he had barely survived a stay in Tokyo!

Our knees were even wobblier from fear by the time we thankfully exited the car at our apartment building on Calle Londres. Our gratitude to feel solid, unmoving earth beneath our feet was immense. We looked up wearily to wave, and saw Tío Pepe being whisked away, blowing fond, airy kisses to us as they disappeared around the bend—on two wheels.

༄

Not long after, Tío Pepe phoned to tell us he had another treat in store for us. He had gotten three tickets to a performance of *Die Fledermaus* at the opera house. We were to meet him at Bellas Artes on the appointed date and time. "Be on time!" he hectored.

We probably would have been, except as we—dressed up and polished—hastened to la Reforma to catch a *pesero* (at that time, a cab that would take you the length of la Reforma for a *peso*, then roughly eight U.S. cents), we had the bad luck to get into an expiring *canario*. (*Peseros* came in two varieties: *cocodrilos*, green with big black-and-white crocodile teeth actually painted around the hood, and *canarios*, yellow as the little birds.)

We made highly irregular progress, our driver pulling over at every fountain down the long Reforma, politely excusing himself, running to the trunk, grabbing a bucket, rushing to the latest fountain to fill it, opening the *canario* hood, and pouring copious water into his water tank!

At the third fountain, we remonstrated with him, knowing that no matter what, we were going to be horribly late. We said we would pay him his full fare but that we would need to catch another cab. I don't know why, but this seemed to upset him terribly. He protested that he himself would get us to Bellas Artes. "Please, *señoritas*," he pleaded. Looking into those inexplicably imploring eyes, we somehow could not refuse. So we bunny hopped from fountain to fountain the rest of the way, wondering if his water tank had any bottom at all.

Pulling up to Bellas Artes, we leaped out, paid and tipped the driver (well, the poor thing!), and ran past the many statues on its little plaza to the entrance where Tío Pepe materialized, looking scandalized. "Come! You're late! It's about to start!" We raced through the lobby on his heels and threw ourselves into our seats. A moment later, the opening notes of the opera rang out.

All was smooth sailing until the intermission, when Tío Pepe suggested we get some fresh air in the lobby. We strolled out, one of us on each of his arms, as usual. When we reached the center of the lobby, a tiny gray-haired woman wearing dark sunglasses and a gray dress came catapulting out of a dim corner and confronted Tío Pepe with the unfettered ferocity of a ground bird defending its nestlings.

"*¡Viejo cabrón!*" she screeched at him as she rushed toward us. "Old goat!" Continuing in equally condemnatory Spanish, she entertained the admiring lobby audience. "A blonde on one arm and a brunette on the other, young enough to be your daughters! You are a disgrace!" she cried. And so on.

"Jeannie," I whispered, pulling her free of Tío Pepe, "I think this would be the perfect time to go to the ladies' room, don't you?"

"Absolutely," she replied fervently.

We rushed off, leaving my great-uncle to do battle. As we sheltered in the bathroom, I speculated that the source of these additional theatrics could only be my great-aunt Sophie. Our family had carefully kept from her the knowledge that I would be in Mexico and forbidden me to see her. So I thought it unlikely that she knew whom she was screaming about.

We peeped out the ladies' room door periodically to see how the fortunes of battle were going. Thea Sophie might be tiny and old but her lungs were certainly strong! Both elderly gladiators were now waving their arms at each other, an angry look creasing Tío Pepe's face. They were surrounded by a rapt circle of operagoers. What an irresistible free show! After a long time, Thea Sophie delivered a parting shot of spleen in ringing tones, indignantly swept her invisible villainess's cape of darkness around her, and sailed angrily out the door.

We returned to a sweating Tío Pepe, dabbing his forehead with a handkerchief. "Well," he said, "at least she still doesn't know who you are, Stephani. I did not tell her. But she knew that we were coming because she went into my mailbox and opened the letter with the opera house tickets. I did wonder when I found that it had been opened. I suspected her but never thought that she would do this!"

We returned, rather sobered, for the next and comparatively less dramatic act of the opera.

⁂

A couple of weeks later, I received a phone call from a strange woman. Her low-pitched, velvety voice speaking in English identified her as my great-aunt Sophie. I stumbled through a hesitant greeting. She made small talk about my studies and quickly moved to an invitation to take me out to lunch. She must have learned who I was from the local Greeks' small grapevine, also realizing that I had avoided contact with her and that I had witnessed her humiliating scene at Bellas Artes. As I gently rebuffed her offer, claiming heavy schoolwork, she persisted in trying to set a date for a meeting. A kind of iridescent green venom seeped into the honey of her fascinating, hypnotic voice as she exerted all her powers of persuasion.

Gently but firmly, I refused. Angry, she hung up. I never heard from her again. A couple of months later, I was told, Sophie took off with the money accumulated while watching over a friend's candy store while this poor woman was far away dealing with a funeral. The friend came home to an empty cashbox. And that was the last anyone heard of Sophie.

⁂

Not long after the milk incident, Jeannie and I decided we could no longer endure living in that apartment with *Señora* and her guavas. We were afraid that another approved apartment might be as bad or worse. So we secretly started hunting on our own and found a simple but nice boardinghouse not far away where we could even have our own rooms for far less than we were paying *Señora* Rook. We moved out at the end of the December trimester and, not specifying our new address to *Señora* or anyone, moved into our new rooms. They were a little chilly but spacious, and we felt free. But not for long. Someone had reported us to the dean of students, who called us in, dressed us down, and threatened to kick us out of the school if we did not move back into an approved apartment. And there was only one possible apartment left.

So began our sojourn with the del Olivares family. Not many days after our interview with the dean, we found ourselves buzzed in on the ground floor and marching up three long flights of stairs to a plain apartment in a nondescript building on Calle Sinaloa where *Señor* del Olivares, a tall, gracious middle-aged man with a sleek dark moustache, welcomed us in the door. Behind him stood a small woman with shortish waved black hair wearing an apron and printed cotton dress, smiling ingratiatingly through her scarlet lipstick. *Señora* del Olivares's black, anxious eyes looked out from dark whirlpools of smudged heavy mascara, which blended into the natural dark pouches under her eyes, somehow giving her the look of a nervous, traumatized cocker spaniel.

The del Olivareses did not speak English, but by that time Jeannie and I had mastered enough Spanish to fend fairly well for ourselves. Our new landlord and landlady quickly ushered us to our room and stood expectantly to take in our reactions. Fortunately, having been in Mexico for some months now and subjected to constant harassment, Jeannie and I had acquired a good command over our facial expressions. So, as we registered the shock of the teeny room with two narrow beds separated only by a tiny nightstand and a big pot with a huge, dark, glossy-leaved plant, taller than us, leaning menacingly forward (we dubbed it the "Potted Peril" and did not enjoy sleeping in its shadow); the small closet already taken up by two vertical bicycles and other family bric-a-brac; and the one tall bureau topped with a mirror reflecting—who knew why?—seven or eight king-sized bottles, some partially full, some empty, of Jockey Club cologne (the empty ones had big red plastic roses stuck randomly in them), with the surrealistic pièce de résistance, a real stuffed skunk set at eye level in the midst of the bottles, we did not wince. "*Muchas gracias,*" we nodded politely, a bit wide-eyed. Smiling and satisfied, they left us to unpack.

"Oh, Jeannie!" I cried when they were out of earshot. "Oh no!" Having grown up with a pet skunk, my reaction to the stiff, taxidermied creature on the bureau was like yours would have been, dear reader, had you moved into a new place only to see a stuffed Fido or Mittens, your childhood pet, callously displayed before your disbelieving eyes on your bureau. My mother had insisted on getting a de-scented baby skunk when I was a child, and Joy (as she named him, after the most expensive perfume in Paris) became a member of our family, sleeping on my bed and consuming his favorite meal of sausage, chocolate, and grapes (he peeled them) in lordly leisure.

So, I could not view with indifference the murdered skunk on our bureau. I immediately stuffed it in the closet. Being as tactful as we could, we got the del Olivareses to reluctantly remove the skunk, the Jockey Club cologne bottles and plastic roses, and the bicycles over the next few days and began to settle in to face the real challenge: *Señora's* cooking. The dean had warned us. This apartment had been empty because *Señora's* cooking was terrible.

In the interest of not giving you sympathetic indigestion, I will not detail *Señora's* menus for you. Suffice it to say that they tended to feature delicacies like coagulated bull's blood. Because she knew of her bad cooking reputation, *Señora* watched us like a hawk at every meal to be sure we ate our food. Jeannie and I had to develop a technique to enable at least one of us at a time to avoid consuming the awful meals. So, we took it in turns to begin animated conversations with *Señora*, using extravagant gestures to catch her eye, while the other, unseen, quickly slipped the food on her plate into the napkin on her lap. On lucky nights, we could alternate and both escape eating, but on some nights one of us would have to be the "sacrificial lamb" and choke down the food. This added a piquant note of gustatory martyrdom to our stay.

We both dated various young Mexican men, most of whom we met at the North-American Cultural Institute where we went folkdancing each week, and, as the months passed, Jeannie even fell in love with a warm and charming man, Ricardo, whom she met there and who adored her.

Somehow, atypically, I wound up going out for a number of months with a rich, intelligent student from Austin, Texas who attended our school. Alan was short with small, neat features, blue eyes, very white skin, and close-cropped black hair. He favored tweed jackets and pipes, probably seeing himself as a fashionable intellectual. He also possessed a sleek red Porsche, and being a bit older than us, was allowed to rent a nice apartment in the Mexico City foothills not far from our school.

One night Alan took me out to a very fancy restaurant. As we pulled down the street for the restaurant, we noticed a large glass store window fronting a big display room of the kind that might hold new deluxe cars for sale. However, nothing was in the display room but a city bus that had pulled halfway through the now-broken window. And, apparently, was just left eerily abandoned there, the kind of troubling, surreal sight that tended to pop up in Mexico City at unexpected moments, giving the city its perpetually dream-like, Salvador Dalí-painting quality.

We paused, nonplussed, and then drove on but could not find parking for the restaurant. Fortunately, there was a bank parking lot just next door. We went upstairs to the restaurant, which had a well-appointed room with very few tables, each centered in its own large space, as if each were a separate galaxy, possessing its own hovering five waiters like planets bound to our personal gravitational field. The people at the other tables were considerably older than we were and all very prosperous looking. I certainly felt out of place, but Alan seemed confident and relaxed. The food was very good, but I found the five waiters at our elbows, staring at us and quick to respond to any slight indication of our needs, disconcerting and could not relax.

After Alan paid the check and left for the men's room, the maître d' came over and, bending down, whispered in my ear in Spanish, "Would you like to take home the leftovers for Mamá?" He obviously thought I was a Mexican young lady out with a *gringo* swell and unaccustomed to such luxury. I was sorry to disabuse him of his notion of my nationality but knew that as soon as I opened my mouth to gently refuse, he would know I was not Mexican. And he did, looking at me in surprise.

Unless I was with blond, blue-eyed Jeannie with her more typically American clothes, I was almost never taken for an American. I wore my long dark hair up, except for a long lock cascading over one shoulder, and my clothing looked more European to Mexicans. Even if I opened my mouth, I was sometimes mistaken for an Italian, as apparently my accent had soft, round vowel sounds as opposed to the flatter American accent. I apparently looked like a respectable young Mexican woman to some, who would even stop to ask me for directions in the Zona Rosa, laughing ruefully when I explained that I was a stranger there too.

Full of a good meal, we climbed into Alan's Porsche and were about to leave when a small, skinny Mexican man ran toward us through the bank parking lot, waving his arms and shouting. He ran to Alan's side of the car, sticking out his hand and protesting loudly. It was obvious he was demanding payment for something. Alan, realizing this was a con, angrily refused. We knew there was no attendant in the bank parking lot at night. My Spanish was better than Alan's, and I tried to soothe the man. But he raved on, and Alan, losing patience, hit the gas pedal. Unfortunately, by then the little man had seized hold of the door on the driver's side and, rather than jumping off, lifted his legs and held on!

To my horror, we were soon speeding down the middle of the ten-lane Reforma with this madman hanging on only inches from the ground. Sometimes he held on with only one arm, waving his other hand angrily in front of Alan's face, still demanding payment. I was terrified he would fall off and be killed and equally terrified he might pull out a knife and stab Alan. I begged Alan to pull over and stop, but, with an angry red flush in his face, he refused. So I continued pleading with the man in idiotically rational-sounding Spanish "But, please, *Señor*, there must be some mistake. . . ."

Part way down la Reforma we saw a policeman standing on a corner, looking on with interest as he saw our strange trio racing toward him. The little man was quick to see him, too, and began shouting to him about how we were cheating him, a poor man. The policeman then began to wave us over. I knew I had to do something right away, as the policeman was unlikely to be sympathetic to our plight and might even further endanger us. I am ashamed to admit this, but I quickly leaned out the car window, calling to the policeman in my most dulcet, appealing tones and shamelessly batting my eyes. The policeman swelled noticeably, began to smile, and straightened his collar, giving me a hopeful, appreciative look.

Alan pulled to a stop in front of him, and I began to beseech this bastion of the law in the prettiest way I could manage. He started to come over, his smile broadening, to my side of the car. This infuriated the little man, and, in a rage, he let go of Alan's side of the car to throw up his arms and protest to the policeman. Alan didn't wait. He hit the gas and we sped off up la Reforma at whatever maximum Porsche speed is (I shudder to think), leaving both the policeman and the con man in the dust.

⁓

Alan had an adventurous nature and one day told me that he had obtained some LSD. Would I like to try some with him? As a matter of fact, I would. Although I had never ingested any kind of mind-altering substance or, for that matter, even smoked a cigarette, I had read an issue of the scholarly semantical quarterly, *et cetera*, on this very subject, and my curiosity was aroused. Because the articles had stressed the need for a very soothing, controlled "Set and Setting," Alan suggested we take the LSD in his apartment, located on a green, quiet foothill. So one evening, we did.

Alan put lovely, calm classical music on his record player, and as we began to "go up," the sounds became ever richer, as if each resonant note were expanding into a whole tapestry of exquisite music that vibrated in our very veins. Even breathing the air seemed particularly lovely, somehow multidimensional, and we became very relaxed. A light, simple snack was indescribably delicious and, when I went into the bathroom, I became rooted to the spot at the mirror, watching the fascinating green-and-brownish spots in my hazel eyes begin to pulsate as if in some kind of kaleidoscope.

Alan came in soon after, put his arms around me, and began to lightly nuzzle me, starting to slowly unbutton my blouse. I quietly rebuttoned it, giving him a mildly reproachful look. I was still a virgin and intended to leave Mexico a virgin. Alan ruefully acceded, and we drifted harmoniously into the living room. The last thing I remember from that trip was standing outside his door, looking at a large, lovely shrub with tiny dark leaves, the door lantern now shining on its glistening, heavy dew like celestial diamonds. It was one of the most beautiful things I had ever seen.

At some point Alan realized we had completely lost track of time. My curfew was eleven o'clock and it was now after midnight. We got into his Porsche and he raced me back to the city.

When I got out I was still quite high and getting into the building and apartment involved navigating four different sets of locks and keys. This became a complex predicament, and, even with Alan's help, getting the first two open turned out to be a major, noisy, and time-consuming effort. Bidding him good night, I closed the door and began to hurry up stairs that seemed to go on and on. I felt as if I must have been slowly climbing for an hour when I heard *Señora's* voice screeching down to me from the second-floor landing. "*¡Estefania! ¡Estefania!* Don't you know what time it is?! It is one A.M.!" And, more urgently, "*¡Teléfono! ¡Teléfono!*"

I had a telephone call? At one A.M.? Oh no! Someone must have died! A stab of fear galvanized me into faster movement, and I soon reached the doorway. *Señora* stood in it, hands flapping me in, looking very worried and understandably annoyed.

Unfortunately, the dining room I had to cross to reach the telephone had one of those alternating black-and-white tile floors, and, as I was still markedly under the influence, the tiles began to pop and dance as if someone was playing lively mariachi music for them. Shakily, I crossed their undulating expanse, *Señora* scurrying along beside me and scolding in my ear, "*¡Estefania! ¡Estefania! ¡No quiere usted que los hombres le respeten?!*" ("Don't you want men to respect you?!") To answer was both pointless and impossible.

I finally picked up the phone and put it to my ear. All I could hear was a woman's voice, sobbing hysterically. Oh no! How could this be happening tonight of all times?! I said hello, struggling to keep my attention away from the dancing tiles. "Hello? Hello? Who is this?"

Finally the sobs quieted and a tear-clogged voice replied, "It's Juanita." Juanita was one of my two high school best friends, and she was stuck at a rudimentary farming-country Midwestern college because, although she was very smart, her sensitive and volatile emotional nature had sometimes taken precedence over her application to her studies, and her high school grades had suffered as a result.

"What's wrong? Are you hurt?"

"Yes. No!"

"Well, what's happened?"

She launched into an odd tale. Juanita had been assigned a roommate who turned out to be mentally ill. She was difficult to deal with, but Juanita had quietly endured her strangeness. One day, however, this young woman had marched to the dean's office and accused Juanita of being a lesbian.

The dean promptly called in Juanita, ignored the fact that she, amazed, told him this was a complete fabrication, and threatened to expel her! He would not hear another word about it! She was, understandably, a wreck, bewildered, unsure what to do, and dreading dealing with her conservative parents.

I tried my best to calm her, expressing my love and caring for her and dragging my eyes away from the pulsating tiles. She refused my offer to call her dean the next day for her. She was sure he would not listen. She was so upset that she just wanted to get away and never see that horrid college again. I couldn't blame her. She calmed down by the end of our call, even managing to make a little joke in her sweet way, so I felt it was safe to finally end the call. (She did leave that school and transfer to a much better school on Long Island.)

Señora was still clucking around me when I hung up the phone. I apologized to her for missing curfew and, viewing with huge pupils the exotic movement of walls and floors around me, stumbled to my bedroom, closed the door, briefly greeted a momentarily wakeful Jeannie, threw myself clothed across my bed, and slept the deep dreamless sleep of the utterly stoned.

⚓

I had asked my mother in September to send me some books I thought I would need for school. This being Mexico, they arrived in May. Not only in May but, rather than reaching the nearest post office, they were abandoned in some teeny, almost-imaginary post office in one of the most outflung districts of the city. Furthermore, I discovered that I would have to take three separate buses to get there. I thought of just giving up the books but hated to lose them. So, stubbornly, I set off one morning by myself to retrieve them.

All the buses were unfamiliar to me. I took a first-class bus out quite a ways, only to find that my next two buses would be third-class buses. That meant the buses would be cheap, probably shared with chickens, and the riders would be mostly Indian, with just a small percentage of mestizo passengers. That was fine with me but I realized I was likely to be heading out into some of the poorer

districts of shantytowns and whole communities where not even
Spanish was spoken, only various Indian languages.

My second bus did come complete with chickens and was very
crowded. So I had to stand in the aisle, looking over the heads of
the petite Indian ladies around me. After a few stops, an amazing
woman got on the bus and stood in the aisle, only one person away
from me and facing me. She was Indian and very old but tall, lean,
and strong. She would have been tall even for an American woman
but here she towered over the other Indian ladies. Her gray hair
hung down in neat braids on either side of her high-cheekboned
face. Our eyes met, with a kind of joyful electric shock. She smiled
an incredible smile that pleated her face with a million wrinkles,
every inch of it. Her bright eyes held mine, and I felt as if she were
looking into and through me with a kind of X-ray vision, seeing
my past, my present, and even my future with wise and kindly
penetration. Then she tilted her head back and laughed, and smiled
joyfully at me again. I smiled back at her, standing there, unable
to move, speechless.

She began to move to get off at the next stop. I struggled within
myself. A good part of me wanted to run after her, stay with her,
study with her. I don't think I knew the word *curandera* at that
time but that's what she clearly was—a wise woman, a healer,
one with knowledge and wisdom beyond the norm. And a great,
light-bearing purity, an almost supernatural-radiance. For a few
moments I considered going after her, even though realizing that,
if I did, it would probably mean abandoning my old life forever,
never coming back—even if she did accept me, which seemed
itself unlikely. Despite my reluctance to leave my old "safe" life, I
did seriously consider it, nonetheless, because of the great draw I
felt to her. But, realizing that I wasn't sure this was a true calling,
and that the risk of a mistake was too great, I quelled my impulse.
I don't know whether it was cowardice or wisdom that won out.
So I rode on wistfully but treasuring and ever after remembering
my few incandescent moments with her, conscious of a sense of
blessing and a lightening of my heart.

꒒

I needed that blessing because at the next stop two young mestizo
thugs in blue jeans got on the bus. Their eyes lit up when they saw
me, and I knew I was in trouble. One pushed roughly past me
where I stood in the aisle, turning around a few people farther on.
Over my shoulder, I saw him face me and pull out a knife from
a sheath on his belt. Looking toward the front of the bus, I saw
his compatriot likewise pull out a knife, grinning at me evilly,

making sure that he had eye contact with me. Each of them began to advance on me, and I was trapped in the middle. Their pace was slow and measured; they were sadistically trying to increase my terror. I saw that I could hope for no mercy from these bullies. They seemed capable of any atrocity. The other passengers melted away to the sides of the aisles, flattening themselves against the seat edges, knowing I was the only intended victim.

I tried to fight down my growing panic. I glanced up toward the driver and saw that he was watching this incident unfold in his mirror, his face creased with deep concern. The bus had gotten very quiet, the poor Indian passengers not unsympathetic to my plight but not daring to confront the bandits.

I wasn't sure, but I thought the driver gave a quick little upward jerk of his chin when he saw me looking at him in his mirror. He suddenly pulled the bus to the side, hitting his brakes hard. All of us in the aisle jolted over, including the thugs. I seized that moment, as I'm sure the driver intended, to push past the thug still off balance in the aisle between me and the door, avoiding his knife hand, and rush past the remaining passengers. The driver slammed open the door as soon as I reached it. I flew down the steps into a hot, dusty, unknown street, hearing the bus door slam closed on my heels. The bus driver took off with a roar and a jolt, giving the thugs no opportunity to descend. He had saved me.

But where was I? I had no idea. I tried to calm the pounding of my heart as I looked around. I seemed to be in a very poor district, its streets lined with worn, crumbling *tiendas* (shops) and flimsy-looking tin-roofed homes that had not been painted in a long time. There were no signs and very few people on the streets. These all turned out to be Indian women who turned blank, unfriendly faces to me when I greeted them in Spanish and asked them where we were. It may have been that none of them spoke Spanish. But, whether they did or not, the atmosphere was distinctly unfriendly. So I started to ramble down the nondescript streets, for I feared to remain still for too long. I could easily find myself in an even worse plight than the one on the bus.

After several streets, I saw a third-class bus rattling along and flagged down the driver. I told him where I was trying to go and that I had lost my way. He shook his head, saying that I certainly had but that he would take me to a place where I could catch another bus that would drop me off at the cursed post office. Gratefully, I ascended the bus stairs and was even able to sit down this time for the bumpy ride.

So, two bus rides later, I arrived at a tiny, dirty, brown-sugar-cube building. The post office. I've seen bigger bedrooms. One idle clerk lounged at the counter within. I explained to him why I had come, and he gazed at me indolently, still leaning on one elbow on the counter. He said he did not think they had my package. I confronted him with the form I had gotten in the mail. Oh, well, yes, maybe they might have it. And he disappeared through a door in the wall behind the counter. Some time later, he returned. A shame, yes, a shame, but there did not seem to be any such package here. And he looked at me meaningfully. Oh. I got it. He wanted a *mordida*, a "little bite," a bribe, to retrieve the package for me—to get me books I no longer really wanted, for which I had foolishly risked robbery, rape, and murder, and for which I now found myself in this outlandish hole in the middle of nowhere, hoping I could get back home before dark, when things would get really dangerous.

I could see that the clerk was dead set on the bribe and so, against my usual policy, I gave him his *mordida*. Whereupon he suddenly remembered that there was one more place he could check. Within a couple of minutes he came back with the books, half falling out of their torn and battered mailing paper.

I strode out of the post office, the unwanted books banging against my hip, and walked to the bus stop the last driver had pointed out to me. Soon a third-class arrived, and I boarded it, beginning the relay race of buses that would finally bring me back, as green twilight descended upon the dark mountains, close enough to walk to Calle Sinaloa, Jeannie, the del Olivareses, and safety at last. On what I had expected to be an innocuous—if lengthy—bus ride I had instead received, from those who crossed my path, searing glimpses of both heaven and hell. Enough and more than enough for one day.

⚓

With other members of the North American Cultural Institute, a mostly Mexican group with whom we folkdanced once a week, Jeannie and I took a field trip. We drove out to a beautiful river in the desert, winding through what seemed like an enormous forested oasis. Relieved that I would be able to go swimming and cool off, I also hoped to get away from the hounding men for a while. Although our excursion group was composed of both men and women, as usual the women would not speak to Jeannie and me, not being willing to risk *gringa* contamination.

Jeannie went off with Ricardo, and I waded into the river for what I hoped would be a desperately longed-for period of cool solitude. But soon I heard loud male cries. "*¡Güera, güera!¡Ai, hermosa!¡ Que linda!*" And my heart sank. These were Mexican men not in our group who spied me at a distance. Calling out that I was "pretty" and "beautiful," they also were referring approvingly to my pale complexion (*güera*). Unfortunately, racism was alive and well in Mexico when it came to skin color.

I dove into the river and swam underwater as long as I could. When I surfaced, the men resumed yelling and were wading my way. I took a deep breath, dove again, and swam underwater until my lungs were bursting. When next I surfaced, fortunately, the men had given up their pursuit.

I got to my feet near a forested bend in the river where another small river with a strong current entered it. A teenage girl from our excursion group was standing alone in the shallow but swift white water of this new river. I looked away for a moment and when I looked back she was gone. Something about it seemed odd to me. She hadn't looked close enough to the bend to disappear so quickly. I decided to investigate.

I walked over and stood in the fast-moving water that only came partway up my shins. Suddenly the amazingly powerful current wrenched my feet out from under me and began rolling me over and over at high speed across the sharp rocks of the riverbed. I realized what had happened to the young woman and that I, too, was now in danger. Stopping was impossible. I pulled my hands and elbows over my face and head to try to protect them from the savage edges of the rocks. I was afraid of being knocked unconscious. Because the water was so shallow, my head came up with every turn and I could usually catch a quick breath. On one of my upturns I got a glimpse ahead—after another sixty feet or so of white water, the river broadened into a peaceful dark-green channel. Then I saw the teenage girl. Hanging on to a stump lodged in the river, she was facing me, her face full of shock and terror. Since there was still white water behind her, she didn't dare let go of the stump.

I desperately tried to angle my body toward the stump. Once I reached it I was able to catch it with one arm and pull my body up against it, the spray breaking crazily over my back and head as if from a high-pressure hose. The water was so loud I had to yell. I told the young woman in Spanish to let go, that there was calm water beyond. And that I would try to hold on long enough for her to get clear. Looking at me trustingly, she did so. Anxiously, I watched the wild foam carry her off. It was hard to breathe from the tension and suspense, as well as the pounding on my back.

She made it! I relaxed my aching arms and let go. The fierce water tumbled me savagely over more rocks, but at last it expelled me into the calm jade water beyond. Thinking only of each other, the girl and I opened wide our arms to hug each other and make sure we were not seriously hurt. I was amazed and pleased by the pure, selfless, compassionate quality of the moment that we so unexpectedly shared. And we weren't Mexican and *gringa* anymore, just two young women who had survived a close call together.

Although calm, the current was so powerful that we did not have to swim at all and just let it carry us past banks too thick with jungle growth for us to climb out. Smiling at each other and sharing a lovely sense of peace, we let the river rest us as it carried us on. Eventually we saw a fallen tree hanging low over the water. Grabbing some of its branches, we pulled ourselves onto its trunk. We sat and chatted, introducing ourselves, thanking each other, and being very grateful to be alive. Sitting there in the sunlight on the log, we saw what the dark water had concealed. We were both bleeding.

Josefa was wearing a black bathing suit with a separate top and bottom sewn together by a crocheted black netting that exposed much of the bare skin of her middle. The netting was torn, and she was bleeding from two- and three-inch cuts along one side. I had a major slit down my left forearm, from below my wrist almost to my elbow, that was bleeding with enthusiasm. We didn't know where we were or how to get back.

Fortunately, at that moment our friend Pedro appeared, swimming with a clean slicing stroke through the dark water. It turned out he had been on the Mexican Junior Olympics swimming team! Noticing our absence, he had come in search of us and wisely skirted the white water before entering the river. The river was almost circular in this area, he said, so if we got back into the water and swam with him, we would soon be close to where we had begun.

When we pulled ourselves out of the water, a small crowd of our fellow excursionists was standing on the shore waiting, including Josefa's grandmother. Josefa enthusiastically introduced me to the smiling gray-haired woman, who grasped my hands warmly and thanked me for helping her grandchild, although really the whole situation had been one of mutual help and I had done very little. Josefa and her grandmother said that to thank me they would like to invite me to come out with them to visit the great pyramids of Teotihuacán, something I had much wanted to do. After so long, I could hardly believe it—Mexican women who wanted to be friends with me! It was a miracle!

Pedro insisted that we needed medical attention for our wounds. But Josefa and her grandmother refused, saying she was really all right, and, after we hugged each other, went back to the bus. Taking me firmly by the hand, Pedro insisted that I had to get my arm wound, still bleeding freely, disinfected and bandaged up. He led me to a strange little hut on the riverbank where he said we would find a nurse on duty.

When we entered the dark hut I was surprised to see a mournful-looking middle-aged woman sitting in one of two chairs at a simple table. A single shelf was attached to the wall behind her. Pedro held up my dripping arm and asked her to help me.

"Aiiiiii!" she groaned, looking away. She jabbered agitatedly at Pedro so quickly that I could not understand her Spanish. He looked at me ruefully and said in English, trying to keep from grinning, "Yes, she is a nurse. But she is afraid of the sight of blood!" I also had to work to keep a straight face.

Shaking her head but resigned, the woman gestured to me to sit in the other chair. Once I had, she pulled three things off the shelf—they appeared to be the only things on the shelf. One was an old box of medical gauze. The second, a pair of scissors. And last was a quart bottle of red liquid that proved to be iodine. Grasping my wrist and pulling my arm out horizontally, she moaned as she saw the blood and, turning her head away, poured most of the iodine over my arm, apparently afraid to look back again. I caught my tongue between my teeth at the stinging.

Pedro grasped her wrist and turned her pouring hand up again before she completely emptied the bottle, took it away, capped it, and returned it to the shelf. Then the "nurse," with trembling hands, wrapped my stinging now-orange arm in gauze like a mummy, cut the gauze, and tied it off in a tight knot. We thanked her and left, getting a safe distance away from the medical hut before we both broke down in hysterics. A nurse afraid of blood! Ah, Mexico!

⚓

Well, I never did go to Teotihuacán with Josefa and her grandmother, though they phoned to invite me again. Part of me wanted to go and be with them but part of me, at the end of this long, trying year, felt too exhausted to do it—especially to begin a relationship I had craved for so long but that I would, after all, have to give up within a couple of weeks. Glad as I was that I had at last broken through the atmospheric plexiglass barrier separating Jeannie and me from Mexican women, I felt that I no longer had the tensile strength to deal with its consequences. The part of me that would have gladly engaged in such new relationships four or five months before was now too drained. I was sorry but certain that I had to let it go.

Jeannie and I took our finals, doing well academically, as we had all year. Perhaps you think it odd, dear reader, that I've never mentioned my studies? The classes were decent but not particularly stimulating, especially compared with my special high school classes. And, of course, the Spanish classes were very good. For the first time ever, the school part of my life was the least interesting and significant part. The true learning, jet propelled, had been on another level altogether.

"Culture is the sea we swim in—" writes the journalist Eric Weiner, "so pervasive, so all-consuming, that we fail to notice its existence until we step out of it." Jeannie and I had been hooked out of the unconscious sea of our bland American middle-class lives and hurled into the wild, thin mountain air of untamed Mexico and its vivid cultures. We had been shaken down, sometimes brutally, from some of our personal and cultural delusions in the process. We were heading home now, changed and ready for a new adventure to begin. For Jeannie it would be in social and political movements. For me it would be in the untamed, mountainous realm of the spirit.

CHAPTER SEVEN

Catechumen II: The Mystery Returns (with Waldo, Waldorf, and Astoria)

The Way Opens

A quiet but powerful vision of God as an inconceivably gigantic white iris of Light opened up in my psychedelic-enhanced consciousness. This flower of transcendent beauty was All That Is. Its shape was that of the Western garden iris with tall and long petals, huge and flowing, rather than the tidier, pointier form of the Japanese or Siberian iris. It was glowing white, except for a tiny rim at the bottom of the front drooping fall, as this petal is so appropriately called (later I thought of its associations with the Fall into Creation, from transcendence into immanence). On that narrow rim were endless circles and globes of many different colors and sizes, shimmering and beautiful, galaxies and universes, infinite in number—the whole of Creation. The rest of the iris, perhaps ninety-nine percent of it, was just God. I had an overpoweringly beautiful feeling that somehow God was so infinitely filled with an inconceivably rich and endless outpouring love that He even "wanted to give to Himself"—His giving and love had no limit.

I'm sorry that I don't have adequate words to convey the strong sensation and deep impact of this image—it was an interior sign that somehow gently, exquisitely, but powerfully quickened my soul into belief, overruling by its radiance and intuited truth much of my previous frozen resistance. "And the desert shall blossom . . . as the rose" (Isa. 35:1). Real change and belief can come in the twinkling of an eye; the mind is a slow tortoise compared to the flying Olympic sprinter of the heart.

I was back on Long Island, working for a year in a bookstore, preparing to transfer to a different university for my sophomore year. I was also still experimenting with psychedelics, and the vision I just described marked a critical change in my attitudes toward God and faith. But this is not an endorsement of taking an experimental approach to using mind-altering drugs. One can have strong, positive, and healing experiences in such conditions, but the Russian-roulette nature of such engagements can also lead to very dark, destructive, traumatizing experiences. There are safer, surer ways to court intimacy with God, if that is what one is seeking. But at the time, like so many of my generation, I didn't know that. And at that point I wouldn't have said that I even was consciously seeking God, Whom I had earlier so thoroughly abandoned. But God found me anyway in the midst of my frivolity and experimentation. Not for the first or the last time, God *happened* to me.

ﷻ

This first experience moved me toward belief, but the next experience made unforgettably vivid to me God's Presence and radiance through His Creation. It was a lovely autumn afternoon, and I had taken LSD with my boyfriend Bruce, a smart, kind premed student I had met in the bookstore. Bruce had brought me an enormous, beautiful bouquet of carnations—white, red, and white-and-red. I put them in a large glass vase, where the slanting golden rays of the late-day sun fell upon them. Already beginning to feel in an elevated state, Bruce and I put Handel's *Messiah* on the record player, its exalted chords thrilling through us. As the magnificent fugue "And He Shall Purify" began, I found myself hearing the chorus singing distinctly, instead, "And He shall *glorify*."

My eyes were fixed on the bouquet of carnations, and I felt that I began to see them moving and gently dancing. The dance was that of their own breath, inward and outward, inward and outward, over and over, rapid and strong but also delicate and ineffably graceful, which my consciousness seemed slowed and awake enough to finally perceive. Each carnation breath expressed itself through a flaring and subsiding of petals, each one in its own varying rhythm and gestures but harmonious with the whole, each one luminous, radiant, semitransparent with the golden light of the sun's slanting rays filling it with fluctuating, fiery splendor. The carnations' petals slowly swirled and flared like dancers' skirts, like dervishes' billowing *tenure* in devotional dance—a deep in-drawing and bowing followed each time by an expansive, complete flaring out, a shining and wholehearted giving forth unrestrainedly without distinction or limitation to everything that was.

Most compelling of all to me was the state of the flowers that were already dying, some of their petals withered and crumpled brown and lifeless. The petals that were still living on such blooms continued to give out to the world their radiance, their healing and joyful breath, with the same complete and selfless giving and zest as did the healthy flowers. The crippled blooms held nothing back for themselves, did not mourn or hesitate or fold in upon themselves in weakness but instead, casting their angelic beauty without restraint upon the winds, the breath of the world, gave as freely as ever what they had to give. They were sunsets, unreservedly vibrant until the very last moment of their lives. They gave completely, as they had in the beginning. Their love was perfect. And their witness struck to my heart.

After this experience, I could no longer deny God's beauty underlying the radiant nature of His Creation, which He had, tenderly and in splendor, infused with intelligence, willpower in its various forms, love, and abundant, overflowing grace.

Sometimes things seen when using psychedelics were just illusions from firing neurons, random and ephemeral as fireworks bursting in the sky, but once in a while you knew that you were receiving a rare view into truth, into the deeper nature of the world, a vibrant view of cosmic greatness that your culturally hypnotized self, walled in with materialism and cynicism, had never allowed you to see before.

ﷻ

First Steps

And so my spiritual search began.

Of course, I still wasn't interested in becoming a Christian again. *Been there, done that, and found it wanting,* my prematurely jaded thoughts ran. But, like for so many of my young compatriots in the New Age of hippie wonders and lively spiritual exploration, Far Eastern religion held a beckoning fascination for me. I read Alan Watts and the *Bhagavad Gita* (well, part of it), assorted books on Zen and Mahayana Buddhism, Taoism, and yoga, and anything else I could get my hands on that described religions of the Far East and their philosophies. I threw yarrow stalks and read the *I Ching.*

A first step for me, ultimately, like for so many of my contemporaries, including the Beatles—aside from dabbling in a little yoga—was being initiated into the Transcendental Meditation of Maharishi Mahesh Yogi. This was accomplished by going to New York City and spending half an hour or so with, of all people, a Norwegian opera singer who gave me my mantra, a specific syllable that he told me to repeat silently twice a day for twenty minutes each time and never to reveal! (Believe me, you're not missing anything; on a scale of one to ten it had a melodious rating of two—or possibly less.) But I found that I did feel more peaceful during and after my mantra meditations.

I was a spiritual baby turtle, newly hatched from the egg, trundling down the big beach, driven to reach the mystic ocean where I could immerse myself in gnosis, the joyful shock of deeper spiritual understanding and growth.

ॐ

But there was plenty to do in the sand in the meantime. After a year clerking in the Long Island bookstore, I transferred to Syracuse University, where I planned to enroll in the Newhouse School of Communications. Syracuse surprised me—it was so big and bustling, overflowing with myriad fraternities and sororities. I suspect the presence of the fraternities led to the Orange Bar, embedded in a small string of stores on campus, having the reputation of selling more beer per year than any other bar in the United States at that time. There was certainly no shortage of drunken fraternity members around.

I escaped the bustle of my dormitory and the teeming streets of newly arrived honking frat boys by climbing a small green hill upon which sat a turreted castle-like brick building, the stately Setnor School of Music. Folding myself before it on the grass in a lotus position, I closed my eyes and began to meditate, silently repeating my mantra. After twenty minutes or so of peacefulness, I opened my eyes to see a dignified short-haired black cat sitting two feet in front of me, staring at me with calm, assessing golden eyes. I got the feeling that the cat had been there awhile. We seemed to be in harmony with each other, but I realized that this elegant feline was easily my superior in meditation. I reached out and gently stroked its head; the cat suffered this patiently, then rose to its feet, stretched and yawned, and trotted away down the hill.

The next day I returned to the same spot for another meditation. This time, when I opened my eyes—and, as Dave Barry would say, I am not making this up!—on either side of me, sitting alertly upright and staring straight ahead, were two large black Labs, each not much more than a foot away from me! I was like a book between canine bookends. I blinked a bit, startled, and pet my two muscular guardians. Well, small wonder that no one bothered me during that meditation! I stood up, and the two dogs went cantering away.

On the third day, I meditated in the same spot again, and when I opened my eyes, there was a six- or seven-year-old black boy sitting cross-legged on the grass, facing me right about where the cat had sat. *God,* I thought, *aren't you carrying this a bit too far?! Is there something I'm supposed to get here? . . . I'm not getting it!* But the boy did look awfully sweet.

He smiled an enchanting, beguiling smile. "Whatcha doin'?" he asked.

I told him I was meditating and, in answer to his next questions, ineptly tried to explain what that was. He took it in noncommittally. When I stood up, he did too. We told each other our names, and he asked me what I was going to do next. I felt that he might be a bit lonely and tried to think of what might be entertaining for such a little boy. I remembered reading that there was some kind of small natural history museum on campus and asked him if he would like to see it. He agreed with enthusiasm. I pulled out my campus map from my backpack, got oriented, and, hand in hand, we headed off to visit the collection.

The galleries were not extensive, but we both enjoyed drifting along past the exhibits, peering into assorted cases. We finally came to a tall case that held a large grizzly bear, standing upright, arms and one huge paw raised.

"Wow!" exclaimed my small friend in awe and excitement, staring up, round-eyed, at the bear.

"Yes, it's huge, isn't it?" I said.

"And," he added with growing excitement, "it's a girl!"

Uh-oh, I thought. *Where is this going?* "Um, how do you know that?" I asked him, a bit tentatively.

He looked at me incredulously, as if he could not believe that I was so ignorant of anatomy and the utterly obvious. "Well, just look at the *nose!*" he exclaimed instructively.

"Oh, yes, yes," I mumbled, quietly sighing with relief. Of course, the nose. What was wrong with me? Didn't I ever take biology? We finished our tour, said our goodbyes, and the boy headed off for home, turning once to cheerily wave at me, before disappearing around the corner.

Not yet as accustomed to being the butt of cosmic jokes as I became later on (though never comfortable with the sensation), I silently asked, *What was that about, God? Were you trying to tell me something? Or just having a yuk?* I never did find out.

My movement from disbelief into belief seemed to initiate a quickening within me on many levels. Expanding toward a belief and relationship with God seemed to stir the smoldering coals of personal blockages and even a cleansing, healing movement—its dynamism not under my command—of childhood traumas, such as:

The Tsunami

Always I had found myself plastered to the floor, soaked in cold sweat, entangled in twisted sheets like a corpse unceremoniously thrown out of a grave by careless plunderers, too terrified to move a muscle. Helter-skelter around me lay my stuffed toys, like soldiers fallen in a sudden enemy attack. Long moments passed before I could even begin to breathe again and take comfort that I was awake, no longer trapped in the devouring nightmare. My shell-shocked body took even longer to unlock its limbs from their spasmed paralysis. Sometimes I lay on the floor for a long time, listening to the hard, fast beat of my heart, before the panic ebbed from my body enough for me to drag myself up and sit trembling on the edge of my bed, staring into the silent dark.

The tsunami dream came over and over again, the wave's massive glassy sheen, higher than a pile of skyscrapers, racing toward me with terrible, incomprehensible speed. I stood small, helpless, and alone on the beach, mesmerized by the ominous wall of towering water filling the horizon, its size and horror increasing with every moment. Everything about it was wrong and strange—an impossibly moving mountain with the glossy sinuousness, the living malevolent energy, of a huge and ancient angry serpent able to reach round the world and consume it.

I could not run, not even move, nor could I ever remember the disastrous moment of impact, but rather always awakened frozen on the floor, just a dead and twisted piece of flotsam smashed and tossed savagely aside by the massive wave.

As I grew older, the tidal wave dream came less frequently—but it still did come at times, and always with its full horror. I spoke of it to no one. I did not know how to oppose it or cleanse it from my system. Weakly, when I was junior-high age, I tried to toughen myself, train myself out of my terror. When my parents drove us through hilly areas, I would try to force myself to imagine that the looming green hills were tidal waves, the motion of the car assisting in the illusion of massive movement. But this futile exercise made no dent in my overpowering fear, only bringing it queasily into waking life. The tsunamis continued to roll on, malevolent and violent in my dreams.

Visiting home from college in my early twenties, one sunny day I was walking along the tidal line of a soft, sandy beach, a fresh breeze lifting long strands of my dark hair and cooling my cheeks. Gentle ripples fanned thinning water like gossamer lace over my toes and empty shells gleamed rosily here and there, catching the cool beams of the young sun. I walked rhythmically, in time with the beat and retreat of the small waves, staring at the ever-changing borderline of sea and sand.

I was musing on some recently acquired knowledge. Having learned a little astrology, I had discovered from my natal horoscope, a kind of inner and outer portrait of the heavens in the day and minute I was born, that the Sun had been positioned in the sign of Capricorn, an Earth sign, and the Moon in the sign of Cancer, a Water sign, at my birth. This formed a powerful full-moon opposition, as that astrological aspect is called, denoting, among other things, an ongoing tension between the Sun, my deepest inner nature, and the Moon, my feelings and soul qualities. I contemplated this new information as I paced down the beach, feeling the gentle tension of the Earth and Water elements where sand and waves met, dancing, tugging, and running away beneath my feet.

Sudden as a dolphin leap out of a placid, faceless sea, an odd little poem surfaced in my mind, keeping time with my rhythmic pace:

> *I feel the pull of sea and land.*
> *Powerless to understand,*
> *I fill my pockets with small deaths*
> *and go.*

Arrowing uncertainly toward meaning, my thoughts turned this verse round and round, like a shell spinning in shallow waves. "Small deaths" might refer to the absent creatures of the empty shells I had scooped up while strolling, now jingling faintly in my pockets. But I had no other clarity, except for the probable astrological associations. As I walked, the cryptic verse rang on and on, persistent and compelling, but stingy of revealing its meaning—a strange little song secret as an underground river, unseen, but nonetheless carving out deep parts of the earth in powerful, methodical, quiet arcs. But I was not the dowser to whom that river spoke. Not yet. Maybe not ever. I felt as if I were blankly watching some other, more skilled person working out a difficult problem I could not hope to understand.

That night, after a long absence, the tsunami nightmare returned in force. Monstrous as ever, the giant, obliterating wave rushed toward me. I stood, sapless, frozen in the same abject terror. But this time something off to the right caught my eye. I turned my head to look. For the first time I was not alone in the dream. On a spit of sand, perhaps eighty feet from me, stood my mother. She was frantic, waving me wildly back from the wave. Would we both be destroyed?

I turned to look back at the immense wave, still racing on, closer now, and suddenly felt a deep conviction that this time I had to actually leap into the wall of water when it reached me. I glanced back at my mother. Somehow she had understood what I planned to do and violently opposed it. She waved me off commandingly, urgently. But I was determined. I knew I must do it. I looked again at the wave, now obscuring the sky with its shiny, moving darkness, so close. So close. Glancing one last time at my mother, I saw her hunched over, arms protectively cradling her head, and realized with a sudden visceral shock of understanding that she was not afraid for me at all but for herself. Not only the mountainous wave threatened her—my decision to jump into it was also a very real threat.

The roaring wall of water was only a few feet away. I gathered myself and leaped up, disappearing into its oblivion. It seemed that only a moment had passed when I found myself lying unharmed on the shore where the wave, mysteriously vanished, had cast me up. Not far from me a motionless body lay on the sand. It was not my mother. It was the dead body of my fear.

Awakening the next morning in a deeply calm state, I remembered it all. And, just as I had known I had to jump into the wave, I knew I must write a letter to my mother about the dream—the last step in breaking the mysterious, dark, umbilical pull of this spell. Returning to college that day, I wrote the letter that night and mailed it the next morning. My mother never ever spoke of that letter and would not acknowledge it in any way. But, hundreds of miles away, I knew when she read it. I felt the powerful bindings, kelp-forest strong, which had pulled and entangled me in her troubled sea tide, slashed in one monstrous stroke from their hidden roots, their malignant strength now crumbling to nothingness—dead, brittle ribbons on some lonely, distant beach.

Often we feel as if understanding—and especially an understanding that frees us from the traumas and powers of the past—must come in a literal form, parsed methodically by the rational mind, after much conscious deep-delving and work. This sometimes helps, yet it is healing at the speed of sound, of words, weighty with a slowness both emotional and intellectual. From a deeper place, the place where music and poetry and the "irrational" impulses well up, can come an undiluted and powerful virgin understanding that heals at the speed of light—a clean sweep. Saints, radiating light, wear their potent halos, and those of us less saintly can nonetheless be swept by such grace and healed of dark hurts by a smidge of information, a few lines of poetry floating on the sea, sunlit ocean lace spilling over our toes, a merciful dream.

The melodies of my sleep changed after that day. Harmonies emerged. The seas became serene and softly rhythmical. And I never had the tidal wave nightmare again.

ﷺ

Dark Currents
The Vietnam War hung over the heads of my generation like a real-life breaking tidal wave, about to sweep so many of us away, many of us into death. Despite our enjoyments, day and night we felt its presence like a psychic dark cloud—and things were bad enough as it was in Syracuse, at that time the darkest city in the U.S. (even Seattle was sunnier). Something terrible was happening on the other side of the world, and we were strangely, intimately, unwillingly tied into it.

We all knew young men sadly heading off to Canada so as not to be drafted. And other resisting young men who focused their creativity on failing their draft board physicals in order to be rejected as unfit, a 4-F, and live with that stigma rather than fight and possibly lose their lives in what they felt was an evil war. The draft-board physical was the prime territory for exerting this strategy. One acquaintance of mine utilized the simple expedient of painting his penis brilliant purple. Unsurprisingly, he was rejected at the physical. Another, an otherwise very normal and "straight-looking" man—small blue eyes, blond crew cut, usually a pen protector in his white short-sleeve shirt pocket, raised his just-full urine sample high in the air at the physical, toasted all the other naked men, shouted "Skol!" and drank down his pee to the last drop. Same result.

A crafty poet I knew decided upon some creative intellectual torture for his draft board.

"Well, I sent them a letter to tell them I had changed my name," he said. "It's the law. You're supposed to do that. Then they called me in for an interview."

"What happened?"

They said, um, "we see here that you changed your name legally to Grim Reaper, yes?"

"That's right."

"Why did you do that?"

"Well, if I liked baseball, I would have changed it to Mickey Mantle."

4-F.

ﻪﻠ

As a generation we had been devastated as youths by the assassination of John F. Kennedy and were now re-traumatized by the murders of Martin Luther King, Jr., and Bobby Kennedy. Grief and outrage were in the air, mixed with flower power, love beads, and flowers-in-gun-barrels sentiments, alternating currents of emotional hot and cool water. We sought the peacefulness of meditation but also burned with the fire of protest. I, too, was afire with both peace and war, demonstrating, marching, and handing out leaflets on city corners and at enlistment centers.

ﻪﻠ

Romance, Desert Cats, and Waldo

So we protested, smoked marijuana and hashish, took mescaline and LSD, danced to Jefferson Airplane and the Grateful Dead, dressed in pseudo-peasant/multiethnic splendor, grew our hair long (both men and women), meditated and did yoga, attended concerts by sitarist Ravi Shankar and other great Indian musicians, meditated during talks by spiritual gurus like Sri Chinmoy, and discovered the joys of "contact highs" with complete strangers when our eyes met in passing on the street. Oh, yes, we also did some academic work (I was thankful that most of my classes were interesting). And engaged in some sexual experimentation. But not me. I was serially monogamous.

Until I met Edmund, that is. Having met in a colorful, fascinating course, "Peoples and Cultures of the Northern Himalayan Regions," we soon found ourselves going out for tea or coffee to discuss the lively classes. A philosophy major, Edmund was also brilliant and charismatic, plus he had some familiarity with spiritual territory unfamiliar to me, such as Sufism. He had himself been a member of a spiritually exacting Gurdjieff Fourth Way group, run by a woman teacher who had been a direct disciple of the famous Greco-Armenian mystical teacher George Gurdjieff. Edmund and I enjoyed each other's company very much and little by little began to fall in love. And I was also still in love with Bruce on Long Island, but the pendulum in my heart was swinging more and more toward Edmund. Painfully and slowly, I eventually broke up with Bruce. And moved into Edmund's apartment with him.

And also with his two large, short-haired silver Abyssinians—muscular and aristocratic desert cats—Brother and Dzitki (that name was supposed to mean "malevolent little evil one" but Dzitki was the opposite, so we just called him "Zeke"). Edmund had inherited these magnificent animals, he said enigmatically, from a "corrupt lawyer friend of mine who had to leave town in a hurry." They were beautiful, smart, and affectionate, with the extra-long back legs of hunters. And very protective.

One night a strange man knocked on our door. I did not know him, and Edmund was only vaguely acquainted with him. We had no idea why he was there, but Edmund courteously invited him in. The cats and I were in the living room as he entered. The cats took one look, raced over to him, and immediately ran up his back, sinking their claws into his shoulders. He screamed. We were horrified. With difficulty, Edmund and I pulled the big cats off his back, and the shell-shocked man ran out of the house as we yelled apologies after him. We had no idea why the normally gentle cats had reacted in such an appalling way. But the next day, Edmund learned why from a mutual acquaintance. For unknown reasons, someone had sent that man over to beat Edmund up! We had been clueless but obviously the cats had known! Wisely, that man never darkened our doorway again! I imagine it took him a while to heal up from his feline tattoos.

ﻭ

During the time I lived with Edmund I dropped out of Syracuse University. I couldn't afford to stay registered because I had not been able to apply for financial assistance, even though my grades were good. The grades of all transfer students were always registered as only C's, hence useless for merit- and need-based financial scholarships. It was also the dropping-out era; many of my compatriots were heading back to the land and/or into the commune or off to the ashram. Edmund and I were subsisting on low-paying jobs, but even these eventually disappeared.

ﻭ

Ineffable Flowers
We reached a period when we were both out of work and had no income at all. It was cold, gray November, bone cold as only Syracuse could be. We could not afford to buy groceries. A kindly neighbor upstairs who worked at Dunkin Donuts brought us a dozen donuts she received for free daily, and that was what we subsisted on for two weeks. It is definitely not a diet I recommend!

One bleak afternoon, I reluctantly walked into our kitchen to force myself to eat yet another donut. There was a donut with a swirly cream top. I looked at it with loathing. It reciprocated. And I could swear the repellent little cream swirl puffed up like a threatening cockscomb! This was the only time in my life that, unaffected by psychoactive drugs, I actually had a hallucination! Though realizing this was probably a side effect of starvation, I still could not bear to pick up that sneering donut and backed silently out of the kitchen. I stared out the living room window for a while. I might also have prayed but I really don't remember.

Then, out of nowhere, a haiku of Basho's floated blissfully, with full meaning, into my mind:

> *If your bowl*
> *is empty,*
> *fill it*
> *with flowers.*

I felt an epiphany, a sudden joy. All my burdens, even the hunger, fell away.

I walked into our bedroom to see Edmund, who had been standing there in despair. Our eyes met. His were suddenly full of light. We were experiencing the same unexpected joy and sense of spiritual lightness. The same inexplicable grace had descended upon both of us. I told him the haiku. We put on our jackets and, hand in hand, smiling, walked out into the twilight together.

We had walked only a block or so when we saw something on the sidewalk ahead, under a streetlight. It turned out to be four one-dollar bills laid parallel to each other, as if by design, across our way. There was no one around, no wallet, and nothing but a bare, empty field alongside it. We stopped, stunned, staring down at the surreal display of dollar bills. Then we bent and picked them up and, with a whoop, ran another block to the grocery store where we bought a loaf of bread and a jar of peanut butter. We hurried home and made sandwiches—the most delicious and nourishing sandwiches we had ever eaten!

And our luck immediately changed. Edmund got a part-time job, and I got work as a proofreader for a weekly alternative newspaper. They published an article or two of mine, and swiftly promoted me to associate editor and reporter. I was one of only two women in the newsroom of the *Syracuse New Times*.

I enjoyed my work there, my colleagues, and the opportunity to write image-rich, long, magazine-style articles. Unfortunately, though, I felt as if my relationship with Edmund was beginning to slowly go downhill; a certain elusive melancholy was permeating our relationship.

Sadly, within a year of each other, both of our cats, died. We cheered ourselves by adopting a ridiculously adorable Maine coon kitten, already named Waldo (after Ralph Waldo Emerson) by our friends, the vassals of his gigantic parents, Skunk and Scudderer. Waldo was a gray-and-black tiger-stripe kitten with a white chin, vest, and paws. He was gorgeous, sweet, and round-eyed—and, as we were to discover, perpetually innocent. The adjective "gormless" might have been invented for him. Waldo was not stupid per se but seemed to have the kind of personality that could never, in any scenario, acquire street smarts. Waldo had a way of just stumbling into situations.

When he became a young cat, I used to take him for walks around the neighborhood with a long, pretty scarf secured around him. He would placidly pad down the sidewalks, sniffing at summer grass and dandelions, and we had very nice outings. One day I was not paying sufficient attention, letting him lead, and Waldo turned right off the sidewalk, heading purposefully up a short stretch of pavement in some stranger's yard to a front porch where he paused on the first step. Just before I bent down to pick Waldo up, I looked ahead to see a lean naked man, probably in his late fifties, standing just behind his porch screen door five feet away, coolly regarding me as he smoked a cigarette. I grabbed Waldo and hastily headed for the hills, determined not to let him be our unsavvy pathfinder ever again!

Another time, when we were living in a second-floor apartment, a cat in heat used to come into the alley below and yowl and sing to him. Although no longer "equipped for action," Waldo would press his nose to the screen, looking down with evident interest. One day we came home to discover the screen missing and Waldo gone. He must have pushed the screen out and fallen or jumped into the alley. Distraught, we called a friend and all three of us began combing the streets, calling for the hapless Waldo. We searched for hours but could not find him. That night, around midnight, we heard him calling to us, almost nonchalantly. He was down in the little alley, lying in a relaxed sprawl, occasionally picking up his head to send up a casual yowl, apparently supremely confident that we, his servants, would come to scoop him up! We did and, despite his daring adventure, Waldo appeared none the worse for wear.

It was also through Waldo we discovered that cats, too, had their very own hippie enjoyments. On our low windowsills I had placed numerous pots of small, brightly colored coleus plants. One day I returned from work to find all the coleus plants eaten to mere stubs. Waldo was lying on his back on our long hall runner, completely blissed out, with his fat white front paws tucked up beneath his chin. He was utterly stoned, as the dilated pupils in his large eyes, rounder than ever, told me. He did not respond to anything I said, just blinked happily up at me. Upon researching the matter, I discovered, as he already had, that coleus plants are psychedelic for cats!

Waldo's true mission in life, however, seemed to be to convert dog people into cat lovers. I can't tell you how many people he converted! It was not just his furry adorableness as he wandered around, occasionally coming to stare soulfully with his round innocent eyes into theirs. His pièce de résistance was that he loved to retrieve pipe cleaners. We would bend a pipe cleaner into a spiral and fling it down our long living room. Waldo would race after it, his paws struggling to gain purchase on our shiny wooden floor. At a certain point he would drop to the floor, sliding on his tummy, with his legs out to either side like a skidding bearskin rug, chin on wood, until he slid up to the pipe cleaner and bumped it with his nose. Then he would pick it up in his mouth, stand, trot back to whoever had thrown it, and drop it at their feet, looking up with a sweet, hopeful expression, eager to repeat the exercise. Even the most ardent cat hater (we had a few) melted—a triumph of extreme cuteness and trustfulness über alles.

ﻋﻠﮯ

Escape

To my regret, I had to abandon Waldo, leaving him with Edmund. Edmund and I lived together for six years, and for the last three I was troubled by a feeling that we were each in some fashion becoming obstacles in each other's relationships with God, despite our shared mystical interests. I kept trying to shove the feeling away but it kept returning, stronger all the time. In that last year or so we were together, Edmund became very controlling and inappropriately jealous. I felt imprisoned.

One night I had a strange dream in which Edmund appeared as Semiramis, an ancient Assyrian queen, on her barge, and as both a man and a woman simultaneously. (Later I learned that Semiramis was said to have dressed as a man after her husband died in order to impersonate her son and lead troops into battle; also, Dante puts Semiramis in the Second Circle of Hell, "among the lustful.") There was a strong feeling of betrayal and treachery emanating from the Edmund / Semiramis of the dream. I felt moved to share this with a friend who regretfully informed me that Edmund had been having an affair with another woman for some months. Ah, so that explained his insecure, dominating behavior! And the dream message of betrayal! I knew I had to leave, and quickly. I realized that Edmund had become too irrational for me to discuss the matter with him. So one cold December night when Edmund was out, I sadly pet Waldo for the last time before calling my friend Graham, who quickly drove over to help me make my escape. I took only my clothes, sleeping bag, and moonstone ring. I left a short note for Edmund telling him our relationship was over and why, but I did not tell him where I was going.

Graham Smith and his wife were Edmund's best friends, which made this move particularly awkward, but the three of us had also become very close. Graham and Katie said I was welcome to stay with them and their two little boys for as long as I needed to.

It took Edmund only about two days to find me. He arrived on a gray, snowy evening. Graham tried to talk reasonably with him through a window but would not let him inside. Spurred to fury, Edmund started pacing around the house, yelling that he was going to take off his clothes and lie down naked in the snow and freeze. Fortunately, he did not make good on this threat and did not return to their house again.

Katie, Graham, and I got along well, and I loved their little boys—a young toddler and a six-year-old. Furthermore, I had the pleasant company of their two cats, Waldorf and Astoria—who were actually Waldo's brothers from the same Maine coon litter! Waldorf was very large like his father Skunk, black and white, and carried himself with the sober, aloof demeanor of an elder statesman. His brother, the orange-and-white Astoria, was just the opposite—equally huge and fluffy but bubbly and friendly, with a Harpo Marx-like air of giddy abandon. In the warmer months, Astoria liked to lie on the grass of the front yard, waiting for some stranger to stroll down the sidewalk. Upon sighting his quarry, he would race to the pavement, throw himself tummy skywards across the sidewalk, and oblige the stymied passerby to either lean down and rub his deeply furry belly at length or to step onto the lawn or into the street in order to continue his stroll.

I appreciated having my own comfortable room at the Smiths', but sleeping there was not restful. I was troubled every night by strange dreams, alarming in their vivid detail. I dreamed that I was an Asian man and saw changing scenes of "my" life—including war episodes and, embarrassingly, even making love to an Asian woman!

One day I mentioned my dreams to Katie. She rolled her eyes.

"Oh, well, a couple of months before you came, our last tenant, who rented your room, left. He had been a captain in the South Vietnamese army!"

I was content living with the Smiths but still grieved at the necessary breakup with Edmund. I tried to bury myself in my work at the *New Times*, grateful that there was sufficient reporting, writing, and editing to keep my concentration away from painful personal matters much of the time.

 مۈ

Return of the Really Real

From editing her art reviews, I had gradually become friends with a talented writer and poet named Carolyne Wright. Both in troubled relationships, we had begun having lunch together from time to time and commiserating about our "difficult" men. Lately Carolyne had been becoming increasingly frustrated and depressed, and I was concerned about her. But one day she walked into the newsroom, her face radiant as the sun.

"Carolyne!" I exclaimed. "What happened?!"

She grinned broadly and beamed upon me. "Holy Order of MANS!"

My heart sank. "Oh no Carolyne!"

"Oh yes! They're wonderful! You must come with me to a class."

"No, no, that wouldn't be for me." I feared she had become entangled with some kind of "Jesus-freak" group. Horrors!

"You'll love it. I know you will!"

"Thanks, no, Carolyne, but I'm glad it's making you happy."

Carolyne persisted in begging me to visit the Order house with her, and I steadfastly refused until, three days after I had left Edmund, feeling sad, worn down, and a bit reckless, I finally said, "Okay, okay. I'll go with you—but just once! I warn you—please don't be offended if I don't like it. This isn't for me."

She gave me a Cheshire-cat grin and said not a word.

The class was in a handsome old house in the gracious neighborhood flanking Syracuse University. We were met at the door by two good-looking Order brothers, about our age, wearing broad, welcoming smiles and long pale-blue cassocks. They helped us hang up our jackets, hats, and scarves, then led us to the dining room, where we were seated at a big round table and offered coffee and tea. A few other people were seated there already—a woman, slightly older than us, and three young men. As we sat drinking our tea, a tall black-haired man, slender and vibrant, entered the room. He wore an ankle-length, bright-cobalt-blue cassock of a heavy material, a clerical collar, a cross, and a serious expression, but introduced himself warmly as Reverend Christopher. Reverend Christopher sat down at the table, closed his eyes, said a Christian prayer, and began the class.

I have no idea what he said. Not only now, after so many years, but even then I had no idea what he was saying—not because it was unintelligible but because my concentration was elsewhere (I think it might have been some kind of Bible study class but am not sure). I was wholly distracted because of my own thoughts, sputtering alarmingly through my head. It felt as if someone had just directed a spotlight onto my mind, and I was suddenly aware of this niggling, petty stream of pointless, judgmental, and often negative thoughts that ran like ticker tape, almost automatically, through it at all times. Yetch! It was horrible, but I could sense that what I was experiencing was real and not some strange figment of my imagination. In my normal casual, busy state, I never noticed this unpleasant, unworthy subtext. To become aware of it was almost unbearably uncomfortable. I could not take my attention off it and could not wait for the class to end so I could race out the door, never to return!

When the class finally drew to a close, Reverend Christopher said another prayer and stood up. So did I, quick as a shot, tossing off a hasty "Thank you! Goodbye!" as I raced for the door. As I was struggling into my down jacket and jamming on my hat, Rev. Christopher came over, smiling benignly and knowingly down at me while standing casually in front of the door. I couldn't get out until he moved but I knew I definitely did not want to look into his eyes. He didn't move. I did the mature thing: held my mittens up over my face.

He chuckled and gently pulled down my mittened hands. "It's all right," he said in a kindly manner, looking into my eyes. And then he said something that offered a solution to a pressing unexpressed problem I had never shared with anyone—forgive me, dear reader, but, important as it seemed at that time, I cannot now remotely remember what it was—that had been bothering me for some time. It was a shock but a lovely shock, a healing shock, if one could describe it so. It was also a shock to realize that, given his phrasing and detailed comment, he had a gift of clairvoyance and had been able to read my thoughts far beyond anything that might have been expressed by my facial expressions and manner.

"Th-th-thank you," I stuttered.

"You are welcome," he said smiling. "Please come again."

We bid each other good night and I staggered out the door, Carolyne grinning by my side. She looked shrewdly at my stunned face. "I knew you'd like it! There's another class this week on Thursday. I'll come by to get you. Good night . . . and Merry Christmas!"

"Good night," I echoed weakly, and headed off toward home, under the glowing moon. I felt an irrepressible joy and, shocking-ly, an amazing presence: a presence who, I knew with surprised certainty, was the Virgin Mary. She filled me to the top and over-flowing with inexpressible happiness.

Gleeful as a Samoyed puppy in its first snowstorm, I started skipping through the knee-high snow, amazed and full of Light. Yes, Light—which had shown up my tawdry thought stream to awaken me and descended in an inner shower to cleanse and bless me. Who knew that, after I'd just left my old, somewhat ship-wrecked life behind, a new life of unimagined possibilities would suddenly open before me?! Of course, I wasn't really a Christian again or anything like that, I thought self-protectively. No, no! I would not fall into that delusion again! And I probably would never even be able to enunciate the words "Bible class." But, um, I guess I would just go back and check this strange place out a little more. Why not? There was, after all, that joy. And certainly that presence . . .

Quantum Christianity

I recounted the experience to Katie the next morning at breakfast, and she seemed pleased. Katie, a humorous and charming individ-ual, was a devout Christian and choir member in a local Episcopal church that performed Renaissance masses. Graham, on the other hand, was a vehement atheist. Hearing of my experience from Katie, he shook his head at me in mock worry, saying, "Stephani, Stephani, you know it's all just rubbish. Don't waste your time!"

But I continued to attend classes and mystical Christian ser-vices at the non-sectarian, non-denominational Holy Order of MANS (Mysterion Agape Nous Sophia—"the Mystery of Love gives Wisdom to the Eye of the Heart," roughly, I believe—founded by Fr. Paul Blighton in the 1960s in San Francisco). The Order offered a powerful Holy Communion service early each morning, as well as evening classes twice a week. I rediscovered the potent guiding presence of Jesus Christ as a tangible and beloved reality, not just a theory. Peace entered my soul—not the anxious, fanatical, forced "peace" of a cult member, but the deep-rooted, free-thinking, marvelous peace of Jesus Christ, that peace that passes understanding. My enduring recognition of Love as a "force" now achieved a clearer, more spiritually productive focus as I encountered Love as a Person. A Person Who knew me intimately, responded to my prayers, and taught me, even beyond all my hopes and conceptions. I became able to call myself a Christian again, inadequate example though I certainly was. And—well, it took some months—I even became able to say "Bible-study class" without gritting my teeth.

To my surprise, quite quickly, as my faith began to grow, it seemed to have a quiet dynamism that affected not only me but the friends I lived with. As I have said before, God is the elephant in the room. Even among those who deny God's Presence and existence, that Presence is felt and affects everyone, nonetheless. When a ripple occurs in one person's relationship with God, others feel it, whether they are cognizant of it or not. Our ties to each other and to our Creator exist in the vibrant quantum field that knows no separation at all. Our sorrows are shared but our blessings even more so; the movement of the tide of Light through which we draw near to God cleanses everything in its path and purges and renews the psyches of those who wish for a deeper relationship with this most dynamic matrix of life. Katie and Graham, sensitive, warm-hearted souls, demonstrated such responsiveness very soon after I began my attendance at the Order classes and services.

ﺍﻟﻠﻪ

Crises of Faith

One day Katie came down to breakfast quite white-faced. "What's the matter?" I asked her.

"Oh, it's terrible!" she replied mournfully. "I've lost my faith!"

"You've lost your faith? How?"

"Well," she said hesitantly. "Last night I realized that God—that God—that God could send me to Iowa! And I don't want to go to Iowa! So I can't believe in Him anymore!"

I put my arm around her and guided her into the living room, where we sat down. She looked fragile.

"So," I said gently, "do you think that God has asked you to go to Iowa?"

"No, no, not at all!"

"So then why—"

"Oh, it's just that if God is real, then He could ask me to go to Iowa, couldn't He? And it would be very bad not to go—disobedient! And I don't want to go!"

Lest you think, dear reader, that Katie is a Gracie Allen-type ditz, let me assure you she is a very intelligent and perceptive woman. But she was honestly confronting a deep spiritual problem that most of us wrestle with continually with greater or lesser success, and are often hesitant to acknowledge: if God is real and He is a Person, He can request things of us. And we can agree or disagree to do what He has asked us and there are, ahem, consequences to our decisions (as the Prophet Jonah found out in a vivid manner during his "time-out"—a temporary incarceration in the belly of a whale!). Katie was staring in the face the possibility of getting divine guidance to do something that, like Jonah, she preferred not to do. She did not apply the convenient personal "statute of limitations" which most of us use to wall off too real and intense a relationship with the Divine, our sliding screens blocking off the possibility of direct guidance that might not be to our taste. Indeed, I have often thought that one of the major appeals of Buddhism to some of my contemporaries might be the relief of getting rid of the annoying possibility of a Person who can ask something of us, as opposed to a Void which cannot/will not! (I add here that such a psychological quirk of resistance afflicts many of us, regardless of religious persuasion.)

Gently, I tried to examine with Katie the likelihood of God asking her to trot off to live in Iowa (No offense to Iowans! We all have our peculiar tastes. I'm sure that Iowans exist who would be horrified at the thought that God might ask them to move to Syracuse, then the darkest city in the lower forty-eight!). Upon consideration, Katie had to admit that the likelihood of this feared possibility was extremely low.

And we also reflected on what she felt God might have asked her to do in her life so far. She had to admit it had seemed relatively unobjectionable up to this point. She had attended a Seven Sisters school for her baccalaureate degree and enjoyed her studies there. She was now happily married with two adorable sons. And enjoyed her choir and volunteer work. What was not to like? As she contemplated all this more calmly, she realized she was holding her belief in God to ransom because of an unfounded fear. She had experienced God's loving-kindness to her and compassionate nearness in so many ways. Why give up those tangible blessings for a stray weird and unlikely thought, likely to have been sent not by an angel of truth but by denizens of darker regions? The underlying issue, of course, remained a real one. But, like so many other challenging spiritual issues, it was best examined case by case, day by day, in real life and not in the abstract. Smiling happily now, Katie gave me a big hug.

"Yes, God is real!" She laughed. "Let's go get some breakfast!"

॰ঽ৽

We passed through Advent and Christmas without further crises, but as Epiphany approached, a totally unexpected one erupted. I came home one afternoon to find Katie in a state of distress. "Oh thank God you're home! It's Graham!"

"Graham! Is he all right? Has he been hurt?"

"No, not exactly. Well, you'll see! He's in the living room."

We walked into the living room to find Graham sitting, staring, in a large armchair. "Hi, Graham!" I said. His eyes acknowledged me for a moment and then moved back to peer wanly into uninhabited space. Graham bore a striking resemblance to a grown-up Charlie Brown and currently looked like the cartoon Charlie in one of his most overwhelmed and despondent moments.

A gentle soul like Charlie, Graham also had an incisive intellect and a generally well-repressed quality of fire in his personality that could, on special occasions, summon up significant vital energy and expression. Where was this fire now, when he needed it, sitting there looking comatose? If we could only rouse it!

When, as a young junior high teacher, Graham had been assigned to an inner-city classroom that appeared to be merely an inadequate storage tank for out-of-control gang warfare (throwing one's opponents out the window was a great favorite—fortunately the classroom was on the first floor), and his first day's futile attempts had not quelled the pandemonium, he realized that he had to try a different approach. On his second day, Graham walked serenely into another session of screaming, cursing, punching teenagers. He stood behind his desk, trying to call them to order. Hopeless! Then, quietly, with an unmoved Charlie Brown expression on his calm, round face, he picked up his heavy desk chair and began to methodically and ferociously smash it to bits upon his desk.

Instant silence—except for the noise of smashing—reigned in the classroom. When, after some time, he had finished obliterating the chair and looked up mildly from its matchsticks into the eyes of the frozen class, they uttered an appalled, "Mr. Smith!" in unison. Then, nervously, each youth took his or her seat, surveying their scary lunatic teacher in alarmed quiet. "All right, today we are studying . . ." began Graham in a peaceful voice. He never had any trouble with them again. The janitor, coming in later and surveying the ruins of Graham's chair on his desk, only chuckled, gave him a knowing wink, and said hopefully, "Didya get any of 'em?" But that wildly inspired Graham was not on view at the moment. He resembled, instead, a deeply pensive iceberg.

"What's going on?" I whispered to Katie as we retired to the dining room.

"Well," she said, sinking her forehead into her hand as we sat down at the table, "Graham has realized that Satan exists."

"What!?"

"Yes, well, you know what a convinced atheist he has been. But somehow, I don't know how, he has come to a conviction that Satan is real. And that was bad enough. But he has also realized that if Satan is real, so is Jesus Christ. He just can't deal with the shock. He's overwhelmed."

"Wow!" I said. "Have you tried talking to him?"

"Yes, but it doesn't seem to do any good. Could you try?"

I did but didn't seem able to evoke any response from the suffering Graham. A few hours passed with no sign of improvement. Our worry deepened.

"Katie, should I see if Brother David can help us somehow?" Reverend Christopher (who had once remarked that atheists were his favorite people: "No one else thinks about God so much!") had been transferred to another Order house out of state not too long after I met him, and Brother David, a bright-eyed, slightly sarcastic, kinetically brilliant man had been brought in to supervise the house until a new priest could be sent. I phoned Brother David and explained. He said he'd be right over.

When he arrived, he told us that sometimes certain people come to faith and belief in God this way, on this "left-hand path," though it wasn't very common. He went in and greeted Graham, who barely acknowledged his presence. "I think perhaps you'd better leave us alone," he told Katie and me judicially, bowing his head in prayer as we walked away.

Two hours later, Brother David joined us in the kitchen, followed by a slightly shaky Graham. "I'm okay now," Graham said with a little laugh. Katie and I threw ourselves into Graham's arms, rejoicing and profusely thanking Brother David. "It was my pleasure," he said with a big smile. "I think he'll do fine now. Please let me know how it goes. God bless you!" Putting on his jacket and hat, he sauntered out into the night.

Neither Graham nor Brother David ever told us what they had talked about, or how Brother David had been able to lead Graham through the mental and emotional maze in which he had found himself entrapped. But from that day on Graham lived as a believing Christian, attending Katie's church and some others, never looking back, and expressing joy and relief in his newfound faith.

ﻙﻟ

Our relief was also great, and particularly so that week because Katie's parents had insisted that Katie and Graham invite some distant and very difficult relatives who were visiting our parts over to dinner. These much-removed cousins were thorns in the side of the whole family, and when they visited, the local family members took turns entertaining them so that no one had to endure too much of them at one time.

"They can't be that bad," I said upon seeing Katie's despondent looks.

"You have no idea!" she said, rolling her eyes to heaven. "Thank God Graham got through that crisis. I can't imagine what would have happen if they'd shown up here tomorrow and Graham had been comatose!"

Early the following evening Katie and I set the table. She had, despite her nerves, been able to cook a delicious dinner. The boys were attired in clean clothes and looked sparklingly cute. Graham stood by the table, anxiously straightening his tie. He had met these dreaded guests before and looked as eager to see them again as he would a mob of attacking Visigoths. How bad could they be? I would soon find out.

The stuffy middle-aged couple strode into the house and seemed to inspect it, critically, as if they had been ordered to file a careful report on its state. The report obviously would not be favorable. They smiled penuriously at Katie, Graham, and me, and nodded at the boys, as if reluctant to spend any of whatever capital of warmth might lie subterraneanly hidden within them. Once the meal began, Mr. and Mrs. Smythe-Graubacher dominated the conversation, and we soon discovered they were both politically a bit to the right of Hitler. This was worse than I had imagined. Any time Graham, Katie, or I, all normally loquacious, tried to gently change the topic, this stern couple would jump down our throats to disagree and cut us off. We sat there, eventually becoming as silent as our chairs. During a particularly glacial silence, Katie nervously suggested we enjoy coffee and dessert in the living room. Looking disapproving, the couple stood up, and as Graham led them into the living room, Katie and I hurried to bring out the dessert and coffee cups. The boys were excused to go off and play.

Soon the five of us were all perched on couches and chairs, uncomfortably balancing our desserts and coffees. Katie, Graham, and I were drained of all potential for speech, like gaping fish laid out in the market. Any attempts on our parts to smile resulted only in strained grimaces. Our guests seemed to believe that smiling was some kind of aberrant liberal innovation and did not condescend to attempt it. The Smythe-Graubachers, not one pleasant word or thanks of any kind having escaped their iron lips, just sat staring at us as if we were lesser life forms they had been forced by cruel duty to associate with. Into this massively gelid silence leaped an Ariel-like form—a unexpected answer to an unvoiced prayer.

It was six-year-old Brian, a sweet blue-eyed, blond boy with an enchanting smile. "Look, Mommy!" he cried enthusiastically as he ran around and around the living room, shooting tampons into the air out of a box he had found in her dresser. "Rockets! Rockets!" As if we were members of a military drill team or the inmates of a cuckoo clock when the hour was struck, Graham, Katie, and I arose in horror and rigid formation and advanced upon the ecstatic Brian. Before we could reach him, one of his high-flying "rockets" landed, with unerring poetry, in Mrs. Smythe-Graubacher's lap. Outrage on her face, she quickly stood up, her rocket dropping to earth's wall-to-wall carpet, and strode to the door, accompanied by her scandalized husband. They let us know in no uncertain terms that they were horrified by our uncivilized display and were leaving that instant!

Katie, Graham, and I dared not meet each other's eyes. We rapidly walked our guests to the door and clustered moronically there. Graham, eyes cast down, quickly mumbled tumbling, unintelligible apologies in a low, breathless monotone, remorsefully addressing his shoes as the mortally affronted guests huffily pulled on their coats. Katie and I understood that Graham was, with an iron hand, holding down a wild urge to express his true feelings and guffaw in their pale, pinched faces. Awestruck and barely breathing, Katie and I silently admired his superhuman control.

But, as soon as the door had slammed shut on our indignant guests, the three of us plummeted to the carpet as if poleaxed, howling with laughter, completely helpless, rolling over and over, our limbs flailing. We couldn't stop, even as we reached the point of pain. We would have made Bedlam look like a Zen temple.

Brian, still clutching his "launching box" came and stood over us, gazing down at us innocently. "Hey, guys, what's so funny?"

After a few weeks of tortured metaphysical distress and drama, the Holy Spirit had, in its quixotic manner, found a way to relax us and keep us from continuing to take ourselves too seriously. A lovely Christmastide present! When we finally regained our strength, we stood up and staggered around collecting the bonanza of "rockets" from the jumbo-size tampon box, one or the other of us occasionally falling down on a convenient piece of furniture in hysterics. Oh yes—that's another big reason some people may be hesitant to believe in God—perhaps I've mentioned this?—His sense of humor.

～ॐ～

The Unheard Melody

I had a bewildering dose or two of the divine eccentric humor on the day I was baptized. Although baptized as a baby in the Greek Orthodox Church, I knew no reason at that time that I should not accept the HOOM's friendly offer of baptism as well.

On a warm summer day, I knelt before the altar in the Order house alongside my dear friend Mindy Lind and a few others who were about to be baptized. Several people were attending the Holy Communion and baptism services in the small chapel; we could feel their prayerful, supportive company behind us. With a sprinkling of holy water and the invocation of the Holy Trinity, our priest baptized the first kneeling woman. She was a visiting sister of the H.O.O.M., wearing a dusky blue robe like the brothers did. The priest, on inspiration, gave her an additional blessing: "Your path will be a straight one," he said softly in her ear. Next was Mindy. She turned to look at me for a moment afterward, and her eyes looked so beautiful, like clear, sparkling stars, full of an almost-supernatural light. Then it was my turn.

As the priest began my baptism, I began to feel overwhelmed by unexpected emotion. Tears ran down my face, followed by, alas, snot (no handkerchief, of course!). I was a mess, and I felt like a mess inside, too—like a shattered vase, a mass of sharp, cutting edges jumbled together, in turmoil. It was terrible! I felt like I was somehow failing my baptism!

Then the service was over. Handsome Brother Daniel picked me up and swung me round and round in the air, laughing with joy. I just wanted to hide away. Then the newly baptized Order sister came over and gave me a long hug. This was emotionally painful for me as I could feel her solid, devoted straightforwardness and purity, setting in high relief my desperate, tortured fragmentation. I grabbed my first chance to escape from the gathering, rushing out the door.

Although it was a Sunday, I had to go to the newsroom to do some work at the *New Times*. A park stretched between the Order house and the large house where our newspaper offices lay. As I stepped into the street that bordered the park, grateful to see that no one was around to witness my grief, something strange happened.

I felt suddenly as if a mysterious unheard melody swept through my soul, a great arcing song made up of the infinite harmonies of every creature and being around me and, indeed, in the whole Creation. Peace and beauty flowed inexhaustibly out of that ineffable chorus, a peace and beauty and harmony of which even I was an integral part. The first notes obliterated the jaggedness and torment in my soul; I rose up, as if from cleansing waters, not only cleansed but given wings to fly within the infinitely spiraling loveliness of all my fellow creatures, one with them and one with God. This great goodness permeating every mote of my renewed being, I marveled as I walked through the park, inhaling its joy with every step and, with a new delighted sensitivity, appreciating more deeply than ever before each being's individual contribution—the grass, the birds, the rocks, the flowers, the bees, the trees, the earth, the clouds, the sky. Walking with this harmony seemed more like light-footed dancing, each step partaking of the indescribable grace surrounding me.

I was halfway across the park when it was as if my soul's sleeve caught on a snag and stopped me dead in my tracks. I heard a very disturbing wrong note. The great harmony still predominated, but this wrong note, a sharp disharmony, was emanating from somewhere nearby. I had to find its source. I plunged farther into the park, determined as a bloodhound on a scent, following the growing loudness, the aching, reverberating sound of that clashing note. Ultimately, I found myself standing in front of a tall oak tree. I could tell that the shrill noise was coming from it, but why? The tree looked perfectly normal.

I walked around the trunk and looked at the other side, catching my breath in a sympathetic gasp of pain. Some enraged person had taken an axe and chopped repeatedly, violently, haphazardly into the trunk, venting his fury on the innocent wood. Both the physical injury and the dark emotions were pulsing out of those wounds on a trembling, suffering note of pain.

I put my hands on the trunk and prayed for the tree. Then I made the sign of the Cross on all its wounds. And laid my hands on them again for a while, eyes closed in prayer for the tree's healing and recovery. Lastly I kissed them, gently hugged the tree, and resumed my walk across the park, deeply thoughtful.

ﷺ

I had hoped to find the newsroom empty, but when I arrived, Michael, our editor in chief, was standing scowling behind his desk. Black haired and black browed, he was an imposing figure, and I found myself hesitating in the doorway. Michael was a fine editor and writer and a good person, but he was subject to frequent dark moods—in which he sometimes even threw things at reporters (never, so far, me)—and he seemed to be stewing, his face like a storm cloud. He regarded me silently, with a bleak eye.

"Uh, hi, Michael!" I said hesitantly, moving into the room and toward him.

He said nothing, just glared.

As I got within six feet of his desk, however, I felt this strange wave come out of me, a golden surge that rolled toward and then over him. As soon as it hit him, he manifested a sea change.

"Hi, Stephani!" he said brightly, almost unrecognizable, his face suddenly aglow with a megawatt smile. "How have you been doing? Nice to see you!"

This cheeriness was so foreign to his nature and general demeanor as to make me gasp. Had the rest of the newsroom staff been there, they would have thought they had witnessed a personality transplant.

"Um, nice to see you, too, Michael."

"Yeah, I just came in to take care of a couple of things," he said, beaming at me.

"Yes, me too."

"Well, I think I'm finished now." Michael picked up his denim jacket, swung it casually over his shoulder, said, "Bye now," with a wink, and headed out the door—whistling.

Whoa! I thought to myself. *What was that?*

کلم

Still somewhat in shock, I mounted the stairs to the main secretary's office. She had just been hired, and I barely knew her name.

"Hi," I said, as I stepped into her office. Our eyes met with an unexpected spark of electricity. And something terrible happened! Somehow—and I can't tell you how I knew this— I suddenly felt two vortices of energy spinning in my ovaries, like two little cyclones of light, Roto-Rootering and cleansing those organs. And, immediately, the same exact thing began to happen to the secretary! This sensation was so forceful that neither of us could stand upright. She struggled out from behind her desk and we both wobbled around the room, leaning on furniture and filing cabinets, unable to speak from weakness and sheer shock. At last she was able to spit out, "What is going on here?!!"

I can't believe you are doing this to me, God! Now what am I supposed to say?!

I staggered toward the door and, leaning against the frame, whimpered, "Uh, sorry—I just got baptized!" And rocketed out, stumbling down the stairs, trying to figure out how I could avoid ever seeing her again!

Trying to get as far away from the reeling secretary as I could, I headed down more stairs to the basement, domain of artists and photographers, normally deserted on Sundays. But my friend Brook Tankle, a photographer, happened to be down there. We were often a team on assignments, she taking the photographs, me writing the story.

"What?!" she said, staring at me. "Hey, don't you come around here shining at me!"

"No—um, what do you mean, Brook?"

"You know what I mean! You're shining, you're glowing! What happened to you?!"

I hesitated. Brook was Jewish.

"Well, it's that I just got baptized," I said apologetically.

"Baptized?" Her eyes narrowed thoughtfully. "Where?"

And the story came out. "I don't know about this," she said, "but I think I better check it out. Where is this place?"

I accomplished my work in the newsroom without any further encounters—or, as I've come to call them, "ring-tailed lemurs." This is my shorthand for uncanny experiences where there is a spontaneous movement of mystical energy that I can neither direct nor suppress, and that often affects others, sometimes even physically. I find them embarrassing in the extreme and impossible to explain (especially as I don't understand them myself!). As they occur unpredictably, they leave a residual anxiety in me that one could pop out at any time. I might just have been introduced to someone and be having a perfectly normal conversation when, without warning, a "ring-tailed lemur" might leap out from "under my cloak" and leave me there, stuttering at the startled person, unable to account for this conspicuously exotic and irrational interruption.

I don't know why this happens (unless, of course, for obscure celestial amusement and/or to embarrass me into humility). As yet an open question. Not that I'm pressing, God.

✺

Two days after my baptism, I returned to the park to visit the tree and see how it was doing. But I could not find it. I knew the area where it grew and I combed through it, over and over. All the trees looked perfect. Then I remembered two trees near it that had oddities in their branching that made them easily identifiable, and from which I could easily triangulate "my" tree's location. There it was. I walked up to the tall oak, as I had the first day. I walked around behind it, gazing steadily at the trunk. There were no wounds on its bark, not even scars. And this was the same tree. I would not blame you for thinking, dear reader, that I was delusional. But I was not. The great energetic harmony that was pouring through me and everything that day must have poured through the tree and given it a complete healing. This amazed me, and I was deeply grateful for it (a gratitude I still could not quite summon up for the energy's effect on that secretary!). I kissed and blessed the tree again, and went home, marveling at the generosity and spontaneous healing power of a loving and untamable God.

How to Fly with One Wing
Feeling the call to work directly with people who were in need, I had quit my newspaper job and, not many weeks after, gotten a job working with intellectually challenged children in a large institution.

Sometimes our clinical unit felt as if, rather than being rooted on mother-ship earth, it was idly circling in the meteor belt deep in space. The twelve severely and profoundly impaired children who lived in its cinder-block and linoleum capsule seemed to ramble—those who could ramble—in a kind of Brownian movement, unfocussed, drifting by walls and chairs as if impelled by eccentric, unseen gravitational forces that sent them hither and thither, reasonless. The children themselves often seemed like lonely asteroids, shot out of the shattered core of some larger planet where parts of them—the parts that gave speech, sight, hearing, linear reason, functional ability, even varying degrees of physical motion—had been left behind. And here they were, still trying to live out their lives—butterflies with only one wing.

Vegetables, some people rudely called them. And inaccurately. Even the least functional child among them, Nina, who was blind, could not speak or move, and lay on her frail side in a fetal position most of the time, would emit small, happy purring sounds, rough and deep in her throat, when her "grandfather," a volunteer older gentleman, would sit beside her and hold her hand or stroke her head, murmuring, "Good girl, good girl, good girl."

The "vegetables" view had a contrasting but equally brutal companion in the fashionable "liberal" policy of 1960s social services called "normalization." Normalization was an attempt to force a blending of this seriously challenged population with the mundane run of society. While certain elements of creating participation in the greater society were workable, others sprang out of a kind of cold-minded fundamentalist cruelty. As in the dark Night of the Teddy Bears, when ninja squads of counselors rushed into adult units, ruthlessly relieving aging grown-ups of their beloved stuffed animals and replacing them, over the shrieks, with "normalizing" wristwatches. A night—and weeks to follow—of weeping and wailing, as adults, some of them with mental and emotional processes revolving at a three- or six-year-old's level, dropped tears on the bland faces of watches affixed to their wrists, and went to bed wretchedly with nothing comforting to cuddle in the lonely dark. Those in favor of this policy said it would make our inmates "look better" to the "normal" population on excursions and be, after all, more "age appropriate."

Most of us, the counselors who worked with the children on the juvenile units, found that social engineering and the big, willful, crude backhoes of enforced lifestyle change were useless in promoting quality of life or even ensuring a successful basic level of functioning. Those of us working on the ground were forced to learn to actually pay attention to these suffering people in a noncoercive way and also to develop more subtle senses and approaches in our interactions with our charges out of necessity, as well as desire. For example, being bathed was upsetting for many of the children; the coldness of the big tile bathing room did not help. We could not control the thermostat, so I would try to pile up towels on counters so that when a child was laid upon them, she would not feel the shock of the cold. But some of them still wailed and jerked when taken to the bathing room, no matter how reassuringly we spoke.

One day I struck upon something that worked for me. I began to sing as I carried an upset child into the bathroom. She calmed and began to smile. Singing proved a soothing magic for each child. The odd thing, though, was that there had to be a different song for each child. No one size fits all, no substitutions, and always the same song for each child, her own particular theme. Or else the usual flailing upset would ensue. I racked my memory for little songs in French, Spanish, Latin, Hebrew, Greek, as well as English—short and cheerful or haunting, depending on each child's temperament. Like a tailor cutting to measure, I had to find the particular melody that matched the mysterious, hidden inner curves of each soul. Even without speaking, without knowing, the children were training me in listening, in inner quiet. Like a kingfisher hovering above a stream, I learned to concentrate until the subtle glint of fish scales signaled me to dive on the particular melody that would soothe and nourish that particular child. Peacefulness, harmony, could not be forced. But instead of resentfully and forcibly making the children submit to being cleaned in order to check another task off the too-long list, I learned to slow down, breathe, and become receptive like the crescent moon, ready to receive any available light that would reveal a workable and healing answer. It would be there if I was in a state of true, and not feigned, patience. It was natural to be gentle in such a state. I felt as if the melody even came through my hands. Each child and I found our own particular and real harmony. And the task was accomplished. Bath time became pleasant for us both.

There was one exception. She was nine years old but had the shriveled, hard-bitten demeanor of an aggrieved ancient crone. Wilma looked as close to a stick-figure drawing of a person as I've ever seen: skinny as a pencil, all awkward angles without an ounce of softening plumpness, she skittered around the unit like a nervous water bug, never making eye contact with anyone, never touching anyone or allowing touch. Her dark, expression-less eyes, tiny and close-set, made her look like a remote, sad android. With a mouth like an almost-lipless slit, smiles were foreign to her. Her hair, chopped a couple of inches above her shoulders, flopped around her paper-white face, thin, lank, and a greasy-looking dark brown. Wilma could move around but not speak. According to the records, there had been a period when she had fed herself, but eventually she stopped doing even that, for unknown reasons, and now waited grimly while a counselor spooned or forked food into her reluctant mouth. At night in the privacy of her room, Wilma would beat herself, tearing with her nails, and emerge in the morning with blood streaming down her face. Even though we were not supposed to, some nights we counselors would tie soft cloth gloves on her hands so that she could not hurt herself as badly.

The one exception to Wilma's no-touch habits involved the sweetest child on the unit. Laurie was eleven but looked younger. She sat upright and motionless all day in her wheelchair, com-pletely paralyzed except for her neck. She had huge, beautiful pale blue eyes that shone with the light of a fathomless love, warming anyone who approached her. And her smile was like a rainbow after storms. Laurie could not speak but she would make a happy "Aaaaaaahhhhhhh!" sound of welcome when anyone approached her. Her dark-blond hair was cut in an elfin pixie style around her pretty face. She was also very slender, like Wilma, but the effect in her case was that of a delicate fine-boned doe.

We all loved Laurie—how not?—and this Wilma noticed. And hated Laurie. Perhaps feeling Laurie's endless outpouring of love and seeing others responding with love to her warm glow made Wilma feel her poverty. She neither had love to give nor allowed anyone to express love or affection toward her. When our backs were turned, Wilma would sidle over to Laurie and pull her hair. We would hear the soft "Aaaahhhh" turn to an anguished "Oooowwwww!" and whip around to see the pained, bewildered look on Laurie's face and the vindictive look on Wilma's as she pulled and pulled.

Although I could get Wilma to submit to bathing, woodenly, I could never find a melody to bring her gladness. There seemed to be a wall or, when the kingfisher side of myself tried to look in, only roiling water obscuring wherever the quick, bright, elusive fish in her being might lie.

We counselors felt that Wilma was getting worse over time. She beat herself harder and more frequently. We resorted to the forbidden gloves more often. I asked advice of my supervisor. Gruffly, he said he didn't think anything could be done and added with a grunt, "Just be sure to cover your ass and write down everything" in the record book. Therapy came a distant second to institutional politics.

A night came when I had put Wilma to bed but felt somehow that I could not leave her. The other bed in her room was empty; she had no roommate. I sat near her in a chair while Wilma sat up in bed, compulsively rocking back and forth, back and forth, back and forth, sucking a red thumb, her eyes hard and miserable. *There must be some way to help,* I thought. *There must be.* I had prayed so many times for Wilma and all the other children in the unit. Once again, I prayed to God for help. Getting quiet within, I tried to reach for whatever that mysterious something was that she needed, my kingfisher hovering over a bigger stream than ever before, where huge fish must be swimming. Somewhere. But nothing. Nothing.

And then, startled, I heard myself, staring fixedly at the girl, say, "Wilma, you must understand—if you want to receive love, you must give love. To receive love, you must give love."

I felt somehow as if I were speaking to her adult soul, craftily concealed in the tortured cave of her rigid body and blocked in most of its outward function. An Eastern sage had referred to impaired people as "beautiful birds in ugly cages." Some part of me was trying to speak to that bird. Some part of me must have believed there was a melody it could hear.

But Wilma rocked on, staring into space, an oblivious, out-of-control marionette. I blushed with embarrassment, feeling despair. Whatever was I doing? That was a crazy thing to say to her. How could she possibly understand? And what would the other counselors think if they had heard me? I was so relieved that no one had. Sighing, I stood up, sadly patted Wilma on the shoulder, turned off the light, and went out.

Three days passed. And then, beyond hope, Wilma came out of the tomb. We three counselors and all the children were in the main room during a time for afternoon relaxation. I was sitting in the big rocking chair. Wilma angled her way over to me and stopped in front of me, like an uncertain heron. She turned her back to me and stood in indecision for a moment. Then, very carefully and slowly, stiff in every limb, she lowered herself into my lap. We were all stunned. All three counselors burst into tears. I wrapped my arms around Wilma, kissed her head, and began to rock her, saying, "Good girl, good girl." She heaved a tremendous sigh of relief, more like a body blast releasing infinite sorrows, and collapsed against my chest, limbs softened and natural at last. It was the first time we had ever seen her relax.

After a good long cuddle and rock and us all telling her we loved her, Wilma clambered out of my lap and made her way over to Laurie. A wave of habitual apprehension passed over the counselors. But, when Wilma reached Laurie, instead of pulling her hair, she tried, in her awkward way, to hug her, holding her stiff arms elbows-up in the air, hands together, in a pointy ring around Laurie's neck. "Aaaaahhhhhh," said Laurie, for us all. "Aaaahhhh!" Wilma was new to expressing and receiving love and perhaps she wasn't very good at it yet, but she had, alone, climbed over the vast bridge from not loving to loving. And now she was giving it all she had, a small shining beacon of beautiful daring.

These children, regarded by some as society's refuse and by some others as pitiable nonentities, had given me lessons that were to fuel my whole life. Laurie's selfless love: its unflagging, unquestioning, glowing radiance, even under daunting conditions, and its great transforming power flowing like sunlight over all of us. Wilma's lessons of courage: the overcoming of what could easily have been described as impossible obstacles, the depth and power of the human soul and its warrior's ardor to live in whatever fullness was possible, both giving and receiving. I have sat at the feet of various spiritual teachers since that time, and for that I am grateful. But among the greatest whom I have ever been privileged to know are these two, Laurie and Wilma—miracle workers who showed you how to fly with one wing.

ﻋﻠﻲ

Let Me Be a Rose
She was coming. I could feel it with every cell of my being.

Living for the first time all by myself, in an apartment I had taken when I started my new job with the children at the institution, I felt my new home and my being itself filling with a subtle radiance, a quiet, inexpressible joy. I didn't want to talk to anyone. I wanted to be alone as much as possible. And I, whose enthusiasm for housekeeping was almost as pitiful as my enthusiasm for higher math (virtually nonexistent), was not only cleaning but dancing as I cleaned, feet unable to stay still for sheer gladness.

I had found her picture in a store, and now she watched me from the wall in a poster-size reproduction of a subtle Leonardo da Vinci drawing of the Holy Virgin, one of his studies for *The Virgin of the Rocks*, I believe. Extraordinarily beautiful, full of grace, her eyes were looking down or perhaps closed in ecstasy, and yet I felt that she saw me—I was with her, enfolded in her sublime presence emanating from the soft chalk lines, luminously compelling. My new life revolved around her as a planet does around the sun.

And I was going to have my first shrine blessing soon. My attempts to find a graceful and inexpensive table or bureau for the shrine had been notably unsuccessful, even in the secondhand stores I frequented. And now there it was, a big and ugly white rectangular hinged table of sorts, my metal "Buick" shrine, or perhaps more like the unfortunate, misbegotten runt offspring of an ocean liner and a refrigerator, taking up most of one end of my room beneath the windows. This shiny cold metal hulk I covered with pretty gold cloth in desperate disguise, but no cloth could hide its graceless, blocky lines. But it was all I could afford and would have to do. Besides, what did it matter, when I knew in my heart that she was coming! That was all that mattered.

The evening of the shrine blessing, eight or nine friends assembled in my bedroom. Two were priests—my local priest, Reverend Jesse, and another HOOM priest, Reverend Frances, visiting from another city. The rest were two Order brothers and friends who attended the HOOM classes and services, as well as Brook, my former photographer colleague at the *New Times*. We gathered before my giant oceangoing shrine with its flowers, one unlit seven-day candle, and a small, lovely reproduction of the Renaissance artist Stefan Lochner's serene *Our Lady of the Rose Garden* upright on a stand in the center.

Reverend Jesse turned to us and spoke quietly, his blue eyes warm, about Our Lady and the goodness of having a shrine in one's home. Reverend Frances, dark haired and lovely, stood beside him, smiling. She was tall and strong looking, with graceful, generous curves, and emanated a reassuring sense of groundedness and peace.

The priests turned to face the shrine, all of us remaining standing. I turned off the lights and Reverend Jesse lit the seven-day candle. It cast wavering red-and-white garlands of light around the shadowy bedroom. We composed ourselves. The priests raised their hands up to receive the sacred, and so did we all. Reverend Jesse began the prayer of shrine blessing, but I'm not sure if he ever made it all the way through. Because she came then, came abruptly and powerfully.

I don't know exactly how it happened, but suddenly all of us fell, in a single fast sweep, to our knees—just dropped to the hard floor but were not hurt. And we were all suddenly singing a hymn to her, completely unpremeditated—and not being led by anyone in a body. We sang other hymns, as easily as waves moving in the sea together, and we prayed. I could only pray one prayer silently over and over in my soul. "Let me be a rose in your garden. Let me be a rose in your garden. Let me be a rose in your garden."

I don't know how long we sang, kneeling in prayer. We were in that deep mystical state where time just disappears. All that mattered was to be with her, beyond time. There were no words for the ecstasy and sense of fulfillment in our souls that being with her in this ineffable way brought us.

Finally, of one accord, the hymns died away into silence. The priests stood up, and we all slowly got to our feet. Quietly, one by one, my friends took leave of me, no one speaking above a whisper, but all still warmly wrapped in the blessed companionship we had felt. Brook looked like she had been hit by a meteor, but a joyful one. Her skin and her deep dark-brown eyes seemed to glow.

"Thank you. We'll talk," she said, with a mysterious little smile. "We definitely will talk. Good night."

The two priests came up to me last of all. "I was almost yanked out of my body!" confided Reverend Jesse in wonder.

"Yes, I could hear his knees knocking together!" said Reverend Frances, smiling, and the three of us chuckled.

They each gave me a warm hug and then headed for the door.

Reverend Jesse hesitated there and returned to me again. He leaned forward, his golden curls almost brushing my face, and spoke softly in my ear. "Um, Stephani, you might want to be careful about who goes near that shrine—um, no one dipsy or fartsy, if you know what I mean? It's very powerful there. We wouldn't want anyone to hurt themselves. God bless you! Good night." And I closed the door after them.

I fell on my bed amid the garlands of light still dancing from the candle. I felt myself drawn into an even deeper state with our Holy Mother. I did not sleep but was in a state so wondrous and deeply satisfying that I did not want to. I felt no tiredness after the long day, only the most pervasive, rich, and beautiful peace.

Hours later, in the early A.M., I heard someone climb the stairs to my second-floor apartment. Whoever it was seized the doorknob in the hall and rattled it, trying to get in. I felt a pang of fear.

I was almost sure this was Edmund, here in the middle of the night and determined to see me. He kept roughly trying to turn the doorknob. Though he never had shown me any sign of violence, I was afraid. But I almost couldn't move. I felt swathed in layers of her grace, like a cocoon composed of thin veils of some kind of living, heavenly fabric. Still lying on my back, I did not try to do anything but only turned to her more deeply in prayer, asking for her protection. I felt that she invited me into that protection simultaneously as I asked for it. I went in deeper, deeper, deeper still until nothing outside mattered and eventually fell asleep. I don't know when the persistent rattling at the door stopped.

I awoke in peace to a sunny, quiet morning, the seven-day candle still burning steadily by her portrait, among all her roses, on my shrine. *I guess I forgot to go down to lock the outside door last night,* I scolded myself. *Thank God I remembered to lock the upstairs door!* I got up and went to pray to her and our Lord at her shrine. Then, on the way to the kitchen to make tea and toast, I stopped and tried the doorknob of my room. It was open, not locked. *Hail Mary, full of grace, the Lord is with thee, indeed.*

CHAPTER EIGHT

Cataract: Not a Caravan of Despair—Arrival of the Magi

*Praise to the Holy Creator, who has placed his throne on the waters, and who has made all terrestrial creatures. . . . Sometimes he causes the dog to go before the traveler; **sometimes he uses the cat to show the Way.***

—Farid Ud-din Attar, from *The Conference of the Birds*

"The grammarian Ibn Babshad was sitting with his friends on the roof of a mosque in Cairo, eating some food," recounts Lorraine Chittock in her wonderful book *Cats of Cairo: Egypt's Enduring Legacy.* "When a cat passed by they gave her some morsels; she took them and ran away, only to come back time and time again. The scholars followed her and saw her running to an adjacent house on whose roof a blind cat was sitting. The cat carefully placed the morsels in front of her. Babshad was so moved by God's caring for the blind creature that he gave up all his belongings and lived in poverty, completely trusting in God until he died in 1067."

Straight Up
Trusting in God—that was what this was all coming down to, though not on the heroic Ibn Babshad level. Just in a small matter but, for us, a vexing one.

It was ninety-three degrees out. Maine is not supposed to get that hot, right? Someone must have thrown the climate rule book out the cosmic window! And, all too horribly, my husband Mark and I had, nonetheless, to climb a mountain. Mount Blue.

We had definitely not planned to do this. On this, the last day of our August vacation in the cheerful Maine town of Weld on gleaming Webb Lake, we had planned to climb a different mountain altogether, a much easier mountain, one with an appealing crater lake on its summit where we could swim and frolic and cool off after what we envisioned as a leisurely, vista-marveling ascent.

However, as happened to us so often, our naive attempt at a carefree vacation was, yet again, morphing into a pilgrimage or, at the very least, a not-greatly appealing obedience.

Fatefully, as we most often did, we had begun the day with prayer and meditation. And during our prayerful silence, we had both received what seemed to be strong guidance from, we believed, the Virgin Mary (to whom we both had a sustaining devotion). Rather than the hedonic-sounding crater-lake-topped mountain we preferred, our holy patroness wanted us to climb the tall, severe, difficult Mount Blue that loomed majestically over Lake Webb. In an inner image during our meditation, I had seen the Virgin Mary standing as tall as that whole mountain in this inland town and absolutely filling it, shining her brilliant light out to the southeast, toward the invisible ocean.

Mark and I discussed this instruction, tried to wriggle out of it, tried to rationalize keeping to our original plan, and failed. We knew in our hearts that it was really a command.

⚓

As we were en route to the mountain in our gigantic low-slung ancient Cadillac, "Big Blue" (bought for $200 from Mark's brother), bumping and jerking along the rutted dirt logging road, our muffler tore mostly off. Ah, wonderful! A great beginning! Just one of those delightful little extra touches that seemed so faithfully to accompany our obediences and pilgrimages! We continued to bump and jerk farther along, only now we were generating the sound effects of an off-key brass band running from an angry roaring bear.

Clanking and roaring, we pulled into the small deserted parking area (who else would be stupid enough to venture on such a climb in this terrible humid heat?), stopped in merciful silence, got out, and walked to the trailhead. Even visually, the path ahead seemed daunting. I remember the bottom of the trail appeared to be a giant staircase of steep, widely spaced railroad ties leading straight up and up, bordered by claustrophobically crowded woods on either side. (In more recent photos of the Mount Blue trail, I see no such railroad ties but only large, plentiful, jumbled jagged rocks—we did have those wildly inconvenient rocks, too, occasionally roped in, as if barely restrained, by large tree roots across the path, like police tape barely holding in check a crowd of stony thugs.) Contemplating our task of climbing over three thousand feet of stairs, full of large fallen rocks, we rolled our eyes at each other. Our shared impulse was to run back to the car immediately and drive off for a cold ice cream somewhere (we were already dripping). But, fortunately, this was not the first challenging guidance we had ever received, so we knew that, no matter what, we had a responsibility to go on.

As we began to ascend, we quickly discovered why other hikers had described the trail as "strenuous, steep, relentless, challenging." We could not have progressed more than a couple of hundred feet before we had to throw our panting, overheated, not-in-condition fortyish bodies down and stare despairingly into each other's tomato-red faces.

"This is not going to work," panted Mark, as sweat rolled into his eyes.

I agreed. But it was guidance. So what were we going to do?

"Well, we have to try something," I replied. "This is really a long shot, but why don't we pray to the Holy Mother again, ask her to help us, and then I can show you how to do the Sufi Earth Walk and Elemental Breath—maybe those might help us with the stress of the climb a little?"

"All right," Mark said with a deep sigh. And so we prayed. And then, a little more rested, rose to practice the Earth Walk.

We were both members of a mystical Sufi Order, now called the Inayati, that initiated people of all faiths, not only Muslims. Since I had been a Sufi *mureed* (student) longer than my husband, I had more training to apply to our current problem. Sufi teachers work with attuning themselves and others to a spectrum of different states of consciousness. They are skillful in the many powerful uses of the breath, among other things, that help elevate consciousness and open up experiences of mystical fields of which we are normally unaware. In my Sufi classes I had been taught a series of special Breaths for the Elements: Earth, Water, Fire, Air, and Ether, plus particular styles of walking that accompanied and expressed each of these. I found these Walks to be interesting and pleasant, even uplifting, but had not had any radical experiences around them as yet, so my expectations were low. But we were desperate.

"Okay, Mark," I said. "The Elemental Breath for Earth is in the nose, out the nose, in the nose, out the nose, with the mouth always closed." This we did. "It might help if we can concentrate on a golden square or cube." (Gold/yellow was the color of Earth in this system, and a square or cube the related shape.)

"All right, now let's move out into the path. The Walk for this Element is done very low to the ground. You're dipping down on your knees almost to a crouch, like the portrayal of Indians stalking through the forest in old movies. We concentrate on our feet, especially on the sole contacting the ground. And we hold our arms out in front, palms down at about waist height or wherever it's comfortable for you, sensing the Earth energy."

We practiced and were surprised and pleased to feel an unexpectedly powerful surge of energy rising up from the earth beneath our hands. We glanced at each other, a gleam of hope now in our eyes.

"Okay, let's try it out."

We put on our small day packs and began the Earth Breath, and Mark fell into step behind me. I discovered that if I moved my hands away from my body and then pulled them back toward me over and over, like the endlessly winding tires of a Caterpillar truck, massaging the air with my palms down, an enormous supporting pillar of Earth energy rose up beneath each hand, thick, cushiony, and dynamic, lifting me up and even slightly pulling me forward at the same time. Mark tried it with the same results.

"Whoo-hoo!" he cried. "This is good!" (And we both added silently, *Thank you, Holy Mother!*)

Despite realizing that it was "impossible," we almost flew up that whole mountain, not even sweating anymore. The powerful Earth energy carried us as surely as would a strong ocean wave if we were surfing it, just as long as we stayed within the discipline of the Earth Breath and its related concentrations. We did find that the compelling current drew us counterintuitively in longer S curves rather than in a shorter straight-ahead tramp. And it carried us up and forward, no matter what the ground was like, even over rocks. Although aware of our feet, we hardly felt the ground. And we moved incredibly fast, closer to running than walking.

I felt as if strong, muscular Mark was powering us ahead, and that I was leading, holding the concentration, "seeing." We felt perfectly paired. It reminded me of a scene in a movie of the opera *The Magic Flute* where Princess Pamina and Prince Tamino have to pass through certain challenging Elemental tests. She leads them, one arm raised before her, seeing what is there, and he follows her, linked, but playing his magic flute, his gaze downward, powering them protectively forward.

We stopped only once, for fifteen minutes, to drink from an ice-cold spring to the left of the trail, and then resumed "flying." Both sides of the trail remained hemmed in by woods, so there were still no vistas, but we were exhilarated.

At last we reached the summit, breaking out joyfully on the stony peak. Mountains and fields stretched away small and color-dappled to impossible distances under a big blue sky, with shadows of random clouds dancing and circling over them. The view was dazzling, a sweet reward.

We climbed partway up an old abandoned fire tower at the top and breathed in the great blue blaze of heady air, feeling free and light as hawks, as eagles. Later, when we were back down in Weld, I read somewhere that the light on top of the fire tower used to be seen far out at sea, to the southeast, and for many mariners that beacon was the first sight that told them they were approaching the Eastern Seaboard. I remembered the meditation then, the image of the Virgin Mary filling the whole mountain, shining brilliantly to the southeast.

Refreshed with a drink and some trail mix, we took our last look at the beautiful vista and began to descend. Given the rocks and steepness, going down looked more difficult and dangerous than climbing up. We prayed and then, with a certain amount of trepidation, resumed the Earth Breath and Walk again. Soon we found that we were actually running down the mountain, swooping in energy-cushioned S-curves, at an astounding pace. Again, miraculously in that baking afternoon, we weren't even sweating. We reached the bottom exalted, filled with amazed gratitude, and said a heartfelt prayer of thanks to our Holy Mother for helping us fulfill the obedience she had so mysteriously set us.

ﷺ

Joining the Magi Caravan

Less than six months after I had, to my great surprise, received Jesus Christ again, a "wise man from the East," whom we shall call Shaikh Qadr, arrived in Syracuse, bearing rich, mystical gifts of Sufic transmission that had come from the teachings of the great Indian singer, musician, and spiritual master Hazrat Inayat Khan, who had, in obedience to his own teacher, brought these soul-quickening treasures from India to the West in 1910. After his repose, his son, Pir Vilayat Inayat Khan, inherited his work, which was also carried on in various channels by some other mystically ripe relatives and senior *mureeds*.

While the leaders of many known Sufi orders claim that to be a Sufi one must be Muslim, the spiritual leaders of some other Sufi groups, such as that of Pir-o-Murshid Hazrat Inayat Khan, have stated that people of all religions can become Sufis while retaining their original faith. These teachers also assert that Sufism was alive and vital in Christian and Jewish times, going back even to ancient

Egypt. Sufism offers the possibility of growing in a transformingly intimate relationship with God through spiritual practices and attunements that stretch our mystical receptive capacities, helping us enter into deeper communion with the many soul-quickening aspects of God's Divine Energies.

ﷲ

On Palm Sunday weekend this American shaikh offered a two-day retreat, and by its end, I felt that I, too, was now following a guiding star leading me to vital, unexplored depths in my own heart in a waterfall of bliss and revelation.

So, naturally, I resisted it. At least at first.

"If you would find Me, you must seek Me with your whole heart."

Jesus Christ seemed to be speaking to me in the depths of my heart as slow, silent tears dripped down my cheeks. A small group of us was sitting in meditation in a living room in Syracuse, considering an offer of *bayat* (initiation) by the Sufi shaikh who had led us through a remarkable light-filled weekend retreat one week before this day's gathering. I was torn—the spiritual depths we had reached in the retreat were remarkable, and the shaikh's profound mystical skills impressive. His manner combined a refined but potent and penetrating spiritual quality with a gently earthy warmth. When working with him through a wide range of mystical practices—chanting, dancing, prayer, silent meditation, the Sufic remembrance practice called *zikr* (or *dhikr*), listening to his well-told enlightening stories, or participating in *sohbet* (spiritual conversation)—I felt layers upon layers of amazing worlds and states opening within me, all underlain with a deep sense of radiating peace and love. Like the swan Leda being wooed by Zeus in a shower of gold, a shower of beautiful mystical states poured upon us, shining and illumining, as veil after veil slipped away, revealing more and more, and yet at the same time only an infinitesimal drop of the blazing heart of love and beauty that is our God.

And, to my surprise and delight, I found that here was Jesus Christ, too, just wearing a different robe this time. But unmistakably Him. "My sheep hear my voice," He said (John 10:27). And "in my house are many mansions." (John 14:2) Among His very first followers were the Zoroastrian wise men, who found Him through their astrology, following His star. They were acceptable to Him, called by Him, though not of the Jewish faith and tradition.

And now He Himself, as I contemplated *bayat*, I believed was calling me on my own doubts and hesitations!

I was experiencing great longing for the shaikh's offered basic Sufic initiation that links one to a specific spiritual guide, the bestower of the *bayat*, and also to the *silsila*, or transmitting body of masters, saints, and prophets of this Sufic line—not a mere ritualistic formality but a powerful act of being linked to a golden umbilical cord from a great family of seekers and lovers of God, both in and out of the body, that passes vital mystical nourishment day and night to the tender neophyte *mureed*. A fight was going on within me between my deep urge to join this caravan and opposing thoughts that battled that urge with warnings that Sufi initiation might conflict with my work with the Holy Order of MANS, not to mention very likely evoking objections from my priest. I felt as if I were caught between two opposing riptides. The conflict raged on and on within me to the point of unbearability, until at last I got up and bolted out of the house, silently sobbing.

The next day, calmed down, I went to see my young priest. After I explained and received Rev. Jesse's expected disapproving reaction, we prayed and meditated together about it. We were also looking at the call I felt to attend a Sufi camp that summer. I felt the call even more strongly in the meditation, and at last he agreed, reluctantly, that I should go, giving me his blessing.

So I met with Shaikh Qadr, and he agreed to initiate me, taking my hand in his and praying to seal the *bayat*.

That brought us to the matter of my name. Sufi *mureeds* most often, though not always, receive a spiritual name suited to their inherent qualities that need calling out and greater expression or less developed parts of themselves that need strengthening. The names are most often—but not always—Arabic. There was just one problem: I already had mine. Stephani Nur. *Nur* is an Arabic word among those called the "Ninety-Nine Beautiful Names of God," each of which reflects some divine aspect or quality. *Nur* refers to the Uncreated Light of the divinity.

"Who gave you your name?" Shaikh Qadr inquired.

"My mother."

"No, no. I want to know who gave you that name," he insisted, beginning to sound a bit irritated.

"My mother," I replied helplessly.

"I really want to know who gave you that name."

"I told you: my mother!"

"That's impossible!" he exclaimed. "It is your correct Sufi name!"

ﷺ

Wading in Roses
My Sufi classmates and I began driving down from Syracuse to our shaikh's home on a farm in southern New York State one Thursday

evening a week for classes. It was a four-hour round trip, with two or more hours of classes sandwiched in the middle. Although tiring, with us returning well into the A.M. on a weekday night, we would not have missed this opportunity for anything. After hours of listening to teachings, doing *zikr* practices, chanting *wazaif* (the Arabic "Beautiful Names of God," each expressing a different aspect of God's manifest beauty and glory) and the mantras of various faiths, and performing sacred dances and walks, we felt, upon our return, still light-filled, cleansed, and imbued with the shimmering, subtle melodies of holiness.

Our shaikh was a profound master of the sacred dances called the Dances of Universal Peace founded by one of his primary teachers, Murshid Ahmed Murad Chishti ("Murshid Sam" or "Sufi Sam," as he was commonly known), an American direct disciple of Hazrat Inayat Khan's, as well as of sacred Walks through which one attuned to a sacred quality, master, saint, or prophet.

I remember one night in a long dim room Shaikh Qadr had us line up closely packed, one after another. We were to put our left hand on the right shoulder of the person in front of us, our right hands on our heart centers (in the middle of our chests), and, concentrating on both our heart centers and our feet, begin to shuffle forward slowly in very tiny steps, gently tossing our heads toward our left shoulders and chanting softly, *"Illa allah, 'illa allah, 'illa allah."* This was the second half of the famous Arabic *zikr* statement, *"La 'ilaha 'illa allah"*—"There is no God / but God.") So, we were affirming the existence of the one God and longing for our God as we walked. And also attuning to the Sufi saint and great poet Farid Ud-din Attar, who wrote, "Sun and Moon, one the day, the other the night, bow to the dust in adoration, and from their worship comes their movement." We now sought to attune the adoration in our hearts for God to Attar's own deep-rooted love, and to let our movement and understanding as much as possible reflect and flow from that source.

"Understand that you are walking on rose petals," Shaikh Qadr said softly, as we slowly proceeded, gently shuffling. "Feel the petals beneath your feet. You are crushing rose petals beneath your feet, and from them a fragrance arises."

We walked and walked for a long time—probably half an hour or more, our chant falling like a light, mystical, refreshing dew upon our shoulders. By the end, I felt so light-filled and exalted that it was as if I could go on forever in an eternal ecstatic movement, like one of the planets singing with inexhaustible love in its effortless, endless orbit, flung in illumining joy into the dancing, circling cosmos by the radiant hand of the Divine. We had been taught that the physical force of gravity itself was a form of *Ishq*, the divine love that embraces and holds all to itself. All things were transformed into a subtler beauty: the shining eyes of the *mureeds*, the exquisitely gentle touch of the floor upon the soles of our feet. And I also felt, to my quiet amazement, mounds and mounds of invisible but tangible rose petals piling up, piling all around, halfway up my shins.

The penetrating tenderness and soft beauty of the practices began to cleanse us, weakening the hard, arrogant shells of our preconceptions, with their misleading pretenses of self-protection. Masters of mystical states, the Sufi "physicians of the heart" like our teacher prescribed practices that gracefully undercut our pincerlike grappling with our own demands and ambitions, drained the swamps of our psychological confusion and, instead, encouraged a gradual, beautiful inner unfolding, like a flower naturally opening at last to the warmth and benign smile of the sun. We were not trying to match God to our prior conceptions. Instead, we were yearning toward Him, allowing ourselves to gently and unpremeditatedly open to that Radiance which sought us earnestly and generously in its turn.

ﻋﻠﻴ

A Different Woodstock

When June's warm days began, it was time for Sufi Camp, to be held that year in Woodstock, New York. Yes, that same Woodstock, but not at Yasgur's farm. Four hundred or so experienced and fledgling Sufis gathered in a large field surrounded by forest, set up tents, patronized the porta potties, and helped arrange the kitchens intended to feed the multitudes for five days.

The first evening, my Syracuse Sufi friend and I having arrived late, we slept tentless in the meadow under the stars, he on a small folding cot and I in its shadow on my sleeping bag, his cot serving as a kind of tent roof for me. Awakening to a sunny day in the fresh, cool morning air was lovely, as was sitting up to see many smiling people wandering among the meadow grasses, graceful in kaftans and prayer beads and jeans and the creatively exotic, beautifully embroidered clothing of the 1960s and 1970s, looking like ladies and paladins from a timeless fairy tale.

I'm glad I enjoyed that cloudless morning because I believe that might have been the last sunny morning I saw at camp. The heavens decided to baptize us all in several days of heavy rain, fortunately falling mainly at night, that soon churned the ground to such a paste of mud that our shoes were sucked off into its depths, and, as a result, the whole camp wandered around barefoot, ankle-deep in mud, like poor but beautifully garbed gypsies.

There were other problems, too, one being the rapid, inexplicable, and indelicate onset of what we had called in Mexico "turista." Diarrhea in the woods with a few hundred other people is not a particularly desirable experience, especially when the lines in front of the porta potties began to resemble queues for sold-out Broadway plays. Those of us who took our turns cooking in the roofed but wall-less outdoor kitchen (I found myself one day standing on a stool for short people, stirring an industrial-size pot of simmering beans with a canoe paddle) were very careful about sanitation, so how had this problem started? Some genius finally figured it out: too much sanitation! After meals we all lined up to wash the bowls, cups, and flatware we had each brought in big tubs of soapy hot water. We then rinsed everything in other tubs of clear water. But the clear-water tubs soon became soapy, and, we all began to ingest dishwashing soap that had not been properly rinsed off and which gave us the runs! As soon as this procedure was corrected, our innards settled into greater serenity, for which we all gave deepest thanks.

Aside from that, there was only one major problem, a more serious one. A dome was being constructed on a large concrete foundation. Headbanded, shirtless young hippie men clutching hammers and filled with enthusiasm were building the dome at a riotous pace every day. I was told that Pir Vilayat, our spiritual teacher and leader, had advised them to slow down and not to build on one particular day, but, confident and maybe brimming over with a bit of machismo, they decided to proceed anyway.

Like most of the camp, I was standing in the meadow below the dome when I heard the sickening crack. Looking up, I saw some of the boards falling from the top of the dome, and two young men plummeting thirty feet onto concrete. Medical personnel rushed to help them, and an ambulance was immediately called. Some masterful teacher got all of us to quickly form concentric rings in the meadow and pray for the men, our arms outthrust toward them, chanting "*Ya Shaffee, Ya Kaffee*" (roughly, "O Healer, O Remedy"), two of the Arabic divine names. We prayed and prayed and chanted and chanted until, at one point, opening my eyes, I was shocked to see my arms without flesh or bone—just two long, fiery streams of flowing light, trembling in the current of powerful energy.

Both men survived, and a rumor even ran around the camp that they miraculously recovered from some of their injuries while still in the ambulance. Whether or not there was any truth to this I do not know, but years later I met the wife of one of those men. She still grimaced remembering the awful event. She said that her husband broke both legs. Pir Vilayat soon addressed a cautioning sermon to us on working prudently with powerful energies.

But mostly the camp was a joy, the kind of joy a young hump-back whale must feel as it breaches, breaking the heavy weight of the water, soaring gracefully into the air accompanied by sparkling diamond drops, entering into a new, exultant sphere of experience. Spending whole days in *zikr* (most often chanting "*La 'ilaha 'illa allah*"—"There is no God but God"—while rotating our heads in a rhythmic circular motion down from left to right shoulder and up, then straight down), swimming in the divine depths of *wazaif* practice, praying, chanting, meditating, singing, doing sacred walks and dances, listening to inspiring talks, we felt the eyes of our hearts opening more and more. More and more light was coming in; we were absorbing it with all the pores of our beings.

This was not a smooth ride, as it was unavoidable to experience an accompanying inner cleansing, the light showing up in new clarity the darknesses and smudges in our own beings, and pointedly illumining what self-protective attachments we each needed to relinquish next. We were being washed clean, not by some forceful outer influence but by the flowing streams of living water arising in our own hearts, a mystical process as natural as the opening of a leaf on a green stalk that has, with its wholesome natural energy, pushed through the fertile earth and out into the light.

علم

Transmission

Of course, mundane cleaning was necessary too. One day I got in a car with two Sufi men, new friends, to go to the laundromat in the town of Woodstock. Near the end of the week, Shaikh Qadr had invited some of us *mureeds* to accompany him to his farm for a few days when the camp ended, so we were in sudden need of clean clothes. It was the only time I left camp that week.

When you are around a spiritual camp of so many earnest seekers and grace-bearing teachers, you begin to become dyed with the powerful vibrational level of that mystical event and resonate with its power. Given this and also, as I have perhaps pointed out less than graciously before, God has a most definite sense of humor, strange uncontrollable experiences can emerge, the dread "ring-tailed lemurs." This particular day, to my dismay, turned out to be a "two-lemur" day.

As we drove toward the town in the wobbly old car, the men sitting in the front seat and I in the back with our laundry, the guys began to discuss the transmission of the car. Well, "transmission" has more than one meaning—*hahaha, God! Yes, a good one!* Bizarrely, every time either man said the word "transmission," an extreme attack of vertigo overwhelmed me, my stomach flipping up into nausea. This happened like clockwork every time and only when they said that word. Desperate to end the unexpectedly disastrous conversation, I would quickly scoot forward on the seat and lean toward them, about to make my urgent request to not say—, only to have one of them say "transmission" exactly at that critical moment, which would send me falling, dizzy and speechless, against the back seat.

This slapstick scenario, with me as a hapless Buster Keaton, played out six or seven times. I grew more and more desperate. And increasingly more annoyed with whatever unseen beings had set up this esoteric comedy and were being amused by it, the little buggers. I never did get to make my request. Fortunately, my two friends eventually switched to another topic, and by then, lolling boneless against the back seat, I was too embarrassed and weak to recount my experience. To this day I have no idea what that was all about! Aside from perhaps entertaining the Unseen on a slow day? That made the ring-tailed lemur count one that morning but at least, mercifully, it had affected only me.

The men and I got our laundry into the machines and split up to do some errands. It was a hot day, and I was thirsty. I found a small café nearby and ordered a large cold Coke. The café had a pleasant, informal atmosphere with locals sitting around four or five round tables and sending up a busy hum of talk. I took my Coke to a high counter against the wall and, with my back to the diners, inconspicuously held my hands above my drink, praying to bless it.

WHOOSH!!! To my trembling shock, I felt a heavy cataract of energy pour down from above my head, jolting through my body and hands into the drink like a silent thunderclap. At first I didn't dare move. So forceful was this silent explosion that anything might have happened. Very slowly, I at last allowed my eyes to creak open, fearing to see some kind of low-budget science-fiction movie transformation of the Coke, as in, say, neon green foam pouring uncontrollably out of the cup! Thanks be to God, it looked normal. What a relief!

But something had changed. What was it? Oh. No. It was now completely quiet in the café. A loud silence, if you know what I mean. No conversation. A strange feeling in my back. I turned around, very slowly. All the people at the tables had stopped their conversations abruptly and were staring at me, unsmiling. Gulping and blushing, before anyone could say a word, I grabbed my drink and rushed out of the café, tearing down the street to find my friends and hide.

Of course, I don't understand any of this. I do have a theory about the second ring-tailed lemur event. My best guess is that the atmosphere of the Sufi Camp was spiritually so high that we were still resonating with it, carrying some of it, when we entered the benign but more dense environs of the town of Woodstock. Prayer was pitched to the heights, and so, when I asked for a blessing on my drink, what came down was an outpouring of the vibrant spiritual attunement of the camp, very noticeable and apparently felt in some startling way by the interrupted diners in the café. I dared not linger to find out how!

بسم

Under the Rose

Many classes were given throughout the day at camp and often into the evening. Even late at night we could hear the bellowing, heavy voices of the Men's *Zikr* deep in the woods, their interior tom-toms pounding away at illusion and blockages, trying to make greater space in themselves for God. Although most *zikrs* were shared by both sexes, we sometimes had a lighter, sweet-voiced Women's *Zikr*, more refined, and several of the women teachers wore white flowing garments to gracefully demonstrate the sacred walks of the Five Elements (Earth, Water, Fire, Air, Ether).

There were also sacred walk and dance classes. One particularly powerful one was offered every afternoon by the young but already mystically potent Shaikh Wali Ali Meyer, who had been the Esoteric Secretary of Murshid Samuel Lewis before his passing. There were often a hundred or more of us in the class, but Wali Ali had us well in hand. Every class of his lifted us into exaltation, but I remember two incidents particularly.

One day, after helping attune us to various walks of different religious traditions and saints and prophets, Wali Ali said, "Now let's see you do some of your own. When you are ready, tell us about the intention of your own particular walk and then step into the center of the circle and lead us in it. Anyone who feels that attunement can then step into the circle and begin to follow the one walking."

So for the next hour or so, different people announced what their walk was about ("This is for Buddhism"; "This is for Zoroaster"; "This is for Judaism" and on and on). With one exception. We were coming to the end of our time and not a single person in this big circle had offered a walk for Christianity or Jesus Christ, the only major religion and teacher not so honored. My insides were clenching in a hard struggle between my great shyness and lack of confidence and my sadness at the implied disrespect and lack of appreciation for Christ and Christianity. It was true that in this group of many who had been raised as Christians, most of them, looking down their noses, had rejected Christianity as "their parents' religion" and patently unsatisfactory. It was in the air, in the winds of the Zeitgeist. Christianity was not cool.

The minutes ticked by, and I knew that Wali Ali was going to end the class. Giving up the hope that someone else would come forth, I concluded that, with trembling knees or not, I myself would have to offer the walk. I raised my hand. Wali Ali called on me.

"For Christianity," I said in a wavering voice. "'Consider the lilies of the field, how they grow; they toil not, neither do they spin: And yet I say unto you, that even Solomon in all his glory was not arrayed like one of these'" (Matt. 6:28–29).

I forced myself to walk out into the huge empty center of the circle. I reached my arms up over my head and forward, apart, palms up, in a lily-like shape, my head tilted toward the sky, and began to take long, slow steps, pleading with the Lord for help and realizing more, with each step, how deeply He was my Sustainer and how deeply, more than ever, I needed Him. Especially now. *Please, please help, Lord!*

It was ominously quiet for what seemed a long time. I felt horribly lonely and conspicuous and yet, somehow, at the same time, oddly comforted. I had made a full circuit of the big circle and still I was alone. When others had done walks, usually a few *mureeds* sympathetic to their attunement would step out after the leader had walked only a few steps and fall in behind him or her. That was not happening now. I swallowed hard and worked to maintain my concentration of gratitude, acceptance, faith, prayerful appeal, and openness, against the buffetings of fear.

And then, suddenly, I began to feel some movement behind me. Someone had stepped out of the circle and was closely following me. And then another. And another. Gradually more and more *mureeds* came in, and by the time we were ready to finish, I saw to my amazement that the whole circle was actually walking in my footsteps, their arms stretched up toward heaven. We finished, crossed our arms over our chests, and bowed. Wali Ali looked at me and said, "Thank you. That was very beautiful."

Another time, we came to one of the last dances of the class. There were so many of us that Wali Ali was able to arrange us in three or four large concentric circles. He had us all practice a chant together and then assigned different parts of the chants to different circles, warning us that he would be switching the chant parts while we danced. Usually, in these dances, the circle moved "in the line of direction," to the right. But in this case alternating circles moved to the left instead. Soon we were all moving, chanting, like great intermeshing cosmic wheels of energy and sound, as if spun out of a vision of Ezekiel's.

There was a crystalline moment when two things happened to me—one was an irrational but deeply felt conviction that this was a Christian dance (especially odd since part of the chant involved the name of the Prophet Mohammed), and the other was a strange vision, interior and exterior simultaneously in a manner I cannot explain. I saw a huge, glorious, open, living rose, easily sixty feet wide, floating ten or fifteen feet above the whole circle like a water lily on water. Its expanse completely covered us all, and its petals waved slowly and gracefully, breathing in and out in a gentle, blessing movement. I cannot now clearly remember its coloring but I think it may have been pinkish and white, soft and shining. Seeing it filled me with such ecstasy that I did not want the dance to end.

But, of course, at last it had to. At the end of class, I went over to Wali Ali and asked him diffidently, "Excuse me, but what do you call that dance?"

"Oh, that?" he said. "That's the Rose Dance."

Really.

ﷺ

Dark Tangles in the Heart
Of course, it was not all ecstasy. I remained my galumphing, all-too-human self no matter how many celestial roses shone above me. And sometimes, befuddled, I had difficulty parsing new and esoteric aspects of this path, ranging from the ridiculous (ever my favorite) to the painful.

During one of the sacred dances where you spent an unusually long time circling with a partner, staring into their eyes, I had a meltdown. I was dancing with Allaudin Mathieu, director of the Sufi Choir, who was a stranger to me. For unidentifiable reasons, a lump suddenly rose to my throat from my heart, choking me, and

I lost all control, sobbing quietly while tears ran down my cheeks. I tried but could not stop.

But neither did I want to break the circle of the dance or abandon my partner. The music, the chanting, went on. So we slowly, gently, kept circling each other, arms upraised, looking into each other's eyes—I'm sure my own must have been dark mirrors of pain—while I sobbed my heart out. Allaudin's eyes filled with compassion, patience, and restraint. We both knew that these kinds of abrupt cleansings could happen sometimes, as old, painful material was unearthed and released. Sometimes you knew what it was and sometimes, as in this case, you did not.

The excruciating dance seemed to last forever but finally ended. I bowed deeply to my partner, quickly said, "Sorry," not meeting his eyes, and rushed off into the woods to hide and let the last waves of my inexplicable interior storm pass. After, I felt drained but oddly peaceful. It never happened again but was one of those things you wished had not happened at all. Of course, no one had ever said that spiritual life was going to be easy . . . or reasonable.

Holy Communion

After several days of illuminating classes and graceful, warmhearted camaraderie had passed, our teacher, Pir Vilayat, surprised us with his crowning gesture. A choir of *mureeds* had been trained to sing a piece of Renaissance or early Baroque music—it may have been *Lamentations* by Palestrina. Pir had assigned this to accompany an actual Roman Catholic Mass! Standing on the top of a hill where an altar had been constructed, Pir Vilayat introduced us to a Roman Catholic priest who told us that, despite his Church's strictures to the contrary, he had felt powerful guidance to offer Holy Communion to our entire camp. And so, despite the risk to himself, he had come to share this precious treasure with us.

Pir, after gratefully thanking the priest, then led us in practices designed to instill in us a quiet, humble, receptive state of mind and heart. He talked reverently about the different stages of the Christian Mass and carefully assured our most deep attentiveness. Some of us were asked to wash people's feet before they ascended up the hill to the altar and the Communion cup; I was among this group. So I knelt on the ground, my long gown gathered around me, a plastic basin of water before me, and white towels piled at my side.

The Mass began with the priest calling out to us and our choir's heavenly singing arising to accompany him. Soon I was washing *mureeds'* feet. This was so absorbing that I never looked up once during the whole mass. Each set of feet was so deeply individual and sweetly vulnerable. I felt a tremendous tenderness arising in my heart toward each person and their own peculiar, striking beauty as I gently rinsed their feet and dried them with a towel. In a way I felt as if I had never seen individual people so clearly before, even though I never once looked into their faces. At some point, a man, probably one of the teachers, put his hand on my head as I washed his feet, and I felt a powerful flow of light-filled blessing cascading down on my head from his hand as if from a waterfall.

In retrospect, my experience of the whole mass I remember as if taking place in very slow motion, as if in a time-altered film—soft and rhythmical with otherworldly grace. Finally, when all had had their feet washed and received Holy Communion, my fellow foot-washers and I reverently approached the holy chalice. We each received a small piece of the Sacred Body (I do not remember now whether it was bread or a wafer, though I suspect the former), dipped it into the few last drops of the Holy Blood in the cup, and in prayerful, grateful quiet consumed them. Back in my tent, I lay down in silence, as if floating in the gentle waves of a warm, mystical sea of light, letting go, letting go, letting go—into the unspeakably tender, quickening embrace of our divine Beloved.

Interestingly, when, over the years, I have met people who were at this unusual Sufi camp, some of them remember the Eucharistic mass and some have no memory of it at all, as if it had never happened. No one had to attend the service, but my impression was that most of the camp did come. Some things are so sublime they actually become hard to remember, the cup of our memory growing too dense and narrow to keep carrying the subtle, refined essence of certain mystical experiences. Or sometimes experiences are erased because they don't fit comfortably into our current worldview. I was there. It happened. And I was deeply grateful for that holy experience.

علم

Bumps in the Road

The rapture of this transcendent Sufi camp was put to the test early in the week following, when some of us *mureeds* visited Shaikh Qadar's lovely farm home. We were stunned to discover that Shaikh Qadar had fallen in love with a member of our class, and she with him. He was already married and had children. We were on his and his wife's property as he broke this news to his wife, and they struggled to come to a good resolution.

The remarkable Murshida Vera Corda was also with us. (Murshid or Murshida are titles indicating a high level of mystical realization.) Murshida Vera was in her sixties, a cheerful, amazing spiritual teacher and artist who could treat other adults as little children without giving offense and who was able to both teach and nurture them with unique, sometimes comic, flair. She was an "Okie" (from Oklahoma) with fire-red dyed hair, customarily clad in white cowboy boots, and had planned and sustained the visionary Sufi "Seed Center" schools of our order.

Murshida Vera was, in her compassion, visiting the farm to help the suffering romantic triangle and, I suspect, to watch over us young *mureeds*, confused and uncertain, swirling on the edge of this unexpected emotional storm. As in so many spiritual groups, rapture is often followed by rupture of some kind—confusion, possible disillusionment, reminders of the all-too-human weaknesses of us all, including teachers. Humility, discernment, compassion, patience, loving-kindness, and forgiveness are required if one is not to abandon the path out of discontent at our inevitable human fallibility while pursuing it. This disillusionment, if not too drastic, can itself be an effective form of spiritual training, seasoning us, bringing about greater maturity, and planting seeds that can grow into more penetrating wisdom and understanding over time.

علم

Out of the Body

The Holy Order of MANS held a weekend regional retreat and conference in Atlantic City, attended by a hundred or more HOOM and Christian Community members. We had Eucharistic services and inspiring talks by our spiritual teachers, as well as times of quiet prayers and meditation. We also had Sufi dancing outdoors, led by a non-Sufi friend and me (per Shaikh Qadr's request, I had been co-leading weekly Dances of Universal Peace in Syracuse). But this opportunity was something I had really longed for: to be able to do the Dances of Universal Peace with a group of committed Christians! We had a huge circle of many people. After a while my friend had to leave, and I was left alone in the center of the circle to lead. The sacred energy had grown very strong.

We came to the last dance, the Kalima Dance. This dance centered on the *zikr* phrase in Arabic meaning "There is no God but God." Normally the chant was sung in a major key with a syncopated counterpoint as all the people in the huge circle came in and out, raising and lowering their linked hands, and then spinning in place individually. Since the mystical energy seemed very high and focused, I felt inspired to do an unusual version of the Kalima

Dance that Shaikh Qadr had taught the Syracuse group. He said that years ago he had been with a Sufi group ending a dance session while, unbeknownst to them, his teacher, Murshid Samuel Lewis (who was in a hospital far away across the country), was dying. The group began to sing, Shaikh Qadr said, in the usual major key, but partway through the dance the melody, and the counterpoint as well, turned mysteriously minor. The result was a hauntingly beautiful and rich but somewhat sorrowful chant. After the dance ended, they learned that Murshid Sam had just passed on.

I taught the group the minor melody, and we began the dance together. Partway through, in the center of the circle, I launched into the extraordinary minor counterpoint chant. Our combined energies became increasingly tighter and tighter, more and more potent and interwoven, like a cyclone of holiness gathering power, winding up and up to a transcendent intensity.

Suddenly the "*hu*," the word at the end of "*La 'ilah 'illa allah hu*" that signified God Himself answering our statement of faith in the preceding phrase, rushed down upon me like a hurricane whirl, the word "*HU-U-U-U-U-U-U-U-U-U-U-U-U-U-U-U-U-U!!!*" more irresistible than a great wind off the sea, vibrating me so strongly that it pushed my subtle body out of my physical body, and I found myself looking down upon the top of my head from eighteen feet up in the air! Astonished, I only lingered up there for a few seconds, fearing that my physical body might crumple down if my subtle body was not holding it up. I retracted into my physical body with speed! The "*HU*" had gone as suddenly as it had come, the wind of the Holy Spirit descending to answer the fervent soul-prayer of the yearning disciples, overflowing into our hearts, and passing on—but not before leaving our hearts mysteriously touched by the divine fire.

Within the Veil of Mary: The Holy Feminine Ocean

> *Sophia [Holy Wisdom] appeared in the vision of saints and illuminated them with knowledge. She often manifested herself as a woman of celestial beauty and was identified by many saints and sages with the Virgin Mary. . . . For Christians wisdom was at once related to the Son . . . and to the feminine principle which was inseparable from the inviolable purity and beauty of the Virgin. . . . In Christianity as in other traditions there is complementarity of the active and the passive, or masculine and feminine elements, in wisdom as in love.*
>
> —Seyyed Hossein Nasr, from *Knowledge and the Sacred*

The power and effectiveness of a given retreat or spiritual event is not dependent upon the number of those attending but rather upon the attunement to which those present respond. Part of the process involves relinquishing whatever self-imposed goals or desires we may be clinging to and, instead, allowing something new to flood in. We often don't know what we most need because we aren't consciously aware as yet that the needed state or quality even exists; we have not entered that particular doorway before.

And one of the things we all most need to encounter is the Divine Feminine, something so heavily suppressed and ignored in modern Western culture that most of us don't even know that it exists and exerts a tangible mystical power and illuminating beauty essential to our lives.

"So God created man in his own image, in the image of God created he him; male and female he created them." (Gen 1:27). Male and female, not male alone.

But how to approach and enter into the dark and luminous waters of the Divine Feminine? How to begin? It can find us if we are seeking it—pouring out of an icon or a piece of music or a sacred landscape or countless other ways. But, if possible, direct transmission through someone who has already awakened to its subtle splendors can most surely quicken our souls and open our spiritual eyes to its power and beauty.

The day this happened for me, I felt like a fish that for my whole life had lain on a gravel beach, and suddenly someone had finally picked me up and hurled me into the depths of the sea, my natural home, where I could truly swim and breathe for the first time. I wish I could describe the qualities I experienced, but for me, it would be like a fish trying to describe water—I was so in it that I could not distinguish myself from it or circumscribe it with thought but was immersed in its transforming knowing. In Orthodox Christian icons, the lips of the saints portrayed are always closed. "Silence is the language of the future age," our holy ones say—direct communication among souls in what is beyond speech to express. Nor can I begin to describe the depths of recognition, relief, and joy I experienced.

With five other women, all of us Christians and most of us Sufis, I was attending a one-day retreat for women at a friend's home in Syracuse. The retreat was led by a remarkable young spiritual teacher, Shaikha Basira Updike, whom Murshid Sam had referred to as "the little seer" (indeed, her spiritual name derived from the Beautiful Name of God, *Ya Basir*, "The All-Seeing").

With our small, pretty shaikha, blond and blue-eyed, we did meditations, prayers, *wazaif, zikr*, walks, and dances (among these a strange and beautiful Armenian folkdance in which, out

in the yard, we each held an edge of a light Indian tie-dyed bed-
spread, slowly circling, while periodically, on command, thrusting
it upwards so that it gracefully formed an ephemeral air-domed
canopy above us as we revolved, chanting). We also sat with the
shaikha individually in darshan, where she prayerfully looked into
our souls, sharing with us the resulting guidance. The practices
flowed from her like melodies billowing forth from a gifted com-
poser, her sails filled with the wind of the Holy Spirit, inspired. All
the time, we were in an atmosphere of the most refined and profound feminine presence, call it what you will—Shekinah, Sophia,
the Holy Mother. All I know is that whatever I absorbed that day
has remained with me all my life and has somehow enabled me
ever since to work more richly with women and girls. I am very
grateful for this gift. Such a short time, such a great teacher, and
such a powerful attunement!

We also had a brief session of *sohbet* (spiritual conversation)
with questions and answers. Questions were often very frank, and
Shaikha Basira's answers equally so. At one point a *mureed* asked
her if she had ever had a male spiritual teacher who treated men
and women equally, without some touch of prejudice against the
women. The shaikha sat thoughtfully, meditatively, with that for a
while. Then she answered forthrightly, "No. I have not. . . . But it
was when I began to question that that I myself became a shaikha."

I was sorry when that nurturing, transforming, and luminous
day ended. I never saw the shaikha again. But, to this day, I have,
so gratefully, carried its imperishable, life-giving gifts in my heart.
Ya Shakur (the divine thankfulness)!

بسم

Rescued within the Veil

Being in a group retreat is rewarding in many different ways, but
individual retreats are also deep experiences, much encouraged in
our Sufi order. Individual retreats can run a day to forty days or
more. Commonly, there are three-day retreats. I was blessed to
be able to take a three-day individual retreat at the very beautiful
Sufi Abode of the Message (now called "an eco-village"), a retreat
center and intentional community, formerly a Shaker village, on
a rural green mountainside in New Lebanon, New York. You can
stay in a small primitive retreat cabin or else a private room in one
of the handsome bigger Shaker buildings.

A retreat guide supervises your retreat and is normally the only
person you speak with once or twice a day, as in most retreats you
otherwise remain on silence except when doing certain practices
aloud. In the morning, the guide brings you a list of your specific

practices for that day, reviews them with you, and answers your questions, as well as checking on how you are doing. The guide will usually check on you in the evening as well. Meals are brought wordlessly to your door. Your retreat passes in an atmosphere of quiet, deep concentration and growing interior intensity. Normally, you can go outside for walks whenever you like, still observing the practice of silence until the retreat is over.

There are many different kinds of retreats, each with its own practices. I chose the option of having a Christian retreat in the Sufic mode. I set up a simple shrine with a lovely blue-and-gold icon of the Virgin Mary and Child Jesus on a small table with my Bible, a candle, and a tiny vase of wildflowers.

That first evening, my Retreat Guide came to meet me in my room, answer questions, and give me a list of practices for the next day. Probably my eyebrows shot up in surprise at times when we were reviewing them—for example, in a certain period of time assigned to "Christian *zikr*," the physical description followed the normal and most common form of *zikr*: that is, while seated, swinging my head to my left shoulder, rotating it down in a circle, coming up to the right shoulder, raising it up, and then bowing straight down toward the heart or solar plexus before repeating the practice. The Arabic version of "There is no God / but God" is the most common accompanying chant. The first phrase is an emptying out and negation, done on the descending part of the circle, and the second half, affirming, is performed on the upswing and final descent. But in this Christian version, I chanted "*Kyrie eleison*" ("Lord, have mercy" in Greek) on the downswing and "*Christe eleison*" (Greek for "Christ, have mercy") on the upswing. I was told that I would experience the presence of the Virgin Mary on the downswing and, on the upswing, the presence of Jesus Christ. *Oh right!* grumbled the cynical part of my mind silently. *Just like that! Easy! Sure!*

But, as with so many unlikely sounding Sufic things, I discovered the next day that there was great and startling power in the practice. Sitting down at the appointed time for this *zikr*, expecting little, I swung my head down—and immediately experienced an overpowering sense of the presence of the Virgin Mary! I almost fell over backward from shock. This was instantly succeeded, on the upswing, by an even more overwhelming and beautiful presence of Jesus Christ! And both of these things happened over and over again throughout the *zikr* practice. My capacity to bear so much love, light, and beauty, such radiant intimacy and sense of limitless power and magnetism from these two holiest of Holy Presences was almost more than I could bear. It stretched me on every level. I had to let go, over and over and over again. And accept, accept, accept the blessing. Being stretched in this way can be rapturous but often is not painless. Sufi teachers sometimes point out that such stretching, reducing our sense of limitation, increases our capacity to bear greater nearness to the Divine and Its holy qualities.

The only significant difficulty occurred at night when I tried to sleep. Uncharacteristically, I found myself tossing and turning, unable to settle down and rest. With bleary eyes, I saw the dawn arrive, still not having slept. I worked doggedly through the day on my assigned practices, but it was difficult—being so tired and sleepy, it was hard to muster enough concentration to perform them effectively.

After I ate my light vegetarian dinner and placed the tray of dishes on the floor outside my door, I looked at the list of evening practices. Rubbing my weary eyes, I knew I could not make it through them without help. So I turned off the lights and, in darkness, lit the candle before the icon on my small shrine. This was a copy of a very ancient miracle-working icon known to Roman Catholics as Our Lady of Perpetual Help and to Eastern Orthodox Christians as Our Lady of the Passion. It portrays the Virgin Mary holding the Child Christ in her arms. He is turning away fearfully from two small angels aloft on either side, one of whom is carrying a cross and the other a spear and sponge.

My version of this icon was done in cobalt blue and gold. I prayed to our Lord and especially to our Holy Mother to help me be able to accomplish the retreat and to cure my sleeplessness. As I prayed intently, gazing at the icon, I felt something shifting around me, as if space itself was somehow stretching and changing. The mantle of the Virgin Mary's protection seemed to float forward palpably, extending to encompass me, and as it did, I observed two ominous dense black clouds float off my back and pass out through the ceiling. Then I felt the Holy Mother pull me into the icon, where there was now an exquisite altar all adorned in gold and cobalt blue and emanating the most heavenly and profound sense of peace and protection I had ever felt in my life. The Virgin Mary was there with me and the altar in some way, but the altar was also within her. We were both within her mantle and her ineffably pure and beautiful, light-filled consciousness. I would have gladly stayed there forever.

In deepest gratitude I came out of the icon, finding myself refreshed and light of heart. The demonic dark clouds having been driven off by Mary's irresistible grace, I was able to apply myself with wakeful clarity to the evening practices. That night I slept a sweet, deep, and dreamless sleep, awakening to a new morning fresh, rested, and feeling deeply blessed.

ﷻ

Murshid Sam

If you look at photos of Murshid Ahmed Murad Chisti—Murshid Samuel Lewis—you most often see a small and scruffy long-haired, bearded man, resembling a twinkling, mischievous elf, wearing baggy clothes that hang on him as if a couple of sizes too large for his compact, slender self. Sometimes he favored a rope rather than a belt to hold up his pants! Murshid had the most amazing laughing eyes. But sometimes, in the more rare serious photos, a deeply rooted, powerful spiritual force emanates from his eyes, mountain-like in strength and purposefulness. He was not only a Sufi Murshid but also a recognized Zen Master, a Christian teacher, and one of the foremost direct disciples of Pir-o-Murshid Hazrat Inayat Khan.

I never had the blessing of meeting Murshid Sam in the flesh. But I did meet with him in two dreams that left powerful impressions.

In the first dream, he and I were alone in what looked like a large old-fashioned British courtroom full of tall wooden "docks" of varying heights. Murshid Sam sat in the tallest dock, like the chief justice. I sat to his left in a somewhat lower dock. I was holding on to one of his fingers—it might have been his little finger. And we were silent but completely, blissfully happy. I was—we were both—experiencing the most profound, unburdened sense of contentment imaginable. And I woke up in joy, but deeply regretful for losing Murshid's inexpressibly dear smiling and serene presence.

The next time, Murshid Sam and I were again alone. This time we were sitting together, side by side, on a small "Chinese couch"—a low, narrow bench with rolled ends, upholstered in red and about the size of a love seat. Again, we were both experiencing a magnificent peace and happiness, a seamless harmony. Then Murshid said to me words I was not very willing to hear and that even seemed preposterous to me: "I have no more to teach you. Now you just have to remember." And the dream was gone.

Murshid Sam also worked with Father Paul Blighton, who had founded the Holy Order of MANS. Good friends, both located primarily in San Francisco, they helped each other. Murshid Sam was actually the first education director of the HOOM, I was told. There is an amazing book entitled (tongue a little in cheek) *This Is the New Age in Person*, with Murshid Sam on the cover. The chapters consist of Murshid's lectures on the Epistles of St. Paul, as addressed to the HOOM sisters and brothers—unexpected, dazzling stuff. I was joyful for this cross-pollenization of the two dominant spiritual transmissions in my life!

ﻋﻠﻪ

Dancing on the Heavenly Ziggurat

I moved to Boston, Massachusetts, the autumn before the infamous blizzard of 1978 that, for weeks, turned the city into a giant impassable igloo where we walked through the snow over the roofs of marooned cars to reach snow-buried friends. I made this move in order to join the HOOM Boston Christian Community and also in the interest of further Sufic activities. Both transmissions continued to push me through desirable but sometimes uncomfortable spiritual changes.

ﻋﻠﻪ

The Cosmic Celebration

Standing on a slender plank a few feet above the floor, I am slowly pacing forward in what I hope are flowing movements synchronized with the ethereal music and swaying steps of other First-Plane Angels single file before and behind me. Feeling the heat of hundreds of watching eyes upon us, I am fighting down panic arising from the fact that I am now completely blind and can see no one at all—nor, for that matter, the wretchedly narrow plank I am dancing upon. Why? Why?! The blankety-blank (speaking as an Angel, you don't really expect me to curse, do you?) costume! Aside from a flimsy tunic and tights in misty colors, the demonically inspired costume designer has devised a gauzy headdress for each of us First-Plane Angels that makes even the most extreme hijab seem a relaxing liberal innovation. A tent's worth of foggy gray fabric falls all around us from the tops of our heads to our ankles, markedly obscuring vision—no eyeholes!—and giving our meditative concentration practice, *Ya Sami, Ya Basir* ("O All-Hearing, O All-Seeing"), an ironic twist, at the very least.

The same genius decided to anchor this mountain of diaphanous cloth with a sparkly, stretchy headband worn across the forehead. Obviously this angelic fashion maven was blissfully ignorant that the choreography demands that we First-Plane Angels, moving sideways, dip our heads frequently and bend our knees deeply while moving forward, with the result that, unknowingly, the person in front of each of us tends to step on and drag down the overlong veil so that the accursed, glittering headband segues into a merciless blindfold—and, in happy elastic torpor, remains smugly and snugly over our eyes! Even in the moments when our hands are not clasped in each other's sweaty, graceful grip, rearranging one's blindfold / headband would clearly lend an unwelcome appearance of hassled dorkiness to the sublime heavens with their otherwise serenely unveiled six planes of Angels above us on ascending levels of the steep ziggurat-stage. Those Angels, unentangled as they are, are beaming in dignified, untroubled splendor at the audience, unaware of our festering troubles in the lower heavens, where the dangers of blindfolded angels becoming fallen Angels are looming large indeed.

When we First-Plane Angels are stationary—but not locked in tableau mode (where we resemble a coral reef in serious trouble, as our prescribed arm movements, never to rise above our shoulders for spiritually symbolic reasons, resemble flash-frozen octopus and anemone tentacles horizontal in a powerful current)—I try, with a couple of fingers, to inconspicuously twitch at the lower sides of my veil in the hope that the distracting dramas taking place on the open stage before us and my closeness to my veiled companions will mask my desperate gestures minutely levering the wretched headband by millimeters off my eyes. Although trying hard to be inconspicuous, I feel like Danny Kaye twitching hilariously in an ill-fated stage number. And worse is yet to come. Worse, that is, than being cued to dance yet again, having the veil stepped on again, having the headband with its attendant darkness descend again . . . but we'll get to that later. I am giving you time to build up your strength.

Yes, can you believe it? I'm in a pageant—again! Almost thirty years old and I still haven't learned! And I'm headdress-challenged again! So, take that, you who smirked disbelievingly when you read about the "The Curse of the Shepherdess's Headdress" in "Christmas Pageant I"! How about this, eh? You don't think there's an element of fate (as well as stupidity) in this sequel? Don't answer that. It's too depressing. Instead, let me try to orient us.

I am one of a cast of three hundred-plus young men and women (including an orchestra and chorus) trying not to shiver too conspicuously in the November cold of Boston's cavernous, drafty stone armory, which apparently was built before the invention of interior heat sources. Most of us are characters in eight three-hour "Cosmic Celebration" performances under the direction and guidance of narrator Pir Vilayat Inayat Khan and director Saphira Linden. It is 1977, and we are all spiritual seekers. In that seeking, one of the treasures we have found to date is Pir Vilayat, an acknowledged meditation master who looks like a spiritual teacher, as they say, sent straight from central casting: regal yet warmly informal in manner and characteristically clad in long robes, white or sometimes soft gold and beige, with a small pointed cap—as if discreetly emphasizing his heavenward orientation—crowning his long, flowing white locks. Small dark eyes, sparkling and penetrating, look out over his elegant hawk's nose that shadows a spouting snowy beard.

Most, though not all, of the cast are initiates in the order Pir Vilayat heads: the Sufi Order International, later known as the Inayati Order. We are also very honored to have the great Nubian oud-player Hamza El Din as a cast member.

Aside from the huge number of participants, the scale of this pageant is indeed cosmic. Although it does focus on the miraculous birth of Jesus Christ like so many pageants, unlike most of them it goes on to His Crucifixion, Death, and Resurrection. Furthermore, it portrays the lives of four other inspirers of major world religions (Hinduism, Buddhism, Judaism, and Islam) and the crucial stages of their lives, all set into the metaphysical pattern of the traditional Roman Catholic mass (Credo, Sanctus, etc.). With a Cecil B. DeMille-like reach on the metaphysical / religious level, it could never be called paltry in conception: it also includes the presence of the Seven Planes of Angels beneath the Throne of God, itself supported by the Four Hayot, known to Christians as the "four living creatures" in the Book of Revelation, and God, surmounting all, represented by a man in a sheltering masculine aspect and God's receptive feminine aspect, represented by a woman with upraised arms. It is universe-spanning.

The casting was in Pir Vilayat's hands. In contrast to his profound stillness when leading us in meditation practices, Pir frequently moved with briskness, purposeful or joyous depending, his quick movements barely seeming to keep pace with the mercurial brilliance of his mind and sometimes punctuated with sudden laughter, like a blaze of sunlight whipping over summer grasses. There was a streak of wildness in his manner, too—not dangerous or chaotic but rather like the fierce but gentle wildness of a hawk or eagle, very much itself and nothing else, accustomed to getting its way through sheer power and speed, most truly at home in the heights and unwilling to be pinned down or chained to anything not true to its nature. Although his manner generally was kind, one felt a disinclination to risk irritating him or stirring up his impatience, which could evoke a sharp eagle glance most penetrating. Indeed, I experienced an unusual variation of this phenomenon.

The night of casting, the three hundred or so of us were milling around inside Boston's Church of All Nations, a spacious round brick structure, as Pir Vilayat darted among us, quickly contemplating each potential cast member and hurling a short descriptive phrase to a somewhat-harried attendant Sufi, armed with a clipboard and pen, scurrying behind him and trying to write down the name and role assigned to each person by Pir. Stopping suddenly in front of one person, Pir Vilayat would bark, "Christian disciple!" The next, "Fourth-Plane Angel!" Then, "Abraham!" "Muslim follower!" "Second-Plane Angel!" "Sita!" "Hindu devotee!" And so on, whirling and churning among us, as if rapidly stirring a boiling pot of exotic mystical presences. But when he came to me, he slowed down a bit and furrowed his brow. Peering briefly into my eyes with his hawk look, he shook his head and swung off elsewhere. A bit later he returned and again gazed into my eyes, this time his eyebrows joining and arching in frustration, as if he couldn't decide. Again he shook his head, uttered a sound between a twittering and a soft growl, and raced off. He soon came back a third time and, with resolution, looked hard at me. Two lightning bolts leaped out of his eyes into mine, pinning me to the spot in shock.

"Ohhh—First-Plane Angel!" he snapped at the clipboard bearer and was off again.

Speechless and motionless, I reeled, trying to take in the vision and sensation of those very distinct lightning bolts—especially as the way I saw them was as two clearly drawn, even unto the black outlines, comic-book-style lightning bolts, rather than as flashes of light. My best guess was that this might have been my subconscious's humorous way of clueing me in to what was going on. It looked as if I had just experienced some variant of what Sufis refer to as "The Glance," with the upshot that I was going to be dancing publicly wearing a tent over my head while silently performing mystical practices and struggling to stay on a slippery suspended plank before hundreds of watchers. No wonder my inner eye sardonically decided to illustrate this in comic-book form! *Haha, God. Yup, you got me again.*

Not that the matter wasn't quite serious, even sacred. Each cast member had a certain *wazifa*—or sacred phrase—that he or she practiced daily during the couple of months of rehearsals, continuously during the actual production, and even before each performance began, in a barely audible hum from hundreds of mouths, as we, the cast, stood in an unseen line in shadow behind the bleachers where the audience was assembling and settling in. These mystical repetitions, reminiscent of Hindu mantras, were mostly Arabic terms expressing and invoking "the Beautiful Names of God." All of God's many manifest aspects, the live energies pouring into the beloved Creation from its Creator, were cherished and reflected in the sacred names, and we cast members strove to attune ourselves to the particular qualities we had been assigned to embody. Most surprisingly, especially during performance, some level of those qualities seemed to arise mysteriously inside us—dimly, as one might expect for such greatness, but tangibly nonetheless—as far as we were able to bear them at the time.

Ya, at the beginning of most of these divine names, is the equivalent of "O Thou." By repetition of a *wazifa*, normally assigned by one's spiritual teacher and changing from time to time, one hoped to enliven and deepen one's real knowledge of particular aspects of God's Presence, be drawn more intimately and powerfully into a relationship with our Creator, the Divine Beloved, and be transformed by this relationship's holiness. As I have mentioned, my plane of Angels silently repeated the *wazaif* "Ya Sami, Ya Basir" ("O All-Hearing, O All-Seeing"), since we represented Angels of cosmic awareness who saw and heard everything in the Creation. The Angels of other planes had different *wazaif*; my tall, handsome, artistic boyfriend Carl, for example, had been cast as a Third-Plane Angel, an Angel of Artistry and Beauty, and was practicing "*Ya Jamil*" ("O Thou Beautiful"). The Cherubim, lofty Sixth-Plane Angels, interiorly chanted "*Ya Azim*" ("O Thou the Highest"). And so on.

We felt some of the power of these meditations and states of consciousness in rehearsals even early on, when we were being spiritually tuned up with group practices like this one: split into two lines facing each other, forty or fifty feet apart, we were asked to—while maintaining our particular *wazaif* and role-specific gestures—lock eyes with a person across from us in the opposite line. On the signal from director Saphira, we were to begin moving toward each other in character, our mutual gaze held throughout, meet in the center, and then continue on to the opposite side. It was an indescribable sensation to begin to flow forward (fortunately, this was pre-veil) wrapped in my *wazaif* of total penetrating psychic awareness and moving my arms like a sea anemone caught in a great current in a mystical ocean, only to also be absorbing the devotional fire and peaceful power in the eyes of a Christian disciple (*Kyrie eleison, Christe eleison*—in Greek, "Lord, have mercy;

Christ, have mercy") coming on toward me, then to pass each other, change places with someone in my old line, and begin again, this time to meet a new person advancing in a different particular beauty and spiritual aspect.

Now swim forward while feeling the exalted concentration shining from the eyes of one of the Sixth-Plane Cherubim coming at me, her arms continually lifting up from her heart, then dome-like over her head and down again, as if carried on an irresistible fountain of shining prayer and adoration (Sixth-Plane Angels could never lower their arms below their shoulders—and I thought I had it bad! Try that for three hours straight in view of an audience!).

Turn again and this time a sturdy Hindu Devotee (*"Jai Ram, Jai Ram, Jai Jai Ram"*—in Sanskrit, "Hail, Lord Ram"), upright, strong, and God-intoxicated, was marching toward me.

Turn again. Now an Angel of Fire, a Fifth-Plane Seraph (*"Ya Hay, Ya Haq"*—"O Life, O Truth") was making his way toward me, his eyes piercing and concentrated as flaming swords, exulting and protecting the sacred with awesome fiery virtue.

Turn again. Next a gentle Muslim devotee, her eyes a rose garden of faithful love (*"Ya Rakhman, Ya Rahim"*—"O Thou Merciful, O Thou Compassionate") drew toward me with soft steps, floating on compassionate peace. And so on.

After half an hour or more of these brief but powerful encounters, both lines reformed. We closed our eyes, folded our arms over our chests, right over left, and stood quietly absorbing all that we could of what we had just experienced, as we had been taught to do at the end of the sacred dances also used as an active meditation practice by our Sufi order. We had, to one degree or another, expanded into the breath of beauty of the subtle universe permeating our own in invisible grandeur and holy illumination— in a manner, as a later Sufi teacher of mine would say, not born of fantasy or "profane imagination" but rather through a sincere guided and attempted attunement to the Real.

Rehearsals were demanding and exhausting but endlessly fascinating. And full of surprises for one and all. I remember standing with all the Angels in our assigned poses on the ziggurat of the Seven Planes when Abraham and Isaac were rehearsing on the open stage before us. As the grieving but obedient Prophet Abraham bent his son over the altar and raised high a knife with one hand, all we angels shouted (in what was really a loud whisper), "Abraham, Abraham!!!"—our arms and hands stretched out toward his back to stop him. He froze. After a long, shocked moment, he turned toward us slowly, white-faced. Apparently no one had told him we were going to do that—perhaps he expected the narrator to just continue telling the story. For a stunned moment or two, our Abraham hadn't known what the source of the voices was—mysteriously external or, even scarier, internal. All the heavens then enjoyed a good laugh! And even Abraham, wiping his forehead, chuckled, a little shakily.

Satan, or *Iblis*, as the Muslims call him—a necessary character in the great stories of the spiritual leaders who overcame him and his wiles—turned out to be something of a problem, as each man chosen to play him found that he couldn't bear carrying for long that malevolent concentration. After two Satans quit from sheer stress, Pir and Saphira decided to split the role between two or three men, so that none of them would have to bear its destructive quality for too long at a time.

At a later production of the "Cosmic Celebration" performed in Harvard's Sanders Theater, my friend Frashoestra (Jim Grant) carried the weighty role of Jesus Christ. As so many of us did in one way or another, he experienced the gamut of the sublime, the ridiculous, and the unexpected in this demanding role. The Crucifixion scene found my tall (six foot four) friend, mostly naked with a cross attached to his back, balancing on a narrow board in a kind of pulpit structure in the theater. If he lost his balance he would fall ten or fifteen feet down, a quite unwelcome prospect. Working hard to maintain his sacred concentration and not wobble, he felt as if he had been up there a very long time as the silent audience looked on. The signal that Christ had died was that he would drop his head to one side, which he did. But nothing happened. He waited. Still nothing happened, and maintaining his balance was becoming even more difficult. So, through the side of his mouth turned away from the audience, the Lord whispered to the lollygagging centurions below, "Get me down!" Silence. Nothing happened. Again, louder, with more emphasis, "Get me down!" One of the centurions looked up and remarked conversationally, "We can't get you down. You're not dead yet." "I'm dead! I'm dead!" he insisted. "Get me DOWN!!!" At which point the on-coffee-break centurions finally complied.

Frashoestra very faithfully maintained his assigned meditative practices to help himself attune to Jesus Christ in a real and living way in his everyday life. A practicing psychotherapist, one day in this period he was called into a nursing home where an elderly woman was having a very difficult time and was quite upset. A volunteer was attending her, hoping to calm her. Just on instinct, Jim went over and knelt on one knee beside her, briefly. She quickly calmed down. Jim soon left, followed by the wondering eyes of the volunteer.

A week or two later, the elderly woman died. Jim went to her funeral, knowing that perhaps no one else might attend. As he slowly passed by her coffin, he extended a gentle hand in blessing to touch it. The volunteer was also present, and a week later, he received a phone call from this woman.

"I don't know how to tell you this," she said, "but when you visited Martha in the nursing home and kneeled beside her, I saw Jesus Christ! And again when you touched her coffin at the funeral, I saw Jesus Christ touching her coffin! I don't understand it but I just had to tell you!" These practices were, as well as healing to those of us doing them, meant as a cosmic doorway for the grace of the holy beings depicted to manifest, sometimes in unexpected places and ways.

But back to the earlier Armory production! Although we angels, after each plane swirled in in consecutive order, dancing, near the beginning of each performance, remained for the most part on our narrow planks, occasionally we descended to participate in the dramas unfolding before us. For example, as the Buddha sat beneath his Bo Tree, having successfully overcome the seduction of demonic attacks of delusion, one Angel from each of the planes flowed down the ziggurat toward him. Oddly enough, I was the assigned Angel from the First Plane. Moving swiftly in our characteristic manners, we aligned ourselves on either side of him and, suddenly, on cue, thrust our arms toward him, fingers out, symbolically delivering enlightenment to him from all the planes at once. During each performance, mission accomplished, as I flowed back to my place on my plank, unappreciative of the fact that "helped enlighten the Buddha" would make a terrific resumé entry, I privately feared that we might perhaps have looked more like an Energizer Bunny demonstration than the graceful, ineffable powers of Enlightenment! Representing higher forces is always such a wild challenge for mere clumsy mortals.

And one never knows how creatively and unsuspectingly one might ruin each sacred opportunity. We discovered from a critic's review, for example, that one of the First-Plane Angels had, as we danced in, spinning and swirling, at the beginning of a performance, somewhat decreased our veiled effect of otherworldliness by wearing a large and conspicuous wristwatch on her extended wrist, flashing it, as she turned, at the audience. While possibly a great branding opportunity for the watchmaker ("the only watch worn by the angels above!"), it had a less happy effect on the pageant.

But the heavenly Timex incident was as nothing compared to the way I came within a hairsbreadth of grenading the solemn peace of the heavenly hosts altogether while in performance. Still going a little white-knuckled at the thought, I relate the tale:

Oysters. Yes, oysters was what it was, although I had no idea of that at the time. My mother had come up from Long Island with her boyfriend to see one of our performances. Neither was a shrinking violet but rather the kind of person who comes under the rubric of "unforgettable character": my mother—very short, kind, dramatic as only proud Greeks can be, flamboyant, and, um, often arrogant—and her boyfriend—very tall, good-hearted, dramatic as only proud Jewish men can be, flamboyant, and, um, mostly arrogant. They insisted on taking my boyfriend Carl and me out to dinner twice. The first time was a semi-disaster since, due to rehearsal scheduling, we had to eat at The Seventh Inn, then one of Boston's two macrobiotic restaurants, due to its proximity to the Armory.

My mother's and her friend's attempts to order meat fell into the faux pas department of such an institution, and their vociferous expressions of shock and bewilderment that a state of meatlessness could exist in a real restaurant did nothing to reduce our increasingly neon profile with the waitstaff and fellow diners. Carl and I were shrinking inwardly—and outwardly, too, so far as possible. We all struggled through the meal—fortunately, a tasty one—and Carl and I were just beginning to breathe normally when the issue of dessert raised its fanged and ugly head like a sudden sea monster, its hot breath threatening to swamp our wobbly kayak just when we thought the storm had finally blown over.

Dessert per se was not actually the issue; its accompaniment— the hot drink of choice—became the unexpected *cause célèbre du jour* or, more accurately, *de l'heure*. Disregarding my attempts to steer them toward realistic possibilities—bancha tea or roasted grain tea were, I think, available—my mother and her friend, giving me looks that seemed to question my sanity, insisted on ordering coffee with cream and sugar (three more black marks in the macrobiotic book) from the now-despairing waiter, whose glazed look was giving way to what might soon shake down into an actual panic attack.

His keen eye alert for danger at sea, the manager sped swiftly to our table, where Carl and I were assessing how feasible it would be to slip beneath it and hide behind the nice, heavy, beautifully ironed white cloth. With a slight smile which didn't even look too forced, the manager gently explained to these fervent but clueless diners that a caffeine, dairy, and sugar orgy was not an option in the culinary purity of this macrobiotic temple— though he put it a bit more politely. This only sparked a great- er eruption of volcanic disbelief with more gesturing, ascending toward arm waving.

Carl and I shot each other a desperate look. We whispered together under the noise of the blasts—"Coffee—no coffee?! How can you have a restaurant and not have cawffee?!!"—and came up with a plan. We stood, suggesting we go somewhere else for dessert and coffee. The manager stared at us with well-restrained inchoate gratitude in his eyes. Still grumbling in disbelief, our hosts paid the bill and we exited. I felt sure that the moment the door closed behind us, the restaurant staff and other patrons would leap up in a Bollywood-style song and dance of wild gratitude, dancing around miso-soup fountains while waving bowls of pick- led cabbage and *hijiki* to the heavens in synchronized rejoicing, all to an exultant bouncy beat. Who could blame them?

Because we didn't feel up to acquiring more PTRSD (Post- Traumatic Restaurant Stress Disorder), Carl and I chose the next day's restaurant (we'd be going between a matinee and an eve- ning performance of our pageant) with great care. Aha, Jimmy's Harborside! About as mainstream as you could get, in a boat, and even owned by a Greek! Mom and her man assented and were quite delighted with the seaside ambience. They ordered oysters for us all, a delicacy I had never tried. They were delicious and the meal was good, if very filling. Our hosts were pleased, and we were thrilled that another semi-disaster had not ensued. Nope, it hadn't. This time it was a real disaster.

Back at the Armory, my mother and her boyfriend settled themselves on the lowest level of the audience bleachers, and Carl and I went to change into our costumes. The pageant soon began and was running fairly smoothly, give or take the occasional attacks of blindness that befell us "all-seeing" First-Plane Angels, when I began to feel rather strange.

I remember feeling Melchizedek, the mysterious Old Testament king of Salem, descending our ziggurat from a high plane. Though our backs were turned to him and his steps were silent, whoever was holding that concentration was doing it with such power that we could always feel him as distinctly as you would a strong tide flowing past you with irresistible pull, rippling down the steps like a pure elemental force of power, peace, and blessing. But my body was not at peace, and this time the blessing seemed distant. I was seriously distracted. My innards sent out aches like hapless foghorns in a pea-soup fog. The aches began to accelerate to severe cramping, accessorized with churning interior motions that made the stage seem more and more like an ocean liner in a gale. Every slow dancing step was now so painful that I found myself biting my lip hard. It was a fight to straighten up after each gentle dancing bend. Bad became worse—much worse. The horrible moment soon came when I knew that dinner was about to come up enthusiastically to participate in the pageant! The churning was overcoming my whole body like an irresistible whirlpool, like a high diver jumping higher and higher on the diving board before that last big plunge.

Forget the *wazaif*! It took every ounce of my will and then some just to hold dinner down, and that will was rapidly disappearing into the rolling digestive tsunami. Compared to the sight of a spot-lit angel loudly and conspicuously upchucking into the heavens (even the miserable veil could not hide that), the wristwatch incident would be a mere nothing! Aside from ruining the pageant, celestial vomiting could raise complicated theological issues! I couldn't believe this was happening! Really!

In agony, I begged wildly in last-ditch prayer to Jesus, Mother Mary, and assorted archangels to save the pageant and me. I didn't seem to be getting through because suddenly the geyser was rising. In my mind I screamed, *Pir! Pir!! PIR!!! Help! HELP!!!* to Pir Vilayat—after all, he was our spiritual teacher and the narrator and producer of the pageant—but I wasn't operating on logic so much as instinct and desperation.

As soon as my silent cry went out, my gorge fell back as if cut off abruptly, and, simultaneously, my whole body broke out in a sweat so violent and sudden that it soaked my tunic and tights within moments. At last I was glad for the tent-like veil. Moving shakily, feeling incredibly weak but still moving, I gasped with overpowering relief as I wobbled along our blasted plank. It felt as if a torrent of poisons had just rushed out of my system and that somehow, consciously or unconsciously, Pir had come to the rescue of both me and the pageant. My gratitude and relief were inexpressible, and they helped buoy my kitten-weak body through the rest of the three-hour performance. By the end of the pageant, when all we Angels and the rest of the cast descended from the ziggurat and stage to join the audience, all of us gently whirling and dancing together, intermingled, and singing the triumphant, peace-filled Pachelbel Canon in D Alleluias in harmonies as varied as the waves of the sea, I was relieved, even happy, but also at the very end of my endurance.

I forced myself to receive my mother's faint platitudes of praise about the pageant and her boyfriend's more vigorous but obviously bewildered ones and excused myself, as I knew that if two more minutes passed and I hadn't lain down, I would collapse on the spot. Quickly, I found an obscure part of the huge Armory and fell down on some raised surface—a long bench, a box, a bale of salt marsh hay—I didn't know what it was and I didn't care. Stretched out on my back, completely limp, I'm not sure that I could have responded if someone yelled, "Fire!" What happened after that was very hazy until Carl found me a couple of hours later.

He said he had been looking all over for me for a long time but that no one had seen me. "There's no color in your face," he observed. "Can you stand up?" Given my blank stare, he took action and gently raised me to my feet. "Can you walk?" I could just, with the support of his arm around me. We had a ride to my apartment. Once there, I said goodnight, telling him I was sure I'd be fine if I could just sleep it off. He hesitated, looking at me doubtfully, but in the end agreed to go.

I fell on my bed and slept like the dead—which onstage, at the time of the crisis, had seemed a preferable alternative to ruining the pageant and also to the level of pain that the apparent food poisoning had been causing. But I was still alive, thanks to God, Pir Vilayat, and the powers that be. The pageant had gone well, despite my in-trouble-again self, and I would, in the next year, discover that it was oysters that I was drastically allergic to. Yes, I found out in a similar fashion but this time on my birthday in the relative privacy of a restaurant's bathroom—it would have to be the Union Oysterhouse!—without the weight of the heavens on my shoulders, not to mention the massive inconvenience of an ankle-length veil. I returned to my friends at our restaurant table relatively cheerful, my innards relieved, the cause clarified, and the heavens—*Alhamdullilah!* ("Thanks be to God!")—untroubled.

CHAPTER NINE
Catapult: Love Comes Flying

Orpheus in the South End

At the same moment, we felt that we stepped over a line from light into darkness and, overcome with foreboding, both stopped walking, without exchanging a word. My friend Mimi and I, new to Boston and unfamiliar with its neighborhoods, had just left behind the busy downtown shopping area of the brightly lit Prudential Center and Copley Plaza, with its giddy crowds and small, flowering trees, heading off in search of the Greek Orthodox cathedral located in West Roxbury—an address meaningless to us at the time. We had taken a streetcar downtown late on the eve of Orthodox Pascha in order to attend the big nighttime Matins service. I was no longer Orthodox, and Mimi never had been, but we were both Christians; I felt a deep longing this night to participate in Pascha once again, and Mimi was interested in pursuing an exotic Easter experience.

I don't remember where we had gotten our directions—but they quickly became meaningless as, overcoming our momentary hesitation, we resumed walking down this shadowy, deserted street of nondescript, mostly windowless blank buildings and quickly became lost. Every turn we took seemed to lead us farther into darkness. The streetlights here grew wan and widely spaced. Pacing under their dim light, we felt a bleak atmosphere beginning to swallow us whole. To counter our sinking hearts, I suggested to Mimi that we sing something. She nodded. Beethoven's "Ode to Joy," cheerfully confident with its masculine all-is-right-with-the-cosmos exuberance, soared gently down the echoing street in our warm soprano and alto harmonies that, we were pleased to note, gave no clue as to our quaking hearts. We felt a bit more secure but still equally bewildered as to where we were heading.

We didn't know that the Greek Orthodox cathedral was located on the borders of the as yet ungentrified South End, and rather than taking the safer, better-known route to reach the church at Roxbury Crossing, we were wandering cluelessly into a ghetto of grimy bowfront red-brick townhouses, crowded elbow to elbow, with trash eddying in the gutters and nowhere a tree or blade of grass.

We stopped singing as we saw people appearing on front stoops, out to enjoy the warm spring night—or for other reasons. We saw young men shooting up on the steps in front of run-down rooming houses, and older men smoking and drinking liquor with their friends, cursing, laughing harshly, and breaking the occasional bottle. We saw not a single white face, and knew that we were trespassing, even though these were public streets. In this time of race riots, waves of hostility, supplemented by curses and sometimes spitting, flared briefly in our wake—or, perhaps even worse, an uneasy, glacial silence settled like ominous snow. There were few women out this Saturday night, and the few that we saw had faces closed to us and quickly looked away when it seemed we might approach them. We felt the danger potential rising like a pot about to boil over and scald us, so, having no other resource besides our silent prayers, we began singing softly again.

"Joyful, joyful, we adore Thee / God of glory, Lord of love," we caroled, passing by scarred gang members and busy drug dealers leaning on lampposts and iron handrails on the stoops' steps. And an odd thing happened. As long as we were singing this old hymn (we were too scared to try anything else), the atmosphere around us palpably softened. These tough men were listening, actually listening, while still doing their deals or muttering to their friends. A startling subterranean wave of warm empathy seemed to flow back to us from them, undercover perhaps, but tangible and strongly tinged with bittersweet nostalgia. So many of these suffering, hardened men had been raised by women of faith, pious grandmothers who regularly attended their Protestant places of worship, and who lived their faith at home, singing the old hymns and praying. Dashed down by the tempest of hard lives and succumbing to dark urges, many of these men yet retained small, living flames in the depths of their hearts, fed and sustained by the persisting, soothing touch of their grandmothers' faith and love. And, I'm sure, their prayers. Regardless of whether each individual man still held any belief, many of them, beneath an unyielding façade, preserved this soft, resilient memory of real love.

As long as we sang, we felt somehow drawn into their hearts, a thin thread of tenderness spinning out from the music, uniting us all, even in this darkness. We walked and sang for over an hour, still hopelessly lost. Getting tired, we stopped singing when we reached a less peopled street. But in a few minutes we heard a deep growl as a drunken older man flung himself out of the shadow of a building, arm and fist extended to punch us. As if someone had suddenly hit an "ON" button, Mimi and I burst into song. And, as the man sailed to within a foot of us, it was as if he hit the force field of the hymn and, however bewilderedly, understood what it was. He quickly jerked himself backward, looking confused, and then his wrinkled face opened in a very pleased smile. "God—bless—you girls," he stuttered, patting the air near us. "God bless you girls! God bless you!" And he stumbled drunkenly off.

After this, we decided it was safer to keep singing, which was what we were doing when a smartly dressed woman in her early forties descended the stairs of a building we were passing. The woman had seen and heard us through a window. She stood in front of us now, her hands on her hips, staring incredulously at the silly young white hippies wandering naively through the urban jungle.

"What are you doing here?!" she exclaimed. "Don't you know you shouldn't be here? It's dangerous here. I can't believe you're walking around these streets!"

We explained that we were lost.

"Well," she said. "I can't just leave you alone in this neighborhood. I'll take you close to where that cathedral is. You need protection! Come with me!"

And we obediently followed our protecting angel. She took us within a block of the cathedral, and we warmly thanked her before she left.

The cathedral was big, beautiful, and crowded. As we were so late, the Matins service was almost over. Mimi and I each got a large golden beeswax candle with a sheltering white plastic cup, moved to a back row, and lit our candles from our smiling neighbors' while we all listened to the beautiful chanting and praise. The air was fragrant with the honey scent of the candles and rich incense; the air itself seemed golden with Resurrectional joy. The faces of the congregation were unusually lovely and serene, filled with that unique Paschal radiance; they all seemed to be softly glowing, as if lit with an interior flame.

Matins came to a close. Some people would stay for the Divine Liturgy that followed, but we had to leave in order to catch the last subway train back to our neighborhood. As we walked back to the narthex, we heard shouting and then a slamming shut of the cathedral's great doors. Ushers, blocking the way, told us that no one could leave, that there was a drunken man outside trying to get in. I leaned against a wall and prayed, feeling how the poor man was trying to get to the Light but could not. He was dragged away, and the doors eventually opened.

Mimi and I exited with our candles still lit with the Paschal flame. I had told her about the custom, and we both hoped to carry our Paschal flames home. But then we got lost again—not in the depths of the tenements this time, but neither was this a wholesome area. We wandered around in the early A.M. through dark, dirty streets like two surreal projections from someone's dream—two long-haired hippie girls in flowing dresses, bearing candles whose bright flames glowed and flickered through translucent plastic cups like pale, ghostly lanterns. We did not sing and saw no one in the almost-deserted streets that it seemed safe to ask for directions. Ambling gormlessly around like misplaced phantoms, we finally stumble upon an obscure MBTA station with elevated trains. It looked deserted. But there was one T employee getting into his car, and we asked him when the next train would be.

"There are no more trains here tonight, girls," he said, looking at us and our candles with amazement. "Where are you trying to go?"

We told him, and he kindly suggested that he could drive us close to Park Street Station where, with luck, if we hurried, we might just catch the last train of the night. We gratefully accepted and asked if it was all right if we got into his car with our lit candles.

"Sure," he said. "It's okay with me. But I don't think they'll let you carry those on the train."

He drove us to the far end of the Boston Common, near Chinatown and what was known in those days as the "Combat Zone," some dreary, decadent streets of strip joints, pornography stores and movie houses, and other unsavory businesses. We got out, thanked him, and started to walk up the Common toward Park Street Station, a couple of long blocks away, trying to figure out how we could keep our candles lit on a subway car.

Suddenly we heard strident shouting. We turned to see four or five young blond, well-dressed men running out of the Combat Zone, yelling lecherously at us. Uh-oh! These looked like spoiled suburban college students, bandits at heart, up to no good. We met each other's eyes. This was real danger. We could feel that sacred music would not touch their empty, selfish hearts in the least; they had no roots, only cravings. These materialists, interested in cars, status, money, and taking what they wanted when they wanted it, were the real wolves.

"Run!" we exclaimed to each other, and we ran. Thank goodness we had a head start. Drunk, they were soon winded. Mimi and I just barely caught the last subway train leaving Park Street Station that night. Of course, our candles had blown out. But we had, despite our stupidity, been protected and guided in our unscheduled Paschal tour through some of the outliers of Hades and even been allowed to share the healing balm of prayerful music with some unlikely, unexpectedly appreciative listeners whose hearts still flamed with hidden goodness. As for those Combat Zone youths—propelled in darkness out of darkness—we felt that, sadly, with them even Orpheus would not have stood a chance.

Hidden in My Heart

The soft glow of the seven-day candle in its tall crimson glass pillar was the only light in the small darkened chapel that night. Having knelt for a while in prayer, I was now sitting on the carpeted floor, its patterned burgundy swirls only dimly visible for a few feet, by the Mary Shrine in the front corner of the silent storefront church of the Christian Community of Boston. Before me, on the wall under a simple peaked wooden shrine roof, hung a Chambers painting reproduction of the Virgin Mary, warmly lit by the candle. Mary was not with Jesus, neither as a baby nor as an adult. She was by herself, standing in graceful naturalness—not an attenuated, mannered Madonna but a real woman, both soft and strong, filled with an inner radiance both gentle and powerful. Her red heart seemed to gleam faintly, with irrepressible generosity, through her white under-robe. Her presence was inviting, its mysteriousness too filled with a reassuring inner light to be in any way alienating or alien. She radiated both kindness and an uncompromising clarity.

I had been there a long time alone, praying and then meditating, sinking into the quiet. So I was startled when a vivid image arose without preamble before my interior eye. Alarmingly, it was of a thrashing tentacled creature—I could only see parts of it— locked in some kind of dim dungeon, behind bars. I saw this only because a gentle, beautiful extended hand held out a ball of golden light, illuminating the scene. Somehow I knew that this was the hand of the Virgin Mary, and that she was gently reproaching me for my poor treatment of the trapped creature, telling me wordlessly that she would treat it with healing compassion. The initial shock doubled as the image faded because I heard a voice distinctly say: "Unearth the blasphemy that holds back the Light! But don't worry. The Spirit will dislodge it."

Oh, yes, right! O my God! Blasphemy! Wasn't that tidily noted in the Bible as the one unforgivable sin, surpassing murder? Sometimes things happen that, though they may seem farfetched to one's narrow, slit-eyed rationality, resound in one's gut as the truth. And this was one of those things. Electrified and deeply worried, I got to my feet and hurried out of the chapel. As I walked home quickly in the dark, the first part of the message kept ricocheting through my troubled thoughts. The second part, starting with "But don't worry," barely registered and gave no tangible comfort.

After a restless night of scant sleep, I got up early, washed and dressed, and hurried out to return to the chapel, where I hoped to find help, consolation, and understanding from our young pastor, Reverend Jacob. He was up and ready for action in his collar and dark-blue clerics, his cross dangling upon his chest. His blond hair was neatly combed and his posture one of zestful anticipation of a day he would shape and mold into fruitfulness through a combination of main force and grace. As he grinned at me with his head to one side, his prominent nose sniffed keenly for what interesting spur had sent me rushing to see him at 8:00 A.M. "So, Steffer [I hated the absurd nickname he gave me], what's up?"

"I need help. Please, can we talk?"

"Sure," he said. "Come sit down."

Leaning forward, his chin resting on one hand, he listened to my strange tale. I awaited his reaction in breathless silence, eagerly looking forward to words of comfort and, I hoped, dismissal of the alarming message as a mere fabrication of my imagination.

Instead, he looked at me, shaking his head, and said, "Gee, you're sure hearing hairy things at the Mary shrine!"

I could have cheerfully strangled him.

"But what is it?!" I blurted. "What is blasphemy?"

He looked at me blankly. "You got me."

I felt that I was about to add murder to my list of crimes.

"You don't know?" I asked, disbelievingly.

"Nope," he said. "Well, why don't I get the dictionary?"

I sat there dumbfounded as he went off to retrieve this unlikely oracle. He returned with a large red book and read a bloodless definition from it, something that didn't touch at all upon my pain and panic, something about showing contempt or lack of reverence for God. It didn't register strongly with him either.

Returning to his chin-on-palm position, he stared at me in silence for a few moments. "Well, Stephani," he said appraisingly, "I've never seen anyone as stuck as you are!" He paused and concluded with, "We'll just have to pray and see."

Feeling myself unable to take in any more "comfort" without resorting to violence, I said a hasty goodbye and rocketed out into the bright sunshine of the street. My atmosphere felt black and heavy as a troubled night, and I could almost feel streams of smoky darkness trailing from me as I raced home, eager to hide in the sheltering refuge of my Boston apartment.

This disturbing sensation did not go away. It persisted for weeks. I found myself avoiding going to the weekly classes at church, skipping most services and leaving those I did attend as quickly as possible so as to not have to talk to anyone (perhaps my atmospheric smoke was tangible, visible). As daily communion was offered, this still meant many hasty departures each week. I forced myself to tend to my responsibilities as a church board member dutifully but with heavy reluctance. I felt myself inexorably sinking, slowly imploding from my own atmospheric density. I was vainly seeking to become a cipher or, better yet, invisible, free from the burden of this painful mystery, but all the while feeling heavier and heavier, as if launched in a space craft subjected to increasing gravity. I felt trapped in a narrow, airless box, slowly, slowly circling in one of the lesser endless rings of Hell. I had not one more inkling of understanding of my predicament than I had had on that first night of revelation, and my fear and frustration were overpowering.

Then, one night, I felt a powerful compulsion to attend the evening class at church. These were held twice a week on many different topics. I had gone to none of them since that disturbing night in the chapel. Now I felt the impulse to go as a driving force that, much as I tried to, I could not resist. I reached the church just a moment before the class started and shamefacedly, head down, slipped into a folding chair in the back row. Reverend Jacob was going to teach. He was a complex man, with a pastoral manner that was at times maddening, as our earlier conversation had demonstrated, and that even at times made him an object of fun. However, he had great spiritual depths that would sometimes manifest with unexpected potency. And moving eloquence. This was one of those nights. I was surprised to hear that his topic would be Mary Magdalene and his theme, "There is no condemnation in Jesus Christ."

His words were striking, both grounded and uplifting. He spoke with true inspiration, arising in him in the moment like a pure fountain and pouring a flow of real, holy transmission upon us all, irresistibly stirring our hearts. I found myself quietly weeping. Tears flowed silently down my cheeks for the whole class, and at its close, I leaped to my feet and ran out the door as if the chapel were on fire.

For four hours I paced through the streets of Allston and Brookline while universes spun and flared inside me. I was being opened and changed. With a powerful shock of recognition, I at last saw my own heart. For years I had thought that I had been running after Jesus Christ, pursuing Him, since I had, to my own surprise, become a believer again. But now I saw that beneath this I had actually firmly closed the door to my heart to Him long ago. This had happened when I was a small child and was shocked by the suffering I saw in the world—a stumbling block to so many. With narrow logic, I had traced the usual weary path: God is all-powerful; there is terrible suffering in the world; so God must be the Perpetrator. And I had slammed shut the door of my heart. "I'll never let You in here, You criminal! Never!" God is not a rapist. He does not force Himself on us. The door I had sealed with my free will, He would not force open.

But He is full of endless compassionate love and mercy, as is His Holy Mother. They did not leave me to suffer in my own blindness but bowed down humbly to give me the opportunity to receive healing for my arrogance and ignorance—for judging God and judging Him wrongly. In that moment I saw that God not only did not create the suffering in the world but suffers it Himself with an exquisite intensity beyond our ability to fathom—and not only the suffering of every human but of every creature, every blade of grass, everything that lives, magnified many times over and intimately endured in the loving co-suffering of His infinite consciousness. I was staggered by just a tiny glimpse of this unimaginable selfless love and faithfulness. And by the realization that we, human beings, had created the suffering ourselves out of the horrid and deliberate misuse of the free will He had given us as a great and pure gift to enable us to be free creatures rather than pets or puppets. And of how He suffered and suffers, uncomplaining and immaculate in love, to allow us this great privilege and honor.

I felt I understood at last the meaning of blasphemy that cannot be forgiven. "Verily I say unto you, All sins shall be forgiven unto the sons of men, and blasphemies wherewith soever they shall blaspheme: But he that shall blaspheme against the Holy Ghost

hath never forgiveness, but is in danger of eternal damnation."
(Mark 3:28–29)

God does not change. He is always loving, faithful, and completely forgiving. But He will not do violence to us, even for our
own benefit. He will never force us to change, force us to open
our closed hearts. The Holy Spirit does not forgive blasphemy as a
means of punishing us for insults or misdeeds. No, the Holy Spirit
always wants to forgive us, entreating us to allow that, but will not
trespass against our free will. It is we, setting ourselves up as little
gods and declaring our own twisted, ignorant boundaries, who do
not allow the forgiveness to take place—we who refuse to receive
it. And that is the only reason the forgiveness that loves and heals
us cannot enter. We condemn ourselves. God does not.

I walked and walked through the dark streets, tears still sliding
quietly down my face, my heart full of grateful repentance and
tender love as it was cleansed in the shower of revelation. In each
person I passed I could see the Light shining from his or her face,
without exception. And I saw, somehow, that for each person, just
living from day to day is an act of faith in God—an act not only
beautiful but not without its reward. Touched by the seamless
beauty of God, I was also touched by the struggling, persevering,
and inherent beauty of humanity. Everything breathed beauty,
mercy, and hope. The Light shone with uncompromising, life-giving brilliance in every mote of humble daily existence. The world
was translucent, filled to the brim and transformed by all-encom-
passing blessing.

Falling on my bed late that night, too exhausted to change my
clothes or even take off my shoes, I slept in deep sweetness, and
when I awoke the next morning, felt myself a new being, both
chastened and blessed. The second part of the resounding message had come into focus and fruition at last: "But don't worry.
The Spirit will dislodge it." The Spirit had indeed, in beauty, in
grace, in mercy, in unspeakable affection. Tender invisible hands
had raised me from the dirty muck of my misconceptions and
cleansed me. And I knew, rejoicing, that my life would never be
the same again. A mountain had been removed from my path. I
had been invited, forever, as far as I could bear it, to walk with the
all-merciful God into the Light.

Changing Appearances

I was working as a "homemaker," a companion who did errands
and light cleaning and cooking for mostly elderly clients at the

Jewish Family and Children's Services agency in the Allston and Brookline areas. The clients ran the gamut from adorable to cantankerous, but I enjoyed most of them. And learned from them, having an intimate view of what had served them well in their long lives and what had not. A preoccupation with material things and status had left some of them almost empty at this time when so many things they had desired had fallen away, like the foolish virgins with their oilless lamps in the Biblical parable. But others, though economically poor and even in physical pain, were rich in spirit, like luxuriant, unfading gardens—wise virgins who had kept their lamps full of the oil of love, kindness, and joy in the simple things of life. And, yes, laughter.

My favorite client was Matilda, a small, lively spinster, who had strong psychic tendencies and a loving devotion to Jesus Christ and her favorite Old Testament prophet, Hosea. She had formerly attended a spiritualist church but did not get around much anymore. Matilda had a portrait of the youthful face of Hosea, wearing a broad white hood that flared out around his head, expansive as a flower's petals, framing a potent, dark-eyed face, both handsome and wise. This reproduction was a detail from the dramatic John Singer Sargent wall mural of the Hebrew prophets at the Boston Public Library. Hosea was sometimes called "the prophet of love," given his unusual character and actions. He was told by God to marry a certain woman, Gomer, and also told that she would be unfaithful to him and ultimately become a harlot. All this came to pass. But Hosea kept treating her with great and forbearing love, even giving money to a scurvy man she was living with so that he could buy her food. Ultimately, Hosea saved her from slavery, tenderly gathering her back to himself, and in the end, Gomer repented and lived faithfully as his wife again. Though very painful for Hosea, this drama was a symbolic demonstration to the Israelites that their God would accept them back with love and forgiveness despite their many sins and betrayals. Matilda was profoundly touched by his magnanimous story and kept Hosea's portrait, beautifully framed, on a small round table next to her armchair, where she would turn to him frequently during the day and, regarding him with loving eyes, sigh affectionately, "Aaaah, Hosea!"

Matilda could be querulous at some times and fussy at others, but on the whole she was a lovely person, often with the sparky, delightful vivacity of a child. I grew very fond of her.

One day it was the end of my shift at her apartment, and I was exceptionally tired. I could hardly wait to get back to the apartment I shared with two lovely Christian Community women and the lively six-year-old son of one of them and lie down. But Matilda started to talk after my shift had ended, and even though I had heard the stories she began to retell, it seemed to me that, for whatever reason—perhaps against loneliness—she needed right then to recount them again. So I wearily settled onto an ottoman near her feet and carefully listened.

Matilda told a few stories and then broke off suddenly with a cry. "You? You there! Who are you?"

She was staring at the air a few feet away from us, to our side. As soon as she said it, I saw something clearly—but not in the usual sense of seeing—it was an image perceived both inside and outside simultaneously. I don't know how else to say it. A tall blond man wearing a long white robe was standing within a few feet of us. He was bending low, close to us, the better to listen to something and observe it. The "something" was a slender cord linking Matilda and me, some kind of warm, living flow coursing through it like gently swirling currents of colored water. I believe it was flowing between our two hearts. It was a cord of patient, compassionate, enduring love that the unearthly being was listening to with great attention, attending to its sweetness and warmth.

"You!" Matilda cried again. "You with the blond hair! Why are you staring at me?" So we were seeing the same person.

"You!" Matilda cried yet again. But this time she had shifted her gaze to me, full of amazement. "You are so good for me! Your face—your face is changing! It is becoming smaller and more oval! Beautiful! Beautiful! And your hair is spreading out like an aureole! You look like a little saint! You are so good for me!" she repeated.

Bewildered, I just sat there silently, and yet I felt flickering changes moving in some mysterious fashion over what must be my spiritual body, perhaps eight inches out from my face. I was feeling whatever she was seeing, but I could not see it myself at all. Or understand it. The only thing I knew was that everything was happening in a deep golden glow of love.

And, I wryly concluded later, I had also met in Matilda someone who could match me, ring-tailed lemur to ring-tailed lemur!

We did not afterward talk about what had happened. I was embarrassed and didn't know what to say. The tall blond man had disappeared from our sight and the visible cord of love as well. I looked like myself again, apparently, thank God. And we never did talk about this incident, but I assume God had some reason for allowing us to see it. It had not seemed delusional—and a shared hallucination would have been highly unlikely. The lingering impression left was of holiness and warmth, reminding us of the richness and nearness of the numinous unseen world.

ﻋﻠﻰ

Illumination

It was a cool summer night, and Reverend Jacob had unexpectedly phoned to ask me to meet him in the chapel.

"Sit down, Stephani. Let's talk," Reverend Jacob said when I arrived, pointing to a folding chair in the first row. He settled down in another chair next to me and leaned forward earnestly to look me in the face.

"I want to talk to you about the Illumination," he said. The Illumination was a mysterious initiation, greatly desired by most of our Community members, said to quicken our spiritual unfoldment. I had heard this was a special dispensation granted by the Lord to our founder, Father Paul, because of the needs of his specific mission that required quickly preparing a large group of committed young Christians to be able to carry out various works such as street missions supportive to those in need, public classes, with genuine authority, love, wisdom, and, it was hoped, purity beyond their years and levels of individual spiritual attainment. Given the vast unpopularity of Christianity among youth at the height of the hippie era, at least in the Northeast, providing such holy troops was a very difficult task. We were told we could not ask for the Illumination, and that Jesus Christ would tell our priest directly when and if someone was ready for that initiation.

Reverend Jacob told me that my time was now, if I was willing to accept it. It was only a couple of weeks since I had received that dramatic healing about the blasphemy. Oh, so that was the meaning of that cryptic guidance: "Unearth the blasphemy that holds back the Light! But don't worry. The Spirit will dislodge it." And It certainly had!

He also explained that receiving the Light and having it sealed within would show up my own faults and shortcomings more clearly to others, the brightness bringing out the shadows. So I told him I thought that I would pass on being Illumined after all; I felt that my own shortcomings were already so glaring that I didn't especially want to shine a further spotlight on them. I could tell by the startled, taken-aback expression on his face that this was definitely the wrong answer! And Reverend Jacob set himself to cajoling me back into accepting.

When I did, he got up and told me to take off my sandals—shoes were never worn in the sanctuary—and pray. An unfamiliar

Order sister in navy-blue clerics appeared out of a back room to help Reverend Jacob set up the sanctuary; she would serve as altar attendant. The electric lights were turned off, and the chapel was now dimly lit only by the red Mary shrine candle, the altar candles, and the three waist-high Law candles set on the floor in a triangular pattern before the altar. In solemn quiet, the semi-sheer ceiling-high curtains that surrounded the sanctuary on three sides were slowly drawn back. These curtains seemed to both concentrate and protect the atmosphere of potent spiritual energy and presence that surrounded the altar.

Reverend Jacob called me into the Law Triangle before the altar. He told me to kneel within it, and I'm not sure exactly what transpired then, as I was concentrated in prayer. At some point he put one hand on my head and one close to my solar plexus, praying. He asked me, at intervals, if I saw the Light. I did not. "That's okay," he said.

Eventually we came out of the sanctuary. I felt good but not terribly different, I thought. The Order sister said good night and left. Rev. Jacob kept glancing at me and finally put two kitchen chairs facing each other, just a few feet apart. He had me sit down in one. He then sat across from me and kept staring at me.

"What is it?" I said. "Is it something bad?"

He looked bemused. "No, no, it's something good. It's good." He added cryptically, "Well, I know whatever I say to you won't go to your head because your spiritual body is so wounded. Your face keeps changing, and I want to watch this for a while."

When he said this, I could feel the transient flickering of something in front of my face and body, again perhaps eight inches out into my atmosphere, as I had so recently with Matilda. This flickering movement, like the movement of light on ocean water, seemed to be fluctuating even faster than it had with Matilda, and seemed to involve the whole front of my body as well. I don't know what Reverend Jacob was seeing, but he was rapt. I think we sat there quite a long time. Perhaps half an hour? I don't really know. I was not tuned in to the passage of time. The staring situation would normally have made me feel quite uncomfortable, but I felt strangely, quietly content just to sit there, even though there was apparently one of those dreadful ring-tailed lemurs sitting on my shoulder with his striped tail around my neck. Amazingly, I just felt peaceful.

At last Reverend Jacob got up. He never told me what he had seen, and I never asked. "You can sleep downstairs in the living room," he said. "I'll get you some blankets and a pillow. I'll be right back." When he came back up the stairs, he was holding a thick pair of men's white socks. "I know these will be big," he said, "but they'll help keep you warm."

I obediently pulled them on, feeling as if they were the most luxuriously soft, silky, cosmically cashmere socks I had ever worn in my life! Aaaaahhhh! Amazing! Lovely.

"Now you just sleep in," said Reverend Jacob. "I'll try not to disturb you. You need a lot of rest after the Illumination. You might even find that you need to nap every day for a couple of weeks. It takes your body a while to catch up with the higher vibrational level."

"Oh no, I can't sleep in," I said. "Do you have an alarm clock?"

"What do you mean?"

"I'm scheduled to be a relief counselor at the Brighton mental health halfway house tomorrow morning. The two regular counselors have the day off."

"Oh, no!" he exclaimed. "Can't you change the day or get someone else to take your place?" He looked quite worried.

"No, I can't. But I'm sure it will be all right."

Shaking his head, he went to get me an alarm clock.

ॐ

The next morning I woke up early because of an intense urge to scratch my feet and ankles. Those cosmically "cashmere" socks? *Haha, God. Yes, you got me again. Is it possible that all this fun is going to continue for eternity?* The socks were woven of lumpy, harsh wool, to which I am extremely allergic. But I had slept peacefully in them all night. My feet were now itching ferociously and if I didn't get these socks off in a hurry, an irritating red rash would begin to pop up all over. I tore them off. *Couldn't you have found another way to prove to me that I was in an altered state last night, Lord? Yes, of course, but this was probably the funniest option, right? Thanks!*

I thanked Reverend Jacob and said goodbye to him. I took a bus to Brighton, grabbed a light breakfast at a diner, and knocked on the door of the halfway house. Although I had worked in another halfway house owned by the same psychologist, a member of our Community, I had never been to this one before.

A grinning Order brother in navy-blue clerics answered the door. "Well, well, well," he said, before we had even introduced ourselves, "how very bright you look!" *Oh, so he knows.*

As I stepped in, an Order sister appeared—the one who had been the altar attendant the night before. "Congratulations," she said. "How are you feeling?"

We went over the house rules, and they explained to me when various clients would be returning from assorted activities. Just then there was only one client in the house, Don, who would be going out in the afternoon.

"If you need to, feel free to take a nap after Don leaves. No one should be coming back for a couple of hours after that." Glancing at his watch, the brother said, "Uh-oh, we're running late. We have to go. You can introduce yourself to Don. He's in the dining room. Thanks again for covering for us!" And they hurried out the door.

I walked into the dining room. And there was Don, a tall black-haired man in his twenties, sitting at a small table. "Hello," I said. "I'm Stephani. I'll be here until the other counselors come back this evening. Is there anything I can help you with?"

As I walked over to him, he turned sideways in his chair, grinning at me in a slightly unpleasant way. He was wearing only pajama bottoms and a thin bathrobe, hanging open, showing his bare chest. Slowly and intimidatingly, he stood up, leaning over me a little too closely. Suddenly I felt Jesus Christ as if He was somehow within me, lightly using my body as His chariot. In a rather ghostly way He leaned forward, between Don and me.

"Sit down," He said softly with my voice—but with His own authority. Don rocketed back into his seat as if he had been thrown.

We gazed at each other in shock, speechless. I recovered first. (Of course, I had not just been hurled back into my chair by the Lord correcting presumption!) "Um, so just let me know if you need something, okay?" I asked him.

"Yeah, yeah. Sure! Thanks! Yeah, thanks a lot!" he replied nervously, his eyes darting around. He looked a little green around the gills.

Leaving him to recover, I went into the office. Don was as mild as a mouse for the rest of the morning. And, when I came for other shifts later on, he was always the most tractable client in the house. That day, hearing him practically tiptoeing out in the afternoon, I chuckled and heaved a sigh of relief. I wondered what he thought about what had happened. But I wasn't going to worry about that. No, not at all. I was just going to—yes!—take a good nap!

ॐ

Love Comes Flying
"Holy shit!"

Those were the first words I ever heard out of the mouth of my unknown husband-to-be. A strikingly handsome stranger was standing in the open doorway of our storefront chapel that Sunday morning with Hale and Stevie Schatz, Community members. Of medium height and a strong athletic build, the stranger had a springing cap of bronze hair above a wide forehead, large hazel-gray eyes that gave an odd impression of being blue, and a bold, confident chin. As the Eucharistic service was about to begin, the fifty or so of us present were already deep in silent meditation and prayer. Just as this man and the Schatzes entered, our priest and altar attendants were drawing open the curtains around the sanctuary, and apparently the Unseen Holy Presence thus revealed had hit the unsuspecting Mark Colby with the force of a spiritual avalanche.

We all burst out laughing. Reverend Jacob stood in the sanctuary in his long cobalt-blue robe, grinning at the newcomer and shaking his head. The new man, a little embarrassed, and the Schatzes were laughing too. Hale and Stevie directed him to a folding chair in the last aisle, the three of them sat, and we all quieted down. The service began.

Thus Mark Ralph Colby, slightly profanely, walked into our community's and my life.

اللّٰه

The Light Unites

Within the year, our storefront chapel moved to a big former Methodist church our Community had purchased, and I moved too. Mark and I both found ourselves living in a large Victorian-style Christian Community house, replete with stained-glass windows and an assortment of fancifully shaped rooms, in Brookline with six other Community members.

Mark and I both had little narrow rooms at the far end of the top hall with two larger bedrooms between us; mine was a charming, if unheated, round turret, fairy-princess-style, overlooking a hill of pink-blooming cherry trees. All the renters had a cordial relationship. The household shared rent, utilities, and meals together—and sometimes prayers. I was slowly getting to know Mark and liked him—he was sharply intelligent and intuitive with a good sense of humor. I enjoyed but was slightly apprehensive of a sunny, swashbuckling air he often possessed—a fiery, stubborn leonine energy that made me just a little bit wary. He could at times be pushy.

All went on fairly normally—and platonically—until Halloween. The week before Halloween I had been kneeling in the chapel one morning, having just received Holy Communion, when a strange stray thought popped into my mind: my female friends who lived in our house and I should dress as Egyptians for the upcoming Community Halloween party. I had not yet given any thought to the party at all, so it was a bit strange to have this thought, and there also seemed to be a peculiar air of forcefulness behind it. Afterward, I told my friends, and we decided to do it, especially as draping white sheets around ourselves as part of the costume would be quite inexpensive.

Halloween night came. Draped in an "Egyptian" white sheet over one shoulder, I was sitting on the floor in my room applying makeup (a rarity for me) using a mirror perched on an old straw chest against the wall. Someone knocked, and I said, "Come in." It was Mark with some question or other. He hesitated in the doorway. As I turned my head and shoulders to answer him, my sheet slipped down somewhat lower on my back, revealing more than I had planned to for the party. A sudden electrical charge flew between us, followed by an awkward silence. He thanked me and left.

Later that night, dancing together at the party, we found that we could not stop looking deeply into each other's eyes. It was becoming distressingly more and more clear, as the minutes passed, that we had fallen in love. This was upsetting because Mark had been dating a friend of mine, Georgiana, for several months. On principle I had always been dead set against ever interfering in a friend's romance; I had once even temporarily broken up with my high school boyfriend because my two best friends were in love with him and I wanted to give them "their chance." I felt full of happiness at the love I felt for Mark and he for me but almost equally filled with sadness and dread by the prospect of hurting Georgiana.

Mark and I met in his little room the next morning to discuss our situation. We were concerned about Georgiana and also as to whether our love was just an infatuation or a sign of God's will for us. We prayed and offered it all up. And ended our discussion tenderly in each other's arms.

Mark had a suggestion to aid our discernment. Somehow he had discovered a miracle-working icon of the Virgin Mary in a Roman Catholic cathedral on Mission Hill in Boston. Our Lady of Perpetual Help (known to Orthodox Christians as Our Lady of the Passion) had her own separate shrine to the left of the altar area in the huge cathedral. Her icon hung high on the wall with sculptured angels to either side; before her lay banks of candles for lighting in red glass holders with a kneeling bar below them. To either side of the Holy Virgin stood tall racks of abandoned crutches that apparently people had limped in with but, healed, had left behind in tribute. The huge cathedral was empty and echoing as we walked toward her shrine one early evening a few days after Halloween.

Mark and I each put a dollar bill through the slit of the little offerings box fixed to the metal rail near the candles, each lit a candle, and knelt to pray in silence. Not many minutes had passed when I heard an odd *thump*. I opened my eyes to see Mark sprawled on his back on the floor with a stunned look on his face. "She pushed me!" he gasped.

"What? What do you mean?" I said as he shakily raised himself from the linoleum.

"She pushed me, she did!" he asserted.

It was rather comical, especially as Mark was notably muscular, a former jock (captain of both his baseball and football teams in his school years) and weight lifter. I had to suppress a giggle at the thought of the demure Virgin Mary giving him a hearty shove and knocking him over.

"Why would she do that?"

"Well," he said, flushing a little and avoiding my eyes, "I might not have been praying respectfully enough."

Hah! I was sure that would never happen again! And it didn't.

Mark knelt again, a little tentatively, on the low bar before the candles, and we resumed our prayers.

We came to this shrine to pray every night for two weeks—a measure of our desperation. We also went to seek counsel with Reverend Karl, a minister who was assisting our priest, Reverend Jacob. Reverend Karl was a wise and warm street-smart former drug dealer, eloquent, lively, and deeply prayerful. We felt that he would not judge us and, we hoped, would help us discern the right thing—the God-pleasing thing—to do. After we laid out our situation to Reverend Karl, the three of us prayed together and sat in meditation. Mark and I felt no greater clarity. And in the following discussion we were even leaning toward giving each other up, despite our feelings, for Georgiana's sake. Reverend Karl said he would not tell us what to do and that he did not know what was the right course. But he did point out that if we cut off our relationship on general principle, we might wonder for the rest of our lives about what might have been.

As the days went by, we ultimately felt that we could not give each other up and decided that Mark should tell Georgiana. She was, naturally, hurt and furious. She did not want to talk to either of us. Mark asked her if he should inform our pastor; Georgiana said that she would prefer to do that. And there the matter lay for some days.

One evening the phone rang in our Community house, and Mark answered it. It was the call I had been dreading—Reverend Jacob. Only a couple of years before, when Reverend Jacob found out about my romance with my fellow Community member Carl, he had done his best to break us up, as he thought we were an

unsuitable match. It had been a painful period, and his inter-
vention was unnecessary as Carl had applied to become a vowed
brother of the Holy Order of MANS, was accepted, and soon
left for his novitiate. I was horrified at the idea of going through
something similar again.

Mark wanted to explain to Reverend Jacob, but our priest
wouldn't let him. "I just want to talk to Stephani," he insisted.

I picked up the phone with trembling hands. "Hi, Reverend
Jacob," I said nervously.

"Hi, Stephani. Georgiana told me about you and Mark," he
said.

"Yes. How is she?"

"Well, she's pretty upset, of course."

I waited for a harangue to descend.

"But you know, Stephani, I think it's great!" I almost dropped
the phone. "I never thought Mark and Georgiana were right for
each other. But you and Mark—I think you were made for each
other! You have my blessing."

"Oh, um, thank you, Reverend Jacob. Thank you very much!"

"Okay. Just wanted to let you know that. I'll see you both soon."
And he hung up.

In a dazed, still somewhat disbelieving state, I shared the good
news with Mark, and we rejoiced together.

But there remained the tormenting situation with Georgiana.

We avoided going to church for a few weeks as we knew that
the sight of us together gave Georgiana pain. But then one night
Reverend Jacob called Mark to offer him the initiation of the
Illumination. He and I were to come to the chapel early the next
evening. Reverend Jacob just had to find an altar attendant for the
service, and all would be in place.

Reverend Jacob called again just before we were about to leave
for the chapel the next night. He sounded worried. "We've got a
little problem," he told Mark. "I've tried all the altar attendants
and only one is available. Guess who? Georgiana. But she did say
she would do it, so I'm afraid we'll have to proceed."

Mark glumly agreed. We set out, full of trepidation.

When we entered the chapel, Reverend Jacob greeted us
warmly. Georgiana stood at his side with a cold look on her face.
She did not respond to our greetings. She and Reverend Jacob went
into the sanctuary to make preparations. The sanctuary curtain was
drawn open, and Reverend Jacob called Mark in, having him kneel
within the Law Triangle marked by three large candlesticks and
candles on the carpet before the altar. Reverend Jacob performed

the Illumination, and he descended from the sanctuary. There was just one problem—our Illumined Mark was in such a state of bliss that he did not want to leave the Law Triangle! He stubbornly but peacefully resisted coming out for some time.

At last Reverend Jacob, stepping farther back into the chapel, ordered Mark out of the sanctuary. As Mark, reluctant but smiling, finally descended, Georgiana and I found ourselves standing next to each other, awaiting him. When he approached us, we all three spontaneously threw ourselves into each other's arms. In that moment, we felt Jesus Christ descend among us like an irresistible force. We all felt a pure and shining love for each other, and all traces of hurt and resentment were erased as if by magic—by grace operating in the twinkling of an eye to heal. This great and merciful healing was to endure. When our Community became Eastern Orthodox Christian some years later, Georgiana honored me by asking me to be her godmother. And she is now the abbess of an Orthodox monastery in Europe. Our Lord had directed all three of us to the paths appointed for us but had also rinsed our hearts clean with His miraculous joy and mercy, so that no unnecessary sorrow would mar our way.

ﷺ

The Proposal

After weeks of sending me bouquets of roses in the hands of stiff, socially impaired engineering students at the MIT psychiatric clinic where I was working as a receptionist/secretary, Mark, in an ugly parking lot in Harvard Square, asked me if I would be willing to make a "lifelong commitment." Changing tactics since I did not then commit, he smartened up and soon swept me off to a charming neighborhood of antique houses and sweeping sea views in Annisquam on Cape Ann where, finely calibrating my softening demeanor, he asked me to marry him. I said yes.

Planning the wedding itself was not a simple matter. First of all, we had to pay for it primarily by ourselves, my parents not being in a position to provide aid. Fortunately, I had inherited a heavy and elaborate antique chain-linked gold bracelet from my Greek grandmother, which I sold to cover most of our wedding expenses. Everything about our wedding was simple and low-key, from the vegetarian Indian buffet at the reception to my modest Empire-waist gown, made by a friend from pale cream silk with a patterned bodice of French figured silk roses. Talented baking friends made our delicious apricot wedding cake as a gift. And our dear capable and efficient friend, Audrey Gordon, took on the enormous task of coordinating the whole wedding, also as a gift. I think all the expenses came to not much over $800 for everything, the limit of what we could do.

A week before the wedding, Mark became seriously ill. He developed severe lower respiratory problems. I convinced him to see our doctor at the university clinic, and she told him her diagnosis: "devil's grip" virus! Not the kind of thing a Christian wants to hear! At home that weekend, his temperature suddenly spiked and his condition worsened on Sunday night. He was soaking through his sheets every twenty minutes or so. I begged him to let me call for an ambulance or at least a friend to take him to a hospital. He adamantly refused. By one o'clock in the morning, feeling desperate, I called up a friend, David Green, who was an acupuncturist. He came right over, tried unsuccessfully to get Mark to agree to go to a hospital, and, having failed, set to work on Mark. At about three A.M., Mark's fever suddenly broke, to our immense relief. David confessed that his hands had been shaking as he worked on Mark. "He was the most critically ill patient I've ever treated," he said ruefully. But his devoted work and the grace of God had saved Mark.

That morning I convinced Mark to at least go in to see our doctor. As we sat in the clinic waiting room, my boss, the head of psychiatry, came dashing in with a small hammer and tested Mark's reflexes right there; when I had called him to explain why I would not be in to work, he had feared that Mark might possibly have meningitis. Then this doctor, a warm and gracious man but not someone you would ever want to displease, went in to see our doctor and apparently excoriated her on her "devil's grip" diagnosis. When we saw her again, she was obviously uncomfortable and insisted that Mark had to go into the small university hospital clinic immediately to be rehydrated and observed. Very reluctantly, he agreed, under pressure from both the doctor and me.

I wanted to postpone the wedding. Mark would not hear of it. In my own prayers and meditations about the nature of Mark's sickness, a certain insight arose. The year we married, I was thirty-two years old and Mark thirty-eight. Mark's father had died of a sudden heart attack at exactly this age, out dancing with Mark's mother, who had not yet gotten to tell him that she was pregnant with their third child. Unfortunately, nine-year-old Mark had learned of his father's death the next morning from the local daily paper in a front-page story, "Belmont Businessman Dies . . ." In shock, he barged into his mother's bedroom to find her red-eyed and weeping upon her bed. The terrible trauma was increased by various adult men close to the family telling little Mark that he was now the man of the family and should not cry and had to take care of his mother. I believe that Mark had always somehow assumed fatalistically that he would also die at the age of thirty-eight.

There appeared to be another layer to his current health scare. His unresolved anguish at his father's death was surfacing in a more intense way as we moved toward marriage. Mark felt that his pain and loss had been unbearable and now, feeling that he loved me deeply but realizing that death could also unexpectedly take me away, part of him rebelled at the possibility of suffering such a terrible loss again. Part of him felt that his own death would be preferable to suffering a second rending bereavement. And his health reflected the profound conflict raging in his psyche.

For his health to be fully restored, Mark would have to resolve the conflict and on some deep level, even if only unconsciously, choose to go on living, even if that meant facing the grief of possibly losing me as he had lost his father. He and I talked about this insight, and this unearthing seemed to ease him. Mark began to mend. And, toward the end of the week, checked himself out of the hospital against doctor's orders and, though thin as a whippet from weight loss during his sickness and still not strong, married me that June Saturday right on schedule.

The wedding ceremony was held in our Community church, officiated by Reverend Jacob and Reverend Karl. As Mark and I drove afterward to the reception site on a church green in Weston, we stopped at a Boston shrine at which we sometimes prayed, Our Lady of Fátima, to offer prayers and thanksgiving. The shrine consisted of a small glass building one could enter within a little grove of trees. There was a large statue of Our Lady of Fátima, surrounded by statues of the three children who had received her appearances and revelations in Portugal in 1917, clearly visible from outside. We stopped, in our wedding clothes, on the lawn to pray. To our surprise, a dark-haired, middle-aged woman came out of the shrine and rushed toward us.

"I just want to tell you," she told us urgently, "to always pray to our Blessed Lady, no matter what challenges you may face in your marriage. She will help! My daughter had a very troubled marriage; her husband was an alcoholic, and the marriage almost broke apart. But my daughter prayed to our Lady, and she intervened! My daughter's husband is no longer an alcoholic, and they have been happily married for many years! So remember! Remember! Always, always pray to our Lady for help!"

We thanked her for sharing with us, and, smiling, she went back into the shrine.

We were thoughtful about this message as we got back into the car and drove out to the reception. We had almost reached the reception area when we both felt something invisible, like a big cosmic bubble, come down over us. It was so powerful that we just drove past the reception, feeling the need to absorb this unexpected spiritual state. It seemed to contain some kind of archetypal pattern of the sacred relationship between husband and wife, man and woman, a polarity and a complementarity that we were being infused with and were meant to explore. It was the opening door of a great mystery that in our whole lives together we might barely begin to penetrate yet was part of our destiny, our journey toward holiness and wholeness. It was deeply beautiful, and so it was with reluctance that we turned back at last to go to our reception with its lively fiddle music, contra dancing, and celebration on a baking church green where it was ninety-eight degrees Fahrenheit!

For two days afterward we mostly slept in our apartment, healing from our exhausting week and Mark's health crisis, before leaving on our honeymoon. We drove to Maine and boarded a mail boat for the hour-long trip to Monhegan Island, twelve miles out to sea—a wildly charming place that Mark had visited but I had never seen.

Cars are not allowed on tiny Monhegan, but a luggage truck carried our things up steep Horn Hill to Barbara Hitchcock's enchanting cottage, Where the Blue Begins, at the top of the hill. A warm and welcoming person, Barbara made us at home in the pretty little cabin with its kerosene lamps and lovely view. Despite the rough beginning of our honeymoon, what followed was sheer delight as we viewed the singing ocean from the tops of 160-foot cliffs rising straight up from the sea, explored the Cathedral Woods with its small "fairy houses" lit by slanting golden rays of sunlight, wandered past lupine-studded meadows and tiny streams lined with wild blue irises, admired the flowering bushes and colorful garden beds of the handsome old New England houses along Monhegan's rustic dirt roads, encountered semi-tame deer browsing in the forests like something out of a fairy tale, and drank in the beauty and elemental wildness combined with a rare homeyness, warm as a hug. We breathed in the sea-pure air and the deep quiet with relief and joy. Mark got stronger, and we both grew happier and happier. Forever after, Monhegan became the place I would fly to whenever I was in deepest need of healing.

و

About a year after our wedding and my having left the psychiatric clinic, we felt moved to take a job together as house parents in a group home for troubled boys in Jamaica Plain. We shared this job with another couple, Peter and Therese Silberman, who quickly became our close friends. They had two small children of their own: an enchanting six-year-old girl, Robin, who drew unicorns and liked to give people healing foot massages, and an adorable, cheerful, and rambunctious toddler, Andrew. There were usually six to eight boys living in our large, drafty old house, ranging from ages six to seventeen. Our boys had emotional problems stemming from living with seriously dysfunctional families that made it impossible to put them in foster home placements. But we discovered that there was great love in all these boys despite their unpredictable acting-out behavior.

The early days were particularly hard. It took us time to adjust to the demanding schedule; each couple had six days on round the clock, then six days off, alternating with three days on round the clock with three days off. However, a huge advantage of this schedule was that we did not have to live nearby, so we joyfully moved to a small, pretty cottage in lovely seaside Rockport, a bit over an hour away.

We also gradually learned that some of the boys had developed almost a science of playing the two house-parent couples against each other, carrying tales—true or untrue—and generally trying to upset the four of us.

"Look," Pete said at one of our house-parent meetings, "can't you see what they're doing? They keep trying to set us all up. There were two sets of other house parents before you two, you know. They each lasted only three months here and both couples got divorced! We have to stay ahead of these boys and keep our communications up to date and clear." United in purpose, we were able to drastically reduce being manipulated by the boys' schemes.

You never knew what to expect from moment to moment from the boys. Many of them were emotionally labile and had difficulties with impulse control. For example, one of the boys who got angry with his roommate set the roommate's bureau on fire in revenge. A boy who was raking autumn leaves for pay in a neighbor's yard simply filled big black plastic bags with her leaves and then emptied them over this woman's white picket fence into her neighbor's yard! And stole her sunglasses while he was at it!

Often crises would erupt that, despite our combined experience in social services, left us unsure what to do. Desperate, we would just stop everything going on, when possible, and sit down to pray and meditate, begging for an appropriate answer. At first the boys would watch us, snickering and disbelieving, but over time came to respect this process, since they saw that it delivered good results. God has better answers than we do to daily challenges, sometimes surprising ones, and I'm sure our desperate need intensified our prayer and receptivity to those answers.

There was inevitably turnover in the house, and when new boys arrived, they often initially reacted sarcastically to Mark's and my seeking answers in prayer. Making noise and mocking comments as we, eyes closed in concentration, were striving to get guidance in prayer, they would suddenly exclaim, "Oof!" or "Ow!" as our long-term boys elbowed them sharply in the ribs, saying, "Shut up! Can't you see that they're prayin' and meditatin'?!"

One night we walked into the bedroom of two of the older boys to find them praying and meditating on their beds. It seemed they had gotten "the feel" from us. "Yep," one of them said happily. "It's great! I can feel the bad energy going out and the good energy pouring in!"

We eventually offered the boys a simple blessing of laying our hands on their heads and giving a short individual prayer for each of them as they lay in their beds before going to sleep at night, to bring them peace and reassurance, as well as needed gentle physical touch. This was completely optional, but every one of them asked for it, with only one exception—sadly, a lovely adolescent boy whose mentally ill mother used to regularly beat him in the name of Jesus Christ.

It became clear to me that the great hunger in these boys' souls was for an ideal as well as for love. I think the drive to discover an ideal to live by was perhaps the deepest craving of all. But between our cynical materialist culture and the destructiveness in the wounded families they were raised with, an ideal to commit themselves to and cherish was desperately hard to find.

The agency we worked for insisted that we take the boys to a house of worship of their faith each week. Since we had no Jewish or Muslim boys, we visited alternating denominations of Christians, including our own Community, which the boys loved, feeling warmly accepted there, and where, to the amazement and in some cases disbelief of their social workers, they always behaved flawlessly.

॰ೞ॰

Our fellow house parent Therese was also a Christian. She had been raised Roman Catholic, and although no longer completely observant, was a woman of strong faith. Her husband Pete, however, was a vehement atheist. Sometimes he looked at Therese, Mark, and me and would say, only half jokingly, "Don't you three come praying around me!"

Pete loved maps and rambling. Our agency sent our boys to summer camp every August and did not pay us in the boys' absence. Therese agreed to allow Pete to go rambling and camping around Europe one August on a very low-budget solo vacation. Pete had heard the three of us animatedly discussing a village called Garabandal located in a remote part of the Spanish Pyrenees. In the 1960s the Virgin Mary had appeared there to four young girls and shared various important spiritual messages with them. We had read two beautiful books about the girls, filled with very lovely photos of them in ecstasy during Our Lady's appearances. Their faces were luminously transfigured at those times, and they were seen walking backwards rapidly over the sharp irregular stones of the village roads, lifting each other effortlessly into the air, raising rosaries above their heads for the Holy Virgin to kiss, receiving Holy Communion from the Archangel Michael, being stuck by doctors with pins to test them for reaction (there was none), and so on. Although Pete ridiculed the idea of these appearances and belief in God in general, he decided that a hike in the Pyrenees to this obscure place might be a lark. So off he went to Europe, and Spain in particular, for a month.

Upon his return, the three of us went to the airport to pick Pete up. He emerged in the terminal, sunburned and hearty and, to our amazement, fingering a string of rosary beads!

"Oh yeah," he said to our disbelieving ears. "I do the rosary all the time now."

His story, as I remember it, is that he actually got lost in the Pyrenees—not a great place to get lost, given the paucity of villages. Not knowing what to do, he settled himself one evening with his light camping equipment on a ledge on a mountainside. As he settled into his sleeping bag, looking out the netted tent opening at the darkening night, he saw mysterious lights spring up on a distant mountainside beyond the valley below. He could not explain why, but suddenly he mysteriously believed in God, Jesus Christ, and the Virgin Mary! He fell asleep in this converted state and awoke in the morning feeling the same way—and very determined to find the source of those lights.

He climbed down the mountainside into the valley, eventually reaching a hamlet on the other mountain. It was Garabandal. The lights he had seen were lights hung in the pines where the Virgin Mary had most frequently appeared to the girls!

Pete had returned as fervent a Christian as he had been an atheist before. He never looked back! But it was weeks before we got over our amusement watching Pete stroll down the sidewalk holding toddler Andrew's hand on one side and praying with his rosary on the other!

✦

Mark and I later actually had the blessing of meeting one of the Garabandal girls. Mari Loli (Mazón) LaFleur was grown up now and living in Haverhill on Massachusetts's North Shore. A Community friend, Liz McNear, unexpectedly invited us to meet Mari Loli one day. Mari Loli was sweet and humble, Liz said, and sometimes troubled by doubts about her Garabandal experiences, but this Liz attributed to her great humility. Liz had become close friends with her and her husband. She said the Virgin Mary had foretold to Mari Loli who her husband would be, and that she would be able to identify him as a man carrying a certain number of a particular color of roses at one of her airport receptions, if I remember the story correctly. They had at that point been married several years and had two little children.

We arrived at a simple suburban house and were ushered in by a shyly smiling Mari Loli. She introduced us to her husband, a good-looking man with a gentle manner, and their two little children, a very young boy and a toddler girl. They offered us tea and light refreshments, but I don't remember much talking taking place. We did not want to be intrusive. And then we began what we had really come for—we all said the rosary together. The atmosphere was pure and peaceful. Even the children did not fuss or grow restless. Our prayer was concentrated but seemed so light—flowing like water and deeply, numinously refreshing. Having drunk deeply of the peace and grace this blessed family drew, we quietly said our goodbyes and left, feeling honored by this contact and very grateful to Liz for taking us. We realized we had just met at least one living saint. Years later, lovely Mari Loli passed away from cancer. In your blessed nearness to our holy ones, Mari Loli, please pray to God for us!

✦

Mark and I remained active in our church. Our beloved Reverend Jacob was transferred to another parish out of state. Although we greatly missed him, the two priests—a couple whom we shall call Reverend Samuel and Reverend Alicia—sent to replace him were fine people and soon won our love and trust. I will always remember vividly a life-changing hour I spent with Reverend Alicia one Holy Week. It happened like this:

◈

Entering through the Locked Door
These confessions were only given once a year, on Holy Saturday, the day before Easter. Our church members spent the whole day, from eight in the morning to eight at night, in our graceful, Gothic-arched chapel, fasting (aside from optional fruits and fruit juices in the church hall below) and praying together. Most of our prayers were done in silence, guided by a couple of sheets of suggested subjects for prayer during each hour, such as praying for everyone we could remember having known, praying for every part of the world and every country, praying for forgiveness for ourselves and everyone who had ever offended or hurt us, meditating on the world filled with light, and so on.

While this was going on, each person would, at some point during the day, leave the chapel where bright motes fell from the high triangular stained-glass windows to the floor like flower petals dappling the quiet contemplatives draped on pews, kneeling on the floor with bowed heads in their hands, some shaded by shawls draped over their heads to intensify the inner quiet, and all deep in silent work, to ascend the stairway at the back and pass through the choir loft to the tiny Mary Room, where a priest would be seated before a small shrine with a portrait of the Virgin Mary upon it and a picture of the adult Jesus Christ. It was my time, and I climbed the stairs pensively, the weight of my life review—which was recommended before confession—temporarily blotting out my ability to think but not erasing the inner tremor of anxiety about the challenges of purification and transformation staring me directly in the face.

The Mary Room door was open. Reverend Alicia was sitting by the shrine, graceful in her cobalt-blue robe with her cross hanging against her chest, her hands neatly folded in her lap. Her features were delicate and refined, reflecting a daintiness from her Swiss heritage. She smiled at me gently and warmly and gestured toward where I should kneel before the shrine. She then said a short prayer and encouraged me to begin my confession.

Like a mule pulling ore-heavy carts up a desert mountainside, I began to unload my litany of mistakes and regrets and sins. Reverend Alicia listened quietly. After I had hauled for what seemed like a long time and finished with confessing various resentments, archaic and recent, toward my parents, I thought I was done and turned expectant eyes on my priest.

"Well," she said, closing her eyes meditatively for a moment, "are you sure there isn't anything else?"

"I don't know, but I don't think so," I replied, baffled.

"Maybe something that happened when you were fourteen?"

Fourteen, I thought. *I don't even remember being fourteen. Fifteen, yes—that was when my grandmother died—but fourteen?* "I don't remember anything."

"Are you sure? Maybe something about your mother?"

"I really can't think of anything."

"All right, shall we try something?"

"What?

"Why don't you just close your eyes and remember a day—any day—when you were fourteen."

This was not a question but a gentle command. And although it sounded ridiculous to me, I obediently closed my eyes. Shockingly, a vivid scene immediately leapt up in my mind: I was fourteen, and my mother was in our small kitchen hurriedly and resentfully cooking dinner and anxious to get out to her evening theater group (her one consolation, as she hated her office day job).

I stood longingly in the doorless kitchen doorway, suddenly needing her in an unnervingly intense way. I didn't understand the dynamic at the time, but I could see it now. I was becoming a woman—no, nothing to do with moon cycles; that had happened years before—and I didn't know how to do that. I desperately needed her help. There was a gulf, a river, I had to cross, was being compelled to traverse, and I could not do it without my mother's help. I was staggered by the intense, unspoken electricity that surged back and forth between us, like being at either end of some unanchored, sizzling power line, snapping and dangerous in a high wind. Deliberately, my mother never met my eyes, only expressing a more emphatic irritation and speed in her cooking gestures, and I, driven but nearly hopeless, did not, could not, speak. Without even words for what I felt, even less did I have the courage to ask her for aid.

On her part, she was in powerful denial that I was becoming a woman. If she could have thrown a barricade across that path, she would have. She wanted me to forever stay the child I had been. Another woman would be uncontrollable, another contending force in the household, something not-her, and, besides, I think my state was bringing up thrust-down memories of her own difficulties and discomforts from the time she herself had faced this intense transition, and she was fighting against the memories coming back.

"What is happening?" asked Rev. Alicia's quiet voice.

I described the scene to her, and I think she felt the pain of my raw and awkward adolescent self hanging in the doorway, unable to ask, unable to go away. "All right," she said. "Now why don't you let Mary enter the room?"

This sounded to me as crazy as her preceding suggestion, but, throwing objections to the winds, I somehow gave an interior assent. And suddenly Mary came into the room. I could not have been more shocked. It was clearly her, but she was shining so brightly that I could not make out her features and only the outlines of her robes. Equally startling, she did not come through the other doorless doorway into the kitchen but rather through the locked outside door, which was barricaded by a large, heavy table.

The Virgin Mary floated smoothly into the room until she stood directly behind my mother, still frantically and somewhat angrily cooking. To my surprise, the Blessed Virgin lifted a large shawl and softly put it over my mother's head. I understood when she did this that she felt compassion and sorrow for my mother, whom she felt was insufficiently sheltered from the rough edges of life. She wished to comfort her. Then she put her hands on my mother's shoulders and gently turned her all the way around, away from the stove and the counters and, instead, facing the small row of windows high on the opposite wall, from which light poured. Mary and my mother stood staring into the Light, and I understood that Mary wished for my mother the peace, refreshment, and nourishing joy of the Light. I felt the Virgin's heartfelt, sheltering love and compassion for my mother. And I was inexpressibly, almost intolerably, heartbrokenly grateful. And completely undone.

Slow, racking sobs burst out of my body. It was an agony to stand in that doorway, so moved, so amazed, and yet so apart, so disconnected from them and myself—all elbows, all edges, a spasming wreck of a not-woman, not-child. A nowhere person, full of pain, like a lost asteroid in the void, not in a relationship of any kind.

Mary then turned her shining head toward me and issued a command, gesturing. She was taller than my mother, who now stood exactly in front of the Virgin, against her chest, the Virgin's arms sheltering but not touching her. Mary wanted me to come to them and put my head against my mother's shoulder. A worse spasm of agony overcame me—my mother did not like physical touch, and the thought of impelling such intimate physical contact with her, and her likely appalled reaction, was frightening. But, if you ever receive a command from the Virgin Mary, you will do it, no matter what. The kitchen was small, but each step I took forward seemed long, aching, and difficult, and I felt my trembling, dissonant, inadequate self more keenly with each movement. I finally reached my mother and the Blessed Virgin. With a great effort, my breath catching in my throat, I summoned my will and began to slowly lower my head toward my mother's left shoulder. When I had almost reached it, my mother disappeared, and I found myself held lovingly in Mary's arms, glowing with light, my head resting in sweetness on her tender, powerful shoulder. I heard a voice. It said, with complete conviction, "Mary is my mother—and she will teach me everything I need to know."

Reverend Alicia asked me to describe what had happened. I did, sobbing. When I opened my eyes, I found I was no longer kneeling facing the shrine but rather with my head on Reverend Alicia's lap. She was tenderly stroking my hair, and we were both weeping.

When we eventually dried our tears, she gave me a gentle absolution and a special blessing. She blessed me to share this story, "like a beautiful red rose," for the benefit of others. I arose, cleansed and renewed in a way I had never experienced before. What I had needed had finally found me, through God's great mercy. Even when the doors are shut, locked, and barricaded, nothing can withstand the divine compassion—and His Mother's bold and tender love that, freely embracing us, heals our souls.

❧

Folly Cove

Folly Cove, just west of Halibut Point, is a small but surprisingly deepwater cove much loved by scuba divers for its lively variety of sea life within easy proximity to the shore. It was summer, and we needed to move out of our Rockport rental cottage so the returning elderly lady could take her customary repossession of it. Through a stroke of luck, a friend had arranged for us to sublet a tiny but very charming cottage, its grassy backyard, along with a small tinkling stream, running right down to the stony beach of Folly Cove. The cottage itself might once have been a miniature barn. Consisting of one downstairs room and one upstairs plus a bathroom, it was almost dollhouse-like—but there was a large floor-to-ceiling window with a gatelike shutter that resembled a hayloft's door in the bedroom upstairs. I loved to sit in front of that huge screened window curled up in a big stuffed chair, looking down the long lawn to the rocky sweep of beach with the singing blue of the ocean lapping at its end. On certain nights the sea wind played in the hollows of the looming rocky cliff on the west side of the cove as if it were an enormous glass harmonica, sending strange, softly booming melodies circling up to the stars.

We had sadly and with reluctance quit our house-parents job. Much as we loved the boys, the many pressures of the work, especially that of an unreasonable administration (although we were blessed with a fine immediate supervisor), had worn us down until we found ourselves exhausted much of the time. The partings from the boys were painful, but we knew we had to move on. Mark continued to work in Boston as a counselor in a couple of halfway houses and group homes, but I found work in Rockport, clerking on weekends in the charming Toad Hall bookstore, a small former bank of gray stone backed by a curving beach of fine sand downtown, and also proofreading a local magazine.

I treasured this quiet time especially because once again I felt as if I were being in some unfamiliar way stretched in my soul. I couldn't exactly put my finger on what it was. One evening as the sun began to sink, I was sitting on some of the boulders that lined the eastern side of the cove, basking in the famous rose-gold Cape Ann light that gave a special warm glow to both rocks and sea. Suddenly I heard a strange, laughing little voice that said, "That rock looks like a rabbit." I happened to be staring vacantly at a particular rock. *No it doesn't!* I couldn't help myself from replying mentally. But the voice just repeated, "That rock looks like a rabbit." I refuted it again, irritated. But the persistent voice intruded mysteriously into my consciousness once again. "That rock looks like a rabbit!"

Annoyed, I stood up. What kind of weird game was this and from whence the bold voice? I turned around only to see not three feet behind me, in a nest of wild grasses perfectly picked out by a broad slanting ray of sun like a spotlight, a small wild brown baby bunny lying peacefully asleep. He was beautiful and perfect. This was completely perplexing! I sat back down on the rock very quietly so as not to disturb him. And set myself to meditative prayer.

An unexpected answer quickly arrived to cast some light on my feeling of being somehow off balance. I felt it was from the Lord. In some fashion He told me He was stretching (my word, not His) Mark and me so that we could move deeper into the respective mysteries of our womanhood and manhood, an inhabitation of more profound levels of those polarities, and of the powerful mystery of these combined mystically in the dynamic sacrament of marriage. I could feel some of what He was nudging me toward, I thought, and though nervous and lacking confidence as I was, I felt I could keep moving in that direction, even if often the rungs

on this experiential bridge sometimes seemed a little far apart. If I
trusted, I felt I could do it. *But what about Mark?* I asked the Lord.
I intuitively felt that he was not quite ready for this and would not
be able at this time to make those leaps. Yet I couldn't wait for
him; I had to forge on in this unknown territory that seemed to
have its own irresistible momentum and critical times of ripeness,
despite Mark and me being so intimately linked in this process.
Don't worry, the Lord seemed to tell me. *I Myself will stand in
that relation to you and support you until Mark is ready and can enter
that state himself.* This was not expressed so much in words as in a
mystical state that the Lord seemed to pass to me. The audience
ended. I got up to go inside. The sunray still spotlighted the nest
in the wild grasses, but the rabbit was gone.

Sometimes there is a need for something to unfold within us
that needs both more time and more psychic space than our perpetually busy, clock-driven, endlessly goal-oriented materialist
culture allows. Such a time was that summer for me, when I had
only a small amount of not-too-time-consuming work to do and
was enfolded in the cleansing elemental beauties of Cape Ann's
embracing seas, forests, and great granite rocks. We most often do
not understand what our urgent inner needs for growth are or the
direction in which our being will be stretched, but these are real
imperatives and important to cooperate with, nonetheless. If circumstances or our own intuitions do not lead us to take such time
away from the whirling wheels of our mundane duties, occasionally
our bodies will take over, demanding a halt through sickness or
accident. It is said in the old Russian Orthodox culture that when
someone became ill, people would hasten to visit that person, not
just to console the stricken one but also to absorb some of the
grace of the event in which "God has visited him or her." Being
taken out of the daily grind unexpectedly could herald a period of
new spiritual opportunity and hinted at the apparent nearness of
transforming grace, despite its possible discomforts.

༄

Community Up Close
We were joyful. Our dear friends Katharine Call and David
Newhouse had fallen in love and were planning to marry. Before
we knew it, the Newhouses were not only in their first year of
marriage, but Katharine was pregnant. David called to give us the
news while we were enjoying our idyllic Folly Cove summer, and
we rejoiced with him. Then he added that he and Katharine were
planning on moving before the child's birth from their Boston
apartment to Waban, part of the affluent suburb of Newton. And

they had decided to ask us if we wanted to live with them there. We were astonished and touched but had no desire to leave Cape Ann. We told David we would think and pray about it and get back to them.

Mark and I discussed this request, and we also tried to pray and meditate about it. We felt that we weren't getting very far with the prayer and meditation, though, because, though we loved David and Katharine, we also deeply loved living on Cape Ann and knew we were very attached to staying on our magical island. So we kept putting off giving an answer until finally David called to invite us to dinner at their place and to ask that we let them know our decision. We could waffle no longer.

We had made our decision, and at dinner Mark opened his mouth to tell Katharine and David that we could not live with them when something strange happened. A distinct presence descended upon both Mark and me—a sweet and lovely presence, accompanied by a sudden compelling conviction that we needed to live with the Newhouses, especially for the sake of this unknown presence. Mark's and my eyes met in this unspoken knowledge. It changed everything.

"Well, yes, David," I heard Mark saying, counter to our script, "Stephani and I would be delighted and honored to live with you and Katharine." And that was that. Guidance often comes in unexpected ways and times—and so often not in line with our own preconceptions and attachments.

Still astonished ourselves at our abrupt wordless about-face, we discussed what had happened as we drove home. We did not know who that presence was but we had both strongly felt it. I speculated that it might be the baby who was coming. I believe it was, indeed.

Babies

We left our beloved Cape Ann behind and moved into Katharine and David's spacious new house in Waban that September.

I also began working as an assistant kindergarten teacher at a Rudolf Steiner Waldorf School in Lexington, a fascinating and creative if often exhausting job. Mark, to his own surprise, was selling solar hot-water systems; although reluctant at first, he soon developed confidence and ease, in a short time becoming the company's most outstanding salesman. He loved the win-win-win aspect of the product: good for the environment, good for the customer (the system paid for itself in energy savings over a few years), and good for us, since he was making a living. Sales contests with trips as prizes especially spurred him on to greater achievement, and he won several of those, which provided us with the great treat of further adventures we could otherwise not afford.

Within a month of our moving in with the Newhouses, two momentous things happened: my mother-in-law, who lived in nearby Belmont, developed colon cancer and had to be rushed to the hospital (after an operation and many anxious months, happily she had a remission), and, after Katharine endured a long and difficult labor, Hope Evangeline Newhouse was born. This beautiful baby, round and rosy, with a smooth cap of dark hair above almond eyes and sweet lips, looking like a tiny princess out of a delicate Persian miniature painting, was to become one of the great loves of my life and my goddaughter, remaining so to this day. Less than a year later, her little sister Lily Amelia was born—in her case, so quickly that a trembling David had to deliver the baby by himself at home in the bathroom, with Katharine overwhelmed by the speed and pain of the labor. Neither the doctor, the midwife, nor I (working in David's new metaphysical bookstore, Skylight Books, in Cambridge) could get to the house in time.

So the four of us lived together there for three years with the two beautiful baby girls. We shared a warm fellowship, but life with infants is inherently demanding. It was an exhausting and challenging period for Katharine and David, and we supported them as we could but also felt the strains of trying to live an independent life in a baby-centered household. I think it is remarkable that we all managed as well as we did, considering the inherent difficulties. Of course, there were conflicts at times.

One upset involved the invasion of our kitchen and surrounds by a species of tiny biting red ants. This was unpleasant for everyone but especially so for our two crawling babies, who were getting bitten all over their tender little legs. What to do? David felt that we had to get exterminators in and let them spray their chemicals to remove the insect menace immediately. Katharine, if I remember correctly, was unsure but desperate to save her daughters from being bitten. Mark and I were very concerned about the toxicity of the pesticides for all concerned, especially the two little ones who would be gamboling over those sprayed floors. We were also concerned about possible allergic reactions among the adults; I was very chemically sensitive. We had numerous meetings and discussions on the subject and prayed together about it. We may have tried some mild natural repellent that did not succeed in eliminating the pests—after so many years I no longer remember. The decision kept getting postponed and postponed until David announced to us one evening, "That's it! I'm not going to let this go on any longer! I called the exterminators today and they're coming by at ten tomorrow morning to spray and get rid of these ants!"

Mark and I protested, and we all agreed to put in one last session of prayer together. We also decided to try to speak directly to the ants this time, explain our reasons, ask them to leave, and warn them of what was coming. We were all feeling the intensity and dangers of the situation and managed to work ourselves into a fairly deep state of prayer. Afterwards, we all felt more peaceful. At the end David said, "I'm going to check the kitchen at eight tomorrow morning. If somehow the ants are gone, I will cancel the exterminator appointment. But, otherwise, we're keeping it."

At eight o'clock the next morning all we adults were in the kitchen. For the first time in many weeks, we saw no ants on the floor. We went around carefully peering in cupboards and around the bases of appliances. Not a single antenna waved! They were gone! We sent up a cheer, and David called to cancel the appointment. And the ants never returned that year or any other. We all felt that we had learned together a valuable lesson about prayer—about the need to enter into it with strong focus and unified intensity, as well as perhaps intriguing possibilities for communicating harmoniously with the wildlife around us. And it definitely expanded the boundaries of our sense of limitation!

Feline Frolics: Enter Sasha and Toshiro

The Gnome Home was picturesquely located on a small hill overlooking Rockport's quaint harbor and breakwater. The little harbor was full of sailboats and lobster boats in the warm seasons, and the sea breezes often carried to us the tinkling chimes of the sailboats' halyards. We had moved back to Cape Ann and into this ridiculously tiny house—seemingly only big enough for gnomes and other small fairy-tale creatures—after three years of living with the Newhouse family. We had become restless, still filled with a deep longing for Cape Ann that only grew stronger over time.

Mark continued to commute into Boston for work at various halfway houses and group homes, eventually taking a job as a full-time mental health caseworker in Cambridge. I had left my jobs at Skylight Books and David's second store, a children's store called The Shepherd and the Lamb, deciding to work from home by opening my own proofreading business. There was also, of all things, an editorial agency right in town that was not only a source of jobs but that eventually hired me as their in-house proofreader as well.

Our little home, which we rented from a lovely older couple whose large home was on the same property, had apparently begun life as an animal manger in the 1600s. In later centuries it evolved into a small sailors' berth with bunk beds for sailors whose ships were in port for a while. In the twentieth century it had become a home for our landlord's elderly Swedish father and, upon his passing, was rented out to temporary tenants. It consisted of a more recent unheated but glassed-in front room with a flat roof, a door with glass panes leading into the peaked main room—only about twelve feet long and eight feet wide at its widest point (a small bathroom took a chunk out of much of that space)—and ended in a tiny low-ceilinged kitchen with a bow window. There were also two petite lofts accessible by ladder and a small black Jøtul woodstove in the main room. Although we were concerned the cottage might be just too teeny for us, we were smitten by its charm, its location, and its reasonable rent. Even the lease was charming: our landlord wrote in that I would make him Greek-style stuffed grape leaves from his own wild grapevines in his backyard (which I did and presented to him on a festive platter adorned with wild roses!) and that he would make us his special award-winning Gravenstein apple pie (delicious!). We moved in and lived there for fifteen years.

The Gnome Home was possessed of a lovely small yard that we eventually bordered with a wild, happy mob of roses, perennials, annuals, and herbs, joining some huge ancient lilacs, rambler roses, a couple of little apple trees, and two substantial silver-berried junipers. Looking out the front-room window we could see the harbor with its huddled dinghies and the long, narrow peninsula of quaint, store-lined Bearskin Neck over the cheerful forsythia hedge at the bottom of the yard. One night, during a big storm, I watched the sea charge over the breakwater and pour two feet of water down the Neck's narrow streets, transforming them into a strange lyrical picture, as if painted by Marc Chagall, passable only by boat: an empty dinghy floated dreamlike down the center of the main road; within moments a rocking yellow bucket followed it, succeeded soon after by a less lyrical floating green propane tank! The sea was beautiful always but we never forgot its danger and formidable power, especially when it breached the breakwater, and the icy freight-train northeast winds shrieked like sirens and shook our small ancient house walls till they trembled like flimsy paper.

My greatest delight was a tall old apple tree that extended its big boughs over the flat roof. Mark and I slept in the tiny loft beside it, and I could climb out the window to enjoy the roof's spectacular sea view. We hung a white macramé basket chair from a sturdy bough, and I could sit in it barefoot, gazing out to the white-capped sea and playing my mountain dulcimer, swinging and singing, listening to the friendly hum of dozens of honeybees dancing through the sweet-smelling cloud of apple blossoms all around me.

The old tree was fruitful and dumped loads of apples on our flat roof, some of them fermenting in the sun and drawing visitors— usually three baby raccoons who climbed up the tree trunk and gamboled about, tasting the high-octane apples with predictable consequences. I would lie on our mattress on the floor by the low window and watch their slapstick comedy as they buffeted one another (the somewhat larger oldest brother especially enjoying delivering corrective cuffs to his two younger siblings) and somersaulted on the roof like roly-poly circus clowns.

One morning I was awakened a little before dawn by a threatening growl close to my ears. The big raccoon brother, his nose against the screen window inches from my face, had caught my scent. "Stop that!" I told him, without thinking, gazing into his bright dark eyes. He looked momentarily abashed, backed up, and went off to swat a little brother, redirecting his moment of aggression—and saving face. Then Big Brother threw himself into buffoonish play with his family until the sun rose, signaling them to stream quickly down the tree and disappear as if by magic.

ₑᏚₑ

Two colorful kittens, both long-haired Maine Coons, also joined our household. We quickly fell in love with the two small balls of fluff, tortoiseshell Sasha and marmalade Toshiro. When new cats come into your life, it's as if they bring fresh colors into your psychic décor—whatever the base tones you and your mate may have been living with are now penetrated relentlessly by the undiluted, nonnegotiable shades of the cats' vibrant personalities—in Sasha's case an electric orange or yellow, in Toshiro's pastel blues and pinks. Sasha was smart, precocious, and initially significantly bigger than tiny round Toshiro, the runt of the litter. We were told that Sasha was a female (as apparently amber and black tortoiseshells usually are) and orange Toshiro a male. Sasha lorded it over tiny Toshiro mercilessly, and it just dawned on us that not all kittens from the same litter are necessarily temperamentally harmonious.

When the kittens had their first vet visits, the vet smiled ruefully as he lifted Sasha out of her case and remarked, "A little feisty, is she?"

"Yes," we replied. "How did you know?"

"The stripe down the nose," he said, pointing out her half-amber, half-black nose. "They always are."

And when he lifted Toshiro out of her carrier, he looked at her face, laughed, and said, "This is not a boy!"

We had gotten the kittens in autumn, and that December a wild, whiteout blizzard descended one day out of nowhere. Although the world was all fanged whirling whiteness outside, and our thin walls shook in the pounding wind, we and the kittens were warm in our tiny shelter, cheered by the friendly flames and red embers in our woodstove flickering reassuringly through its glass door. The winds died down later that night, leaving only the faint dry whisper of thickly falling snow to accompany us as we went to bed.

In the deep, snow-padded quiet of the night, I abruptly awoke and sat up. Our Gnome Home suddenly seemed like the stage of the Metropolitan Opera, featuring a deep-bosomed coloratura giving her favorite aria her best, most resounding shot. Impossible, melodic notes were booming away in the dark in our tiny house!

"Wake up, Mark! Wake up! Something is in our house! It sounds big enough to eat the kittens!"

Mark sat up groggily, and his eyes widened when he heard the sonorous singing pulsing as if through a bullhorn right beside us. He and I crept to the ladder hung against the loft (only I was short enough to stand up in the center peak of the roof), flashlights in hand, and pointed them toward the living room floor. Both kittens were standing side by side at the bottom of the ladder (they were too small to climb it yet), gazing up at us in round-eyed fear. They had come to the same conclusion as I had: the singer definitely sounded big enough to eat them!

Mark and I hastened down the ladder and quickly searched the whole little house. No sign of anyone but us and the kittens, and yet the happy, high-volume arias, following a basic pattern of "who-cooks-for-you" but with further elaborate embellishments as the singer was inspired, rang on. Finally it dawned on us that the rhapsodic singer must actually be under the floorboards of our house! There was no foundation, only a four-inch crawl space. This singer must be a sizable bird with a florid musical personality who had managed to escape from the storm by scrunching itself under our floorboards and, comfortably sheltered, was probably now enjoying the luxurious bonus of a mouse delicatessen as it took its ease. Our kittens were not in danger after all.

At last we went back to bed, the continuous arias circling around us like glowing sonorous curlicues in the air, and finally fell asleep. We woke the next morning to a blue sky and the tangible silence of deeply mounded snow. It seemed our diva had gone off on tour. As we made breakfast, I put on a tape of birdcalls; the odds seemed great that our serenader was an owl, given the volume and majesty of her song—though how she fit beneath our floorboards was a mystery. Sure enough! Although the singing on the tape did not match our singer's in splendor and improvisatory embellishments, the call was distinctive. Our visitor had been a barred owl, a largish medium-size owl. Further research indicated that these birds occasionally took shelter in barns and other convenient human habitations during storms. Given the joyous exuberance of its calls, we figured we had probably now achieved a five-star rating in the owl B and B guide!

ℓ

All cats teach lessons by the undiluted purity of their distinct personalities and individual approaches to life. Sasha, who never grew very large, was determined to make up for her unimpressive size by sheer persistence and pugnaciousness. When she wanted something, the word "no" did not exist in her universe. For example, if Mark and I were trying to have a quiet dinner in our tiny kitchen and had latched the pine door to keep the cats out, Sasha would run the length of the living room and hurl herself at the door, crashing into it repeatedly and sounding more like a small rampaging bear than a cat. And not stop, despite our yelling at her. "Never stop" was her heartfelt motto. With this credo and her own scientific method, she also figured out how to open the sliding screen door in our front room. She would rush up to it, slap the screen on three separate pressure points, and whisk it open in a flash.

She was also exceedingly smart—kind of like a small, impatient rocket scientist wearing a fur coat. Sasha carefully studied how we got water to run through our water filter in clear hopes of mastering this act, but, fortunately for us, pressure had to be applied to two points she did not have the ability to span.

Sasha did not like her sister, the inoffensive Toshiro, or, for that matter, any other cat. She would attack any cat who ventured into her territory, her battle plan being to have the advantage of surprise at least, if she could not intimidate by size. But she became best friends with a neighbor's tiny dog, and they used to joyously chase each other around the yard (sadly, the little dog was later killed by a car when it dashed out into the street). Then Sasha took up with a new playmate. Going to the door one evening to call Sasha inside as I always did around sunset, I opened it to see Sasha playing with a frisky new friend—a skunk. They were both hopping (yes, cats can hop) in a small circle about five feet wide on the grass, going happily round and round. I diplomatically withdrew, reluctant to disturb their frolic prematurely!

Sasha also had a taste for revenge. After Mark's and my first prolonged absence on a trip (brave friends had come to stay with our cats), I got up on my first morning home ready to set to work on some galleys after a light breakfast. I put water on for tea and bread in the toaster, pushing down the lever. Sasha had been sitting on the floor, watching me with what seemed like extra intensity. A strange odor began to fill the air—unpleasant but somehow familiar. What was it? NO?!! Hot cat pee?!! Sasha dashed away and hid under the couch. She knew my morning routine and had planned this little surprise for me to let me know exactly how she felt about our absence. With a gymnast's skill, she must have squeezed herself into the small space between our low wall cabinets and the toaster, positioning herself perfectly to pee into the slots! We had to throw the toaster out, of course! And I didn't feel too keen on toast for quite a while.

When we were gone for six weeks one summer, the cats were pampered by an expressive ensemble of colorful friends (among them, John Link, a.k.a. "Swami-ji"; John Pettibone, known as "John-San," given his Orientalist leanings; and artist Cindy Bromley) staying with them. This quixotic crew left a dazzling fantasy literary log about the cats' alleged activities, including pen-and-ink illustrations—Sasha and Toshiro digging escape holes through the floor wearing boots and lit miners' helmets and clutching shovels or arranging museum exhibits of their abstract expressionist poop sculpture, the scenes meticulously drawn, even unto the corded museum exhibit barriers. One contributor still had enough leftover verbal energy to remonstrate about the "cheap Chablis" in the refrigerator. Meanwhile, Sasha again planned punishment. We arrived home our first night to find that Sasha had dropped several large poops into a big pot sitting on the stove. "But how did she know which night you were coming back?" asked our bewildered cat sitter.

꧁

It had to be admitted that Toshiro was a considerably dimmer bulb than Sasha. Not an intellectual giant, Toshiro at least did turn out to be a physical one. A long-legged, long-bodied orange girl, her growth unfurled suddenly and copiously like a flag suddenly slapping open in a breeze—to the horror of Sasha, formerly dominant but now forever shrimpy and, at least when it came to the food bowl, usurped. Fortunately, Toshiro had a gentle temperament— kind of like a feline version of Ferdinand the Bull sniffing flowers in his meadow.

Among our neighbors' cats was a very unpleasant fellow—a huge, ridiculously muscular Siamese. We forgot his name and just called him Darth. Darth would come muscling around, growling and showing his fangs, lusting to beat up all the neighborhood cats. Until he met Toshiro.

I saw Darth, revving up his chain-saw growl as he crept out of our hedge one day, fangs flashing, only three feet or so from Toshiro. I was afraid to move with him so close to her, worrying I might set him off. Toshiro peered at him with interest, batting her long eyelashes over pale eyes that always seemed as if they should be sky blue. Darth added big chopper motorcycle sounds to give a further bass-register nastiness to his voice. Toshiro only blinked at him again and, lowering her head near the ground, crept a few steps closer to him, sniffing interestedly in his direction. Darth started to get a strange, confused expression on his face. When Toshiro crept a couple of more steps toward him in a most friendly, gentle way (she was purring sweetly, I'd bet), his face became a mask of not-very-bright cat consternation at being confronted by a cat who did not even play by the most elementary rules! He was threatening her with sabers and the terrors of his overpowering countenance, and she was offering him tea and petit fours on an antimacassar, smiling with gentle interest! Intolerable! Impossible! With a look of pure panic, Darth broke and ran. He never darkened our yard again. I contemplated this act of emotional judo, as disciple to sensei, for years.

Toshiro's tender heart extended to people. Due to a grief I cannot even remember, I was sitting one day in my rocking chair, sobbing. Toshiro leapt up and flung her long orange self around my neck, hanging down over my chest on both sides like a large apricot floral piece on a winning horse. She was doing her loving best to console me, and I did stop crying, mainly because I was touched but partly also because she was a lot of cat to carry around my neck.

Sadly, Toshiro died suddenly at the age of eight; our vet suspected an aneurysm. Despite our sadness, we felt a lovely peace in the moments of her passing—a gentle gift from our gentle companion.

A wild and free spirit, Sasha lived to the age of fourteen. She loved to be given rides in our wheelbarrow, the faster the better, up and down our little green hill, her eyes keen and sparkling. One otherwise calm and sunny summer day, three low miniature cyclones wended their way from the ocean onto our front lawn. I jumped at a loud crash behind me. One mini-tornado had whimsically lifted a large, heavy window box, overstuffed with alyssum and big pink geraniums, off its supports on our wall and dropped it smartly on the ground, barely five feet behind me. I turned back again to see two smaller wind devils turning a few feet from me, one of them sweeping a delighted Sasha two feet into the air, who, unconcerned, even thrilled, was playfully batting at the rising column of leaves swirling all around her. Heart beating fast, I swiftly snatched her out of the air and rushed into the cottage with her, spoiling her fun but saving her from being blown out to sea!

The vividness of cats' lives and personalities marked my early life growing up in the droning, anesthetized 1950s where, in suburbia, hardly anything else seemed real. Cats have continued to be a wake-up call—small, furry Paul Reveres of the psyche, varyingly cooperative but never really tame, their colorful, undiluted personalities flaming through the dark mists of social conformity and paved-over nature, the power of their authenticity jarring and awakening me, both a blessing and a needed warning in the night.

I have lived with several Zen masters. All of them cats.
—Eckhart Tolle

CHAPTER TEN

Catechumen III: New Eyes

Come to the Waters

The dawn summer mists wrapped silent Ponkapoag Pond in trailing filmy scarves. A lone canoeist paddled softly in solitary reverie until, at the shock of a disembodied voice trumpeting through the fog, he stilled his paddle abruptly.

"Here! Come here! Come! I need you!" The voice's timbre was not ghostly but robust. And, improbably, it had a Russian accent. As some of the mists began to clear, the bemused canoeist saw a large monk in a long black robe and brocade priestly cuffs and stole running along the shoreline, his long hair and skirts flapping behind him in the breeze.

"Yes, you! I need you!" the monk cried again, and gradually the canoeist began to see ranks of bathing-suit-clad men, women, and children standing behind him on the sandy shore, staring hopefully at him.

The canoeist looked nervously over his shoulder to see just whom the mad monk could possibly be shouting at. No one was there. Hesitantly, he pointed to himself with a questioning look.

"Yes, yes, you!" shouted the monk. "Come now to help me!"

As if still uncertain if he were dreaming or not, the canoeist slowly turned the canoe and paddled tentatively toward the big monk. As he got closer, he could see that the monk had a long thin beard and a slightly Asiatic look, as if there were a Mongolian strain in his family tree. He was now beaming with joy at the canoeist and shouting, "Yes, yes! Thank you, thank you!"

The canoeist pulled up on the shore. The monk leaned down, patted him warmly on the shoulder, and explained that he needed the canoeist's help for a while in order to baptize in the pond the crowd of forty or fifty people waiting on the shore. The baptisms, done in the ancient Orthodox tradition, would be full immersions, but the monk had discovered, upon their arrival, that there was no dock from which he could lean down to the water. As officiating priest, the monk said, he was required to keep his stole and cuffs dry. So, if the good canoeist could just take him out a little ways in the canoe? Rather numbly, the canoeist nodded his head in agreement. The monk climbed in, and the canoeist paddled him out into the pond, followed by a steady stream of candidates for baptism like a huge brood of obedient ducklings.

Marveling, the canoeist watched as the priest said baptismal prayers and pushed each catechumen three times under the pond's dark waters. A quiet jubilation began to rise all around like an unseen mystical mist. When all had been baptized and the canoeist roundly thanked, he left his canoe on the shore and lay down on his back under a tree, looking dazed. Asked by a newly baptized man how he was feeling, the canoeist replied, "This was the ultimate experience of my life!" And, understandably overwhelmed, fell asleep. When he awoke, the shore was empty again, as if his experience had been an exotic dream.

ه

Baptisms
If anyone had told me a year before this that I would become an Orthodox Christian again, I would have told her she was crazy. My personal dogma had, I thought, permanently eliminated such a possibility. *Yes, haha, God. You really got me this time!*

After the passing of the charismatic founder of the Holy Order of MANS, Father Paul (Earl) Blighton, in 1974, his successor felt it necessary to examine more traditional forms of Christianity less dependent on a charismatic leader and more deeply rooted in the ancient Christian spirit and traditions. The tragedy of the mass suicides and murders in the Jonestown cult had also sent a shock wave through the larger culture. Any less traditionally conforming spiritual expressions were being examined with a harsher eye, and accusations of such groups as cults flew indiscriminately and vitriolically through the air. A stability in Christian mystical tradition and transmission and the amplification of the basic Order minimal liturgical structure were being sought by those entrusted with our leadership. The "wild olive tree" (Rom. 11:17) wished to be grafted in an appropriate way into the hoarier tree of holy tradition and faith.

So, for a number of years, the Order priests, sisters, brothers, and Community members set about studying Christianity in reverse historical order—first Protestantism, then Roman

Catholicism, and, last, Orthodox Christianity. We read books and journals, went to conventions and talks, and attended classes in the first two denominations over a period of years, familiarizing ourselves with the likes of Dietrich Bonhoeffer, C.S. Lewis, Tony Campolo, Thomas Merton, Henri Nouwen, and many others. These studies were enriching, but we still felt like a homeless Jewish tribe wandering in the desert, searching, searching. When our teachers, studying ahead of the rest of us, came upon Orthodox Christianity, however, many of them experienced a powerful resonance with this deeply mystical stream of ancient Christianity and at last smelled the oasis perfumes of "home" being carried to them on an Eastern desert breeze.

One of only two cradle Orthodox in the roughly two thousand or so members in the Order and its communities (the other was a man in the Midwest), I was shocked. And worried. I wrote our long-suffering director general a twenty-one-page typed letter about my fears of what we could lose if we became Orthodox—our warm, spontaneous spirit, our close-knit and family-like communities, our reverent but informal nature and tone, our vital mystical meditative qualities, our women priests, etc. Not to mention the possibility of adopting a cultural overlay of misogyny, fossilized (as opposed to vibrant) practice, and a stiff, pompous hierarchical atmosphere.

I'm sure I was not the only person who rained dissension on Father Andrew. And so he sent his most effective answer around in the person of the tall, warm-hearted Russian Orthodox abbot whom we shall call Father Jeremiah. This monk, in his fifties with hair and beard just beginning to gray, was incandescent with a deep-seated spiritual joy. As our community sat with him in hours of classes about Orthodox history, dogmatics, apologetics, practices, and hagiography, peppering him with our probing questions, to our amazement a very beautiful inner spiritual landscape, luminous and profound, began to open up. With his unfurling erudition and descriptions of vivid, traditional practices to guide us into an atmosphere of increasing blessedness, I began to understand Orthodox Christianity as never before. And to crave it. I felt a quickening and I wanted what I saw. Enough, even, to begin to wrestle with some views of my own that might stand in the way. However, I was still not an easy sell.

☙

Our beloved former pastor, Father Jacob Meyers, came back to Boston for a visit while all this transformation was fomenting. Mark and I went out to lunch with him in a Northern Italian restaurant in Harvard Square. As we Unfold our white cloth napkins as we prepared to eat, I could not hold myself back anymore.

"Well, what about reincarnation?" I asked Fr. Jacob, somewhat challengingly. I had had some experiences that seemed to imply this possibility, and, although it was not dogma in the HOOM, many members believed in it.

"What about it?" he replied.

"Well, is it true or not?"

Surprisingly, as he was often quick in response, he just sat there quietly for a moment and then closed his eyes in silent prayer.

A few moments later he looked at me penetratingly. "The reason why you are asking this question is not because you are concerned about reincarnation—but because you don't trust God."

I felt a shock in my chest as I received the unwelcome truth of these words. I saw in a flash of light that I was resentfully clutching at the doctrine of reincarnation for exactly the reason Father Jacob had identified—I was angry about the suffering in the world, and reincarnation seemed to me the only relatively reasonable explanation I had ever heard for it. I did care less about its reality and more about exerting what seemed to me some degree of intellectual control and personal sense of justice about our crazy world and its maladies. God obviously could not be trusted to tend such things in His mysterious ways—look at the mess!—so I set myself up as a petty queen to judge what might seem rationally (though perhaps inaccurately) satisfying. No matter how I justified it to myself, my view was hollow all through. Realizing that my sins of pride, resentment, and compulsion for control needed much more to be dealt with than this specific issue of metaphysical reality, I repented and let go of the whole thing, feeling the stinging but healthy relief of receiving a revealing impact of truth, stimulating further purification in my heart.

This is not to say we shouldn't pursue metaphysical truth around such questions but merely that caution is needed about our own real motivations every step of the way. We can especially be easily blinded by the autointoxication of wanting to be right. Being neither a theologian nor a saint, I can stake out only tentative territory regarding this question. As of now, I personally don't accept the doctrine of reincarnation, but I don't absolutely know this for sure. An Orthodox priest once told me he had had experiences that seemed like reincarnation, but he thought they were probably the result of dipping into the great cosmic memory of the universe somehow and being impressed by experiences of people who had gone before him that he resonated with so strongly as to completely identify with their experiences. The great Sufi teacher Hazrat Inayat Khan explains reincarnation sensations similarly, as resulting from the passage of our souls through the heavenly spheres as we come into incarnation, with souls ascending and descending past us on Jacob's ladder, and our being particularly impressed by some of these, resonating with them in our new impressionable souls as strongly as if their experiences were indeed ours. He also explains child prodigies this way. Certainly, quantum mechanics with its complete interconnection of everything created, and the sensitive reaction of all parts that exist anywhere to all the other parts that exist lays out a scientific possibility for such unseen but powerful connections. The remarkable modern Irish Christian mystic Lorna Byrne, who claims that she has seen and communicated with angels continuously since babyhood, states that she has been shown that reincarnation is very rare—but can sometimes happen for some special needs. Traditional Christianity, so far as I know, does not accept reincarnation as a metaphysical reality.

ﷺ

Father Jeremiah offered us the possibility of becoming Orthodox Christians under the leadership of a Greek-American bishop in New York City, whom we shall call Metropolitan Gerasimos. Some months of individual and collective soul-searching followed. Members left because they felt they could not proceed on this path, but many of us, the majority, decided to take the steps into Orthodox Christianity. No one was pressured. We each made our own decision individually—I think most of us ultimately out of conviction but probably some because they did not want to leave the warmth and security of our community life. Among the many changes were Reverends Samuel and Alicia transferring to a parish in another state. Succeeding them was another couple whom we will call Father Zeno and Presbytera (the honorific for a priest's wife) Laura.

Among the essential first steps were receiving, in imitation of Jesus Christ, the sacrament of baptism, followed by chrismation. Most often these days, when non-Orthodox Christians convert to Orthodox Christianity, they will receive only chrismation, the anointing with special holy oil, symbolic of the individual's personal Pentecost, to be accepted into the Church. But that can only be if they have been previously baptized in the name of the Holy Trinity: Father, Son, and Holy Spirit. If not, they must receive a full-immersion baptism. This raises certain awkward logistic issues. Until recently, adult baptism has been relatively rare in the Orthodox Church since babies born into Orthodox families are baptized as infants. Unlike Anabaptist Protestant sects, that delay baptism for many years, wishing to wait until the catechumens can intellectually and emotionally assert for themselves their acceptance of Jesus Christ, Orthodox Christians accept that the grace of the Holy Spirit is something transfiguring that works and protects far above and beyond intellectual conviction. Hence the practice of putting the baby actively into the hands and under the initiatic, transcendent blessing of Jesus Christ as soon as possible through the sacrament. Baptism is not regarded as merely a respectful, symbolic act of remembrance, a formal rite, but as a deeply powerful, transforming mystical act implanting a very real and dynamic sacred seed of new life in Christ, encompassing but beyond the realms of the rational.

In recent years, as there has been a large and increasing number of converts to Eastern Orthodox Christianity, there has been a new spotlight on adult baptisms. In our church, some people seemed to be uncertain whether they had actually been baptized in the name of the Holy Trinity, and we also had many ethnically Jewish members, so a pragmatic decision was made to baptize just about everyone. Except me, as I had been submerged in an Eastern Orthodox baptismal font as a baby. I felt a bit disappointed to be left out. Little did I know at that time that not many years hence I would be standing in the Jordan River, the ultimate baptismal font, in a flowing white baptismal robe about to be immersed three times for the renewal of my baptism!

Since our priests had not attended Orthodox seminaries, they had not been instructed in all the details of the services, as well as many other practices. Father Jeremiah and the bishop began to train them but could not be on-site much of the time. So, as the lone cradle Greek Orthodox, I was appointed to be the researcher, getting detailed instructions from the bishop on how we were to proceed. From his cathedral in New York, the bishop preferred to talk on the phone from 11 P.M. to 1 A.M., which he and I did on many nights as I furiously scribbled notes. The bishop was meticulous in delineating details, including the practical ones. For example, the challenge of finding water-bearing containers that were large enough to submerge full-grown adults was a dilemma (pond baptisms not being an option in New England winters). Some churches resorted to children's pools or horse troughs. It was necessary to be inventive!

"Not a problem," the bishop asserted briskly. "Here is what you do: get the largest jumbo-size Rubbermaid garbage cans made. Don't get any other brand—Rubbermaid is the only brand strong enough! Run a hose from the sink . . ."

I moaned silently. My work as a messenger was never exactly pleasant, but I shuddered at the likely reaction of our priests to the directive to baptize our congregants in large garbage cans!

But we did. Hapless sacristans struggled to attach gold cloth around the outside of the huge round rubber garbage can set out before the sanctuary, but as the rubber was slippery, more often than not, during the holy moments of the baptism, some of the cloth would slip down and a black Rubbermaid logo would emerge surrealistically into the sacred décor, like the ridged eye of a rising crocodile. I could only comfort myself by thinking that being baptized in a garbage can might be of some benefit to a person's humility (always a slippery quality at the best of times)!

There were so many things to learn, large and small. Sometimes details were important, like learning not to stand to the west in the church narthex while catechumens and their godparents were "spitting on Satan" (symbolically inhabiting the west, away from the rising light and altar in the east) during the exorcism, the first part of the baptismal sacrament. And what to wear? Apparently in ancient times catechumens went into the font naked (one of the many reasons for retaining women deacons, who baptized the women). So what to do? Men wore bathing suits, but somehow this did not seem to us like quite the right garment for women. What would that be?

While we were still trying to work this out, my dear friend and goddaughter Anna Elisabeth Higgins was ready to be baptized. She wore a tank top (it is important to not be too covered up so that the priest and godparents can thoroughly anoint the candidate with holy chrism oil) and shorts. Standing in the narthex with me, she also wore a terry-cloth robe, its belt untied per instructions (nothing was supposed to be knotted or buttoned, symbolic of no obstruction in the path of the movement of the Holy Spirit during the exorcism). We spoke the Nicene Creed, rejected and spat on Satan and his ways, and thus completed the exorcism.

We then walked up to the front of the church to the "baptismal font." Altar servers had already filled it with water, and the perennial gold cloth was hanging gamely if tentatively around its circumference. A small three-step wooden footstool stood just outside the font. Anna took off her robe, and the priest and I helped her climb up the footstool and into the font (which also had its own little interior footstool). So far, so good. Cantors were sweetly singing the appropriate hymns. The big moment of immersion arrived.

I was surprised to see Father Zeno hesitating. He beckoned to me, and we leaned over the font so he could whisper in my ear. "Unsnap Anna's shorts," he commanded.

"What?" I responded dumbly, not believing my ears.

"Unsnap her shorts—nothing should be tied or bound when the Holy Spirit is moving."

"Father Zeno, her shorts will fall off!" I had horrible visions of Anna emerging from the font sans bottoms.

"No, they won't," he declared. "Just stick your fingers through her belt loops and hang on."

I stared at him incredulously. The jumbo Rubbermaid garbage can rose higher than my breast level. How could this possibly work?

"Just do it!" he ordered.

Leaning over the font, I plunged my arms into the sacred waters and unsnapped Anna's shorts, desperately hanging on to her belt loops as I balanced on tiptoe.

"All right," said Father Zeno. "Hold on!" And, proclaiming the Holy Trinity, he pushed Anna down into the font three times. Each time I almost had to dive in headfirst myself to retain my tenuous hold, and each time her loops slipped further off my fingers until, the last time, I was barely hanging on by my fingertips. With great relief and aching arms I at last gained permission to re-snap her.

Despite the contentious whispered conversation buzzing by her ears while she was in the font, Anna Elisabeth, clearly in a transcendent mystical state, heard and registered none of it. She came out of the font glowing like a rose. As I helped dress her in her new white baptismal robe, I was so happy to see that our galumphing comedy of errors had not disturbed her in the least. She radiated peace and joy, the renewing light of baptism shining through her as through an alabaster lamp.

(Soon after, our community settled on sleeveless jumper-like dresses for women to wear into the font.)

༄

My husband, raised Congregationalist, was baptized Orthodox on Pentecost with six others. Each baptism was, of course, individual, but the group was considered henceforth to be "brothers and sisters of the font." Our faithful, optimistically adorned jumbo Rubbermaid garbage can awaited them as they approached, one by one, with most of our congregation present to pray for and encourage them.

I don't know why, but the two officiating priests chose my husband as the second or third candidate to be baptized. About average in height but with a wrestler's muscular body and big bones, Mark said that, as he was pushed down for the first time, "In the name of the Father" ringing in his ears, and came up, he heard a surge of displaced water leap over the font rim like a wave suddenly liberated from a dam and splash down loudly on the priests' shoes! As he came up from the second immersion, he heard one priest whisper hoarsely to the other, "Next time let's take the big ones last!" Despite our errant human comedy, Mark was deeply moved by his baptism. God is generous and is able to hold space both for our frequent ridiculousness and for the transcendent mystical experiences He grants us, without harming the latter. As the psalm says, "He knows whereof we are made."

۶لی

The ritual immersion of baptism aroused a host of intense, often deeply buried psychological issues for many people. Its dramatic symbolism was so unambiguous that it struck hard at individuals' core visceral conflicts, especially those relating to the sense of trust. To go into the font, lightly clad and thus vulnerable, submitting to the guiding hands of the priest and your godparents like a baby, and to "die" there where you could not breathe, only to be mysteriously reborn in Christ, was a challenging act, especially when taken most seriously—as most of our mystical group, by temperament and devotion, were inclined to do.

Father Zeno asked me to work with the candidates preparing for baptism—basically, to try to help them over the common bumps and fears. I found that even the thought of being reduced to such infant-like vulnerability sent a wave of panic rolling through many people's hearts because it brought up childhood and babyhood emotions and memories of feeling insufficiently protected or worse by their parents. As the projection of the personalities of the parents often underlie the child's fundamental assumptions about the nature and character of God, this contamination by association often devolved into an unspoken but deeply held fear of not being able to trust God—a conflict that had to be worked out at least to a sufficient level to enable the catechumen to enter the font and "put on Christ."

The other major, related issue that surfaced was people's horror at the suffering they experienced and viewed in the world and their fear and resentment that God must be somehow complicit in it—perhaps only in inexplicably allowing it or, worse, as a possible perpetrator and cause.

Allowing these painful issues to come to the surface, and to talk and pray about them together, was therapeutic. And also about related issues of forgiveness—toward parents, toward those who had hurt us, toward ourselves, and even toward God. It was not necessary to be completely healed to be able to commit oneself to enter the font and engage sincerely in the act of turning oneself over completely to Christ—one needed to have just that degree of healing, particular to each person, that allowed that one courageous step to be taken with sincerity and hope. In the deep cleansing and downpouring of grace upon the newly illumined, the Holy Spirit would take the healing on from there.

ﮩ

Vigil

Many of our members, a wholeheartedly mystical group, spent the night before their baptisms partly in vigil and prayer, partly sleeping, in the chapel. In the case of one of my godchildren, a college student, I spent the night in the chapel with him, laboriously sewing a red braided cross on the back of his white baptismal robe. Tall, slender Michael McCormick, with a springing crop of black curls, alternately stood and sat for most of the night near the sanctuary, reading aloud the entire Gospel of all four Evangelists— something he felt deeply moved to do. It was an extraordinary experience for both of us, to hear all four Gospels read aloud consecutively—extremely powerful. We felt immersed in the Lord's life in a new and profound way, and in some manner intimately participating in it. Michael periodically took short breaks to lie down for half an hour or so and rest his voice but always soon got up again to resume reading. Just as the first beam of dawn came slanting in through the stained-glass windows and I took the last stitch on his cross, Michael read the last word of the last Gospel. The moment was crystalline and holy. Then Michael lay down again and we communed in sacred silence. Soon he entered into the deeply felt beauty of the mystery of baptism.

ﮩ

A Split Screen

Although I could not be rebaptized, the bishop decided to re-chrismate me, as I had not been an Orthodox Christian for some years. He, and our former pastor Father Jacob, who was visiting, decided to surprise me with this decision one Sunday morning as we were waiting for divine liturgy to begin. An altar server came to tell me that Father Jacob wanted to see me at the sanctuary. My pocketbook still hanging on my shoulder, I walked up and knocked on one of the angel doors. A grinning Father Jacob opened it and motioned for me to wait. The bishop, fully garbed in his impressive regalia and crown, stepped up behind him.

"Stephani," His Eminence said, smiling down at me, "I want to re-chrismate you now."

"Now? Here?" escaped me.

"Yes. But I need you to answer some questions for me." He asked me about my belief in Jesus Christ. And then if I had ever belonged to another religion.

"No," I replied. And then added, "Well, Sufism."

"No, no, I mean another religion," he clarified. I was dazzled that he apparently understood what Sufism was—that it is indeed not another religion but rather an inner spirit and state common to all revealed religions in their depths.

He then motioned to an altar server, who brought him the holy chrism oil. Then and there he anointed and blessed me. A moment later I went staggering away, and divine liturgy began.

Aside from being startled by the whole thing, I found that I was very unexpectedly having a spiritual experience: I saw my own consciousness as a large movie screen that had been split in two. One side was what you might call my genuine life (and here the Church was, too), and the other side was separate and different. But it was not some other religion. The second screen consisted of my secular materialist life with its mundane values and preoccupations—something foreign to my true and spiritual self, and an enervating distraction from that truer self, a split in my attention and consciousness. Under the impact of the chrismation blessing and holy oil, the second screen dissolved, the two screens becoming one and whole, my spiritual self restored to primacy. After this healing and cleansing, I felt suddenly charged with energy and joy.

I went looking for my husband and found him downstairs in the church hall. Before I could say anything, he took one startled look at me and exclaimed, "Whatever happened to you? You look different, radiant."

I told him.

During divine liturgy an altar server emerged from the sanctuary to tell me that the bishop commanded that I receive Holy Communion that day. I was reluctant. I had not received Orthodox Communion since my teens, and only one other person, a newly chrismated priest's wife, would be receiving that day. I preferred to wait until my brothers and sisters in the church community could also receive. But the bishop insisted. So, near the end of liturgy, I found myself walking up the aisle toward the chalice when suddenly my heart started pounding wildly. Even from afar I could feel a powerful, awe-inspiring holiness emanating from the contents of the chalice, and such an indescribable Presence that it made me shake in my boots. This may have been the only time I ever understood viscerally why it is important to prepare to receive Holy Communion, and to engage in a certain amount of preparation beforehand (one of the reasons that the Eastern Orthodox Eucharist is not open to all; Saint Paul warns against the possible negative consequences of not receiving in a prepared and appropriate manner). I did experience "the fear of the Lord" as I received. This is not an ugly or intimidating kind of fear but rather the "beautiful fear," a species of awe, of a mere mortal being received into that light-filled, all-powerful, and immaculate Presence.

After the service, I noticed our two priests staring at me. "Congratulations," one said as I came up to them. "The bishop said that something happened when you received."

"What happened?" I asked bewilderedly.

"I'm not going to tell you. I don't want it to go to your head."

༄

Holy Tradition

I was startled to find myself, in my midthirties, a newly minted pilgrim in my old faith. And finding it a rich, exciting adventure! Despite Eastern Orthodoxy's seemingly constraining, even forbidding, formal lineaments, I found vast, uncharted mystical expanses within it and felt like a dolphin probing and leaping endlessly into a sea of wonder and fresh, intimate experiences with God. The forms and practices carried painstakingly forward from ancient tradition were an ideal cradle for sheltering and nurturing that vibrant new life. The life-bearing Mysteries (Sacraments) and holy feasts of the Church both spring out of the rich, vital soil of Holy Tradition, as well as Biblical belief. Not an unrooted addition, Holy Tradition is rather the shared mystical context and transmission coming down through the ages from believers. It was through the discerning lens of Holy Tradition that such matters as choosing which of the extant Biblical books should be accepted was determined (Orthodox and Roman Catholic tradition additionally accept a few Biblical books left out of the Protestant canon), as well as the composition of the believers' creeds of the early Ecumenical Councils. Holy Tradition creates both an orienting atmosphere and a fertile, evocative context in which such potent spiritual practices as the meditative Jesus Prayer ("Lord Jesus Christ, have mercy upon me") could evolve.

Critics of Holy Tradition as an essential element in Christian transmission complain that it is fossilized dinosaur of the culture of certain eras and that it continues practices of "unnecessary froufrou" (my preferred theological term) that distract from a spartan intellectual/emotional belief in Jesus Christ, deemed in itself sufficient to ensure sanctification and salvation. Though the latter is possible, an active, conscious, and rewarding spiritual life is more likely for most of us, I believe, when guided and inspired by the rich atmosphere and practices of ancient Christian understanding, artistry, and transmission. And Holy Tradition, despite some of its more formal, venerable elements, is not a dead thing.

Paired fruitfully with Holy Tradition is its heavenly sibling, *oikonomia* (economia), carried on the wings of the unconventional, ever-freshening Holy Spirit. This formal recognition of the "divine economy" encompasses the changes and deviations from convention and tradition that God may bring forth in the moment for anything (short of the tenets of the Nicean Creed) to help fend off stagnation. Its unconventional action is an antidote to our strong gravitational pull toward spiritual sleep and the heavy, closing eyelids of convention. Although the formal definition of the term is a narrow one exclusively involving the prerogatives of a bishop, the spirit of economia breathes through the Church as a whole. This is one of the reasons, for example, that even before an official canonization is declared by the church hierarchy, local parishioners may begin celebrating and acknowledging a local saint, their expression of faith rising up the structural steps of the Church rather than only descending from above. Economia is freedom but not license, and so is not invoked frequently. But it does manifest at times. I love the idea that the Church honors this idea of fresh and sensitive manifestations of the Spirit to address changing needs as a living approach.

Standing at midnight in the oil-lamp-lit darkness beneath the enormous dome of the Holy Sepulchre—the great ancient church in Jerusalem that houses both Calvary, the site of Jesus Christ's crucifixion, and the Tomb from which He was resurrected—having prayerfully attended a Greek divine liturgy, I waited in a line of quiet, awed pilgrims as we slowly advanced toward the cup of Holy Communion. This golden chalice was closely held by a young, dark-haired, dark-bearded Greek bishop of the Holy Land, his gaze fixed upon it, almost as if it were a holy Baby he was embracing lovingly in his arms, the Babe's radiance reflecting upon his face, illuminating it with an unspeakable tenderness and mystical Light. He stood just within the entrance of the Edicule, the small and beautiful carved marble shelter surrounding the Tomb of Christ. Suddenly, out of the silence, and from an invisible source, strong, reverent masculine voices rose in a hymn of unearthly beauty that took our breath away. Although it was not formally part of the liturgy, we learned later that this was a hymn of devotion to the Virgin Mary penned by a twentieth-century Greek saint, St. Nectarios of Aegina. This holy bishop endured a life of persecution but had a deep and abiding love for the Mother of God, composing many hymns for her. This one, "O Pure Virgin," has moved many hearts—as ours at that moment, even though we could not understand the Greek words—and so, though not formally enshrined in any of the services of the Church, this hymn has begun to appear often in places where there is retained a flexibility of content within those services, a manifestation of economia. It is becoming a part of living Holy Tradition, its sanctity borne witness to by the faithful, like those monks in the Holy Sepulchre raising its ecstatic verses to heaven.

CHAPTER ELEVEN

Catbrier: Thorny Experiences on the Path

Being Present at Feasts
Put off thy shoes from off thy feet, for the place whereon thou standest
is holy ground.

> —God's words to Moses as he stood before the
> burning bush that was not consumed (Exod. 3:5)

*I*t was Holy Friday, and I was in a grumpy, distracted mood. It was not even Pascha yet, and I was already exhausted and worn out from having to superintend the hundreds of details of the Holy Week services in my post as liturgical coordinator. Usually, I remained reverent and more or less focused despite these burdens, but today I found myself repeatedly off-center.

I tried to pull myself together as our line of parishioners advanced toward the Tomb of Christ, where we would have the opportunity to venerate our sacrificed Lord as depicted in a long fabric icon, His head in His mother's lap and grieving apostles and angels all around. The icon lay in the Holy Tomb, that resembled a small canopy bed below its low dome completely covered with hundreds of fragrant fresh flowers—a small oasis of mystical purity. From where I stood I could see a part of the icon where a female disciple in unquenchable grief was throwing her arms high above her head and wailing. It struck me as a little too much, bringing to my judgmental, nitpicking mind a memory of my mother and aunt having a discussion in which they disapprovingly described my notorious great aunt Sophie's contortions at a funeral. She had arrived with her nylons rolled down, tearing at her clothing, and wailing as she tossed her arms above her head. I had the impression that perhaps Sophie did not know the deceased well, and that my mother and aunt felt that her inappropriate antics were for show and attention, not to mention in bad taste and disrespectful (although they acknowledged that this was probably the approved style of an earlier age).

Unfortunately for me, I happened to be thinking about this discussion as I performed two full prostrations before the Holy Tomb and arose to step to where I could kiss the Lord's naked, nail-pierced feet in the icon. Leaning over the icon beneath the perfumed dome, from the corner of my eye I disapprovingly caught a glimpse of the "excessive" female disciple with her outflung arms. In that fatal nanosecond of supercilious judgment, an unseen being struck me, and struck me hard.

The resonant thump on my back was delivered with a kind of etheric density and exactitude right over my heart chakra. I had never received such a blow before. And while stunned that someone unseen, a rebuking angel, could deliver such a powerful physical chastisement, I was even more overpowered by a perception smiting its way through my being like wild, rolling lightning, searing my understanding: the woman disciple's response was completely appropriate. If anything, it was understated: We had crucified God! We had crucified *God*! That such a thing could happen, that we His creatures could perform such a terrible act, was a horror almost beyond the mind's and heart's strength to bear! But it smote me with the same overpowering certainty as that of my childhood experience of all the glorious Creation issuing out of the almost-naked figure of Jesus Christ hanging on the Cross above the altar.

Having kissed the Lord's feet with unfeigned, deep repentance, I staggered away from the Tomb. As I numbly tried to get back to the pews, my legs failed me and instead I fell on the floor, hunched over with trembling shock, weeping uncontrollably. I could not get up. The epiphany kept roaring through me like cannon fire, blotting out everything else. My grief seemed as great as the ocean, huge and merciless as its most towering waves. My being suffered in every mote and cell with this ultimate of cosmic tragedies. Of the Unthinkable. The Impossible. Now Possible. Done. By us, mere creatures.

Eventually a few of my goddaughters tenderly scraped me up off the floor and folded me into a pew, holding my hands and trying to calm me. But I could not stop weeping for a long time. Although I had neither the capacity nor the desire to stay submerged within this epiphany for long, I now understood how a number of saints, individuals of much greater purity, submission, and capacity, had ultimately blinded themselves with months and years of weeping from acute spiritual insights. The Crucifixion, I saw now, was even worse than global cataclysm because it was a fierce, blind, vicious striking at the Source of all that is and all that is beautiful and good, trying to destroy and root it out. This was the full-fanged beast of nihilism raging at its most destructive—mad emptiness trying to annihilate Life and Love at their foundation.

I had invited this sharp but merciful lesson by straying into the immaculate territory of the holy while still unconcernedly wearing the casual and coarse thoughts of my lower nature—dead animal skins on my feet like clumsy shoes insulating me from sensitive understanding, humble respect, and real participation in the mystery.

۵

Darker Forces

Our very first Great Vespers fell on the December feast of Saint Nicholas of Myra. It was almost as new to me as to my fellow parishioners since this was the first Vespers I had ever attended that was celebrated in English. Although it was a little awkward and halting as singers new to this music struggled to offer it smoothly, the service was still quite beautiful, and I was surprised at the sense of a very distinct presence I felt of Saint Nicholas himself: warm, kind, wise, and deeply mature, strong in the best paternal sense, gently gathering us all under the protection of his powerful, encompassing mantle. As we neared the end of the service, each person, one at a time, approached Father Jeremiah, now standing in front of the sanctuary, to receive his blessing. Somehow the atmosphere became very intense for me in a strange way. As each person reached him, Father Jeremiah would ask his or her name and then politely shake his or her hand, realizing that most of our group were too new to Orthodoxy to understand and be comfortable about kissing a priest's hand (this act is not personal to him, but represents kissing the hand of Christ). I felt a peculiar irrational conviction that, when I reached Father Jeremiah and he asked me my name, I had to answer with my actual baptismal name, "Stephania"—and that he would then know, given this Greek form of my name, that I was Orthodox. For unknown reasons, the thought of revealing this filled me with such a strange terror that it felt as if my bones were melting. I was rooted to the spot by inarticulate panic.

The pew in front of me was emptying. What could I do? Rosie, a six-year-old girl of whom I was very fond, was in that pew. Just before she left, she turned around and fixed me with her large, serious eyes. She said something to me—I cannot remember what— but it seemed more like the remark of a wise adult with spiritual sight. Somehow it freed my feet, and I was able to walk up and join the line before Father Jeremiah.

The moment of confrontation came. "What is your name?" the big monk whispered in my ear with his heavy Russian accent.

I gulped, summoned my courage, and whispered back, "Stephania."

Father Jeremiah threw his arms into the air and cried, "My compatriot!" And then he gave me a big hug. I could feel a vast inflow of father-energy from the Holy Spirit descend like a gust of wind through him and into me. I started to cry. Fr. Jeremiah looked concerned.

"What is your problem?" he asked gently.

"I—I—I don't know!" I sobbed.

"Good girl!" he cried and hugged me again. This time also I felt the downflow of healing father energy pour powerfully into me—perhaps the needed influx that my own father, lost in his troubles and disbelief, had been unable to give me in my youth. Fr. Jeremiah hugged me one more time, and I went stumbling off and, stunned, fell into a pew. For unknown reasons, someone wordlessly put a baby into my arms.

From this point on, something seemed to have broken open in the service's atmosphere. Every person who came up to Fr. Jeremiah after this he hugged and they hugged right back, happy smiles on their faces. After the Vespers ended, as I sat there with the quiet baby still in my arms, two people came up to me separately. One, Lennie, said he had been suffering and struggling all through the Vespers. Of Jewish extraction, he said he could not stop thinking with horror of the Russian pogroms against the Jewish people and the awful violence of the Cossack attacks. His fear and hatred of this nightmarish history was separating him from the warmth of the service. "But," he said, "as soon as Fr. Jeremiah hugged you, that was all swept away, and all I could feel was the spiritual sweetness and healing beauty of the Vespers and I was just so grateful to be here."

After he left, the wife of a priest, *Matushka* Melissa, came up and sat down next to me, a warm and loving look on her face. She said that when Fr. Jeremiah hugged me, she had an interior vision of me—of a dark and empty place within me. Suddenly the sun shone upon that place, the rain fell upon it, and flowers began to sprout and blossom there. She had been praying, praying, praying. "But then," she said, "I could only weep with joy." And she gave me a gentle hug before leaving.

Mark collected me, tolerantly assessing his bemused wife. We went out and got into our car for the hour-plus ride back to our Gnome Home in Rockport. All was well until we reached the intersection before the Tobin Bridge in Boston. There Mark miscalculated and drove through the beginning of a red light. Very quickly, a police car followed us up onto the bridge and pulled us over. Two officers got out and started questioning Mark. The policemen had strange expressions on their faces—almost as if they were a bit hypnotized. Their eyes were dull, their faces almost expressionless, and there seemed to be a compulsive quality to their questions. We told them we were just returning home from Vespers, but they seemed already convinced that that was not true and that Mark must be drunk, although he was acting perfectly normal. They made him get out and walk a straight line, which he did without any difficulty, and yet they still seemed to want to arrest him.

Sitting in the front seat, I was about to speak again when suddenly, to my shock and horror, I felt a distinct presence of one or more hostile beings sitting on my chest and exerting great pressure, strangling my ability to express myself. I struggled, wildly praying to the Lord and the Archangel Michael to free me. The pressure suddenly lifted as if ripped away, and I cried out to the policemen, "He's fine! Just fine! We are just coming from church! From church! He just made a mistake!" The two policemen suddenly looked different, as if someone had abruptly slapped them awake from a deep sleep. Some expression returned to their eyes. "Well, all right, okay," one said confusedly, "we'll just give you a warning this time." And they allowed Mark to get back into the car. As we drove home, though, I felt as if a mocking presence accompanied us, jeering that if we liked attending Vespers so much, we had better be willing and able to deal with additional troubles.

Darker Yet

Mark and I were attending a church board meeting on a warm spring afternoon. We had both been on the church board numerous times (in all I served either one- or two-year terms on eleven boards), and Mark was also ultimately the president of the church twice, for four years. Normally one or more of our priests were present at board meetings, but this time there were only the board members plus one parishioner who, having some free time while hanging around the church, decided to attend.

We were still very early into our entry into Orthodoxy. I was, with the priests' blessings, writing lessons for our parishioners about the various services and their meanings and history, and other practices of the church. This board meeting had gone on for some time when I started to feel a strange concentrated heat, as if a fire were burning close to my left side. The guest parishioner was seated there within a couple of feet of me. Turning to find the source of this disturbing blowtorch blast, I looked at him. A terrible hostility was beating out of him toward me in blasts of psychic heat, and, where his eyeballs and pupils should have been, I saw instead awful fiery lights—the ugly, inhuman orangey-red eyes, lava-bright and implacable in their hatred, of a horror movie. I caught my breath in shock as I connected with this demon gaze. Just then the man burst out angrily: "Why do we have to have all these services?! It's too much! We don't have to have them! It's Stephani's fault! We have them because of her, and we should stop them!"

Of course, this was completely untrue. The Church rubrics prescribe the services; we don't choose them. But I certainly functioned within our community as a support for them. All present were shocked into silence, and a peculiar clay-like atmosphere stole over the meeting, suffocating normal responses. I calmly explained why we had the services, but it was as if this normality did not register with anyone there except my husband and Jim Higgins, the board chairman, who looked incredulously at the attacking man, and denied his charges. Nonetheless, the man raved on, refusing to agree or be silent. I sat there in shock. I could see Mark restraining himself because of the delicacy of the atmosphere. A wrong move or remark could have bad consequences. Finally, Jim warned the man to be quiet or he would personally eject him from the meeting. Sullenly, the man at last consented and sat there in a sulfurous stink of resentful anger. It was hard to endure having that infernal fever heat beating away so close to my side. I could only try to collect myself, endure, and pray.

The meeting ended. Shaken, I went up alone to the chapel. Standing in front of the Lord's icon on the icon screen, I prayed—and complained. I was not absolutely sure if He said anything at all in response, but I had a fleeting impression that He may have said, "When I was scourged, I was silent." Not a comfort.

Mark and I drove home in a disturbed state, deeply eager to reach the safety and peace of our cottage. We parked in the driveway and started to walk up the small green hill to the Gnome Home.

But, instead of the usual wave-washed quiet, shrill, angry screams rent the air with violence. Walking ahead, I was the first to see the injured squirrel running back and forth along the edge of the flat roof of our front room. Blood was pouring from his mouth. Still running, he fixed his eyes unwaveringly on mine as I came up, pouring out his fury and agony as if I had been the wretched, hated cause of all his suffering. Mark and I were filled with horror and pity. How could we catch the raging squirrel and bring him to medical help? I had to steel myself to go closer, with the squirrel's mad eyes still locked on mine as he leaned toward me over the roof edge as if he wanted to leap at me and tear me. Still he ran hysterically back and forth, back and forth along the rim. He ignored Mark. As we got really close, he disappeared. We ran to the sides of the house to find him. We searched all around there and in the yard. There was no sign of him, and now we could hear nothing beyond the normal wind in the trees.

We called the animal control officer, and he told us sadly that he thought there was nothing we could do for the squirrel, even if we found him. He said that, given our description, he probably had bitten into a power line and suffered internal injuries. We hung up the phone sadly and sat down in our living room, deeply despondent. This horrible scene, piled on top of the ugly shock of the meeting, pushed me into despair.

It is always a terrible blow to experience evil up close. And sometimes the worst part of it is when it surfaces in a person whom we like and think of as—and who mostly is, actually—good. The man who had accused and verbally and psychically assaulted me at the board meeting was a friend, usually a kind, rather sensitive, and artistic man, though subject to depression. I knew he had some problems, but he also had virtues. That he had lent himself so deeply, if unconsciously, to that vicious demonic presence was extra horrifying to me. And it echoed some other recent dismaying experiences I had had with otherwise kind people running amuck and my having to reluctantly deal with the psychic violence they expressed.

I went to bed deeply depressed. When I woke in the morning, I could hardly drag myself out of bed. I didn't want to talk and I could barely pray. Mark had to go off on an unavoidable errand. Later that morning I heard a knock at our front door. It was our paperboy, looking distressed. "Please, come help!" he said. "There's a hurt bird."

I only had to follow him a few steps to see a handsome blue jay lying stunned on the ground. Going back inside, I got a shoebox and ripped off one side, filling it with soft cloths. Taking a bottle of Rescue Remedy—the Bach Flower Essences emergency formula—in my other hand, I returned to the boy. Very gently we shifted the blue jay into the box, where he lay on his back, panting. I knew the jay might have already suffered internal injuries and did not know what to do for him. "I have this," I said, showing the boy the little bottle. "I don't know if it will help, but shall we try it?" He nodded anxiously.

Very carefully, I eased two drops of the Rescue Remedy tincture into the jay's open beak. He immediately flapped his wings powerfully, startling us both, and flew about eight feet straight up in the air, still on his back, as we gaped up at him as if spotting Superman. Then the jay neatly righted himself in mid-air and flew about forty feet down to a big juniper in our front yard. He landed on its lowest branch, a good ten feet up, and huddled next to its trunk.

The boy looked up at me with round eyes, exhaling in awe. Uh-oh. I could see a "white witch" projection coming on. "Um, well, this is just a simple kind of herbal remedy, really," I said, showing him the little bottle again. "Sometimes it can help with shock, but I don't know if this time . . . Er, would you like to have it?" He nodded eagerly. I told him I would try to keep an eye on the jay, and he said he would come back tomorrow to check on it. He left, holding the little tincture bottle in his hand and gazing at it as if it were the Holy Grail.

I looked up at the motionless jay on its branch, and my heart felt like stone. I really knew then that, despite its acrobatic performance, the bird was going to die. And that I would have to face a very sad boy the next morning too. I felt too crowded with sorrows, as if their load was breaking my back. I knew from past experience that either Rescue Remedy tincture or the homeopathic remedy *Arsenicum Album 200c* could briefly revive a dying animal with a last burst of energy and strength, as if one breathed on a dying flame that then leapt up in one last magnificent flare. All the rest of the day I kept returning to the doorway every hour to peer at the huddled, unmoving jay, and each time I felt my heart sink deeper and deeper into some terrible, unseen pit. The last time I checked, the bird was barely visible, fading away into the dark.

Mark was delayed getting back. It was long before he came home. I didn't want to eat or talk. I went to bed early. When I got up in the morning, I went directly to the front door and looked out. The dead jay was lying like a stone at the foot of the tree. My heart felt like ice. When the boy came, I apologized. He was heartbroken. So was I. After he left, Mark and I buried the cold bird.

I sank into a dark night of the soul. I didn't want to eat and soon found that, not only did I not want to talk, but I actually could not talk. Words just didn't seem to form and be utterable. And now I couldn't pray—not even mentally. A worried Mark fussed over me but could get no response. The daytime did not seem that much different from the darkness of the evening. I went to bed, wordless still, moving as if already in a lightless dream.

The next day Mark urged me to come out for a drive with him, hoping to distract and cheer me. He drove us to wild, beautiful Maudslay State Park in Newburyport. We wandered along its rhododendron avenues, broad meadows flanking the Merrimack River, crumbling Italian gardens, tall pine bluffs, and little forests. I was still mute. We entered a small, dry valley without underbrush but studded with slender young trees. It was very quiet there, and felt oddly deserted, almost like an empty stage set. I don't think I even heard any birdsong. I walked on numbly and stopped about twenty feet away from Mark. Furious squawking erupted over my head. Suddenly two blue jays, so completely entangled in fighting each other that they formed an interlocked circle with their outspread wings, plummeted to the earth just a foot away from my feet. As I stood frozen in shock, they continued their furious combat as if I were not there, turning and turning in the dirt, a violent whirling mandala of blue and white. Unable even to move away, I stared down at them in quiet horror. Mark looked at me in amazement. "Oh no," he said. "Maybe this wasn't such a good idea." And he came to me, took my arm, and led me away.

That evening Mark coaxed me to sit at our shrine with him. He prayed and tried to help. After a while I seemed to see something trailing along in the air in front of the shrine, a few feet above my head. Peering at it, I saw that it was Jesus's long bare feet, slowly walking, and the bottom of his robe. I knew that He wanted me to reach up and touch His feet, but I was so paralyzed in my pit of darkness that I could not move even to do it mentally. So He kindly, gently, humbly lowered His feet to my hands, and I felt the hem of His robe slipping over them. Suddenly I could talk again and I could pray, though I remained very shaken.

It was some weeks before I returned to normal. I didn't want to see or speak to anyone. I ate a little and I could pray a little. And I kept reading over and over bits of two books that sustained me, their words seeming to pour a slow, patient healing into me, like a freshly emerged underground spring spreading new life into a dry riverbed. One was *Wisdom from Mount*

Athos, the lyrical, heartfelt, faith-drenched writings of the great modern elder of Mount Athos in Greece, St. Silouan, whose many sufferings only sharpened his love for God. The other was a chapter, "Of Herbs and Stewed Rabbit," from Tolkien's *The Two Towers*, describing a wild and lovely land, Ithilien, that had been attacked by the evil enemy Sauron and, though damaged and under assault, yet managed to retain some of its independence and natural loveliness—all the more poignant because of its embattled state. The beleaguered hobbits Frodo and Sam, who had already experienced great torment, were passing through Ithilien's unexpected refreshment with deep, startled gratitude, and yes, now so was I, so was I:

> *The dusk was deep when at length they set out, creeping over the westward rim of the dell, and fading like ghosts into the broken country on the borders of the road. . . . A single red light burned high up in the Towers of the Teeth. . . .*
>
> *For many miles the red eye seemed to stare at them as they fled, stumbling through a barren stony country. . . . At last, when night was growing old and they were already weary . . . the eye dwindled to a small fiery point and then vanished: they had turned the dark northern shoulder of the lower mountains and were heading southwards.*
>
> *With hearts strangely lightened they now rested again. . . .*
>
> *The growing light revealed to them a land already less barren and ruinous. . . . All about them lay a tumbled heathland, grown with ling and broom and cornel, and other shrubs that they did not know. Here and there they saw knots of tall pine-trees. The hearts of the hobbits rose again a little in spite of the weariness: the air was fresh and fragrant. . . . It seemed good to be reprieved, to walk in a land that had only been for a few years under the dominion of the Dark Lord and was not yet fallen wholly into decay. . . .*
>
> *So they passed into the northern marches of that land that Men once called Ithilien, a fair country of climbing wood and swift-falling streams. The night became fine under star and round moon, and it seemed to the hobbits that the fragrance of the air grew as they went forward. . . .*
>
> *As they walked, brushing their way through bush and herb, sweet odours rose about them . . . . The hobbits breathed deep, and suddenly Sam laughed, for heart's ease not for jest.*

A long list of wonderful plants, appearing in the middle of this passage, acted like a beautiful incantation, restoring my battered soul as if by rhythmic shamanic song, slowly knitting up the ragged, bleeding tears within me. I felt as if I breathed in the wholesome, delightful airs of this oppressed but unbroken land as I read; as spring broke through the damage and decay in once fair and free Ithilien, so it began to break through in me, tender sprouts growing stronger each day. Even rereading these words now, so many years later, I feel the same thrill, the frisson of delight, that at that time coursed through me like new blood.

So, what did I gain from this difficult experience? I could stare evil in the face, at least to some degree, and survive it, through grace. And experience the grace to be restored from the trauma. I grew somewhat in understanding of the piercing paradox that evil was not just a discrete monolith, but also could exist where there was good and even a kindly nature, given its destructive entry by people's unexamined weaknesses and compulsions. And I gained some visceral knowledge of the internal state of those undergoing such a trial. Thus, I was able to help two friends in the next two years who faced similar scourgings: one, a medical scientist whistle-blower who, reporting falsified data in an ongoing study at a major university, was turned on and attacked; the other a mental health professional working for a narcissistic, mentally unwell, and sadistic boss. These two could feel that I knew in my bones the nature of their distress, could genuinely empathize with them, and thus allowed me, in small ways, to help them, when they felt that there was no one they could turn to who would really understand.

When we are in a certain kind of confrontation with evil, we feel utterly alone in a very extreme way, even if it is only a small trial, like mine. Certainly, there are unseen (and often unsensed) angelic presences hovering and protecting. And yet the experience itself takes place in a terrible kind of loneliness, and no one can join you there or alleviate its horror and pain. It's like being dropped down a well. Despite this, we can still feel a delicate and knowing sympathy from those who have faced the same trials. They can't pull us out of that well or fight the demons for us. But it is as if they are able to keep strumming a certain tone, a certain chord, on an inner lute—the chord of having been there and having survived the experience. Although the strings of our own instrument may be mute with shock, our dead strings yet feel that hopeful whisper of sustained vibration, a slender thread of the possibility that we can come through this darkness too and, though it may feel impossible in the moment, yet make living music again.

A sharp gift, dear Lord, but an invaluable one.

Sing unto the Lord

Sing unto the Lord, all the earth; show forth from day to day his salvation. . . . Glory and honour are in his presence; strength and gladness are in his place. . . . Give unto the Lord the glory due to his name: bring an offering and come before him: worship the Lord in the beauty of holiness. (1 Chron. 16:23, 27, 29)

In all my school years, the only class I was ever thrown out of was a music class. My fourth-grade teacher, Miss Lily, was an intelligent gray-haired woman, probably in her early fifties, who had inspired my awed admiration by daringly taking a trip to the Amazon jungle by herself during what my nine-year-old mind could only regard as her frail dotage. Miss Lily had a sharp mind and a sharp tongue when irritable, as I discovered that particular day. Very musical herself, she was attempting to teach our class to sight-read music. She walked from student to student, standing beside us while each individual wrestled with notes and staffs. I couldn't do it at all. I tried but had some kind of block—I could not make the interior connection between the abstract symbols on the paper and the varying tones they represented. I was quite hopeless, even after repeated tries, and embarrassed and blushing to boot. Miss Lily resented this. "Get up!" she snapped. "Go out into the hall and stand there! You are too smart not to be able to do this!"

Numbly I stood up and fumbled my way into the hall, standing there for the remainder of the class. At one point our kindly school principal came by. He stopped and stared at me, eyebrows raised in surprise. "You're out here?" (I was a notorious good girl.) "Why?" I explained, and he walked on down the hallway, shaking his head.

Although I liked to sing, things just didn't seem to work out for me musically. Almost everyone was in the school chorus, both in elementary school and junior high, but not me. I had a lisp and so instead was forced to attend dreary, frustrating speech classes that no amount of hand puppets could ever make helpful or even tolerable. Sometimes alone, sometimes with two or three other similarly handicapped students, I had to struggle along with the boring rote exercises that never seemed to correct that lisp. And, of course, I missed all the singing.

Later, as an adult, I acquired a friend who was a speech specialist. With a laugh, she explained, "The kind of lisp you have is not correctible!" Now they tell me!

Anyway, out of sheer frustration and lisp-correcting fatigue, I finally broke down one day in a junior high speech class (scheduled, of course, during chorus) where I was the only pupil that day. If I had to pick up one more finger puppet, I probably would have torn it to bits with my teeth! The kindly teacher gazed at me compassionately as I sobbed.

"Oh, I'm so sorry, dear." She paused and added delicately, "Do you have problems at home?"

A light bulb lit up in my head! I nodded emphatically yes. (Of course, I did, but that was not the precipitating issue.)

"All right," she said. "I'm excusing you from class, and you don't have to come back anymore."

Oh joy! Maybe she thought I needed more time alone? Yes! But it was still too late to join chorus! And by the time we were in high school, I felt too intimidated and behind to even try out.

Furthermore, my mother did not like me singing at home and discouraged it. I did not sing badly and had a good ear, so why? Well, sometimes I probably sang too high in a squeaky soprano, and there I couldn't blame her. But my best guess was that it just brought an alien element into her consciousness—something strong and undiluted that was not her—right into the heart of her realm. Perhaps she did not care for the reminder that there could be a different personality and approach to life even within her zealously guarded domain.

Nonetheless, I did eventually have a few guitar lessons and learned a handful of chords. As teenagers, my friend Bird and I, along with Juanita, would take our guitars down to the beach on summer nights, build a small bonfire, and carol "Mr. Tambourine Man" and "Puff the Magic Dragon" to the stars, the ocean waves playing bass as we sang our hearts out. This was more like it!

But I didn't begin to really sing until I became involved with Sufis as a young adult. In my particular Order, descended in large part from the musical Chishti lineage of India, singing and chanting were not optional. Many of our meditation practices were sung. So, I gradually learned to be less self-conscious and raise my voice with the others.

I also learned Protestant and Roman Catholic hymns in Christian services with the Holy Order of MANS

But I didn't yet know that a voice was lurking within me—furtive and invisible, evanescent as glimpses of a lynx padding through the snow-clad trees—that possessed its own secret power and drive. Unbidden, this voice would emerge without warning sporadically in future years, shocking and sometimes healing me and others as it seemed to convey a numinous pulse from beyond. Walking with Christ, we never know what we will encounter—externally but also from within ourselves: hidden gifts, unfamiliar sides of our own beings—sometimes shocking but always a stretch. He constantly enlarges our own sense of ourselves. I was no exception.

By the time we became Orthodox Christians, I had progressed enough to be trained and ultimately tonsured by a bishop as a *Psaltria* (Psaltress / Reader / Cantor)—as in the case of subdeacons, this is technically regarded as a lower-clergy position in the Orthodox Church. My husband also was soon ordained as upper clergy, one of our two deacons. Although I still could not read music and had an untrained voice, I gradually learned the dozens of melodies, involving the basic eight Tones (similar to modes) plus other special melodies, that were necessary to cover the fundamental chanting of the long services that were almost entirely sung. We had to know these melodies cold—well enough to look at a paragraph of hymn verses for the first time and be able to sing them immediately, unrehearsed, to Sticheron or Troparion or Canon Tone 3 or Tone 7 or whatever the specified melody might be. They were sung a capella, without guiding musical instruments. It took me the better part of three years to learn these basics, and even then I knew that I was barely touching the surface (for example, trained in the Russian style as I was, I learned that a gentle, penitent Kievan Tone 8 was quite different in mood and melody from, say, a more triumphalist Carpatho-Russian Tone 8—and the Greek Byzantine Tone 8 of my childhood was entirely different from either of these).

I also learned some striking pieces in the Byzantine style. Instead of the (ideally) four-part harmony of the Slavic music, the Byzantine style featured elaborately wrought, haunting melodies undergirded by the *ison*, one or more long, sustained tones thrumming beneath the melody line, creating a sonic atmosphere of mystical tension and depth far more complex than one might expect from only two parts. Sometimes, when there were particularly skilled cantors serving, a double *ison* with two sustained notes an octave apart might be chanted, increasing the sense of mystery and drama. I heard the *ison* once explained as representing the Uncreated Light always shimmering everywhere beneath the surface of the Creation.

Even though it was anxiety-provoking and difficult—and the *kliros* (or Readers' Stand) turned out often to be a place with a magnetic attraction for what we called "unseen warfare," various forms of trouble all too often becoming seen—I loved serving in this way. It was inexpressibly beautiful to participate together in our rich, intertwined vocal adoration of our beloved God.

The Orthodox services are long. At the church where I was trained, the full primary Christmas (Feast of the Nativity) service, held in the middle of the night, consisted usually of Great Compline, Matins, and Divine Liturgy. That was about six hours of mostly singing and chanting. Of course, Holy Week and Pascha, with their twenty-one services, were a vocal marathon. But these lengthy services provided a priceless opportunity for us to marinate in the feast, draw its ineffable elements into ourselves to the extent that we could bear them at the time, and often to experience a mystical interior quickening.

Even though there were many painful moments—us being the fallible and contentious individuals we are—in my many years of sacred music ministry, there was also enduring joy and blessing. And, of course—how not?—unintentional comedy.

During one of our first divine liturgies, for which our choir had learned, a bit shakily, a particularly exquisite polyphonic Cherubic Hymn to sing during the dramatic Great Entrance when the priests, deacons, and altar servers process through the whole congregation bearing in honor the bread and wine that would later become the Body and Blood of the Lord, in memory of His carrying of His Cross to Calvary, the unexpected happened. For reasons I can't remember, there was a drought of sopranos, with only two of us at the *klíros*. As the holy procession paced solemnly down the aisle, the other soprano, a sensitive, artistic type, suddenly fell to her knees, mystically moved, and stopped singing. I was overcome with confusion. Should I also not be singing at that point, I wondered? Stupidly, I stopped to try to figure it out.

At that moment my friend Anna Elisabeth, an alto standing next to me, lifted a rolled-up calendar (where did she get that from?) and slapped me hard on the forearm with it. Simultaneously, unpremeditated, without my conscious cooperation, the next notes and words soared out of my mouth, thus averting an awkward and embarrassing musical blank space during the procession. I have no idea how and why this worked, and Anna was unconscious that she had slapped me and had no memory of it later on in the service! God does provide, though often not in our preferred manner! On such embarrassing amusements must a certain mischievous class of angels thrive—perhaps the same ones who recommended rubber garbage cans for our baptismal fonts? It's nice to know that we were making someone happy.

Eventually I was able to put together a small team of Readers, all women, to sing the Presanctified Liturgy, combining both Russian and Byzantine Greek music, once a week during Great Lent. This beautiful service seemed particularly exquisite and moving, in the candle- and oil-lamp-lit darkness, when sung by the sweetly chiming voices of our women.

For years I spent many hours preparing these and other services and in practices with other choir members and Readers. One of my most cherished hymns was "The Great Doxology," in Byzantine Tone 1. It appeared in Matins, most often at the end of two or three hours of a long Saturday-night vigil consisting of Great Vespers and Matins. Most people had gone home by then, but those who remained had been soaking in the ambient holiness for hours, their "spiritual molecules" becoming more and more subtly churned and changed. Usually I sang this swooping, soaring, heartfelt piece with Anna Elisabeth or one of my other goddaughters, Gabriella (memory eternal), singing the accompanying *ison*. It had power—and some nights especially so. One night a couple in our congregation told us after Matins that, upset with certain things about our church and our priests, they had decided to quit it. But they had been so deeply moved by that Great Doxology that they completely changed their minds and were staying after all.

Another night at the end of a long vigil, only Anna and I were left in the chapel, with just a priest and altar servers in the sanctuary. But as we launched into the Byzantine "Great Doxology", we did so with all our hearts. "Glory to Thee Who has shone forth the light, glory to God in the highest, and on earth peace, good will among men. . . ."

At the end, when we looked out into the chapel, there were two strangers sitting there, a young curly-haired woman and a slightly older bearded man. Sitting bemusedly in a pew, they were staring fixedly at us with big smiles. They had been out for an evening walk and, on a whim, wandered into the church's open doors from the street and up to the chapel. Their eyes looked like stars, twinkling with sparkling light. As Anna and I prepared to leave the chapel, the two rose to greet us, thanking us for the beauty of the chant and saying that they were deeply moved.

"Where do we sign up?" the man asked. We stared at them, startled.

"We knew from that hymn that this is the place for us," said the woman.

It is forever amazing how music travels like lightning from heart to heart, a powerful unseen messenger, carrying fire from being to being, quickening a deep and wordless understanding. The great poetry of the Church combined with that firebird of ecstatic music can bring us into subtle and unseen but very real worlds. We feel them in our breath, feel their shining tides pouring through us in a mystical reign of light, beyond conscious understanding, awakening hidden, secret knowledge in our blood.

I was also beginning to discover that my voice, though often paltry and awkward, at times blazed with a strange beauty that I could not control. Ring-tailed-lemur-like, sometimes it jolted listeners, even as they relished its sound.

One evening I entered our chapel to attend Vespers and found it full of priests from all over the country, along with our bishop, as we were hosting a national conference. The service was supposed to start in ten minutes, but, to my horror, I saw that no Reader stood at the *klíros*. And, indeed, no Reader showed up. The young man who was assigned to lead had simply gone AWOL without a word, apparently due to some obscure inner conflict. Fr. Zeno and I frantically consulted, realizing that I would have to act as lead Reader for this service without preparation—not a good thing! We quickly threw together the necessary papers and books, and I scanned the rubrics—the order of the service—checking for potential "crashes." No time for anything else!

Our Bulgarian bishop gravely began the opening blessing of the Vespers. And, as I began to chant the beginning Trisagion Prayers, my voice broke away from me like a wild, beautiful raptor, soaring into the Gothic rafters of our church. My belief in what I was chanting and praying remained sincere, but I was also caught up in a state of fury. Furious at the deserting young man, certainly, but also just furious to find myself abandoned in this dreadful, embarrassing, and very public position. And the rage flamed off some remaining inhibitions on my voice that I had never realized existed. A few times in my life now anger has unexpectedly dissolved unknown bindings on my vocal power.

Within the sanctuary, unseen by me, someone was reacting to my prayer offering. "Who is *that*?" exclaimed the visiting Fr. Lucas.

"That's Stephani," Fr. Zeno replied.

"Yes, that's my *diaconissa*," my husband, serving in the altar, added proudly, as the bishop later told me. (*Diaconissa* is the honorary title for a deacon's wife.)

When the service ended, I felt as if I had run a marathon and wanted to get out of the chapel as quickly as possible. But Fr. Lucas came flying out of the sanctuary, ran to the *klíros*, and grabbed my wrist. "We have to talk," he said intensely and led me over to a pew.

"Sit down," he said. "I was in the sanctuary and the service was starting and I heard this incredibly beautiful woman's voice and I was amazed. They told me that it was you. Was it?"

"Well, I chanted the service," I admitted reluctantly, "with help." I had been joined later by a few assisting Readers, but they had already left the chapel.

"How? How?" he asked me, brow furrowed. I could see that he was struggling to understand both the impact and why, since he had known me casually for years, he had been unaware that I had such a capacity. Well, I had been unaware of it too. He was a priest with a penetrating kind of mind, and I could feel his restless determination to somehow get to the bottom of this small mystery, like a fierce hound on an obscure trail. The odd confrontation was becoming increasingly uncomfortable. I didn't know where this would go, but I didn't think it could go anywhere good. White-witch, ring-tailed-lemur territory, it looked like. I had the feeling he might want to try to "figure out" and tame something not tam-able. I needed to quickly abort the conversation. Turning away from his piercing eyes, I stood up.

"The bishop will be blessing dinner any moment now. You'd better go down right away or you'll be late," I said.

Fr. Lucas stood up, still staring at me intensely. He shook his head twice and left. I felt in some strange way, which I cannot explain either to you or to myself, as if I had had a close call.

✦

Drive-by Death

In much of current Western culture, traditional observances around death seem to be dwindling, disappearing down a funnel of vagueness and distance. Memorial services are often held at some fuzzy TBA date far from the actual time of passing. Cremations often replace the more lingering and immediate confrontations of burials. Headstones lie flat with the ground in some cemeteries, leaving the identity of the deceased mostly invisible and the cemetery itself looking like just another park. If a funeral takes place, it is often very short, with little processing time for the mourners. Increasingly, only a work crew is present when the deceased's coffin is actually placed in the ground, family and friends having been shunted away beforehand. Even the bereaved are often expected to get over their grief in an abbreviated period of time. This trend seems to reflect a desire for the uber-critical passage of death to be handled with the brisk dispatch of a fast-food drive-by window. We demonstrate that we are growing more and more uncomfort-able with almost every aspect of death as we increase a cultural tone that is clinical, distant, and as little felt as possible around death. In so doing, we ignore and deny the needs of both the mourners and the traveling soul itself during this drastic passage.

But, traditionally, we Orthodox Christians do death long. And thoroughly. And I have learned there is wisdom in this slow, sensitive, sometimes gritty approach.

From the moment of death, aside from a short service of supplication and blessing, ideally there is someone reading the Psalms beside the deceased person, a reading continued as much as possible for three days and three nights. Like traditional Jewish people, observant Orthodox Christians are not embalmed. At my old church, family and close friends, with the aid of the clergy and clergy wives, would wash, fragrantly oil, and prepare the body (a process not without its challenges). The dead, lovingly clothed and anointed, would then lie in an open coffin in the church nave. People would sign up to read or chant the Psalms beside the coffin round the clock until the funeral itself. Our understanding was that the person's soul was likely to be wandering nearby for roughly three days, visiting loved ones and loved places. Family and friends read the Psalms aloud so that the journeying soul would not feel alone and also have the benefit of the wise, faith-filled guidance of the Psalms.

The funeral service itself is long, long, long (did I say long?) and full of in-your-face realism, though in poetic form, almost all of it is chanted and sung. In the voice of the deceased, the chanters sing:

> As you behold me lie before you all speechless and bereft of breath, weep for me, O friends and brethren, O kinsfolk and acquaintance. For but yesterday I talked with you, and suddenly there came upon me the dread hour of death. But come, all you who loved me, and kiss me with the last kiss. For nevermore shall I walk or talk with you. . . . But I beg and implore you all, that ye will pray without ceasing unto Christ God . . . that He will appoint unto me a place where is the light of life.

Here the great, soulful music of the Church comes to our aid, mixing spiritual honey with the bitter gall of grief and dissolution. Rather than such a frontal approach being cruel and difficult, I have seen it—especially if offered at full length and not unwisely abbreviated (the impatience of an always-rushing age!)—to be deeply cathartic and healing to the mourners. It does not demand that people who need to mourn stuff their grief away. The service itself expresses this grief without trying to tone down its tragic and difficult aspects, and gives the mourners spacious time to dwell in it—but with the difference that we are all together in that grief, our collective consciousness, our group prayers and singing, supporting each person in his or her private grief, leavened by an ancient deep faith and understanding. A startling spiritual buoyancy arises from this strangely intimate group sharing, and we gradually feel more and more of the enduring light at its core.

Things happen during those three days of prayer. There is a reason that people are standing watch and chanting in prayer. It seems that not all souls have an easy passage. Or that, at least, some parts of a soul's passage may become rough. I was standing in prayer one night in our chapel not far from the coffin containing the first person to die in our community—a woman in her forties, dead of cancer—when the man reading the Psalms for her stopped and came over to me.

"Stephani, I keep feeling that something is wrong with her, that she's having a hard time. I can really feel it. What can we do?" We gathered the five of us in the chapel together and went over to the icon of the Virgin Mary on the icon screen, where we began to pray for our dead friend in a more intense fashion. I, too, now that my attention had been drawn to it, could feel an invisible storm she seemed to be caught up in. But as we all wholeheartedly prayed for her, we began to feel this oppression lift. We soon all felt that she was out of dangerous waters, and we were able to return to our former activities. We were glad to have been there for her.

Our tradition teaches that after death there is an approximately forty-day period in which the soul travels locally for about three days, then passes through "tollbooths" for the remaining time, where it is confronted about its earthly life, supported by its guardian angels, and accused by fallen spirits. At roughly the fortieth day, the soul comes before God for its personal judgment, where it receives its placement in the cosmos until the last judgment comes. So, during these sensitive forty days, families and friends often pray extra prayers for their loved one, have liturgies offered, and give charitable gifts in his or her name in order to bestow additional grace and merit on the traveling soul at this critical time.

For priests, the Gospels, rather than the Psalms, are read. A well-loved priest died after suffering much and long from pancreatic cancer. There was an atmosphere of grace around him in his coffin that was like golden spiritual honey. To my husband and me it seemed tangible. A good thing for many reasons, but especially because, due to an unexpected gravediggers' strike, the funeral had to be postponed by one day. And there was, meanwhile, a wedding scheduled in our chapel for an out-of-state couple that could not be moved. So, as our choir sang, the bride and groom, candles in hand, led by the priest and accompanied by their two witnesses, circled three times around the open coffin in the middle of the chapel. Perhaps it sounds gruesome and inauspicious, but actually it felt blessed and beautiful. There was a deep atmosphere of peace and quiet radiance, and even of harmony, as these great sacramental passages came together and mingled in dignity and great love in our chapel.

This priest's actual funeral itself was challenging, in part because his parents were vehement atheists and hated anything to do with God and the Church. The mother's anger and resentment were particularly intense, to the point where she could not bring herself to even walk up the stairs to our church but stood outside, grief-stricken and furious. When advised of this difficulty, our wise and kind Bulgarian bishop went out himself and took the distraught mother's hands into his own. He spoke softly and lovingly to her, telling her that he would bring her into the church himself, and that she could stay only as long as she wanted to. His gentleness moved her, and so he was able to bring her within.

We chanters felt extra pressure to make the service as beautiful as possible, and we worked our hardest. I think that we tuned up higher when we saw our bishop bring the suffering mother into the packed chapel and gently settle her in a pew with her husband and her other son, also a priest. We gave it our all. The heavily attended funeral service went on for hours. I spoke with her son at the reception afterward.

"It was a miracle," he said, referring to his mother and shaking his head. "She was so angry at first and could hardly bear it, but after a long while, she turned to me and said, 'This is amazing! I don't feel any hate and anger in my heart anymore! It's as if it's been all washed away. I just feel comfort—and peace.'" The wise, ancient, unrushed ways of the Church, filled with love, can send gentle healing streams through the most parched and stony lands of the heart.

☙

When the woman who was the first in our community to die passed away, her body was gently prepared and clothed by some of the women of our church. When four men began to carry her coffin up the stairs from the first floor to the chapel, I tagged along behind. I had a strange but strong feeling that she was walking behind her coffin, perhaps still bemused by this shocking transition. And quite alone. So, ignoring the fact that it might look foolish, even crazy, if anyone saw me, I held out my hand to her. And walked up the stairs, feeling that somehow we actually were walking together hand in hand, and that it was cheering and comforting for her.

On the morning of her funeral, I came early to say goodbye to her alone. We had not been particularly close but shared the pleasant friendliness common to our community. As I knelt next to her coffin and gazed at her now-peaceful face, I had a sudden intense spiritual experience of what I could only identify as heaven. The power and beauty were so overwhelming that I felt as if the greatest earthly beauties of Nature and of humanity that I had ever experienced were nothing in comparison—just dust and ashes, and no more, compared to this staggering, inexpressible, magnificent, ineffable beauty. It was one of only two experiences like this that I have had in my life and was deeply strengthening to my faith. I felt that it was a gift from the deceased woman, a very great gift in return for a very small gesture—because I had stretched out my hand.

Eye hath not seen, nor ear heard, neither have entered into the heart of man, the things which God hath prepared for them that love Him. (1 Cor. 2:9)

رَبِّ

Calling on the Saints

I had an experience of the glories beyond conception and the marrow-deep peace of heaven once again in my life when, several years later, I had a dream about St. Paraskevi, the holy martyr and healer to whom my childhood church had been dedicated. Nothing actually "happened" in the dream. St. Paraskevi was merely present, standing there beaming at me in every sense of the word—so much light!—and her beauty alone was so great as to, again, make me reflect viscerally on all earthly beauty, even the greatest, as only dust and ashes. If I could have stayed gazing on her forever, drinking in the exquisite majesty and unutterable goodness of her being, I would have gladly and gratefully done so. But at last I had to wake up. Nonetheless, for many hours that day I still felt her deep, healing peace.

When in need, we may ask earthly friends for help, but, sadly, too often we neglect to ask as well these powerful holy ones, who are beyond the veil and thus positioned far better to give us aid.

Sometimes this is because we simply don't believe in them but sometimes because we think it better to just pray directly to God, as if we were visualizing the spiritual life as a major corporation where we must reach the CEO directly, without reference to those around him. But the Body of Christ is not like a corporation; it is like an exceedingly sweet though awesome family, all its members entwined round and round the blessedness of God. The saints listen. They hear and will help. They will magnify our prayers. We are not in some way disrespecting God or settling for a lower level when we pray to the saints. The purpose of their lives is to be our helpers.

Which does not mean that the saints are tame. Nothing truly of God is ever tame. If we wish to seek their guidance and help, we must be willing to engage with responses beyond our comfort zones. They may respond in unpredictable, unconventional ways.

Most people have seen photos of Saint Basil's, the elaborate Russian Orthodox church on Red Square in Moscow that is roofed with a jubilation of onion domes looking like giant ice cream cones covered with brightly colored sprinkles. So it can come as a shock, after the full-tilt-bougie decorativeness of its exterior, to see the very plain icon of the saint to whom the church is dedicated. St. Basil is portrayed as a slender, completely naked man. He is a saint of the type we call a "fool-for-Christ," owning nothing and, in his case, wearing nothing. He lived during the reign of the tsar Ivan the Terrible, and even defied that murderous monarch to his face, reproaching him for his violence—and for not paying attention in church! Nonetheless, Ivan the Terrible served as a pallbearer at the saint's funeral.

Fools-for-Christ live in ways that defy convention, both in their actions and their manner, and their strange symbolic gestures often have prophetic significance. Many of them have been seen, barely clothed, praying all night in the fields in all weathers. Some may curse at and even strike people—but later on, it is always shown to be for good cause—for healing or to awaken a sleeping soul to its danger or to offer up the sins of the people. They often show up at odd moments with strange messages, as, for example, when the great fool-for-Christ St. Xenia of Saint Petersburg dropped into the home of a young woman and ordered her to immediately go to a certain cemetery where "your husband is burying his wife." Obediently, the young woman leaped to her feet and hurried to the cemetery, arriving to see a coffin being placed in a grave. A young man, the husband of the deceased, fainted into her arms. She gently revived him and they became acquainted, falling in love. Eventually, he proposed to her.

In more recent times Blessed Theoktista Michailovna of Voronezh, a small, skinny woman with noble features, walked around in huge soldiers' boots with untied laces, splashing through puddles until the boots filled with water. She would slosh on, leaning on her cane. One man who knew her said, "She would walk and be swearing a blue streak—but at the same time she would be looking with the kindest eyes." In the big public square in Voronezh, lined with official buildings and Chekist guards, there were also monuments to Lenin and Stalin. In front of everyone, Blessed Theoktista went up to these statues and peed on them, making a puddle. Promptly arrested by the outraged guards, she was taken to the office of the commandant in the Chekist headquarters. Seeing his desk covered with his official papers, at a time when thousands of innocent people were being murdered by decree, the little saint climbed up on his desk and pooped on his business. The stunned chief detained but then released her as "abnormal." He undoubtedly wanted to get as far away from her as he could!

Saint John Maximovich the Wonderworker of San Francisco, Paris, and Shanghai, a contemporary saint, was both a bishop and a fool-for-Christ, an unusual combination. When he was archbishop of Paris, he customarily went around barefoot, thus offending some of his fellow bishops who thought it undignified. They complained to Saint John's superior, who promptly wrote him a letter instructing him to wear shoes. But the letter was in French and utilized the verb *porter*, which means "to wear" but also "to carry." So, Saint John obediently began going around—though still barefoot—carrying his shoes in the crook of one arm!

In our church we regarded Saint John Maximovich as our "spiritual grandfather," as our spiritual father had been one of his disciples, and we often prayed to him. We found that he would still respond to prayer, sometimes in a quixotic, fool-for-Christ fashion.

A headhunter once interviewed my husband for a sales position (on the heels of his having been the top salesman for a solar hot-water company). The position was with an insurance company in, of all places, Ohio. We were interested in neither the job nor the location, but the company was willing to fly Mark out for an interview. I didn't think that Mark should pursue it, but he was determined to, in the hopes of being able to lift us out of poverty at last, given the quoted salary.

Of course, we prayed about it to many saints, including *Vladika* (a respectful and affectionate term for a bishop) John. I would sit down at the shrine and pray about the job offer, while meditatively contemplating *Vladika* John's icon.

Startlingly, he seemed to shout at me from his icon, "No! No!"
"What?"

"No! No! NO!!!" silently reverberated in my head. Once could
have been just a freak event, but after this had happened a few
times, I became seriously alarmed. Mark did not have any negative experiences in prayer about this job pursuit, but I also think
his mind was made up and left no space for reconsideration. I
was worried and begged Mark not to go to Ohio. He would not
budge. And, coward that I was, I stopped praying to *Vladika* John
altogether and slunk by the shrine, avoiding eye contact with his
icon!

Three days before Mark's flight, he came down with a bad cold
and got very stuffed up. Two days before, while we were at a gas
station, he managed to mysteriously smack his face into a pole after
he opened his car door (to this day I cannot figure out how it was
possible; it seemed like an acrobatic feat).

He developed a lovely shiner on one eye as a result. Now I
begged him—I really didn't think that the "accident" was acci-
dental—to please cancel his interview and trip. "Don't you think
that *Vladika* John may be giving you a hint? You're hardly in good
condition now for an interview!"

Mark remained adamant. Although, through utilizing alternating homeopathic remedies, I was able to get rid of most of the dark
bruising around his eye, on D-day the area was still swollen and,
between that and his stuffed sinuses, gave him a bit of an enlarged-
brow Frankenstein aura—hardly ideal for a business interview.

Mark flew off to Ohio and spent the day in the field with a
supervisor, seeing how the company did business door to door
and in the office. Toward the end of the day he went to his interview with the CEO. Their conversation went well at first; my husband's sales record was impressive, and he could speak with an
easy, engaging charm. The CEO began to indicate that the job was
Mark's if he wanted it. Did he have any questions?

"Yes," Mark said. And the conversation went downhill from
there. Mark had observed some company practices that he felt
were ethically dubious and he wanted an explanation. The CEO
quickly became icy and distant. It was clear that they did not want
anyone with such questions working for them. Mark flew home
without the job but with his integrity intact. And, had we listened
to St. John, he could have been saved much time, pain, trouble,
and, I believe, a shiner! When you call on the saints, anything
can happen!

ॐ

The People's Republic of Cambridge Meets the Saints

My dear friend and goddaughter Anna Elisabeth and I sometimes offered women's evenings at our church, which were often classes on women saints, along with group prayer, contemplation, and hymn singing. It was remarkable and inspiring how different each saint was, especially when read in the often quite detailed hagiography of the Orthodox Church. The idea of a pale pasteboard "saint type," bland and wan, as if manufactured on some kind of dull metaphysical assembly line, could not have been further from the truth. And coming to know each unique personality a little better and approaching them in prayer brought great joy.

After a while Anna and I began to feel that we should spread this joy beyond our church, into the spiritually thirsty world— and decided to try to offer similar classes at Cambridge Adult Education in Harvard Square. We realized that in this venue it would be more in keeping to offer classes on Marxism or art appreciation or fine-tuning one's espresso-making skills, but we applied anyway, were accepted, and, by the time we reached the evening of our first class, found that there were eleven women enrolled in our first "Women Saints" class.

Anna and I prepared the room with dozens of icons on tables covered with beautiful cloths and small vases of flowers, each icon with its own small candle. Between us on a little table was a tall cast-iron candelabra bearing twelve long candles. We planned to have the lights completely off for our two-hour classes, even using tapers to read our notes, as we had found that the nervous jitter accompanying electric lights tended to make it harder for our participants to let go and enter a meditative space, unlike the welcoming embrace of soft candlelight. We turned on a lovely tape of Orthodox nuns chanting hymns as our first students entered our gently lit room, breathing in the delicate fragrance rising from incense in a burner that Anna carefully superintended. Yes, all this was against fire regulations, but we had gotten an informal nod to proceed from an official, with us swearing to be very careful.

Once all were settled in, Anna and I said a short prayer and launched into a beautiful hymn with a haunting minor melody. Just as our voices soared in gentle exaltation, we all became privy to the disconcerting fact that, on the other side of an extremely thin wall, dwelt an Italian class, awakened suddenly as if by a cymbal crash to charge into loud, vigorous verb conjugations, sounding like a phalanx of robust Roman warriors yelling war cries as they fell upon invading Goths. These high-volume conjugators blew us right out of the water. Even before we all stopped laughing unto tears, Anna and I knew that our second class would definitely have to be in a new location.

We asked our participants to introduce themselves, giving their names and saying something about themselves and why they were there. The mix of people was broad, both age-wise and temperamentally. For example, we had an older woman with a Harvard Divinity School PhD and a college student who introduced herself as a "Jewish lesbian atheist." We were dubious about what the appeal might be for the latter, but she turned out to be a faithful student. Once, when we asked her privately how she was managing with potential worldview conflicts, she said she was doing fine—and added that she actually didn't care what we said specifically; she just "loved everything that came out of our mouths." We could only account for this by a possible sensitivity on her part to the spiritual beauty of the Holy Spirit, who, despite our mangling, often seemed to visit our class.

We taught the classes on and off for about three years, even gaining a couple of faithful male students, and a small group that wanted more and different types of classes (for example, on the sacraments); we held these privately outside the school.

I also gave a slideshow talk on icons for the school's public lecture series, and Anna and I held two full-day seminars: one on St. John Maximovich the Wonderworker (my "No!"-shouter), and the other one on the life of the Virgin Mary. In keeping closer company with the saints as we shared their lives and presence, it was as if a tangible cloud of witnesses, a white-hot lightning-like blaze of light, began accompanying Anna and me in daily life—and demanding its own purifications on our parts in order to be able to endure such blessed but high-octane companionship. The saints are "available", but keeping company with them leads inevitably to changes within ourselves—often not comfortable but ultimately an enrichment, a healing, and a blessing. And its own wild ride. Yes, definitely not tame at all.

੭ೊ

The Saint Mary of Bethany Society

Sitting on my low backless storytelling chair under a pink draped canopy crowned with a wreath of flowers, I looked out at a room of ten young girls pretty as flowers themselves, their dresses spread around them like graceful pastel petals on chairs and floor cushions. Candles were lit on shelves and tables before icons. A long dining table beautifully draped in damask was set for the celebratory meal that would soon follow. We were gathering in a special place, our own festive set-apart place, since we had special things to talk about together.

This was a meeting of the Saint Mary of Bethany Society, an organization for Christian girls ages seven to seventeen, founded by *Diaconissa* Mary Seraphima Williamson and me. Our group met in private homes, holding five-hour monthly "theological teas" where we prayed, sang, told and listened to stories, studied Scripture, learned the lives of saints and stories of the feasts, contemplated meaningful fairy tales ("not true on the outside but true on the inside"), asked theological questions (for which we did not always have the answers), worked on related craft projects, and shared experiences. Two dedicated adult women from our church assisted us, and two gifted artists generously designed our handsome craft projects.

We always had an open time for questions, telling our girls that we might not know the answers but that we could research them and also later consult with our priests. We committed ourselves to an atmosphere of unconditional love, supportive to each girl individually and to the whole group. The atmosphere was pious but also fun, refreshing, and relaxed. No one was ever mocked or made uncomfortable. This lovingly positive (but not saccharine) atmosphere was an important part of our program, and created an encouraging foundation of safety, freeing the girls to explore. As Marilyn McEntyre points out in her wise book, *Caring for Words in a Culture of Lies*, "we inflict corrosive kinds of irony even upon the very young. From Sesame Street onward, sarcasm, mild insults, and ironic banter take the place of story or sustained conversation." We wanted to have a shared conversation with each other untainted by such subtle but widely accepted poisons. We wanted our girls to experience the real life-giving joy of a genuinely Christian, openhearted gathering.

Like so much else worthwhile in my life, I had also resisted founding this group. After I had been on a pilgrimage to the Holy Land and Greece and then spent six weeks in an Orthodox theological academy in California, I came back feeling as if I needed to respond to a calling to found this group. The calling had been present for three years—ever since I noticed a certain glaze on the eyes of some of our church's girls and recognized it as "cradle Orthodox tuning out," the phenomenon of being raised in a religion but not yet making it one's own. As a cradle Orthodox myself I was uniquely placed to perceive this and work with it; the girls' parents, converts having come to Orthodox Christianity with zeal, did not always realize that their daughters needed to make the very same journey to a deeper personal relationship with their faith.

Although I felt this calling, I had also felt inadequate to lead such a group, due both to my ignorance and my personal deficiencies. Who was I to try to help young and pure souls? But after those pilgrimage journeys, while staying at Saint Xenia's monastery in the rugged Northern California mountain woodlands of Wildwood, I felt as if St. Xenia herself gave me a kick: "Do it now. The need is there. God will help you and give the increase." So I did.

And now I was sitting in this gathering of smiling girls, looking into their trusting flower faces, as one bright-eyed girl raised her hand with a question. "Yes, Evgenia?" I said.

"Well, what I always wanted to know was why they cut off Jesus's hair around his private parts?"

I sat in stunned silence, looking desperately at the faces of my three adult colleagues, who were barely containing big grins as they discreetly savored my moment on the dreadful hot seat. As their twinkling eyes told me, they were obviously not going to offer an answer! Traitors!! *Why me, Lord?* I silently whined.

The girls gazed at me expectantly, the silence was lengthening, and I was aging fast. *Help, Lord! Saint Mary? Anyone?*

I didn't want to embarrass this child and I didn't want to shock or scandalize anyone. And I certainly didn't want to use the "p-word"! So, after a rather curt silent prayer, I heard myself, as if summoning up a dry-as-dust file from a remote government bureaucracy, embarking on an opaque, not-too-specific description of circumcision (since this was my best guess of what she was probably asking about. *Please let it be that, God!*). A standard encyclopedia description would have been wildly more exciting than my colorless offering! Lamely, I ended my "explanation," thinking she would never be satisfied with such a dull, vague response. But, to my surprise, Evgenia just smiled at me and said, "Yes, thank you. That's what I wanted to know."

Thank you, thank you, for small miracles, Lord.

Our society thrived for six years, and once a year we spent a day at a local Greek Orthodox women's monastery, a cherished outing. The nuns were wonderful to us and took the girls through the convent, showing them the iconographers at work, the nuns sewing vestments, the beeswax-candle makers, the nuns making prayer ropes and buttons with the icons of saints, and generally sharing their life. We worshipped with them in their beautiful chapel and ate in the refectory, listening to a nun reading saints' lives, as is the tradition, during the meal. The girls looked forward to an hour in the afternoon spent with the abbess, the gracious Mother Seraphima, who, accompanied by the kindly steward, Mother Martha, would give us a fine homily and then answer the girls' questions. Mother Seraphima had a beautiful voice with an unusual rich patina resembling the warm tone of a violin, and we enjoyed hearing her lovely chanting, along with the other nuns, fine singers all, during the services. Mother Seraphima was humble and shy, and seemed to feel that she was "not good with children"—but she was actually quite good. As the date of our visit approached and I contemplated our usual session with the abbess, I thought about little Evgenia's question and wondered if the child had truly been satisfied with my answer. I felt a frisson of horror about this challenging question possibly popping up again at the convent. I debated whether to write Mother Seraphima to give her a heads-up, just in case. Finally, I did so.

When we arrived at the monastery that morning, sharp-eyed Mother Thecla met us at the door. "Welcome, welcome, girls!" she exclaimed. "Welcome, Stephani!" And leaning over their heads, she whispered, "Which one is Evgenia?" Ahem. I saw that all the nuns, or at least the senior ones, had enjoyed my letter! Thankfully, that afternoon Mother Seraphima was spared this tricky question and had only to answer questions about whether, if you became a nun, you could watch TV, have cats, and visit your family. God is merciful.

Our society also took an annual weekend retreat at the home of Jeanette Robinson, one of our adult helpers. The girls were enthusiastic about visiting Jeanette's lovely home in a shady woodland and participating in a more intensive retreat. Each retreat had a theme—for example, Celtic saints, fools-for-Christ, saints and animals, angels—which we explored in various media.

I think we especially enjoyed the retreat on angels. I showed the girls the enormous volume, more than two inches thick, of *The New Strong's Exhaustive Concordance of the Bible* ("You have to be strong to pick it up, and it's exhausting to hold"), pointing out that there were more than three hundred entries about angels in the Bible. I then handed out slips of paper with assorted Biblical verses about angels and asked various girls to read them out loud. Invariably, they read that people fell down in awe and fear when encountering an angel. Then I whipped out a syrupy card with simpering cherubs on it and held it up. "So what's wrong with this picture?"

They laughed, but they also recognized that our culture trivialized and thereby denied the existence of angels. I wanted them to take this in but had no idea that I could thereby be creating spiritual vigilantes! One girl, a priest's daughter whose mother loved cherubs, went home after the weekend and started ruthlessly removing cherubs from their home's décor! Her mother called me, bewildered, as her chubby-cheeked winged tots disappeared from view, now stashed deep in dark closets. Her daughter, embarked wholeheartedly on cherubicide, could not be deterred. One of the most faithful of our members and a generous girl, when the time for her birthday party came around, she actually asked her friends to, in lieu of presents, make a financial contribution to the St. Mary of Bethany Society! I was deeply touched.

We had fun as we studied together, even as we probed deep subjects like eschatology, or "last things"—death, judgment, the final destiny of souls individually and collectively, the "last days" (which many of the girls turned out to be preoccupied with). The Orthodox Church encourages its members to read the Book of Revelation, but it is never read in church, out of a prudent concern that it can be open to many different interpretations, alarming to parishioners. I figured that if we didn't read it in the St. Mary of Bethany Society, the girls might never get around to it. So, armed with two guidebooks (one by the great Archbishop Averky— memory eternal!) and cautioning all that we couldn't interpret its verses definitively, we took the plunge into the Apocalypse—an adventure that the girls found fascinating.

One day as I worked at home on our next eschatology class, I read the verses about the angels blowing their horns and the terrible destruction around the Apocalypse. When I reached the section about the world's waters being poisoned in thirds—"And the second angel sounded . . . and the third part of the sea became blood; and the third part of the creatures which were in the sea, and had life, died; and the third part of the ships were destroyed. And the third angel sounded, and there fell a great star . . . upon the third part of the rivers, and upon the fountains of waters; And the name of the star is called Wormwood: and the third part of the waters became wormwood; and many men died of the waters, because they were made bitter." (Rev. 8:8–11)—I decided I had had enough horror for the afternoon. Getting up to make a cup of tea, I casually flipped the radio on.

A man's heavy, solemn voice rang through the Gnome Home kitchen: "We now know that two-thirds of the earth's waters have been poisoned."

I almost dropped the cup! NPR was broadcasting a special report on the state of the world's waters. Talk about knowing the signs of the times! (Later I was also to discover that the translation of the name Chernobyl is "wormwood.")

෧

The society was named for Saint Mary of Bethany, the sister of
Saints Lazarus and Martha. I dedicated it to her because I wanted
to emphasize the devotional and mystical, as opposed to outer-ser-
vice, nature of our group. The young St. James of Borovichi, a
doozie of a fool-for-Christ saint (even among fools-for-Christ),
was our secondary patron. Just before our very first session, one
of our adult helpers, whom we will call Veronica, had a meltdown
ten minutes or so before the girls were to arrive. "I can't do this!"
she cried. "Why am I doing this? I don't even like children!" (Not
actually true.) She was semi-hysterical. We could not calm her. I
prayed and grabbed the icon of Saint Mary of Bethany, making
the sign of the Cross over Veronica with it. Instantly she calmed
down. And we were able to proceed. For the next six years.

But each year we four adults had to recommit ourselves to
another year of this labor because we found that, as well as extensive preparation time, we were regularly punished by hostile unseen
influences obviously displeased with our efforts. We all found
that one to two weeks before each session, many things would
start going wrong with our lives, and unforeseen problems arose.
Sometimes they were small and petty—for example, my going to a
copier store to copy multiple pages for the girls for our next session,
only to find four copy machines breaking down, one after another, as I tried to use them. The clerks in this store started viewing
me as if I were Typhoid Mary, and I had to make a hasty retreat.
Not long after, Mary Seraphima, also trying to copy for the society at a different store, had three copy machines break down, one
after another. The timing of the unwelcome, unexpected events,
including people being gratuitously nasty to us, made it clear that
someone was trying to discourage us, along the lines of "no good
deed goes unpunished." But this low-level harassment, really further proof that what we were doing was worthwhile, only made us
more determined to endure the lumps and continue our project.

Although our emphasis remained on our inner lives, as was the
case with our patroness who sat at our Lord's feet and was one of
the two women to anoint them with her tears and dry them with
her hair (Orthodox tradition allows for two women and two incidents, rather than just one), we did do one work of material service,
Saint Martha-like: we held several bake sales to raise funds to buy
our church a pair of beautiful tall angelic fans, *exapteryga*, used
for processions and to guard the altar and Gospel. When we had
saved up enough money to purchase them, one Sunday our girls
processed into the chapel, singing, to present the shining brass

fans on long varnished poles, their gleaming circles portraying the many-winged seraphim, for the altar. To my surprise, it felt as if, like some kind of tiny mystical army, we were being carried forward on a huge wave of dense and powerful archangelic presence, formidable as a Bay of Fundy tide. We felt the reverberating blessing to our toes. Never doubt, never doubt, that the unseen ones are with us. And that even our smallest gestures are well received.

·ℓ·

Travails of the Veil: The Enclosed Garden
I was annoyed. I had heard a rumor that women in a sister parish out of state, converts to Orthodoxy (as in our church), were starting to wear head scarves in services. Head scarves! That symbol of oppression! My blood went on slow boil.

When I was a child, the women and girls in my Orthodox church did wear head scarves—mostly attractive lace mantillas. Yes, they were aesthetically pleasing, but for me they became the resented symbol of every inequality I felt I had witnessed perpetuated against women in the Church. Hearing that women in former Holy Order of MANS Christian Communities might be starting to don them enraged me.

So I phoned the priest of the congregation in question, an old friend. "What's this I hear about women in your church starting to wear head scarves?" I asked, an edge of hostility in my voice.

"Well, yes," he answered mildly. "It wasn't my suggestion but some of them just took it up."

"Why?!"

"I don't know exactly. Maybe because it's a tradition."

"How does it benefit them in any way?"

"Well, that's the interesting thing. They have been finding that it makes them feel more . . . uh . . . graceful. Graceful and graced."

This observation was so out of left field that it left me speechless. Despite myself, very reluctantly, I could feel some undertone of truth vibrating through his remark.

"Oh."

After I further reassured myself that there was no pressure, especially from men, being exerted to further this scarf adoption, I hung up the phone and sat in silence for a while, perplexed.

·ℓ·

On Pentecost Sunday I was in the chapel early before divine liturgy. My husband was to be baptized that day, along with some other parishioners. He was busy somewhere else in the church, and I was sitting alone in a front pew, praying. Suddenly I felt as if there were a large number of unseen holy angelic beings churning in dense clouds before me, in constant movement, filling all the space between myself and the sanctuary.

As I sat there, dumbstruck, a faint aching began on top of my head, in the crown chakra area. Then a strange thought marched through my mind: *I wish I had a nice solid piece of cloth to put on my head.*

Yerch!!! Who said that?! A sudden interior vision appeared, as if on a movie screen: outlined in light were subtle diagrams representing inner structuring in men and women. The male image was a convex shape, a kind of dome, while the female image was a concave shape, like a chalice. Communicated along with these images was a thought that because of this inner structure, women were inherently more receptive than men and thus could be subject at times to an overly intense and destabilizing reception of downpouring mystical energy. And that this instability could be offset by—yes, dadgummit!—a physical covering on top of the head! *Grrrrr!* But it just felt true. As I sat there, the pain on top of my head increased. And was with me at any time I prayed for weeks afterwards, except—of course—when I put a piece of cloth on my head, protecting the cranial tenderness! In self-defense, I began wearing a head scarf at times of prayer, both public and private, and even began to appreciate its sheltering aspect psychologically over time.

Later I heard an American Mevlevi Sufi shaikh mention that this particular female receptive susceptibility could be an issue for certain women learning to do the Mevlevi turn (think whirling dervishes), but these dervishes had at least the protection of their *sikke* (tall hats).

The wearing of scarves and veils are hot issues in our times, from the tent-like hijab of certain Muslim women to the shorter scarves of a number of other religious groups. In either case, this veiling element can be viewed as an oppression, a negation, and a hindrance, or, conversely, as a protection, a refuge, and an act of modesty and independence. It's not possible for us to explore this surprisingly immense subject here, and given its large spectrum of variation, I don't want to generalize about it. I will say that, as in anything else involved in the spiritual life, I think it is beneficial to try to get out of knee-jerk reactions to what cloth on the head might mean in different situations and for different individuals, realizing that differences of opinions are not necessarily contradictions nor easy to unravel.

Beyond this particular issue, the veiled aspect of the Feminine, which should be regarded with the deepest respect, is neither a punishment nor an imprisonment due to inferiority but something unique in its own right: a protection and a concentration of powers; an undiluted purity. This condition should not be and cannot be something imposed from without but rather must be something arising from within, treasured in each individual woman. Its power is related to the phenomenon of the "enclosed garden."

One time, in a Christian women's group I belonged to dedicated to prayer, contemplation, singing, and sacred dance that met monthly for three years, we came up with, out of prayer and meditation, a theme for our next meeting: the Enclosed Garden. When we met that time, a new woman joined us, saying that she felt she had to come because of our chosen theme. Recently she had had a dream about an enclosed garden. The garden was within her; it was small and round, surrounded by high hedges, with a beautiful statue of the Virgin Mary at its center. She felt extraordinary peace and loveliness within it. It occurred to her that she should shorten the hedge so that more people could see in and enjoy it. She was about to start clipping the tall hedge down when an authoritative angelic voice stopped her, forbidding her to do it. The voice told her, instead, to grow the hedge even higher. She was left in perplexity and had come to our group seeking an epiphany about this—to her—strange counsel.

In the course of our group contemplation, it became clear that keeping an inner core in our hearts uninterfered with and undiluted by even the polite attention of others, and unknown to anyone but ourselves and God, creates a well of pure, living water, feeding deep inner richness and creativity, as well as an authentic, wordless sense of ourselves. Exposure can only weaken that inherent power and authenticity, like roots torn out of moist soil and exposed unnaturally to the hot, drying sun. In our noisy, restless, tell-all culture, we are too often ignorant of the benefits and power of contained experience that is shared only with the Highest and His immaterial spiritual servants. Perhaps also, we, especially women, may be influenced by a feeling that we have to justify our existence by explanation, by what we construct as an act of sharing, whether we are prompted to it by our deepest instincts or not—that we are not good enough just as we already are to have a rightful and accepted and honorable place in the Creation without such gestures. But, within the enclosed garden, we are whole and sufficient, infinitely reachable by the wise and tender touch of the Holy Spirit. And the enclosed garden is full of fertile if unseen life, as in the womb which is itself both a veil and an enclosed garden of creation.

One of the ninety-nine beautiful names of God noted within Islam is *Ya Batin*, "the Veiled One." It means "the hidden treasure." In the brilliant *Physicians of the Heart*, the authors state that "Another way of saying this is to say that God is the inward, without being inside of anything. . . ." In other words, this aspect of God is infinitely spacious, despite its sheltering containment. The potential for everything, limitless depths, lies beneath the veil.

I think this is a possible clue to the feminine aspect of God. Yes, God is not a guy. Though He contains "guyness." In Genesis, we are told that God created humans male and female in His own image, so both are part of the inherent nature of God. He encompasses them but is not defined by either. The name "Allah," and its Aramaic and Hebrew antecedents, is neither male nor female. And Christians in the Middle East were using the word "Allah" for God (as well as the Arabic word "*Quddus*," Holy Spirit) for hundreds of years before Islam ever arose. And do so to this day.

So, why "He"? It has been the default general pronoun in both English and Arabic since well back in history and can be used as a generalized indicator (as in "brethren") rather than a strictly masculine one. But can also mislead us into the idea of a male singularity, a "male" God.

However, one of the reasons I don't mind using it, for lack of an acceptable alternative, is that I associate the masculine to some degree with outward-moving force and the feminine with inward-concentrating force. These are equal in power and authority but not necessarily recognized as such by a relentlessly outward-concentrated society. To our loss.

But, if such is the case, then we don't meet the Great Feminine in the out-reaching gestures of God; rather we must go inward, descend into its luminous mystery, to begin to absorb its true nature and meaning. This does not limit women's temperaments to a particular "type"—the Great Feminine's nature is veiled but unconfining—warrior or temple virgin, choleric or gentle, and anything imaginable can take genuine roots from the concentrated but unlimited depths of the authentic feminine aspect of God. But this "She" aspect is mystically interior—while "He" does, "She" draws us into her depths—a different direction of movement. And this veiled and potent nature is something we hunger to know, whether we recognize it or not.

I have been a feminist since the late 1960s, but I try not to surrender to the seduction of being too simplistic in my feminism. Yes, God is also She. But it would be an impoverishment of mystical conception to automatically assume that the She part looks and functions identically to the He part. And, really, it would be illogical—as well as, um, boring—to expect them to be the same.

And so why am I, who spent many years in a Christian congregation that had women as well as men priests, now with a Church in which priests are only male? There are several parts to the answer. The first is out of obedience—feeling so strongly that inner call to where I feel God wants me to be and which brings peace and joy to my soul; I feel that real obedience (as opposed to a simulacrum forced on us by others) is part of the Gospel "precious pearl of great price." Second, I have not found the magnitude of spiritual treasure carried by the ancient Eastern Orthodox Church equaled elsewhere in my experience. I feel it would be foolish not to drink in these living waters. Last, the ordination of women deacons still exists in the canons of the Orthodox Church and was for centuries an active ministry. Strong movements, which I fully support, are currently working to revive this important spiritual expression. Now it remains for some of our bishops to stand up and have the courage and integrity to ordain women deacons, as the great St. Nectarios did during the twentieth century. I feel that that day will come. May God grant!

And as to women priests: my own experience with the Holy Order of MANS indicates to me that the Lord did not disdain or flee from women as liturgical celebrants or pastors. I could feel nothing deviant or inadequate about these priests' offering of the Holy Eucharist; rather, I experienced great blessing. But as to whether there should eventually be Orthodox Christian women priests, I must honestly say that I do not know the answer to that question. What may seem obvious answers to either viewpoint may not always be the God-pleasing answers. Perhaps time and the Holy Spirit will reveal. May God's will be done.

☙

Oh yes, and let us not forget about the cats. Most often women do not go into the sanctuary behind the icon screen (except, often, elderly ladies blessed to clean—hmm, why is that?). I should add that women can enter at need with a bishop's blessing (which I and a number of women I know have). However, female cats can enter—and male cats are excluded! How can this be? Cats are valued for keeping mice away from the holy bread; they are little warriors and protectors. But since male cats spray, ironically their stinkinesses are not welcome in the sacred precincts. Hah!

Many years ago in my old church I was resting quite alone

in our main room when there was a knock on the church door. Answering it, I looked down upon a small group of men in black robes on the outside stairs. In the center stood a tiny wizened old man with a bishop's staff. He did not speak English, but one of his accompanying entourage explained that he was an Old Calendar Greek bishop who wished to visit our church and see our chapel. I asked them to please wait while I phoned Fr. Zeno. They entered but, insisting they had no time to wait, asked that their bishop merely be allowed to view our chapel. I could hardly refuse and so brought them up the many stairs to our second floor.

Entering the nave a few steps before the bishop and his entourage turned the corner into the chapel, I stopped, frozen with horror. Like an aerialist playing showily to the crowd, our church cat Buffy, a benign, slightly portly gray tiger-striped feline, was high-stepping daintily and slowly all the way across the very top of our icon screen, chin high in dignity. Oh no! Perhaps the bishop would be shocked and think we were aberrant cat worshippers or some other variety of weirdness! I shuddered at the thought of having to explain this cat exaltation, not having any explanation to begin with. But, just as His Grace stepped into the chapel, Buffy, her prescient cat instincts lighting up, smoothly leapt down and disappeared, unseen by our holy tourists. I breathed again. After a short tour, the bishop and his entourage left. And, finding Buffy, I settled down with a sigh in a pew to give her a very grateful cuddle.

⟨ornament⟩

Lost in the Desert: The Dueling Dragons, Power and Love

> *Maybe we simply don't want our leaders to have needs. Maybe it's not only the leaders who think they should be perfect; maybe it's also their followers who expect them to have it all together. Maybe we want the people who care for us and lead us not to be like us, to not struggle like us, because if we realize they, too, are hurting and needy, then maybe the spell—the illusion that we're okay, that we're in good hands—breaks.*
>
> —Pastor Nadia Bolz-Weber

Joining a church is like diving into the sea. You enter an unpredictable vastness, surging with strange tides and swirling with both beauties and dangers. Just keeping afloat will make you use interior muscles you didn't even know you had—sometimes to the point of exhaustion on every level and what can feel like the brink of ruin—until you find yourself saved by strange graces, like that dolphin back rising unexpectedly under your drowning body to carry you up to the sweet air. Disconcerting confrontations also arise in these tides where you are swirled around so strongly with others, one of the most difficult being when your pastor seems untrustworthy, perhaps overwhelmed in a rogue wave of his or her own unexamined inner weaknesses, and its stunning wave-weight descends upon you or those you love.

There were up to four priests at one time in my old church. They were all very different personalities. And each of them was kind, loving, intelligent, generous, and helpful to my husband and me at various times. For which I was and am grateful. But there were also painful conflicts, with fallout often devastating to us and to others.

One night I was the lead Reader during a vigil (Great Vespers and Matins), assisted by my friend and goddaughter Gabriella. A priest whom we shall call Father Zaccheus was serving. Father Zaccheus was a kindly man but also suffered from emotional instability and insecurity. I don't know what was tormenting him, but he had, a few times when he was serving alone, tried to end a vigil mid-service, even when the chapel was filled with worshippers. The Reader who trained me (and who is now a Ukrainian Orthodox deacon) and I felt that we could not just stop the service dead when so many people were deep in prayer and the Holy Spirit seemed so much with us all—the very thing, I suspected, that was putting so much interior pressure on Father Zaccheus and perhaps spurring him to flee. So, the times our celebrant hurried precipitately out of the chapel, my mentor chanter and I simply continued the vigil as a Readers' service (an acceptable form, with the priest's and deacon's parts left out, and some small alterations), so as not to disturb the congregation's worship unduly.

The night in question I was chanting in the dimly lit chapel when I felt a psychic bolt of anger directed toward me come flying out of the sanctuary like a venom-bearing rocket. As it hit my atmosphere, the bolt seemed absorbed by a coating of impermeable green light that protected me from the shock and, though I was alarmed, allowed me to keep chanting uninterrupted. When I finished the verse, another Reader took up the next verse, and I was able to take a shaky breath. Gabriella, her face very white, looked at me and said, "Just then—when you were chanting—I suddenly had this terrible vision of Father Zaccheus's face. It was peeling off, like in a nightmare."

Holy Week and Pascha came soon after, and this sacred time,

always a challenge, turned out to be particularly difficult. Father Zeno and Father Zaccheus had long resented my necessary work as liturgical coordinator for Holy Week and Pascha; as they had neither attended seminary nor studied closely over years with a bishop (the two standard ways to be trained for Orthodox priesthood) in order to absorb the massive amount of information and spiritual formation involved in Orthodox Christianity, they needed help they could not easily get elsewhere. And, unfortunately for them and me both, I was mostly it, at least as far as the services went. (It should be said that they had been priests in the Holy Order of MANS for years and already had a flock that they were tending. Full-time caring for their congregation, as well as their family situations and low pay, did not allow them to take up seminary studies, had they wished to, as some other HOOM priests with inheritances or other connections had ultimately been able to do.)

One Pascha when the lead celebrant was Father Zaccheus, we experienced a strange chaos. Something must have come over him on Holy Saturday night because, as we were finishing chanting the Midnight Office in the chapel, darkened in preparation for the emergence of the Holy Light of the Resurrection at midnight, he sent out an altar server with a message to me on the *klíros*. The message left me gaping. He said he was not going to take the *Epitaphios*, the fabric icon of our dead Lord, into the altar nor have the altar servers put the bulky Tomb of Christ itself, the formerly flower-bedecked canopy bed in the front of the chapel, into the side altar at the appointed time. Why, and what was he thinking?

I went up to an angel door and knocked lightly on it. Father Zaccheus answered and, despite my protest, refused to change his mind. The result was that, at midnight, he emerged from the sanctuary into the chapel with the Holy Fire, announcing the Resurrection, alone (as he had forgotten to give the deacons and altar servers a blessing to come out with him), and raced forward, knocking against the Tomb as he manically lit people's candles and grabbed volunteers to carry banners for our procession outdoors. When Father Zaccheus banged into the Tomb, he inadvertently knocked off the top canopy part, which rested on a table base. Sitting in a front pew, our Sacristan Katie Stell leaped up and threw her body across the canopy section and icon to keep it all from crashing to the floor. All this drama threatened to turn the service into a circus.

Dumbfounded as we were, the choir and Readers were still forced to follow our impulsive priest outside, singing the processional hymn. Anna, who was singing beside me and also had a supervisory role for the Paschal service, alternated "Thy Resurrection, O Christ our Savior, the angels in heaven sing . . ." with "I'm going to murder him! I'm going to strangle him!" " . . . enable us on earth to glorify Thee with purity of heart. . . ." "I'm going to kill him!"

In the early A.M. of that night I lay down on the floor in one of the church rooms to get some sleep at last but not without a few frustrated tears and a strange plea to Saint John the Evangelist and Theologian, a saint whom, along with Saint Paraskevi, I regarded as one of my two personal mentors (I was born on his day on the Roman Catholic calendar). I felt shredded and worn out and angry and was surprised to hear myself shout interiorly, "*Saint John! Help me! I'm a woman and I need protection, and you are my protector! So please do it! Protect me!*" Feeling suddenly as if a huge weight had been lifted from my shoulders, exhausted, I fell directly asleep.

Our next Paschal service, the Agape Vespers, was held at 5:00 P.M. that Sunday. After the service, we had a dessert feast (a treat for everyone after the fasts of Lent). Father Zaccheus made his way over to me and asked if we could speak for a few moments. I was wary but agreed, and we found a quiet corner.

He said, "You know, I woke up early today and was reading the accounts of the Resurrection in my Bible. I began wondering why did the Lord appear first to the women after the Resurrection? Then I realized, of course, He did it because they were weaker."

Oh no, I thought. *This is beginning badly, and can it get worse?*

But, to my surprise, Father Zaccheus then looked me in the eyes and said, "And then I realized that I was jealous—jealous because He had come to you—and not to me. . . . I'm sorry."

I was stunned by his honesty and insight, and the courage and love it took for him to confess this weakness to me. We reconciled with a hug. And yet within me there remained a sadness; I could feel that his epiphany was as yet unstable in his being and might be swept away by older and darker forces.

&

When we first came into Orthodoxy, there were many matters, large and small, to sort out. One question was whether our Greek-American bishop would tonsure women Readers. "Tonsure" refers to the symbolic act of the bishop cutting off four small pieces of hair in the pattern of a cross on the head of a candidate during a service to give that person a blessing to take on some kind of spiritual office. It symbolizes becoming a willing slave for Christ. A similar cutting of hair takes place during the sacrament of Chrismation when a person commits herself to Christ. Two of my goddaughters felt especially strongly about being called to receive the Reader's tonsure and were thinking about leaving our church if it was denied. (One of them is now the abbess of a convent.)

So I called Father Zeno to ask him if he knew if Metropolitan Gerasimos tonsured women Readers.

"Oh, I don't think that he would do that," he said.

"Did he tell you that?" I asked him.

"No. But I don't think he would."

"Well, would you please ask him so that we know for sure? It's important to some of the women."

"No, I'm not going to ask him," he said huffily.

"Why not?"

"I'm just not going to. It's not necessary." End of conversation.

So I called Father Jacob, my former pastor, now in charge of a church in Atlanta. I knew that he was close to the metropolitan regarding organizational matters and thus might know. "No, I don't," he said. "But I'll call and ask him."

Within a day Father Jacob called me back and said that, yes, the bishop did tonsure women Readers. Before I could pass on the good news, I got an angry call from Father Zeno.

"Stephani, how dare you, how dare you go above my head to Fr. Jacob about the Readers' tonsure?"

"I didn't go above your head. He's my old pastor."

"I know that! This is my business! Don't ever do that again!"

It was painful to see how threatened Father Zeno felt by the relatively innocuous recognition and empowering of women as lower clergy, and how callously indifferent he was to whatever the women's own feelings might be about this—for them—important matter.

One of the hardest things to come to grips with in Church is the imperfections of our pastors. We often want the pastor to be "Perfect Daddy" (or, in some sects, "Perfect Mommy/Daddy"). And, due to our fear and weakness, we will often go far to preserve this illusion, even unto, at times, throwing our conscience and innocent lives under the bus. We will refuse to see the devastation that a misguided and unconscious or tempted pastor can wreak. A friend of mine was married to an Episcopalian minister who was a former Vietnam vet and an alcoholic who went into drunken rages and beat her. Finally, unable to bear her mistreatment, she confessed this situation to their rural congregation.

Rather than admit that their pastor had problems and take steps to seek help for him and for his wife, the whole congregation except for one woman turned their backs on the wife and cruelly ostracized her.

The misuse of pastoral power is a terrible thing, and I am not speaking here of sexual abuse only. Abuse comes in many forms, always devastating, whenever it sins against the holy dignity of the individual or the institution. It is a misuse of power. The pastor Tony Campolo suggests that there is a continuum that exists with Love at one end and Power at the other. The closer you get to one, he says, the further you are from the other. Think of Herod and think of Jesus on the Cross.

As Bishop Kallistos Ware points out in his essay on the spiritual guide in Orthodox Christianity:

> In the Orthodox tradition at its best, spiritual guides have always sought to avoid any kind of constraint and spiritual violence in their relations with their disciples. If, under the guidance of the Spirit, they speak and act with authority, it is with the authority of humble love. Anxious to avoid all mechanical constraint, they may sometimes refuse to provide their disciples with a rule of life, a set of external commands to be applied automatically. . ."the spiritual father is not a legislator but a mystagogue." He guides others, not by imposing rules, but by sharing his life with them.

"Do not force people's free will," said the Elder Barsanuphius. "The task of our spiritual father is not to destroy our freedom, but to assist us to see the truth for ourselves; not to suppress our personality, but to enable us to discover our own true self, to grow to full maturity and to become what we truly are."

A great temptation lurks for pastors to become a law unto themselves, inherently insular. For Orthodox priests, especially unseasoned converts dazzled by the accounts of *startzi* (holy elders) demonstrating holiness and spiritual gifts such as clairvoyance, there can be a temptation to become heavy-handed and even condescending in dealing with their flocks, both individually and as a group. In their insecurity, such pastors, taking to themselves the unwarranted status of elders of great insight and holiness, can begin to indulge themselves in a "my-way-or-the-highway" approach. As they take unto themselves a level of authority that is not truly theirs, they wreak damage upon the sensitive souls of their congregation. Both Bishop Kallistos Ware and the Reverend Deacon John Chryssavgis have written warningly about this species of pastoral sin. But too often these priests are not within reach

of a spiritual counselor able to reveal to them their error and problem. Parishioners leave such clergy situations crushed and often
wounded in their faith. Recently I talked with two teenagers who
left a church because the pastor, when hearing their confessions
(which is a sacrament of release, purification, and blessing), rather
than lifting them up and giving them hope and inspiration, only
increased their sense of guilt and heaviness of heart. They left the
freeing mystery of confession feeling far worse than when they
had come in! It was clear that the priest's own heavily judgmental
nature was interfering with both the nature of the sacrament and
the spiritual unfolding of these young lives.

At my old church we had additional difficulties. We learned
over time that there were serious problems with our bishop, one
of many being that he had perhaps not been totally honest with us
about the manner of his own consecration. The issue of dishonesty
aside, he was becoming revealed as uncanonical. This and other
conflicts led to our former HOOM parishes reluctantly breaking
with him en masse.

The arduous search for a new bishop began. Until we came
under the mantle of a successor, our priests could not perform
the sacraments, since formally they do this under the authority
of a bishop. For six long months our Sunday services consisted of
Typika (a type of nonsacramental worship held in place of divine
liturgy) and fervent *molebens* (an intercessory service, often to St.
John Maximovich) and *paraklesis* (the same to the Virgin Mary).
We were like the Israelites wandering in the desert, with the painful knowledge that we had sick members of our congregation who
might even die while we still had no sacramental home. But our
passionate desire for a "righteous home" made for beautiful, intense
prayer services, and God heard our prayers.

We were introduced to a seasoned, "very canonical" Bulgarian
bishop who was willing to consider taking us under his care. He
had spent many years in Communist prisons in his homeland.
Our congregation spent three days with him, listening and asking
all the hard questions (including, yes, that he tonsured women
Readers!). We could see that he listened carefully and openly. We
all began to fall a bit in love. The bishop decided to receive us, and
we decided to accept him.

Due to the uncanonical status of our first bishop, our new metropolitan insisted on redoing almost all religious initiations: ton-
sures and ordinations, marriages, and even a reconsecration of the
church building itself, an immense task. Clergy and their wives
were flown out to Ohio so that all our own "do-overs" could take
place in what the bishop felt was a properly consecrated building

before we reconsecrated our own! He was careful and meticulous. And warm and loving. And, as he said in his charming, somewhat original English, we soon found ourselves "in symphony" with one another.

ـﻟﮫ

The Forgiveness

"Let us embrace each other! Let us call 'brothers' even those who hate us and forgive all by the Resurrection!" These words from Paschal Matins are being sung very softly by the choir as all the members of our church stand in the aisles, bowing down or even prostrating to each other individually, both asking and giving forgiveness. This special Forgiveness Vespers marks the first evening of Great Lent. We are taking our first penitent steps on the stony road to the Passion, the Cross, and beyond, into the Light of the Resurrection. The forgiveness offered and received here is not conditional. It is offered to friend and stranger alike because we have all sinned against each other by both commission and omission, what we have done and what we have not done. No one is completely untouched by our iniquities, their fallen vibrations swimming out in the human atmospheric sea, and no one, including ourselves, is beyond the generous forgiveness that pours in loving purity from the immeasurable heart of God. So, I say here earnestly to all of you, those who read, those whom I have written about, even those I will never meet, *Forgive me, a sinner. I forgive you. God bless us all.*

CHAPTER TWELVE

Catching on: Subtle Conversations with Plants, Birds, Animals, and Spirits

The Tipi Quest

The mountainside shook with thunder. Blasts of lightning wrenched its unfamiliar contours—and that of the sweeping valley and mountains beyond—in and out of darkness. Although it was an August night in the Green Mountains of West Roxbury, Vermont, the air, cold and fiery with this unseasonable storm, felt like chilled metal laid against our skin. But we were too mesmerized to pull on sweaters, hypnotized by the erratic, strobing detonations of light so bright as to negate color. The starkly revealed trees and grass blades, painted icy blue-white by each violent slap of lightning, looked like hundreds of skinny New England farmers caught frozen in their long underwear by the same hyperactive flash photographer. Peculiarly, although every detail and fleck was made visible by this X-ray light, all individuality seemed blotted out at the same time, a paradox I had no time to contemplate as I bent over our crumpled directions with a dim flashlight. Squinting vainly through the monsoon, Mark cautiously steered our little tin can of a car around the shipwrecks of fallen tree limbs and potholes aspiring to pondhood.

Crescendoing crash-and-rumbles blotted out half our conversations so that they seemed like interrupted Morse code messages in which too often only the unimportant words stood out: "The *crash–bang–bang–rumble* isn't *crash–crash*, right?"

We crept more and more slowly along the lonely dirt road that was rapidly condensing into pudding, a road we had never driven before, a lightless road lined with wild woods, a road that held somewhere in a crook of its arm the lost little meadow we were seeking. What had driven us out into this raging, sorcerous night that had extinguished the white pinnacles of the Vermont churches in their serene green valleys like weak candle flames and, changeling-like, substituted this wave-tossed Wagnerian darkness—silver-streaked, percussive, knife-edged, and bitter as a glance from Ahab's eye?

Yes, *guidance*—of course.

Dear reader, I know you are very surprised.

It was our unpaid month off from the group home. Not only that but we had to vacate our Rockport cottage every August to accommodate an elderly lady who had used it as a summer retreat for years. But, as usual, God had His own big plans for us while we were in our temporary vagabond state. It had all started so quietly and innocuously.

The Eleventh Commandment Fellowship was an ecologically oriented program of the Holy Order of MANS. Our Boston chapter met once a month for informative ecological programs, the formulation of group and individual action steps in aid of the environment, and prayer and meditation. During the prayer and meditation at the end of one such meeting, I heard a clear interior voice that said, "Everything begins in the medicine tent!" and was immediately struck by a strong conviction that Mark and I were supposed to live in a tipi at some point, possibly quite soon. This startled me, especially as there had been no mention of anything Native American that whole evening. Even though this seemed likely to be just imagination, it made me nervous all the same.

Trying to be casual, I asked Mark how his meditation had been. "Oh, fine," he said. "But I did keep getting this image over and over of you and me sitting in a tipi with some people."

Uh-oh! This could not just be coincidence. So Mark and I started praying about it and asking God whether this was an actual obedience or not.

He answered in His usual colorful, quixotic fashion.

A couple of days later Mark and I went to a favorite local Audubon sanctuary, Drumlin Farm. As we entered the meadow beyond the parking lot, we stopped short. There before us stood a good-sized white canvas tipi near the meadow's split-rail fence. We hadn't seen one there any other visits. We looked at each other with round eyes and walked silently over to it. Stepping through the oval opening and entering, we still couldn't speak.

Inside we felt overwhelmed by a sense of purity and holiness. We soon stepped out again. We looked at each other wordlessly and stepped in again. Within moments we had an argument, as if out of nowhere. This tipi was a very potent environment, and perhaps these moments were full of foreshadowing. We stepped out again and apologized to each other.

The next night we went to babysit for some friends. Still musing on our possible guidance, we asked the husband, David Green, if he happened to know anything about tipis.

"Do I know anything about tipis?!" he exclaimed. "Just sit down here and give me a minute!" He fetched a photo album from another room and plunked it in our laps. It was full of photos of him and his wife Gean standing in front of a tipi—one that they had been married in and had lived in for a year.

"Wow! Do you still have it by any chance?"

"Well, yes and no. I don't have poles anymore but the cover is stored in a box in a barn in West Virginia. It probably needs repairs. Why?"

We explained, and David offered to send for the cover.

We visited our pastor, Reverend Samuel, to talk and pray with him about this challenge. Originally from the Midwest, he had some interest in Native American traditional ways and said in surprise, "You don't know what the medicine tent is? Why, it's the sacred tipi, the altar of the Indians." And though he seemed slightly amused and may have thought our intent a little harebrained, he gave us his blessing on our quest.

I began to research tipis. Getting poles was the biggest challenge. For a sixteen- to eighteen-foot-diameter tipi cover, seventeen long straight poles twenty to twenty-four feet long and about three inches in diameter at the butt end were needed. Not only were these hard to find, but how could one transport them? And, also, where could we set this tipi up?

We began asking everyone we knew about poles and potential places to set up a tipi. Friends gave us leads in Massachusetts, Vermont, and New Hampshire for farms and other possible locations, but none of them panned out, although we were racing all over for several months, checking out places.

Eventually, we asked a Wampanoag medicine man, Medicine Story, whom we had previously contacted to help a half-Native American boy in our group home, for advice. He put us in touch with Slow Turtle, a prominent Wampanoag spiritual leader, medicine man, and the first executive director of the Massachusetts Commission of Indian Affairs. Slow Turtle was kind and said he'd try to help us locate poles but that August would be a hard month because so many people wanted to use their poles at powwows then.

In the meantime, true to his word, David had sent for the tipi cover. It was in pretty good shape except for a number of holes, especially near the bottom. I'm not terribly handy but realized I would need to patch the tipi. I contacted an old sailmaker in Gloucester who thought that even the sanitized version of the story I shared with him was pretty bizarre but, nonetheless, agreed to help me. At his house I watched him repair a sail while he explained to me that just using a needle and thread was not sufficient because water would come through the needle holes since the thread did not completely block the spaces. He had a mixture of some strange goop that had pine tar, beeswax, and some other mysterious ingredients in it that he would draw the thread through before stitching. The goop—each sailmaker had his own secret formula, he said—would swell around the thread and fill the needle hole, blocking any water from coming in. Shaking his head about my strange project, he kindly gave me a supply of his personal goop for my work. I used colored canvas to make large patches in suitable shapes to cover the tears and holes—a butterfly, a snake, and other creatures. Time was passing. Slow Turtle was not finding any available poles, and we still didn't have a place. One day we rushed up to a New Hampshire farm on a friend's suggestion, but it turned out to be unsuitable. You need a surprisingly wide, level space to set up a tipi, and also we needed to be reasonably close to a source of water. We were feeling worn out from the long months of our unsuccessful efforts as we watched the farmer's wife, who had been very nice, walk away from us down the dirt road. She was extremely pregnant and swayed from side to side, accompanied by two companionable, also highly pregnant goats who strolled with her on either side, all of them picturesquely swaying in unison.

Despondent, I told Mark that I just couldn't go on anymore pursuing the elusive tipi. So much fruitless time and energy had gone into it, and we were becoming a laughingstock among our friends; even our pastor was chuckling.

"One more prayer and meditation, just one more—and that's it for me!" I warned Mark.

We stepped aside into a little wood by the road. We prayed and meditated. To my despair, all I got was an image of a waterfall. *Oh great,* I thought. *Must be spiritual greed!* (I had hoped we could find a tipi spot near a stream, and now I thought I was "upping the ante"!) Mark did not get anything concrete but felt a strong, reinvigorated conviction that we should continue to pursue this quest. I threw up my hands.

A few days later, after our Sunday church service, we heard a friend calling our names during the fellowship coffee hour. Racing up to us, she exclaimed, "Mark! Stephani! I've just seen the most beautiful waterfall and I really feel that you should go see it!"

Oh no! A waterfall! It was halfway up the state of Vermont!

But we felt we had to try, just in case. The problem was that we were supposed to start a three-day shift in the group home that evening. We called the other house parents, Pete and Therese, and they said they could cover for us but for no more than twenty-four hours. We jumped into our rickety car and raced to Vermont, arriving just as the sun was setting. The waterfall was beautiful, its waters red gold in the evening light, with warm rays slanting down through the pines on either side. But our hearts sank. Its banks were too steep to admit even a toy tipi. What to do now?

After staying overnight in an inexpensive B and B, the next morning we went from store to store in Randolph, asking about places to pitch a tipi and poles. We had to leave by noon in order to get back to Boston in time for our shift. But we had no luck, although the local people were nice and, in these rural environs, didn't even seem particularly taken aback by our strange requests. The clock was ticking and it was now almost noon. At 11:45 we stepped into the Vermont Castings woodstove store, where our "waterfall" friend Marilyn had gone for a training not long before. This was our last-ditch hope. Marilyn recommended we see a man who worked at the store who she thought could help us. We went to the counter and asked for him.

"Oh, sorry," said the clerk. "He just left on a three-week trip to Europe yesterday. But"—looking at our sad faces—"maybe I could help you. Exactly what are you looking for?"

We told him, and he shook his head. "Sorry, I have no idea."

After our mad trip to Vermont, this failure felt especially crushing. We thanked the clerk and, feet dragging, turned around and headed for the door. Mark's hand was on the doorknob when suddenly a new voice cried, "No! Don't go! Wait!"

We turned in surprise to see a man, probably in his thirties, coming through a door behind the counter. He looked oddly as if he were being dragged out the door, almost fighting against something. When he spoke, his remarks were reluctant and halting, as if compelled.

"I, uh, heard what you asked. And my wife and I, uh, we have a farm where you, um, might be able to set up a tipi in a field. Of course, I'd have to ask her if it's all right. We're expecting our first child in August. If it's okay with her, maybe we could do some kind of barter thing—like you help us at the farmers' market one day a week or something.

"And, oh yeah, maybe I could help you with the poles. It's the darnedest thing, but when we got married, a friend of my wife's gave her a set of tipi poles as a wedding present! No cover, just the poles! Just crazy! What a weird gift! I couldn't understand it. And they've been sitting in our barn ever since. We've never used them, but you probably could."

The tipi adventure was on!

Which is why, on this howling August night (it actually snowed only thirty miles away), we found ourselves in our elderly car packed to the roof with tipi cover, Coleman stove, gas lantern, axe, shovel, pup tent, and other camping supplies, not to mention clothes, food, and sundries, crawling through rain so violent and thick that we could barely see through it. The raindrops were coming down so hard that they bounced back up eight inches or more in a crazy tattoo in our headlights. Finding the entrance to that forsaken meadow somewhere in the tossing, wind-racked forest seemed an overwhelming task. Lightning was striking madly all around us, bringing down trees with reverberating cracks and crashes.

Perhaps had we known about the Thunder Beings, the powerful storm spirits of Native American tradition, we might have been somewhat comforted. They are said to manifest powerfully before times of great spiritual initiation and growth, and to bring you blessings. That is, if they don't kill you in the process, which apparently sometimes happens. Well, maybe that knowledge might not have been so comforting after all!

We decided to try to creep to our host's barn, reportedly at the end of this road, and find shelter there for the night.

Nope. A huge tree, the kind of big-mamoo tree that shows up in Tolkien stories, was lying completely across the road. No way we could shift it or climb around or over it in the dark. We were stuck out here in the middle of nowhere, all alone in the murderous night.

Muttering a few choice words under his breath, Mark began to back the car, inch by inch, as there was no room to turn around. Peering myopically into the dark, we at last saw what looked like a shadowy entrance to a meadow framed by large trees (their trunks—as happily we could not see that night—were full of bullets!). We turned off there and pulled up a wet slope of low, darkly shining grass. Around this innocent-looking expanse was dense forest that currently sounded like the site of embattled armies, its soldier-trees groaning, creaking, losing limbs, or even falling thunderously beneath the cannon fire of the skies. It was so scary, like one of those novels you don't ever want to read right before bedtime. But now it was bedtime and there was no way to close the pages of this book!

We stopped in the middle of the field, feeling naked and vulnerable as the highest thing in it. We didn't know if we were really safe there, and the car was too packed for us to stretch out within it. Cramped from long hours of driving, we knew we would have to get out of the car, leaving the reassuring insulation of its rubber tires. Reluctantly, we decided we would have to pitch our little pup tent in the meadow, despite electricity-conducting metal cleats and poles. The pup tent was a true antique, probably languishing unused since Mark's Cub Scout days.

Pitching the tent in the light of our headlights in the gusting wind and rain was a struggle, our ponchos flapping like berserk bats as we tried to wrestle it into shape. The tiny tent was the old canvas kind that, if you touched the inside when it was raining, created a small leak into the tent itself; soon it was filled with polka dots of moisture the size of our fingerprints. Careening back and forth between the tent and our car, we finally got our sleeping bags, a canteen of water, and a few necessities, all, like us, very damp, into our pocket-handkerchief tent. Exhausted, we fell on our sleeping bags, scrunched together in the wobbly little shelter, its roof so low that we could barely sit up.

Although seemingly impossible, the storm now escalated. Thunder banged and roared every half minute. The shuddering landscape was lit up by white-hot strobes, visible even through the coarse gray fabric of the tent. Even the ground began shaking from the force of falling trees. What next? An earthquake? I couldn't believe this!

Looking at Mark's face, blue in the sickly flashlight glow, I could tell that he was scared too. But then, to my surprise, in a brief hiatus of the thunder, I saw a maddeningly philosophical smile spread smugly across his face. Quite calmly he said, "I guess it's up to God whether we live or die tonight, isn't it? Since it's completely out of our hands, I'm going to go to sleep. Good night!" And just like that, he dropped off to sleep.

I felt outraged but then realized finally that my reaction was the more ridiculous one. Unable to close my eyes, I lay on the trembling earth, praying and wincing at every new thunder roll and hot glare of sky-fire. There was the terror, the shaking, the loud bangs, the fierce glare, and then somehow suddenly, miraculously, there was sleep.

I awoke to a serene morning, feeling deeply rested and wondering where I was. The air was fresh and sweet, and Mark snored peacefully beside me. Even through the dull weave of the fatigued tent fabric I could tell it was a beautiful, sunny day. Birds sang extra lyrically, as if auditioning for a Snow White movie production. I lay there, stunned and grateful to see another day, especially this Pollyanna-pretty one that seemed to deny that anything like the bowels-of-hell night that preceded it could possibly have existed. *You must have been mistaken,* it seemed to flute at us. *You must have been confused. Look at how sweet and peaceful and sunny and innocent everything is. . . .* Then I heard a strange concentrated hissing sound somewhere near at hand.

"Mark! Wake up! Wake up! There's something outside!"

Mark woke quickly, looking well-rested. "Best sleep of my life." He grinned and then heard the hissing sound. "What's that?!"

He jumped up and went outside. I heard him yelling abuse, and I rushed out to see a big yellow dog running fast out of the meadow.

"That bastard was pissing on our tent!" Mark cried in indignation. "He better not do it again!"

So much for Pollyanna. The dog did do it again, carefully anointing our tent every morning until Mark rushed out in a fury to chase him away. Mark tired of this game, and one morning I came out of the tent in time to see his new solution.

"What are you doing?!" I cried.

"As you see, pissing on all four corners of the tent myself! That should get rid of that hound!"

And it seemed to work. Ever after we saw his yellow hide infrequently and always at a distance. But Mark still felt it necessary to re-mark his "territory" every few days, preventatively. And just as much, I'm sure, for the kick of it.

We had no more violent weather for the remainder of our stay on the mountainside—just occasional chill rain. We were high enough up that the white puffy clouds blowing by swiftly on the fresh winds seemed very close to us, almost as if we could reach out and touch them in the calm, intensely turquoise sky.

Our first day we walked down the road to visit our hosts in their home, clambering awkwardly around the huge tree in the road that men with chainsaws, a backhoe, and determination soon removed. We admired our hosts' beautiful new baby, Amber Crystal, and confirmed that we would help them one day a week at the local farmers' market in exchange for our stay. They had a large organic vegetable garden and said we could help ourselves, leaving some money in the can by the shed for whatever we took. The woods would be our bathroom, but we could bathe in a small but lovely icy-cold waterfall a little ways off the road, not far from our meadow. It was idyllic.

But there was still the matter of getting the tipi set up. We did have a booklet of directions. However, our friend David had advised us not to try doing it without help—"at least three or four other people, if possible." Our hosts knew nothing about tipis but had acquaintances across the valley on the next mountain who often lived in a tipi and who they thought would be willing to help. And thus we made the acquaintance of the deeply delightful Dan and Dana Hugg, just as charming as their names. Dan was a handsome forester in his twenties, Dana a graceful, accomplished artist whose drawings of flowers were so ineffably beautiful and "speaking" that she made her living from selling them, with no need to advertise. They were not only very knowledgeable about tipis and quite willing to help but had been praying to meet some other Christians with whom they could do Bible study and contemplation! So soon the four of us were sitting contentedly in their tipi, Bibles in our laps, praying and seeking inspiration. It was the scene that Mark had seen in his Eleventh Commandment meditation!

However, the Huggses said that even for them the business of setting up a tipi was a bit of a challenge, and they thought it best to call in more expert help. And so we met Billy, a grizzled, weathered-looking man ten or twenty years older than the rest of us. Billy was short, lean, and sinewy, with a dazzling, broken-toothed grin. We liked him right away, and a certain odiferousness floating around him was quite tolerable.

Billy's story was tragic. Dan and Dana told us that he lived in an unheated barn with his goats all year round. During the frozen Vermont winters he burrowed among his goats to stay warm. All the food he ate was simple and uncooked because he had neither cooking facilities nor electricity. He was living a life of repentance as severe as any desert father's.

A number of years before, Billy had lived in a little cabin in the woods. One day he saw movement among the trees and thought it was a deer. Hoping for venison, he took out his rifle, aimed, and shot. When he hurried to collect his quarry, he found no deer. Instead he found his best friend lying on the ground—a young pregnant woman who, unbeknownst to him, had been coming to visit him. Both she and her baby were dead. Billy never recovered from this shock and his unbearable remorse.

Billy was not sent to prison because it was so clearly all a terrible mistake, but from that point he ceased to live a normal human life of minimal comforts, instead treating himself as an animal of the fields, or rather worse. Billy did occasional odd jobs for local people in order to survive on the most rudimentary level. I was happy to cook up as much hot food on our little camp stove as he would eat. We enjoyed his company, which despite the Greek tragedy he was living out, seemed full of a natural, cheerful grace. Billy had Native American blood and knew a lot about tipis. He was happy to help us. I just needed to finish the repairs on the tipi cover, and then we could all get together and put the tipi up. These repairs became strangely difficult on an emotional level. I remember sitting in the meadow grasses, needle and thread and patches in hand, the huge tipi cover spread around me, crying quietly and uncontrollably as I felt that I was somehow reliving previously unremembered but strongly felt experiences from when I was about twelve years old. (Later I discovered that, at the same time, Mark found himself uncomfortably processing heavy feelings from when he was junior-high age.) We were going through an involuntary purification, it seemed.

At last I finished the patches, and a day was appointed for Billy, Dan, and Dana to meet with us in our meadow to raise the tipi. Tipi-raising was a complicated process that involved all of us carefully coordinating our movements with the long poles and then the tipi cover as if we were all in a kind of ballet or maypole dance. But after a few hours of effort and concentration the tipi was up—white, multicolored near its patched hem, and very beautiful, shining in the afternoon sun, its shape truly holy, evocative of harmony and goodness. We felt great joy and satisfaction. We all had a good meal, laughing and joking together, and as the early stars appeared, we thanked our three helpers. Smiling and waving, they left us in our new home.

Sleeping in the tipi on our low camp cots unexpectedly resembled being on a ship at sea. The poles, ropes, and canvas creaked to and fro, singing in the night wind. It felt wonderful, though—like a kind of primal embrace, a safe harbor, and I loved seeing the bright stars shining down on us through the smoke hole.

We had some halcyon days, both with the weather and our spirits. One day, lying in the grass together beneath the joyful, soaring clouds, Mark read me the entire book of Psalms, one after another, in his warm, resonant voice—a rapturous, deeply inspiring experience. At night Mark often liked to lie in the grass outside the tipi, watching the stars and looking at my shadow outlined by the lamplight on the tipi walls as I played my guitar and sang inside. We ate the fresh vegetables, full of invigorating "Vermont juice," walked in the woods or on the dusty road to the diamond-bright waterfall to wash off and get cool, carried our hosts' baby in a backpack or sold vegetables in the cheerful Farmers' Market, and spent peaceful hours with Dan and Dana, sharing our lives and our spiritual hopes. It was a magical interlude.

We did not see our hosts very often. Once in a great while I'd walk down the dirt road and knock on their kitchen door, next to a glorious bank of lilac water lily-like autumn crocuses with gold stamen hearts. On one visit I saw that the wife's eyes were red and swollen and that she was clutching a handkerchief in one hand.

I asked her what was wrong, and she told me that their pediatrician had detected a bad heart murmur in Amanda Crystal, severe enough to necessitate surgery. If the baby had not outgrown it by the next week, he would insist on an operation. Both parents had a bad feeling about the operation.

I tried to comfort her and told her that we would ask people to pray for the baby and them.

When I returned to the meadow, I told Mark. We both prayed, and then he drove into town to call our church, explaining the situation and making sure that everyone in the prayer chain would understand the stakes. This was on a Friday. On Monday the sad parents took the baby to the doctor again.

"Well, this is impossible!" the doctor exclaimed, looking at them with his stethoscope pressed to the baby's tiny chest. "There is no more heart murmur at all! Certainly that can happen with minor ones, but never with any this major!" He kept rechecking, shaking his head, and finally said, "I don't understand it, but she's just fine. No surgery necessary!"

We celebrated with Amanda's parents in their cozy kitchen. Between ourselves, Mark and I wondered if this was why we had been sent to Vermont—so as to gather prayers for this beautiful baby at a critical time. Of course, we couldn't know for sure if the baby's cure had come through God's response to the many prayers rising to heaven for her sake, but past experience told us that the odds were good. By itself, this and our connection with the Huggses would have been plenty of reason to justify this adventure, but as usual, God had more threads in this weaving.

ﷺ

Mark and I, even living so simply, soon ran out of money. To say we were underpaid in our house-parents job would be putting it mildly. Our combined salaries were far less than one "normal" person's low pay. We needed very little—gas, vegetable money, and occasionally a few basic groceries—but we couldn't survive the month with no pay. Reluctantly, Mark decided that he needed to return to Boston for a few days to work as a relief counselor in group homes for mentally ill and developmentally disabled residents. He called in and was asked to cover three days' shifts. We weren't happy about this but felt we had no choice.

On the afternoon when Mark was supposed to leave, as we frantically tried to pack what he needed and make plans, he accidentally locked his keys in the car. We couldn't get it open. He quickly trotted down to our hosts' but they couldn't help us either. The husband suggested that Mark call "Jed," a local man who he knew could get the window open—for a price. Mark was reluctant; we had met this brusque, overbearing man, who we knew had threatened to kill a friend of ours who had annoyed him. But we didn't know what else to do. So Mark called Jed from our hosts' house. Jed agreed to help for a fee that was large for us and that we would have to pay later on.

Jed, burly and unsmiling, soon pulled into the meadow in his truck and curtly set to work getting our car window open. A large handgun sticking out of his back pocket did not improve the atmosphere. We thanked him, he bluntly reminded us about his fee, and was off.

Mark was already running quite late. He should have left more than an hour earlier to be on time for his shift in Boston, but we had still more delays. We were both concerned about my staying alone in the isolated meadow. We had by then discovered the many bullets in the trees at the entrance to the meadow that "good old boys" driving by had pumped into them. Furthermore, the tipi could be seen clearly from the road by that entrance. One thing we still hadn't done was to hang the more than head-high lining in the tipi. This now took on a certain urgency, since the lining made it impossible to see the lit-up outlines of anyone in the tipi at night. The moving silhouette of a young woman alone in the glowing tipi in the lonely meadow seemed like it could be an invitation for trouble.

So we set to work hurriedly hanging the lining. This was time-consuming, since ties had to be wound round and round each pole. Spooked by both Jed's unsavory presence such a short time ago in our "sanctuary" and also the fact that it was desperately late, we were working too fast in a strange, driven atmosphere. Suddenly, Mark accidentally caught one of my supporting hands against the tipi pole as he rapidly wound the rope around it and pulled it taut.

"Mark, stop! Stop! My hand!" Strangely, although our heads were only a couple of feet apart, it was as if he, in his fierce concentration, could not hear me. "Stop! Please stop! It hurts!"

But he only wound the rope tighter and tighter, cutting into my hand until I thought I would scream with pain. In desperation and panic, since I couldn't seem to reach him any other way, I slapped his face. He looked at me as if he didn't know me and, dropping the rope, which fell away, backhanded me hard across the face. I flew backward across the tipi, falling out through the entrance hole. I was lying on my back on the ground, cradling my swelling lip and crying unbelieving tears, when Mark rushed out to pick me up and cradle me in his arms.

"I'm sorry! I'm so sorry! I don't know what happened there! What came over me?! I just reacted instinctively. Oh my God, how could I do that?! Please forgive me! This is crazy! I'm so sorry!"

I sobbed against his chest. "I'm sorry I hit you, Mark! You didn't realize you were hurting me, and I couldn't get your attention any other way. I was desperate! I'm so sorry!"

Twilight was washing over us like a tide, and we felt as if we were stranded on a besieged little island of shock and grief in its swirling midst. Everything seemed dreadful, dangerous, and wrong somehow. Threatening. But nonetheless, in minutes, Mark absolutely had to leave. We forced ourselves to get up and go inside the tipi, still shaky but able somehow to properly affix the lining to the last two poles. Staring hopelessly at each other, still grief-stricken, we said anguished goodbyes. A prayer and a long hug, and then he was gone. I watched the car's taillights disappear between the trees.

I was alone in the darkening meadow.

Somehow my shell had been cracked, and everything was different now. Almost too exhausted to move, with great effort I dragged myself across the field to put our cookstove and equipment away and relieve myself in the shelter of the woods.

Every step seemed strange and uneven, exaggerated, as if my progress was being shot with a jolting handheld movie camera. I kept fearfully glancing over my shoulder, hoping no one was driving by to glimpse me staggering across the tufted field. No one did.

The darkness came on like a great wave, and I turned my flashlight on and headed back. Suddenly the landscape became strangely bright. I turned my flashlight off and turned around. And screamed.

An enormous light was hanging in the sky, seemingly much too close, bright white above the dark meadow trees and the looming flank of a neighboring mountain. It felt as if this impossibly huge rising ball might roll right down on me. It took me several horrified moments to realize that it was only the moon, the full moon—but the moon as I have never seen it, before or since, easily five or six times normal size. I have since learned about rare supermoons with their gigantic magnifications, but at the time I had no idea that the moon could appear in such an awesome way. I felt foolish and relieved that it was "only the moon," but the sight of such a titanic moon was still uncanny, and uncanniness was most unwelcome after the strange events of the day.

I jolted back to the tipi and lit the lamp, throwing myself down on my sleeping bag, too fried to get out of my work clothes. Eventually I turned off the kerosene lamp, lying awake a long time listening to the loud creaks of wind-pulled canvas and wood. Just as my eyelids were at last closing from exhaustion, I sat bolt upright from another shock. The most terrible rending screams I have ever heard were coming from the woods near at hand. It was hard to tell if they were animal or human—they seemed something in between. They were loud and wild, as if ripped from the bowels of agony. It sounded as if someone, something, was being violently, slowly tortured to death. I could not move for horror, pity, and fear. I knew I would be unable to help whatever that was and could only pray for it and myself for protection and relief. Finally, the screams stopped, abruptly cut off. Just like that. Hoping that whatever was causing the screams wouldn't come for me in the dark, I at last fell asleep. (I never found out what had caused the screaming. I've heard that mating bobcats can sound ghastly, and that great horned owls can make the most appalling and terrifying screams when so inclined. Since I found no signs of a struggle or remains the next day, I was grateful that the cause was probably benign. But there had been no such soothing realization on the night of the monster moon.)

"Stephani! Stephani, wake up!" called the gentle voice. It was bright morning, and Dana, wispy in a pale blue peasant-style dress and big green Wellington boots against the heavy morning dew, was standing looking down at me inside the tipi. She was a ringer for Heidi, especially with the pretty young white doe-goat standing beside her, whom she introduced as Elsa. "Mark called us and asked us to look after you. Are you okay? Dan and I want you to come have breakfast with us."

I quickly pulled myself together. Due to the efficacy of the homeopathic medicines I had taken the evening before, my fat lip was now only slightly swollen and tender. I went in a daze with Dana, had a pleasant breakfast with her and Dan, and then, returning, realized that it was Farmers' Market day. I met our hosts at their house and helped at the market in the normal way but felt as if I were sleepwalking through the whole thing, slightly removed from it all. The next day our hosts were going on a trip and would be away for several days. And then I would really be alone on the mountain.

Dan and Dana had planned to check in with me on the succeeding days, but unexpected events kept them away on their neighboring mountain. So there was no way Mark could reach me to let me know he had to stay on the job for five days rather than three. I moved around as if being carried on the current of an unseen river, and—except for some fear and anxiety when Mark did not return as scheduled, but which reflected on in prayer did not seem to indicate that he was in any danger or trouble—I was strangely peaceful.

I spoke to no one, and no one spoke to me, unless it was "all my relatives" around me. I trawled like a fisherwoman in nature's delights, finding gooseberries and currants gone wild in the tapestry of hedgerows bordering the road. I saw the plump, exquisite blossoms of the purple-flowered raspberry, its mauve beauty becoming a symbol of this precious time. I tasted the fine flavor, dry and sophisticated, of its mounded fruit. I sat and listened to the waterfall's music and plunged under its thrumming, cold, pure showers. I felt the warm dirt of the road cradling my bare feet, wrapped my arms around trees and listened to their high voices singing and tossing in the wind, heard the fluting calls of birds as if they were wreathing me round in bright, joyful ribbons, lay in the silky embrace of the meadow grass looking into a boundless sky. I felt something settling out of me but I could not give it a name. I only felt a simple, deep happiness in the companionable silence of those magical days.

And, although cars did pass on the road, oddly I was never in sight when they did. Always I was at one or the other side of the field, invisible from the road. I had to chalk this up to angelic protection.

On the fifth evening, Mark returned. He got out of the car, and we ran to each other with joy. After we hugged and kissed, he held me out from himself, looking deep into my eyes. "What is this?! This is amazing, this is wonderful," he breathed. "Whatever happened to you while I was gone?"

Connecting with him, feeling the reflection of what he saw, I could now feel it myself. Power was pouring out of the earth into me and pouring out through my eyes and every pore, pouring blessing on him and everything around. I was at last in my true self, connected intimately and lovingly with the Creation, with its ineffable radiance now shining through my eyes. I felt and was part of the profound, ever-flowing strength and joy, the harmony of the elements, the creatures, the plants—the immense dancing circle of all life spun in potent, speaking, intimate splendor out of the heart of God.

"This happiness not only lit up the interior of my soul, the outer world also appeared to me to be filled with beauty, everything called me to love and pay homage to God. The people, the trees, the plants, everything was like family to me," wrote the nineteenth-century pilgrim author of the memoir *The Way of a Pilgrim.* In my own small way, my heart was dancing with a like joy.

It seemed to us that God had sent us to the tipi and Vermont for many reasons, but one of them apparently was to put me on a kind of vision quest, not knowingly connected to a medicine person or other guide and yet very real and well-orchestrated including its shocks to my superficial personality shell and the healing that poured into my unguarded heart from the loving embrace of Nature—and from a special holy "medicine tent" on a holy mountainside in the deep green living sweetness of magical Vermont. A friend of mine once said, "Vermont? Why it's the breast of Mary!" We drank deep of that grace.

Meeting in Council

> *A man's attitude to the nature around him, and the animals in nature, is of special importance, because as we respect our created world, so also do we show respect for the real world that we cannot see.*
>
>   —Thomas Yellowtail

Many years later I attended a lecture given by a Mohawk woman who said she had lived for years with the Mayans in Chiapas, studying their medicine ways, and also studied with Mongolian shamans as a medicine woman. Her talk occurred during a time when many people were anxious about the reported "end" of the ancient Mayan calendar and its possible implications for global catastrophe. The medicine woman drew two circles on a blackboard with chalk while explaining to us that the Mayan calendar was not about an ending but rather described major repeating cycles over vast time periods. She said that Mongolians had an almost identical calendar, and that in both cases our current time period was marked as one of significant change. She had drawn one circle, much smaller than the other, inside the bigger one, and located it not in the center but near the bottom of the large circle. Both circles represented related but independent cycles. Only a narrow pathway existed between the closest edges of the two circles. She pointed at this space, saying, "This is where we are now in the cycle, in this narrow part." She explained that this energetic "squeeze," like tidal waters being forced through a narrow channel, created an atmosphere of intensity and pressure that people instinctively felt and that often brought out our fearfulness and unresolved issues, as well as a sense that time was speeding up and that things were happening too fast to be able to deal with. She told us not to be surprised if we saw a great deal of public violence and freaking out as people felt the pressures and just panicked. And that this period, a kind of purging, would last for quite a while.

"There are only two ways to survive this period well," she said, looking soberly at us. "One way is to have a talking relationship with our Creator. And the other is to have a talking relationship with the Creation."

There are constant conversations going on between ourselves and everything else in the universe. Quantum mechanics has demonstrated how intertwined the existence of everything is and the great sensitivity—and malleability—of even the subtlest mutating particles/waves. Merely the act of being observed can change their characteristics; two different people contemplating the same particle/wave alter it by the differing qualities of their attention. Communication is not bound by what we think of as traditional boundaries; a virus that mutates in North America can suddenly show an identical mutation in China without any direct contact. Our large and sensitive electromagnetic fields interact with each other's in subtle but powerful communication. Studies have shown the positive influence toward healing of prayers for the sick and those recovering from operations—not only for those prayed for before and during operations, but also those prayed for afterward—an indication that the chronological reach of the field of time itself is altered when dealing with such subtle energies.

I am not a scientist and do not have a deep grasp of these principles, but as a human being, I have seen over and over again how fundamental our subtle conversations with everything that is are to our existence and our deeper nature.

Everything Speaks
In my bumbling way, I had been more or less in a talking relationship with the Creator for some time, its potency varying with my capacity for true openness and God's grace. But a talking relationship with the Creation? I have had some experiences I could probably describe in this way, but I know I need to go so much deeper.

Most of us grow up in a world of strangers. Not only do our families and modern Western culture tend to be insular and distrustful socially but the natural environment more often than not is regarded as either a threatening "enemy" or "dumb substances" to be coldly utilized for our goals and enthusiasms of the moment. We too often act as if we were the only creatures to have sensitive, feeling, breathing life. Nothing could be further from the truth. God created everything "alive" in the most profound sense, each creature and "thing" possessing its own form of intelligence, dynamism, and receptivity. In traditional Eastern Christian theology, as in the works of Saint Maximus the Confessor and Saint Gregory Palamas, recognition is shown for the *logoi*, the "little words," that the great Word, the Logos, infused into every aspect of His Creation and which can reveal Him to willing human perception through grace. "Sometimes he causes the dog to go before the traveler; sometimes he uses the cat to show the Way. Sometimes he gives the power of Solomon to a staff; sometimes he accords eloquence to the ant," writes the wise mystical poet Attar. Sufis and traditional Eastern Christians alike do not believe in pantheism—that Nature is God—but rather in pan*en*theism, that God fills Nature in every dimension and every particular and can reveal Himself to us through every element of His Creation if we do not psychologically barricade ourselves away from His messages to us.

Growing up in twentieth-century suburban America, I was taught to regard all wild plants—or indeed any plant—not safely specified as food, as dangerous and toxic. Walking out into the woods or meadows, you were surrounded by "enemies," threatening to your very life—alien and strange. But, beginning in my teens, I started investigating herbalism and coming to know how many benign and healing plants surround us at all times. As my studies progressed, when I walked outside I suddenly found myself in the midst of friends, not enemies. What had been just a blur of green with threatening hidden toxins now became specific plants with specific personalities full of healing power and, yes, compassion. Dear friends. Not that I wasn't cautious. Certain plants themselves and certain parts of other plants can kill you. You have to know what you are doing—but it is not impossible to learn and know such beneficial things.

The more I learned, ultimately apprenticing myself to herbalists, the more joy, as well as knowledge, I gained. I was blessed to study with the gifted herbalists Tommy Priester and Madelon Hope and also at times with Matthew Wood, Margi Flint, Phyllis Light, Stephen Harrod Buhner, and others. A whole new world opened up, and my growing understanding of the generosity of Divine Providence filled me with awe. A fourth-generation Appalachian Native American herbalist explained that her herbalist grandparents never brought medicinal herbs with them when they went out to treat patients in the growing season. They knew that the particular medicinal plants those patients would need would be growing within sixty feet or so of their own houses! God provides. As I began to pay attention to the yearly change of wild plant varieties outside the places I lived, I was stunned to see how much the plant life varied from year to year—and its correspondences to the types of illnesses each particular year brought.

Most herbalists teach a protocol for approaching plants that encompasses more than not picking too many of any one variety, not picking within one hundred feet of roadways, and other such practical acts. It has to do with approaching the plants with true respect, recognition of their intelligence, and humble gratitude. You explain why you need the plant and, if possible, for whom. You ask the plant's permission and wait to hear the answer in your heart. If it is no, then you move on. If it is yes, you then offer a gift of thanksgiving—traditionally tobacco, cornmeal, or pollen. However, if there is a need and you have none of these at hand, you also can offer some of your hair (a nutrient) or even spit (life-giving moisture) by the plant's roots. Plants are generally gracious; it is part of their purpose to heal, and if we are respectful and receptive, they will "speak" to us in their own way. Sometimes with words, sometimes with images, sometimes with just a certain sensing. How do we learn to distinguish the plant's "voice" from the voices of our own imaginings? As the great

modern herbalist Stephen Harrod Buhner says, "Practice." Keep
practicing until your discernment for the difference between
authentic communication and mind noise is quickened and
strengthened, he advises.

ॐ

Rescue by the Elderflower Spirit

One year my husband and I were afflicted by an unusual and
terrible flu. A dominant symptom was extreme dizziness with
attendant nausea, as well as respiratory illness. I could barely stag-
ger around, and my poor husband could not even sit up. He was
becoming extremely dehydrated, and a friend and I had to bring
him to a hospital. After an eight-hour wait, he was admitted and
spent four days there, hooked up to IVs. I was so sick that I could
not go back to the hospital.

On the fourth morning Mark returned home unexpectedly,
having checked himself out against doctor's orders, rehydrated
but still very sick and dizzy. I had awakened from a strange dream
that morning. In the dream I was sitting across a small table from
a slim man with long straggly hair who looked rather like Baba
Ram Dass on a bad day. He told me he was going to put some
elderflowers in a medicinal soup for me.

Hmmm, I thought. *Why not try it?* I had elderflowers in my
herbal collection and knew of no contraindications. So I made
mugs of elderflower tea for both Mark and me. Having each drunk
one mug, to our astonishment we found our dizziness drastically reduced. A second mug of tea brought me further dramatic
improvement; I was almost normal again. The second mug also
improved Mark further but did not take him as far along as it had
me. We soon purchased a homeopathic compound remedy for
dizziness that cured the rest of his vertigo. I can only assume that
elderflowers must have been the specific antidote for that particular
virus; viruses and bacteria can quickly mutate to counter pharma-
ceuticals, which are relatively simple chemically. Herbs, though,
have dozens, sometimes hundreds, of chemical compounds in
their makeup, making their potent healing forces most often much
more challenging for viruses and bacteria to counter effectively.
(However, there can be dangers with herbs as well; it is recommended that advice from both your regular doctor and a knowledgeable herbalist be sought before any sort of self-treatment.)

We all need more knowledge of our brethren of the plant kingdom, not less, and ideally, as much as possible, open dialogues
with them.

Possible dialogues tend to be limited by how we ourselves frame
our questions and by our own belief systems that restrict the kind

of answers we can receive. Certain habitual terminology can itself be toxic. Such a term is the dread "anthropomorphizing"—a term that makes many modern people, and especially a certain breed of scientist, leap up on their intellectual hassocks in fear like agitated Victorian ladies encountering a mouse. This knee-jerk reaction, with its concomitant fears of being regarded as naïve, ignorant, and sentimental by others, is a real block to understanding the natural world and to exploring its powerful and subtle but very real intelligent nature.

All of Nature is a great council in which we are only members, though members with special responsibilities. A council can only be fully effective if its members communicate, and there are modes of approach to opening the subtle sensitivities that make this sharing possible for us at need or inspiration. We are not strangers and alone but part of a great family of beautiful beings created in wisdom by the hand of our God.

࿇

Owl Gifts and Keewaydinoquay
In the dream I was standing on a narrow dirt path, bordered by low thick shrubs, in a forest. Suddenly, perhaps thirty feet in front of me, a dense flow of birds of all sizes and types crossed the path from one shrub border to the next. They were all on foot or flying very low. The thick ribbon of birds, though not hurrying, still moved rapidly. Suddenly they were all gone except for just one. It stood motionless and staring at me in the center of the path. An owl. It may have been medium-sized and brownish but I am not sure. I awoke with its presence and concentrated gaze strong in my mind.

That day I went to my job as a clerk at my friend David Newhouse's children's store, The Shepherd and The Lamb. My new church friend Anna Higgins, also a clerk, met me with a smile. "I have something for you," she said, handing me an envelope. I opened it, and on the enclosed card a photograph of an owl with a penetrating stare was gazing at me from a hole in a tree. Inside the card were two credits for workshops at an educational retreat center for holistic studies in New York State. I stared at her in open-mouthed amazement.

She said, "I hope that you can use these." They were made out to Anna and her former boyfriend John. "I looked in their catalog and couldn't really find anything I wanted to go to this summer. John is gone and can't use his. I know that you were interested in attending something there this summer, and I didn't want to have them go to waste. So it's a pleasure for me to be able to give them to you. Please accept them and enjoy your workshop."

I showed them to Mark that night—an answer to our prayer. We had noticed that this holistic retreat center was going to offer a five-day program with Native American elders consisting of mornings spent in a large pavilion with all the elders and afternoons with the teacher of our choice. The teacher I wanted to be with was named Keewaydinoquay (Woman of the Northwest Wind), an Abenaki herbalist, ethnobotanist, and teacher of traditional ways. I had been studying herbalism on and off for years and felt a calling to learn from her, though I knew nothing about her. Mark could feel that calling in me, too, but, as usual, we had no funds, so we had been praying about it daily, hoping that some way would open up to make it possible.

And the solemn-eyed owls had brought that very opening. Anna's two credits covered the program fee exactly to the dollar. Thank you, Anna, dear God, and wise owls!

                                     ॐ

I camped out in a small green dome tent in the woodsy camping grounds at the center. Mornings were spent with the whole group in a large wooden pavilion, roofed but open-air, raised a few feet above the ground. Five Native American elders, most of them men, taught us and prayed with us there. Whenever Keewaydinoquay prayed in these gatherings, I keenly felt the presence of God.

Afternoons were a treasure as thirty or so of us retreatants spent time imbibing Keewaydinoquay's herbal teachings and wisdom. Small and stocky, with large, speaking eyes, Kee also shared gifts with us from the women of her tribe, like bags of fresh balsam twigs that we would sew into pillows during our session and print with spiritually significant designs.

Kee, called in her early days Margaret Peschel, had a colorful life story, including eventful encounters with animals. As a toddler her parents found her in the woods gathering blueberries, her little hands in the fur of two bears who were also scoffing the berries! That's where she got her childhood name, "Walks with Bears." Bears, knowledgeable about the healing qualities of various plants and roots, are greatly honored by Native American herbalists. Some say that if you dream of a bear, it is a sign that you should dedicate yourself to the study of herbs.

Kee also had a lively childhood friendship with a mother otter and her six pups who lived, fished, and played in a nearby stream. This romp of otters, as the collective is so fittingly called, would glide down mudslides with little Kee, and they would all fish together. Kee's communication with the mother otter finally became so honed that Kee was able to invite the otter family to her own yard for an outdoor tea party, set up with plates, cups, and floral centerpiece, as if for dolls. To Kee's mother's shock, the otters showed up at the appointed hour and settled themselves in to enjoy the bits of fish on their plates. When Kee's family was about to move, and she had to bid farewell to the otters, her family came home on their last day to find seven fresh fish tucked neatly into their screen door—farewell gifts, one from each otter!

Although Kee was a preserver of the old native ways, she was also a Christian, she told us. But she had never formally joined a church. "Well, I just never found one where I liked the way they treated their children," she said sadly.

Not long into her classes, Kee told us sorrowfully that she could not share with us the fullness of her teachings because the holistic studies center had not given her tobacco, the traditional gift of respect to a native healer, that helped open the way into the teachings. And, also, for that reason she would not be returning here again.

How could this be? After class I went to the center's office and explained the situation. To my surprise, I was met with indifference and told that they would not be bothering with the tobacco.

So I decided to try to do something. In the faint hope of finding some tobacco, I went to the little store on campus that sold snacks and small necessities like combs and toothpaste. And lo and behold! Enough old-hippie-era ambience lingered that they carried some packets of loose, roll-your-own tobacco there! I bought a small fat packet and contemplated it back in my tent. It just did not seem respectful enough to hand Kee the tobacco in its logo-emblazoned crackling cellophane package. So what should I do?

As I had left home, I had, for unknown reasons, thrust an embroidery needle, pins, and pink and purple embroidery thread into my pack. Maybe I could sew a pouch of some kind? But I had no fabric.

Then the image of one of my favorite plants, mullein, with its soft gray felty leaves, floated into my mind. Yes! A couple of big, soft leaves from a first-year mullein rosette that I could sew together would make a perfect pouch! Mullein is an herb used for the healing of the lungs and is especially noted for treating inner ear infections. How appropriate to utilize it for an "unheard" need!

Looking around outside for mullein plants, I only found a few scattered plants, all of them with the tall yellow-blossomed flower stalk, candelabra-like, that showed that they were second-year plants. Their basal leaves, as a result, had grown very large but too thin and papery to sew. At last I did find a big stand of mulleins in front of one of several small white cabins raised a few steps from the ground. But every single one was a second-year plant! I prayed and looked for the "grandfather" or "grandmother" plant that would likely be the head of the local tribe. The tallest one in the center felt right. I sprinkled cornmeal (an acceptable honoring gift) around its roots, politely and silently explaining my need of a first-year rosette.

To my surprise, it felt as if the grandfather mullein immediately replied with an authoritative *Go over there*. I turned around to look at where it had told me to go. There was nothing there—just lawn ending in bushes and woods. Not mullein territory. Disappointed, I turned back to the grandfather mullein. *Go over there*, he repeated.

Reluctantly, thinking it was all my imagination, I obeyed. I got there. Still nothing. Assuming it had all been just my own vain mind games, I turned to leave. And froze. From where I was standing—and only from that spot—I could see that, under the floor of one of the raised wooden cottages, in shadow, three mullein plants were growing. Two of them were first-year plants with soft, perfect, felted leaves!

Mentally thanking the grandfather plant, I rushed joyfully over and knelt to offer cornmeal, ask permission, and gather two good leaves and two spares for my pouch. Then I also saw an opportunity to help. The second-year mullein there had a problem. It had sent up the usual cheery yellow-flowered stalk but had met the obstacle of the cottage floor and had grown bent, still trapped in the shade. I gently eased the flower stalk out from under the floor so that two or three inches were now in sunlight and could grow straight up. What a clever grandfather mullein! Not only had it granted my request, it had arranged for me to aid one of its tribe!

Back in my room I sewed two of the soft gray mullein leaves together with my pink and purple embroidery thread, leaving one end of the oval pouch open. I stuffed it with the loose tobacco, said a prayer over it, and went out to look for Kee.

Finding her alone in our classroom, I thanked her for teaching us and respectfully offered her the tobacco. Her face lit up and she exclaimed, "Well, I thought I'd seen everything that could be done with mullein leaves but I've never seen this before!" And she thanked me with shining eyes.

We got to talking about how I had come to study with her. After I told her the owl story, she pointed out that some tribes fear owls as harbingers of death, but others have more positive associations with them. She said there are some people for whom owls are particularly good and gave me a copy of a lovely traditional story about a young girl who is badly treated and unappreciated by her tribe but whose virtues impress the local owls so much that they carry her off to lead a joyful life with them.

The Golden Eyes of the Marsh Hawk

Halibut Point is the northernmost mitten-top curve of the island of Cape Ann and its towns of Rockport and Gloucester. The name derives not from the fish but from "haul-about"—the necessary work of mariners who were sailing around this rocky shore with its tricky currents. Halibut Point is now a small but very beautiful state park radiating out from a hilltop crowned by a deep and handsome quarry pond (spring- and rain-filled since the granite quarry was abandoned), framed like a bezel in a blue ring of ocean, sloping down to a wild shoreline of rugged boulders. Blueberry and waxy-berried bayberry bushes, fluffy low shadbush trees like scraps of cloud caught in twiggy branches, fragrant sweet fern, arrowwood, sweeps of shining wild grasses, and many other wild-flowers and plants tumble down in a froth beside narrow dirt trails that end at tide pools and cresting sea waves. Birds of all kinds sing and soar in its fresh ocean airs, especially during spring and autumn migrations.

On clear days, when standing on the overlook by the quarry, you can see distant shoreline views extending as far as Mount Agamenticus in Maine. Halibut Point is a place for shaking off the doldrums, for rapturous rambles of the windblown, fancy-free kind, in a landscape that kicks up its heels in tousled beauty.

One afternoon Mark and I were wandering a trail not far from the bounding waves along the shore. As we were passing among low boulders, out of the corner of my eye I saw something large and brown nearby on the ground. I took one more step and halted.

"Mark!" I whispered as loudly as I could. "Stop! Look!"

He stopped, turned around, and also paused. Not fifteen feet away from us a big beautiful hawk was standing on a boulder flush with the ground, calmly eating another bird—perhaps a catbird, given its size and color, but now minus its head. The hawk's feathers were a rich brown on her back and wings, but her face and chest were a glorious speckling of brown and white on buff gold. Her eyes were yellow and bright as two topazes. I'm sure that she was aware of us but gave no sign. Over the next hour or so, with aching slowness, we silently inched our way closer to her, bit by bit, amazed that she did not startle. At last we wound up sitting cross-legged on a low rock within five feet of her. The hawk continued daintily plucking out and dis-carding the bird's feathers and tearing off tiny scraps of meat to eat while showing no sign of objection to our presence. Feeling amazement and unfathomable gratitude, we were full of wonder at her magnificent beauty and that she clearly accepted our companionship.

At one point the hawk paused in her dining. Her fierce golden eyes suddenly looked straight into mine. A powerful shock of electricity raced through the marrow of my being, like interior lightning. I felt both shaken and that I had received a gift—some kind of profound direct transmission. The hawk then calmly resumed her eating.

A couple came rambling down the narrow dirt trail and stopped within about twenty feet of us and the hawk. They stared at the three of us in surprise.

"This is impossible!" exclaimed the man softly. And to my amazement, shaking their heads, they just walked off, as if we were all some kind of hallucination.

We had sat with the hawk well over two hours. The sun had set, the air and the stone we sat upon were growing cool, and the first ripples of twilight began to spread over the rocky field where we lingered in a kind of dreamlike, meditative state with the hawk. Another couple came down the path, preceded this time by a running five-year-old boy. At his noise, the hawk decided to finally seek a less public dining room, spread her broad wings, picked up the bird's remains, and sailed into the air, turning to fly low over some larger boulders and settling behind them out of sight about thirty feet away. Her white rump patch combined with her coloring and considerable size identified her as a female marsh hawk, or northern harrier.

The couple on the path stared at her, lofting into the air with her dinner, in amazement. "That's impossible," breathed the man. It seemed that both couples were reading from the same unlikely script!

After they left and no one was around, Mark and I got up and walked over to where the hawk had first appeared. We stood respectfully on that spot and gave a prayer of thanksgiving for the blessing, a prayer for her, and prayers to the four directions. For years afterward, we would return once a year to stand again on "her spot," feel our gratitude for her accepting and blessing company, and offer up those prayers afresh.

༄

Urban Raptors

I was putting change in a soap-vending machine in a laundromat in the densely populated suburban town of Belmont, bordering Cambridge, Massachusetts. There were a number of quarters, but one of them kept falling back out into the coin catcher. I picked it up and stared at it idly. To my surprise, the design of a beautiful falcon gleamed on its silver surface. Was it perhaps a state bird? The other state coins had registered in the machine but not this one.

I put the coin in my pocket, poured the soap in a washer, started the machine, and strolled out the door into the afternoon sunshine. Just round the corner I paused at a busy intersection of five streets, including a main road. As I hesitated, trying to decide on the best way to cross, a sudden *whoosh* rushed by my right ear, stirring my hair with the wind of its passing. Open-mouthed, I watched a robin-sized falcon speeding across the traffic intersection like a feathered bullet. It had swooped low to sail by my ear but now it was arcing upwards incredibly fast. As it reached a tall tree across the road, an explosion of thirty or forty sparrows leaped into the air like ardent fireworks. The falcon disappeared in pursuit. The whole incident struck me as some kind of unspoken poem, a strong, swift message, striking but unsortable with my rational mind.

After Mark's second stroke, when we had to move closer to the Boston hospitals, we found ourselves living in a low-budget part of densely populated Belmont. As well as two elaborate "groundhog condo complexes" (at one point sheltering a mother and eight rotund babies) in our side yard, dark, thick evergreen trees lining the back of our building's small parking lot helped bring Nature up close. Behind the trees, a train ran; on the far side of the tracks lay a swamp and public park. Given the urban environs, an unusual amount of wildlife showed up. One evening, as we were dining at a small patio table outside, a self-possessed, slender young mother fox holding a motionless baby rabbit, her pups' dinner, in her mouth, trotted past within three feet of us without a blink. As I was getting out of a car in front of our house after a meeting one night, my driver's quick restraining hand was all that kept me from colliding with a speeding skunk around the size of a tractor trailer. Huge and mostly white, its wild fluff inches deep, Moby Skunk looked like a brakeless parade float racing downhill at accelerating speed. Had its spray been commensurate with its size, it could have decimated the entire neighborhood.

And there were, of course, the owls—quite an assortment of screech owls, tiny, invisible in the dark trees, fierce, and vocal. I often responded to their whinnies with an incompetent amateur version of my own. But they did not disdain to respond, and often we would share extended conversations. I learned over time that I could utter "our whinny" quite softly in our apartment, and the owls, with their extra-sharp ears, would still hear it and respond.

I was amazed at the different pitches and timbres and tempos of the owls' whinnies—so many different voices; it's a mistake to think that birds of the same type always sound alike. I don't know how many small but obviously confident owls lived in the evergreens, but there seemed to be quite a lot of them. One early evening I stood in our little backyard, waiting for Mark to drive us to church. Under my breath I was singing a special piece I offered as a solo in a service once a year, the psalm "By the Waters of Babylon." Suddenly, at a time when he would normally be asleep, a screech owl started screaming and raving ferociously. Sounding like he had a megaphone up his tree, he vented his fury at a shocking decibel level. I realized with a jolt that he was yelling at me, having, amazingly, recognized my sotto voce voice. Rough translation: "WHAT are you doing?!! You know what our song is! That is the WRONG song! Stop it at once! At once, I say, at once!" I did, feeling as abashed as a schoolgirl reprimanded by a stern school principal. When I stopped my misguided musical solo, he stopped shouting, and huffy, offended silence prevailed.

This peculiar relationship with screech owls went on for years in various locales and continues today. One of its more odd and embarrassing aspects I blush to recount. Occasionally, when for inexplicable reasons I am not seeing the obvious (amazing, given my dazzling intellect) but finally crash-land somehow into the correct conclusion, no matter the time of day, midnight or midday, a screech owl will, out of the blue, make one to three very loud jeering cries. As if to confirm, "Yes, stupid, you got it at last!"

One of the times this happened was when I was afflicted by what I thought were spider bites on my scalp that woke me with their stinging in the middle of the night. The next day a nurse friend at church examined them for me but could not tell me anything about them. The day after, fortunately, I had an appointment with my Chinese acupuncturist, Dr. Liu. Although he was uncertain about the bites (shingles is apparently hard to diagnose in its early stages), he did observe, rather admiringly, "Spidah bettah acupuncturist than me! Bites right on gallbladder meridian points!" But the rash got worse and more painful as the week went on. Finally, on Saturday afternoon, almost a week later, the light dawned on me. "It must be shingles!" Three loud, mocking screech owl cries immediately confirmed my tardy diagnosis!

ﻝ

Contemplative Hawk

One Pascha morning, having been up all night at our church's Easter services and feast, we slept a few hours at Mark's mother's in Belmont and then, having gathered coffee and croissants, headed to nearby lush Mount Auburn Cemetery to tour its gently rolling hills studded with flowering trees, splashes of spring blooms, and elaborate carved gravestones and mausoleums. As we cruised very slowly down a quiet lane, I noticed something large on top of one of the gravestones and asked Mark to stop the car. We got out and walked toward the big dark shape hunched motionless on top of an old carved granite headstone. As we got closer we saw that it was not a stone embellishment but rather a handsome broad-winged hawk clutching the top of the gravestone firmly in its talons. Unlike some of the more slender types of hawks, this medium-size buteo projected a solid, football-player kind of massiveness, reminiscent of sepia photos of dignified, big-boned Indian chiefs from the 1800s. But its dark eyes and manner were gentle. Very slowly and quietly we walked closer and closer. It watched us peacefully. When we got within five feet, I began to worry. It didn't fly away. Could it be injured? Was something wrong with its wings or its feathers? We began to talk gently and softly to the hawk, and it seemed to have no objection. As we talked I began to edge to the side of the big raptor so I could see its back and tail. Everything looked all right, even as I got within a foot of the hawk. We were amazed that it seemed to accept us so companionably.

Suddenly we heard harsh cries. Looking up among the nearby trees, we saw two crows flying hurriedly toward us and the hawk. The hawk drew its brows together like a man in an old Excedrin headache commercial. Oh no. Crows! As the black cawing birds approached, diving toward our raptor, the hawk opened his powerful wings and launched himself into the air, disappearing into the trees with the black-feathered posse in hot pursuit. He seemed fully functional. And had, to our joy, brought an extra grace to our grace-filled Pascha day.

Omens

Red-tailed hawks seemed to be particularly Mark's birds, though I also felt an affinity with them, as I did with all raptors. We saw them fairly often even in urban areas. One day as we were driving by Cambridge's Mount Auburn Cemetery during a busy rush hour, Mark spied a large red-tailed hawk standing in the middle of the street, eating some roadkill. Cars were rushing by on either side, barely missing it. Mark pulled up directly behind the great hawk and stopped our car—and much of the traffic as well. Annoyed honking drivers had to pull around us, but Mark was unperturbed. He had the hawk's back, and no one else could get near it. The hawk continued calmly eating, and Mark did not try to hurry it off. We sat there until the hawk finally decided it had had enough, spread its huge wings, and soared into the sky.

On Mark's sixtieth birthday, our dear friends Jim and Anna Higgins planned a barbecue celebration for him in their backyard. We were touched but not in the best of moods during the party. Within a couple of days I would be leaving on a pilgrimage to Bulgaria with our Bulgarian bishop and a small group of parishioners, a gift from generous friends. Mark was not well enough to travel and resented that I was going, and that I would be gone for the two weeks of the pilgrimage. Given his dicey health, he felt that I should not be leaving him. But I was worn out from caretaking and felt a deep need for a drastic, if short-lived, change. And this was a rare and precious opportunity. I felt in my heart that Mark was going to be all right, and even our pastor counseled him that he thought I should go.

So, as we sat and chatted and ate delicious barbecue and salads in our friends' backyard in the shade of a very large and beautiful pine, to our amazement, two red-tailed hawks arrived. They began to circle quite low over the urban backyard, a very unlikely hunting ground, especially given that it was full of people. The big raptors flew around and around, calling out with high-pitched, sharp cries. Suddenly one flew down and stood in the lowest crotch of the pine, only about ten feet over our heads. The other continued to circle low, as both kept calling, each as if urging the other to stay—or to go. I couldn't help but think of Mark, like the hawk perched in the tree, complaining, and me, like the hawk circling in the air, refusing to settle, ready to fly on. After quite a while, both hawks flew off. More often than we would like to admit, our lives are reflected in Nature's looking glass of signs.

At Mark's funeral, six years later, the mourners were in their cars, waiting for the cortege to form up. Our friends the herbalist Tommy Priester and acupuncturist Karen Maguire, both of them very involved with traditional Native American spirituality, were startled to see "a huge red-tailed hawk, the biggest one we've ever seen—and we've seen many" fly very low over the hood of their car. It flew across the street from the church into that busy urban area of bars, eateries, and small stores, alighting on the low parapet of a funky antique store. There it turned to stand at attention and, like a dignified honor guard, watch the funeral cortege. Once Mark's hearse began to move and the other cars to follow, the redtail spread its great wings and sailed off, disappearing into the sky. I was grateful to hear that one of Mark's raptor friends had given him a send-off. So, that time in Jim's and Anna's yard, perhaps I was the hawk in the tree after all, calling out in sorrow, and Mark was the hawk in the sky, getting ready to truly sail on. That's the thing about omens—they are open to more than one interpretation—and more than one can be right.

ﻬ

More Omens

Years earlier, one grim November day, I looked out a window of the Gnome Home to see a huge peregrine falcon standing on the ground less than ten feet away, holding a small dead bird with the big yellow talons of one foot and beginning to consume it. I must have just missed the famously fast hunting dive of the peregrine. This scene was heartbreaking, though. The dead bird was one of the pair of mockingbirds that nested in our yard. Its mate, distraught with grief, was leaping back and forth around a bare multiflora rose bush's black curling branches, just inches from the big raptor's head and cruel beak. Its body language showed that it wished somehow to save its mate, and that it was overcome with shock and panic. The raptor ignored the hysterical mockingbird, calmly concentrating on its meal. I felt as if my heart was being squeezed inside my chest, out of pity for the victim and especially for the recklessly grieving mate, darting wildly around the huge elegant predator's head. This did feel like an omen to me: that Mark and I would not die together but one of us first, swiftly and shockingly—and that it would be him, not me. Sadness drifted down over me like a smoky veil, dimming the bright autumn day.

Despite some of the darker interpretations that sometimes came to mind at these raptor appearances, I also always felt a certain joy. I so loved their beauty and their grace, their quick, keen eyes, their majestic soaring. And, in Native American tradition, hawks are associated with the east and illumination. But there was one bird that, despite its natural beauty, began to give me the shivers at its appearance: the blue jay. Although interpretations vary, in some Native American traditions the blue jay is regarded with suspicion as potentially "bad medicine," a possible ally of sorcerers. I don't know about that, but the jays certainly seemed to have an odd connection in foretelling sad and difficult incidents in my life. I have already mentioned the three blue jays whose atypical appearances coincided with my breakdown after a disastrous church board meeting. After that, at least three different times, blue jays acted very strangely around me, actually flying to the stairs at our door, perching on the iron railing as close to the window as possible, staring into my eyes and screeching and screeching and screeching with their harsh, hysterical voices. The first time this happened, it turned out my father had died the night before. The second time, my closest childhood friend had fallen down the stairs that morning and, though fortunately she survived, had to be rushed to the hospital and received many stitches in her head. A third incident also presaged harm befalling someone close to me. What was striking in all these cases was that the blue jays did not act normally. They came right up to our windows, stared into my eyes, and screamed at me—a fact my amazed husband witnessed. That's the thing with omens—odd behavior on the part of creatures adds extra weight to the possibility of there being some kind of a foreshadowing. We are interconnected with the world around us on all sorts of strange, subtle levels. My challenging relationship with blue jays also was not helped by a horrible incident when a couple I worked for one day insisted that I look out their apartment window with them and watch a blue jay ferociously tearing a live, featherless baby sparrow limb from limb and eating it in front of its horrified parents.

Which is not to condemn blue jays. They are intelligent, lovely-looking birds. Like the rest of us, they are subject to the difficult, chaotic conditions of a fallen world. But I admit that I tend to breathe a bit less easily now when they come close by.

༄

Animal Communication

Mindy and I walked into the Gloucester Petco en route to hunting for our mythical El Dorado, a healthy brand of canned cat food that our cats would actually eat. As we strolled past the banks of terrariums my glance fell upon a couple of cute baby iguanas in one of them. Because, basically, I don't like seeing creatures caged and feel compassion for them, I "threw" a little prayer/blessing in the iguanas' direction. But I was stunned and stopped in my tracks as I felt them "catch" the blessing and lob it back to me, complete with their own additional "psychic text message." I could have pointed out to you spatially the exact spot where their idea-message hit my extended subtle atmosphere and translated itself into words: "We are not happy with the atmosphere of our terrarium." Whoa!

This was a new one for me! Nervously, I told Mindy what had happened. We had a warm relationship with the delightful manager of this Petco, Caroline by name. I asked for her but she was not in that day. For another two days at home I stewed about the iguana interaction. Was it just my imagination? I really knew in my heart that it was not. Embarrassing as it was, I owed it to the iguanas to try to help them out. So I gathered my courage, phoned the store, and asked for Caroline.

"Caroline, it's Stephani. I, um, have something a little strange I need to tell you."

"That's okay. I do strange."

And I told her about the iguana incident.

"Oh," she said. "That's all right. I'm a little that way myself. I'm glad you told me about it. You know, the iguanas are molting right now, and they usually like more moist conditions for that. Let me take a look at them."

A slight pause and then, "Oh my God! Oh my God!"

"What?!"

"I can't believe it!" she said. "Since you were here the other day I put in three more baby iguanas. When I went to look at them, all five of them turned around and pointed their heads at the humidity gauge, staring at it! I'll get on this right away! Thank you for telling me. Please always tell me these things if they come up."

I know, I know. But that is just how it happened.

As I told Caroline, I am not an animal communicator. But I feel the potential for all of us to be animal communicators. There seems to be a zone we can tune in to that helps open up that "channel." A couple of times I have slid close to it. Once it was with my majestic, lord-in-charge cat Winston; the look of unbelieving shock on his face as I got into that psychic vicinity was extraordinary. I hastily backed off. Another time I was in an art gallery. A big, beautiful greyhound reclining on a large, soft cushion stood up and came over to me, assessing me with intelligent eyes. Very gently she put her elegant snout into my hand and looked up at me hopefully. I could feel that she sensed it would be possible for us to converse, and that she had something she really wanted to say. For a moment I balanced right on the edge, but then my cowardice overcame me and, apologetically, interiorly I turned away. It was hard to see the disappointment rise in her beautiful eyes. She returned to her cushion and lay down.

I have been reluctant to get engaged with animal communication, even though it appears to me probably to be real and a good thing to do. I do fear becoming constantly "on call" to every creature around as one possible effect. Although sometimes strange things happen to me, I do not feel at home with every variety of uncanniness, even the benign ones. Perhaps I will have to grow in compassion and love before I take a more deliberate step into this particular kind of conversation.

My friend and housemate Mindy is a fine-jewelry artisan. We both work at home, occasionally in the company of uninvited fellow laborers like spiders. One day Mindy noticed a small spider who seemed attracted to watching her work. Perhaps her fine-motor manipulations resembled delicate spider-leg movements to him? Anyway, Reginald, as she came to call him, would come down and get as close to her fingers as he could and just sit there and watch her. She became fond of him over the few days of their acquaintance but was concerned that he probably didn't have anything to eat or drink. So—and I saw her do this—from time to time she took a little spray bottle and put some drops of water on the edge of a mirror on her wall. She pointed the drops out to Reginald and told him to drink. Before my eyes, he gamely climbed off her worktable, went up her wall, and over to the water droplets. Within a few days Mindy felt that he needed to get outside in order to catch some food. She pried open a corner of the screen in the window over her bed and kept tapping it and calling him, explaining that he needed to go out and why. I watched as Reginald climbed over her bed, up her headboard, and out the open corner of the window!

I've noticed that spiders seem to be especially sensitive and subtle. Most insects ignore your attention unless you actively pursue them. But I have seen many times that, most often, as soon as you see a spider, it will freeze. It is as if it feels the "weight" of your attention and stops cold until it knows your intent. I have found it helpful for removing spiders from the house to let my attention "lie gently" on them and explain mentally why I am putting them out, that I will not hurt them and that they need not be afraid. Usually they will then let me put a container over them without their scurrying or making a fuss. In Native American tradition, spiders have "writers' medicine." They certainly create much beauty from their small selves.

How to get into that animal communication zone? I can't tell you, except that I suspect we can tune in to that level of transmission by being around and studying with someone who is already doing it. Even reading about it can help. But I suspect we would need to be pure in our motives of love and compassion. Any desire to be manipulative, or the crosscurrents of mental or emotional imbalance, are likely to get in the way. The animal communicator Amelia Kinkade writes, "'God is love' as a thought is nonsense. 'God is love' as a feeling is a revelation. Clairsentience travels through a tunnel of love."

For anyone who would like to see a deeply moving—and

persuasive—short video on a striking instance of animal communication, I recommend "The Incredible Story of How Leopard Diabolo Became Spirit" on YouTube. The film recounts the tale of a ferocious formerly abused black leopard who is brought to the Jukani Predator Park for rehabilitation and life in a supportive home. The angry, frightened leopard resists efforts to calm him until, despite the unbelieving attitude of the park owner, the animal communicator Anna Breytenbach is brought in to listen to the leopard and talk to him in gentle silence. She learns much, sharing it with the park personnel, and a deep and beautiful reconciliation occurs. Incidents like this show that there is so much hope for mutual understanding and improving the lives of the creatures around us.

Our cultural secular materialism has often rendered us crude and tone-deaf in relation to the natural world and its creatures. Rather than being obsessed by a brooding fear of "anthropomorphism," we need to adjust our perceptions to recognize what some writers characterize as "anthropocentric hubris"—assuming that only human beings feel and think, especially as so much evidence is accumulating to the contrary.

Some traditional cultures, living closer to the land, retain a greater sensitivity and efficacy in relation to animals. The stunningly beautiful movie *The Story of the Weeping Camel* is a mind-blowing documentary about a mother and baby camel in Mongolia's Gobi desert. After a difficult labor, the mother gives birth to a rare white baby but, traumatized by her first labor, refuses to accept and feed the calf.

Although a kindly Mongolian family hand-feeds the baby, all know it will soon die if the mother does not begin to nurse it. Buddhist rituals are offered and ultimately a special musician is sent for. The man, with his quiet face and manner, plays a simple stringed instrument with a tone somewhat like a violin. He places the instrument on one of the two humps of the mother Bactrian camel "to establish a sympathetic magical linkage between the mother and the state of harmony represented by the instrument." Then, the instrument removed, the lovely young mother of the family begins to stroke the mother camel very gently and sing a haunting, beautiful, and melancholy song, eventually accompanied by the musician—a song specific to the camel's difficulties and handed down through the generations as an instrument of compassionate healing. Eventually, tears begin to flow from the mother camel's eyes, and the family knows that she will now accept her baby, and they bring it to nurse from her, successfully. So much more is possible in healing than we usually allow.

Invisible Waters

When it was time to leave the tipi, Mark and I decided that we would like to spend a little more time exploring gorgeous Vermont before returning to Massachusetts. We took a leisurely drive up into the picturesque Northeast Kingdom. As we entered the pleasant hamlet of Danville, we were surprised to see a billboard reading: "Welcome, dowsers! We needed the rain!" We had arrived the evening before the start of a five-day annual dowsers' convention. So, naturally, we decided to stay and check it out.

> I know very well that many scientists consider dowsing as a type of superstition. According to my conviction this is, however, unjustified. The dowsing rod is a simple instrument which shows the reaction of the human nervous system to certain factors which are unknown to us at this time.
>
> —Albert Einstein

The story behind the billboard was that the Northeast Kingdom had been having some drought, and the local townspeople knew from past experience that whenever there was a dowsers' gathering, it rained and rained and rained! Not only could the dowsers find water, they attracted it! And it did rain, almost every day, while we were there.

Most housing was already taken, but we were fortunate to get hooked up with a kindhearted older couple, Dottie and Emil, who were willing to rent us a room in their home. This smiling pair were the parents of six daughters, all grown. Emil and Dottie exuded a kind of warm grace, reminding me of mature, silver-barked trees, sheltering anyone in need within their gracious shade. We loved staying with them.

The conference itself was endlessly fascinating, with many different workshops running throughout the day—water dowsing, health dowsing, missing-people and -things dowsing, geomagnetic pollution dowsing, animal veterinary dowsing, etc.—and participants were taught to use Y-rods, L-rods, pendulums, and what-have-you as helpful tools.

In one workshop, some men offered to teach us Y-rod water dowsing. My instructor, a chunky middle-aged man, put his arms around me from behind as I held a forked wooden Y-rod in both hands. Having followed directions as to setting up the mental questioning needed to bring forth reactions through the dowsing rod, I suddenly felt a remarkably powerful surge pull the raised rod dramatically toward the earth. Unfortunately, simultaneously, I felt a twin surge of intense lust from my instructor—a bewildering, distressing combination. I separated myself from him as quickly as I could and followed the path of the subterranean water vein I had located, also trying to elicit yes/no answers from the motions of the rod as to its depth, width, and flow per minute. It was exhilarating to feel such a close and speaking kinship with the elements!

Over dinner with Dottie and Emil that night, we discussed what we had learned. They were not dowsers themselves but had a positive attitude toward the craft. We told them about the health workshop we had attended that day where we had been told that it was unhealthy for people to sleep over water veins, disturbed sleep and arthritic conditions often resulting from that confluence. And that dogs avoid sleeping over water veins but that cats love to sleep on them (it figures!).

"You know," Emil said. "Ever since we changed our bedroom a few years ago, Dottie hasn't been sleeping well, and I've developed arthritis. Do you think you could try dowsing our bedroom?"

Mark and I went into their ground-floor bedroom with our new copper L-rods, did our mental preparations, and began to dowse. We were startled to find two substantial water veins beneath their bed, and apparently not very far underground. Being so new to the craft, we were reluctant to credit it, but the results had seemed strong.

"Maybe we better change bedrooms," mused Dottie thoughtfully.

"Or get Paul to move the water veins!" suggested Emil with a smile.

Paul was a Danville resident and president of the American Society of Dowsers. He was a very accomplished master dowser. We had already met two members of the Danville Public Works crew in a café downtown who claimed that, when asked, Paul could actually move water veins mentally. "Very convenient," one of them said. "If we have problems with a broken pipe, we can just ask Paul to move the water vein until we make the repair and then move it back again! It's great!" Emil confirmed that he had heard that same assertion from credible others.

Learning we could have a dialogue with, or at least a deep awareness of, water added yet more richness to our sense of communication and understanding of the natural world, linking us up more intimately with the Kingdom of the Elements.

ॐ

Lightning Rivers
I was bent over the body of the woman lying peacefully on the massage table, my hands extended a couple of inches above her side as, with the other three members of my Reiki healing team, I made myself available to healing energy flowing through me to her during our clinic. As peaceful music streamed from the CD player, I slowly moved along her body until my hands were over her lower abdomen, where I received a shock—a delightful one but nonetheless a shock. I had not known that this woman was pregnant but suddenly felt a startling, energetic fountain of joy leap up forcefully, like pure light, from the little baby girl in her womb as the child reacted to the healing energy coming through my hands. I later confirmed with my teacher, the leader of our team, that the woman was indeed pregnant. Years later I read in a book by a Mohawk medicine woman that in some tribes toddlers were kept away from the vicinity of pregnant women's wombs because of a strong "wind" felt to emanate from the baby in the womb that could somewhat discombobulate them. That emanation did feel like a wind to me. I was enchanted by the baby's pure, luminous delight.

Our next client was a tall, handsome man in his thirties. Though so young, he suffered from advanced prostate cancer. As we worked on him, I began to feel an activated polarity between his genital area and his throat. I got a strong impression that he was such a kind and gentle man that he had heavily suppressed things he needed to say for fear of hurting someone or some people. There is a marked relationship between the sexual organs and the throat—as we see in the change in boys' voices at puberty—and they are both organs of expression and creation. Much of the healing energy passing through our group was working to relieve the strain and tension between those two afflicted centers. Had I been treating the man privately, I probably would have spoken to him about the impression I was receiving, but it did not seem appropriate in the group setting. After the clinic was over, I shared this with my teacher. She said that she was going to also be seeing the man privately and that she would tell him.

A youth, over six feet tall and clanking with silvery metal hardware on his black leather garb, was our unlikely next client. This reluctant sixteen-year-old goth, sent by his mother, regarded us with suspicious eyes. But he did finally climb on the table and settled in stiffly with all his armaments. We silently prayed and began. By the end of the treatment, he was completely relaxed and brimming with surprised happiness. He practically embraced us when he got off the table and thanked us many times.

There were so many lovely harmonies in the Reiki clinic. It was inexpensive, and we received people of a great variety of ages, ailments, and types. We Reiki practitioners were like a string quartet playing a piece full of compassionate love in harmony with each other and the patient to bring about healing guided by the universal healing energy (Reiki) of God and the client's own innate unconscious inner wisdom, on whatever level it was most needed.

I had first learned about Reiki from my pastor's wife, *Popadia* (the Bulgarian honorific for a priest's wife) Laura. An experienced nurse and a loving, compassionate friend, she had visited Mark and me during one of Mark's longer hospitalizations following a stroke. I was staying with him, sleeping in a broken hospital chair next to his bed. We had been in the hospital for days and were as drained and exhausted by its fluorescent glare, beeping machines and noise, relentless routines, and chemical smells as by Mark's sickness itself. We both felt completely worn out and low on hope.

"You two look terrible," Laura said, taking in our white and weary faces. "Let me see what I can do for you."

She told us to just relax and do nothing while she worked. She closed her eyes in prayer and concentration and then began to make slow sweeping passes with her hands a couple of inches above our bodies, sometimes lightly resting them upon us as well. Within twenty minutes or so, we began to feel deeply refreshed—as if we were new people, just awakened from a good sleep. We also felt optimism and hope. It was like a miracle.

"What was that?" we asked her earnestly, after having thanked her. She explained that Reiki was a form of healing with subtle universal energy; this method had been developed by Dr. Mikao Usui, a Japanese man, in the early 1920s. Through earnest prayer and meditation he had received an attunement to be able to focus the universal healing energy that is all around us in a helpful, effective way and was able to transmit this attunement to others.

Reiki is one of many different forms of working with what is commonly called "energy medicine." Like the rivers we can see veining the earth when we fly high above them in an airplane, in our bodies there are the microcosmic rivers of our circulatory and nervous systems and, beyond that, normally invisible but potent fine-energy meridians and chakras, like the myriad geomagnetic energetic pathways in the earth, that channel vital energy. As we experience a change in our perception of the rivers when we are flying above them, so, given the correct inner attunement, we can also experience an altered perception and enhanced awareness of these subtle but vital interior currents, and learn to work to relieve them of impeding blockages, thereby stimulating balance, restfulness, and healing for the suffering.

Impelled by an instinctive response to want to relieve suffering, I had already developed a hands-on style of energy healing I called "soft-sound, gentle-touch," where I gently laid my hands on or above clients' bodies and, as I worked to balance and smooth their energetic bodies by "feel," would at times quietly sing some sounds, most often vowel sounds, and sometimes even encourage the client to sing them with me. The sounds seemed to enhance dissolving energy blockages. A sick lady of delicate constitution whom I worked on for a number of years sometimes needed multiple treatments of this kind in a day to alleviate her distressing symptoms. Although I was willing, after a while I began to feel weaker and unwell. Because I was drawing on my personal chi (vital energy) to help her, I had begun to suffer from a condition that the Chinese, long experienced in energy-healing modalities like Qigong, call "Running Fire." In Running Fire your personal chi can become drained and diminished, and you may even start to take on some of your patients' illnesses. Fortunately, I soon learned two effective energy-healing modalities that bypassed my personal chi and instead drew only on the endless pool of universal chi. One of those was Reiki.

My husband and I were fortunate in finding two excellent Reiki Masters, Ulrike and Denis Dettling Kalthofer, to attune, initiate, and train us in the first and second levels of Reiki (Reiki II empowers you to perform distance healing). When Uli lifted her hands from my head after giving me my Reiki I attunement, she whispered in my ear, "Something came to me as I just did that. Are you interested in hearing it?" I assented. She continued, "This doesn't mean anything to me but perhaps it will to you: 'Pentecost, the dispersion of the Holy Spirit.' Does that mean anything to you?"

"Oh yes, it certainly does! Thank you, Uli." And, I reflected, was this why so many subtle-energy forms of healing had sprung up in recent years? The generosity of the Holy Spirit overflowing to bring healing and relief to the suffering in simple, direct ways? I flashed upon the words of the Old Testament Prophet Joel:

And it shall come to pass afterward, that I will pour out my spirit upon all flesh; and your sons and your daughters shall prophesy, your old men shall dream dreams, your young men shall see visions: And also upon the servants and upon the handmaids in those days will I pour out my spirit. (Joel 2:28–29)

I myself received much healing at the hands of warmhearted Reiki practitioners and, given the attunement and training and the grace of God, was able to help relieve suffering people with Reiki, at least reducing their distress. Encouraged by an insightful herbalist/psychotherapist to whom I was apprenticed, I opened a part-time energy-healing practice (composed of Reiki, my personal method, and providing Bach Flower Essences—the last something I had done for many years) and rented an office part-time from my Reiki teachers.

𝓮𝓵

Working with Dolls
The energy-healing modality I learned soon after and came to use the most is called Tong Ren ("Bronze Man" in Chinese). A remarkable healer, acupuncturist, and Tai Chi and Qigong Master named Tom Tam developed this method. As I remember the story, one day he was leading a Tai Chi class when one of his students had a sudden disabling attack of sciatica. She was in severe pain, but Tom did not have any clean acupuncture needles with him—only some dirty ones in his pocket. Trying to cheer her up, he kidded the aching student, pretending to draw her on a piece of paper and then sticking the dirty acupuncture needles on the meridian points in the drawing that he would have used in an actual treatment. Immediately, her pain stopped. She and Tam looked at each other in amazement, and he realized he had stumbled upon a phenomenon with great potential.

Tom eventually developed a method of effective indirect healing using a small plastic acupuncture doll with meridians and points drawn on it and a slender magnetic hammer. The doll, as Tom explained in his Tong Ren certification classes, was merely a "language," a point of focus, that helped us tune in to the currents of universal healing energy around us and make a direct connection with the body of someone we were treating. We would use the small hammer to lightly bang on the doll following the sequence of points typical of a certain disease or imbalanced state, opening blockages and activating the freer flow of chi, which also prompted increased blood circulation that healed and relieved pain.

Most of the time this was remarkably effective. Distance was in no way a barrier; I treated people from Paris to Hawaii with good results. It even became a surprising instrument to open the heart of my embittered father in the last year of his life. Dad and I loved each other but were not close. After I left for college, he and my mother split up, and he took up with another lady whom he seemed reluctant to let me know about. He had never demonstrated any interest in my life; I think it may have felt like territory that was too foreign to him. After my wedding day, I didn't see him for another twenty-five years or so. In our infrequent phone conversations, I felt that he seemed nervous and not welcoming.

My brother, in a rare call, let me know that our father was seriously ill. He had advancing diabetes and other ailments. I called Dad, and he was frank enough to tell me that he felt great pain and anxiety that his meds were not controlling. Given how desperate he seemed, I plucked up my courage and offered to treat him with Tong Ren over the phone. At first, as expected, he was outraged. An aeronautical engineer by training and angry against God, if He even existed, my father had no toleration for such airy-fairy nonsense. But I begged him until he, still sputtering with indignation, agreed for us to give it a try. I think he experienced one of the greatest shocks of his life as, in the course of an hour on the phone, the Tong Ren treatment was able to bring his pain level from eight, on a scale of one to ten, down to two. He didn't know that such things could happen in the cold, atheistic, "scientific" universe he believed in. I think that not only did it open a door for physical healing for him but also another door, one leading out of his despair. So I treated him once every week or two over the phone for about a year with good results, but his illnesses were already far advanced when we began. Eventually he had to go into the hospital, and I came down from New England to Long Island to be with him and try to help.

He was not doing well. Although I could relieve him temporarily of some of the pain and anxiety, he was clearly sinking. I was concerned about his bitterness of soul and decided that I had to risk mentioning the elephant in the room to him at last.

"Dad," I said gently, "God is real."

"I know that, Stephani!" he said sharply. This was news to me.

"If you are willing, I'd like to anoint you with some holy oil, give you a blessing, and say a prayer," I said quietly, trying not to show my trepidation.

To my great surprise, he said, "I'd like that, Stephani."

I got up and moved closer to him. Taking the small bottle of holy oil out of my pocket, I anointed him with the sign of the Cross on his forehead, laid my hands on his head, and prayed aloud for "the servant of God Joseph Miles." He seemed to drink this in like a thirsty plant receiving healing rain. He thanked me quietly and warmly. An atmosphere of peace and grace had settled on us both and upon the room. I hoped that this was his reconciliation with God. I think that his discovery that healing could come to him so unexpectedly "out of nowhere"—that there was indeed an ineffable divine mercy—had created a crack in the cement wall beneath which he had been denying God for long years. If this could happen, then anything was possible. His body was failing but, so unexpectedly, at the same time, Hope had entered his spirit.

مِلَه

Around this time I was also distance-treating a friend in Maine. Pregnant with her second child, she was finding it impossible to keep food down. Losing weight at a dangerous rate and fearing for the survival of her baby, she had asked for help at various local clinics and social service agencies without success, despite being very low-income. The evening I first treated her was the first time she was able to keep a meal down in several days. I treated her a few more times, and as her system settled down, she retained her food and began to gain weight again.

I distance-treated another friend, this one in New Hampshire, suffering from a foot that went curiously numb at unexpected times. She would stumble going downstairs or fall in the fields of her farm without notice. One treatment reduced the numbness significantly, but it took nine treatments altogether to completely alleviate the problem.

How any practitioner perceives the fundamental states and actions of a client's health in energy-healing treatment varies. Some "see" images, some "hear" indications, some "feel" the problem and are able to alleviate it by compassionate subtle contact—some experience all three modes, singly or together, at various times. This is the case with me, though the predominant impression for me is usually "feeling." This also often includes feeling the actual physical pain of the patient within my own body, though often mercifully "damped down" so that, although my awareness is sharpened, the pain does not overwhelm me. This sometimes includes pains or blockages not reported by the patient, most often because the primary pain dominates his or her awareness. But these subtler blockages often seem to "wave their hands" at me, signaling with relief that they need to be attended to—and, especially as they are often contributing to maintaining the primary pain, are important to bring to awareness and unblock.

Once I was at a conference and a member of our group, a doctor, was sidelined by intense abdominal pain. I asked him if he would like a treatment (I had brought my Tong Ren doll and hammer along), and he eagerly assented. During the treatment we chatted a little, and he told me about his good "friend," a surgeon, who had operated on him many times for hernias. "He says he thinks his hernia patients should have another hernia operation once a year," the doctor said, chuckling. I could not even smile at this wild assertion as I was getting one of my rare but, in this case, very vivid interior images: his abdominal area looked like a crazy quilt to me, with various areas stitched together at odd angles in a chaotic fashion. The feeling was horrible, and perhaps doubly so for me since I, too, had had a hernia operation, so it was uncomfortably close to home. I felt like I was staring right at awful malpractice but would be unable to say a thing as I knew the doctor was completely invested in his surgeon's competence. And I, after all, was only an energy healer. So I just prayed and treated him as best I could. With the doctor's pain level significantly relieved after the treatment, he was able to return to attending the conference.

ॐ

In Danger

I woke up one morning in the Gnome Home in the most excruciating pain I had ever experienced—worse even then the strangulated hernia I had once had that made it impossible for me to stay still. This pain was many times worse—an agony that made it impossible for me to move at all. When I was finally able to look in a mirror, I saw an unrecognizable, sallow face: the right side of my face was hugely puffed out and extended. I looked more like a close-up two-page spread of a fish photo in *National Geographic* than a human being. I also could barely open my mouth. All I could do was sit, stunned, emitting a low moan.

Mark was horrified when he saw me and wanted to call an ambulance. It seemed as if I must be suffering from a runaway infection in my face—a very dangerous condition, especially if the infection traveled on to the brain, which could be fatal. And yet, struggling to speak, I begged Mark not to call an ambulance. I had heard an interior voice when he first made the suggestion. It warned me not to take the ambulance and implied that, if I did, I would die before I reached the hospital; there was a suggestion that my condition was so delicate that any jolt on the road could push the infection further on, fatally.

Discerning guidance had been an important part of my life for many years; when there were "voices" involved, I experienced different degrees of conviction, depending. Sometimes voices seemed "casual" to me, and I usually assumed they were just "mind noise" (sometimes they were, but sometimes they did turn out to be actual guidance); sometimes the voices seemed "deeper," and I was more careful to pray and meditate about those; and once in a great while a voice came that I knew irrefutably was the truth. This time I knew that this was the rare, bedrock "truth" voice, and I would ignore it at my peril. Unlike voices that may come in mental illness, feeling like an outside attack or an inner compulsion, the voices of real guidance come from a source of genuine knowing deep within, stemming from our truest self and its deep, inviolable living connection with the Spirit.

It was hard for Mark to agree to not calling an ambulance. Only his many years of life with me and our working with guidance helped him trust me enough not to do it. I did have him call our dentist, though, since I figured the odds were great that this was some kind of runaway dental infection, and request an antibiotic and a painkiller. Our dentist was worried and tried to convince Mark to bring me to his office—an hour away. Out of the question, but he did call in a prescription for the antibiotic, which probably saved my life, and a painkiller, which, regrettably, did not have a strong impact on my massive pain. The pain level turned some of my hair gray overnight.

I didn't lie down for six weeks, as the pain in my face would increase astronomically whenever I moved my head at a lowering angle. For two weeks I couldn't eat more than a few very soft noodles and broth spooned into the thin crack that was as far as I could open my mouth. Living with the pain was exhausting and draining. Fortunately, Mark was kind and patient.

Slowly the enormous swelling went down and the pain reduced. Eventually you could not tell from my appearance, except from my looking so pale and washed out, that anything traumatic had happened. But I was very slow to recover my strength. A friend had read in a homeopathy book that the remedy *Carbo vegetabilis* could be used when you felt that you were having difficulty recovering from an illness. I had thought of it only as a digestive remedy but decided to give it a try. After taking *Carbo vegetabilis 30c*, I was surprised to note that I did feel better. So I soon took *Carbo vegetabilis 200c*, a stronger potency, and felt a marked immediate improvement. It had been as if I were trying to rebuild a house but only its wall frame was standing. With this remedy, I felt suddenly as if the "floor" had been put solidly in place and that I could begin to build more rapidly from there.

Soon after I made a few short excursions from the house with Mark. We learned that a group of classical Turkish musicians associated with the Mevlevi Sufi order were going to give a concert in Cambridge. We both greatly wanted to attend and decided to risk the hour-plus drive. The concert was beautiful and full of a penetrating mystical energy. Afterward, out on the street where the early-spring leaves were just starting to form on the trees, I felt caught up in an inexplicable special state, almost as if I were somehow twirling in peace and starry joy in a twinkling harmony with the gradually unfurling leaves. That night when I got home, I anointed my gums, as I had for some time, with healing oil from St. John Maximovich's shrine but this time felt a new, positive, and intense sensation, as if spiritual energy was itself twirling in my gums in the anointed areas, healing powerfully and dynamically.

Soon after, I saw a dental specialist recommended by my dentist. When I told him what had happened to me, he said that there would be visible signs from that level of trauma, and he could see none. I could only think of the twirling healing of the Mevlevi concert and the Saint John's oil, when I felt that something fundamental physically, as well as spiritually, was changing in my mouth. Perhaps it had.

Over time I gained strength and began to live a more normal life, but there still seemed to be a big energetic deficit that I could not come back from. Mark and I began to pray about it and felt that we got guidance that I needed to go to Monhegan Island in Maine by myself for five days, mostly on silence, in order to more fully recover. But, chronically low-income as we were, we did not have the funds. The months passed and I seemed to only be barely holding my own.

We decided to offer a forty-day canon to the Virgin Mary about it. This involves chanting or reading nine odes of an intercessory prayer each day during a specified period and is a frequent aid to Orthodox Christians who wish to implore her help. We began it at the very end of summer, concerned that I somehow get out to Monhegan before the cold weather came on.

In September our church had an annual harvest festival with crafts, music, storytelling, food, and also a yard sale and raffle. We always bought raffle tickets but, as the years went by, never won anything. This year when the ticket for the top prize was pulled—a mountain bike—our name was on it, to our amazement. Some grumbled, thinking the Colbys would not use a mountain bike, and so it would be a waste. But not so—we saw the Holy Mother's hand in this unexpected win. We sold the mountain bike, which provided most of the funds I needed to get to Monhegan. We were overjoyed and continued to pray the canon. On the fortieth day of the canon, I was on the mail boat from Port Clyde, heading out into the cold dark blue Atlantic waters, our prow pointed toward Monhegan.

The weather was unusually fine, sunny and warm, for Monhegan after the first week of October. I had lovely days silently wandering the great sea cliffs and spreading meadows, the enchanting trails in the spruce forests, and listening to the soothing, invigorating music of the waves. I got to walk gently through forests where wild deer munched tree leaves near me without startling, and reminisced about the beauty I had seen in Monhegan during other rare autumn visits: Monarch butterflies in migration getting inebriated on fermented tree sap and brawling with each other like drunken ballerinas; living garlands of monarchs lining the gravelly cliff paths, perched like great orange flames on candles of cobalt-blue gentian blossoms. I had found all the feathers (but no bones) of a yellow flicker on a cliff, a raptor's gift; the flicker is associated with healing. Rafts of thousands of big eider ducks floated like foam below the cliffs and could be set off by a seal's startled snort, ascending into the skies rapidly, their wingbeats sounding like hundreds of bolts of heavy silk being flapped open in the wind. One night every meter of the sky was covered at sunset with a dozen shades of glowing crimson. I was lost in beauty and, day by day, being healed. At the end of the five days, Mark came to spend the weekend with me. We had a glorious time—and even one night, a huge looming angel stood in the center of a sunset sky completely awash in myriad shades of gold, its wings unfurling over us in glowing glory. We felt blessedness and with great joy offered prayers and toasts to our Holy Mother who had made me whole.

A Quiver Full of Arrows

I respect contemporary conventional medicine but not with the monomaniacal worshipful fixation our culture encourages us to cultivate in ourselves—as if no other effective healing modalities can be of use. My life has been saved and I have been healed of sickness by both conventional medical and alternative/traditional medical practices, and I am grateful to both. However, the fear- and profit-fueled medical model that dominates our culture today often does not operate in the best interests of the patient. Sometimes gentler, far less expensive interventions, more finely tuned to a given individual's condition, that stem from alternative and traditional medical approaches, can be the most effective aids to health. So-called "scientific studies" of these alternatives often seem to be set up to fail, whether through the ignorance of the experiment designers or deliberate bad intent—for example, studies of the herb echinacea as a cure for colds where the dosages prescribed are far below those known by trained herbalists to be effective, or reviews of homeopathic medicines fatally using inappropriate pharmaceutical, rather than the correct homeopathic, protocols.

Herbalism, homeopathy, and aromatherapy have been great helps to me. You might say that the herb itself is the "medium" state of the plant; naturally chemically active, it can heal or harm, depending on appropriate usage. In homeopathy, the plant or other natural substance is so diluted and succussed (shaken) that, although it can be powerfully healing, it can rarely do any harm; it is theorized that its healing action may be more in the nature of an electronic signature. Essential oils, the distilled and thus most intense state of the plant, can be very healing but, due to their great concentration, can also harm; essential oils are rarely taken internally in the U.S. (and must never be confused with "fragrances," toxic synthetics that may mimic them). These modalities can bring healing and comfort in many different forms.

In my first editorial job I learned the old proofreaders' trick for tired eyes: lying down, closing them, and putting cotton balls lightly soaked in pure rose water on the eyelids. The anti-inflammatory quality of rose water reduced swelling and refreshed the eyes. Herbally, the rose plant, among many other uses, has an affinity for the female reproductive system. The essential oil of rose also has a calming effect, among other virtues. When my husband was recovering from his strokes, I noticed that putting rose essential oil in our candle-warmed diffusers always relaxed him. But I was also surprised to note the more powerful action of the oil of centifolia roses over that of oil of damask roses for putting Mark to sleep quickly. Research indicated that centifolia roses contained a significantly higher percentage of sedative chemical constituents than the damask, though both were helpful. Every type of plant is different, with its own individual virtues.

I always carry essential oil of lavender with me since there is no way to know when I or someone in my vicinity might get a burn. It is one of the few essential oils that can usually safely be used neat on the skin, without a more neutral carrier oil. One night my husband and I were dining in a Vietnamese restaurant and found ourselves waiting an inordinate amount of time for our waiter to return with our dishes. A distressed hostess eventually came to tell us that our server had badly burned his arm in the kitchen. I told her I had something I thought could help him and to please send him out. When our waiter arrived, he was cringing with pain and his forearm was lobster red from the burn. He had run cold water over it but was hurting badly. I asked him to let me pour lavender oil over the burn. His pain diminished in a few minutes. I gave him the bottle of lavender oil to reapply when needed. I also gave him a few pilules of homeopathic *Cantharis 30c* orally. He was shocked at how quickly he experienced relief, and had no blisters or scarring, as we discovered a few months later when we visited another Vietnamese restaurant owned by the same family, and the waiter treated us like beloved long-lost family.

At the other end of the spectrum from the strong essential oils, homeopathy brings us the plant (or other natural substance) in its most refined, delicate, and diluted form, but one that is nonetheless very powerful. Founded as a systematic medical modality in the 1700s by the great German doctor Samuel Hahnemann, homeopathy follows the ancient Law of Similars (promulgated by Hippocrates and Paracelsus, among others) that "like cures like." The Greek *homoios* means "similar," and *pathos* means "suffering."

In the nineteenth century, homeopathy actually became the modality favored by the more educated classes. Mark Twain, Nathaniel Hawthorne, Daniel Webster, Harriet Beecher Stowe, Henry Wadsworth Longfellow, Charles Dickens, Goethe, Yeats, the prime minister Disraeli, and Pope Pius X were all homeopathy supporters, not to mention the British royal family. I remember wondering as a child when reading *Little Women* why their beloved Marmee was always prescribing arsenic and belladonna for her sick children. I knew they were poisons! But clearly she was prescribing the homeopathic versions, where what would have been toxic in its raw substance became powerfully healing in its dilute and succussed homeopathic form. Henry James also paid homage to homeopathy in his novels.

Members of the young AMA (American Medical Association), furious at the large market share of patients who preferred homeopathy to the AMA's relatively brutal medical approach in the 1800s (the domain of the "barber surgeons" with much indiscriminate bloodletting with leeches, among other things), began a ferocious campaign to stamp out homeopathy and, over the years, almost succeeded, forcing the many homeopathic medical schools and hospitals to close, despite their notable success in saving lives in the infectious epidemics that swept the country (death rates in homeopathic hospitals were often one-half to one-eighth those in the standard medical hospitals).

Although homeopathic remedies are often made from plants, they are also made from minerals, animals, and other substances. The *Cantharis 30c* I gave our burned Vietnamese waiter is made from Spanish fly! I try to keep it in my kitchen because it is such an effective oral burn remedy.

And I always carry *Arnica montana* 200c. Made from a daisy-like plant that is rather toxic in its basic substance and thus not taken internally, Arnica is useful in bringing down swelling and inflammation in contusions.

℥

Flower essences are a particular form of homeopathy that can be used for physical healing but tend most often to treat emotional states. In the 1930s a remarkable Welsh doctor, Edward Bach, investigated the making of simple essences from nontoxic flowers set in water in sunlight and then removed. He developed an array of thirty-eight essences, each keyed to a different emotional affliction—e.g., Mimulus for specific fears, Red Chestnut for fears for the welfare of others, Agrimony for tension and secret suffering disguised beneath a smiling face. He also combined five flower essences in a great emergency remedy he called Rescue Remedy.

These remedies have helped thousands, both people and animals; more and more veterinarians use them, a good sign of their efficacy, as you can't talk animals into manifesting a placebo effect!

When I was in a five-day Bach Flower Essences training, one of my fellow students kept a shelter in her yard and home for "traumatized roosters." She said she had a good cure rate with these abused animals by using Star of Bethlehem flower essence, the chief trauma and shock essence in Rescue Remedy.

"I always know when they need another dose too," she added. "They'll all fly onto the railing on my deck and hold their beaks open until I go down the line, dropping a couple of drops of Star of Bethlehem into each beak!"

Flower essences do not cure by suppression but rather by infusing the sufferer with the positive personality of the plant and thus encouraging them to retune to a more wholesome vibration. There are now hundreds, perhaps thousands, of flower essences. Some are better vetted than others. I have been a practitioner of the Bach system for many years but have also done some exploration in other flower essences. The most striking discovery I've made to date is finding that the flower essences of Self-heal (in the mint family) and Violet together seem to be a specific for healing the pain of bereavement. Like other forms of homeopathic remedies, flower essences are nontoxic and gentle, not interacting with herbal or pharmaceutical remedies. I am deeply grateful to be able to utilize their subtle but powerful healing.

Certain homeopathic, herbal, and aromatherapy remedies I experience as if having a helpful collection of arrows in my quiver that I can use to help myself and others. Although I don't have extensive training in any of these areas, I feel that the Holy Spirit often brings an unknown remedy to my attention just before someone presents with really needing it. I am well aware of the pitfalls of dilettantism in health care and tend to err on the side of caution. However, in a country where every household used to have its pantry full of useful and well-vetted home remedies, it seems criminal that our right to treat ourselves medically in even the most basic ways has been ripped out of our hands and transferred legally and mechanically to a medical-industrial complex. Without even being able to use the simple remedies with which our Creator has surrounded us, no wonder we feel more and more alienated from the natural world and from our own capacity to help ourselves and others. We lose our natural inheritance and place of communion with the plants and other beings on the council through this unnatural separation.

Acupuncture is also a modality I have greatly benefitted from, and it helped my husband recover from his strokes in a time so short as to astonish his therapists.

Even astrology can be medically—and otherwise—useful. I realize that some will gasp with horror at reading this "daring" assertion, but too often there are knee-jerk reactions of resistance to this topic so that it cannot even be rationally considered. One can misuse astrology like anything else, but this unique combination of art and science can show us much about the natural world and its cycles. For Christians and others who may fear that it is demonic and forbidden, it would be well to distinguish between a misused form where individuals believe that they do not have free will and that the planets control them and their lives (and leave God out of the equation altogether) and a rational form that takes account of certain cyclic energetic influences that may or may not be caused by (but come in tandem with) certain celestial patterns. On a day when I have some important events scheduled, I might check an astrological ephemeris to learn what macrocosmic stresses and helpful energies could be moving through our universe that day, like checking the prevailing winds before going out on a sail. The winds will not make something happen, but their influence will be part of the equation, and a wise sailor will be forewarned.

Then there are those who react against astrology because they feel that it is superstitious and "not scientific"—ideas that have probably been drummed into their heads since childhood.

Thoughtful investigation is the best answer to this accusation. I became interested myself through gardening and planting by the moon, as is done in many traditions. I learned that plants planted when the moon is in Water or Earth signs, regarded as fertile, tend to thrive, while those planted in Fire or Air signs, regarded as barren, don't do very well. So I tried to set up an experiment. I planted two small gardens side by side, one on a day shown as a Water Moon and the other on a day shown as a Fire Moon in a Farmers' Almanac I had picked up. Well, they did grow dramatically differently! One garden was lush and green with big, healthy plants. The other was puny and slow to grow. But, to my shock, these results appeared to be opposite to the traditional indications—the Fire Moon was the lush garden and the Water Moon the pathetic one! Then I discovered my error—I should have used an astrological ephemeris, not a Farmers' Almanac. For reasons not worth describing here, their identification of the timing of Moon signs is different. When I got an actual ephemeris, I discovered that the dramatic difference in growth and health of my gardens corresponded perfectly with the appropriate Water and Fire sign characteristics. And I had both an unintentionally double-blind experiment and another helpful insight into the natural world and its wonders.

ﷺ

Demons

> The best definition I have for Satan is that it is a real spirit of unreality. The paradoxical unreality of this spirit must be recognized. Although intangible and immaterial, it has a personality, a true being. . . . Satan's personality cannot be characterized simply by an absence, a nothingness. It is true that there is an absence of love in its personality. It is also true, however, that pervading this personality is an active presence of hate. Satan wants to destroy us. . . . The spirit of evil is one of unreality, but it itself is real. It really exists. To think otherwise is to be misled. Indeed, as several have commented, perhaps Satan's best deception is its general success in concealing its own reality from the human mind.
>
> —M. Scott Peck, from *People of the Lie:*
> *The Hope for Healing Human Evil*

The first time I remember feeling a soul entrapped by demonic possession was on Pascha night during my first year in Boston. As I've related, a friend and I had gotten lost in a dangerous section of downtown Boston close to midnight and had been rescued by a kind middle-aged woman who led us out of the gang-infested area to the Greek Orthodox cathedral we had been seeking. Inside the great church everything was light and joy; we were relieved and grateful to be there.

Soon, after Orthros ended and before divine liturgy began, we started to make our way out of the church, as a number of others were also doing. To our surprise we heard loud yelling and raving. The ushers suddenly closed the huge doors of the church and stood against them, letting no one leave. They said a drunken man was on the cathedral steps and the police had been sent for. No one could leave until he was removed. I closed my eyes, leaned against the wall, and began to pray. An impression came through that wrung my heart with pity—that the man was not drunk but possessed, and his soul was fighting heroically, trying to get to the awakened Light he could feel filling the cathedral and those there. The demon fought him compellingly, trying to drag him away, and what we heard was the noise of their combat. I prayed so hard I could barely stand for the weakness in my knees but to no avail. I had not the virtue, authority, or power to effectively help the imprisoned soul. At last he was taken away, never having been able to enter.

ﷺ

For a period of about three years, I seemed to have an increased sensitivity to people suffering from demonic possession. I don't know why this occurred. At that time, we were doing a lot of prayer and meditation practices with Light in my Christian Community. We trained ourselves to respond to negative presences with the thought *Stand in the Light of Christ or leave!*—testing the spirits, as St. John the Evangelist recommends in his Gospel letters. This seemed effective even in dreams, at least to some degree.

But for me personally in waking life, if a possessed person approached within a block or two, I would start to feel a light electric current running over the surface of my skin. At that moment I would become aware of both the person and the demon—and they would become aware of me. We could feel each other's approach. For unknown reasons, this tended to happen most often around Coolidge Corner in Brookline.

Once a large possessed man, his face contorted with the demon's rage, chased me into a store there. We spoke no words. Though most such contacts were equally negative, even if nothing overt happened but an unpleasant, subtle mutual recognition (I usually crossed to the other side of the street when possible), one day a small youngish woman, obviously suffering from a certain degree of Down syndrome, who was standing next to me waiting for a subway train and giving off that possessed electricity, looked up at me with deep, mournful eyes and said sadly, "There are two persons inside of me." I could only look at her in sympathy and say a quick silent prayer for her before we left on our trains.

We are far too quick to relegate the idea of the reality of demons, and demonic possession, to ancient myth. As Dr. Peck has pointed out, such an attitude gives these fallen spirits too much latitude to deceive and potentially entrap us. The famous exorcist Malachi Martin points out that disbelief in the reality of Satan gives it and its demons an enormous advantage in relation to us—"the ultimate camouflage. Not to believe in evil is not to be armed against it." Mental illness can involve but—given my own admittedly limited experience working for a few years in a major university's psychiatric clinic and also in halfway houses for the mentally ill—rarely does involve demonic possession. Having seen thousands of psychiatric patients at our clinic job, a strongly intuitive Christian colleague and I felt that we had seen only one possessed patient—oddly, an eleven-year-old boy. Which is not to say that I believe our identifications were infallible, either way. But merely that it is important to distinguish between actual mental illness and the imprisoning domination of a human soul by a fallen spirit.

As to how someone might come to be possessed. I have read that sometimes conditions of severe shock, physical and/or emotional, might open a person to the possibility of that awful slavery, but that a certain degree of willing cooperation is also essential. Aside from trauma, Dr. Peck mentions, in two of the cases he witnessed, a loneliness that predisposed the individuals to heeding voices and presences that at first seemed friendly but grew increasingly more menacing. Not knowing the causes, we should not judge as "weak" a person who has become possessed—we do not know what that person has been through, and it is even possible in some cases the person has been singled out because his or her inherent virtue is potentially a threat to satanic powers. A gradually increasing possession can even begin in childhood. Involvement with the occult can also be a factor, Dr. Peck states. And I would imagine that certain states of debauchery and negativity might open a door, slowly or quickly, into the darkness. Apparently free will is also a factor in the situation; what motivates the possessed individual to increasingly accept the sometimes-disguised demonic suggestions and allow that influence to grow until it dominates him or her is something at times revealed to exorcists during a successful exorcism, according to the literature.

Exorcism and the regaining of spiritual freedom is possible but rare, difficult, and demanding upon everyone involved. I have been grateful that my only contacts with such tragic situations have been brief and glancing.

◆

I was sitting on a crowded Boston subway train when a short, chunky, dapper traveler stepped briskly into our car. Late middle aged, dressed in a three-piece suit and fedora, this man craned his large-nosed face eagerly around, gazing with a crow's sharp, hard-glinting eyes at his fellow passengers. He grinned and, with a raconteur's ease, began loudly and clearly talking, talking, talking. What he said was not nonsensical but neither was it relevant in any way, and yet he seemed to hold his listeners spellbound.

When he came aboard, I had groaned silently. I had seen this man before on the T. Feeling the prickly electricity shimmering again over my own skin, I knew I was once more in the presence of the possessed. And one who was deliberately impinging on the consciousness of everyone traveling within his reach. I was tired and irritable, distinctly annoyed at being confronted with this malefic phenomenon. Poor me! Grudgingly, I started to pray silently, but my heart was not in it. The words were "correct," asking help for the besieged soul, but the emotional content was just an annoyed "Get rid of him!!!"

As soon as I began to "pray," the little man broke off halfway through a sentence and walked over to stand directly next to me, holding the pole by my seat. "You know, folks," he said slowly and deliberately, as if pondering, "there are still witches around!" And he glanced quickly down at me.

I knew he was referring to me and what I was doing. Quite right too! Aaaargh! Rebuked by a demon! How low could I go?! Because the fact was that I was not genuinely praying, just going through the motions, without compassion, without love, with only the manipulative intent of getting rid of this nuisance as quickly as possible. Manipulation on inner levels is what we call sorcery, and, by my casual coldheartedness, I was indeed functioning as an inept "witch."

Instantly I felt convicted and repented. How could I be so stonyhearted? I made myself think of the suffering soul inside that demon-dominated body, and suddenly it wasn't so hard to feel compassion anymore, along with my shame. I prayed to the Lord Jesus and especially to our Holy Mother Mary, with sincerity and sadness for the captured soul. The possessed man had resumed his usual inane patter, but suddenly, as I began to feel the presence of the Virgin Mary entering our car as if on floating clouds of gentleness, he broke off his shtick again and cried out in alarm, "Oh! Oh no, folks! I'm in trouble now! I'm getting into hot water! It's boiling here! I gotta get off! I gotta go! I gotta get out of here!" The train stopped, the doors opened, and he leapt out.

Another day I was also on the T, this time on a very crowded streetcar that stopped at the long traffic light at the corner of Harvard and Commonwealth Avenues. There were so many of us standing that five or six other people and I were crammed into the area between the windshield and yellow floor line where no one was supposed to stand. As we stood at the red light, I felt electricity shimmer over my skin and knew that a possessed person was near. Suddenly a man started barking loudly; you could tell that it was not really a dog. Looking over my shoulder, I saw a bald, middle-aged, blocky man standing on the corner, throwing his head back and barking. A cocky teenage boy who had just gotten off our streetcar walked up to him and barked back into his face. The man's expression of shocked, indignant response before he resumed barking again was comical. The boy drifted on.

Facing away from the disturbed man, I began to pray to the Lord and especially to the Virgin Mary for him. I did begin to feel her presence. As soon as that happened, the possessed man stopped barking and yelled in a cold and lucid voice, "Stop telling her to do that! Don't tell her to do that! Stop telling her to do that!!!" I noticed that all the people clustered around me were staring at me strangely. Peeking over my shoulder, I saw that the possessed man, continuing his rant, had extended one arm fully from his shoulder and was pointing distinctly right at me as he yelled with an intense, vindictive expression on a face grown crudely menacing. I was so rattled by this very obvious public calling-out that, startled, I broke off praying. At that moment, as the streetcar jolted into motion, moving away, I heard the man give an ugly laugh and scream aloud in demonic triumph.

Clearly the presence of our Lord Jesus Christ and the Virgin Mary is intolerable to demons. Most of us appear to be protected from the worst effects, as well as a consciousness of demonic forces most of the time. But we need to be awake to their existence and our occasional encounters with them, availing ourselves of the protection also of the Archangel Michael. This is one of those situations in which having a talking relationship with our Creator is critical to mental health, spiritual protection, and survival.

༄

Angels

As it is important to be awake and wary of negative spiritual influences such as these, it is even more important to be aware of the loving, unflagging aid of the angelic presences, sent by God to help us on every level of our lives. Once a year in the Holy Order of MANS we used to have an "angel class" where we chanted individually the names of the seven archangels and meditated upon them.

The practice of chanting the archangels' names came in handy one cold winter night when Mark and I were returning to Rockport from Boston. We were about halfway home when an unanticipated snowstorm whirled in, quickly becoming a whiteout blizzard. There were only woods, and occasional obscure exits, along this stretch of highway, and we could see nothing at all through our windshield—just matte white, as if a fluffy blanket had been pulled tightly over our car. Even when I opened the door as we cruised along at a walking pace, I could see no more than three inches from the car. We didn't dare stop for fear that someone, blind as we were, might crash into us from behind. But we also didn't dare drive at more than a crawl for fear of hitting an unseen someone ahead of us.

We had a long way to go, including passing over a steel-arch bridge high above the Annisquam River. The dangers of our situation were all too vivid, and the blizzard showed no sign of clearing. As we felt fear clutching at us, Mark and I decided to pray to the Archangel Michael and then chant his name. We did this, and quite soon, after beginning to chant "Mi-cha-el," we felt a kind of bell jar descend over us, full of a powerful sense of protection, peace, and safety. This feeling did not waver, even though it took us four hours, rather than the usual half hour, to get home. We even somehow—thanks be to God and the Archangel Michael!—were able to drive over the four-lane bridge safely, though completely blind, without making a fatal plunge into the river far below. A short time after we had traversed the bridge, the storm began to thin slightly so, joy and relief rising in our hearts, we could begin to faintly make out certain landmarks. Not long after, we were at last home. We never forgot the calming, guiding power of the great Archangel Michael.

CHAPTER THIRTEEN

Catacombs: Finding the Forgotten in Journeys to the Ancients: England, Greece, and Turkey

England: Changing the Stories

Every man's life is a fairy tale written by God's finger.
—Hans Christian Andersen

We were circling above the British countryside, our jet like a lazy raptor riding high thermals. What we saw below us had a mythical glow—hilly fields of green and gold and purple joined in squares and rectangles like a rumpled quilt, a delicate embroidery of lacy hedgerows stitching them together. Slanting rays of densely golden sunset light poured over them like manna, magnifying their beauty, which somehow managed to be at once magnificent and cozy—Tolkien's Shire unexpectedly spread out in splendor beneath us. Since our landing at Heathrow had been delayed, while patiently hovering we were given this fairy-tale landscape as our enchanted introduction to England.

I wondered, as I had several times during the flight, in the still-active little-girl portion of my mind, what it would be like to meet an English person who would whisk us away to stay in their castle with them! To see such a magical landscape below seemed to invite the possibility, embarrassed as I would have been to confess my hopeful desire aloud.

But, as in any fairy tale, we did not remain in bliss. The woman sitting across the aisle from me whipped out a bottle of perfume and sprayed herself heavily. And I had my usual allergic reaction to synthetic fragrances but worse this time, my throat and sinuses instantly filling with a heavy fog. Mark and I were exhausted and sleep-deprived from packing and dealing with pre-trip home responsibilities, both drooping like drought-stricken plants, and now, perfume-poisoned, I drooped even lower.

But we were very excited about this trip—in my case, my first to England—taken to celebrate our twentieth wedding anniversary. Funds from the sale of his late mother's house enabled us to make this journey, and Mark's stroke the year before, from which he was almost entirely recovered, had spurred us on to take a chance on realizing one of our dreams: to visit the world-famous Mottisfont garden of old roses at its June peak of bloom.

We reentered the unenchanted world at Heathrow, including pacing for what seemed miles down an allegedly moving walkway that did not move. When we finally reached the baggage terminal, we discovered that it was afflicted with the opposite problem: the machinery was hyperactive, as if some unobservant technician had left the controls on triple speed. Luggage was whizzing by us as if ambitious to break the sound barrier. Mark, strong as he was, had to leap forward to grab our luggage and was dragged along by our suitcases as if he were a cowboy struggling with a willful, speeding heifer at a rodeo. It took a few manic passes to effect the rescue of our things. If we were in a fairy tale now, it was by Lewis Carroll, and our looking-glass environment was getting more and more crazed with each passing moment.

We had planned to stay overnight at an airport hotel and handily found two large shopping-cart-like trolleys for our luggage. Pushing them to the hotel through tall hallways unexpectedly involved going up hills and down valleys—bad enough but made much worse by the fact that the wheels of the willful carts seemed to have their own convictions about the direction in which they would be pleased to roll (seldom in accord with ours and even sometimes disagreeing among themselves!). We were dragged back and forth, up and down, by their quarreling weight, sometimes crashing into passage walls. By the time we reached the hotel desk, we looked as if we had just survived, barely, a World War II battle.

As we staggered into our hotel room, I discovered that I had suddenly developed a shocking cold, both nose and chest engaged. I poured assorted homeopathic and herbal remedies into myself and, sneezing and hacking, crawled into bed, where I slept for eighteen hours and, thanks be to God, mysteriously awakened well.

In the meantime Mark had rented a car for us and had begun his harrowing attempts to drive on the opposite side of the road from what he had all his life. As we departed the airport, we had assorted adrenaline-rush adventures, like driving toward a moving bus in its lane (the wrong one), and Mark nearly taking out a couple of tanks at a gas station. This did not do his still-recovering-from-the-stroke nerves any good and scared me half to death.

But somehow we finally arrived at the "self-catering cottage" we were renting in lovely Hampshire in southern England and were warmly greeted by two older British ladies and their beagles, who led us to our charming terraced apartment. Soothed and settled in comfortably with a working fireplace, small conservatory, and pretty backyard garden, we exhaled. And, over the next several days, discovered the sensationally vivid charms of the over two hundred square mile New Forest (new since William the Conqueror declared it his personal hunting park in 1079), lush with huge ancient trees, flowering heathland and moorland, fields of maroon foxgloves in full bloom, sparkling water meadows, and quiet hedgerow-lined roads where semi-wild ponies, donkeys, long-horned Scottish cattle, and several varieties of elegant deer wandered at will (not to mention the substantial sounder of pigs we had to make way for as they were gently urged along the road by a pig herder!). Gaping at the million shades of green that embroidered the landscape, I watched slack-jawed as we leisurely drove past gorgeous thatched cottages with a surf of foaming cottage gardens breaking in rainbows against their walls and realized that people were actually living in them—this was not Disney World! This was the real thing, still alive in our decadent days! We ate good meals at warm-timbered pubs and drank local elderberry brandy and ate Stilton cheese by our dancing fire in the evening.

We went to the Mottisfont rose garden three times and almost perished from terminal delight. It was all glorious, but the farthest back of the brick-walled gardens surpassed my imagination in painting an ideal fairy-tale princess's garden. Long rows of bushy lavender framed extravagant tableaus of burgeoning roses in all colors, set off by choirs of white foxgloves and tall Madonna lilies, surrounded by a dazzling mix of other flowers, and leading to a frothy, bloom-decked gazebo in the center. Thickly garlanded rose climbers hung the walls as if to adorn a wedding feast in heaven, and the dramatically changing skies even granted us a big double rainbow on our last visit there. Not to mention the black currant juice and pink rose-petal ice cream at the café. *Aaaaahhhhhh* . . .

We also got to visit the amazing Hawk Conservancy Trust, a conservation and rehabilitation center for raptors, where we sat in a wildflower meadow while show-off falcons, hawks, owls, and eagles flew right over our heads, clearly enjoying the amazement and applause of their audience.

I soon got to visit my first European cathedral, Salisbury, with its gigantic spire towering over the countryside. We took in Evensong there, beautifully sung by a girls' choir.

The next night we went to magnificent Winchester Cathedral and attended a somewhat longer Evensong, gracefully sung by a boys' choir. Afterward we realized we were quite hungry, but as it was growing late and this was our first time in Winchester, we had no idea at all of where to eat. As we stood on the sidewalk across the broad green lawn that fronts the cathedral, we decided to pray for direction.

It happened to be the eve of the feast of Saint John Maximovich, one of our favorite saints. Orthodox feast days are usually the death dates of given saints—or as the Sufis more cheerfully say regarding the saint's reunion with God, his "wedding night." I had actually been praying to *Vladika* John quite a bit during that Evensong, especially around the puzzling question of what we were really doing in England. This trip had been thrown together in barely three weeks with some strange "coincidences" happening that allowed us to make such a last-minute journey at the height of the tourist season. Suspicious.

Also, we were still quite exhausted from the events surrounding Mark's mother's death, his stroke, the clearing out and sale of his mother's house, and so on. Physically, we were not really up to travel just then—but this trip had a certain energy of inevitability about it, almost as if we had been forcibly shoved out the door.

Plus, our concept of this trip had been suspiciously "vacationy"—a luxury that seemed not to be in our usual repertoire. Our characteristic mode, will we or nill we, tended to be obeying odd guidances, effortful pilgrimages, or, er, nothing. *Hmmm* . . . But my prayers and meditation during Evensong had yielded nothing specifically incriminating toward the divine Suspect. As yet.

We closed our eyes and prayed to the Lord, our Holy Mother, and *Vladika* John to guide us to a suitable place to dine (and, in my case, to show us what the heaven this was really all about).

ﻋﻠﮯ

Owls and Castles
Just as we opened our eyes, a lone figure, striding briskly, emerged from the cathedral and onto the sidewalk. As he approached, we thought he looked the quintessential Englishman—tweed jacket; sporty red bowtie; handsome gray beard; distinguished face with a strong, slightly imperious nose; frank blue eyes; and a jaunty air. We hailed him as he came near us, and he stopped, greeting us with a warm smile. Even his voice had the character and depth of a Shakespearean actor's!

When we explained our plight, he shook his head sadly. "I am so sorry, but I don't know what to tell you. I'm a stranger here myself. I've only come for the university graduation of my daughter tomorrow, the eighth of my children." He paused. "But I'll tell you something! Don't go to my hotel—the food is bad, and the service is worse!"

As we all chuckled, he asked if we had attended the Evensong. Upon finding that we had, he asked if it was our first one. We explained that we had experienced one at Salisbury the night before. He asked how the two compared. I said they were both lovely but that we had actually enjoyed the Winchester one a bit more because it was longer—and that we were Orthodox Christians and enjoyed longer services.

"You're Orthodox!" he cried eagerly. "Well, so am I! Actually, I'm Archpriest Benedict Ramsden!"

We stared at each other, all rather stunned. The odds of running into an Orthodox priest on the street in England were rather like those of winning big on a scratch ticket. *Hmm* . . . A divine ulterior motive was perhaps tiptoeing into view! When Father Benedict then discovered that my husband was a deacon and also worked in the mental health field (he was a caseworker at that time), he insisted on taking us to his hotel to meet his wife, *Matushka* (the Russian Orthodox honorific for a priest's wife) Lilah.

We had an amazing conversation en route, discovering that he and his wife were converts; that he had been ordained by the great Metropolitan Anthony Bloom of Sourozh, whose books we had read; that through most unusual happenings he had received relics of early British saints (most of those having been sadly destroyed during the sixteenth-century Dissolution of the Monasteries by King Henry VIII); and that he and his wife had run major programs for people suffering from mental health problems for over thirty years.

At the hotel we were greeted with a kind smile by the willowy, dark-haired *Matushka*; this hospitable couple treated us to a cream tea while our animated conversation flew on. And then it happened: Father Benedict insisted that we come to stay with them in the fifteenth-century stone manor house in Devon in which they were living (my castle! Yes! Or pretty durn close! Sometimes "random thoughts" can be on the mark after all!) and visit their program.

Father Benedict said he would send "his man" to pick us up and drive us from Hampshire to Devon. Still dazed with our good fortune, the next afternoon we wandered off to enjoy one last day in the New Forest. One thing we had hoped to see there was a rare white hart—a white male fallow deer. The tawny fallow deer, medium sized with huge, graceful, chalice-shaped antlers, wandered through the forest, occasionally putting in appearances in the dew-heavy meadows. We had seen some, but inquiries among the local people revealed that, to their knowledge, there had not been a white hart born for a number of years. It seemed that this celebrated animal would have to remain a creature of fairy tale and legend for us.

Nonetheless, as the sun was setting on our last day, we lingered in the Forest, leaning on a split-rail fence enclosing a field streaked red and gold with the fading sunlight. We waited and waited but there was no sign of any deer. Birds sang and flew overhead, settling into their nighttime roosts. We would have to go soon. As we began to turn sadly away, sorry to have to leave the magic of the New Forest, something unspoken turned us quietly around again.

A tall, beautiful creature, white as a bright moon, was stepping his lordly way out of the darkening forest. He bore a huge, majestic chalice of antlers, scalloped as elegantly as any medieval prince's sleeves. The white hart took a few steps into the meadow and paused there, raising his head high. Perhaps he sniffed us on the breeze. There were no other people. The woodland prince then looked straight at us, assessing. Having decided, he came forward calmly, a train of winsome hinds wandering after him to partake, under his protection, of the sweet grasses. His large harem spread out around him while he held the center front. As they grazed, he kept his handsome head up, proud and watchful.

We stood there a long time. Toward the end the deer became dim and hard to see, but the white hart still shone among them, like the moon behind a thin cloud. At last he turned, regal and certain, and led his obedient herd in a stately pavane back into the shadowy fernbrakes of the forest. Then it was just us and the rising moon and the sweet evening scents in the meadow. We smiled at each other in wordless joy, and taking each other's hands, strolled back to our car.

ℓ

True to his word, Father Benedict sent a lovely man, Stephen, to pick us up the next day. This was all so unlikely that, stepping into his car, I felt like Cinderella stepping into her pumpkin coach. Stephen talked pleasantly about the area, the Ramsdens' programs, and English life as we sped down multiple highways. At one point I was startled to see Stonehenge itØself flash surreally by us as we passed, as if it were just some kind of prehistoric highway truck stop.

Within a couple of hours, we found ourselves facing the huge wooden doors of the great dark-stone Sortbury Manor. Stephen helped us go in, and we found ourselves in a large entry hall, in its center an immense glass case filled with a variety of handsome stuffed owls! Owl medicine had found us yet again! Lilah later told us that dozens of tawny owls lived in the vast attics of the manor, and that she had once pulled out by the talons one who had managed to get caught in a woodstove pipe, placing the ruffled owl on a bed where it and a two-year-old grandson bemusedly contemplated each other for a while.

Father Benedict and Lilah came down the stairs, welcomed us, and showed us to our lovely room, its old-fashioned casement windows opening on green hills where fleecy sheep floated like clouds. Neat shiny-leaved topiaries lined the windows, and a beautiful stuffed barn owl, white and gold, stood on a column in one corner. We did not discover until the next day that it was their own room they had given us and insisted we keep, over our protests. Although the manor was large, much of it was used exclusively for a special program that one of their sons was running for several residents.

We enjoyed the Ramsdens' lavish hospitality as they fed and entertained us. We found ourselves swept away in eager conversation with much to share. After dinner, Father Benedict, a virtuoso, played on various harpsichords and antique organs he owned, to our delight. Lilah showed us her prized dark-green Agha, on which she cooked, the following morning, the most delicious scrambled eggs, freshly laid by her own hens.

We discovered that this vivid, engaging couple had been raised Anglican. Ramsden had been a private school professor and Lilah the daughter of a wastrel aristocrat who had "thrown away at least a couple of fortunes." Lilah had inherited from him an ancient building called the Priory in Totnes, a dissolved monastery handed over to an ancestor lord by the king. They had already begun a family when Ramsden encountered Russian Orthodox Christianity and was inspired to convert. Not long passed before he was ordained a priest, and in the meantime, Lilah had her own private conversion experience. As they began raising a family that would ultimately number eight children, sometimes just scraping by, they were yet filled with gratitude toward God and wondered what they could offer Him in thanksgiving and in service. One night, they recounted, the two prayed to God together, telling him, "We know that we are not much, Lord. But at least we can offer you the Priory for your work."

He heard their prayer. Not long after, while Father Benedict was away one night during a ferocious thunder storm, Lilah heard a violent pounding on their doors. Nervously, she went to the door and opened it. Amid the downpour and crashes of thunder a strange man was standing there, sobbing uncontrollably, soaked to the skin. Lilah said, "I knew then that God had answered our prayer. And I was terrified!" In that decisive moment, Lilah bringing this unknown, grief-stricken man in out of the storm was to change the Ramsdens' life forever.

Lilah gave the man clean, dry clothes and food and settled him into a room. The man turned out to be mentally ill and became the first of dozens of such afflicted who would live with the Ramsdens and their children for long years as part of their household.

The Ramsdens brought a simple yet radical approach of Christian love to their hospitality for troubled, marginalized people, enveloping them in a warm and colorful family life in contrast to the cold, depersonalized institutional life more likely to befall them. Lilah characterized their approach, at least in part, as "creative domesticity." They felt that, no matter how poor or how wealthy a mentally ill person's background might be, some essential spiritual and societal elements were probably missing from their lives. Such emptinesses spurred many of these anguished people instinctively to gain attention the only way they could—by acting odd and ill, spotlighting their inner discomforts. So the Ramsden family worked at filling these tragic gaps by giving their guests a daily life rich in beauty, culture, positive human interactions, humor, and healthy activities. They created a living environment in which problems and disabilities were no longer the defining elements for those in their care but, rather, a joyful engagement with others in a supportive egalitarian community with many cultural and educational outlets.

Sometimes the Ramsdens worked with redirection. "If, for example," Lilah said, "a man began to say, 'I'm hearing voices! I'm hearing voices!' I would say, 'Well, don't mind about that now. Here, the baby's diaper needs changing—could you help me?'"

A famous story in a magazine article about them recounted a startling interaction between one of their adolescent daughters and a troubled resident. As I remember it, the young man, holding a knife, walked into a living room where the child was and declared that he was going to slit his wrists and commit suicide. The girl looked at him and said, "Oh, don't do that here! Mummy will be so displeased if you get blood on the rug. At least go into the kitchen and use the sink." They both walked into the kitchen, where he stood for a moment at the sink, holding the knife. The absurdity of it all must have struck him because he put the knife down, walked away, and never mentioned (or tried to commit) suicide again.

Founded on a deeply Christian view of the worth and beauty of every soul without exception and a need to transcend labels and stereotypes as a result, the Ramsdens' program grew and was highly successful. Dozens of such sufferers passed through their home, eventually formalized as the Community of Saint Antony and Saint Elias, and many of them left cured—able to marry, hold jobs, and live satisfying lives. The Ramsdens did not try to take their residents off their medications but worked hard to enrich their daily lives. When the number of residents required that more houses be established, the Ramsdens ensured that each house was attractive and of a homey size, that each resident had his or her own room in colors pleasing to him or her, that the staff ratio was high so that residents always had someone to help them or to turn to, and that staff and residents together did the domestic chores that kept the households running without the intrusion of a janitorial staff, thus fostering a family feeling. Residents received gentle, positive encouragement to engage in the many cultural and artistic activities available, as well as sporting and outdoor pursuits. This loving and joyful approach worked wonders.

Soon the Secretary of State for Health and Social Care in the UK got in touch and began to send the Ramsdens clients, especially people who could not be placed elsewhere because they could not be insured—arsonists, the criminally insane. Over the long years, there was never a violent incident or a suicide in their program.

Although Father Benedict performed regular services in the tiny chapel at the Priory—the living heartbeat of their program—religion was never preached to residents, nor were they even encouraged to attend services. The Ramsdens were aware that religious associations could tip off certain kinds of mania in particular sufferers. Yet some of the residents found their way to the chapel and drank in the services' healing beauty. A troubled woman and her small daughter used to come often. The daughter had been regarded by the authorities as severely impaired and was not expected to ever speak. However, one day as Father Benedict was celebrating divine liturgy, he heard a strange gurgling noise in the chapel. He eventually realized that it was the little girl and calmly continued with the service. But suddenly the gurgling changed to words: "L-l-l-ord have m-m-mercy-y-y, L-l-ord have m-mercy, Lord have mercy!" Those were her first words.

After this breakthrough she rapidly learned speech and also showed that she was not suffering from a cognitive deficit but was quite intelligent. By the age of ten she was attending school like any other girl her age.

As the program expanded at the Community of Saint Antony and Saint Elias, so did officialdom's interest. A government department ordered the Ramsdens to give up the Priory's big old-fashioned upstairs-downstairs Victorian-style kitchen and change to a typical institutional kitchen. The Ramsdens refused. Lilah took the department to court over the order. She argued that the patina and ancient homey loveliness of the kitchen was itself an intrinsic part of their healing program. Lilah won. Mark and I sat in that very kitchen with the staff one day to have tea and scones. It was a delightful environment, right out of a BBC costume drama. Stephen, sitting next to me, handed me a huge mixing bowl full of Devonshire cream for my delectation. "Cholesterol!" he quipped with a wink.

When a donor gave a substantial financial gift to the program, instead of pouring it into infrastructure as a more conventional program director might do, Father Benedict decided to take the residents and staff to Venice, to have a superb experience of drinking in beauty. There was one man, a former artist, whom he had rescued from a dark basement in another program, who suffered from a terrible condition where he could never be still, his body always in constant movement. Although it would have been too difficult to bring this man around with them as they visited the various sights, Father Benedict found a most beautiful room with a magnificent view of the buildings and water traffic of Venice from a balcony where the man could sit and gaze to his heart's content.

The program had a strong framework of activities, but even details were tended with care. When Lilah heard that in one house the staff were beginning to make afternoon tea with tea bags and rather hastily, she instructed them to return to using loose tea and offering tea graciously, since that would be more healing and enriching for the residents.

Father Benedict drove Mark and me across the moody expanses of Dartmoor to visit the program's houses in Totnes and Plymouth. The three of us and a few others began the day with a divine liturgy in the Priory chapel, both my husband, as deacon, and me, as Reader, serving, along with Father Benedict's Reader. Father Benedict then immediately swept us into a full gathering of his staff. It turned out that this day was an anniversary of his ordination to the priesthood and a significant date also for the program. We were met with flutes of champagne that, fasting as we were due to the liturgy, quickly went to our heads. Through that sparkling mist, we heard Father Benedict announce to his staff that Father Deacon Mark would now address them with a talk on the state of mental health in America! We both nearly choked. *Do you find this amusing, Lord?* But, with only a few minutes to pull himself together and both of us praying fervently, Mark managed to compose himself and, mightily assisted by the Holy Spirit, gave a good talk. Over a festive brunch and on house tours later that day, we got to meet with enthusiastic staff and smiling residents.

Back at the manor, we later were able to attend services in the beautifully painted "house church." The Ramsdens generously invited us to come again and stay with them as long as we wished, training in their programs should we so desire. It was hard to finally take leave of this warm and fascinating couple who had left upon our troubled society such a loving, creative, and healing mark.

England had been a joy and a refreshment—and for me, a connection with ancestral blood, as my father's family had apparently been in England for centuries, though their root was Germanic. But most of all it had been a great lesson in hope, as seen so vividly in the Ramsdens' programs—in not letting preconceptions block healing and natural unfoldment, and in the power of beauty, love, faith, and creative imagination to heal up old wounds and free the spirit. Even of those widely thought to be incurable. With God and with love, all is possible.

Greece: A Sacred Spirit Song
A rich, seductive fragrance awoke me. Sleepily I opened my eyes to see graceful curls of sweet, resinous-smelling smoke circling around my head, like delicate dancing snakes lit silver by the early-morning light.

"Frankincense," I breathed in wonder. "Mark," I said, patting his arm. "Frankincense!"

"What?" he mumbled. "Why—what?" He opened his eyes and sat up. "Oh!"

Getting quickly out of bed in our tidy *pensión* room, we rushed to our windows, their shutters of beautifully carved golden wood hanging wide open. Looking below on the shapely terraced hills of the island of Patmos, wave-washed and humped like the backs of dreaming whales, we saw that the incense was streaming up to us from a shining censer swung rhythmically by a dark-bearded priest in green-and-gold raiment standing within the open doors of a tiny, snowy private church. Beside him our neighbor, a small white-haired, black-clad widow, owner of this little family chapel, stood with smiling satisfaction as the priest began to chant prayers in a mellifluous Byzantine style. We listened, enchanted.

"Ah," I sighed with satisfaction. "This is the way to start the day! Forget alarm clocks forever!"

A month before, I could not have dreamed that this could be happening, that I would find myself in Greece, my ancestors' land, breathing in its fresh sea breezes and intoxicating frankincense. But then there was no way to apprehend in advance the whims of the Holy Spirit or of my husband and especially—Lord, have mercy!—of the two of them combined.

Around that time on a chilly, rainy New England night, at an hour favored only by owls, my husband sat bolt upright in bed and exclaimed, "We're going!"

"Whah?" I gasped, one eye barely opening.

"We're going! We're going to Greece!"

"Mark, what are you saying? Silly, go back to sleep!" And I pulled my pillow over my foggy, disbelieving head.

But I discovered in the morning that this had not been a freakish dream. I had heard right. And Mark meant what he said. As he explained it to me later, he deeply felt that I needed to connect directly with my roots in Greece, my ancestors' homeland, and had been carrying in his heart for a long time a prayer that this journey happen. And now he thought he saw a way.

Mark had seen in a newspaper that a major airline was opening a new route from New York to Athens at an unbelievably low price. And Mark, then employed selling solar hot-water systems, had just won a big sales contest. The prize was a trip for two to Disney World. He quickly called his bosses and asked them to check on whether he could trade in the Disney World trip for tickets to Greece. The answer was yes! We still had no money for the actual travel, but, inspired and obviously helped along by the Unseen, Mark broke all his company's sales records in the next two weeks, supplying us with more than enough funds for our Greek adventure.

჻

I was thrilled and had to pinch myself to believe that I was not dreaming as within weeks we found ourselves on the Athenian Acropolis, walking up a hill among tumbled marble blocks and wild red poppies and daisies to the actual, for-real Parthenon, just as beautiful in person—no, more beautiful—than in the thousand photos I had seen, despite the construction staging lining one side. As we gradually overcame jet lag and adjusted to the rising May heat, having drunk in the colorful culture of Athens, we prepared to go on our first excursion: fabled Delphi, home of the oracles.

But we couldn't seem to figure out how to get there with our maps. So we went to the offices of the Greek equivalent of AAA for some help. I remember the building as round—is that possible?—and of several floors, with a wide, open space or atrium in the center ringed by crowded desks and many busy people. We were on perhaps the third floor, and a kind English-speaking man was trying to help us plan our trip. But he was running into the same problems we had: it seemed that due to construction and other changes, every route heading west toward Delphi was blocked off. With a creased brow, he said, "Let me ask my supervisor."

He did so by yelling across the open expanse to a chunky broad-shouldered woman on the far side. He explained the problem. She answered with a curt explanation in Greek.

"But—" he objected.

"No buts," she declared.

"But—" he remonstrated.

"No!" she cried. "Eet ees seemple!" And curling her arms up in front of her, her hands in ardent, imploring fists, she shook them, yelling, "Break the law! Just break the law!!!"

As Mark and I took in this unusual bit of official advice in startled silence, our helper gazed down at the map again. "Well, yes," he mused philosophically. "You see here where it shows that you can only turn east? Just turn west instead. I think that is what my supervisor is advising." So we did. We, um, broke the law, no one was hurt, and we did get to Delphi.

This was our introduction to Greek-think in regard to official pronouncements. Laws and formal policies often seemed optional. For example, there was the rule we saw prominently posted in large letters all over the Athens airport—each passenger could have no more than two carry-on bags. When Mark and I boarded a plane to the islands, each with only our two officially sanctioned bags, we were amazed to see Greek ladies jostling down the aisle with three, or even five, hefty bags. Bewildered, we asked a flight attendant about this inconsistency. She beamed upon us with an unselfconscious smile and said, "Of course, yes, we have the rule because that makes people who want this rule happy. But we also allow people to bring on as many bags as they like because otherwise *they* will be unhappy. So, this way, *everyone* is happy." And, having disposed of this philosophical Gordian knot in one hefty irrational saber swing, she left us eating her dust in the aisle. I should have known better. After all, I did grow up with them.

ﻋﻠﻰ

Delphi—Mystery's Citadel
We hung out giddily on our *pensión* balcony in stunning Delphi over a series of endless valleys, dipping many miles from the base of Mount Parnassus all the way down to the distant azure waters of the Saronic Gulf. We felt like eagle chicks nesting in a gigantic aerie suspended over a landscape so dramatic as to seem unreal. Strong sunlight and the fleeting shadows of clouds raced over the ruins of elegant ancient temples, tall exclamation points of dark

cypresses, the wind-brushed silver of olive groves, verdant patches of untrimmed grass, and a mad riot of spring flowers that leapt from every nook and cranny on the narrow terraces of this enormous mountainside, delicately and imperiously holding their places despite dwelling in a terrain racked by earthquakes and landslides.

Across the strait, white-capped mountains of the Peloponnesus reared up, as if in a striking answering chorus to the mighty cliffs on which we stood.

Although inhabited by various cultures for thousands of years, Delphi, sacred center dedicated to the god Apollo, yet preserved an air of wildness and freedom. After the day-tripping tourist buses left at sunset and the early stars began to shine in the vast sky, Mark and I would wander hand in hand down the dirt roads ribboning past the dramatic ruins of the huge Temple of Apollo, its few remaining pillars still powerful against the night sky, with the graceful circular Tholos of Athena with its three elegant columns, framed beautifully among the trees, hanging over the great gulf like the lovely nest of a sacred bird. We would draw our hands through the cool waters of the Castalian Spring, where the Pythia, the ancient oracular priestess, had come to cleanse herself before delivering her mysterious prophecies to questioning seekers within the Temple of Apollo. Mark and I wandered the quiet roads with a sense of being both beyond time and deeply content.

I felt myself drenched in beauty, as if sacred ancient songs, their melodies and numinous words both new and yet strangely familiar, were pouring up out of the earth through my feet and my whole being, playing me like a reverberating string, making vibrant chords with the quickening counterpoint of the Greek language now spoken everywhere around me, both night and day— the language from my first two years of life, when I lived in my grandparents' house, where the music of conversation was Greek and Greek only. Mark was right—my thirsty soul roots needed this bathing in ancient waters of land and language, and the culture shaped from them. I breathed with new freedom, feeling that I was in my heart's home.

Samos—Ancient Emerald in a Sapphire Sea

Samos is a large green island in the Dodecanese only a short distance from the Turkish shore, popular with tourists in season. But for me it was a real homecoming as Mark and I tried to find the building in the gracious port of Vathy (also known now as Samos) where my Yiayia had sat on a balcony sewing and singing as my enchanted grandfather had followed the lovely voice from the public park and, unexpectedly, laid delighting eyes on the woman who was to become his wife and the mother of his children. We photographed a number of possible building candidates but were never sure that we had located the right one.

However, we were sure that we had found her ancestral village, Vourliotes, a charming mountainside town spreading out from a small public square like the improbably pretty stage set of an Italian operetta, nestled in the glorious greenery of cypresses, velvet-gray olive groves, and pastel flowering fruit trees of Samos's romantic north shore, where mountains rose up from the beaches so full of plashing waterfalls and nightingale songs that it was referred to locally as "Paradise."

We strolled the cobblestones of the lovely curving harbor of Pythagorion, where Cleopatra and Mark Antony had also walked in their last assignation together. From time to time we dropped into the bright blue chairs of this or that taverna, admiring the graceful fishing boats rising and falling on the gentle swells, sipping bitter Greek coffee in tiny cups, and people-watching the flow of smiling strollers, both Greeks and travelers from all over the world.

Above Pythagorion on a hillside is a little cave church called Spiliani. This is dedicated to the Virgin Mary but in pre-Christian times was the cave of a Sibyl, a pagan priestess named Feto. She is still remembered, thousands of years later, for having proclaimed the One God. In some of the very old churches in Greece and Bulgaria you will see in the wall frescoes not only Christian saints but the pre-Christian Righteous, as they are called—not only such persons as John the Baptist and Forerunner but also Plato and Socrates and, in their soft, slightly pointed caps, the lithe pagan Sibyls who were faithful to the mysterious urgings of the divine Spirit and who bore witness to the One God before His time of incarnation.

I wish that this beautiful acknowledgment appeared more often in the Orthodox churches of the New World as a healthy celebration beyond labels of all who loved and worshipped God.

In lighting a candle in the tiny building close under the slanting roof of the dripping cave, you honored and joined with the endless Light passed down through the centuries by grateful hearts, from Feto to the Virgin Mary and beyond.

Patmos—The Holy Cave of Fire and Prophecy
The swift hydrofoil carried us in a matter of hours from the red-roofed villages of Samos to Cycladic-style sugar-cube homes piled in spilling geometric heaps dazzling white in the strong sun upon

the hills of the small seahorse-shaped island of Patmos. Our eyes traveled up the sweep of the big hill rising from the port to the huge ancient stone monastery of St. John the Theologian on the hilltop, established there in 1088. It dominates the scene, a hulking gray shepherd sheltering a flock of white cubic buildings, the dwellings of the people of the little town of Chora.

Halfway down the hill, other white buildings mark the small monastery of the Cave of the Apocalypse. The Apostle and Evangelist Saint John had been exiled here when the Roman Emperor Domitian's attempts to kill him, first with a cup of poison and second with a public boiling in oil, both spectacularly failed (the latter leading to an immense number of Christian conversions by witnesses in the amphitheater). Too dangerous to keep around and too dangerous to be set free, John, the apostle who had lain upon the Lord's breast at the Last Supper and who had stood by His Cross at His death, was sent off to a remote, quiet island in the hopes that he would not survive a stay in such rustic surroundings. John not only survived but converted the island's population to Christianity and also, in a small cave on a hillside that you can still visit today, received the staggering, apocalyptic Book of Revelation from the blazing presence of Jesus Christ as the Ancient of Days, His eyes "as a flame of fire," in His mouth a "two-edged sword," and His face "as the sun shineth in its strength" (Rev. 1:14, 16). Thousands of pilgrims through the centuries have journeyed to visit this awe-inspiring sacred site, we among them.

You can take a bus or walk up the hill to the cave. It contains two small church naves and icon screens fronting two sanctuaries, as well as folding wooden chanters' seats against one wall, some simple benches, and, at the entrance, a place to light a candle before a beautifully carved analogion with an icon of Saint John, venerable with a curl of white hair upon his high forehead and a pensive, benign expression. Otherwise, you are surrounded by low-ceilinged rough gray cave walls, with a curious three-pronged split in the ceiling caused, it is said, by the power of the voice of the Alpha and the Omega Himself descending upon the apostle. Saint John in Revelation states that he fell down at this appearance, and in the cave there are silver half-circles beaten into the wall marking where his head and hand struck, miraculously softening the stone that took their imprint, according to tradition.

The icons in the screens are exceedingly beautiful—powerful and elegant in design but also rich and vivid in color, especially the one of St. John prostrate before the fiery Lord, the seven candlesticks of the seven ancient churches glowing between them. We felt joyful and peaceful being there, just quietly soaking up the pervasive atmosphere of grace, and settled into two chanters' seats to pray and meditate.

Places remember what has transpired in them. The rocks, the very earth, hold like a low, quiet, constant song the vibrations that have thrilled through them, even from ancient times. People are not the only beings with memories. Were this not true, there would be little point in pilgrimages. We absorb through our skin, through our breath, the living experiences impressed upon holy places that have been the sensitive containers of unparalleled experiences. They expand us on levels beyond the rational—essential nutrients of the spirit in which we are scarcely aware we are deficient until they begin to flood into us like a quickening tide of deeper life. Sometimes we feel this and recognize it right away but sometimes not until later, maybe even years later, when some seemingly unrelated incident unexpectedly throws our previous experience into a new high relief, and, stirred by the Spirit, we gain a glimpse of what we were unconsciously absorbing at a then-unrecognized but truly precious time.

We took a number of photos in that holy chapel. Oddly, although the cave photos were in the middle of the roll of film, only they—and not the ones before or after them—were overexposed. Everything could be seen clearly but was overlain with what looked like swathes of red and golden light.

الله

Our visit to the cave the next day was not so solitary—nor so quiet. We returned to attend the Divine Liturgy there. We sat on simple wooden benches not far from a small group of adolescent local schoolboys, the only other congregants. For unknown reasons, over the subtle fragrance of incense blared a malodorous barnyard stench apparently emanating from one of these boys, which had to be gasped to be believed. Had the Greeks been able to employ it against the Turks in the War of Independence, they would definitely have gotten rid of the Ottomans much sooner! Unsurprisingly, the boys were nervously giggling.

They quieted down when the Divine Liturgy began. The white-bearded celebrant, a frail, elderly hieromonk, was assisted by a complacent brown-haired monk in his thirties. Plump, sleek, and rounded, the younger monk reminded me irresistibly of a well-groomed, well-fed, and very self-satisfied seal.

The Divine Liturgy was well underway when we were startled to see a meandering line of thirty or forty tourists, many of them dressed inappropriately in shorts and skimpy tops, file into the chapel, staring around themselves with a slightly bored, gum-chewing gaze. They ambled past as if there were not even other people present, much less people engaged in a sacred rite. I could barely keep myself from waving my hands in front of their faces to see if they would blink and actually be able to distinguish us from a carving or a candlestick. We learned later that cruise ships determined the schedule of these rude entries, arranged by businessmen unconcerned with the dignity and rights of the locals. How would you feel if strange tourists strolled in and out of your place of worship during your own services, oblivious to what was going on?

The tourists left, the Divine Liturgy ended, and even the boys (and their accompanying stink) departed. We had not presumed to receive Holy Communion but went up in the customary way to receive *antidoron*—blessed bread—from the old priest standing in front of the iconostasis. The younger monk startled us by shooting his arm out in front of the old monk to keep him from giving us blessed bread.

"Are you Orthodox?" he asked us abruptly in English, a disbelieving sting underlying his words.

"Yes, we are," we replied. (Our understanding was that it is not necessary to be Orthodox to receive blessed bread, but we had no wish to argue the point.)

"Prove it!" he snapped, raising his chin and folding his arms.

Mark and I looked blankly at each other. How to prove it? In the absence of documents or tattoos or anything tangible to attest to our affiliation, we were not sure what would convince him. We had run into Greeks who thought that if you could not speak Greek, you could not be Orthodox. Although we did not judge the insolent monk to suffer from such naiveté, we were not sure that even reciting the Nicean Creed in English would convince him.

Hmmm, let me see. Ah yes, I had it!

"Mark, let's sing the Great Doxology in Byzantine Tone 1," I suggested. He nodded, rolling his eyes. We had both learned it from a CD.

We launched into this unmistakably Greek tone, watching the monk's scowl dissolve as we rolled out the lengthy, beautiful hymn until he was actually beaming at us and even joined in, swaying from side to side with barely restrained enthusiasm. We all three ended our glorification on a final rousing note.

"You're Orthodox, all right!" the monk congratulated us. Turning to the bewildered hieromonk, he curtly directed him to give us blessed bread.

Despite the holiness of both the rite and the place, between the invasion of the insensate, lightly clad cruise-ship Huns, torture by stink, and the cross-examination by the local Inquisition, we both felt the need to go lie down at once to recover from this fraught ecclesiastical experience.

∼ℓ∼

Patmos possessed that slightly too-intense-to-be-real beauty of so many places in Greece. Standing in the entrance to the village of Chora on the hilltop and turning around to gaze down at the port of Skala spreading white and sparkling in the turquoise embrace of the caressing sea, we involuntarily gasped at the island's loveliness. We sometimes sat in a taverna perched on the edge of that hill and enjoyed a delicious breakfast of eggs saganaki—eggs fried with melting gobs of kasseri cheese—served with tea, toast, and jam, to begin our day with both good food and a rousingly gorgeous view.

It was unusually cold in Patmos that May, so, on a night of chill rain, we moved from our first unheated *pensión* to a lovely new place, well-heated—a dreamy room overhanging the more northern hills of Chora. It was here that we were awakened by the chanting priest and his frankincense, and we never tired of the view of the little cascading hills, many terraced with a foam of flowering rose gardens, that wended down to the sea. In the distance, a small mountain arose, capped with a white church of St. Elias on its summit, and in the evening the haunting melodies of multitoned bells from invisible goat herds being guided home down its flanks would float over to us like a drifting evening lullaby. There was a clean shared bathroom, and the other room was then occupied by a lively young Frenchman, full of bonhomie and intellectual energy, the curator of a small, obscure museum in Paris. We got along well, and when he left, I found on the terrace table a lovely poem he had written for me, a pressed red poppy in its folds.

∼ℓ∼

We explored the handsome island on a motorbike and demonstrated typical tourist stupidity by traveling in the heat of the day, when sensible Greeks were enjoying a shady siesta inside. We visited the various attractive beaches, including one, Lambi, that was covered with small gorgeous stones marvelously patterned in white, black, caramel, and beige, as if thoughtfully provided by a designer volcano with a sophisticated line for upscale home décor. Mark groaned, hefting our bag of stones onto the bike. We stood in hilltop fields of foot-high wild roses, the air heavy with their intoxicating scent, and the contented bee music all around us as loud and vibrant as a symphony. We stopped in cultivated rose gardens where individual blooms spread wider than my hand. And, of course, we visited the many churches and monasteries sprinkled all over the island, omnipresent as a primary agricultural crop in other countries. The whole island was seeded with holiness; most traditional families had at least one small family church that they themselves had built. Of course, we also visited the huge monastery of Saint John and admired its venerable frescoed icons, telling the story of their patron and more besides—and also their museum of manuscripts, ecclesiastical regalia, and antiquities.

We attended a few services there, but our favorite church was Evangelismos, the church of the Annunciation, near the sea on one of the lower slopes of Patmos. It was also a thriving women's monastery, founded by a great saint of the twentieth century, Elder Amphilochios Makris.

We were sweetly greeted by a tiny bird-boned nun in her eighties who had set up a card table in the Evangelismos courtyard with Orthodox spiritual books in many different languages, including, to our surprise, some printed by the California Saint Herman Press. Her name was *Mitera* (Mother) Paraskevi, and she was as friendly and bright-eyed as a child.

Some of the awesome depths of her spirit, however, were only revealed to us when we attended Orthros. In the lengthy segment known as the Six Psalms, a section that some chanters will gallop through at a daunting rate, *Mitera* Paraskevi, serving as *Psaltria*, rendered that reading—or rather recital, as she clearly knew all the words by heart—unforgettable. "Kyrie"—"Lord"— she would say with a gentle, aching tenderness as if involved in a slow and tangibly intimate conversation with the Lord—and "Kyrie," again, with a delicate, searching pause. She offered each psalm like a precious, unhurried gift, leading us deeper and deeper into the Holy Presence. It was as if a curtain had been lifted on an inner chamber of her soul, and we had somehow magically been transported within. Although we did not understand the Greek, Mark and I were quite familiar with the Six Psalms and their content. I had chanted them many times myself—but never like this. We felt as if veils between this world and the great one beyond were being constantly lifted in gossamer, shimmering waves, as if we were being invited into the Song of Solomon to witness the love-entwined conversation between the Lover and the Beloved, invited into an intimate scene in Mother Paraskevi's soul that we felt unworthy to attend but so deeply blessed to witness at whatever level we were capable of receiving it.

Elder Amphilochius himself had said:

There is no other way of purification and sanctification than by inner prayer. Psalms are also good, but we say them in order to attract and touch the people. We must speak to the King directly. Those who chant resemble people who are outside the palace of the King, and shout praise to show their enthusiasm. Of course, the King is pleased by them because they sing for Him, but He delights and pays more attention to the people of His court, those who speak secretly in His ear.

Elder Amphilochius was clearly not the only saint of that shining little monastery. After that Spirit-filled Matins, we left Patmos with our hearts full.

જી

Turkey—Meryem Ana

Thanks to an eighteenth-century bedridden Roman Catholic German nun, her head and other parts of her body swathed in bandages to cover bleeding stigmata, Mark and I were on the ferry heading from Samos, Greece, on the hour-and-a-half run to Kusadasi, Turkey. Blessed Anne Catherine Emmerich had been a mystic and ecstatic who described amazingly detailed visions of the life of Jesus Christ and also of the Virgin Mary, which were written down by her contemporary, poet Clemens Brentano. Among Emmerich's accounts was a minutely specific description of the location and architectural layout and details of the small stone home in the vicinity of Ephesus where the disciple St. John the Evangelist was thought to have taken the Virgin Mary during the apostolic era. This home was high on Bülbül Dağı—Nightingale Mountain—where other Christians seeking to escape persecution had also made simple homes, some of them in caves, in a scattered settlement.

In the late 1800s, some skeptical Roman Catholic priests, urged on by nuns living in Turkey, had hiked up the mountain in teams to check out the site specified by Emmerich. The priests were shocked to find the ruins of a small dwelling from the first century on the exact location she described, and which were later shown to conform exactly in size, placement, and design to her description. Furthermore, they learned that Greeks in a nearby village, descendants of the early Christians of Ephesus, had for generations made a difficult annual pilgrimage up the roadless mountain in August on the Dormition of the Virgin Mary, the Orthodox Christian equivalent of the Assumption, to pray there. Further archaeological investigation revealed not only the early origin of the partial four walls still remaining but stones from a fallen early basilica surrounding it.

Eventually, Meryem Ana Evi, or the House of Mother Mary, was reconstructed from the tumbled stones and roofed per Emmerich's description and became an unusual site of pilgrimage for both Christians and Muslims, where members of the two religions prayed to her, wonderfully, side by side. Although it was not given ultimate official status and remains a subject of controversy regarding where—Ephesus or Jerusalem—the Virgin Mary was taken up into heaven at her earthly life's end, Pope Leo XIII declared it a place of pilgrimage in 1896, and three Popes have visited and prayed there. Capuchin monks oversee its care as custodians. Muslim volunteers are also involved in helping run a souvenir store there and helping in the site's care.

Mark and I had felt an irresistible draw to visit this remarkable holy place and were greatly looking forward to it. But we weren't quite prepared for the hustle of tourist-town Kusadaci where we disembarked, with merchants ready to physically drag us off the street while forcibly trying to sell us their wares. Even the popular music blaring from radios had a cruder, earthier, belly-dance beat, unlike the air-and-fire, flying, dancing syncopations of the Greek music we left behind. It seemed not just a different country but a different world.

ُﻞ

The Hills of Heaven

Driving up the winding road on Bülbül Daği late one morning, we felt lifted by a light and peaceful spirit. The farther we drove, the more pastoral the scene became—green meadows elegantly punctuated by a great old grandfather tree or two where flocks of sheep or goats slowly rambled, accompanied by shepherds and goatherds dressed so simply as to add to the strong sense of our becoming effortlessly enfolded in a Biblical narrative. Views of the blue and distant sea opened around many verdant bends, making us feel less and less earthbound. The crassness of Kusadaci and the camera-crowded, tourist-swamped marble lanes of Ephesus dropped away as if they had never been, and we found ourselves instead breathing pure, revitalizing air in an atmosphere of welcome simplicity and peace. We did not have to ask ourselves whether there was grace here.

We parked on the mountaintop and joined many other pilgrims visiting the holy site. But there was no noise and crowding—just a seemly, gentle fellow-feeling of being blessed to be in this special place at this time. There were some small stores selling souvenirs and such, but even they seemed to fit in quietly. There were special fountains fed by a local spring from which pilgrims could

take water. Simple seating was arranged for outdoor services. Just
then an outdoor Roman Catholic mass was about to begin, and a
warmly smiling priest was asking any pilgrims who would like to
receiving Holy Communion to raise their hands. We found ourselves, without thinking or questioning, lifting ours and gratefully
received Holy Communion outdoors on that sacred soil with a
deep sense of blessing.

Soon after, we approached the handsome but simple little stone
house, the fruit of Saint John's, Anne Catherine Emmerich's, and
various priests' and nuns' efforts to preserve the living memory and
grace of this site so intimately touched by the Virgin Mary. We
entered its arched doorway and found places to kneel to pray before
the altar, glowing with candles and surmounted by a handsome
statue of the Holy Virgin, at the far end of the room. I sank into
the rich spiritual quiet as if descending through fluffy layers of
pure white feathers, floating above interior hills of heaven, serenity
wrapping around me like a numinous, embracing shawl. At one
point I opened my eyes and saw, in the smaller room to my right,
a young Muslim woman praying, doing soulful prostrations on her
brightly colored prayer rug. My joy was complete.

Years later, I read with a kindred joy in his moving memoir, *The
Last Barrier*, Sufi teacher Reshad Feild quoting his teacher Hamid
as the latter prepared him for his first sacred visit to Meryem Ana
Evi:

> *There are many paths to God, but the way of Mary is the sweetest
> and most gentle. . . .*
> *. . . Mary is the blue of the flame, and Mary is the matrix of
> all divine possibility in form, here, in our world. It is necessary
> that she be recognized. Learn to love God with all of your being,
> every part of yourself, your heart, your mind, your soul, and then
> we may all be granted the understanding of the meaning of the
> virgin birth. Learn to pray and your prayers will come back from
> the very matrix that forms the child. . . .*
> *Mary was chosen to bear Jesus because she kept her purity
> intact. Simple people call this her "virginity," but those who know
> understand that to be pure means to be completely adaptable, to
> flow with each moment, to be like a running stream cascading
> from the waters of life itself. To be pure is to spread joy, and joy is
> the unfoldment of the knowledge of the perfection of God.*

Joy is the unfoldment of the knowledge of the perfection of
God. And there is no end to the depths of the being of Mary, our
holy Mother.

As I knelt there with my husband in her blessedness, communing with Roman Catholics and praying with Muslims, we were lifted up—not in a mindless ecumenism but rather a recognition of the vibrant, touching oneness of God at the center of all, and our acceptance of the healing arms of our Mother Mary reaching out to us all, without exception, each and every one.

On our last day driving around in Turkey, we got lost. Not only lost in a series of meadows of high grasses without any road signs or streetlights, but lost, unfortunately, as sunset rapidly approached, darkness in its train. Our lostness earlier in the day had been profitable—we had stumbled upon a monadnock-like cave lonely in the center of a big field with a sign in several languages declaring it to be the Cave of the Seven Sleepers. We knew of these saints, honored both in Christianity and Islam. They were, among other things, the patron saints of the sleepless. These third-century saints, all young men, were sealed up in a hill cave by the Roman emperor Decius because they refused to worship idols. Three hundred years later a farmer opened up the hill, and all seven young men were found to be still alive, thinking they had slept just one night. They were shocked to then see crosses in public places and citizens speaking openly of Jesus Christ, as it was now the reign of the Christian emperor Theodosius. They and the local bishop and citizenry praised God for the miracle. Soon after, however, "they laid their heads upon the ground and died," having requested the emperor to leave them thus, rather than interring them in jeweled coffins, as he had wished. Their relics were later taken away to other places.

Early Christian catacombs are also to be found in this cave, and a fifth-century church had once been built over them. The odd, isolated little hill still stands with haunting emptiness and its deserted graves over its stark field, an enigmatic historical presence. The cave's sign states that the body of St. Mary Magdalene once rested there as well.

Not far from this area we had, to our astonishment, stumbled upon the extensive ruins of a graceful six-domed basilica dedicated to the Apostle and Evangelist Saint John! We were the only people wandering around the remaining columns and walls of this enormous cathedral, backed by a few much more recently constructed crude walls papered, surreally, with huge posters of militaristic-looking Turkish men's faces and slashes of red banners. The basilica itself was built above the resting place where, at an advanced age but still alive, Saint John had had his weeping disciples lay him in the ground in a cross-shaped grave, cover him with earth and his face with a sheet, and leave him overnight. When they returned in the morning, the grave was empty. The traditional understanding was that Saint John, like the Virgin Mary, was assumed bodily into heaven. From that time on, every May 8, a fine dust would rise from his grave; collected by devotees and pilgrims, it is reputed to have wrought healings and miraculous cures.

The great basilica was built with its central altar over Saint John's grave, and pilgrims could go into the crypt beneath the altar to gather the blessed dust. Despite the church having been mostly destroyed, the four lovely columns marking the raised slab on which the altar sat are still in place, and the holy crypt beneath it exists as well. But, although one can go down the few steps to reach it, the Turks have put a padlocked iron-grill door over the entrance, making it impossible for the faithful to enter and collect the miraculous dust.

Coming back up, we were struck by the poignance of this savaged beauty and sacredness with its enormous nave and its separate octagonal baptistries where the baptismal candidates would walk naked down into a pool from west to east for their immersion into new life in Christ. Now the ruined cathedral was ringed by the crude murals of power and war of a more contemporary society, its representative images ones of violence and strongman control.

We were touched by stumbling on this remarkable complex, never having heard of it before, and especially because, even before our visit to Patmos, we felt that St. John was our particular patron.

But on the drive back to our *pensión*, we got lost among fields of high grass, without streetlights or signs. The car was an unfamiliar make, and Mark had pulled off on the side of the road so we could consult the driver's manual in order to discover how to turn the headlights on. We pulled the little book out of the glove compartment only to discover that it was written completely in Turkish! Uh-oh! Mark tried various esoteric knobs and buttons, all to no avail, and we sank into pitch darkness, no moon or stars lighting our lonely field, no streetlights on the twisting dirt roads. What now? We prayed.

"I know this is crazy, Mark," I said, "but can I just run my hands over the dashboard and see what happens?" As I am a non-driver, we knew that the odds of my finding the lights were remote. Wearily, he nodded. As if reading Braille, I ran my fingers over the various protuberances on the dashboard and randomly pushed one. The headlights came on! Thank you, Lord!

ᒷᒐᒷ

The next day we returned to Athens, but something was very wrong. My insides seemed to be in a state of complete rebellion, and I spent hours in the bathroom, miserably upchucking. At the last place we had eaten in Turkey roadside signs had cheerfully informed us that "Mutti" (German for "mother," to attract the many German tourists) cooked there. Well, Mutti must have been slipping up on her kitchen hygiene because I left Turkey with a wretched case of food poisoning, alleviated only by the consumption of restorative homeopathic *Arsenicum album 200c.*

On top of this, Greece was embroiled in the furor of national elections, and there were noisy marches in the streets at all hours of the day and night, loud arguments, and the occasional fistfight, right below our hotel windows. A restful recovery was not in the picture! So we were relieved when, my insides calmed down at last, we got into a cab to go to the Athens airport. Our cabbie, also completely caught up in election fever and driving wildly as he turned to exhort us about the worthy policies of his conservative candidate, had some narrow misses with other cars and roadside curbs. Released at last from this campaign-crazed driver, we stumbled into the airport, grateful to be alive.

Many hours later we arrived at LaGuardia airport in New York but had to travel to JFK airport to catch our flight home to Boston. Wearily we piled into another cab. Due to the sometimes vicious humor that descends from on high—or, perhaps, rises up from below—our new driver was also a Greek. And also passionately involved with the election. But from the opposing party, of course. So, as this one swerved back and forth over the roads as he peered excitedly into our eyes in the back seat, preaching to us about the radiant virtues of his candidate Papandreou and actually tossing pamphlets in both English and Greek at us, we began to feel as if we might be destined to meet our Maker inter-airport in a shroud of political papers. To our unspeakable relief, our cabbie in Boston was Irish.

In a health-food store later that week, we met a friend we had known from church who is Turkish, Hale. Told about our trip, she became very animated. "That's great! You know that road up Bülbül Dağı to Meryem Ana? My father was the supervisor of the work crew that built that road up the mountain! He said it was the best thing he had ever done in his life!"

CHAPTER FOURTEEN

Catena: The Ancient Songs Go On: The Holy Land, Greece (again), and Bulgaria

The Holy Land: The Sacred Center

Sequestered behind tall stone walls on top of the Mount of Olives is a rare, little-known place called Small Galilee. And Mark and I were about to be married there. Small Galilee was the place where the Lord first appeared to His apostles after His Resurrection. I was told that the mother of one of the apostles, among other Galileans, had owned a small house on this site, and that the men had all fled there after the Crucifixion, in hiding from the authorities. And there the Lord had entered, although all the doors and windows were shut, and first brought to them the eternal life and radiance of His Resurrection.

When the wall gates closed behind us that May, we found ourselves high above the spreading pale gold-tinted walls of the old parts of the great ancient city of Jerusalem, the gold of the Dome of the Rock shining below and various other domes and religious spires poking up from the faith-dense streets like an intensive garden bed of the Spirit. Before us lay flowering spring meadows bright with poppies and daisies, where wandering dirt paths between silver olive trees and cultivated flower beds lent an almost rustic, pastoral quality to the land—and bore witness to the resident animal life with an occasional impressive cowpat. But the feeling there was unique—indescribable, ethereal but also solid; this place was drenched with Pascha, an unfading Pascha that did not end or give way to anything else. A stable Pascha. I felt as if I breathed Light with every breath and as if I were walking lightly, the spring of the Resurrection in each step.

Churches and chapels seem scattered like jewel boxes in the meadow of this summer residence of the Greek Patriarchate in Jerusalem. Two Popes and two Ecumenical Patriarchs have met here for prayer and discussion but there seems a veil of privacy over this place. There is a large two-level church dedicated to the apostles and a small, charming church of the Theotokos, Virgin Mary the God-bearer, dedicated to her feast of the Dormition, her "falling asleep" and being carried to heaven by her Son at the end of her life. We were told that the chapel was the work of a Russian elder who lived there many years, and, indeed, the icon frescoes are wrought in a soft, nineteenth-century realistic style, full of tangible devotion. It was in this lovely chapel that our wedding was to take place.

Small Galilee is just across the road from the site of Jesus Christ's Ascension—a site now owned by Muslims, so Christian services can only be held there once a year. The spot is marked by a small octagonal Romanesque domed chapel in the style of the Knights Templar, and pilgrims can put a lit candle in a sandbox on the floor near what looks like the imprint of a large masculine foot, said to be where the stone softened beneath Jesus's foot as He began to ascend.

In the small chapel of the Virgin's church hidden behind the wall across the way, a stone a couple of feet wide sits directly beneath the altar. Upon this stone the Holy Virgin used to kneel to pray to her Son, gazing toward the place of His Ascension, we were told. We were permitted to venerate this stone, which has two long parallel shallow troughs, said to be the impressions of her knees and her shins where the stone here, too, softened from the spiritual intensity of her prayerful interactions with Christ. Tradition tells that the tall trees around this spot used to bow down toward her when she prayed, and even now, many of the tall trees surrounding the little stone building slant noticeably toward it, as a flower might toward the sun.

We were greeted by *Mitera* Agni, Mother Agnes, the tiny gray-haired nun who oversaw Small Galilee. I had heard about her from nuns in the States; she had a reputation as a seer and was highly honored by them. She warmly welcomed our small pilgrim band, a potpourri of twenty-three older Greeks, middle-aged convert Americans, two Russians, two Australian Greeks, and a Ukrainian. Our Greek-American bishop, Metropolitan Gerasimos, served a liturgy in the small church of the Theotokos, during which he also ordained one pilgrim, our friend John, as a Reader and another as a subdeacon and then deacon, and afterward we prepared for the wedding. *Mitera* Agni later told our pilgrims that she saw the Virgin Mary kneeling at the altar during the divine liturgy. The already-married members of my home church, newly converted to Orthodox Christianity, had been asked to renew our vows in an Orthodox marriage ceremony, and Mark and I couldn't think of a better place to do so than in the Holy Land on the Mount of Olives. So our dear *koumbaros*, our witnesses, John and Mary Williamson, who had already generously given us the gift of this pilgrimage, patiently carried our white-flowered wedding crowns—joined by satin ribbons and handmade by a friend—all over the Holy Land, just waiting for this moment.

The bishop had Mark take off his long black *ráso* (cassock) and put on a tie with his dress shirt and khakis. I wore a long white Mexican cotton dress thickly embroidered with twining purple flowers and vines and had a patterned gossamer scarf to wear like a veil beneath my wedding crown. The bishop began the marriage service, our Greek woman cantor began to sing the verses, and before we knew it Mark, John, Mary, the bishop, and I were traipsing with lit candles round and round a central analogion in the chapel, performing the ancient "Dance of Isaiah." Photos of that sacred wedding dance show, by the altered expressions on the faces of all five of us, that we were deeply affected and traveling in those moments somewhere "beyond." The atmosphere was beautiful but so intense that, during the vows, both Mark and I wept uncontrollably. It was as if several rivers of hidden inner sensitivity were converging in a powerful white-water of feeling, with a painfully sweet, almost unbearable, sense of blessedness. Mark's and my love for each other; and our deeply committed mutual tenderness despite the many challenges of our marriage, temperamentally and otherwise; our adventures and pains in our small, struggling attempts at service for our Lord combined with the enormous grace pulsating in this unearthly place filled and overflowed our souls piercingly. Being married in the chapel of the Holy Virgin Mary, Mark and I felt, was one of the greatest moments of our lives.

Afterward, *Mitera* Agni held a little impromptu wedding reception for us in her cell, a cozy tiny house with a wall completely covered in icons. John, as best man, had run from our hotel into the markets of Jerusalem early that morning to purchase pastel Jordan almonds, a much-enjoyed Orthodox wedding favor, to give to our guests. He also poured them wine we had gotten from the holy site in Cana where Jesus had turned the water into wine at the wedding. I felt as if I were drifting on a cloud of happiness. Even going out to use *Mitera* Agni's little outhouse turned out to be an experience of beauty—it was completely surrounded by orange trees in full, passionately fragrant bloom!

As we all sat on her low bed and benches in her cell, comfortably talking, *Mitera* Agni's eyes and mine met, and we both smiled. Suddenly there was nothing but Light, as if we had both been subsumed into an annihilating radiance, raised up in an unexpected glory. Though it passed in a moment, this glory left its mark on my soul. *Mitera* Agni smiled again and said something in Greek to the bishop and some of the pilgrims. They nodded. "She said," one of the pilgrims told me, "'See how much grace the bride has.'" The same thing—the igniting glance and smile and blaze of light—happened to me years later in America with a woman Sufi teacher. Such moments you cannot forget. An opening into heaven.

Needing to push on with our itinerary, we left around noon. *Mitera* Agni bid us a gracious farewell. I looked back as we all walked away and was surprised to see, as she stared fixedly after us, her expression change to a worried, deeply troubled one. Might she be seeing the trouble soon to come with our conflicted bishop and our controversial ecclesiastical situation? I do not know.

ﻋﻠﻰ

Up in the Swallows' Nest with Elijah and the Ravens

> *And the word of the Lord came unto him, saying, Get thee hence and turn thee eastward, and hide thyself by the brook Che´rith, that is before Jordan. And it shall be that thou shalt drink of the brook; and I have commanded the ravens to feed thee there. So he went and did according unto the word of the Lord: for he went and dwelt by the brook Che´rith, that is before Jordan. And the ravens brought him bread and flesh in the morning, and bread and flesh in the evening; and he drank of the brook. (1 Kings 17:2–6)*

I was sitting on a low wooden bench, polished and smooth, in a cave hundreds of feet above the lush spring-fed Wadi Qelt, the former brook Che´rith, a narrow green exclamation mark far below in an otherwise overpoweringly monochromatic landscape of dry beige rock. The little cave was clutched in the grip of the Judaean desert's towering, contorted rock hills and canyons that resembled nothing so much as the great swirling muscles of an enormous dancer suddenly frozen in stone. I was alone—except, perhaps, for the spirits of the departed who had left their indelible grace

and spiritual imprint in this very cave—among them, the Prophet
Elijah and St. Joachim, father of the Virgin Mary.

The local tradition claims that this was the very cave where the
Prophet Elijah was fed by the wild ravens when he was in hiding
from the murderous rulers, Jezebel and Ahab. And it is, according
to tradition, the cave to which St. Joachim had fled after he had
been publicly insulted by the high priest of the Temple because of
his and his wife Anna's childlessness, considered a grave sin for the
Jewish people of that time. Without even telling his wife, Joachim
hurried out into the desert and climbed to this cave, weeping and
bemoaning their state before God. He stayed there forty days and
nights, pleading in prayer. On the fortieth day, the Archangel
Gabriel appeared to him and told him that he and his wife would
conceive, and that she would bear a special child, a blessed maid.
To confirm this, Gabriel told Joachim to hurry back to Jerusalem,
where he would meet his wife in front of the Golden Gate. The
archangel also appeared to Anna, sitting in her garden and grieving for her husband, and reassured her, telling her of the child
she would carry in her womb and instructing her to rush to the
Golden Gate, where she would meet her missing husband. There
are wonderful icons of this encounter, the joyous couple clasped in
each other's arms before the gate, the wind of their passage streaming their clothes out from their bodies. In the Eastern Orthodox
tradition, they soon conceived the Virgin Mary in the natural way.

This cave is part of the Greek Orthodox monastery of St.
George the Chozebite, which hangs dizzyingly, like a complex
of swallows' nests, with pale chapels and colored domes midway
up a high cliff pocked with caves that were formerly the dwellings of hermits. Parts of the old Roman road linking Jerusalem
and Jericho edge the frothy green of the wadi below, where palm
trees, olive trees, cypresses, evergreens, and various deciduous trees
and bushes shine bright emerald and silver in the strong sunlight.
The monastery's predecessor was a small lavra formed by John of
Thebes, an Egyptian, with five Syrian hermits who had settled
around Elijah's cave in the fifth century. The formal monastery
was founded in the sixth century by Saint George the Chozebite
and through the centuries survived attacks (the Persians, in 614,
killed all fourteen monks), abandonment, and various reconstruc-
tions and renewals to the present day. As is the case at so many
sacred sites in the Holy Land, there are only a small number of
monastics to continue the life of prayer, keep up the sacred places,
and welcome pilgrims.

Sitting in the small cave by myself, I was deeply happy.
Although the lower walls are whitewashed, the rough rock of

the low-roofed ceiling is uncompromisingly gray and knobbly. Despite the efforts at making a semi-tame chapel, with two benches, framed icons here and there on the walls, and a stand holding sand for lit candles, the overall impression is of encroaching, enfolding wilderness. You are not really inside. Inside and outside merge seamlessly. A tile floor, pale gray with large diamonds outlined in narrow bands of black, spreads from the completely open entrance—indeed, if a raven wanted to fly in to bring you food, it would have no problem—to the narrow back, not much larger than the altar beneath the hanging oil lamps, barely set off from the rest of the cave by a low, airy metal gate.

And it is dry. Dry as bones that have lain in the desert a long time. At least on the day I was there. And it was hot—definitely not my favorite thing, but, oddly, that day I was loving it: both the heat and the dryness. The air was so thirsty that it swept away your sweat before it could dampen your skin. The spiritual atmosphere of the cave also had that kind of comforting suction—as if it swept away rambling thoughts, knotty problems, besetting sins, idle fantasy effortlessly and left you sitting very still, deeply composed, and breathing in a pervasive peace with every cleansing breath. In a profound way, it was the cleanest place I had ever been, and, by sympathy, it made me, at least for a little while, clean.

I am trying to describe how it felt and know that I am not succeeding. Even though we may not always notice them, each holy place has particular atmospheric qualities peculiar to itself alone, just as each individual person has. The singularity of Elijah's and Joachim's cave seemed particularly prominent somehow.

Years later, while I was attending a service in the small chapel of The Priory in southern England, my attention kept being drawn back to one of several icons hanging on the wall. The icon was very old—so old that the paint was blurred and both the lettering and saint depicted had become quite indistinct. But there seemed to be so much power emanating from it. Not only power but a familiar power. What was it? Yes—*that's it!*—it felt just like Elijah's cave.

When the celebrant came out of the altar at the end of the service, I led him to the icon and asked him if he knew who it was. "Oh, yes," Fr. Benedict replied. "That's Elijah." Indeed.

ॐ

The monastery has other singularities, such as that the bishop's chair in their main chapel does not bear the usual icon of Jesus Christ but rather that of the Virgin Mary. This anomaly is not Mariolatry but, as a monk explained to us, because St. Joachim had received the news of the coming conception of the Virgin Mary in their cave, and the monks felt that this holy event created a special connection for them with the Panaghia, the All-Holy one. "So, you see, she is our bishop," the monk said, smiling.

Getting to the monastery requires deep motivation—and stamina—on the pilgrim's part. There are hundreds of steps up (and, yes, down) and a rough, rocky path. One must first descend from a high cliff where the buses can park, then cross a wide gulf of air from the monastery to the walking bridge far below over the coursing waters of the Wadi Qelt itself, followed by many stairs—did I say "many"? Rank understatement!—most of the way up the cliff face on the opposite side. Some can ride donkeys (the poor creatures!). I don't believe that the donkeys were available during our pilgrimage in 1993, but even if they were, we walked.

Yes, and provided a little unexpected theater for the climbing pilgrims of all nations who were also working their way up to the sacred swallows' nests. Because Mark, Mary, John, and I walked with our fellow-pilgrim Vicki—the one and only amazing, fabulous Vicki!—an Athenian lady, possibly in her seventies, with a heart condition and abundant flaming red hair. We knew that her doctor did not recommend such exertions for her, but Vicki was determined to live at least to see the monastery. She was quite a portly woman and carried a gigantic shoulder bag that John, who often kindly offered to carry it for her, called "the Cannonball." Sweetly and tactfully John would beg Vicki to take one or two things out before our next expedition to lighten the load, but, mysteriously, the Cannonball actually got heavier every day. John, tall and strapping, eventually had to carry it across his chest in the interest of not dislocating a shoulder.

"Why don't you ask her if she would please leave the Cannonball in the bus?" I asked him one day.

"No, it's okay," he groaned, adding with conviction, "it's for my sins."

So John carried the Cannonball and Vicki grasped the forearms of Mary, Mark, and me alternately as we slowly descended to the wadi and climbed up the opposite cliff. We were probably the slowest pilgrims on the cliff—even hobblers seemed hare-like compared to our halting tortoise pace—particularly as Vicki insisted on a certain unique declaiming style of climb. Leaning on our arms, she would walk eight or ten steps, stop, throw her head back, and implore the heavens, "Help Vicki! Help Vicki, God! God, help Vicki!" ending, for reasons best known to herself, by bellowing, with outstretched arms, "GOD BLESS AMERRRICA!!!" So, in this colorful fashion, we eventually found ourselves entering the first gates and courtyards of the monastery lined with beautiful small gardens of blooming roses and bougainvillea.

Winded and heated, we made our way finally into a long cool room with small balconies hanging out over the great emptiness below. We sat on metal folding chairs looking down at the distantly sparkling wadi beneath our feet and drank achingly cold spring water.

We were charmed by the clever way this was provided, without ice cubes or refrigeration. There was a waist-high blue wooden shelf surrounding one of the large pillars supporting the Romanesque-style arches in this airy room. A water faucet in the pillar kept the tray-like shelf full of water. Standing in the tray were earthen pitchers containing water. They absorbed water from the tray, and the intense desert heat would draw water to the outside of the porous water jugs, dramatically cooling the water within them by evaporation. Such delicious water and such a staggering view! Not to mention some young multi-patterned black-and-white cats who rolled, played, and twirled on the speckled black-and-white linoleum floor like an Escher drawing in motion. As we did at every site, we held a short service in the lovely monastery and venerated its relics (including a bodily incorrupt saint). Repaired in spirit, eventually even our muscles recovered, in a few days, from our gymnastic climb to the holy swallows' nests.

ﷺ

Mar Saba—Drama in the Desert
The afternoon following Mark's and my wedding—after a stop at the monastery of Saint Theodosius, where our bishop tonsured Mary Seraphima, a Reader—we came to the great grim fortress-like monastic complex of the Holy Lavra of Saint Sabbas the Sanctified, Mar Saba in Arabic. The monastic buildings, far larger and more numerous than those at Saint George the Chozebite, draped like a huge wasps' nest down a high cliff above a deep ravine. Mar Saba bristled with dark-gray domes, red roofs, and different shapes and sizes of beige flat-roofed buildings, all surrounded by a high, thick wall of sand-colored stone. The surrounding area of dry hills and barren canyons was scoured of all vegetation, mercilessly bleak to the horizon.

One of the oldest continuously inhabited monasteries in the world despite many historical attacks, Mar Saba was founded in 483 and overlooks the Kidron Valley halfway between the Old City of Jerusalem and the Dead Sea. It holds the relics of St. Sabbas and St. John of Damascus, among other illustrious saints. It also is famous for developing the TypiÔkon, or order of services, used throughout the Orthodox world to this day. At its height the monastery had three hundred monks but now fewer than twenty.

Mar Saba is a very strict and traditional monastery. Among other things, no woman is allowed within its gates. I don't have a problem with given monastic communities barring the opposite sex from their enclosures—issues of distraction and temptation aside, I can understand wanting to live with and explore the pure essence of one's own sex in an environment of worship—a kind of powerful distillation of a certain aspect of being, aside from its likely and more importantly being a calling from God. As long as the same right is granted to women monastics—and it is—I have no objection.

But, that said, Mar Saba turned out to be a very unpleasant experience for our women pilgrims. Although some of the monastery's relics were brought to its gate for us women to venerate, during the long hours of the men's visit within, we were left sitting in the sun on a low wall in the outer courtyard. A tall, lean, dark-haired monk with a saturnine face and manner, probably in his forties, was left to watch over us—a duty that he clearly disdained. We were surrounded by local adolescent Palestinian boys who swarmed us, begging for money. The sour-faced monk yelled at them and periodically chased them off, but the boys always returned, pressing close to us and demanding. The bored monk stopped paying attention. We smiled at the boys but faced an insuperable language barrier. One of the boys was walking a pigeon along the top of our wall, gently holding its wings upright. I gestured to him why didn't he let it fly away. He gestured to his mouth—because he and his family would eat it.

Our bishop had warned us strictly not to give in to the boys' requests for money, but after some time, one of our softhearted ladies succumbed and handed a boy a dollar bill. This incited a surge of importuning boys, and one or two other ladies handed over dollars. The boys became bolder, even snatching at purses now. The disgruntled monk studiously ignored them. But then one urchin, perhaps nine years old, lunged at the first woman who had given money and ripped the gold cross she wore from her neck. This awoke the near-drowsing monk like an electric strike. He leaped forward, ran, and grabbed the small boy by his shirt collar, dragging him roughly to the stone wall. Then, yelling, the monk started to bash the little boy's head against the stones. A few other ladies and I leapt to our feet in indignation and shouted, trying to call off the monk's brutal excess. He resented our objections but stopped, giving the boy a solid kick, and made him return the cross to the forgiving lady. Disgusted, the monk then seemed to wash his hands of us altogether and for the rest of our visit just stood like an unseeing post against the wall.

After a short period of quiet the boys rushed back in again like predatory seagulls hovering around a boat full of fish. Again there were attempts to snatch purses that were putting some of our older ladies into such a nervous state that they wanted to return to the bus, hot though it was likely to be. To do this, you had to walk up a slope where, for a few minutes, you were hidden from view by two steep hillocks on either side. One of our older ladies who had disappeared in there cried out. I leapt to my feet and ran to the path. When I saw the boy trying to drag her shiny black patent leather handbag away from the frail, cowering woman, I shouted and ran up, waving the boy off with a ferocity that surprised even me. He fell back, astonished. I accompanied the thankful elder lady to the bus and, returning, escorted another lady up there also. There were one or two boys who stalked us at a safe distance but, when I turned my burning, minatory look on them, retreated from dealing with me. In the Judaean desert, I had found my inner samurai!

The last time I walked one of our ladies up to the bus, one of the older adolescent boys kept pace with us at a safe distance. I can't explain it, but there was something about him that I liked. I think he might even have been a little amused at a small Western woman brandishing her arms and fixing him with the fierce and implacable gaze of a hunting hawk whenever he drew near. I signed to him that, if he left our ladies alone, I would give him something before we left. He then politely withdrew.

Finally our bishop and men came out of the monastery gates, and we all walked back to the bus. That young Palestinian boy reappeared, edging diplomatically close to me. I quickly handed him a dollar bill and nodded curtly at him. He nodded back, smiling in a friendly, grateful way. We waved goodbye to each other.

We had not been long on the bus when my fit of unfamiliar ferocity evaporated. It had been such an overwhelming, intense day! The wedding in the paradise of Small Galilee in the morning, and the hot, painful afternoon outside Mar Saba, feeling and witnessing some of the poverty, incivility, and cruelty rampant in the area. I could not wash away the image of the tall, unfeeling monk taking ugly satisfaction in smashing the little boy's head against the stone wall. I started to cry and could not stop for a long time.

The Holy Sepulchre—Heart of the Holiness

Overwhelmed as we were by entering the enormous stone basilica in Jerusalem containing both Golgotha and the Lord's Tomb, not to mention numerous other sacred sites on different levels—and sometimes jostled in the streaming crowds of pilgrims and tourists, including a large group of Japanese people in hot-pink baseball caps swarming around like a school of vivid fish—Mark and I were gobsmacked by the intense and powerfully living sense of holiness that vibrates like an enormous, endlessly tolling bell throughout the sacred complex. Within minutes we both expressed a desire to chuck our old life in order to become guides at the Holy Sepulchre and breathe it in every day. It's that kind of place.

In the fourth century, the newly Christian king of the Byzantine Empire, Constantine, and his devout mother, Helena, wished to recover holy relics and establish Christian churches, especially in the Holy Land. St. Helena spent two years uncovering the holy sites. Having demolished a temple of Venus that the Emperor Hadrian had built over the top of the hill of Calvary in Jerusalem, Helena's workmen came upon three crosses buried in the hill. We are told that Helena had a woman near death brought to the site and laid upon each of the crosses in turn. Nothing happened with the first two, but after lying on the third cross, the woman arose healed and well. And so the Church of the Holy Sepulchre, also known as the Church of the Resurrection, was built on this site, housing the True Cross and also the Holy Tomb from which Jesus arose. Earthquakes, fires, and Muslim troop invasions repeatedly damaged and destroyed the church over the centuries, but it was repeatedly rebuilt and renewed. Its current appearance has not changed substantially since the twelfth century.

Romanesque stone arches witness to the rule of the Knights Templar from 1099 to 1244. The Templars arrived with the First Crusade and, rather than leaving the small, connected churches on the site as is, put all the holy places under one roof for the first time. There are two big domes, and under the largest, the Edicule—the small building surrounding the Tomb of Christ—is centered, clad in an elegant exterior of flowing marble swags and holy reliefs reflecting the Ottoman Baroque style of 1810, when it was built.

The Holy Sepulchre is owned by the Greek Orthodox, Armenian Apostolic, and Roman Catholic Churches, with the Greek Orthodox predominating. To a lesser degree, the ownership is shared by the Coptic Orthodox, Syriac Orthodox, and Ethiopian Tewahedo Churches. Repairs often remain undone due to conflict over ownership between these Churches.

The courtyard outside is plain and dusty looking. People come tramping up from the Via Dolorosa, the stony route on which Jesus Christ carried the Cross, and from the nearby roofed souq, full of rugs, clothes, olive wood and brassware, icons, jewelry, and every kind of Holy Land souvenir. You enter the church through a huge arched door and soon find yourself by a long polished reddish stone, rectangular and perhaps twelve feet long, set in a marble holder raised a few inches from the floor. Hanging above it are eight large white-and-gold oil lamps, and tall candles and candleholders stand at either end. Often there are red rose petals strewn upon it, and a fragrant oil like myrrh coats its surface. Called the Anointing Stone, it is believed to mark the spot where the lifeless body of Jesus Christ was washed and anointed for burial. Pilgrims kneel next to it, pressing prayer ropes against it, collecting rose petals, and praying.

When you walk farther into the vast stone halls, you come to an open stairway to your right. At the top is a small but gorgeous chapel, vibrant with richly colored icons and shining with gold and silver oil lamps and candlestands. Jesus hangs on the Cross in its center with the Virgin Mary to one side of him and the young Apostle John to the other, and beneath the altar in front lies the rough rock of Calvary. This was where St. Helena found the True Cross. There is a hole in the rock that is believed to have held the Cross, and pilgrims crouch down to put their hands in it and venerate it. There are other altars and chapels on the same level.

But if you descend the stairs again you pass through an area with the big Greek *katholikón*, or church, and its large icon screen, jewel-colored and golden, and then directly on to the Rotunda, the giant basilica, three tall stories high, its immense dome surrounded by a sunburst of figurative sunrays with the real daylight peeking in at the top. In the center of this vast space is the Edicule and, within it, the Tomb of Christ.

On the Holy Saturday afternoon before Pascha for hundreds of years now, a miraculous Holy Fire has descended on the worshippers packing the huge basilica. This fire glows blue white at first and for some time, perhaps even half an hour, will not burn skin or hair. I have seen films of people holding their hands in the flames of their lit candles and even "washing" their faces with the fire. The rite that evokes this ancient miracle begins when the Greek Orthodox patriarch, wearing a simple robe patted down by guards, formerly Muslims but now Israeli Jewish police, who check that he has no matches or means of starting a fire, is allowed to enter the Edicule. Going into the innermost chamber, he says traditional prayers and rubs the surface of the stone where Jesus arose until a white mist begins to form. Then the sacred fire rushes down and flames on a small unlit oil lamp, and from that the patriarch lights his two candle bundles—thirty-three narrow tapers each, one for each year of the Lord's life. He rushes to the entrance of the Edicule and emerges with his candles held high, crying "*Christos anesti!*" and begins to light the candle bundles of all around him. The Holy Fire, however, has a mind of its own and flies around the great basilica, lighting oil lamps and certain individual candles on its own, before the flame from the patriarch's candles can reach those holding them.

In the year 1579, the Armenian patriarchate conspired with the Turkish overlords to block the Greek patriarch and his people from entering the Holy Sepulchre at all on Holy Saturday, the Armenian patriarch instead taking his place within the Edicule. Time passed and the Holy Fire did not descend. The Orthodox Patriarch Sophronius IV was in the courtyard, leaning on the closed great door, weeping, surrounded by his people, when suddenly there was a loud noise and the column next to him cracked open, the Holy Fire issuing from within it. With joy he lit his candle bundles from it and passed the flame to the crowd, crying "Christ is risen!" Inside the Holy Sepulchre they heard the noise and someone was sent out to check. Upon his report, the doors were opened and the Armenian patriarch came out and prostrated before the Greek patriarch, apologizing and proclaiming that they would never do such a thing again.

You can still see the more than three-foot-long crack in the column; a lovely fragrance issues from it. In the twenty-first century, two scientists, fracture specialists in the strength of materials, carefully examined detailed images of the crack and concluded that it could only have been caused by a strong electrical discharge combined with seismic pressure, something not technologically possible at that time.

လ႕

In the daytime, you wait on long lines for a chance to step into the small, precious jewel box of the Edicule—Christ's tomb. Going under the low arched doorway at last, you find yourself in a tiny room, bedecked in gloriously carved marble, and with nothing but a low carved column in its center into which is set a square box with a chunk of marble stone beneath its glass cover. This, tradition teaches, is a piece of the huge stone that the angel sat upon and rolled away from the Tomb for the women disciples. Then you walk into a second tiny room, narrow and only long enough to contain maybe six people. On your right is a low slab of marble, long as a tall man, marking the spot where Jesus was laid and rose from the dead. Dozens of gold and silver oil lamps hang from the ceiling, casting their glow over the slab and sparking light out of the *rizas*, the gold and silver coverings on the icons resting on a narrow shelf above the burial slab amid gleaming candlesticks, their candles lit, and small vases of fresh flowers. An icon of the Virgin Mary holding the church hangs on the narrow back wall. The icon is hinged and when opened allows you to touch the original rock of the Tomb.

The first time I knelt to kiss the burial stone, breathing in the sweet fragrance of the oil in which it was covered and basking in the golden glow warming every surface, not only did I feel the deepest joy, but even my physical heart, overwhelmed by a happiness and sense of freedom more profound than the body could contain, began to leap and dance in new rhythms. The shocking nearness of the Beloved opened me to my core and filled me with ecstasy and exaltation. Here was the heart of all the holiness, in a Tomb, but warm, tender, aglow with life!

We came back after dark for a midnight liturgy. This time the huge church was quiet, a vast dark contained universe lit with glowing hanging oil lamps and huge candles atop giant shining candlesticks for stars. We walked silently, small mice in a big house. There were very few people there—such a relief after the daytime crowds. And the quiet was deep, beautiful, and soothing. We heard the sweet jingle of small bells and saw a young deacon in shining brocade raiment swinging his censer as he sped, like a planet on its orbit, swiftly around the basilica. Another deacon appeared, of a different Christian group, and they stopped, bowed to each other, censed each other, and then, like angelic holy dancers, swept on.

The Divine Liturgy had begun at the altar in the Edicule, over the Resurrection stone. As it was performed by a young, dark-bearded bishop of the Holy Land, with shining eyes, we fell under its mystical spell, even though his honey-voiced chanter was singing the verses in Greek. Reverently, we lined up in front of the Edicule, each quietly preparing to receive the Holy Body and Blood of Jesus Christ. I couldn't believe my blessedness, my good fortune, to have the opportunity to receive the Holy Eucharist here, on the spot where it all began, where the Resurrection first unfurled its wings of light, fire, grace, and new life. With eyes closed, I breathed deeply of the fragrant incense and the pervasive sense of sacred blessing.

"Stephani," a slightly sharp voice said near my ear. "Stephani, I want to talk to you."

I opened my eyes in surprise to see an Orthodox American nun, now a sister in the lovely Russian Orthodox monastery of Saint

Mary Magdalene on the Mount of Olives. I had met her once briefly before. She had been a sister in the Holy Order of MANS in the old days.

"What about?" I asked, surprised. "I'm waiting to receive."

"The canonicity of your bishop," she remarked irritably. "We need to talk about that."

I couldn't believe my ears. "Not here, not now!" I responded, horrified.

"Well, then soon," she snapped and walked away.

I walked up a few steps with the slowly moving line and was just recovering from this dissonant confrontation when a lovely young Australian Greek woman, who had joined our pilgrim group with her mother in the Holy Land, walked up to me and moaned in a grief-stricken tone, "Oh, Stephani, I'm so *ashamed!*"

You're kidding, Lord, right? I'm fifteen steps from the Edicule and the chalice and this young woman is about to go to pieces in front of me? What could this possibly be?

"What is it?" I asked her gently, fearing some kind of drastic revelation of personal tragedy and sin.

"You know that the bishop told us to wear head scarves," she whispered urgently. "I just didn't want to, and now I'm so ashamed that I disobeyed." I was relieved this was not a darker revelation! It is true, however, that the Orthodox canons stipulate that women should wear covering on their heads when receiving Holy Communion, and, this being such an ancient and traditional place, every other woman there had done so. "What shall I do?!"

Now we were only eight feet or so away from the Edicule and the chalice. I tried to calculate if I could receive and then whip my head scarf off and pass it to her but decided this would be too awkward and probably not appreciated by the celebrant. Mary Seraphima was behind me, and I turned to consult with her. I was relieved to learn that she had an extra bandanna in her backpack, and she swiftly pulled it out, handing it to our young friend, who gratefully received it and tied it on her head. Crisis averted.

Three steps from the Edicule and the chalice. I was next. And, with the grace of God, I breathed deep, collected myself, and received.

۔ؤ۔

Waters of Grace
Water carries memory and grace, too, just like rock and soil. It can carry the imprint of holiness in the wild as well as in carefully blessed basins in churches. We pilgrims went to the River Jordan to renew our baptisms in the waters blessed by the baptism of Jesus Christ Himself, the event that revealed the Holy Trinity to all.

Not all places are safe for entering the Jordan, apparently—for both physical and political reasons. A certain area has been set up for pilgrims with a stone-paved area from which stairs and white-painted metal guide rails aid you in descending into the cool gray-green waters of its flow. A tangle of wild trees and bushes line the river all around on its banks.

We each wore a long white baptismal robe with a red cross on the back. Some of us, like Mark and me, had brought our own, but those who had not, ironically, could buy them at the store run by the local Jewish kibbutz! The bishop stood in the water with four of the men and, one by one, we descended, were grasped firmly but gently by the men, and lowered backward under the waters three times as the bishop pronounced the baptismal consecration to the Holy Trinity.

Mary Seraphima and I had to sing the special troparia and kontakia for the Baptism of the Lord while our pilgrims were undergoing this rite. Fortunately, there was a Greek woman chanter present for the more complicated services. Music worrying my mind, I was perhaps less present than I should have been for this special experience, but I do remember the freshness and gladness our pilgrim group felt as, newly washed in the great river which had received our Lord, we all stood together for a commemorative photo.

One of the happiest times of my life, however, was out in a boat on the lilting waves of the Sea of Galilee. The waters shone gold and silver in the rich sunlight, and a feeling of freedom and joy swept over me as if I suddenly possessed the wings of a gull. Pretty pastoral fields rife with wildflowers adorned the shore, and it was not hard to imagine a tall, bearded, long-haired man standing there and calling out to frustrated fishermen in a small boat to let down their empty nets just once more and pull them up, bursting with fish—and with their souls shockingly awakening to faith.

A Troubled Land

We visited the Holy Land during the last year of the six-year-long First Intifada, the Palestinian uprising against the twenty-year Israeli occupation of the West Bank, Gaza Strip, and East Jerusalem. While the Palestinians engaged in general strikes and boycotts and the throwing of rocks and Molotov cocktails, the Israelis used heavy violence against them—tear gas, rubber bullets, beatings, and live ammunition. Thousands of Palestinians died or were injured. Israelis were also killed or injured but in much lower numbers. The Oslo Accords put a temporary end to this terrible chapter, but with the basic problems of a divided nation unresolved, conflicts continued to arise, as we see, to the present day.

Our bus was stoned by young Palestinians at one point—the closest we came to the violence. Our guide was a careful and experienced Palestinian man, and he kept his ear to the ground, rerouting our itinerary to avoid each day's hot spots. Since many of the holy sites were in the West Bank, this was a very real concern. Naïve and unfamiliar as we were with the area, he regularly steered us out of trouble. Father Zaccheus had asked me to pick up for him a hand-painted icon he had ordered from the Saint Mary Magdalene convent, and, with the blessings of the bishop, I was about to set off to get it when our guide forbade me. "No, no!" he exclaimed. "It is not safe! There is much drug dealing around the base of the Mount of Olives! You cannot go there!" Our whole group later picked up the icon when we visited the Russian Orthodox Saint Mary Magdalene convent with its golden shining onion domes and lovely terraced rose gardens and offered a short service there.

It was hard not to feel pushed to take sides, especially when we watched bulldozers demolishing Palestinian homes and trees to make way for Israeli settlers.

We stayed in a Palestinian hotel near the Old City, an area only about a third of a mile square, yet containing Jewish, Christian, Armenian, and Muslim quarters enclosed in close to three miles of enormous defensive walls, sixteen to forty-nine feet high. Built by the Turkish sultan Suleiman the Magnificent in the sixteenth century, the sand-colored walls are ten feet wide at their base and marked by many famous huge gates. Our hotel was simple but comfortable, with a pleasant staff. Some of the Palestinian waiters were stranded in the hotel because of the Intifada and the violence happening around Gaza and the West Bank that made it impossible for them to return to their families in these areas. Even in our hotel, it was not possible to escape from the tragic division of the land.

Bethlehem—The Place of the Star
Our pilgrimage actually began in Bethlehem, with us awakening to a handsome landscape of sweeping scrubby hills with pale stone buildings picturesquely sprinkled over them like ornaments.

Early that morning our bus rolled past the Shepherds' Field, where the angel had appeared to announce to the shepherds the wondrous tidings of the Messiah's birth, and on to the Church of the Nativity, an immense basilica and the oldest major church of the Holy Land.

Traditional memories can be very strong, and the local people were able to show the ever-active Saint Helena the cave in which the blessed babe was born and even the exact spot where his manger bed had lain; she had the first church built over it in 327. It was later destroyed by fire during a revolt, and the Emperor Justinian had it rebuilt in 565, and in 614 even the invading Persians decided to spare it, a mercy they showed to no other church in the Holy Land. The reason? Their commander saw over the entrance—a very low door called the Door of Humility (built deliberately small so that no conqueror could insolently ride a camel or horse into the sacred space)—a representation of the Three Magi, dressed in Persian Zoroastrian priestly garb, and thus he apparently assumed some kind of Persian ownership or presence.

The main church is an extraordinarily long basilica with twelve large Corinthian columns in five aisles supporting its immense roof. Though impressive, it also looked worn and weather-stained. Funds for upkeep did not seem to be readily available, despite its importance and holiness. After our group performed a brief service in front of the iconostasis, an older monk who was one of the custodians there addressed us tearfully in Greek, our bishop translating. The old priest said that there were very few custodians to care for the Christian holy sites, and that their lives were very difficult. He had not even been able to leave to attend his own parents' funerals in Greece because of the lack of help here, something that broke his heart. Like many of the monastics we encountered at other sites, he begged us to return to this church and to the Holy Land as often as we could, and to support the sacred sites' preservation. You could feel his faithfulness, which struggled relentlessly on beneath exhaustion and disappointment. Our bishop made a donation from us all for this shrine, as we did at many other holy places. The monk blessed us, and then we headed down the worn marble stairs, misshapen from hundreds of years of pilgrim footsteps, to the sacred cave.

The cave is divided into proprietary areas among the Greek Orthodox, Armenian Apostolic, and Roman Catholic groups, as in the case of the Holy Sepulchre, the result of a nineteenth-century sultan's firman establishing what is known in both instances as "The Status Quo." For the Greek Orthodox, a handsome fourteen-point silver star set into a marble floor marks the place where Jesus was born, fifteen silver oil lamps hanging low above it, their flames glowing through red glass, while brocade tapestries and curtains surround it above and to the sides. The Roman Catholics have a smaller altar area, regarded as the site of the manger bed. The Armenians share the use of the Greek Orthodox altar. But pilgrims entering the small cave can enjoy the presence of all of these and venerate as they see fit. Despite the crowds, the sad condition of the great church, and the knowledge of conflict among the holy custodians, I felt a great sense of refreshment after venerating at the star—a bit of the newness one can feel in the quiet of Christmas Eve as something fresh and wonderful makes its mysterious way into the world.

Cats, Great and Small

"Charm" is not usually the first word that comes to mind when thinking of a monastery, but in the gold-domed church and monastery of Saint Gerasimos of the Jordan in a green and flowering oasis frilly with the spreading fans of palms, dappled shade of fruit trees, and lacework of vines, we pilgrims experienced the epitome of charm. Leaving the hot desert sands and walking through a cool open tunnel passageway, we entered the monastery's courtyard rife with greenery, blossoms, and many delicate hanging cages of sweetly trilling birds around a central well, an air of enchantment and hospitality pervading all.

Located in the bleak, rugged desert of the lower Jordan Valley a couple of miles southeast of Jericho, a cave now beneath the church floor is where the Virgin Mary and Saint Joseph stopped with the infant Jesus on their flight into Egypt, according to tradition. This crypt chapel now holds an icon of the Virgin nursing the Baby Jesus and many glass-covered display cabinets with relics, most of them the bones of monks martyred by the Persians. First established in the fifth century, the church has been destroyed and rebuilt many times, the latest repair taking place in 1885. However, some of its structure still dates from the thirteenth century, and the second floor has an airy open colonnade with arches above the courtyard, reminiscent of Knight Templar architecture.

We were greeted warmly by the young abbot, Father Chrysostomos, bearded and barefoot in his black robe, with long brown hair flowing down his back and a lively sparkle in his large, intelligent brown eyes. We gathered in the nave of the main church, where he welcomed us in English and told us stories about this sacred site. In Arabic it is called Deir Hajla, the Monastery of the Partridge. Father Chrysostomos told us that when the Holy

Family was fleeing Herod and stopped here overnight, migrating Bedouin tribes came upon them and were struck by the beauty and sweetness of the Holy Virgin and her babe. As they regarded the partridge as the most beautiful of birds, they named the spot the "Place of the Partridge" thereafter in her honor. And still used this designation to arrange meetings on their migration routes. We did see quite a few clusters of the black goat-hair Bedouin tents out in the desert during our pilgrimage.

While researching this book, I discovered that at a far earlier time, as noted in the Old Testament Book of Joshua, a location in this area north of the Dead Sea was known as Bethhoglah—the "House of the Partridge" in Hebrew! How these two stories align I cannot say!

The monastery was founded by Saint Gerasimos of the Jordan in the middle of the fifth century. This saint is famous for taking pity on a big lion he found roaring with pain by the Jordan, a large splinter deep in his paw. The saint pulled out the splinter, cleaned the wound, and bound it, expecting the lion to then go on its way. But instead the grateful lion followed the saint back to his monastery and lived there for five years, becoming a close companion to Gerasimos and serving the monks who named him "Jordanes," by guarding their donkey and camels. When Saint Gerasimos died, the lion threw himself on his grave, roaring inconsolably, and there died of grief, tradition tells us.

Another lion figures in the life of the other major saint associated with the monastery, Saint Mary of Egypt. A nymphomaniac turned penitent, Mary went out into the arid Judaean desert in this area and was not seen for forty-seven years. Then a priest-monk, Zosimas, wandering in the desert during Lent, came upon her. Overwhelmed by her sanctity and seeing her walk upon the waters of the Jordan, he became her disciple. She asked him to return in a year and bring her Holy Communion, which he did. After she received, she asked him to come back the following year. He did, only to find her dead, lying incorrupt upon the sands. Wanting to bury her but having no tool, he struggled hopelessly to dig in the sand with his hands. Feeling another presence, he looked up to see a huge lion standing near him. He was terrified, but the lion did not touch him. Instead, it took over the digging with its massive paws and soon had dug a grave for the holy Mary. Then it wandered back off into the desert.

"Are there still any lions here?" asked one of our pilgrims.

"No," the abbot said, smiling. "When people became more fierce than the lions, the lions left."

Felines deserve great credit. Here lions were the helpers and protectors of saints, but even our more humble felines, the house cats, have been effective protectors of sacred places.

The remarkable and indefatigable Saint Helena, in her quest to establish and protect as many holy Christian places as possible, went from the Holy Land to the island of Cyprus, where she and the governor of the island ordered construction of a monastery to Saint Nicholas in 327. Unfortunately, Cyprus had been suffering from drought for some years, with the effect of a proliferation of venomous adders everywhere. The poisonous snakes were so numerous that they drove off the builders of the monastery and even locals. Saint Helena, a determined problem-solver, imported one thousand cats from Persia and Egypt and deployed them to battle the snakes. The cats learned to come to two bells rung at the monastery—the first to hunt and destroy the snakes and the second to come to be fed by the monastics. The cats got the snake problem well under control, but as with so many holy places, the monastery itself was destroyed and rebuilt many times, the cats wandering away over the island. In 1983 the remaining buildings were given to a group of Orthodox nuns, who discovered—how history repeats itself!—that there were too many venomous snakes on their property. Remembering Saint Helena, they imported one hundred cats to live with them. Again, the valiant cats warred upon the snakes and dramatically reduced their numbers. In gratitude for the centuries of feline protection, the nuns decided to take in and care for any cat in need. The cats—and the nuns—are there to this day, at the monastery known as Saint Nicholas of the Cats on Kavo Gata, the Cape of Cats. As well as a very few, probably by now quite cautious, snakes.

When I first came to Jerusalem, I felt like it was my heart's home, "my" city. I was surprised to see this sentiment echoed by a Christian, a Muslim, a Jew, and even an atheist whose impressions of this remarkable city I read. I felt as if the air was dense with holy happenings, the historical and spiritual events being so powerful as to still be ringing in the air—we walked through them, into their livingness, gathering conscious and unconscious impressions amplifying our consciousness as an exploring honeybee gathers pollen until its breeches are so encrusted with the new gold of life-giving pollen that it can carry no more and must return home to its hive to share. At last we, too, had to take our reluctant leave. But, thanks to the generosity of John and Mary, before we returned to America, the four of us were going to Greece.

Samos and Patmos, Reprise

We had all been there before, though not together. We arrived on Samos, my grandmother's island, fried and exhausted from our beautiful but tough Holy Land pilgrimage, where we were up early (often awakened by the electronically amplified predawn Muslim call to prayer from nearby minarets) and to bed late, often traveling for hours, climbing or standing for hours, often waiting too many hours between sometimes skimpy meals (a quick falafel on the run), offering services in our shaky, uncertain voices, as we charged along under the lash of a demanding itinerary, a determined bishop, and the desert heat. We all four were fervently looking forward to a chance to exhale in Greece, where we could at last decide what to do and not do and when to do it—and rest.

Mark and I had had our treasured trip to Greece years before, and our enthusiastic praise had inspired John and Mary to honeymoon on Samos and Patmos, which they had loved. The only thing they had not loved was experiencing Samos, and particularly Pythagorion, during a particularly hectic tourist invasion, with crowded buses clogging the streets, which resounded with noise from the frolicking visitors. As a result, in the airport we four crisped pilgrims had our first major disagreement. For various reasons, Mark and I felt that we should find a *pensión* in nearby Pythagorion, so as to rest as soon as possible; we did not feel that we had the tensile strength to explore new possibilities right away. John, remembering their unpleasant experience before, vetoed that. I don't remember Mary venturing an opinion. The only certain thing was that all four of us were dropping with exhaustion. We needed a quick resolution.

Tempers began to arise alarmingly between the men, and they fixed each other with implacable, steely gazes. Mary and I prayed. I suggested we just take a cab and see if the driver might be able to help us. There was reluctant agreement.

Fortunately, the first Greek cabdriver we found spoke English. "Where do you want to go?" he asked.

"We don't know," I said, unhelpfully. "We need a *pensión*. Please just take us somewhere green!"

Oddly, he seemed to have no trouble understanding this cryptic request. "Okay, get in. I know a place."

Soon he pulled up by a sidewalk on a small side street in Pythagorion just under the hill that contained the holy cave of Spiliani. "Let me do the bargaining," Mark warned the three of us as he paid off the cabdriver and walked forward to greet the *pensión* proprietor, who had come out from a very pretty low white wall and fancy tall iron gate to meet us. Mark was obviously working at looking dubious in the hopes of getting lower room rates, but Mary, John, and I had looked through that gate and over the wall into a wildly beautiful formal garden, packed with roses, lilies, delphiniums, zinnias, and every imaginable type of glorious flower and greenery. Not a smidgen of doubt remained in our minds. Cost be damned, this was where we were going to stay!

While Mark was still bargaining and making disapproving faces at us, John, Mary, and I, in unwavering solidarity, were dragging our suitcases through the gate of this unbelievable paradise. Mark had no choice but to follow, accepting the proprietor's charges with an annoyed scowl in our subversive direction.

Soon we were in cool, pleasant, clean rooms that opened on a nice patio backed by a silvery olive grove. *Aaaaahhh . . .*

I dropped flat across a bed for a few moments, relieved down to my aching toes. And then got up to use the en suite bathroom. All good until I tried to leave the little bathroom. No matter how I turned the knob and jiggered the lock, it just would not open. I called Mark for help, and he tried to open the door from the other side. He called John to help him, but our two bulls could not disengage the door. Mark then went for the proprietor, Angelos, who also tried to force the door open. No good. Nothing worked. What to do? Angelos had to send for a locksmith.

And then I lost it, sitting on the toilet seat and sobbing away inconsolably, finally cracking from the rigors of the pilgrimage, the alarming confrontation at the airport, and now a strange fit of unbearable, exhausted claustrophobia in the tiny bathroom. I wept and wept, quietly hysterical, and couldn't stop.

When the locksmith arrived, he told Angelos they would not be able to get the lock open. The only possibility was to take the door off its hinges! So, a couple of hours after I had entered the bathroom, after a long session of enduring the loud masculine batterings of hinges and wood at close quarters and assorted cursing in Greek (here my linguistic ignorance was probably a benefit), I was finally able to leave my prison as the door fell away, emerging like Lazarus from the tomb, only in my case wrung out like a dishrag, a very used-up pilgrim.

However, just a few days spent in that pleasant *pensión*, being served Continental breakfasts and sipping Greek coffee from demitasse cups on the handsome white portico opening on the wall-to-wall magnificent flowers of the front garden with no particular schedule to obey, was effective healing balm on all our psychic wounds, mine included.

و۵

Battle of the Font

We exchanged pleasantries with a nice family on the hydrofoil bound for Patmos—an American father, a Swiss mother, and their very beautiful six-year-old daughter, Lilah. There seemed to be an incredible chemistry between Lilah and me—the moment we laid eyes on each other, she flew into my arms, and with great pleasure I sat with my arm around her most of the trip to Patmos. Once we arrived at the island, Mark and I were able to get our same lovely room at the Chora *pensión* and settled in, still weary but recovering.

Lilah's parents sought us out the next day. The child had announced to them that she wanted to be baptized here, on St. John's island, and she wanted me to be her godmother. Her family was Christian and lived in Switzerland, worshipping simply, in a Protestant style, at home. The father's father had been a minister in the "Church of Saint John"—perhaps the Baptist—in the States. Neither he, his wife, nor Lilah herself seemed troubled by the fact that the only way she could be baptized on Patmos was as a Greek Orthodox Christian. So we went to talk to Papa Pavlos, Father Paul, a venerable white-bearded priest who had been close to the great elder Amphilochius. Fortunately, he spoke English.

Although gracious, it was clear he was quite surprised by this request. Lilah's father was as black as dark coffee beans—something probably rarely seen on this island—and Lilah herself a lovely coffee-and-cream. Lilah's mother was fair-skinned and red-haired. Interracial marriages were something else probably rarely seen on this island. More of an issue, however, was the couple's Protestantism. And also whether I was really "Orthodox enough" to be Lilah's godmother! After all, I didn't speak Greek!

Papa Pavlos mulled all this over, prayed, and decided to proceed. The baptism was set for the next morning in the large, gorgeous church of Panaghia Diasozousa with its miracle-working icons. This church in Chora was reached by a series of white zigzag stairways graced with torrents of lush pink roses and fragrant gold-and-white honeysuckle bushes tumbling over its handsome balustrades. Upon reaching the courtyard in front of the church that morning, Mark and I were surprised to see that there was already a pretty big crowd waiting, mainly German travelers who returned to Patmos year after year in a spiritual sympathy for, and varying degrees of commitment to, its Orthodoxy. As we walked up, a hysterical screeching rent the morning air.

"*Protestanti! Protestanti!*" shrieked an elderly woman's voice. Black-haired (probably dyed!) and clad in black, she was facing off with Lilah's father, who, with rising temper, was asserting, "I'm a Christian! I'm as much a Christian as you! Church of John, I was raised in!"

"Who is that?" I asked a knowledgeable German lady.

"Oh, she's Papa Pavlos's sister!"

And she turned out also to be the "other godmother." Apparently Papa Pavlos was hedging his bets, just in case I turned out not to be the real thing! We were quite a pair, she clad in black from head to toe, and I likewise in white, it being the joyous Paschal period.

I gently stepped in between the two religious disputants. "It's okay," I reassured Lilah's father. "Don't worry." And turning to the fuming Greek lady, I said, "*En daxi, en daxi.*" "It's okay, it's all right." She simmered down but still kept throwing doubtful looks at Lilah's parents.

Fortunately, Papa Pavlos arrived then with two other priests and calmed his sister, and our whole crowd swept into the church. We did the preliminary prayers of the "exorcism" in the narthex of the church. Papa Pavlos, looking a bit dubious, handed me a small prayer book with the Nicean Creed in English to read. I could have sung it without a book but didn't know how that would have been received and also was aware of the danger of blanking out in critical places when under pressure. I took the book but pointedly chanted the Creed, as opposed to just reading it, to add a little more evidence to my assertion that I was Orthodox. We proceeded to the font.

Lilah, looking extra-beautiful all in white, put herself trustingly into Papa Pavlos's guiding hands. We two godmothers, the white and the black, helped her strip down to her snowy undershirt and underpants. We and the priest anointed her with holy oil. Papa Pavlos, after the necessary prayers, gently lifted her into the baptismal font and immersed her three times in the name of the Holy Trinity. She was a cooperative lamb throughout the whole baptism, submitting to its strangeness as if it were the most natural thing in the world. We godmothers dried her off with a fluffy towel, and her mother took her off to dress her in dry white clothes. Then, led by Papa Pavlos with a censer as a cantor sang "Those Who Have Been Baptized in Christ" in Greek, Lilah and her two godmothers, all of us carrying tall lit candles, slowly circled three times an analogion stand bearing a holy icon. Lilah was radiant. Her parents' faces were also glowing with joy.

Lilah's baptismal name, as decided by herself and her parents, was Christine. Her mother became very nervous when it was suggested that she would be named, Greek-style, Christina. She said that the bureaucracy in Switzerland could be very difficult to deal with about anything official, like names, and felt that she didn't dare even change one letter of her daughter's baptismal name to alter it from the normal Swiss form, and so it appeared with an "e," officially impeccable, on her baptismal certificate. But when Christine lifted her head up to receive her first Holy Communion, a godmother on each side of her, and the brown-bearded priest asked her name in Greek, I replied, "Christina Ioanna." "Christina Ioanna," he replied with satisfaction, tipping the chalice into her mouth. Christina Joanna. Christina of John. After all, she had deliberately chosen John's island!

Lilah and her parents were very happy. The other godmother's perturbations had subsided. There was also general rejoicing among the Germans, some of whom had taken beautiful photographs of the whole occasion. Lilah's father gave a generous donation to the celebrants, and the crowd finally dispersed.

Lilah's parents insisted that we and John and Mary come out to breakfast with them at the Vangelises' taverna. We all celebrated together, still in the luminous glow of the sacrament. At last we all dispersed, Mark and I finding ourselves strangely exhausted. We staggered back to our *pensión* and, entering our room, with deep sighs threw ourselves down on the bed with enormous relief.

A moment later, there was a knock on the door. Who could this be? It was Mr. Vangelis with three workmen, all bearing a new carved pinewood window frame and window to replace the one in our room! Oh no! We asked if this could please take place later, but Mr. Vangelis insisted it had to be done now—but not to worry! It would be quick! Our hearts sinking, we watched this amazing team move in and, to our astonishment, with the grace and coordination of ballet dancers, take the old window out and set the new one in, as if to music. It could not have taken more than fifteen minutes. We couldn't help ourselves applauding, and they nodded, smiling, as they walked out the door. Then we collapsed. And slept the deep dreamless zonked sleep of the repeatedly blessed.

※

Bulgaria: The Wood Nymph and the Great White Sharks
Our Bulgarian bishop decided to make a pilgrimage to Bulgaria, inviting his spiritual children to join him, and, thanks to the generosity of my dear friends, I was able to participate in this rare opportunity to visit the sacred places of another Orthodox Christian culture and, as always on a pilgrimage, to gather grace.

Sadly, my husband Mark's questionable state of health made it impossible for him to go along. But there were many of my friends among our twenty or so pilgrims, many of us Orthodox cantors, and even Father Zeno came along.

Bulgaria came as a shock—a vibrant paradise of verdant, ravishing landscapes of dramatic mountains and valleys merged with a gray pall of Eastern Bloc Communist architecture, statuary, and lingering unease. It had only been ten years since Bulgaria had received a democratic constitution and only about twelve years since the first election in which Bulgarians could vote for a choice of parties. For every charming green parklet jeweled with fountains in the capital Sofia there seemed to be a score of ponderous all-hail-to-the-workers metal statues, leaning into their grim tasks with clenched fists and determined brows, pursuing relentlessly the complete eradication of humor, grace, tenderness, and any such frivolous things that might threaten the State or comfort a human heart.

Mountain drives past enchanting if dilapidated red-tile-roofed villages with black and white storks nesting on big straw halos on their roofs would yield to plains of horrid, decaying substandard Soviet-style apartment buildings where the occasional pitiful pots of geraniums could not overcome the depressing effect of parking-garage-style living quarters for human beings. Gorgeous old churches and basilicas—many-domed and some of them robed externally in gleaming floral tiles with gold lacework edging in an exquisite Russian style—and elegant neoclassical buildings gave way to big Soviet "tanker-style" official buildings, supposed to be grand but merely achieving terminal oppressiveness.

Even inside, these fortresslike structures suffered from a strange glut of humongous chandeliers, as if invasions of huge, crystallized mutant jellyfish had suckered themselves threateningly to the ceilings, while the felt presence of invisible great white sharks of despotic surveillance cruised menacingly among them. Walking beneath the chandeliers' glowering weight, you felt as if the alien jellyfish might suddenly drop down and snuff you out if you did anything inappropriate, like smile.

In the cities, gangs of ragged Romany children would follow you and thrust their hands in front of your face, hampering your every step until you gave them some money—and, after that, they would hamper you even worse, making you all too aware of the persistent existence of the impoverished Romany underclass. But, given their many economic reversals and crises over hundreds of years of invasions and drastic political transitions, there was plenty of poverty to go around for all Bulgarians.

Our young tour guide, Darina, was vivacious, endearing, and frank. As we stared gloomily from our van windows at the miles of ugly apartment buildings—it is true, once or twice, unaccountably separated by small farm fields being plowed by a man with an ox!— she told us that these disintegrating complexes cost about $50,000 per apartment (a fortune, given that at that time in Bulgaria, she said, monthly income ran about one hundred dollars). And that the apartments were so badly constructed they were not expected to last more than thirty-five to forty-five years. Homelessness was a looming problem in the Bulgarian future, Darina said sadly.

But, nonetheless, Bulgaria was wildly gorgeous, a great fertile wood nymph, her roadside skirts a lavish tapestry of wild apricot and plum trees dropping golden and purple-velvet fruits into a tangle of fragrant blooming plants, her emerald-green mountain bodice nesting glorious ancient churches in its steep, heavily forested folds, her woodland sleeves embroidered with delicate pale-rose miniature cyclamens and a host of other graceful plants, and her gown endlessly rich with pink-flowered tobacco fields, cornfields full of beaming sunflowers, and small orchards with their bountiful apples just beginning to turn yellow. Bulgaria was beautiful and, on the whole, I must say, its women the most beautiful I had ever seen—small-boned, curvy, and slender, with dark, glowing eyes and hair and graceful, delicate features.

Unfortunately, the pleasantness of this overall impression was somewhat spoiled by the tendency of many of the younger women—unlike their babushka elders with the potato-sack bodies easier for me to identify with—to wear the briefest and most clinging of clothes and the heaviest makeup.

This style of apparel was distracting in church, at the very least. When, during a very holy ceremony at a big church feast, a pretty young blond Bulgarian woman fecklessly joined our cantors on the left *kliros* wearing a crocheted "sweater" consisting of windowpane-like holes outlined in infrequent narrow ropes of stitches that left her basically standing in front of us in her bra—reminiscent of the old "I went to a sacred church service in my Maidenform bra" print ads of the 1950s—our beleaguered choir director turned to me with a despairing gaze and moaned, "I don't know where to put my eyes!" I couldn't advise him because, just at that moment, a sleeping, long-boned Bulgarian farmer who had also inappropriately loped into our cantors' section of the church and plunked his tired body down in a cantor's chair set fire to his hair with his torch of thirty-three bound slender candles. I dashed toward him, reaching for a blanket that a television crew had left there (this service was a big deal, and even featured the king reading the

Creed), hoping to extinguish the fire. However, the flames in his longish side-parted hair awakened him and he just casually slapped them out with one huge hand—and then went back to sleep. Did I tell you that a certain amount of surrealism haunted my Bulgarian experience? And not just the street and building signs, which gave me a disturbing sense of being caught up in a dream with Greek, Cyrillic, and occasionally English letters all mixed together, giving me the illusion that I almost understood what I was reading. But never, ever, actually did.

Our bishop was quite pleased to have a number of his singers along as he was determined to have us demonstrate that Orthodox Christianity was alive even in the distant materialistic United States of America. He determinedly pursued this agenda by having us sing and participate in services all over the country, sometimes a number of times in one day, with a sublime indifference to the fact that we were horribly jet-lagged, exhausted, often dehydrated, and pushed to the edge of our endurance by the August heat, hovering mostly in the high nineties and sometimes over one hundred degrees Fahrenheit. The luxury of air-conditioning was just that: a luxury, available only at certain, rarely visited hotels. This did not surprise us, given that a number of places where we stayed did not even have window screens but only patterned lace curtains to confuse the bugs.

The day after we arrived, following a daylong tiring trot of ecclesiastical sightseeing in Sofia, our bishop blithely informed us, cross-eyed though we were, that he wanted us to help conduct a Vespers service in the second-biggest church in the Balkans, the multi-domed Alexander Nevsky cathedral, a behemoth that can hold ten thousand worshippers and which has its own professional Russian-style choir. Andrew Kalford, Ben Stell, and I, to whom it fell to lead the singing group, looked at each other with the eyes of those in a lifeboat that has just been rammed by a whale. *Surely he jests? No.* Oh yes, and he cheerfully added, "And prepare an encore for the end of the service, in case!"

Ongoing repairs necessitated elaborate staging outside the church and inside as well. Our bishop positioned us on the left *klíros* and, sweeping Father Deacon John and our priests with him after giving us a list of pieces he wanted us to sing, disappeared into the sanctuary. We were abandoned in the vast space with its welter of multicolored marble, onyx, and alabaster columns and carvings; omnipresent bright icons; and enormously tall carved and gilded icon screen, all hemmed in at odd angles by raw wooden panels and construction scaffolding. To our surprise, no cantors appeared on the right *klíros*, the primary place of the leaders. And, to our horror, we discovered as the Vespers began that the technically perfect, ripe-voiced Russian-style choir was instead in some invisible choir loft far away in this behemoth church that could swallow multiple football fields and not even notice it.

We felt like musical mice alternating with the musical elephants of the professional choir. We got through the Vespers but, tense and exhausted, certainly did not sound our best. There were some worshippers present, and at the service's end, Mila, a young Bulgarian woman who had attended St. Vladimir's Russian Orthodox seminary in New York, rushed up to us to say how deeply moved she had been by our singing, especially by our encore, the Great Doxology.

"This is so beautiful, really beautiful," she said, with her hand over her heart. I apologetically indicated the contrast to the well-oiled, high-volume professional chorus. "Pah!" she retorted. "They are nothing! Just paid professionals. You don't understand what it is like to hear believers sing!"

I did myself feel a certain atmospheric coldness in the cathedral. Darina told us that the basilica was used mostly for state occasions; no ordinary people could have baptisms or weddings there; there was no parish. Physically it was beautiful, but it seemed to lack the most essential thing: spiritual warmth. The church seemed more like a monument than a holy house to nurture souls.

ﷻ

We staggered out of the jaws of the mammoth cathedral like Jonah escaping from the whale. Our hopes to go collapse in our rooms in the air-conditioned hotel were immediately dashed as we were herded into our touring van, the one where the air-conditioning never worked. We were swept up, up, up, and up the dark-green lushly forested mountain slopes, past partially constructed homes of the rich ("They build as much as they can until they run out of money and then they abandon the site until they have enough money to build again," said Darina) that added a kind of offhand Salvador Dalí tweak to the otherwise pastoral views. But, as we ascended, we breathed in the blessed green coolness of the higher altitudes with gratitude and were soon deposited at a self-consciously rustic restaurant with traditional décor for a "folkloric dinner."

We were seated on benches at joined tables lining a narrow room. Red tablecloths woven with bright folkloric patterns covered the tables, which were set with charming pottery plates and bowls slip-glazed brown with appealing designs of blue and gold melting through them in rhythmical patterns—a distinctive Bulgarian style known as Troyan. We were to see throughout our trip that the Bulgarians are a very artistic people, and that their artisans do especially fine work in silver, pottery, embroidery, and wood carving in striking designs rarely seen in the West.

Waiters brought tasty food to us, a notably good course being the first one: a flavorful bean dish, a savory eggplant puree, a delicate coleslaw, and assorted other appetizers, followed by courses of good-enough cabbage stuffed with mushrooms and meat, popovers, and the like. Bulgarian cuisine was a cheerful medley of influences from the many cultures that had invaded it over the centuries—Slav, Greek, Persian, Turkish, etc. A big hit was the dessert of a subtle ice cream accompanied by large chunks of sweetened smooth frozen heavy cream.

While we ate, three musicians on a rug-covered dais—a guitarist, an accordionist, and a drummer with an ethnic drum—played traditional Bulgarian melodies for us. Bulgarian folkdancing is famous for its athleticism, and, sure enough, two young couples soon came leaping in, performing very up-tempo and vigorous folkdances, occasionally rushing off to change costumes—sometimes elegant, sometimes garish—before leaping back like spawning salmon to deliver the next impressive dance. All good but the evening started to deteriorate when the dancers insisted on conscripting "volunteers" from our group to join them.

After some of our group had been pulled into a few line dances in the narrow space, a zaftig costumed Bulgarian lady sashayed onto the dais. This singer had loosely piled dyed white-blond hair with three-inch dark roots, fluorescent pink lipstick, and an ululation they could probably hear in Romania. The sound system had obviously been turned up to the maximum, and our ears rang with her high-pitched songs. While we were still poking our ears, a Bulgarian man in national costume strode onto the dais and, to my horror, launched into the opening notes of "Bésame Mucho"! At least half an hour of international musical mayhem, including—yes, I do not lie!—Swiss yodeling, followed. Mary Seraphima and I looked at each other with mute, suffering eyes. That recurrent surrealism attending this trip, now amply reinforced musically, made me feel that perhaps this was just a weird dream, and if I were lucky, I would soon awake in my comfy bed at home. No such luck. At last let out of that deafening international-music prison around 10:30 that night, we stumbled like zombies to our van.

We were up early the next morning because Mila, our new Bulgarian friend, had invited our group to sing the Divine Liturgy at her parish church, the Protection of the Mother of God, to be followed by a group discussion with the congregation about what is involved in living in a vital community of Orthodox Christian life. Having been repressed, as well as sometimes infiltrated, by the Communists for so many years, many churches were just feeling their way out of the enforced numbness of living under a hostile dictatorship. Although the circling great white sharks of that unblinking domination were no longer externally visible, in the Bulgarian psychic ocean the currents of their anxiety-generating presence could still be felt.

Short on sleep, still jet-lagged, and breakfastless (since we were about to do a Eucharistic service), we regretfully walked out the doors of our Swedish-owned hotel, which had provided us with a nostalgically remembered lavish breakfast buffet the day before. Even the early-morning air was uncomfortably hot. ("Most people who can leave Sofia in August," Darina told us, "to escape from the heat." Yes, indeed. Not an option on our pilgrim path!) We dutifully sang our way through the liturgy, hanging on with our musical fingernails, and then, like the *Titanic* approaching the iceberg, we came up against the sermon. We loved our bishop, a loving and zealous man, but we did not realize that he was competing in the *Guinness Book of World Records* for "longest sermon in life-threatening heat." His homily—all in Bulgarian, of course— might have been an hour and a half long. It certainly felt that long. And the Bulgarians stood all the way through it. Which meant we had to also. Orthodox etiquette in some places is to stand through sermons, but it is often not observed; however, in this old-country setting, we didn't dare to offend. Sitting here appeared to be out of the question.

Partway through the sermon, Ben whispered to me in a strangled voice, "Stephani, I think I'm going to faint!" Fortunately, there was a chair near where we stood. I grabbed his arms and eased him into it.

"Open your mouth," I said. He obediently opened it. I dropped four drops of Rescue Remedy tincture into it and then pulled a water bottle from my bag and handed it to him. "Drink," I said, standing in front of him to block him from view, as drinking even water before Holy Communion is generally disapproved of. I looked back at him. He had been white, but some faint color was coming back into his face. He gave me a grateful, grim little smile.

Ben was one of our more stalwart, physically strong people. If he is going down so soon, what is going to happen to the rest of us? I wondered.

The long liturgy was followed by an even longer, somewhat contentious group discussion by parishioners. Clearly in uncertain territory after the repressive Communist years, various young people, especially, were feeling their oats about certain religious topics and trying out ideas with the vehemence of the young and inexperienced, such as should one, as was done traditionally, dress up for church to honor God or come wearing old T-shirts and any old thing to testify that God takes us and loves us as we are? I'm sure that topics of much more depth were discussed, but I draw a complete blank, as our heat-bashed crew, dehydrated, having fasted since the night before, and subsisting on the light "brunch" offered of bread with marmalade, bread with a kind of ketchup, *loukoumi* (sticky sugar-powdered Turkish delight), and some nectarines, struggled to follow the translations of the intensely argued discussions. We crawled back into our heated-tin can van around 3:00 P.M., wondering if we might wind up leaving our singers' bones in Bulgaria.

Fortunately for us, our next stop took us a two-and-a-half hour drive up into the emerald-green Rila mountains, their highest peak about nine thousand feet, to possibly the most magical place I have ever visited: the Saint John of Rila Monastery. Backed by sixty-five-foot stone walls, an enclosing curl of monastic buildings, arcaded on four levels and strikingly banded in red and black, protectively enclose a huge courtyard of cobbles and flagstones centered on an enormous domed church, its exterior walls gorgeously frescoed with religious scenes in glowing, singing shades of rose, gold, heavenly blue, and soft green. Nestled cozily and improbably in a verdant valley among very steep thickly forested mountain slopes, the monastery looked less like ecclesiastical buildings and more like a fairy-tale secret treasure hidden by highly artistic giants. But this remote monastery and its founder reflect the heart and soul of Bulgaria, and are most highly honored by Bulgarians. The monastery is also a UNESCO World Heritage Site.

All this warm splendor is the result of the life of a very simple man, Saint John (Ivan) of Rila. Born in 876 in the Sofia area, the pious boy was orphaned early and, to survive, hired himself out as a cowherd. His wealthy employer beat him when a cow and calf were missing, then was later shocked to see the downtrodden boy, through prayer and a miracle before his very eyes, bring the cow

and calf back. Frightened, the man paid John off generously and
sent him on his way. John went to barren places to live a life of
asceticism dedicated to God, and at some point he was tonsured a
monk. He moved around as he had to, often living in caves and at
last in the hollow of an oak tree in the remote wilderness of Rila.
Having endured temptations and confrontations with the Evil
One, beatings by robbers, the kidnapping of the beloved nephew
who had joined him (the boy died of a snakebite on the road), and
many sorrows, he achieved a level of sainthood and healing ability
that drew people to him from near and far. At last he accepted
monastics who wished to live near him, and they built a church in
a cave he had formerly dwelt in. Saint John himself lived out on
top of a rocky outcropping without shelter for many years, and even
after he died, his incorrupt relics continued to work many miracles.

I could feel the presence of the saint, I thought, throughout the
whole area—a remarkably soft presence, even tender. On the last of
the three times we were able to venerate his unveiled relics in the
enormous gilded church, I smelled a distinct, exquisite aroma of
roses that my friends did not smell (so I know there was no added
physical perfume). At one point I felt as if St. John was gently patting my cheek. I can't explain it. It was just a joy to be in his aura,
under his mantle, in the flow of grace he had left in this blessed
place that seemed steady and unwavering as a great river. One did
not have to deserve the grace; one did not have to struggle for it.
The grace was freely given, overflowing, from a sanctified heart
that knew no bounds.

Loveliest of all was our visit to Saint John's tiny house-church,
more like a pleasant peasant's cottage, and mysterious cave high
up on the mountainside above the monastery. It was a fairly challenging hike for those of us who were out of shape but doable,
passing through the fertile slopes of a handsome beech wood with
mixed conifers and deciduous trees farther above. The bishop himself cut me a walking staff and encouraged us all upward. When
the huge monastery looked like little children's play buildings far
below us, we came to the small stone-and-stucco Church of the
Dormition of Saint John of Rila. His body had originally lain in
the cave alongside the tiny church, our guide told us, but had also
been kept inside the little church; his relics had been transferred
to various places near and far many times but now lay in the big
monastery below.

The whitewashed inner walls of this church were covered, floor
to ceiling, in beautiful frescoes painted in warm tones. I was happy
to see icon frescoes of a large number of Unmercenary Healer

saints (healers who do not charge) filling a small side room, an unusual sight. There was a lovely icon of Saint John himself centrally located, carrying the same sweetness that his ineffable presence seemed to bear; even though he was standing still, the icon was not static—there seemed a movement like music, as if the folds of Saint John's robes were gently swaying to the music of the spheres, the background of blue sky studded with stars sharing with him and thus with us, his spiritual children, a glad chorus of light.

So much could be said of Rila with its rich spiritual and historical heritage, but I find I cannot—because I am overwhelmed with a personal sense of longing that I have never felt for any other place. Saint John's presence, the beautiful monastery and churches, the lush abandon of nature spilling up mountainsides and down meadows with a fertile intensity that struck my soul with a sense of exaltation—and perhaps having all this in an area so far from crowded human habitations, where the ratio of Nature to humans seemed to be a healthy million to one—made my spirit feel like a harp struck by unseen hands rousing an unfading song of deepest delight.

To the side of the little church was Saint John's small, damp cave, irregular stone steps leading you into its narrow opening below a slanted triangular ceiling. Maybe fifteen feet long in all and not very wide, the rough cave has a small ledge with icons and lit candles among its rubble and rocks on one side. You walk slowly and carefully past it on the irregular stone floor in semidarkness. A little light pours down at the end of the cave, picking out a wooden ladder leaning into the six-foot-long tunnel you must climb up to come out into the sunlight and fragrant forest again.

There is a tradition about Saint John's cave that it has a special blessing on it whereby if you can go through the narrow tunnel hole and out, your sins up to that point are forgiven. But not being able to fit through—and not everyone does—is a bad sign. Our bishop was worried, fearing that my portliness might keep me from making it through the hole; one of our accompanying priests, not heavy but a tall, big-boned man, was also worried. Apparently the bishop had had two plump women pilgrims with him the last time he visited, and they wept inconsolably when they couldn't get through.

I don't know, but I just couldn't get worried about it; I felt deeply calm. And when I climbed the ladder and entered the challenging tunnel, I felt like something happened to me, almost like being catapulted into another universe or level of existence, my consciousness briefly altered—the hole suddenly seemed to grow huge, and I myself felt like a little marveling hobbit, enchanted to be in it and with plenty of room to spare. As I emerged into the sunlight, men reaching out to help me up, there were cheers. As there were for each one of us. I don't know what the nature of the blessing was in Saint John's magical hole, but that there was a blessing, a very real and enduring blessing, I feel in my bones.

We were able to take water from a holy spring there and see the great rock on which St. John prayed, day and night, through the seasons. I was sorry when we had to go; I would have loved to spend the night in the little church. But, at least, my accommodations down below, two minutes' walk from the monastery, were also enchanting. I had my own odd little room in a picturesque red-tile-roofed "folkloric" hotel with swallows nesting in its eaves, above a rushing stream with a full, joyous, effervescent song. I liked to think of it singing through my dreams. Across a narrow rocky road were huge assorted conifers of great beauty, crowded together like a group of enormous, benign bishops in conference. The breeze, when it flowed from their direction, carried a delicious, delicate cedary scent.

The room, though simple, seemed to have been staged by Franco Zeffirelli with an eye to a bit of drama. The furniture was plain and wooden, but blankets in dazzling woven patterns had been folded vertically into the bedsheets in an idiosyncratic manner. My little bed ended just a few feet before the room's angled glass door fronting a small pie-wedge of balcony shadowed by a huge conifer. The whole end of the room was hung from ceiling to floor with rococo white lace curtains and, over them, heavy ten-foot maroon velvet curtains. It looked so improbably operatic that I asked my friend Monica to come sing a few bars from an aria on my balcony. She obliged, and it seemed entirely appropriate. After that, there was just soaring birdsong and the chanting of the vigorous river. And my own happy thoughts. More than enough.

اگ

We sang in services at the main church; met and received hospitality and small gifts (icons, postcards, etc.) from the *igumen*, the abbot; visited the monastery museum with its miraculously small carvings of scenes from the life of Christ on a wooden cross, sumptuous embroidered vestments in subtle glissades of shimmering shades, richly ornamented bulls from Ottoman emperors, and more.

We were taken up into the most ancient part of the monastery, a five-story-high fortified stone tower built by a local feudal lord in 1334, designed to allow its guardians to throw rocks and boiling liquids down on invaders. Um, including a creatively designed "toilet," carved out of the stone so as to allow one's backside to hang out over the open air and potentially poop on unsuspecting enemies! One would have to keep an eye out, though, I would think, for enemies with bows and arrows! There were chapels on certain floors and an unusual domed chapel dedicated to Holy Wisdom, portrayed as a woman in a sleeveless robe with a triangle behind her head. Around the dome's border were seven winged little babies, lightly swaddled and representing the Seven Gifts of the Holy Spirit—all of it done in a light, airy, almost fanciful style—quite a contrast to the grim practicality of the stone tower.

At last we had to say a sad goodbye to Rila and continue our whirlwind musical tour, mainly traveling from monastery to monastery but occasionally with other stops, like visiting our bishop's village and church. We saw a number of powerful miracle-working icons, such as Our Lady of Bachkovo at the beautiful Bachkovo Monastery with its ancient frescos that included the pre-Christian Righteous: Plato, Socrates, and pagan Pythia priestesses. Of course, we sang there, and then a tiny hieromonk wearing the usual long black *ráso* but also a green velvet cap that gave him an elfish look came out, stating (in Bulgarian) that he was so moved and pleased by our pious women wearing our head scarves (we usually did in services), that he wanted to give us a gift—the blessing of our bus. Father Zeno would have liked to pass on this, as we were already hours behind schedule, with the *igumenos* at another monastery waiting for us, but the little monk insisted. He may have performed the most thorough blessing of a vehicle with holy water ever. Slowly and conscientiously, he sprinkled and blessed each seat and every inch of the bus interior and then went outside, opened up the motor, and blessed each part of the engine! Not to mention the whole outside of the bus. By the time he was done, Father Zeno, who had some responsibility for schedules, was just about tearing his beard out, but the little monk smiled at us beatifically and waved fondly at us as our bus pulled out in haste.

We visited a couple of small women's monasteries also, both with just a handful of nuns. We were received warmly and sat down for coffee and sweets with them in their gardens, bright with phlox and dahlias. In one case, the nuns ran an orphanage for Romany children, and they brought out their star singer, a small six-year-old boy, who belted out Romanian Romany songs with great panache.

In both cases the *igumeni*, the abbess, was notably short in stature. As we were departing from one, the *igumeni*, actually a dwarf, rushed back to me and took my hand as we walked, saying urgently, "*Popadia! Popadia!* Stay! Stay!" "Stay" was apparently her one word of English, and she didn't hesitate to use it to try to recruit nuns! Our bishop barked at her with unusual gruffness. I heard him in Bulgarian correcting her that I was a "*diaconissa*" (deacon's wife, rather than a *popadia*, priest's wife) and obviously telling her to back off and that I was not going to be a recruit! She patted my hand with a regretful smile.

ᴥ

We visited ethnographic museums; in the charming town of Arbanassi explored lovely old houses painted in strong, rich shades and with elegant carved ceilings inspired by the artistic waves of the Bulgarian National Revival period of the eighteenth and nineteenth centuries; visited a natural history museum with stuffed boars as high as my shoulder and a variety of other impressive if inanimate wildlife; and tried out our voices in the huge ancient amphitheater recently uncovered in the city of Plovdiv. There we stayed in a hotel that was like an outtake from the early 1960s; the rooms were basically white but with life preserver-orange bedspreads and domed bright-orange plastic lamps; we would not have been surprised to see a Jane Fonda-esque maid in miniskirt and go-go boots materialize to offer us Tab and Twinkies. Shielding my eyes from the glare, I shoved my bedspreads out of sight in the closet and joined my compatriots milling around nervously in the hall. Someone unwisely asked Fr. Deacon John, being an artist, his opinion of the hotel's interior designer. "He should be taken out and shot!" exclaimed John, uncharacteristically violent. I agreed with him.

Our bishop at last released us one hot, dusty afternoon to do some shopping for gifts to bring home. We were in a major city, but the area we were in seemed dull, with little to buy. I wandered back to our bus and stood outside it with the bishop. On the way there I had had to pass through a broad sunken plaza. I had steered a bit away from a young dark-haired woman there who was hopping around on one foot and talking excitedly in Bulgarian to any passerby. She was pretty, wearing a printed yellow full-sleeved blouse, many crosses, and very tight jeans. I said a prayer for her, feeling sympathy for the plight of her mental illness.

Standing by the bishop, both of us a bit somnambulant in the heat, I struggled to find something to say. What popped out of my mouth was, "Do you still have any fool-for-Christ saints in Bulgaria?" He looked at me like I was crazy.

"Sure!" he announced firmly. "There! Slava!" and pointed at the young hopping woman.

Oh no! I had worried that if I ever actually met a fool-for-Christ, I'd miss it! Yup! It was a lesson. Why hadn't I even considered that possibility? Ah, I know, the tight jeans! So much for my nonjudgmental mind! A good learning experience about the danger of assumptions, especially those welded to notions of propriety!

When I pointed out to some of our returning pilgrims that there was a fool-for-Christ right before us, Monica rushed back down the stairs into the square. Slava was leaving now, but Monica dashed like an Olympic sprinter to catch up with her, exclaiming, "Pray! Pray!" as she tried to stuff dollar bills into the tiny pockets of the too-tight jeans! Despite the language barrier, I'm sure the young fool-for-Christ got the message!

ﷲ

We traveled on, visiting the famous damask rose fields in Kazanlak, which supplies most of the world's attar of roses and rose absolute—but no roses bloom in August there. We sang with a welcoming choir of young men both liturgically and informally later in the room of an inn where we all refreshed ourselves with watermelon, plums, and nectarines. We were given gifts of paper icons and small wooden bottles of rose oil and felt a real sense of celebration with these warmhearted people who truly loved their music and loved to share it.

As we traveled around, we occasionally had to make restroom stops. In one somewhat old-fashioned hotel where we briefly halted, a tiny old lady was sitting in the lobby at a card table—selling toilet paper by the square.

Individual Bulgarians we most often found to be friendly and kind. But, as anywhere else, there are always exceptions. Going out for a little ice cream break with Darina one day, I could see that she was very upset.

"What is it?" I asked.

Her eyes filled with tears. "It's my mother!" she choked. "She is in the hospital."

"Oh no!" I said. "What happened?"

"Well, it is like this. My mother noticed that her priest and his deacon were involved in an active homosexual relationship with each other, and she went to see the priest to complain about this. The next day the priest and the deacon came to her house and beat her up so badly that she had to be admitted to the hospital!"

"That is terrible! What will happen now?"

"Oh, nothing. Nothing will be done," Darina said resignedly, wiping her eyes.

"But that's wrong! Surely something must be done about such violence. Let's talk to our bishop."

Darina told our bishop her sad tale, and he shook his head sympathetically but said, "I am sorry. There is nothing I can do. They are not under my authority."

We finally convinced *Vladika*, our bishop, to get in touch with the bishop who did have authority over those particular men. He agreed with reluctance. Afterward he said, "I told him about it. But that is all I can do." Neither Darina nor her mother ever heard from the men's bishop, and, at least while we were still in Bulgaria, no action, legal or ecclesiastical, was brought against them. I don't know for sure but doubt that they were ever brought to trial. That this kind of unchallenged brutality could happen even under the mantle of the Church, as well as the state, showed that those great white sharks cruised with abandon anywhere that there was an imbalance of power and unchallenged authority.

⚓

The brutal heat continued unabated. I felt as if I were trapped in a furnace. I had had heatstroke twice before, and one of its consequences was that my metabolism was so altered that my body could not shake off heat in the normal way. After a few days singing and trekking with the temperature in the low one hundreds, we came at the end of a long, broiling day to a simple hotel in Arbanassi late in the evening. It turned out to have only one air-conditioned room—and I didn't get that room. Unable to sleep and feeling as if my skin was roasting, I went to the desk and begged them for at least an electrical fan. They acted as if this was an odd and unreasonable request (bear in mind that it was still in the nineties), and it took them about two hours to produce one and set it up. Its effect was negligible. I hardly slept that night.

The next day we forged on. We had a long day singing at monasteries and touring traditional houses. We arrived late, at 7:00 P.M., at Dryanovo Monastery, tucked neatly in the lap of soaring gray rock cliffs and striking butte-shaped outcroppings. The kindly *igumenos*, Archimandrite Nikodim, had been waiting for us for two hours in his vestments. His handsome young helper, the monk Nestorius, rang the church bells to welcome our bishop, but a restaurant not far away blasted out disruptive rock music while he did it. Ben suggested, through gritted teeth, that a grenade might solve that situation! We were all a little frayed around the edges by then. The *igumenos* and the monk swept us into their church dedicated to the Holy Archangel Michael for a formal ceremony of welcome and then graciously showed us to our rooms in their guest quarters.

A long rectangular building across the flagstone courtyard from the church ran alongside a chuckling river, the waters flowing right up against its thick walls of gray stone. The second story was gleamingly whitewashed with multipaned windows in varnished brown wood frames, topped with a roof of gray-brown tiles and frequent white chimneys outcropping like young mushrooms. The interior was invitingly clean, with beautiful folkloric scatter rugs warming the shining wood floors. I fell bonelessly on my bed in the little double room, simple but cheerful with bright blankets and lace curtains in the unscreened windows that opened up over the river and its surrounding woods. Although the supports of the bed mattresses looked like a strange kind of chain mail, they were comfortable enough. But I was in very bad condition.

The heatstroke, like a runner I had been trying to outrace during the long, busy day, finally passed and overcame me. I felt separated from my body, as if it were a strange burning desert completely unfamiliar to me to which I was only tentatively joined. Weak and dizzy, I was aware of Laura, a nurse, repeatedly feeling my forehead and consulting in worried whispers with Monica, also a nurse. They put cold wet cloths on my face and pulse points and brought a bucket of ice water for me to put my feet in as they tried desperately to bring down my temperature. We added soothing lavender oil to the water too. Fortunately, I had homeopathic *Veratrum album* 200c with me, an excellent remedy for heatstroke, especially of the pale, unsweating kind, and took it repeatedly. And I drank and drank and drank water. When the bishop came to see me to cheer me and give me a blessing, I still felt restless, burning, and tormented and unexpectedly burst into tears. He was patient and kind and told me that our pilgrims were earnestly praying for me. As the evening progressed, I began to feel a little better, though very weak.

Having finally slept through the night, I awoke feeling somewhat better but too shaky to go out on our group's activities. The bishop told me that, for my safety, the *igumenos* wanted me to stay in the guesthouse and keep it locked all day while they were out and to let only our group in during the late afternoon. Light, pleasant meals (I later learned that the faithful *igumenos* had been up for three hours before the morning service, preparing the breakfasts himself!) were brought to me and stored in my room. And then my group departed.

I was so weak, it was lovely just to lie still, breathe the

mountain-fresh air, and listen to the bright sounds of the river. The weather changed drastically that day, to my unspeakable relief—dropping from the low one hundreds into the seventies!

The bishop later declared this radically cooler weather a miracle, evoked, he believed, by our pilgrims' fervent prayers. The day passed quickly, and in the late afternoon I heard a knocking on the outside door. Taking the key and having ascertained that the knockers were our pilgrims, I tried to fit the large, strangely wrought key into the lock and turn it—to no avail! I just couldn't get it to work, as I explained to those without. What to do? Soon after, I heard rapid footsteps and looked up to see the *igumenos*, his black robes flying, advancing down the hall. He came to my side, transfixing me with the kindest eyes and smile. Archimandrite Nikodim had a picturesquely carunculated and high-bridged nose, oddly attractive; thatched gray-frosted black eyebrows thrusting up and out like furry butterfly wings; and long tumbling hair and beard. In his tall monastic hat, with his merry, twinkling eyes, he was a perfect Gandalf! Indeed, I felt a kind of magic in his atmosphere as he gently took my hand and tried to help me get the key to work, laughing and shooting me humorous glances. It took quite a bit of jiggling on both our parts, but at last the door opened, and we stood there grinning at each other like co-conspirators who had just pulled off a prank as the pilgrims poured in. Though still shaky, the next day I was better and even able to take a short walk in the beautiful woods behind the monastery, the ground paved with blooming wildflowers. The temperature had begun to ascend again right away, however, so I soon returned to my quiet, restful room.

One of our last visits was to the magnificent old monastery of Troyan, the third largest in Bulgaria. A jewel set in the northern Balkan Mountains, it was founded more recently than some of the great monasteries, reputedly by a small group of hermits near the end of the seventeenth century. Like all the monasteries under the Turkish yoke for so many years, it was destroyed and rebuilt periodically. Also like Rila, Bachkovo, and Dryanovo, it had been a secret meeting place for the Bulgarian revolutionaries plotting to overthrow the Ottomans. This was an especially soulful visit for our bishop, who had formerly been *igumenos* of Troyan Monastery himself.

We arrived a few days before the matronal feast of the monastery: the Dormition of the Most Holy Mother of God on August 15. In the meantime we were honored (and slightly terrified) by the fact that the Patriarch of Bulgaria himself was present at services when, at 7:00 A.M., we sang the Great Doxology and offered almost the entire Divine Liturgy, with the regular Troyan choir doing only a few parts. Our bishop told us later that His Holiness liked the sweetness of our singing and was very pleased with it, that he said that our Typikon was "perfect," and that he blessed us to reach out in America to give the gift of Orthodox Christianity to others.

At that time attendance at such a great sacred feast day as the Dormition, despite the many years of Communist rule, was taken up with more enthusiasm by Bulgarians than going to major sports events. When the day arrived, the church and streets were full of people—twenty thousand Bulgarians, as reported by the newspapers—most of them offhandedly carrying bundles of thirty-three slender bound candles. Many of them were soon packed into the basilica, and our choir surveyed them nervously from the left *klíros*, where our bishop had stashed us before taking off to join the Patriarch, five fellow bishops, and eight priests for what turned out to be a spiritually warm and beautiful Great Vespers on the eve of the feast. Although we pilgrim singers were on the left *klíros* again, we didn't serve but this time just got to drink it all in—very lovely, aside from the fact that the glowing-torch candle bundles of the Bulgarians made the church look like it was the Bastille about to be stormed by a packed mob of fiery sansculottes. How they managed not to set the church on fire that night or the next morning, when we and the many thousands arrived again at 6:30 A.M. for the Divine Liturgy, I do not know.

The *plaschanitsa*, the finely embroidered velvet cloth bearing an icon of the Virgin Mary in repose, was now brought out and carried reverently in procession as we worshippers poured out of the church and circumambulated it counterclockwise, stopping at all four corners for prayers. As we returned to the chapel, the *plaschanitsa* bearers held it up high in the doorway between the narthex and the nave so that all the worshippers could walk beneath it, receiving the grace and blessing of the Holy Virgin and her sacred feast. Throughout the services there was a conspicuous media presence that intensified when the king (who was at that time also the prime minister) arrived. He read the Creed with dignity and simplicity during the Divine Liturgy, camera flashes illuminating him where he stood. One of our pilgrims was also taking photographs, watched with interest by a little old Bulgarian lady who had wandered up on our *klíros*. Seeing her interest, he leaned down to show her the image of the king in the photo he had just taken. Impetuously, she grabbed the camera from his hands and planted a loud kiss on the king in the photo.

We were blessed to receive Holy Communion, and we were all

pretty happy, aside from being too hot and rather squashed and somewhat nervously preoccupied with avoiding being toasted by jauntily held candle torches. At last we processed out, accompanied by the twenty thousand Bulgarians, to go to a nearby holy well associated with the large and beautiful wonder-working icon known as Our Lady of the Three Hands that sat in its own gold-and-silver shrine in the church.

Our Lady of the Three Hands has an ancient history. Saint John of Damascus, of a Syrian Christian family but living under Ottoman rulership, inherited a high public office as chief financial officer for the eighth-century caliph Abd al-Malik. Eloquent and extremely well educated, John wrote many hymns for the Church and also expounded on theological topics. In 726, the fundamentalist Byzantine emperor Leo the Isaurian issued his first edict against the veneration of icons. John wrote a powerful and widely circulated refutation. Very angry but unable to touch John since he was under the caliph's protection, Leo devised a wicked plan. He had a copy of one of John's hand-written works given to a forger and instructed him to write a letter offering to betray Damascus into Leo's hands, signing it with John's signature. Feigning brotherly concern, Leo sent this letter to Abd al-Malik. The enraged caliph, who took the bait and thought he had been betrayed, turning a deaf ear to John's claims of innocence, ordered that John's right hand be severed at the wrist. This was immediately done.

In an agony of pain, the weeping John fell before an icon of the Virgin Mary in his home, propping his severed hand against it and imploring her aid. He swooned or fell asleep there, and when he awoke, his hand was reattached to his wrist. It worked perfectly, the only reminder of the incident a thin red line marking the cut. Rejoicing, he rushed to the caliph, who, staggered by the miracle, apologized and offered him his position back. But John asked that he instead be released to become a monk. The caliph acceded, and John joined the monastery of Mar Saba in the Judaean desert. But he also had a silver hand made and attached to the icon in thanksgiving for his healing—hence, "three hands."

This icon itself, as well as many of its copies, has a reputation for being miracle-working. The history of the local icon at Troyan revolves around a monk coming from Mount Athos in Greece in the seventeenth century, bearing the huge icon. He was trying to go to Wallachia with it but always found himself somehow returning to Troyan. Eventually he gave up trying to bring it and left the icon with a Bulgarian monk who gave it to the monastery.

This icon continued to have a mind of its own. At a later date there was an attempt to take the icon to Romania. I was told that it was loaded into a wagon pulled by horses but had not traveled very far down the road when the horses dropped dead. New horses were brought for the wagon, but they also dropped dead in the same spot. The decision-makers made a prudent decision to forget Romania and bring the icon back to the Troyan monastery. They also commemorated the incident by building a little shingled roof over a wall-less enclosure housing a holy well at the spot by the road where the icon had stopped. We and the twenty thousand Bulgarians now all tried to reach this sacred spot at once, with the effect that we pilgrims had to grab each other's clothing so as not to get separated as we were pushed and shoved and squeezed. As we got near the shrine, we were in danger of being elbowed off a low cliff; below it I saw thornbushes. I didn't remember how to say "No!" in Bulgarian, but at that point my survival instincts enabled me to bellow "NO!!!" in a manner unmistakable in any language. Father Zeno said he heard me from the other side of the field. The Bulgarians stopped pressing us quite so hard. A kind young sub-deacon named Alexander caught sight of us and led us through the press to the holy well, where we were asked to sing. TV reporters were also there, with the result that we were filmed and appeared that night on Bulgarian television. Unbeknownst to us, our bishop was waiting back at the church with the king, who also wished to hear us sing. Hot, tired, hungry, thirsty, and smooshed, most of us opted for a rest, and only a few straggled back to sing, so we lost our one chance at serenading royalty.

We did get to venerate the huge, numinous icon again before we left, however. Our bishop was moved to tears as he venerated the Holy Virgin of the Three Hands. "When you look at the icon of the Mother of God, you see how strong she is," he said. "At first you see strength, but then her eyes start to change—and you see a little smile."

ﷺ

Caterpillar Pilgrims

The desacralizing of the world is . . . a modern phenomenon. Only the United States and a few other countries have no integral mystical tradition that is given cultural recognition and support. The human tendency to experience the sacred is not lost but in such cases, it becomes a debased and furtive experience. Those people who have mystical expe-rience have no cultural guidelines to direct their development, no elders. They cannot be overtly recognized for their condition (being in contact with the sacred) nor can they bring the knowledge and renewal of life energy they gain from such direct spiritual experience to their communi-ty—one of its main purposes. As a result, the culture itself begins to lose a sense of meaning and direction and the land on which the culture is

founded becomes increasingly degraded. For a society to remain viable,
its members must frequently renew their connection with the REAL.
—Stephen Harrod Buhner, from *Sacred Plant Medicine*

Why do we go on pilgrimage? One reason is the hope to offer more powerful intercessory prayer for some need of our own or another. Another is curiosity about the unknown, both physical and metaphysical. Perhaps the most fundamental one is a persistent itch in the soul, a need to allow oneself to be propelled into a new stage of development by as yet unencountered forces—a caterpillar seeking just the right circumstances, beyond its own design and control, that will aid it in finding a supported place to begin its slow metamorphosis through the guided bewilderment of a veiled chrysalis into the ultimate triumphant alchemy of a winged butterfly, master of the freedom of the air and a seer and seeker of new and greater horizons.

This expansion that occurs on pilgrimage, sometimes ecstatic but often uncomfortable, this blending with the character and vibration of different places and beings, shakes loose our old habitual containers of thought and feeling, loosening our constricting caterpillar skin. Stephen Harrod Buhner says:

> *The ancient Greeks called this heart exchange with other living organisms 'aesthesis.' It literally means 'to breathe in.' The Greeks recognized that this moment of entrainment between two organisms . . . [was] an exchange of soul essence, when the thing that was more than the sum of its parts, that thing that came into being at the moment of synchronicity, that thing that is our soul, was touched by the soul in something outside the self.*

Everything speaks, if we have the ears to hear. Everything remembers the momentous events that have taken place within its territory. Everything reaches out to us with the generosity of goodness inherent in its making. The Really Real awaits us, dear readers. Let us not refuse the gift.

> *And the Spirit and the bride say, Come. And let him that heareth say, Come. And let him who is athirst come. And whosoever will, let him take the water of life freely.* (Rev. 22:17)

Amen.

CHAPTER FIFTEEN
Catharsis: The Purge—
Life Falls Apart

Guardian at the Gate

Lord Spudley, resident woodchuck and baron of both The Mound and Falling Granite Mansion (after Frank Lloyd Wright), surprised us by his un-rodent-like social demeanor. When Mark and I arrived to take a look at a particular apartment for rent in a somewhat run-down part of Belmont, he was standing upright and facing us by the cracked sidewalk near the front door. He was an enormous woodchuck, his prosperous bulges suggesting a sumo wrestler crossed with an indulgent Regency squire clad in a resplendent palomino-gold waistcoat. The self-possessed woodchuck surveyed us with interest and expectancy as we got out of our car. We felt that he was just about to invite us to his backyard barbecue when, hearing an inaudible summons, he dropped to all four feet, turned, and swiftly disappeared.

We figured that Lord Spudley, as we immediately christened him, was probably a sign, an omen, as animals acting atypically often are. This was probably the place. And it was: sunny, relatively inexpensive, small, and worn down. As were we, after years of sickness, hospitalizations, homelessness, and angst. So we set up our housekeeping next to Lord Spudley's manorial park: a traditional three-foot-high mound roofed with wild herbs and grass and the more nouveau-riche "Falling Granite" mega-home: a big pile of cement slabs and granite chunks dumped every which way on top of each other, affording excellent multilevel entrances for enterprising rodents.

What we didn't know was that the animal medicine associated with woodchucks was that of life and death due to their yearly hibernation and renewal, and that this handsome woodchuck might just be a genial harbinger of death.

It's a good thing that Spudley was land-rich as he soon brought home an enchanting bride, the big-eyed Spudelina, about half his size. Spudelina was also very pregnant, and, upon the arrival of eight babies, Lord Spudley suddenly remembered pressing affairs he had neglected on the Continent that demanded his immediate attention. "I thought it was just going to be you and me, babe," he must have said in bewilderment to Spudelina, "but, can't be helped, must leave and swim to France to check on our vineyards. Right away. See you later, dear." But the magnificent Lord Spudley never returned! Couldn't imagine why, with eight little babies, each portly pup looking like a miniature Hindenburg, rolling around on the grass, bouncing off each other and falling over in unsuccessful attempts to wrestle, given spherical tummies and too-short arms. Or trying to squirm under and overturn their mother in order to nurse when she was desperately trying to get a few bites of grass for herself, her chest planted firmly against the ground.

I felt sorry for Lady Spudelina with her overwhelming responsibilities and AWOL husband. I tried to help a bit by leaving fresh broccoli for her in the main run into the Mound. Once we almost ran into each other as I laid my tribute down. Spudelina's startled eyes, though brown, looked to me just like Hayley Mills's, round and haloed with eyelashes so humongous as to look pasted on. She may have been grateful for the broccoli but not sufficiently so as to keep her from mowing through a big tray of my pansies.

Although we enjoyed the babies' cuteness and funniness ourselves (and learned to sprinkle Epsom salts on any green growing thing we did not want to have voraciously consumed), we were especially grateful for the coterie of woodchucks as theatrical entertainment for our new rescue cat, one-year-old Winston Nicholas, a huge, beautiful gray-tiger Maine coon with opulent ruffled white vest and paws. Lonely Winston, an indoor cat only, would sit for hours with his nose pressed to the window, watching the absurd woodchuck babies flopping around in the grass as if busily auditioning for a Marx Brothers movie. Or appearing and disappearing on the Falling Granite ledges, finally arraying themselves, each on a different ledge, like sunning vacationers on a multistory resort in Ibiza. You could imagine them each wearing tiny sunglasses with a celery-juice cocktail, complete with paper umbrella, clutched in one paw.

Within six months we adopted another young Maine coon cat from a different shelter to be company for Winston: an exceptionally gorgeous two-year-old tortoiseshell female with the loveliest, most luminous sea-green eyes I have ever seen on a cat. She was sweet but quite self-possessed and clearly a lot more grown up than Winston. Mirabai (as we named her) had been owned by someone who bought her from a breeder, had her chipped, and, when she was a year old, abruptly thrown her out into the woods where the little cat had to fend for herself and, apparently, soon for two litters of kittens as well. Signs of trauma showed up in her fear of men (except for my Mark, with whom it was love at first sight) and how terrified she would get if anyone came in wearing a hat (perhaps she had seen some animal attacked by another animal jumping on its head?). Mirabai loved women's energy, and if a female friend was sitting on the couch with me, she would lie down exactly between us, purring and absorbing our energy like sunlight.

In the beginning, her feelings toward Winston were, unfortunately, not so warm. His gentle, friendly overtures she spurned with growls and sharp fangs. If he persisted, she became hysterical. Initially amazed, he soon became resentful of his rejection and began slinking around, looking like a Chinese villain from some old 1930s opium-den movie, his eyes narrow, scheming slits, and his muscles tensed in anticipation of giving her a good whap on the head when proximity allowed. Their relationship eventually did warm up, but Winston still nursed his resentment for some time. I would be reading on the sofa with both of them next to me, and Winston would be sweetly grooming Mirabai while keeping one eye on me. As soon as I got absorbed in my book, he'd abruptly slap her on the head with one huge white paw. As my head swung back toward him, he'd resume licking her fur with a saintly, innocent expression, telegraphing to me, "Look how I love her and how kind I am! Just cleaning her up! Dutiful, too!"

Winston grew into a magnificent creature, large even for a Maine coon, his lordly yet gentle temperament having only one big character flaw: his inability to tolerate rejection or even anyone not acknowledging his kingly, leonine presence. And he did not endure such disrespect and lack of appreciation quietly. For example, a friend came on a visit and stayed with me for about twenty-four hours. Pete completely ignored Winston—never pet him, never said his name, never even looked at him. I noticed Winston's face, which usually bore a noble, gracious expression, turning ominously colder and stonier hour by hour. Just before Pete was about to leave, Winston loped by and, swiftly dipping down by Pete's feet, deposited two big turds on the floor right in front of his toes. I was momentarily speechless. Pete, about to take a step, looked down and exclaimed, "Hey! I could have stepped in that!" Exactly. Winston had given him an eloquent don't-bother-to-come-back-again departure gift! From that day on I became a bit paranoid about making sure my visitors, especially men, always at least greeted His Highness King Winston!

Egyptian Plagues
Less benign relations with creatures also entered into these difficult years of sickness and sadness. While still in the Gnome Home, we had an invasion of rats. Living right by the waterfront as we were, this was always a possibility. It happened when our landlord, a lovely man but suffering from increasing dementia, had failed to have the bales of salt marsh hay removed from around our house in the spring, despite our reminding him a few times. In the winter, given that we had no foundation but only a four-inch crawl space beneath our tiny home, the hay bales helped greatly in keeping the rattling and roaring northeast winds from freezing our floor and us. But, because they were not removed in the spring as usual, they became the launching pads for the rodent invasion.

At first I saw just a few ruffled-up-looking mice hanging around inside, like small-time toughs in a seedy bar. They weren't like the sleek, smooth mice of our previous acquaintance. These strange mice were clearly hoods, with their disagreeably fluffed-up dull gray fur, beneath which they probably concealed tiny tattoos—"Death to cats!", "Cheese for me!", "Mightiest Mouse!", etc. They were bad enough, but these punks disappeared when the gangster kings, the big, sharp-nosed rats, appeared, whale-huge compared to their dolphin size. We still had Sasha when this all began but she soon died, and rats seem to know anyway that an old cat will not fight them. We put her food bowl on our kitchen table to keep her above the fray, but a few times I saw her almost nose to nose with a large rat on the table, who seemed about to challenge her for her food.

Mark had his second stroke, and we had to immediately move out. He could not function in a house where you had to climb a ladder to your bedroom. While Mark was recovering in a Boston hospital, with me mostly living there on a cot in a shared room with him and his tolerant elderly roommate (who, as I gladly emptied his urinals for him, referred to me fondly as his "second wife"), I also worked on getting packed up and moved out of Rockport. This was a horrible experience. I felt devastated by the earthquake of change—Mark incapacitated again and depressed, our slim pocketbook almost empty, the backbreaking struggle of packing and moving, the frightening knowledge that we had nowhere to move to, and that we could not afford market rents—all laced with that *soupçon* of Egyptian plague-ish *je ne sais quoi* in the form of the omnipresent sharp-toothed rats who seemed as scarily aware of me as I was of them, running by me or sitting still as a sphinx, staring hard at me with calculating eyes. Without the love and help of wonderful friends who went far beyond the call of duty, I would never have survived this challenge that I seemed to struggle through so clumsily and ineptly, lurching and falling down, as if I were a foundering stroke victim myself.

Ultimately, I realized I would have to poison the rats. I agonized over this, not wanting to harm any creature and realizing that the poor things would die in pain. But I felt I had no choice. Sasha was gone, and I could just go stay for a few days in the hospital with Mark, as I had been doing. So I steeled myself and set out the poison and let it work. When I returned with friends to do the moving and cleaning, there were dead rats scattered around, as if our little home, already far from its presentable best, had been transformed into the back alley of a Dickensian slum. When John and I went up the ladder to roll up and discard the mattress and bedding where Mark and I had slept, a poisoned black rat lay with his head just on my pillow, his body slightly curled around it, like death trying to enter my dreams. When I insisted on offering up my killing of the rats in Confession, sobbing desperately, Father Zeno could only shake his head, mystified.

ॐ

Magic Needles and Russian Roulette Rehab

We had learned after Mark's first stroke that Chinese acupuncture can be very effective for treating this condition. Our friend Jeanette referred us to Dr. Liu, who said that if a stroke patient begins acupuncture treatment within four weeks of the stroke, his recovery can be rapid; even later, acupuncture can help. But ideally the patient should receive acupuncture treatment every day for the first eight days. So when Mark had his second stroke, we contacted Dr. Liu. Loving friends offered to pay for these treatments, and thus Dr. Liu referred us to a small Chinese woman acupuncturist who came daily to treat Mark.

Of course, the hospital didn't want to allow this, but I read the patient's bill of rights and saw that we were entitled to proceed. We insisted, and they couldn't stop us. Sometimes medical staff hung around for a while, watching the acupuncturist. Mark always made a great jump in function during each treatment and seemed to retain around eighty percent of his gain each time. The observers couldn't believe their eyes—and often rushed off, as if unable to deal with what they had just seen. Chinese physicians had had several thousand years to work with this problem and had developed an excellent protocol. Mark improved by leaps and bounds.

ॐ

Medicine with the Marx Brothers

When Mark's second stroke first hit, we were sitting in a Boston-area restaurant near his chiropractor's office, having brunch. He had been adjusted for bad neck pain that came on the night before and, though we didn't realize it, must have been the beginning of the stroke. Tired and hungry, we were relieved to be in a quiet restaurant. We placed our order with the waiter, a dark-eyed man in his thirties with a head of big black curls whom we eventually discovered to be Moroccan. He seemed fascinated by Mark and came back around the table a few times, filling water glasses and fussing. At last he leaned closer to Mark and said, "Tell me, are you a man of prayer?"

Surprised and unsure of what to say but at the least having to admit to being a deacon, Mark said, "Yes. You could say that."

To our surprise, a few strangers in public places seemed able to pick Mark out as clergy, even when he was not wearing anything to indicate this.

"I knew it! I knew it!" the waiter cried. "Will you please pray for me and my wife?" And he explained, with tears in his eyes, that he and his wife had been childless for many years but greatly desired a child. Mark asked his wife's name and said he would pray for them. Our waiter expressed ecstatic thanks.

A few minutes later, Mark began to feel very unwell. I called 911. The waiter, seeing Mark suffering, became upset. I explained that Mark had already had one stroke, and that help was on the way. The waiter rushed into the kitchen and returned exclaiming that in his own country he was a medical person and knew what to do for strokes. He was carrying a big pitcher full of ice cubes—and promptly poured them down Mark's back! Except for a big gulp of air when the ice hit his skin, Mark and I were both speechless!

In moments the EMTs were running in the door. They were checking Mark's vital signs and lifting him onto a stretcher. Meanwhile the only other customer, a large, heavy bald man sitting at a table a few feet away, directly facing us, kept placidly munching on his toast and staring at Mark as if my husband's distressing situation was just a bland TV show on a screen. In contrast, the waiter, almost hysterical now, was wringing his hands. I kept hoping he would not rush in with any other creative first aid—coleslaw shampoo or some other unlikely fix!

These EMTs would not let me sit near my husband in the ambulance, unlike other EMTs I had dealt with. I had to go in the cab part of the vehicle. We took off, and I saw that two men with movie cameras, sitting between my husband and me, were avidly filming Mark and the EMTs.

"Hey, what's going on here?" I asked angrily, well aware that they were sitting where I wished to be for my husband's sake. They were filming some kind of publicity movie for EMTs. I was furious!

"You never even asked our permission! What do you think you are doing here?! We'll never give you a release, never! How dare you!"

‮ولی‬

Spruce Island Miracle Medic
After Mark and I had spent several days in a big Boston hospital, I needed to go home briefly for a change of clothes for both of us and to collect the mail and check on things. Our dear friend John gallantly drove me back to the Gnome Home late at night and waited while I collected what I thought was necessary—including many large poster-size icons from calendars and tape and scissors to trim them and put them up all over Mark's room. I knew that the sterile, fluorescent hospital environment was increasing his depression, and I wanted to give Mark this enlivening beauty to gaze at, as well as the hope of celestial help from these holy beings.

By the time I had gotten all the icons up, it must have been one or two A.M. I was seriously exhausted, having been pushing hard without much rest for days. Feeling sick in some strange, unaccountable way I cannot describe, I fell on my cot and went unconscious. All during the night I woke up periodically, especially as nurses came and went on their inexorable rounds. I found that I could not move, not even a finger, much less get up. This was terrifying! What had happened to me?! Now I was paralyzed. I could not make my mouth function to call for help, though I tried hard. I would have completely panicked except that an unexpected gentle, reassuring presence wafted over me repeatedly, enfolding me in its calm. I even recognized the presence—it was St. Herman of Alaska, a Russian monk whom Catherine the Great had sent to Alaska in a mission with nine other monks in 1794. The monks found that the native Aleuts were being abused in many ways by resident Russian fur traders and began to vigorously defend them,

St. Herman most of all. The Aleuts deeply loved Herman, and even when he moved from Kodiak to little Spruce Island to live as a hermit, many of them moved and settled there so as to be able to remain with him. When asked how he could bear to be alone in the forest, he replied, "I am not alone. God is here. God is everywhere."

And now St. Herman seemed "everywhere" with me!

I had first encountered his presence while walking down a forested hill in Santa Rosa at the six-week intensive Valaam Missionary School in California that Mark and I attended after our return from our Holy Land pilgrimage. Very tired, I was late for Father Jeremiah's evening lecture. I did not know what his topic would be. But I felt such a strong presence, characterized by the most meltingly beautiful but powerful emanations of gentleness. When I arrived at the lecture hall, I discovered that Father's topic was St. Herman of Alaska.

Since that time I thought I had perhaps sensed a bit of Saint Herman's presence now and then, and I did pray to him in a list of saints whom I often importuned. But I did not have a special devotion to him. So why was he so strongly with me, shielding me somehow, while I lay sunken in this strange paralysis? I did not know but could only be inexpressibly grateful. Periodically, Saint Herman seemed to wrap me in a kind of numinous golden mantle that surrounded him and carry me off, under his strong protection, to deep, dark-green spruce forests, moss-quiet, filled with a sense of renewing, flowing life. I felt cradled and sustained, nourished, tenderly blessed. This went on all night, whether I was sleeping or waking. In the morning I found that I could speak and move again. There seemed to be no residual impairment.

Later that morning I began opening the mail that I had stuffed into a small suitcase. The suitcase stood right by my cot all night, the mail in the upper corner next to my head. One letter was plump, containing something more than paper. Opening it, I found a little plastic bag filled with earth from Saint Herman's grave, an unexpected gift from Saint Innocent's Academy on Kodiak, a school we occasionally supported. The dirt from his grave and the oil from the lamp hung over Saint Herman's burial place were reputed to be wonder-working and healing. So I believe it was this blessed, vibrationally infused earth's physical proximity to me that helped bring this great, loving, and gentle saint to me when I was most in need. Thank you, dear Saint Herman. Yes, God is everywhere—even, and sometimes especially, in a handful of earth in the cold sterility of a faceless hospital room.

༄

Homeless

We were devastated. We no longer had a home and could not afford market rents. Mark, partially incapacitated, had by then been diagnosed with a benign pituitary tumor and had suffered two strokes (each time, paralyzed from the neck down on one side) and a heart attack. There had been multiple additional traumas; the most recent that his insurance company illegally refused to pay out his long-term insurance (it would be a few years until a disability lawyer would succeed in suing the company for us, and an indignant judge would angrily order restitution at last). Unable to pay Boston-area rents on my salary alone—I worked part time as a helper and companion for a sick woman, needing also to be a caregiver to my semi-paralyzed husband—we were dependent upon the charity of others for a roof over our heads. We stayed with friends and cat-, fish-, and apartment-sat in various places while our possessions sat expensively in storage. Sometimes we did not know until the night before where we would be moving to the next day, or for how long.

Finally, a dear friend through her connections got a property owner to agree to have us as his part-time roommates in a handsome third-floor apartment in Boston's Jamaica Plain neighborhood; our landlord only stayed there occasionally. It was well below market rate at the $500 per month plus utilities he charged us but still very difficult for us to manage. The apartment was lovely, but our room was a teeny windowless walk-in closet, just big enough for a mattress and a tiny bureau, lit by a small skylight. The biggest drawback was that he would only guarantee us staying there for two weeks at a time. This sword of Damocles constantly hanging over our heads was a tremendous strain on us, particularly on my husband's stroke-shattered nerves. But we wound up staying there in the endless insecurity of these strange two-week installments for a whole year and a half.

༄

Healer's Hands

Have you ever had a doctor with healer's hands? If you have, you know what I mean. I've only had two that I know of. One was a Danish MD but primarily a homeopath. She had a healing atmosphere too. As soon as I came into her office, I would start to feel better just from the glow of the caring magnetism of her atmosphere.

My current primary care physician also has healer's hands. He is a youngish regular MD, with little knowledge of alternative and traditional medicine as far as I know, but you can tell that caring compassion drew him into medicine in the first place, and that the sensitive gentleness of the instinctive healer vibrates through his fingers.

Hospitals are primarily designed by engineers, the makers of machines. That coldness is not conducive to healing, does not encourage the natural resilience of the patients' bodies to leap up to be renewed, as does the healer's touch. Although I am also grateful for the technical aspect of modern hospitals and for how they have saved my husband's, my, and other people's lives, they tend to be experienced as a kind of arctic hell, all cold glacier walls and damaging (as well as health-preserving) sterility.

Over nine years Mark and I spent a great deal of time in hospitals and, like most people, hated it. The sense of impending coldness began to run so deep that I would get a urinary tract infection (which I otherwise never got), the acidic balance of my system apparently veering steeply into anticipated grief, just walking under the lintel on yet another new hospital visit. And Mark, not inclined to weep, began to burst into tears whenever he heard an ambulance siren. We can do better than this.

༄

The Witch Trial
Can Satan heal or only God?

If you are a secular materialist, you should probably just take a time-out right about now, but, believe me, in certain social circles this is a very real question. I can viscerally vouch for that.

The day after I turned sixty, I had a witch trial.

Encouraged by an insightful herbalist/therapist to whom I was then apprenticed, I had opened my own rather low-key energy-healing practice specializing in Bach Flower Essences, my own soft sound-gentle touch method, Reiki, and eventually Tong Ren as well. In the normal course of things I had gone to my pastor for a blessing on this enterprise. I felt that this healing work was a calling I had from God, so I was stunned that not only did Father Zeno object, but objected forcefully. We argued and were still at an impasse when I left, shaken.

As I prayed about it later with my husband, we still felt that this was a calling from our Lord. When I then composed and sent out a letter about the practice, I also sent it to my many friends in our spiritual community, our church. Father Zeno called me in, furious. Among his many objections was that I was "too influential." We wound up both standing up, shouting at each other, in his office. I flew from the room and raced upstairs to the chapel. He apparently came up the alternate way, and soon we found ourselves facing each other again, tellingly, on either side of the *pannikhida* table, a low table near the icon screen where people came to light candles for their dead. Jesus Christ, His tormented body on a cross affixed to the back of the table, hung mutely in the air between us.

There was a terrible silence as we, just a few feet apart, stared at each other.

"I see." I heard the words break from me, hesitatingly, seeming to echo in the silence. "You want to get rid of me . . . . I am in your way."

He did not deny it. We both turned and raced out of the chapel, each in our opposite ways.

Father Zeno immediately escalated the matter, calling in our Bulgarian bishop to judge. Our bishop, in many ways a humble man, took a bus from New York City to Boston in order to sit down and talk with me alone, as well as with my pastor. The bishop and I spent more than two hours discussing my practice, how I had gotten into it (the bishop was startled to learn that I had learned about the Reiki portion from my pastor's own wife, who now denied her part in it), and what it actually consisted of, theologically as well as practically speaking. I thought I answered his searching questions well enough, but there were moments of semantic impasse—English is not a terrific language for describing subtle spiritual states, and we had my nonexistent Bulgarian and the bishop's not entirely fluent English as obstacles as well. We reached the crux of the matter when he at last asked about those I treated, peering intently into my eyes. "So, tell me, do you touch their souls? If you touch their souls, then it becomes my business!"

I thought I knew what he meant but was not positive. In Bulgaria, witchcraft still occurs. Well, it does in the United States too. It does everywhere and anywhere human beings use their free will to try to influence another by force. It is the psychic equivalent of blunt force on the physical level—in both cases, a terrible misuse of free will. Too often, given our secular-materialist naiveté, we do not realize that the concentration powers of the mind itself can be honed and sharpened just as a physical knife can be to wield a powerful, even deadly, influence upon the psyches and lives of others. We are often so busy patting ourselves on our own shoulders in compliment to our "superstitionless" modernity that we block out the awareness of very real psychic dimensions potentially dangerous to ourselves and others.

No, I answered the bishop, I did not "touch their souls"—assuming that our bishop meant trying to forcefully influence them on subtle levels to comply with any personal intent of my own, even of healing. The energy-healing work I did more resembled playing a musical duet with the patient, each free in our own parts, with me trying to help the patient retune his or her own inner strings that may have gotten too tight or too slack from stress and shock as closely as possible to an ideal pitch that vibrated with health and healing for that patient.

The bishop liked me, was fond of my chanting and voice, and we had gone on a warmhearted Bulgarian pilgrimage in my company. He loved my husband. I could see that, though in earnest, he was not eager to create problems in our lives. His next step was to suggest to our pastor and the church board that they meet with Father Zeno and me to see if they could help us work out this problem. For Father Zeno, I believe it was a triumph. For me, it was a disaster.

At the Stake

We met in the cold of late December. Given his precarious health, I would not let Mark attend, much as I wished I could have him there for support. There were the seven or so members of the board, our pastor, the assistant pastor, Father Deacon John and his wife (a board member), and a supportive friend of mine. We sat down at tables in the church hall and began, the president reading the bishop's letter aloud.

Interestingly, the question of whether people were recovering, sometimes or at all, when I treated them was regarded as completely irrelevant by Father Zeno, as he framed the discussion. The issue was rather, he observed, was God healing them or was Satan, through the training and techniques I used, craftily relieving them temporarily of sickness so as to lead them astray in some other way? Even now I feel ill typing these words. Father Zeno clearly felt it was better to leave people unrelieved in their pain if there was any chance that the removal of that pain might somehow leave them more open to sin. If he had, as I had so often, felt some of their pain in his own body, I don't think he would have so glibly dismissed the matter of their relief on purely theoretical metaphysical grounds.

Father Zeno's trump card in the matter, which he unfurled with the support of a board member who had traveled to Mount Athos in Greece with him the year before, was that a holy elder they visited in his hermitage there had declared the Tong Ren I practiced "sorcery"! Anna, who was on this board, and I looked at them in stunned astonishment, our jaws dropping. "What?" we both exclaimed in unison. "The elder knew about Tong Ren?"

My accusers nodded their heads in vigorous affirmation. "Yes!"

"But how?" I asked.

"Oh, we told him about it."

Anna and I looked at each other with sinking hearts. Of course the elder would think banging on a doll with a magnetic hammer was bound to be witchcraft. From an old-country perspective, looks like a duck, sounds like a duck, must be a duck. Even though it was not a duck. That elder had not gotten his "insight" from an angel but from an already ignorant and biased description by visitors that could only lead him to that one deadly conclusion.

In further support of his point, Father Zeno quoted from a modern Mount Athos elder who asserted that demonic forces could remove illness in order to soften up a soul to make him more vulnerable to their influences. And read a brief account of a young man, the spiritual child of this elder, who suffered from terrible migraines. As I roughly remember it, the young man had an operation that cured his migraines, and he returned joyfully to his elder with the news. The elder was appalled and told his spiritual son that the headaches had been working toward his salvation and that he had now ruined this benefit—and that the elder refused to be his spiritual father anymore.

I countered with quotes from the great Saint John Chrysostom, who asserted that Satan never would or could relieve an ounce of sickness or suffering from a human being.

After three hours or so of this argument, we adjourned. Although most present had been kind, and a few had even tried to defend me, the opposing forces were heavier and more strident. I felt as if I had been beaten with clubs. As the group departed, I began to cry, and sobbed, sobbed, sobbed, uncontrollably, for half an hour.

I knew that somehow I had lost, even though there was not—and could not be—any official decision. As is so often the way, the "fear-of-Daddy factor,"—parishioners' reluctance to disagree with the father-figure pastor—would hold sway for many, if not all, concerned. Mark and I had carefully kept this conflict as quiet as we could, not wanting to upset and divide our community.

Now a written report would be sent to the bishop by the board, probably written by the president. My precious spiritual community of thirty years, my precious church, seemed to be slipping away, like I was trying to grasp water in a storm's tidal rush, and I could do nothing to stop it. I also felt deeply betrayed. Father Zeno and my husband and I had been close friends; we had helped each other in our various ways, and Father Zeno and his wife had often acted in kindness toward us. Their friendship had been precious. Now I felt that, were it an earlier age, he would probably, regretfully but stonily adhering to his conviction, have me led to the stake to be burned.

ﷺ

The Voice from the Icon

Sitting on the edge of the bed in our small bedroom, I was staring, mesmerized, at the beautiful icon on top of the bookcase, less than an arm's length away. The lovely Virgin, long faced with melting eyes, was holding the infant Jesus, who seemed to stand upright in her tender arms and, in the Eastern style, looked more like an angelic youth, his face expressing a mysterious sobriety, than a baby. The exceedingly graceful icon in this photographic reproduction had been clad in a *riza*, a covering of white pearls and gold and sky-blue enamel over all but the faces and hands of the two holy ones. Designed with a fine artistic sensitivity and harmony, this *riza* not only did not detract from the icon but swept one further into a feeling of heavenly beauty, of the dazzling sense of white cloud in a pure blue sky, made even more magnificent in a luminous unseen inner world than in the natural one.

Orthodox Christian icons are deliberately designed to help us move beyond the normal veils obscuring the holy from our sight. Rather than being depictions of dead-end stories, they are regarded as doors that can open into living light. Icons are avenues of grace that can take us beyond the trite linear pathways of our minds into a deeper world, transcending our left-brained tightness and helping us make a leap into an intuitive right-brained openness to deeper things. Icons are signposts, not walls.

It was January, nearly Christmas on the old—or Julian—calendar, which our particular church followed. It was about a week after the witch trial when I sat down on the bed that afternoon, gazing into the calm beauty of that icon, my heart sore. Suddenly, startlingly, I felt the holy entity of the feast of the Nativity of Our Lord—Christmas itself! —inexplicably flowing out of the icon to me and suffusing me with intense, exquisite spiritual joy and peace. A feast had never come to me in this way, descending upon me like a refined but potent dewy cloud, unbidden and before its time. Amazed and overjoyed, I felt infused with the particular special beauty and illumining grace of this great and precious feast: the miraculous entry of our Lord incarnate, glorified by the angels to all who could hear, into our grieving world. This experience was not of the intellect but tangible; overpowering yet gentle—an ineffable, ecstatic singing in my soul.

Even as I drank it in, rejoicing, part of me was standing aside, wondering, *Why now? The feast of the Nativity is less than a week away, January 7.* As if in answer, a short time later a distinct inner voice spoke, seemingly also from the icon, these mysterious words: "One can only come to the Nativity through suffering." Although the words may sound harsh, at the time, in the stream of holiness pouring through the icon, they seemed only sober, steadying, guiding, even though I did not understand them.

Three days later I did.

It was a bitterly cold New England morning, only fifteen degrees with a sharp wind. Mark and I were arguing. He was insisting on taking out two heavy bags of garbage and would not let me do it instead. I was angry with him, knowing that someone who had had a heart attack and now had four stents in one artery should not be out breathing the icy air, which could constrict the arteries further, much less doing physical work. He ignored my objections and dragged the bags outside.

When he came in, he was tired and sat down, weary and despondent, in a rocking chair. A few minutes later he cried out loudly and, his face distorted with shock and pain, began to topple from his seat. I tried to get beneath him to break his fall, but he was too large a man for me to hold up and, despite my efforts, landed facedown on the floor. He cried out loudly again, his body spasmed twice powerfully, and then he lay still. I rushed to the phone and called 911, a friend to call others for prayers, and my Tong Ren teacher for whatever he could do, if anything.

Our two cats were also witnessing this tragedy. Mirabai, panicked and distressed, ran from the room, but our big male, Winston, stood rooted to the spot. I watched his eyes traveling up from Mark's prone body into the air. I had the distinct feeling that he was watching Mark's spirit separate and rise from his body. Suddenly all the long hairs on Winston's body stood on end, like an electrified lion's mane. As the EMTs burst in, he ran from the room.

After they worked on Mark, with me shunted into the hall, they took us both to Mount Auburn hospital, the very same one in which Mark had been born sixty-six years before—but they could not revive him. He was gone. Twenty-eight years of marriage ended abruptly. I would never see my dear husband in this world again.

ॐ

First Visit

Father Zeno tried to talk me into having a friend stay with me that night, but somehow I knew I had to be alone. It was early evening, just the cats and me sitting quietly, when Mark came. I couldn't see him, but I could feel exactly where he was as he sped around the room with the grace of an ice-skater. And I could hear him exclaiming in joy, "I'm not sick anymore!" He felt so restored—whole, with the irrepressible vigor of youth.

I was filled with gladness. And great relief. More than anything I had needed to be reassured about the state of his soul. Mark had grown so depressed in the last couple of years, especially since the heart attack, that he had become increasingly testy, even refusing to pray with me for much of that time; this was crushing to me as, with our often overwhelming problems, shared prayer was really all we had. I knew, though, watching him devotedly serving in the altar at the times when he had sufficient strength to do so, that his faith was still intact. And here he was, almost flying—I couldn't see his luminescence but I could feel it—with the joy of new life!

As with any wife, no one knew my husband's shortcomings better than I. But I also knew Mark's secret sacrifices, his devotion, and his willingness to put himself on the line for what he believed was right and would help our community. This last he often paid for dearly; the stress took its toll on him. He also had great compassion and administered our church's charity account for many years, quick to rush to the aid of a parishioner or a stranger off the street. He sincerely felt a deacon's traditional responsibility to look after widows, and he helped a lot of our church's teenage boys as a consistent needed friend and coach. I felt that God recognized and was now rewarding Mark's greatness of heart and the suffering he had endured.

Mark's brief visit deeply comforted me. But then he was gone. Then I felt the overwhelming sorrow of his loss, the loneliness of the empty apartment. Then was the time for me not to be alone, as my dear friend Katharine Newhouse well understood. She phoned that evening to tell me that she would be driving from Pennsylvania the next day to stay with me for a few days. And that the oldest of her four daughters, Mark's and my much beloved goddaughter Hope, would also be with us.

Hope, an actor with a degree in French, was about to return to her life in Paris the day that Mark died. Oddly, he had insisted on phoning her, knowing that she was in a car en route to the airport. "This is important," he declared. So they got to tell each other one last time just how much they loved each other. Before she boarded her plane, Mark was dead. Hope cancelled her flight, and she and Katharine joined me the next day, immersing me in their love.

We all grieved together. Katharine and Hope were like angels, comforting me and coaxing me to eat, doing the piled-up dishes in the now-messy kitchen, helping with the flood of tasks that rushed in on the tide of this devastating event. My beautiful friends and whole community pulled together to help me and provide Mark with an inspiring funeral. Knowing that Mark and I had no funds, generous friends even paid for the funeral. Clergy and a few other male friends gently washed and anointed Mark's body and arrayed it in his deacon's robes to be buried, one of them chanting the Psalms for him throughout. Hope and I later went to visit Mark, lying in his brocade vestments among the icons in his coffin at church. He looked so peaceful—as if he were deep in a much-needed sleep after a long, hard struggle.

Word of Mark's departure traveled swiftly. The abbess of the convent where we used to take the Saint Mary of Bethany girls wrote me a very beautiful, uplifting letter and sent me icons, candles, holy oil, and an incredibly delicious big loaf of bread baked by the nuns. For a while it was the only thing I could bear to eat. It seemed full of love and blessings.

✒

Although I would have spared my community if I could, the bishop declared that my husband's funeral would be on Christmas Day, January 7, and that he would preside.

"One can only come to the Nativity through suffering." Now I was learning something of the meaning of these mysterious words of warning and prophecy. This year I would have no Christmas at all in the usual sense but rather, on that day, the prayerful, painful, beautiful acknowledgment of my husband's passing. So, out of our Lord's exquisite and inexplicable compassion, Christmas had come to me early, powerfully and undeniably, so that, regardless of every impediment, I should not be without it. Even in my dazed and grieving state, my heart was deeply touched and grateful for this sublime and delicate mercy, a cradling gentleness infusing the deep ache within. Christmas is not so much a day as it is a state, and, in our need, can come to find us, fortifying and uplifting us in a way beyond the ways of this world. "Peace I leave with you, my peace I give unto you: not as the world giveth, give I unto you" (John 14:27).

I was heartbroken, but I also knew that I was not alone. The love and help of my friends washed over me in a great, comforting wave, but I knew also that One stood beside me through all, One who had anticipated my deepest needs, both spiritual and mundane. The Beloved Himself, in His humility and tenderness, consoled me for the loss of my beloved.

☙

The chapel filled up fast the day of the funeral, and the Readers on the *klíros* were led by a young man who had been particularly close to my husband and who gave the wonderful service his heartfelt all.

I rode to the burial hand in hand with Hope. I confessed to her that this was often where I lost it at a funeral. Seeing the coffin committed to the earth seemed so final. She was surprised. "Oh really? It's my favorite part!"

"Why is that?"

"Because it always seems to me like a seed being planted in the ground, with new life to spring from it."

"Verily, verily, I say unto you, Except a corn of wheat fall into the ground and die, it abideth alone: but if it die, it bringeth forth much fruit" (John 12:24).

With my lovely goddaughter's words, my inner orientation shifted away from momentary despair into life-affirming hope.

At the burial, we all sang with enthusiasm and love, especially *"Christos Anesti,"* "Christ is risen!" We sent Mark on his way to his new life on a wave of the Resurrection!

A delicious memorial meal followed, kindly offered by Father Zeno and *Popadia* Laura at their home. There seemed to be so much Light at the funeral and afterward, so much love, that I felt lifted and carried on its peace like on a strong tide.

A few days later, Hope and Katharine had to return to their normal lives, but they had helped carry me in their loving arms through the dangerous early emotional surf of bereavement with a tender faithfulness I can never forget.

☙

Winston and Mirabai were also bereaved. Almost immediately Winston came down with a terrible cold, and Mirabai showed signs of so much pain that I had to take her to the vet. She had suddenly developed huge bladder stones, it turned out, and while we decided what to do—I could not afford an operation for her—I could not sleep for very long at a time, needing to get up frequently to give her pain medication. My herbalist friends came to the rescue with herbs and good advice. I found myself syringing cooled corn silk tea into her mouth several times a day. Amazingly, not too many days later, X-rays showed that her stones had dissolved!

But the cats were miserable, so intensely missing Mark. I gave us all Bach Flower Essences that took off some of the edge, but we were all still deeply depressed. I decided to try an experiment. A psychotherapist named Dr. Roger J. Callahan had developed a surprisingly effective system of tapping certain points on the body primarily to relieve difficult emotional issues. He called his method Thought Field Therapy, and I had his book, *Tapping the Healer Within*. I sat down with the two cats to give it a try. I tried to include them in my own emotional atmosphere and energetic body as much as possible. With this approach you need to first experience the emotion you are trying to heal. I focused on our collective grief. The living room seemed suddenly to fill from the floor to the ceiling, like an enormous swimming pool, with sorrow. Then I began the tapping and other techniques. Our grief eased, step by step. We all received significant relief, as our relaxed postures eventually demonstrated. By the time I was done, the three of us were able to cuddle in contentment and peace. It had helped. I was so grateful!

Each day's emotional states were as wild and unpredictable as New England weather: sometimes gentle sadness; sometimes a feeling of peace and freedom pervaded with a sense of relief at not having to struggle with our combined wills and problems anymore (hard to admit but quite real); sometimes a visceral anguish so rending that I could only sit on the floor and howl like a wounded wolf.

⚭

The Tenth Day
In Orthodox Christianity, the funeral is not the last time formal prayers are offered for the dead person. They also occur on the tenth and fortieth days after death, and often annually thereafter.

I arrived at church early on the tenth day, as I wanted to offer a confession with Father Gregory, the assistant pastor, before our *pannikhida* service. Father Zeno had been withholding the sacraments from me once we had plunged into disagreement about my healing practice. That was bad enough but worse was that he also began often withholding them from Mark, a deacon and a sick man ("unconscionable," said a priest I later met), because Mark fully supported my continuing with my healing work.

The day of Mark's funeral, the bishop sat down with me to talk privately. He was kind and loving and, while acknowledging the unsettled state of my affairs due to the controversy over my healing practice, said that, nonetheless, he blessed me to receive Holy

Communion and did not want anybody "bothering" (his word) me about it during the forty days following Mark's death. I was overjoyed; it had been a very long time since I had received. So on the tenth day I arrived confident that this confession would open the way to my receiving the Holy Eucharist.

Partway through my confession, Father Gregory interrupted me to say, "You know, Stephani, I am not going to absolve you."

I thought I must have heard him wrong. "What?"

"I am not going to absolve you."

"But why? The bishop blessed me to receive!"

"Well, that's not how Father Zeno and I understand it. We feel he meant that you could begin to work toward receiving."

"What? That makes no sense!"

"That's how we see it," he said firmly.

I couldn't believe this was happening to me. It seemed like both madness and cruelty. And Father Gregory was one of my oldest friends in the community. I had known him long before he became a deacon and priest. He was known to follow Father Zeno's lead in most things, but this seemed excessive. Looking at his stony face, it was hard to recognize it as that of a friend who was well aware that I had just lost my husband. How could this be happening?

Father Gregory remained immovable. I felt as if he had, out of the blue, stabbed me with a sword. I burst into tears and ran sobbing out of the chapel. He did not try to stop me and, despite our many years of friendship, never contacted me in any way again.

I ran into the street, somewhat crazed with grief. I called Anna Elisabeth. She was supposed to be the Reader for Mark's tenth day memorial service so she was already on the way. Furious about what had just happened, she swung by the bus stop where I was waiting for her and picked me up. We drove to my apartment, with her vividly excoriating the priests all the way there.

We were hungry so I put out some cheese and crackers and red wine for us. What to do? I decided to phone the bishop, who was now back in New York. I got up my courage and dialed. A strange priest answered the phone. I had never met him but knew that he was greatly respected by our bishop. The bishop had even had him read a long typed letter I had sent explaining and defending my practice. This priest had liked the letter, thought it was good, and apparently was impressed that I didn't insult and condemn my priests! They must play much rougher in Bulgaria, I thought, when the bishop reported this to me.

Anyway, the bishop was not there. But the priest wanted to talk with me a bit longer. I knew he had spent many years in solitary confinement in Communist prisons; he was a kind of martyric hero. He mentioned his imprisonment and the pains that tormented him as a result of that confinement.

"*Diaconissa*," he asked gently, "do you think you could do anything for my condition?"

A bit stunned, I automatically repeated his question. Anna, sitting on the couch across from me, sputtered, laughing, and almost spit out her wine. Ah, the irony!

"Well, I don't know, Father, but if you like, I can try."

"Oh, *Diaconissa*," he said happily, "your voice is so sweet! But I bet all your patients say that to you, yes?"

I excused myself to get my hammer and doll as Anna rolled around on the couch, trying to stuff down her mirth.

I treated the long-suffering priest, and, thanks be to God, he experienced significant relief. I also treated him a few times later on. The priest even became interested in trying to learn the technique himself. He was a lovely man.

و

The Fortieth Day

The next day I phoned our bishop again. This time I reached him, but it quickly became clear that our priests had already gotten to him. His voice was cold. When I brought up the issue of my receiving, he told me he could not contradict what my confessor had told me; he was powerless to change that. I did not really believe that but could see he was under a lot of pressure. As happens all too often in great institutions, the old boys' club had mercilessly closed ranks, regardless of collateral damage—in this case, me.

The bishop sent me a polite letter telling me I must choose between continuing my healing practice and remaining a member of our church, and that I should make my decision by Pascha. There was no question that I would leave the church, painfully, regretfully, after so many years, but nonetheless leave. Viewing my healing work as a calling from our Lord and feeling incapable of abandoning suffering people whom I could help—at this point including my own dying father—what choice was there? I stopped going to church except for arriving on the fortieth day for my husband's memorial service.

In the meantime, a strange thing happened. I woke up several times in the early hours one night, each time feeling distinctly that there was an angel standing at the foot of my bed, saying "Let not your heart be troubled, neither let it be afraid" (John 14:27), and a great aura of peace filled my room.

When Father Zeno gave his homily at Mark's fortieth day

ceremony, he said he wanted to share a text that he wished Mark could have heard as a little boy (knowing how traumatized Mark had been when his father died suddenly when he was nine). The text was, it happens, "Let not your heart be troubled, neither let it be afraid."

I also wanted to say something for Mark that night. With tears rolling down my face and my tall honorary godson Reader Aaron Friar standing with his arm supportively around me, I told a brief version of Oscar Wilde's poignant story "The Happy Prince." I knew that Mark felt like a failure by the end of his life, and perhaps there were some who would judge him so. But I knew that he was not. In the story, the gold- and jewel-crusted statue of a little prince stands high on a hill overlooking the many sorrows and sufferings of those in his city. He convinces a swallow, already late for migration, to begin stripping off his gold and jewels and taking them to those in need. This the swallow, out of love for the prince, faithfully does until the fierce cold comes and he falls dead between the prince's feet. Stripped of all his finery, the heart of the now-shabby prince breaks. The statue is junked and melted down. Its broken heart is thrown on a dust heap next to a dead bird, the swallow. God sends an angel to bring Him the two most precious things in the city. The angel rightly flies back with the heart of the prince and the dead swallow. I felt that the cracked heart of my poor husband, who felt most like a battered old failure at the end of his days, would have been nestled with them right in the angel's arms.

CHAPTER SIXTEEN
Katavasia[1]: *The Brush of the Phoenix's Wings*

Mark's Return

After his death and first visit, Mark returned twice more.

I do not have the powers to describe his second visit. He came as I was lying in bed. The best I can do is share part of a poem I tried to write about his visitations called "Three Seeds":

> *The second time*
> *you returned*
> *after your death,*
> *we were overshadowed*
> *by the wings of Paradise,*
> *as you hung mere inches above me*
> *from four to six in the morning,*
> *two hours beyond time*
> *and the comprehension of earth.*
>
> *Everything unfulfilled*
> *in our relationship*

---

1 *Katavasia*: a sung verse in a liturgical canon that ends and sometimes also begins an ode; derived from "to descend," referring to when two antiphonal choirs come down to join together in the center of the church. The term was also used for hymns that were especially festal or solemn. "We do not only go up to God as in the Hymns of Ascent; God must also come down to us and *katavasia* is the Greek word for descending especially into the realm of death." (St. Nicholas Orthodox Christian Church, Arkansas)

filled,
scars healed,
wordless words spoken as,
perfect as the yin/yang circle,
we clasped each other's souls
blooming,
level after level,
universe after universe
in our selves,
our souls sharing the breath
of eternity,
a single breath,
pulsing in light,
filled
overflowing
with lost harmonies
gathered up
in the arms of angels.

We knew each other
without grasping,
in the giving so deep
there can be no giving at all.
We unfurled.
All our fragrances rushed out
in a dance deeper-breathed than the waves of the sea,
petals forever entwining, entwined, entwining,
contained and boundless,
the heartbeats of all seeds.

We cannot begin to anticipate all that God can and will do for us in this life and beyond. Through the Hebrew Prophet Joel, He said, *"And I will restore to you the years that the locust hath eaten"* (Joel 2:25). How can years eaten by ravening locusts be restored? We cannot imagine. But God can. And perform it as well. When Mark visited me the second time, it surpassed all my imagination and hopes. The ecstasy of our union was unspeakable; as well, I felt profoundly fulfilled—the word falls so far short of expressing it— on every level as a woman, in the flowering fullness of that aspect, as well as a soul. Who could imagine such a thing? Certainly I could not. Nor the tenderness and generosity that brought it pouring out of the life beyond, embracing my beloved and me in new depths of unplumbable mystery and in the deepest, inconceivable repair and healing of our deep but worn and tattered relationship.

It is hard for me to write about my experiences—not many, but they do exist—of people visiting me after their deaths because of the pain, frustration, and longing it may arouse in some bereaved people. I am sure that many more people feel some touch of a loved one after death than will admit it. But some feel desperate for that kind of reassurance, for a glimpse in whatever fashion of a loved one they have lost, and yet that sign may seem to them never to come. I did not and do not seek such visits. I leave the matter in God's hands, Who knows better than I whether such a visitation is really for the best. Both my mother and my brother visited me after their repose, but I have not had the slightest trace of presence or sign from my father, that I know of, and that makes me sad. Not everyone's afterlife is a happy one, I believe, and I would love to be reassured for his sake. Many people do, apparently, at the hour of their own deaths, see their deceased loved ones and are warmly greeted by them, if deathbed and near-death accounts are to be believed. So, if this is a subject of pain for you, dear reader, I am sorry and can only advise you to keep praying, asking, and offering it up as often as you need to, with the knowing that someday, at the right time, the veil over this mystery, too, will be lifted, to your joy.

Mark's Third Visit

God and Mark both like variety. So, after the exquisite ethereality of his second visit, not to be predictable, Mark came next as if triumphantly celebrating a successful Red Sox game, almost with etheric beer and hot dogs in hand!

I had just treated a friend on the phone for painful kidney stones and was happy that the friend felt relieved. The minute I put down the receiver, I felt Mark rush into the room, shouting, "Do it! Do it! Do it!" He sounded like a berserk heavenly sports coach (in his life he had coached baseball and football). I felt as if he were grinning, and I could only take this as yet another affirmation that I was doing the right thing by continuing my healing practice!

Where from Here? Enter the Good Samaritans

My life had taken a fateful turn, and now I had to begin rebuilding it. But how? My worst moments were that January and February, as I found myself wandering about numbly in the snow, trying to find a suitable new church. I felt like a lost sparrow, stumbling around on foot in the cold buffeting wind and drifting snow, feeling more alone and helpless than I ever had in my life.

A friend, hoping to alleviate my sorrow, recommended I call an Orthodox priest whom we shall call Father Zosimas. Father

Zosimas had skillfully intervened in a crisis for a friend of hers. By now it was Lent, and the Presanctified Liturgies on weekdays had begun. I talked with him on the phone, and he agreed to see me, suggesting I come to the church where he was serving at that time. I took a train out from Boston, and when I descended at the proper station, saw the tall priest in his long black *podrasnik* waiting expectantly beside the tracks.

Greeting me warmly, he seated me in his car, and we drove to the church. He listened carefully as I told him my story. I asked if he would hear my confession. He graciously agreed. It was such a relief to confess to this gentle priest and to feel his stole and absolving hand upon my head at its end. I felt such grace!

He asked me if I had fasted—which I had, in the hopes, however faint, of perhaps being able to receive Holy Communion that night at the Presanctified Liturgy. It had been a very long time! He then blessed me to receive the Eucharist, saying, "If I'm going to go to hell, I'd rather it be from being too merciful than from being too strict." So like Saint John Chrysostom: "Mercy imitates God and disappoints Satan."

Receiving the Precious Body and Blood of our Lord that night in the deep quiet of the beautiful little candle- and oil-lamp-lit church was wonderful. I felt such a deep peace. And Father Zosimas's healing kindness had deeply touched my fractured heart.

When the problem of getting back arose, Father Zosimas refused to let me take the train and insisted on driving me all the way back to Belmont with the aid of his indefatigable GPS, "Martha." He kept up a stream of relaxing, pleasant conversation all the way back, pooh-poohing my apologies about his long round trip.

⳾

I was more than relieved that there were also many other Orthodox Christians waiting with open arms. Even before I had to leave my community, I had gotten in touch with a brilliant theology professor at the Greek Orthodox Holy Cross seminary linked with Hellenic College in Brookline, Massachusetts. A much-published author, scholar, and psychotherapist, this professor was pulled by a thousand responsibilities and yet made time to discuss and explore with me the theological issues underlying Father Zeno's attack. Seemingly in Saint John Chrysostom's camp in regard to healing, the professor basically assessed my priests' assertions as "bad theology."

This professor went out of the way to comfort and help me, taking me out to lunch repeatedly and making it possible for me to attend some classes at the seminary.

My Good Samaritans' kindnesses were like the sun's warmth beginning to thaw a frozen plant. I began to feel as if I were slowly returning from a great distance, coming back from an icy landscape of trauma and shock where I had almost ceased to breathe. I met many other lovely people at Holy Cross. It all made me feel less like a leper. The pain of exile is hard to understand, I think, for anyone who has not experienced it. In such banishment it's as if something is ripped out of the ground floor of your soul. Finding your footing again is not an easy matter.

ﷺ

He Is with Me

Eventually I found a large Greek church I could reach by bus. I went to see the young pastor. Given the circumstances under which I had left my last church, I felt it would be unfair to attempt to join a congregation without making a clean breast of my situation to the priest in charge. He listened compassionately, praying on his prayer rope throughout (which I took as a good sign). At the end of my tale, he smiled warmly and welcomed me to his church. The only thing he wondered about was if their church might be "too Greek" for me—the services were largely in Greek. But I did begin attending services there. The Greekness was actually comforting, given my childhood background, and, being a trained Reader and having the relevant texts, I could still follow the services fairly well. The services were beautiful, the people warm and friendly. There was even someone I knew there, a redheaded convert named Timothy whom Mark and I had met when Timothy was working at Barnes & Noble and had commented on Mark wearing his *ráso* when we were there one night on the way back from services. Timothy was kind, pleasant company, and often gave me rides to and from services.

Entering my first Lent, Holy Week, and Pascha in a new church, far from the spiritual home and community where I had been so intimately entwined with these feasts for so long, was challenging. One day as I stood in the large group of worshippers during a service, I felt as if the Lord was pointing out to me a certain singularity I was inhabiting and telling me that I was to be "as a renunciate" among them—something that immediately aroused my fear and resistance, even though I didn't entirely understand what that meant.

Holy Week was just as intense as always—it exists like its own floating country in a dimension beyond. Its evocative services lift us into this untamed spiritual territory just as surely as if we had set foot on a pilgrim ship traveling far upon the ocean. Late Holy

Friday evening, after the Funeral service, I found myself standing alone in the narthex, awaiting Timothy by the empty Tomb. A few stray gardenias and small maroon dendrobium orchids still lay upon it. I took them gently into my hands. I had been trying to stuff down my longing for my old church and how much I was missing Mark all week and, doubly deceptive, trying to fool myself that I was not stuffing it down. I heard a voice. The Lord was calling my bluff.

As my hand, cupping a small gardenia, lay upon His bare Holy Tomb, He said to me, "He is with Me. And I am with you."

I got it. Yes, He knew my pain. And was forcing me to admit to it, for my own good. But also consoling and reassuring me that Mark and I were not really apart—we were united in Him in a very real way. And would be forever.

ﷺ

Spiritual Nest

I liked my new church, but it could not compare for me, of course, with the church I had been in for more than thirty years or with the community in which we had lived with such intimate intensity and focused prayerfulness together—not the usual parish, where interpersonal connections were often lightly drawn and mutual commitment tended to be low. I knew I was just treading water at this Greek church, but, at the least, that seemed better than the alternative.

Then our bright young pastor got promoted, and a somewhat older priest, proud with academic degrees like intellectual epaulets weighing down his shoulders, came to replace him. I could tell within one or two sermons that this pastor would not work out for me, a fact soon emphasized by a rumor that he did not approve of Mind/Body medicine even in hospitals. Oh no, not again!

I went out searching for a new spiritual home. And found one, in the place my theology professor friend had suggested to me from the beginning: Saint Mary's Antiochian Orthodox Church in Cambridge, Massachusetts. I had not gone there at first because I knew that, like my old church, it was about half converts, and I feared the similarity might be hard to bear, especially so soon after being ripped away from my old congregation. Also, Mark and I had gone to a service or two there many years before; at that time the chanting was in a rather heavy nasal Arabic style delivered by male chanters, which did not much appeal to us. Well, much had changed.

I found this to be an enchanting church, full of the Spirit, with a warm and loving congregation, delightfully interracial, reverent but also able to laugh, an outstanding choir, both male and female chanters, and an exceptionally beautiful and heartwarming pastor. In short, a glorious spiritual nest! I was welcomed with open arms, and Father Antony Hughes even graciously gave a blessing for my healing work. I hadn't dared to hope to be this happy in a new spiritual community and church ever again. It made me see yet again how, with God, all things are possible!

☙

Back to the Beloved Place

About a year after Mark died, my dear friends Katharine and David Newhouse suggested to me that I move back to Cape Ann to live in a cottage they owned in Rockport. I could hardly believe my ears and was overjoyed. The only drawback would be moving so far away from my new church. However, it would be possible to reach it on public transportation—more than two hours each way, it's true, but worth it to me when I could manage it. There was no Orthodox church on Cape Ann, much less one fitting my particular needs. Besides, I knew this special Cambridge church to be a rare treasure.

The move was difficult, as all moves seem to be. It forced me to go through and throw out over a hundred big garbage bags of Mark's things; anything good of his—and there was not much—I had already given away. About two weeks before I was supposed to move on May 1, I came down with an unusually severe case of bronchitis. I was so weak that I could hardly function, and the chest infection showed no signs of improving. I had to get permission to postpone the move by two weeks.

My friend the acupuncturist Karen Maguire came to visit me and was concerned at the state of my health.

"I was just at a Qigong training this weekend and learned some things. Shall I try some of them on you?"

I readily agreed. We sat on two chairs close to each other. Karen fixed me with her soulful, beautiful eyes and told me to breathe. I closed my eyes and breathed. Opening them again, I saw that Karen was making graceful passes with her hands just a few inches from my chest. Suddenly I was aware of my heart chakra in the middle of my chest and the tremendous tightness and grief within it, keeping me from breathing. Moving would, on some level deep in my being, mean losing Mark again. I could not face leaving the last place I had been with him. But the moment I saw it, I began to be free of this inhibition. Karen's gentle hands were still dancing in front of my chest, removing the subtle, tangled energetic bindings. I took the best breath I had taken in weeks and told her what I had just discovered. Peace flooded in. We rejoiced together. I began to mend rapidly.

ـ۞ـ

The kind people I had worked for, who had also so generously handled the costs of Mark's funeral, paid for a small crew of young Romanian men to move me. Other friends came and helped.

By the time the day's move ended, I felt half dead. But it was already deeply refreshing to be back in the wild beauty of Cape Ann. To my joy I also soon learned that in my absence a local TimeBank had been established. TimeBanks are organizations where members freely trade their time and skills with each other on an equal basis—one hour of doing dishes for someone or explaining nuclear physics have the same value in this system— and no money is involved. Unlike barter, members exchange labor freely through the whole organization with all members rather than in specific exchanges. Joining TimeBank made it possible for me to get rides around Cape Ann and elsewhere, solving much of my transportation problem, as well as bringing some beautiful new friends into my life along with a joyful sense of community.

ـ۞ـ

SoulSong
I did miss the singing. No longer engaged as a cantor, as I had been for so many years at my old church, I felt as if I had laid my voice aside like an instrument I no longer played—an additional sadness.

Michael O'Leary is a traditional singer of Irish, Scottish, and maritime songs and ballads. Originally from the Midwest, he has lived on Cape Ann for over twenty years, gives concerts and leads *seisiún*—Irish music fests—all over the cape, and also led a highly creative "song circle" that I joined.

"SoulSong," as Michael had named his group, met once a week at a local wellness center. Three to ten of us sat down in the dimly lit room while Michael lit white sage in an abalone shell and passed it to us so that we could smudge and purify our personal atmospheres with the sacred smoke. Then we would go around the circle doing a "check-in," where each person could briefly tell what had been happening to them or reflect aloud on some matter. The trick was that you could not speak your contribution—you had to sing it. It is amazing what kinds of things come out of a person when the vehicle is melody. One less hand on the inner controls! This did not lead to emotional outbursts but rather seemed to encourage a kind of gentle emotional flowering once you could drop the initial self-consciousness and let your singing voice carry to the surface whatever thoughts and feelings were brewing in you.

Ideas about performance quality and musical inhibitions began to drop away in the circle, where each person was appreciated and supported for his or her truly unique voice, without judgment or demands. Michael was a beautiful leader, sensitive and strong, his golden voice drawing us on through short songs, often seasonal, that we learned to improvise with as rich, unexpected harmonies built among us. The second half of each evening, following a brief break, was kept for individual improvisation. You would step into the center of the circle and see what arose that moment spontaneously out of your own voice. You could also ask someone else— or even two people—to improvise with you. Unexpected harmonic beauties would rise swirling in the air as you, and perhaps your partners, let go and sang and sang and sang.

SoulSong was freeing and healing. My ability to work with spontaneous harmony increased rapidly. I knew I was making a breakthrough with this on an emotional level when I discovered that I could suddenly harmonize below the melody line as well as above it—something I had always found impossible before. I felt as if this new ability and I were like a strong, sunny dandelion pushing its way through concrete paving, working its joyful way into the sun. Something deep inside was healing. Every SoulSong evening, as we ended by smudging with sweetgrass, traditionally an invitation to blessed presences, we also prayed silently or aloud, and I felt the gentle dew of blessing falling upon me, refreshing my soul.

Michael became a close friend and my local hero. He is one of those rare people in whom a deep inner goodness reflects powerfully in his voice. An online recording (https://soundcloud.com/ michael-o-10)of his singing of the Irish ballad "The Lakes of Pontchartrain," which two friends listened to separately, evoked the same unusual remark from each of them: "Dangerously beautiful."

not!

⁂

The Magi Caravan Returns: A Snowy Oasis
Due to guidance that Mark and I received early in our marriage, even though we were both Sufi initiates, we had ceased participating in Sufi activities and practices many years before, instead dedicating ourselves exclusively to our Christian Community. So much was new in my life now that I felt it was time to see if perhaps particular past guidances might no longer apply, including the one discouraging my active involvement with the Sufi path.

So, one cold, snowy evening a year after Mark died, I found myself at the Abode of the Message in New Lebanon, New

York—a rustic long-standing Sufi community on a mountainside in a beautiful old Shaker village. An enormous hemlock and two huge old willows dominated a courtyard where clean-lined Shaker buildings stood, now festooned with icicles and swags of snow. My old teacher, Shaikh—now Murshid—Qadr, was scheduled to teach there that week, and I had arranged a short private appointment with him between his classes. We hadn't spoken to each other in eighteen or twenty years.

Except for being more gray and grizzled, he looked the same, his dark, intelligent eyes sparkling perceptively. We sat down in the small kitchen of one of the houses, and I told him what had happened. He received it kindly, and we both sat in silent prayer and meditation for a short time, contemplating what new direction I might take. Truly, neither of us got any clarity. It just felt as if we were, perhaps, trying to take still slightly unbaked dough out of the oven too soon. We stood up. He gave me a warm hug and the assurance of his continued prayers. And I walked out into the snow, as mystified as when I went in. Children came tumbling and laughing out of the school, throwing snowballs at one another as they crossed my path. I felt as fragile and uncertain as the colliding snowballs.

I had paid for a room overnight and dinner was included, so I headed to Razzaq, the refectory, for the evening meal. My dear friend Mariel Walters, living on the West Coast, had called her friend Rabia Longworth, who lived at the Abode, to ask her to watch out for me. As I walked into the toasty dining hall, full of the cheerful smells of good food, a beautiful, lean, silver-haired lady launched herself from a bench by a nearby table and grabbed my hands, exclaiming, "You must be Stephani Nur! Mariel told me you were coming. Welcome, welcome!" Her face shone with light, and I could hardly look away from her intensely bright eyes.

She guided me to a food line, we filled a couple of plates with savory vegetarian food, and, like a conscientious sheepdog, she herded me back and settled me at one of the polished picnic tables. After we ate a bit, she wished to hear my story. I wasn't sure how much I wanted to share with her, but I found that, bit by bit, Rabia seemed able to draw much of it out of me, and at last I found myself sobbing in her comforting arms. I felt as if I were being held by an expert healer who was delicately drawing all the poison out of my system while simultaneously infusing me with light, an amazing operation. It was as if she was gently squeezing all the last remaining badness, tucked in dark corners where I hadn't even seen it, out of my system. I stopped crying.

And felt as clean and light as the first fine crust of untouched snow. Rabia and I threw our arms around each other and laughed and laughed. There was such joy. So this was why I had had to come to the Abode this time, to receive this sweet and powerful healing at this wise woman's hands. I left the Abode still uncertain but hopeful and renewed.

اللہ

I called an old friend, a Sufi teacher on the West Coast, to see if I could get any greater clarity about my direction. Shams was helpful, filling me in on much that had developed in our Order in the years I had been away. What he said about Zira'at, one of the five particular "Activities" of the Order established by our founder (the Esoteric School, Universal Worship, Kinship, the Healing Order, and Zira'at) especially interested me. As formally described by the Inayati Order: "Zira'at is an activity which uses symbols and processes of agriculture to promote an understanding of the earth's sacredness, and to describe and facilitate growth in the inner life, bridging both the material and spiritual worlds." It involved both a practical and mystical approach to ecology, to being in right relationship with the earth and preserving the sacred community of Nature, Shams said, and had flourished in these last years. He gave me contact information for the head of Zira'at, Sharifa Felicia Norton. I e-mailed her.

اللہ

A Golden Flower and an Etheric Temple
Sharifa e-mailed me back quite promptly. As I began to read her note, I felt as if a golden warmth rushed out to me, like being enveloped in the petals of a glowing flower. Sharifa was gracious and helpful, very welcoming. She sent me Zira'at links and information.

I got up from the computer and was stunned to immediately feel another presence, very distinct and potent. It was that of our spiritual father, Pir-o-Murshid Hazrat Inayat Khan. Not only did I feel his presence, I seemed somehow to be in his presence, actually within it, walking around inside it, no matter where in the house I was. His atmospheric mantle—perhaps the very beauty of his personality itself—was manifesting as an enormous and exceedingly beautiful temple or palace with many glorious rooms and halls, arches and columns, both exquisite and magnificent in which I could wander, breathing in a majestic, unearthly peace. This bemused and blessed sensation lasted for a couple of hours, even while I was doing dishes. The best way I could describe it to myself was that it seemed like the heavenly Platonic archetype of the Earth Element. Weeks later I happened to get to see Murshid's natal horoscope: he had a preponderance of planets in Earth signs.

I wrote Sharifa back right away. "I think I've gotten a go-ahead!" I was climbing back on my camel in the Magi's caravan!

بسم الله

Ploughing and Harrowing

Before long I attended a weekend Zira'at retreat skillfully led by Sharifa and her husband, Muinuddin Charles Smith, at the Abode. The retreat spanned from attuning to and learning the breaths and walks of the different Elements to participating through meditation, contemplation, and chant in the fertile stages of an alchemical retreat. It was very beautiful and inspiring. And Sharifa and I quickly connected on a deep level. I decided to ask her if she would be my Sufi guide; if she agreed, I would, as a courtesy, write Murshid Qadr for his blessing. Despite her busy schedule as an international soloist dancer and teacher of dance in Manhattan, and despite already being responsible for a number of *mureeds*, Sharifa graciously, with a glowing smile, assented.

We were offered initiation in Zira'at, if we wished to receive it. My goddaughter Lydia Hutchinski and I accepted the first level of initiation: Plougher. There are subsequent ones: Harrower, Sower, Reaper, Thresher, Garnerer, Farmer, and Experienced Farmer. A watchword accompanied each of these initiations—for example, "Toil" for the Plougher and "Hope" for the Sower. Having over the years passed through each of these levels through Farmer, I never stopped being astonished at how powerfully each one shaped the next year of my life in the kinds of things that happened to me and issues I faced. This was true for my friends also. There was an unseen mystical river in the Zira'at transmission with its own compelling current that cleansed and brought hidden things to light and fruition.

In the first four years or so of these annual retreats, we also participated in a Universal Worship service in the Abode meditation hall on Sunday mornings, led by Sharifa and Muinuddin, that celebrated all the major religious traditions with prayers, readings, stories, singing, and chants. Sharifa suggested that my goddaughter and I supply a reading and hymn or two for the Christian part of the worship. This we gladly did. Lydia Raphaela is a pure-voiced soprano with a music degree, and we had been singing together as cantors for years in my old church. I don't remember the reading we used, but we did then sing three very short hymns. The last one was the *Troparion*, or festal hymn for the feast of the Holy Dormition, or Falling Asleep of the Mother of God:

In giving birth, thou didst keep thy virginity,
And in thy repose, thou didst not forsake the world, o Theotokos [Greek:
    the God-bearer],
For thou art the Mother of life and, having passed over into life,
Through thine intercessions, from death thou dost redeem our souls.

I sang the haunting Byzantine melody, and Lydia sang the shifting, shimmering *ison* that throbbed beneath it. It was one of those rare moments when everything was perfect: the tone of our voices, the shift of light, the breeze, the angle of our hearers' heads—I can't explain it, but on the last lingering note of this hymn, I knew that something very special had just taken place, something beautiful had slipped frictionlessly into a place just made for it.

Sharifa came over to Lydia and me a bit after the service with a gentle, lingering smile. She told us she had been concerned about one of her *mureeds* who was attending the retreat but who had been in a state of deep despair. This woman's daughter, in her twenties, had died of late-stage Lyme disease that year, and the mother felt unable to recover from this tragedy and was very depressed. She felt that the retreat was not reaching her through her immense sorrow, but Sharifa had encouraged her to stay anyway and to try to be gentle with herself.

This woman had been at the Universal Worship. Suddenly, when Lydia and I sang the troparion, something had broken through to her. "Passing over into life"—at those words she had a flash, a deep conviction, that there was life after death and also that her daughter was actually in life now! Her sorrow fell away, and she felt filled with a new joy. The perfection of that moment had been designed for this grieving mother—God and our Holy Mother, who knew so well a mother's grief, had reached out healing hands to her. Lydia and I were filled with gratitude to have been used to help this holy and healing purpose. We left the retreat that afternoon on a wave of joy.

ॐ

Back at the Ranch
I was settling in comfortably at the pretty Rockport cottage. With my dear friend and mentor Elianne Linda Obadia in California coaching me and helping me make new connections, I began freelance copyediting and proofreading again. I was glad to be able to earn my bread working from home. I was also supported by Mark's small but significant Social Security payments. Had he died one

week earlier, before I turned sixty, I would have had nothing at all. Sixty, however, was the magic number for receiving survivor's payments. Again, I had been looked out for in a mysterious way.

The first year back was difficult, though, in having so many Cape Ann people asking me where Mark was—and my having to tell them. And deal with their upset. One lovely woman cried out, "Oh no! How can that be? You two were like one soul!"

Many evenings that first year I would ramble sadly down to Old Garden Beach, a charming curve of sand and rock at the base of a twenty-foot stone wall, to sit on a bench on the beach-rose-bordered green parklet atop the wall and watch the misty twilight roll in over the soothing, chanting waves of the Atlantic. Despite the beauty, I felt as if I wore a heavy cloak of grief. But many different consolations came about as a result of my living on Cape Ann again, among them finding vibrant new friends who became loving and inspiring sisters to me, Dana Jamila Watt and Karen Nur Khabira Pearson, both also drawn irresistibly to the mystical magnetism of wild Cape Ann.

ﻋﻠﻰ

A Prophetic Alpine Meadow
One July day I woke up, went into the kitchen, and opened the door into our small yard. The sun was shining brightly, and I almost reeled back from the glare reflecting into my eyes. The yard had been transformed into an alpine meadow of cascading white blossoms. The lawn had not been mowed for some time, and this had given a host of hidden flowers a chance to send up shoots and bloom. This gorgeous sight cheered my heart. The flowers did look somewhat familiar, and I went out to examine them more closely. Yes! They were Star of Bethlehem, a wonderful herb and in the Bach Flower Essences one of the five Essences in Rescue Remedy. As an Essence, they were a specific for treating grief, trauma, and shock.

Later that day, it occurred to me to wonder why the Star of Bethlehem blooms had made their appearance just now. From years of observing what wild plants made their entry in my own yard each year, I had come to see, as my herbalist teachers taught, that needs soon to come were foreshadowed by the entry of particular plants in my vicinity.

Oh no! Did this mean I was about to have an experience of shock, grief, and loss? Yes. Within three days of the alpine meadow's appearance, Mirabai became quite sick. Although only eight years old, she had developed a large tumor in one lung. With my faithful friend Katharine at my side in the vet's office, both of us shedding tears, we laid tender, soothing hands on Mirabai as the vet gently put her to sleep.

‿◡‿

Max

Winston needed a friend. He was inconsolable for the loss of Mirabai. However, it took some time before I could find a suitable companion. Dana, one of Winston's willing slaves, decided to help him out. She found a lovely young Maine coon cat, less than a year old, in a local shelter. He was even a gray tiger with white touches, like Winston. She brought him over. Dana and I sat down on the couch, eager to watch these cats' first contact. They sniffed each other interestedly through the wire of the cat carrier. As Winston was a great gentleman, mayhem did not seem likely. I opened the carrier, and Maximilian shot out like a rocket, with Winston in instant pursuit.

Max ran around and up and down the cottage, exploring it continuously, for three hours, Winston closely shadowing him. There was an odd, twisting little stairway between floors, and Max often launched himself in the air off it midway down, sailing a couple of feet above the living room chairs, looking like a little biplane with the furry dirigible of the immense Winston also airborne just a few feet behind him.

There were never any spats in those early days, and the two cats settled into a mostly gentle friendship, often sleeping together. I did feel, though, that sometimes Winston gave me a considering look when the little guy began to annoy him that said, "Couldn't you puh-leeze have gotten a girl?" They were both handsome cats, and Max had amazing eyes that were so pale they would reflect any color near him. We have lovely photos of him lying next to a hydrangea bouquet on a table, his eyes the identical intense blue of the flowers. A real pinup boy. Anna, admiring them one day, said, "Max is the Johnny Depp of cats, and Winston is the Sean Connery."

Temperamentally, though both genial, they were quite different. Max would run away and hide whenever anyone entered the house. Winston, on the other hand, would advance toward the newcomer in order to display his magnificent self for adoration. Winston also wanted to be involved with (and apparently supervise) any project, including—so un-catlike!—vacuuming.

When my friend Mindy soon joined the three of us as a loving roommate, she felt that one day Winston "said" to her, "You wonder why I am always overseeing what happens here? It's because I am the man of the house and it is my responsibility."

Winston definitely stayed on top of everything, including some-times Max, whom he would thus squeeze out of an appealing new cardboard box, all the while making it look like he was only affectionately cuddling with him. Bit by bit, Winston moved into the box, and Max somehow found himself on the floor.

Winston also liked to entertain with his very own "party tricks," such as first making quite sure that all our guests were watching him and then diving headfirst into a ridiculously small blue plastic basket on the floor. Twisting and turning, he would eventually get his immense self completely stuffed into it, to general applause. He also liked to lie on the floor and have Mindy put ten or twelve small toys all along his body, like a proud old general displaying his medals.

But, before Max was full grown, tragedy struck us again. Although neither cat had ever been let outside, both came down with serious flea infestations and manifested a severe allergy to their bites. Mindy and I were horrified to learn from the vet that fleas and ticks could hitchhike in on people's shoes and thus attack inside-only cats. Our boys were suffering terribly, and Max even lost all the fur on the bottom half of his body (Mindy felt that he "cat-talked" to her one day, telling her that he was so ashamed of his bare bottom!).

Some natural attempts at flea control didn't really seem to work, and I finally let the vet talk me into using one of the standard topical poisons that were put on the back of a cat's neck to kill fleas. But Max had a terrible reaction, hyperventilating and trem-bling until I could administer a dose of *Arsenicum album 200c*, after quickly rinsing his back off with soapy water to rid him of the poison. Also, I called my friend Dana, and we both gave Max an energy-healing treatment that calmed him. Oddly not long after, the fleas began to disappear from the scene. Max recovered and even regained his lush fur pantaloons.

But our beautiful Winston never really recovered. He grew weaker and weaker, and at last the vet said it would be cruel not to let him go. Dear Katharine, who has been so incredibly faithful in facing death with me—of my husband, and of my cats—took me to the vet. We both said goodbye to the exhausted Winston, looking into his wise eyes and, crying, with our hands on him, let him go to the vet's merciful injection. He passed away peacefully.

I have loved all the cats whose lives I have shared down the long, rich years, but of them all I was closest to Mirabai and Winston. There is still a hole in my heart where their presence used to be.

Missouri Mystics

Anna and I were in Kansas City, Missouri. I had sold Mark's and my gold wedding rings, as well as saved up for several months, to finance this adventure. I felt that Mark would have approved. Experience is more precious than gold, especially spiritual experience.

I had never been in the Midwest before (does Ohio count?). Anna, originally Jo Alison England (marriage and baptism having converted her name to the unrecognizable) from Ann Arbor, Michigan, had grown up there but in parts far more northern in every sense of the word. Now we were in the sultry southern Midwest, a new and foreign territory to us both. We had been drawn by the irresistible opportunity to spend over a week with the great Sufi teacher Murshid Wali Ali Meyer in a general weekend retreat and then a six-day *wazaif* intensive where we would concentrate on working with the Beautiful Names of God.

We were enthusiastically welcomed by the friendly local Sufi community, and, after the first day of the general retreat, full of dancing and chanting and inspiring wisdom stories told by Wali Ali, we were swept away by a kind Sufi couple, Batina and Jamil, to spend the next few nights with them in their amazing earth-bermed home. Their dwelling was partly covered by a curving grass-and-herb roof like a little hillock, complete with rabbit footprints all over the skylights! It was like a wizard's house of odd but charming room shapes and varying windows. The enchanted effect was further enhanced by bowls and open chests of beautiful necklaces of semiprecious stones, handmade by Batina that spilled out of them like Aladdin's treasure. The earth-bermed walls did not feel at all claustrophobic—if anything, the opposite, like a deeply peaceful and quiet embrace. Our magical surroundings matched the spiritual magic beginning to open up in our souls as the retreat unfolded.

Going Deeper

After the general retreat, we moved, along with forty retreatants or so, out of Kansas City into the country to a plain but adequate retreat center of sprawling redbrick buildings for the intensive *wazaif* retreat. We each had our own private room, or cell, where we would be alone most of the day and evening doing our assigned practices. Each of us had been assigned to a particular "stream" of practices following private interviews with Wali Ali and his assistant, Murshida Tawwaba Bloch. Our groups, divided into the particular streams, would meet with Wali Ali and Tawwaba each morning for instruction. Following this, all of us, on silence except for when we were doing our practices, would return to our individual rooms or find a place to work outside.

There was an optional group class with Wali Ali in the evening, and Dances of Universal Peace were also scheduled. Several hours during the day were available for private consultations when needed with Wali Ali and Tawwaba; a wise provision, as the many hours of intensive repetitions of the assigned *wazaif*—a single *wazifa* or pairs—1,001 times aloud, with repetition continued silently on the breath alone for hundreds of times, and finally time spent without words at all in the state evoked by that particular *wazifa* for hundreds of breaths, often took you into deep spiritual waters for which you needed the help of an experienced guide.

Like icons, *wazaif* are passages into the towering realities of the spiritual world but gain that access through sound rather than our visual capacity. Both Sufism and Orthodox Christianity posit that we can directly know and contact God through His Divine Energies. Such contact reveals us more deeply to ourselves in the power of that divine light, purifying and healing. Our capacity to bear greater life and gnostic depth is stretched by these contacts that vibrate through our whole being on directed currents of sound.

In the quiet of my room, I quickly found myself caught up in the revelatory swirl of the *wazaif*. Because I have since misplaced my notebook, I cannot now tell you what particular *wazaif* combination I was using when I became uncomfortably aware that I was carrying resentment toward God. The hidden is often revealed in Sufic practice, especially what you have hidden from yourself.

This buried anger had to do with a role I felt I was sometimes asked to play in disrupting people's comfort and complacency, letting sometimes-unwelcome fresh air into a situation of stagnant energy. I was shrinkingly averse to hurting people, even briefly and in a good cause, and I also did not enjoy the hostility that often came flying my way as a result. I knew that I felt impelled to such acts at times by the Holy Spirit, but, rather than develop a mature view and come to terms with this recurrent challenge, I had simply blamed God.

As I chanted, with one hand moving the sandalwood and amber beads along my long *tasbih*, or prayer rope, a bright image flashed by of a surgeon wielding a knife. I felt as if I were, in my stubbornness, being argued with reasonably by an unseen being. The message seemed to be that it was better for people to suffer temporary pain and discomfort than to remain unhealed of greater sicknesses. If that job should sometimes fall to me, it was my duty to accept it without repining. Although ashamed of my reluctant self-interest, I still did not like the nudge. I went to see Wali Ali and Tawwaba to consult.

Wali Ali basically dressed me down in a kind way, pointing out that since gentle people don't want to hurt others, they often refuse to accept their own God-given power. "Accepting the power is half of the whole thing," he said—and reiterated it to all in our evening class. I'm sure I was not the only one struggling with this sharp point of discipleship. "It's your dharma," he said to me. "You can't know what will happen to people if they don't get this kind of shock when they need it. Only God does. Just check to see if your ego is in it—and if not, do it! With your whole heart."

ﷲ

Visitors

As the days passed, our group of retreatants swam deeper and deeper in the mystical river. One evening as I began my practices, I didn't know I was about to be caught up in a little sea-surge in that river. I was chanting "*Ya Wakil* (the Trustworthy, the Protector), *Ya Muhaimin* (Protector of the essence)" hundreds of times, breathing in and out with its sonorous tide. Suddenly I felt the presence of two men in long robes in my room with me. They each put their hands on my head, giving me a blessing, and then there was only Light. I had completely lost any sense of my body, my personal identity, or any earthly sight or orientation. There was just Light, beautiful, blazing Light. This, I later realized, must have been an instance of what the Sufis call "*fana*"—the extinguishing of the personal ego as it is subsumed into a higher manifestation.

When I came back to myself, it was almost as if my eyes had changed into those of a raptor's—I could see an incredible amount of sharp detail all over my room, and even the regular light seemed to have intensified and increased. Although it was the end of a long day, I felt full of energy and as if I could run all night!

The next day I went to check with Wali Ali, in hopes that I hadn't been delusional. He asked me several questions about aspects of the experience. "No, you weren't delusional," he said. "That was a visitation. Don't you know that when you chant '*Ya Muhaimin*' you call upon the *silsila*?" (I didn't and shook my head. The *silsila* is the saintly group of our spiritual lineage through the ages.) "Well, you called on them, and the *silsila* sent those two to you." I was overjoyed to learn about this aspect of *Ya Muhaimin*— to think of those beautiful, powerful intercessors unseen but so close at all times!

بسم

The Box of Shadows

Cleansing, of one sort or another, must accompany any healing. To my surprise, as I chanted yet another series of *wazaif*, a long rectangular shadowy box seemed to rise to the surface on the subtle body of the right side of my torso. I recognized it. It had happened to me many months before while I was attending a memorial service in a private home for a recently reposed much-beloved former member of my old Christian community. I did not feel that my banishment barred me from attending such an assembly of prayer, as it was not in the church proper, even though I knew that one or two present in the group were likely not to feel kindly toward me.

I had kept a low profile in the back of the room as we chanted the memorial prayers, but periodically I experienced a wave of psychic assault, as if someone was trying to extinguish my voice, pressing down hard on my throat chakra. That long shadowy box also formed on my chest, like a narrow psychic coffin. The only way I could cast off this oppression was by silently chanting *"Kyrie eleison"*—Lord, have mercy—or *"Ya Wakil,"* the Protector. They were both effective, but whenever I stopped, the disturbing sensations returned. I was eager to leave that night when the service ended. Once I was away from that room, the oppression lifted.

Now I was distressed to find that that "box" was still somehow within me. I went to see Wali Ali and explained what had happened. He put our two chairs close together and leaned forward, looking into my eyes and, seemingly, deep into my being. I couldn't help focusing more on one of his eyes and had a strange sensation that it grew enormously in size as we gazed at each other. I realized that he must be using some advanced version of "The Glance" to diagnose my trouble, like the good physician of the heart that he was.

He sat back, looking troubled, and confirmed that there was something amiss, that some kind of subtle damage did exist.

"Well, what can we do?" I pleaded.

"I'd recommend an exorcism," he replied thoughtfully. "I saw Reverend Joe Miller do one once, but I don't know how to do them myself. But I can teach you a protection that Murshid Sam taught me." He told me to chant *"Ya Qawiyy"* ("O Thou Mighty") many times and then eventually to start alternating that with *"Allahu Akbar"* ("God is great"). He said that *Allahu Akbar* protects on all the planes of existence, and that *Ya Qawiyy* is the unconquerable might of God against which nothing can stand. He explained the paradox of the overwhelming strength of *Ya Qawiyy* in that it is completely formless—which, in our culture, we would tend to think of as inherently weak by definition. But its indomitable strength derives from that very formlessness—there is nothing for a resisting force to grab onto to initiate a struggle; opposition is an impossibility.

At my new church I heard "*al Qawiyy*" chanted every Sunday in the Divine Liturgy. My church, in the Antiochian Orthodox jurisdiction, had been founded by Syrian, Jordanian, and Palestinian Christians, so we had chanting in Arabic and Greek as well as English. Indeed, the names Allah and *Quduus* (the Holy Spirit) appeared in every service. "Holy God, Holy Mighty, Holy Immortal, have mercy on us." "*Quduusun allah, Quduusun al Qawiyy, Quduusun allah di la yamut irhamna*." The unopposable Mighty, triumphant in all circumstances and all contexts.

I followed Wali Ali's advice and experienced relief, continuing the practice when I returned home. Perhaps I did not continue it quite long enough as, a year or so later, when chanting a practice new to me that my guide had given me but that had long been used by our Order, I suddenly fell on my bed as if clonked on the head with a cudgel and fell into a heavy sleep for three hours, though it was only early afternoon. I awakened feeling deeply refreshed and cleansed and, strangely, with the certain conviction that the last taints from that psychic invasion had finally been completely cleansed from my system. Upon lookingx up the practice online, I was shocked to see that the Arabic words had to do with the Evil Eye! I called my guide, and she explained to me that our Pir had recently updated this practice into a more correct form, which she then passed on to me. However, so surprisingly, the "wrong" form had brought me a profoundly thorough healing. The Ineffable's ways are mysterious, and yet again He had provided for my need in an odd and unpredictable way.

اَللّٰه

A Robe for the Christian Sufis
Anna Elisabeth had attended many Sufic events with me but was not yet initiated in the path. In Missouri she decided to take that step. Wali Ali recommended that she ask Tawwaba to be her guide. So the four of us, Wali Ali, Tawwaba, Anna, and I walked down to the edge of a pond near the retreat and arranged ourselves in a little gazebo-like shelter. Tawwaba put on a simple, rustic-looking robe that Wali Ali handed her. She took Anna's hands in hers and followed Wali Ali's instructions as the ceremony of *bayat* began. Soon it was over; we were all full of joy.

Tawwaba gave the robe back to Wali Ali. It was now folded

and hanging over one of his shoulders. Out of nowhere I heard myself asking him, "Do you still have the robe that Murshid Sam was given for the Christian Sufis?" He grinned down at me and pointed to the robe on his shoulder. Impulsively I stood on tiptoe and kissed it. When Murshid Sam had been traveling in Pakistan, he had a dream in which he was given a robe—a mantle of authority—for the "Christian Sufis." The next day an unknown shaikh—a cabdriver?—presented him with that very mantle in waking life. And here it was.

Anna, now Anna Azima (*Ya Azim*, "O Thou Magnificent"), was radiant as we walked back to the retreat building. After many hugs, we separated, returning to our own rooms to rest and absorb the wondrous experience in solitary quietude. I sat on the edge of my bed and felt such overpowering happiness that I could not move! I had experienced physical agony so great that I could not move in the past, but this was the far other end of the spectrum! Who even knew that it was possible—to be immobilized by overwhelming happiness? Part of it may have been my joy that Anna Azima Elisabeth, so inexpressibly dear to me, was now under the protection of the *silsila* and with her feet on the path to potentially ever-deepening happiness. And perhaps part of it was the touch of grace of Murshid Sam's robe for the Christian Sufis. I didn't have to know the cause, though, when every breath was a joy.

The Wind That Erases Footprints

Even this grace-filled retreat had to end. The last day in the last dance class, our farewell class, it happened that I got to demonstrate the "Forgiveness" couple dance with Wali Ali. Among the Beautiful Names of God, there are four specifically dealing with forgiveness in gradations of magnitude, from the first, *Ya Ghaffar*, continuous and repeated forgiveness, to the last, *Ya 'Afuw*, a forgiveness so complete that no trace of any offense, no forgiver or forgiven person—or even the act of forgiving—remains. It is the perfection of divine forgiveness that we strive to enter. *Ya 'Afuw*, says *Physicians of the Heart*, "can be compared to the wind completely erasing the footprints in the desert sand, as if no one had ever walked there."

In this exquisite, moving dance, you chant four *wazaif* with corresponding gestures, receiving from and offering forgiveness to your partner (your partner will change as the circle moves on). To perform this with Wali Ali was deeply moving. He is a man of profound humility and great warmth of heart. The word Wali has to do with the true Friend. I felt honored and touched to be dancing with this true and great Friend of God and of us all. As our circle moved on, I saw face after face shining with light, eyes pouring forth and receiving holy forgiveness.

By the time we reached the last dance of the session, the tone filling the room had become lofty and elegiac. I was not the only one dancing on with quiet tears running down my face. We had all grown so close together in our absorption in the pathways of practices leading to our Beloved. We would never all be together again, each one shot out alone into the world, like a seed bearing our collective blessing. But, though separated and invisible to each other, we would all be blooming—and sharing that blooming with others—from the deep roots of our intertwined hearts.

ﷺ

Turning

During these years of rebuilding my life, I also had the blessing of attending some weekend retreats led by another great Sufi teacher, like Wali Ali also of the Ruhaniat lineage—in fact, its head, Pir Shabda Kahn. Pir Shabda is also an accomplished singer and musician and director of the Chishti Sabri School of Music.

Aside from the retreats being musically beautiful, given Pir Shabda's particular gifts, I seemed always to learn so many useful and inspiring things. Pir Shabda was warm and frank, a master of sound and of the breath. He was also daring—as in having the whole group together chant "*Ya Tawwab*" (another forgiveness *wazifa*) 1,001 times, and then silently in *fikr* and *fikr a siir* many times. This was the first time I ever chanted "*Ya Tawwab*," and it immediately yielded a surprising revelation for me.

The root of *Ya Tawwab* has to do with turning—turning toward God and/or, curatively, showing you what you may be turning away from God toward. As we chanted "*Ya Tawwab*," I found myself sinking into a forgotten early memory: as a child, I had felt a sense of blessedness on a certain level all the time. I knew I hadn't earned and "didn't deserve" this lovely feeling and, over time, noticed that most of the people around me didn't seem to feel that way. This seemed unfair and, well, cruel. Obviously, God had messed up some way, my child self reasoned, so I would jettison my sense of blessedness as a backhanded way of "being more fair" to the others who palpably did not feel this way! A childhood sin! Yes, there are many. Although I don't think we should overemphasize the word "sin" and use it as a club with which to bludgeon ourselves, neither do I believe we should ignore it and act as if it doesn't exist or doesn't matter. This was a sin of pride—I was judging God and finding God wanting! But now I saw it in the gentle light of *Ya Tawwab*, where there was no condemnation, only truth. Where I had erred, turning away to my own ignorant judgment, I now turned back toward God. I repented, asked forgiveness, and agreed within myself to take up my obedience and let myself feel blessed again. And I have ever since. Much better for me and for others! Feelings of blessedness are contagious.

اهو

The Suluk Caravan

When I came downstairs from my tiny room in the Abode's Meditation Hall on the first evening's session of the Gulzar class of the Suluk Academy, I paused halfway down the stairs to breathe in the beauty of what I saw before me. Delicate sitar music was playing, and forty or so people of all different ages, my fellow *saliks* (male travelers) and *salikas* (female travelers), were sitting on the floor with backrests or on chairs, their eyes closed, quietly meditating. Though strangers, their corporate loveliness seemed overwhelming to me.

It was as if I breathed in the numinous fragrance of fine incense. The long hall, which I had been in many times before, even in my twenties, seemed more handsome than ever. Sunken somewhat into the hill, it was yet sunny during the day and had a subdued beauty from its golden wood floor, enlivened with large Oriental carpets, and its dark beams and white walls embraced by a base of strong gray stone. There was a large framed photograph of our founder, Pir-o-Murshid Hazrat Inayat Khan, hanging in the center of the far wall and, loveliest of all, a graceful stained glass window with intertwined roses over the altar, reading in fluid script, "Enter unhesitatingly, Beloved, for in this abode there is naught but my longing for Thee."

The sense of deep quiet and spiritual gorgeousness was so profound, the patient souls waiting in gentle meditation at that moment pure as a dell of snowdrops, that at every subsequent session I skipped the first evening's dinner in the refectory so that my first contact with my class would always be like this, and I could revel in undisturbed quietude in their mystical purity, delicately tangible to inner senses. On one such night I felt especially strongly the presence of Hazrat Inayat Khan. As part of me questioned that, I felt that he etherically stepped into the center of the room and all of us, answering, "But where else should I be but in the hearts of my disciples?"

اهو

The Quest

We are here not to add to the sum of our knowledge, nor to collect more facts, but to undergo a different kind of experience, an experience of travel, a journey within, moving through the terrain, the landscape of our own mind, within our own heart, within our own soul, to return to the center of ourselves.

—Pir Zia Inayat-Khan

Suluk means "journey." And the Suluk Academy involved a special journey taken for two years with Pir Zia Inayat-Khan, grandson of Hazrat Inayat Khan and head of the Inayati Order, and other spiritual teachers in eight intensive six-day sessions of study on-site at the Abode of the Message. With the help of a scholarship, a financial gift from friends, some small savings, and a burning desire in my heart, I was able to attend.

More than forty of us met as the Suluk Gulzar class for two years. We were of all ages, though with a substantial contingent toward the older end. Each session we began with morning meditation, followed by two long concentrated classes given by Pir Zia with a break, or one class by Pir Zia and the other by a guest teacher. We were not allowed to take notes, the intent being that we absorb the teaching deeply with our whole beings.

The curriculum was structured on chronological mystical building blocks: Concentration, Contemplation, Meditation, and Realization. It was assumed that we could not progress to the next level without some essential mastery of the prior one. There were books to purchase and read, homework essays to write, practices to perform. This curriculum was rich and challenging. And then there was the "karma yoga"—the rotated never-ending kitchen cleanup!

Afternoons, following lunch and a brief rest break, were spent first with our mentor group (the class was divided into three such groups, each with its own additional mentor) and next with our "pod" (the mentor group was itself divided into groups of six or seven for the small pods). In both these groups we did further practices, asked questions—especially of our mentor (in my case, happily my own guide, Sharifa)—and explored somewhat more intimately the topics we had covered that day. I enjoyed my mentor group very much; Sharifa has a gift for handling challenging topics in a manner both light and lively—we were often laughing—but at the same time subtle and deep.

My pod, which met after our mentor class, exceeded all expectations. The very first day I fell completely in love with the whole group. What radiant faces! We immediately decided we would try to go deep with each other from the start and open up our hearts and our secret joys and troubles. We became very close at dazzling speed. Our ages ranged from the thirties to late sixties: Batina Janess Sheets, Misbah Noor Humera Afridi, Jalaluddin

Joseph Losavio, Tajali Jan King, Tarana Sara Jobin, Zakir Amin Ron Povich, and me.

During our first pod meeting, Tajali, having heard me sing at some Zira'at Universal Worship services, asked me if I was going to sing at Suluk. I said no, as I preferred not to sing alone and did not have any of my usual partners with me. The last member of our pod, a slender, fresh-faced young woman with a ponytail and a beaming smile who looked like she could not have been more than twenty-three, volunteered eagerly, "Oh, I'll sing with you! I love to sing with people!"

Only after I accepted her kind offer did I discover who she was: Tarana, who looked dramatically younger than her actual years, was a professional opera and orchestra conductor! I practically went into shock. With my untrained voice and inability to read music, I had just agreed to sing publicly with an opera conductor! *Why me, Lord? Surely you jest? Again?*

But singing with sweet-voiced Tarana, and for a time as well with the velvet-voiced Fatiha Alexis, became one of the great joys of my Suluk years. Kind, warmhearted, sensitive, and full of fun, Tarana made every occasion a delight. And she was very tolerant of those, like me, who could be all thumbs with music. Every Suluk session ended with an evening *sema*, a freelance devotional service with a Chishti-like emphasis on music, and we sang at every one of them in English, Arabic, Greek, Latin, and Quechua.

As the Suluk sessions proceeded, it was as if we were all accumulating fine layers of numinous silken gauze on our humble forms, mystical butterfly wings that would eventually be strong enough to carry our caterpillar selves up into gnostic flight. Pir Zia taught quietly, potently, drawing us into deeper realities through his eloquence and realization. His writings, too, were elegant and deep, inviting and thought-provoking.

Crises came and went for us all—deaths, births, marriages, divorces, injuries, healings, changes of occupation or of residence, everything imaginable. The griefs we felt as a collective body blow, so sensitive and attuned were we becoming to each other; the joys filled us with irrepressible sunlight. A great upheaval arrived midway through our classes that shook us all; the Abode itself went into both financial and psychological crisis.

Abode employees were fired, right and left, gracelessly. Some of these people were our classmates, and our hearts ached for them, seeing them turn quickly away, dashing tears from their faces. There was conflict and disagreement between those living at the Abode and the Inayati Board of Directors. The Abode community, once a healthy group of people of all ages, babies to elders, had shrunk—the school was closed, there were many fewer children, the elders had begun to die off or had to move to more supportive environments. The embracing sense of community was disappearing. And communications from the board seemed cold to those of us watching on the sidelines. Scary ideas were suggested: selling the Abode and its historical Shaker buildings to become a spa— and worse.

Our Gulzar class met and rallied. We decided to do what we could—we prayed, fund-raised, and wrote a public letter to the board about the importance and inestimable value of the Abode. Ultimately, the Order and the Abode separated their governing and financial ties. The Order center moved to Virginia. The Abode, now called an "eco-village" and continuing to remain an important source of Sufi *baraka* (grace), began to rebuild itself. This process, a difficult and sensitive one, is still underway.

At last, in June 2015, our Gulzar class's graduation arrived. We traveled to the top of the mountain above the Abode, a double rainbow rising above us. We prayed and sang and felt such love for one another, standing among the tall green trees glowing in the midday sun. Pir Zia, beaming, blessed each one of us individually and handed us our graduation certificates and blessed prayer beads. Two of our special teachers, the wonderful Aziza Scott and— hurrah!—the imported, radiant Wali Ali, hugged us and handed us roses. Our dear mentors, Kainat, Khabira, and Ruhya, poured poems and rose petals upon us: *Ishk Allah Mahboud Lillah.* "God is Love, Lover, and Beloved." Without knowing that this was to be the theme, Tarana and I had also chosen to sing this particular phrase for the group as we stopped near Pir Vilayat's former meditation pod partway up the mountain. I sang the Arabic as a counterpoint to Tarana's singing "What Wondrous Love Is This." It felt, in a way, like the Sufic and the Shaker elements combined in joy to rejoice together in the true Beloved of us all.

> *What wondrous love is this, O my soul, O my soul,*
> *What wondrous love is this, O my soul?*
> *What wondrous love is this that caused the Lord of bliss*
> *To send His perfect peace to my soul, to my soul,*
> *To send His perfect peace to my soul?*

ﷺ

Terrible as an Army with Banners
>   *Who is she that looketh forth as the morning, fair as the moon, clear as*
>   *the sun, and terrible as an army with banners?* (Song of Sol. 6:10)

I don't know when the idea first came to me to try to offer a retreat focused on the Virgin Mary at the Abode, but over time this inspiration became more and more compelling. I envisioned it as a pouring out of Christian and Sufic richness—with music and chanting from both traditions, mystical dancing, sacred stories and contemplation, Biblical readings, spiritual walks, and poetry, encompassing the story of her whole life as we knew it primarily from the Eastern Orthodox tradition and evoking her loving, gracious presence among us. I asked three of my goddaughters, cantors all, to help present it and they agreed. And I wanted to ask my guide, Sharifa, if she would co-lead the retreat with me. I knew I was not qualified, especially in dealing with the Sufic practices and approaches, to do it without her expertise and spiritual wisdom and maturity.

I hadn't yet had a chance to ask Sharifa if she would be willing when I saw that, at the current Suluk session, I was scheduled for a private appointment with Pir Zia. Each session every one of us had such a *sohbet*, or spiritual conversation, either with our Pir or the other major teacher for that session. I always found Pir Zia to be kind, polite, and gentle. His manner was dignified, with some of the Earth Element gravitas of his grandfather, our Murshid, but Pir Zia's dark eyes could also easily sparkle with laughter.

After an initial prayer, as we settled into comfortable chairs in his office, we soon found ourselves engaged on a topic of concern to me: what seemed to me the slightly suppressed or, perhaps, just neglected, status of Christianity in our Order's activities, and the Ruhaniat's as well. So many Inayati *mureeds* had grown up in Christian homes and churches and seemed to want to get away from them as far as possible, either identifying exclusively with other faiths or, at best, expressing what traditional Christians such as myself could only view as a highly revisionist version of our faith. Even such things as holding Universal Worship most often on Sunday mornings implied that there was no need to attend Christian services usually held at that time.

If this were the case, Pir Zia asked me, what did I think might help? He had a couple of years before, he said, encouraged Jewish, Christian, and Muslim *mureeds* to form their own online support groups. Only the Jewish and Muslim *mureeds* had done so, but even these groups had eventually faded away. Impulsively, I brought up the idea of the Virgin Mary retreat, explaining to him my willingness and credentials, such as they were, but that I had not had a chance to ask Sharifa.

Little did I know that at that time, outside on the dirt road not many feet from this office, Sharifa was having an experience of the Virgin Mary!

Pir Zia prayed, thought about it, and said yes, if Sharifa agreed. He felt that this event could be regarded as within the Universal Worship department of the Inayati Order. I left happy, with his blessing.

Sharifa (whose name around that time Pir Zia was changing to Kainat as a result of guidance), a free spirit in so many ways, readily agreed to do the retreat with me. I alerted the cantors, and we contacted the programs director to search for a date.

ﷺ

Storm at Sea

Just as we were opening up our sails for this mystical voyage, a typhoon struck. Kainat and I were called into her office by a very angry senior Sufi Inayati official. The person who, so far as we knew, bore the title of Program Director, was not the program director, this woman insisted. She herself was, and how dare we try to proceed without her notification and approval! She said that it would be impossible for us to do the retreat in the next year—possibly in three or four years, depending upon other programming necessities. I pointed out to her politely that, being in my sixties already, this was not easy to hear. She blew me off. And, being completely resistant, was, I'm sure, glad to see our backs soon going out her office door. Later on, meeting privately with poor Kainat, she scolded her for, among other things, allowing a "mere *mureed*" to suggest such a thing! It made me feel as if we had suddenly swung into an *Upstairs, Downstairs* episode—and, for sure, I was downstairs.

Eventually, I did get to check with Pir Zia. He was apologetic but said that, as this woman was in charge of many aspects of the organization, he would have to defer to her about the retreat.

One thing I had not shared with Pir Zia was that I felt—I could not tell you how or why—that there was some inimical force that did not want the Virgin Mary's presence to be strongly invited into the Abode, especially in the Meditation Hall. It did not seem to emanate from a particular person, was merely a noxious hovering, to my perception, in the subtle air. And this despite the fact that I'm sure the Virgin Mary was acknowledged in that hall at many times—especially in the Universal Worship, where she might be invoked in both or either the Christian or Islamic portions. And yet I felt it there, a little shadowy node of metallic iciness protected from notice by its hiddenness, chanting "no, no, no."

Suluk was like a finely woven celestial spider's web, all its fine strings quivering and responsive to every interior spiritual tug and shiver of all its members. With such a conflict as Kainat and I were experiencing with the official, it was not realistic to expect that no signs would emerge in others. Among the most mystically attuned in our class was red-haired Parvati, an extraordinary tiny woman in her seventies, a fabric artist and energy healer, who had wed and buried three husbands, and now, still indomitable, attended our Suluk classes using a walker and with a patch over one eye. She stopped me in the Meditation Hall's large shared restroom, fixed me with her penetrating eye, and said with meaningful emphasis, "I saw the Rev—"

Someone walked into the room, and she stopped. Then we had to hurry off to an evening class.

The next day, we repeated the same scene in the same place. "I saw the Rev—"

Again someone came in, and Parvati went silent.

The day after that I met Parvati in the hall. She stopped me and, putting a restraining hand upon my arm, said, "I saw the Reverend Mother on your face. You have the authority!!!" And she shuffled away on her walker while I stood dazed and staring into space. I was grateful for her kindness and respected her authority but was not overjoyed to have a ring-tailed lemur popping up once again! I wondered what that face change looked like! But was just as glad not to know. Despite its weirdness (what else was new?), I regarded it as a sign of encouragement.

Kainat and I talked and prayed. The cantors prayed. The official was both immovable and quite unpleasant to Kainat; me she would not even communicate with any longer, feeling that I was really beneath her notice. Weeks passed with this storm cloud swirling around our heads as we plugged through one and then another Suluk session.

It happened that the co-teacher with Pir Zia for this particular session was a man with whom I immediately got off on the wrong foot. With no shred of the prized Sufi *adab*, or exquisite politeness of manner expected of all *mureeds* and teachers, this man, who had barely told me his name, began with a kind of geeky gracelessness to immediately bore into my eyes with his own as if he were entirely entitled.

I objected, and he resented the objection. But I had to admit that he did know some things about inner processing. Under his tutelage, as he guided my class in working in pairs to discern, through a certain kind of dialogue, deeper levels of what was passing internally within us, I began to notice certain things for the first time. I became aware that somehow around the core guidance I thought might be coming through, there were other little thought forms flitting around near the edges. Like butterflies, these graceful little things, frothy and often strange, I chronically dismissed as my imagination. But somehow becoming more aware of them as we went through this intensive inner process, I began to wonder whether they really were just insubstantial lacework on the fringes or not. I decided to take a chance and try an experiment with them.

That evening I went quietly into the shadowy Meditation Hall around midnight. There was just one other person there—a dear friend from my pod, sitting on the floor intensively doing practices. I sat down at the far end of the room and put on a ledge a beautiful icon of the Virgin Mary with a battery-operated candle before it. I prayed many prayers to her and to our Lord about the Virgin Mary retreat and for others' needs. Then, hesitatingly, I tried out the butterfly guidance: I prayed aloud to each of the Seven Archangels by name (some of their names vary, depending upon whose list you use): Michael, Gabriel, Raphael, Uriel, Salathiel, Jeremiel, and Barachiel. Something seemed to shift on an inner level. Then I felt I had to sing a certain hymn to seal this offering. Very softly, so as not to disturb my fellow *mureed*, I sang "Now the Powers of Heaven Serve Invisibly with Us," a haunting Byzantine hymn from the Presanctified Liturgy. At the end, I felt a distinct closure—and a lovely peace—descend. I went upstairs to my room filled with an inner quiet.

Early the next morning, I awoke from a refreshing sleep. Oddly, there were already a couple of e-mails on my phone. One was addressed to Kainat but also cc'd to me. It was from the resistant official; she was suddenly completely conciliatory and had swung around in her attitude 180 degrees! She suggested that she and Kainat communicate as soon as possible to enable this "wonderful retreat idea to be scheduled soon."

Unexpectedly, within a couple of weeks, the official abruptly retired, disappearing from the scene. At the next Suluk session, Kainat and I went to talk to her replacement. This pleasant, keen-eyed woman leaned forward across her desk and said, "I feel that my job is to try to find out what the Spirit wants to have happen here. And to help it happen!"

"That's just exactly what I've been waiting to hear!" I cried. She helped Kainat and me set a date for the Virgin Mary retreat at the Abode for May of 2015.

~~Ω~~

Walking with Mary

Our exceptionally gorgeous flyers of red, gold, and blue, designed by the artistically gifted Dana Jamila, read "Walking with Mary / a mystical journey / Who is she? / And what does she mean for our lives?" We said that we were offering "a meditative immersion in the story of her luminous life as we explore it from prophecies before her birth through its challenges and triumphs, to her ultimate transcendent glorification. Reflecting together upon the different passages of her life, we will contemplate them as keys to our own personal inner life, throwing light upon our individual paths while also drawing us into an increasingly powerful and intimate relationship with Mary herself."

More than thirty other people joined us for the retreat, despite our having little time to publicize it. We were very fortunate to have the gifted dance leader Nizam Ellen Ash join our team to draw us into periodic wonderful Dances of Universal Peace. The cantors and I had brought a couple of hundred icons of various sizes, handsome tablecloths, candles, vases, and bouquets of flowers to transform the Meditation Hall into an appropriate spiritual nest. It took us hours just to set up before our program began on that Friday evening. Many people were working to make this retreat as beautiful as possible. Dana Jamila and Qudsiya Carol Rodrigue had baked some special treats and made wonderful teas with rose petals floating in them and, for that matter, put rose petals and pretty bowls of special small gifts everywhere.

Although our retreat would draw primarily from the traditions and practices of the Eastern Church, as well as Sufic ones, after our opening prayers, introductions, and explanations, we ended our first evening with a gesture of love toward the Western Church. Tarana and I sang a beautiful ancient song, a Cantiga de Santa Maria from the venerable Spanish pilgrims' route to Santiago de Compostela, that joyously welcomes May and Mary in her month.

We then asked everyone to stand and form a circle. As the cantors, Tarana, and I began to sing another Cantiga with a haunting harmony, "Stella Splendens," about the Virgin Mary as the "splendid star" of the mountains, we all began to slowly walk in the circle as if embarking on a physical pilgrimage, putting ourselves as much as possible into the hands of the Virgin Mary. Each person picked up a pretty scallop shell on a long red cord as they passed by a full basket, putting over their heads and on their hearts this sacred symbol of the pilgrimage of Santiago de Compostela. As the singing ended, we all stopped, bowed deeply to each other in the circle, and silently returned to our rooms.

The weekend passed in a whirl of laughter, tears, beauty, and glory. And much music: we cantors sang at least forty-six sacred songs. The retreatants were from a wide variety of backgrounds: Sufic, Orthodox Christian, Roman Catholic, Episcopalian, and others, including no particular faith. For some it was their very first retreat ever while some others, very experienced, were senior Sufic teachers. Yet we united deeply and almost seamlessly in the strong, sweet, and powerful presence of our Holy Mother, the Virgin Mary.

During the Universal Worship on Sunday morning, Nizam offered a Native American segment, telling the story of Our Lady of Guadalupe. Tarana and we cantors sang "Hanacpachap cussicuinin," a lovely ancient processional for the Virgin Mary in Quechua, the Mayan language, in a Spanish Baroque style combined with some Mayan musical elements and rhythms. Nizam then led us in a wonderful circular Dance of Universal Peace for the Virgin Mary, "Altissimo Corazón," "Highest Heart." This dance was both lively and uplifting. As we got underway, Sher Arifa, her years of training in the Mevlevi tradition rising to the inspiration of the moment, slipped into the center of the circle and began skillfully performing the elegant, heart-opening Mevlevi turn. With Sher as its whirling center, we all got higher and higher as we danced on in the circle, singing in Spanish, sometimes turning in place, sometimes holding hands pacing forward and back. We did not want the dance to end. But when it did, I noticed one of our cantors, her expression radiant, walking away from the circle looking stunned, tears of happiness running quietly down her cheeks.

In another inspired section, Kainat guided everyone in taking turns with all the other people people in attuning to the Archangel Gabriel delivering the news of the Annunciation to the Virgin Mary or attuning to the Virgin Mary receiving it. Nothing was compulsory in our retreat, but we all did this. In either role, you got to know yourself better, as well as the holy personage invoked, and to see the great beauty shining from each of your partners.

I was very moved to see realized a particular inspiration I had received for this retreat. In the section on the Crucifixion of Christ, we had a man, a Sufic senior teacher, stand with his arms outstretched as upon the Cross. The women made two tight circles around him like the faithful women who had stood by the cross, each of us with one hand on the left shoulder of the woman before us, our right hands free. The four other men stood at a little distance from the circles in the four cardinal directions, one man attuning to St. John the Evangelist, the only male disciple to stay at Jesus's side through the crucifixion, and the others attuning to the angelic presences or to the other grieving male disciples. As we settled into our concentrations, the women began to take tiny steps forward, chanting, "*Ya Shahid*" ("O Thou Witness," with our hands pointing down to the ground), "*Ya Habib*" ("O Thou Dearly Beloved," looking upward with our right hands raised up to heaven in grief and love); the men chanted too. This practice was exquisitely moving, and its intimacy, both painful and transcendent, especially acknowledged the love, strength, and faithfulness of the women disciples on that terrible day.

I'm not saying everything went smoothly. We presenters had our bumps, and I'm sure many of the retreatants must have had theirs as well. But the overall effect was enormously positive, and the feedback we got back later was one of rejoicing and requests for more such retreats. One man wrote us, "To see you and the 'holy women' up there was a confirmation to me that the dispensation of the Word continues in modern times, that there continue to be keepers of the holy flame among us, pure vessels dedicated to bringing the cup to all who thirst. It was a love letter to Mary and the message of her Son. It still resonates in me."

Others thanked us for helping them transcend the "distance" between their concepts about Mary and her actual living, loving presence. She had become real for many of them and vitally entwined into their lives. We were exhausted but transcendently happy. In her great graciousness she had come to us, she who "lookest forth as the morning, fair as the moon, clear as the sun, and terrible as an army with banners." And dearer than all.

اللہ

The next morning I awoke happy but exhausted—and feeling physically like I had been in a bar brawl. Everything that could ache seemed to be aching. And yet streams of inspiration for the next Virgin Mary retreat were coming down upon me like monsoon rain. Feeling like I had been thrust half-awake into a full-force mystical needle shower, I began mentally crying out "Cut! Cut! Cut!" like an agitated director. "Back off! Can't I have even one day—just one day!— ONE DAY!!!—of rest?!" Pathetic. I could hear the etheric laughter. Yet again I understood viscerally St. Catherine of Ávila's famous remark, "If this is how You treat Your friends, it is no wonder that You have so few of them!" But I, um, noted down the inspirations all the same. Just in case, you know.

CHAPTER SEVENTEEN

Cattail Marvels

Glory in the Swamp

You can stroll through a swamp, casually noting its cattails, bul-
rushes, marsh marigolds, and plethora of flora, and completely
miss the wonders surrounding you. Take the common cattail, its
innocuous cob-topped stalk gently stirring in the afternoon breeze.
Visually it provides pleasant architecture, but in its outer simplicity there is no hint of the many marvels it contains. If you slit its
green stem in the spring, you find a tasty vegetable: a white inner
core of crunchy "Cossack asparagus" that tastes like an unusually
delicious cross between cucumber and asparagus. Young shoots
are edible, and the lower parts of the leaves can be used in salads.
In midsummer, the yellow pollen dust on the head can be flour for
baking. In fall, the rich roots, cooked, provide starchy nutrition.
In late autumn, after the heads have burst open, their light, puffy
dandelion-like seeds can be used like down to stuff jackets or as
excellent tinder. And there are so many other uses—the long leaves
to weave mats and baskets, many traditional medical uses, and the
stem with its cob can be dipped in fat to make a reputedly excellent
torch. The humble cattail is a hidden multifaceted treasury. As are
our lives, of which we can never say that we have come to the end
of a situation, a meaning, or a new possibility. The eyes of wonder
and discovery, and the eye of the heart, never cease opening to
look upon marvels.

The Really Real at a Funeral

Anna and I were on our way up to Maine. A dear friend had called
and asked us to chant the funeral of her husband, formerly a well-
loved member of our old community. The wife was temporarily

a member of a local Greek church but wanted her husband to have the full-length funeral that Father Jeremiah had taught us to observe, complete with the traditional three days of round-the-clock prayers by his body. She feared the local priest might instead do a truncated form. So she had gathered her own servers. Anna and I were traveling north, service books and stacks of music piled on the car seat, to try to fulfill her wishes.

I was to be head Reader, and we were to be assisted by some very competent Readers from Maine, Faith and Seraphim. As we would be chanting in the Russian style, we were particularly delighted to have Seraphim's fine bass to round out the harmony.

However, I was worried. Three priests would be concelebrating this funeral: the local Greek priest, a convert Russian Orthodox priest who was starting a mission that our friend was involved with in Maine, and . . . Father Zeno, from the Boston Bulgarian jurisdiction. I had not seen Father Zeno in the four years since I had left my old church. Offering a funeral service that involved working with three priests of different jurisdictions, with almost no time to meet and work together on the rubrics and all involved, was in itself very daunting. Adding to that having to meet and work with the priest who had expelled me from my old community seemed over the top in terms of stress. But it had to be done.

Rising early at our friend's house the morning of the funeral after very little sleep, we walked to the church, just a few blocks away. Crossing myself as I entered the church door, I also tried to pull myself together, knowing I would soon see Father Zeno. He was already there. We looked at each other across the church nave. There was a moment of silence. And then we ran into each other's arms. The Really Real was intervening across our disaffection. Nothing in the situation had changed. We still each felt the same way about the issues that had come between us. There was no alteration. I could not go back to my old church. But the way we really felt about each other, beneath all the conflict—the deep love we truly felt—could not be held down. It was real and pure. After we hugged each other a few times in gladness, I left to sit down in a pew to quickly review the service with the Russian Orthodox priest, who would be the lead celebrant.

After the long funeral's end, we went to a memorial meal in the church hall. I asked the Greek priest if his congregation, heavy in their attendance, had been okay with the way we had done the service. "Oh yes," he said. "Many of them are saying it was the most beautiful service they have ever attended. But now," he added glumly, shaking his head, "they are all going to want the same thing!"

I was glad that Anna and I were able to help and honor our friends. And I was overjoyed that God had seized this opportunity to remind both Fr. Zeno and me of the Really Real, of the blessed and fundamental substrate of our relationship, the love and forgiveness that are there—and that will still be there—when all our dissensions fall away into dust. This was not a quick fix and, really, not a fix at all. Nor was it a social Band-Aid briefly applied to decently cover a wounded relationship on a demanding public occasion. It was a brief dive into the true depths of our relationship. In the Really Real we were always, and always will be, of one heart.

⳥

Wings

Looking back three years before this trip to Maine, it was Clean Monday, the first day of Lent. I had passed through the first anniversary of Mark's death just three months before. Having just left a theology class at Holy Cross / Hellenic College, I was taking a break on the campus's high, breezy hill, seated on a park bench in the brick-paved courtyard outside the seminary's small cruciform church. Surmounted by a little golden dome and cross in its center, the church, with its lovely beige and russet tiles set in a traditional style, would not have seemed out of place among farm fields in the Greek countryside. Managing to look both coolly elegant and warmly approachable at the same time—a striking architectural feat—the chapel was the heartbeat of the school, where life revolved around the celebration of services evoking the changing feasts of the year. But it was quiet right now, the students in their classes or working hard in the library.

The night before, I had attended the Forgiveness Vespers at my new church, each one of us in the congregation personally asking forgiveness of and offering forgiveness to each other member. It had been a very beautiful and moving service, rich with love and humility, both cleansing and uniting for us all. Lent, though penitential and restricting in certain ways, was also a new beginning, a chance to make amends, to go deeper, and to meet the waves of grace that arose to carry us strongly upward in support of such blessed choices.

I felt the embryonic potential of the beautiful dove of the Holy Spirit that would, several weeks from now, break out of the restrictive Lenten shell in a blaze of glory and winged life on Pascha, but for now that bird of light and fire was quiet, hidden in the mute, shadowy womb of its meditative shell.

I was missing Mark and missing my old community, much as I found that I also loved my new spiritual nest of Saint Mary's. I felt the old loneliness. A cold breeze arose, and, despite my light jacket, I was chilled. I wanted to get up and leave, but when I tried to, something held me down. This was not an inner hesitation—something, someone, outside myself, was actually holding me down physically on the bench! Ah, more mischief from the Unseen! I could tell that if I really wanted to I could force my way up, but that would seem somehow to be churlish. Maybe this was just a joke but maybe not. *All right*, I thought at my captor, *I'll wait—but not for too long!*

Just as I mentally consented, an enormous peregrine falcon flew low over the dome of the church and alighted, standing upright, with huge bright-yellow talons clasping the golden cross. Had I left when I wished to, I would have missed this marvelous sight, which I felt I was meant to see. The falcon was breathtakingly beautiful, her white breast blazing in the sunlight, her slate-colored wings, even in repose, graceful arcs in the air. I felt a wonderful shock beholding her in her heraldic stance, like the eagle representative of Saint John the Evangelist, like a mythic messenger from beyond proclaiming through all the levels of existence the glory and triumph of Jesus Christ. My heart soared and sang with the joy of this gift. As I gazed at her, the church doors opened, and a priest in a long black *ráso* stepped out. It was my own dear pastor, Fr. Antony, whom I had never encountered on campus before.

"Father Antony, look!" I called out, pointing to the magnificent falcon on the dome. He hurried forward, and just as he did, a second falcon flew gracefully over us and, with the refined delicacy of a dancer, touched just the end of his wing tip to one of the standing falcon's and swept by. Receiving his gentle signal, the first falcon turned, smooth and quick as a dervish, in a swirl of wings and the next moment was gone, pursuing her shared life with him beyond the trees and our sight.

The restraining force gone, I stood up, still breathing deep of the beauty of the gift. Father Antony came forward. We shared a rejoicing hug. I was pleased at the synchronicity of this dear and grace-bearing priest's unexpected appearance just one beat after the prophetic falcon. It was Clean Monday. The world was full of hope. Life, unexpected, radiant, and touched by the Ineffable, was beginning again.

EVERY FOOT A SHRINE

Every creature has a religion. Every
foot is a shrine where
a secret candle
burns.

Every cell in us worships
God.

Every arrow in the bow of desire
has rushed out in hope
of nearing
Him.

—Saint Thomas Aquinas,
Translation, Daniel Ladinsky

ACKNOWLEDGMENTS

*W*ithout the steady help and loving support of a wonderful group of friends and editorial professionals, this book would not now exist. I cannot thank them enough for being such patient midwives to my literary labors and sharing so much good advice, professional wisdom, financial support, willing ears— and still being able to laugh and remind me to as well.

Great thanks to Katharine Call Newhouse for her unflagging friendship, generous contributions, and listening heart. Also, to David Newhouse, Juanita Wetherell, Carol and Merritt Lipsky, Dana and Mark Watt, Rev. Deacon John and *Diaconissa* Mary Seraphima Williamson, and Liz McNear, gratitude for keeping my impecunious boat afloat through some very challenging times.

To my beloved beta readers, Dana Watt, Joseph Losavio, Helen Gioulis, Naomi Halima Rose, and Celia and Phil Devine, my great gratitude for their shared inspirations, suggestions for improvement, and loving encouragement. And to Anna Elisabeth Higgins, Mindy Lind-Terk, Lydia Hutchinski, Karen Pearson, Elianne Obadia, Sher Gamard, Mariel Walters, Janess Batina Sheets, Jan Tajali King, Misbah Noor Humera Afridi, Sara Tarana Jobin, Ron Zakir-Amin Povich, Iris Taj a Nur Grant, James Frashoestra Grant, and other friends for their sustaining warmth and prayers. To Fr. Antony Hughes, my beloved Inayatiyya Guide Kainat Felicia Norton, Pir Zia Inayat-Khan, Shafayat Mahdiah Esther Jacobs Kahn, and Senior Teacher Risala Laird for ongoing spiritual inspiration and the blessing of their prayers, great thanks.

To publisher Dede Cummings, cover artist Asha Hossain, editor John Tiholiz, copyeditor Claire Thomas, advisor Charita Cole Brown, publicist Ben Tanzer, and the remarkable wizard/

all-round publishing professional extraordinaire of When Words Count Retreat, Steve Eisner, I offer several bush loads of roses in thanks for all. But to my wise, loving, and delightful chief editor, Peggy Moran, I would give the Tuileries or the Mottisfont rose gardens if I could, in thanks for her excellent suggestions, apt criticisms, and unflagging, often humorous encouragement through even the most difficult passages, both of the book and my personality and life.

To my readers, I thank you for entering this adventure with me. I hope that my story may have been in some way of some help to you. Any mistaken views and any errors are exclusively my own, and I'm sure there are likely many. For these, please forgive me. I am not a spiritual teacher and clearly not a saint but just a regular person occasionally intoxicated by God, as we all can be at times when grace and our own openness allow. As your raggle-taggle gypsy sister, trudging along the pilgrim road, I am honored that you have allowed me to share some stories from my worn travel bag with you. I wish you every joy and every blessing and real divine guidance upon your quest. May you find your heart's desire in this journey.

Lastly, I would like to acknowledge the wisdom of the frequent warnings against sharing spiritual experiences found in many religions and paths. There are so many potential pitfalls for both writer and reader. But I felt compelled to set my small account down, due to the despair I see so much around me regarding the existence of God and the value of religion and spiritual transmission. I wrote to encourage hope and the breaking down of barriers that can lead to spiritual sterility and stagnation where it need not exist. Also, two of my spiritual mothers encouraged me to share some of these stories. I thank them for their guidance and prayers.

Oh, and how could I forget to thank them—the cats! Fluffy Angel Face, even you Jezebel, Albion, Fenris, Zeke and Brother, Waldo, Waldorf and Astoria, Sasha and Toshiro, Buffy, Winston and Mirabai, and now Maximilian and Fiona, you have brought a great vitality and a deep richness to my life, an unfailing authenticity even in the most anesthetized of circumstances. For your natural fidelity to the Really Real, I am forever grateful.